P9-DXI-311

Library
Justice Institute of BC
715 McBride Boulevard
New Westminster, BC , V3L 5T4

Stress Management in Law Enforcement

481.22.

Stress Management in
Law Enforcement

Third Edition

Edited by

Leonard Territo
SAINT LEO UNIVERSITY

and

James D. Sewell
FLORIDA DEPARTMENT OF LAW ENFORCEMENT (RETIRED)

CAROLINA ACADEMIC PRESS
Durham, North Carolina

Copyright © 1999, 2007, 2013
Leonard Territo and James D. Sewell
All Rights Reserved

Library of Congress Cataloging-in-Publication Data

Stress management in law enforcement / [edited by] Leonard Territo and
James D. Sewell. -- 3rd ed.
    p. cm.
Includes bibliographical references and index.
ISBN 978-1-61163-111-1 (alk. paper)
1. Police--Job stress. 2. Police--Mental health services. 3. Stress manage-
ment. I. Territo, Leonard. II. Sewell, James D., 1950-

HV7936.J63S77 2012
363.201'9--dc23

                            2012023670

CAROLINA ACADEMIC PRESS
700 Kent Street
Durham, North Carolina 27701
Telephone (919) 489-7486
Fax (919) 493-5668
www.cap-press.com

Printed in the United States of America

Dedication

For my wife, Elena, the kindest and sweetest woman I have ever known, and our children, Lorraine, Sergei, Kseniya, Illia, and our grandchildren, Matthew, Branden, and Alexander.
—Leonard Territo

"For Kate ... who faced the demons of The Job ... and survived ...."
—James D. Sewell

Contents

Preface

There is considerable evidence suggesting that more law enforcement officers are likely to be killed by job-related stress than are killed by criminals. For every police officer slain by an assailant in the line of duty, countless others succumb to the insidious, long-range effects of job-induced pressures including alcoholism, drug abuse, domestic violence, post-traumatic stress disorder, and even suicide.

The stress imposed by the physical hazards of policing is well known. Few occupations require employees to face the kinds of dangerous situations that police officers may encounter as part of their daily routines. Popular television shows have familiarized viewers with the more obvious dangers police officers encounter in protecting society from the lawbreaker, especially hot pursuits, stop-and-search situations, domestic violence calls, violent political demonstrations, and terrorist attacks such as those on the World Trade Center. The continual observation of incidents of injury, death, and inexplicable acts of cruelty over time can take a terrible toll on the psychological and physical well-being of police officers.

Both editors of this volume have been extensively involved in training and writing about police stress for the past 30 years and, over that time, have witnessed major changes in the ways law enforcement agencies and their leadership respond to this critical problem. Since police stress became a focus of academic and professional concern in the mid-1970s, we have seen the creation and expansion of progressive programs which specifically address issues associated with job-related stress. Throughout this time, training in this area has also been vastly improved and has resulted in saving the careers and even the lives, health, and psychological well-being of many police officers.

We recognize that a wide variety of groups are interested in the topic of police stress. To this end we have designed this book toward meeting the interests of four audiences: first, academicians who have a scholarly interest in police stress and who may also teach the subject; second, police administrators who must deal with the negative effects of stress on their officers on a daily basis; third, police officers who work on the streets and are regularly exposed to the stress to which we have already alluded; and, lastly, students of law enforcement who wish to understand and carry out research relating to the impact of stress on law enforcement officers.

This book is divided into ten sections in which we address matters of intense current interest among law enforcement personnel. We have accomplished this by the careful selection of articles and research papers written by the leading scholars in the field of job-related stress in policing, and each of this volume's ten sections focuses on particular areas of police stress. Each section has a list of key terms. In addition, each article/research paper includes discussion questions which can be used by instructors to enhance the engagement of students in the classroom, as well as for the creation of essay examination questions in regular college classes.

Part One—What Is Stress All About? provides the reader with an orientation and introduction to the topics of stress and some of its principal psychological, physiological, and social consequences. It acquaints the reader with basic concepts and terminology relating to stress.

Part Two—What Does Stress Mean for Cops? examines some of the basic issues of stress that affect law enforcement officers, looking at symptoms and causes throughout the profession, as well as focusing on the unique effects caused by the location and size of the police agency.

Part Three—Are There Ways We Can Tell It Is There? presents a number of research studies which have empirically analyzed and quantified police stress and its impact on police officers.

Part Four—What Are Some of the Bad Effects of Stress on Cops? discusses two of the most destructive maladaptive manifestations of stress in police work: addictive behaviors and suicide. The selected articles will assist the reader in understanding why cops are driven to drink or drugs, why police suicides occur, and what can be done to prevent both.

Part Five—How Does Stress Impact the Cop's Family Life? examines the toll extracted from spouses, children and relatives of law enforcement personnel as a result of the stressful aspects of police work. The alarmingly high rate of marital discord too often includes violence in the police family, events which sometimes culminate in the murder of a family member by a police officer, followed by the officer's suicide. Other less extreme effects on the family include; chronic family bickering and divorce; disruption of the family-centered activities due to irregular work schedules; and school and adjustment problems among the children of law enforcement officers.

Part Six—How Does the Worst of the Worst Affect Cops? focuses on those features of police work that often expose officers to trauma as a result of critical incidents in which people are violently killed or injured. This regular and consistent contact with the effects of cumulative career traumatic stress may, and often over time does, result in signs of traumatization as well as overt manifestations of post-traumatic stress disorder.

Part Seven—What Is the Impact of Foreign Wars on Our Cops? America's protracted wars in Afghanistan and Iraq have taken their toll on American law enforcement personnel serving in military reserve and National Guard units that have been activated for service. Police officers returning from a combat deployment and combat veterans seeking first-time employment as police officers both face the potential impact of psychological issues resulting from their combat experiences. Perhaps more frightening, recent research indicates an increased risk of suicide among returning combat veterans and among police officers. Additionally, law enforcement in the future will find itself dealing with wartime veterans as consumers of police services as those wartime experiences manifest themselves in homelessness, domestic violence, substance abuse, and violent behavior acted out "on the street."

Part Eight—What Are the Tools that a Cop Can Use to Better Handle Stress? looks at the methods by which individual officers may better handle the stress of their law enforcement world. These include increased stress management training, professional counseling for officers and their families, peer support, and required fitness standards and programs.

Part Nine—What Support Is Available for Cops? examines some of the individual techniques and more successful programs recognized as providing effective police psychological services and support for officers under stress.

Part Ten—How Can the Bosses Better Help Their Cops? reflects on the role of the organization and agency managers in identifying, confronting, and reducing stress among an agency's law enforcement personnel and includes recommendations by the Police Psychological Section of the International Association of Chiefs of Police for the psychological support of American law enforcement personnel.

Acknowledgments

We wish to express our thanks and indebtedness to the many distinguished scholars who allowed us to use the results of their hard earned labors. Without their dedicated efforts, this book would have never come to fruition. We also wish to thank the many publishers who allowed us to use the materials from their books and journals. However, we wish to give special thanks to a number of individuals who wrote research papers specifically for this book. These are: Dr. Laurence Miller, psychologist in private practice in Boca Raton, Florida; Dr. Michael Arter, Associate Professor, Pennsylvania State University at Altoona; Mr. Allen Kates, author and journalist; Ms. Karen Oehme, J.D., Director; Dr. Elizabeth A. Donnelly, and Mr. Zachary Summerlin, Institute for Family Violence Studies, Florida State University; Dr. John M. Violanti, Research Associate Professor, University of Buffalo, New York; Dr. Richard F. Cipriano, psychologist in private practice in Tampa, Florida; Dr. Carol Logan, Chief Psychologist, Austin, Texas, Police Department; and Ms. Teresa Tate, Founder, Survivors of Law Enforcement Suicide (SOLES).

Typing and other numerous clerical services were also provided by our hardworking secretary Sharon Ostermann, whose constructive comments and long hours of work are very much appreciated. We also to wish to thank her assistant Shari Allen, whose dazzling speed on the computer keyboard helped to keep us on schedule.

Lastly, we want to thank our publisher, Keith R. Sipe, for sharing our conviction that this book, like previous editions, will continue to make a significant contribution to the law enforcement profession.

About the Editors

Dr. Leonard Territo is presently a distinguished professor of criminal justice in the Department of Criminal Justice at Saint Leo University, Saint Leo, Florida, as well as Professor Emeritus in the Department of Criminology, at the University of South Florida, Tampa, Florida. He has previously served first as a Major and then as Chief Deputy (Undersheriff) with the Leon County Sheriff's Office, Tallahassee, Florida. He also served for almost nine years with the Tampa Florida Police Department and had assignments as a patrol officer; motorcycle officer; homicide, rape, and robbery detective; internal affairs detective; and member of the police academy training staff. Dr. Territo is the former chairman of the Department of Police Administration and Director of the Florida Institute for Law Enforcement at St. Petersburg Junior College (now St. Petersburg College), St. Petersburg, Florida. He has also been teaching and writing about the topic of police stress for over 30 years.

He is a graduate of the United States Secret Service "Dignitary Protection Seminar," the nationally recognized University of Louisville "National Crime Prevention Institute," and the Saint Leo University Institute for Excellence in Criminal Justice Administration "Non-Verbal Communications/Detecting Deception."

He has coauthored some of the leading books in the law enforcement profession including: *Police Administration*, which is in its 8th edition; *Criminal Investigation*, which is in its 11th edition and is by far the bestselling book of its kind in the United States (both *Police Administration* and *Criminal Investigation* have recently been translated into Chinese for use by Chinese criminal justice students as well as Chinese law enforcement officers and administrators); *International Sex Trafficking of Women and Children: Understanding the Global Epidemic*; *The International Trafficking of Human Organs: A Multidisciplinary Perspective*; *Crime and Justice in America*, which is in its 6th edition; *Stress and Police Personnel*; *The Police Personnel Selection Process*; *Police Civil Liability*; *Hospital and College Security Liability*; and *College Crime Prevention and Personal Safety Awareness*. His books have been used in over 1,000 colleges and universities in all 50 states and he has had numerous articles published in nationally recognized law enforcement and legal journals. His books have been used and referenced by both academic and police departments in Australia, Barbados, Belarus, Canada, Chile, China, Czechoslovakia, England, France, Germany, Israel, The Netherlands, Poland, Saudi Arabia, South Korea, and Spain.

He was selected for inclusion in "Who's Who in American Law Enforcement," selected as Florida's "Outstanding Criminal Justice Educator" by the Florida Criminal Justice Educators Association, cited for ten years of "Meritorious Service" by the Florida Police Chiefs Association, given the "Outstanding Teacher Award" by the College of Social and Behavioral Sciences, University of South Florida, Tampa, Florida, cited for 25 years of teaching and meritorious service to the Tampa Florida Police Academy, and awarded the Saint Leo University, Saint Leo, Florida Outstanding Publication Award.

He has also been qualified as a Police Policies and Procedures Expert in both state and federal courts in the following states: Alaska, Arizona, District of Columbia, Florida, Georgia, Illinois, Iowa, Kansas, Kentucky, Louisiana, Michigan, New Jersey, Ohio, Oregon, Pennsylvania, Tennessee, Virginia, Washington, and Wisconsin.

Dr. Territo has served as a lecturer throughout the United States and has instructed a wide variety of police subjects to thousands of law enforcement officials.

Dr. James D. Sewell retired as Assistant Commissioner of the Florida Department of Law Enforcement in February 2005, following a 32-year career with university, municipal, and state law enforcement agencies in Florida. Since his retirement from active law enforcement, he has provided training and management consulting services to a number of law enforcement and social services agencies, not-for-profit organizations, and professional associations.

Dr. Sewell received his B.S., M.S., and Ph.D. in Criminology from Florida State University. He has published two textbooks and over fifty journal articles and book chapters, principally on law enforcement management and law enforcement stress. He holds Diplomate status within the American Academy of Experts in Traumatic Stress and is a board-certified expert in traumatic stress and in stress management by that body.

Dr. Sewell is a graduate of the Florida Criminal Justice Executive Institute Chief Executive Seminar (Eighth Class) and F.B.I. National Academy (114th Session) and is a Life Member of both the International Association of Chiefs of Police and the Florida Police Chiefs Association. In 2010, he was named to the FPCA's Wall of Honor for contributions to the Association and the law enforcement profession.

Stress Management in
Law Enforcement

Part One

What Is Stress All About?

Over the last several years, society in general and a number of professional fields in particular have shown increasing concern over the concept and visible manifestations of the phenomenon referred to as stress. Broadly defined by Hans Selye, the recognized "father of stress," as the "body's nonspecific response to any demand placed upon it," its effects have been linked to hypertension, coronary heart disease, alcohol and drug abuse, and a deterioration in normal interpersonal relations. In the business world, "stress has moved from the nether world of 'emotional problems' and 'personality problems' to the corporate balance sheet ... stress is now seen as not only troublesome, but expensive" (Slobogin, 48).

But exactly what is this phenomenon of stress which has caught the concentrated attention of the professional and academic communities? Selye has amplified the parameters of his definition, saying that:

> ... stress is essentially reflected by the rate of all the wear and tear
> caused by life ... Although we cannot avoid stress as long as we live,
> we can learn a great deal about how to keep its damaging side-effects,
> "distress," to a minimum (Selye, xvi)

It was as a result of his research into the effects of stress on the body's homeostatic tendencies that Selye hypothesized the existence of the General Adaptation Syndrome (G.A.S.). Defined basically as the manifestations of the body's adaptive reactions to stress, the G.A.S., or stress syndrome, " ... evolves in time through three stages ... (1) The alarm reaction, (2) The stage of resistance, and (3) The stage of exhaustion" (Selye, 38).

Selye pinpointed a number of indices of stress which he felt were indicative of an acute impact on the stressed individual, including (Selye, 174–8):

- General irritability, hyperexcitation, or depression
- Impulsive behavior or emotional instability
- Emotional tenseness and alertness
- Hypermotility

- Pain in the neck or lower back
- Insomnia
- Increased smoking
- Alcohol addiction
- Psychoses
- Free-floating anxiety

Holding that it is an individual's "ability to cope with the demands made by the events in our lives, not the quality or intensity of the events, that counts" (Selye, 178), Selye attributed a number of physical and psychological ailments to inappropriate or excessive bodily adaptations to stress. Among these "diseases of adaptation" were cardiovascular illness and heart attack, renal disease, hypertension, inflammatory or allergic diseases, sexual difficulties, digestive disturbances, metabolic problems and nervous/mental disorders.

It is within the parameters first suggested by Selye that the authors in Part One provide their contributions. Their discussions are critical in establishing the framework for understanding stress, especially as we will later apply it to policing.

Miller reflects on the history of stress in general and trauma in particular and provides a linkage between these psychological concepts and the experiences of emergency service workers. His work, an updated version of an original work from the Second Edition of *Stress Management for Law Enforcement*, will give the reader an understanding of the phenomenology, symptomatology, psychophysiology, neuropsychology, and main principles of treatment for stress reactions and traumatic stress syndromes. Of particular usefulness to the reader will be his concluding discussion on psychological treatment of stress and trauma syndromes.

Palm, Polusny, and Follette focus their attention on vicarious traumatization, a form of post-traumatic stress response sometimes experienced by those, such as police officers, fire fighters, and emergency medical workers, who indirectly are exposed to traumatic events. They examine how such reactions are experienced, and may vary, across professions and offer organizational and individual considerations for effectively dealing with such issues.

Yet, the final two authors in this section caution against crediting too much negative manifestations to stress. As Carmichael notes, Selye wrote about two types of stress, distress, or the "bad" kind that takes its toll on one's health and mental well-being, and eustress, the "good" kind that serves to gear one up to effectively handle danger and a hostile environment. Stress is a natural part of life, our dealing with change that is normal to us as human beings. It is how we respond to stressful situations and to the accumulation of stress and, particularly, the amount of control that we perceive as having over our lives that determines its ultimate impact on us.

As Komaroff explains, Walter Bradford Cannon was the first to describe the "fight or flight" response critical to the concept of stress and argued how certain stress reactions are harmful to the individual. As more recent research has shown, the relationship between stress and disease is not always as clear or as pronounced as some physicians, researchers, or even the public would expect. As Komaroff concludes, "the facts are that stress can worsen the symptoms of any disease and stress management can offer relief. Stress, however, is rarely the sole, convenient explanation for a patient's suffering."

Additional Reading

Braham, Barbara J. (1994). *Managing Stress: Keeping Calm Under Fire.* Burr Ridge, IL: Irwin Professional Publishing.

Charlesworth, Edward A., and Nathan, Ronald G. (1984). *Stress Management: A Comprehensive Guide to Wellness.* New York, NY: Ballantine Books.

Coleman, James C. (1973). "Life Stress and Maladaptive Behavior," *The American Journal of Occupational Therapy*, 27(4), 169–180.

Jacobs, Gregg D. (2001). "The Physiology of Mind-Body Interactions: The Stress Response and the Relaxation Response," *The Journal of Alternative and Complementary Medicine*, 7 (Supplement 1), S-83–92.

Levi, Lennart (1967) "Stress as a Cause of Disease," in L. Levi, *Stress: Sources. Management and Prevention.* New York: Liveright Publishing Company.

Selye, Hans (1967). *The Stress of Life (Revised Edition).* New York, NY: McGraw-Hill.

Slobogin, Kathy (1977). "Stress." New York Times Magazine, November 20, 48–55.

Thomas, Rhiannon B., and Wilson, John P. (2004). "Issues and Controversies in the Understanding and Diagnosis of Compassion Fatigue, Vicarious Traumatization, and Secondary Traumatic Stress Disorder," *International Journal of Emergency Mental Health*, 6(2), 81–92.

Key Terms/Names in Part One

Acute Stress Disorder (ASD): A diagnostic category in which ASD is defined as a reaction to traumatic stress that occurs within four weeks after the immediate trauma.

Alarm Reaction Stage: The first stage in the General Adaptation Syndrome. During this stage, the body's physiological defenses mobilize to recognize and respond to the assault by the stressor.

Autonomic Nervous System: The body's emergency "generator;" that system which controls the body's "fight-flight syndrome."

Chronic stress: Stress that builds up cumulatively over time and produces a slower, wearing effect on an individual's ability to cope.

Distress: Harmful or unpleasant stress.

Epidemiology: The clinical science that studies the spread of diseases and their effects within a population.

Eustress: Positive stress that motivates and stimulates an individual,

General Adaptation Syndrome: The manner in which the body responds to stress. Selye held that it occurs in three stages: the alarm reaction; the stage of resistance; and the stage of exhaustion.

Hans Selye: Born in Vienna, Austria, in 1907, his lifetime work on the study of stress and its effects on the human body, including the identification of the general adaptation syndrome, has resulted in his being called "the father of stress." Dr. Selye was a physician and endocrinologist who authored more than 40 books and about 1700 articles and served as Director of the Institute of Experimental Medicine and Surgery at the University of Montreal. He died in Montreal in 1982, where he had lived for about 50 years.

Homeostasis: A psychological state of equilibrium within an individual.

Hypothalamus: Selye first described the system by which the body copes with stress, the hypothalamus-pituitary-adrenal system. The autonomic nervous system has its most important centers in that portion of the brain known as the hypothalamus; during stressful situations, the hypothalamus calls for the secretion of adrenocorticotrophic hormone (ACTH), triggering the body's response and linking the autonomic nervous system and the endocrine glands.

Mental Stressors: Those stressors, such as financial insecurity, poor interpersonal relationships, or fear of failure, which present themselves as social or psychological dangers.

Milieu internal: Bernard's term to describe the self-regulating mechanism that every healthy organism utilizes to maintain a constant physiological state.

Parasympathetic nervous system: The second part of the autonomic nervous system, this system is more active during times of emotional/physical equilibrium, building up and storing the body's reserve energy.

Physical stressors: Those stressors, e.g., diseases, accidents, or bacteria and viruses, which directly affect the body's functioning.

Posttraumatic stress disorder (PTSD): A syndrome of emotional and behavioral disturbance that follows exposure to a traumatic stressor or set of traumatically stressful experiences that is typically outside the range of normal, everyday experience for that person.

Sham Death: Also known as immobilization reflex, this term refers to a response to stress in which the victim "freezes" and inaction predominates.

Stage of Exhaustion: The third stage in the General Adaptation Syndrome. At this stage, the body has been unsuccessful in its response and is unable to respond or adjust to the stressor. In dealing with the stress of most occupations, the "worst case scenario" is death, either through physical disease or suicide.

Stage of Resistance: The second stage in the General Adaptation Syndrome. At this point, the body draws upon its natural and learned skills to confront or adjust to the stressor.

Stress: According to Selye, stress is the "body's non-specific response to any demand place upon it;" he also referred to it as "the rate of wear and tear in the body."

Sympathetic nervous system: A part of the autonomic nervous system, this system is activated during times of emotion or threat and increases the heart rate and blood pressure and assures distribution of blood throughout the body.

Syndrome: In clinical psychology, a set of symptoms and signs that occur in a fairly regular pattern from patient to patient, under a given set of circumstances, and with a specific set of causes (even though individual variations may be seen).

Vicarious traumatization: Post-traumatic stress reactions experienced by those who are indirectly exposed to traumatic events.

1

Stress, Traumatic Stress, and Posttraumatic Stress Syndromes

Laurence Miller

Introduction:
Stress, Chronic Stress, and Traumatic Stress

Feeling stressed? What exactly does that mean? How about *really* stressed? How about really, *traumatically* stressed? Let's begin with a little terminology. As typically used by mental health professionals, *stress* generally refers to one of two things. *Acute stress* typically takes the form of a traumatic critical incident that strikes relatively suddenly, catches the nervous system by surprise, disrupts the person's emotional equilibrium, and may leave an emotional scar in its wake. Examples include a motor vehicle accident, criminal assault, sudden natural disaster, or news of a traumatic loss. *Chronic stress* usually builds up cumulatively over time and produces a slower, wearing effect on the person's ability to cope, such as in an oppressive job setting, economic stress, relationship disruption, or persisting health crisis. Obviously, there can be some overlap; for example, when months of nerve-racking chronic stress over an ongoing company downsizing is punctuated by an acutely traumatizing episode of workplace violence committed by a disgruntled employee (Miller, 1998a, 2008c).

Many law enforcement and emergency service professionals know this process all too well. Chronic departmental pressures and creeping burnout may suddenly be compounded by a critical incident such as an officer-involved shooting or line-of-duty death (Miller, 2006a, 2007b). Add to this a dose of domestic discord and family stress (Miller, 2007a; Miller et al., 2010), and the cumulative pressure can overwhelm the coping resources of most officers.

9

Mention traumatic stress today, and almost every American will evoke September 11, 2001. Ironically, however, by the time that tragic event occurred, trauma psychologists and emergency crisis workers already knew a great deal about how to treat stress disorders and traumatic disability syndromes (Miller, 1998a, 2005), preventing even greater fear and ignorance from adding to the confusion and horror of that event. Accordingly, this chapter will describe the history, phenomenology, symptomatology, psychophysiology, and main principles of psychological treatment for stress reactions and traumatic stress syndromes.

History of the Stress and Trauma Concepts

Historically, the pendulum of interest in stress syndromes has swung back and forth between military and civilian traumas (Evans, 1992; Holbrook, 2011; Pizarro, 2006; Rosen, 1975; Trimble, 1981; Wilson, 1994). During warfare, rulers and generals have always had an interest in knowing as much as possible about factors that might adversely affect their fighting forces. To this end, doctors have been pressed into service to diagnose and treat soldiers with the aim of getting them back to the front lines as quickly as possible. In times of peace, attention turns to the everyday accidents and individual acts of mayhem that can produce stress, pain, and trauma in the lives of civilians.

The ancient Greeks and Romans wrote eloquently about the trials and travails that could afflict the warrior mind (Sherman, 2005). One of the first modern conceptualizations of posttraumatic stress was put forth by the army surgeon Hoffer who, in 1678, developed the concept of *nostalgia,* which he defined as deterioration in the physical and mental health of homesick soldiers. The cause of this malady was attributed to the formation of abnormally vivid images in the affected soldier's brain by battle-induced overexcitation of the "vital spirits." Here, in effect, was one of the first attempts to explain how a psychological event could affect brain functioning and, in turn, influence health and behavior.

With the 18th and 19th centuries came the giant machines of the Industrial Revolution to crush, grind, sear, scald, and flay scores of hapless workers who toiled nearby. At about the same time, a new form of high-speed transportation, the railroad, began strewing many of its passengers about in derailments and collisions. All too often, after the physical scars had healed, or even when injury to the body was minor or nonexistent, many factory or railway accident victims showed persisting disturbances in thought, feeling, and action that could not readily be explained by the conventional medical knowledge of the day.

In 1882, Erichson introduced the concept of *railway spine*, which he attributed to as-yet unobservable perturbations in the structure of the central nervous system caused by blows to the body. Other physicians of the time considered the strange disorders of sensation and movement to be due to disruptions in blood flow to the spinal cord or even to unobservable small hemorrhages.

While these organically minded physicians were squinting to discern structural microtraumas in nervous tissue, others expanded their gaze to view the origin of posttraumatic impairment syndromes as a psychological phenomenon, albeit straying none too far from the home base of neurophysiology. This was expressed in Page's (1895) theory of *nervous shock* which posited that a state of overwhelming fright or terror—not physical bangs and jolts—was the primary cause of traumatic impairment syndromes in railway and industrial accidents. Similarly, at around the same time, Oppenheim (1890) theorized that a strong enough stimulus perceived through the senses might jar the nervous system into a state of disequilibrium.

For his part, the great French physician Charcot (1887) regarded the effects of physical trauma as a form of *hysteria*, the symptoms arising as a consequence of disordered brain physiology caused by the terrifying memory of the traumatic event. In postulating the impact of a psychological force on the physical functioning of the brain, these late 19th century theories were reminiscent of Hoffer's conceptualization two centuries earlier, except that electrophysiological impulses now had replaced vital spirits as the underlying mechanism of the disorder.

Attention, however, soon shifted back to the field of battle. The American Civil War had introduced a new level of industrialized killing and, with it, a dramatic increase in reports of stress-related nervous ailments. Further advances in weapons technology during the First World War produced an alarming accumulation of horrid battlefield casualties from machine guns, poison gas, and especially long-range artillery. The latter led to the widely applied concept of *shell shock*, a form of psychological incapacitation initially believed to be caused by the brain-concussive effects of exploding shells. This wartime stress theory was actually not too different from the earlier concept of railway spine. In both cases, undocumentable effects on the nervous system were postulated on the basis of observed disorders in behavior.

To this end, physicians continued to marshal new findings about the role of the nervous system in regulating states of arousal and bodily homeostasis. Wilson and his colleagues (Frazier & Wilson, 1918; Mearburg & Wilson, 1918) described a syndrome in traumatized soldiers they called *irritable heart*, which they attributed to overstimulation of the sympathetic ("fight-or-flight") branch of the autonomic nervous system.

Even Sigmund Freud got into the act. No stranger to neuroscientific theory and practice himself (Miller, 1991), Freud (1920) regarded the tendency to remain mentally fixated on traumatic events as having a biological basis. But recurring recollections and nightmares of a frightening nature seemed to fly in the face of Freud's theory of the *pleasure principle*. Consequently, he was forced to consider a psychogenic cause—that traumatic dreams and other symptoms served the function of helping the traumatized person master the terrifying event by working it over and over in the victim's mind.

The persistently annoying failure of medical science to discover any definitive organic basis for these debilitating stress syndromes led to a gradual, if grudging acceptance of psychodynamic explanations, as the Freudian influence began to be felt more generally throughout psychiatry. This contributed to the replacement of shell shock by the more mentalistic-sounding term, *war neurosis*.

With this conceptual leap, physicians now no longer felt compelled to tether their diagnoses and treatments to ephemeral defects of nervous tissue. Accordingly, Ferenczi and his colleagues (1921) elaborated the basic model of traumatic neurosis that is still largely accepted today among psychodynamic theorists (Horowitz, 1986). Ferenczi's group described the central role of anxiety, the persistence of morbid apprehension, regression of the ego, the attempted reparative function of recurring nightmares, and the therapeutic use of abreaction and catharsis. For the most part, the patients themselves seemed to do well with the kinds of psychologically ventilative and supportive approaches that were provided by caring counselors, ministers, or nurses.

Continuing research and clinical experience expanded the theoretical base of trauma psychology. After surveying over 1,000 reports in the international literature published during the First World War, Southard (1919) concluded that shell shock, war neurosis, and similar syndromes were true psychoneuroses. Kardiner (1941) followed a group of patients with war neuroses for more than a decade and concluded that severe war trauma produced a kind of centripetal collapse of the ego that prevented these patients from adapting to and mastering life's subsequent challenges. Kardiner elaborated a conceptualization of trauma termed *physioneurosis* that is quite close to the modern concept of posttraumatic stress disorder (discussed on the following page). The features of Kardiner's physioneurosis included persistence of a startle response or irritability; a proclivity to explosive behavior; fixation on the trauma; an overall constriction of the personality; and a disturbed dream life, including vivid nightmares.

The experiences of the Second World War contributed surprisingly little to the development of new theories and treatments for wartime trauma, except for its redubbing as *battle fatigue*. In fact, resistance to the very concept of battle fatigue, with its implications of mental weakness and lack of moral resolve, was widespread in both medical and military circles. There was a war on, plenty of good Joes were getting killed and wounded, and the army had little sympathy for the pusillanimous whining of a few slackers and nervous nellies who couldn't buck up and pull their weight.

But it was becoming apparent that wartime psychological trauma could take place in circumstances other than the actual battlefield. In WWII, then in Korea and Vietnam, and most recently in the Persian Gulf wars, clinicians began to learn about disabling stress syndromes associated with large-scale bombings of civilian populations, prisoner of war and concentration camps, "brainwashing" of POWs, civilian atrocities, terrorism, and the threat of wholesale nuclear annihilation.

Today's daily media relentlessly continue to churn out more than ample examples of every imaginable species of human tragedy: war crimes, industrial injuries, plane crashes, auto accidents, rapes, assaults, domestic violence, child abuse, earthquakes, hurricanes, fires, floods, toxic spills, terrorist bombings —the list goes on (Miller, 1994, 1995, 1998a, 1999, 2000, 2005, 2007c, 2008b). In 1980, traumatic stress syndromes were finally codified as an identifiable type of psychopathological syndrome—*posttraumatic stress disorder* (PTSD)— in the American Psychiatric Association's official *Diagnostic and Statistical Manual of Mental Disorders* (APA, 1980, 1987, 1994, 2000).

Posttraumatic Stress Disorder

In clinical classification, a *syndrome* is defined as a set of symptoms and signs that occur in a fairly regular pattern from patient to patient, under a given set of circumstances, and with a specific set of causes (even though individual variations may be seen). By this definition, *posttraumatic stress disorder,* or PTSD, is a syndrome of emotional and behavioral disturbance that follows exposure to a traumatic stressor or set of traumatically stressful experiences that is typically outside the range of normal, everyday experience for that person. As a result, there develops a characteristic set of symptoms (APA, 3000; Meek, 1990; Merskey 1992; Miller, 1994, 1998a, 2008b, 2012; Modlin, 1983; Parker, 1990; Weinter, 1992).

Table 1—Posttraumatic Stress Disorder (PTSD)

Criterion A—Precipitating Traumatic Stressor: The person has been exposed to a traumatic event in which he/she was confronted with death or injury to self or others and which involved the experience of intense fear, helplessness, or horror.

Criterion B—Persistent Reexperiencing Symptoms: The person persistently or repeatedly re-experiences the traumatic event through waking recollections, disturbing dreams, dissociative reliving experiences ("flashbacks"), and/or psychological or physiological hyperreactivity to stimuli that directly or symbolically resemble the traumatic experience.

Criterion C—Persistent Avoidance Symptoms: The person: (1) behaviorally avoids a range of situations which remind, resemble, or symbolically represent the traumatic event, leading to a constriction of social activity; and/or (2) experiences a psychological numbing to outside stimuli which constricts his/her emotional responsivity and interpersonal interaction.

Criterion D—Persistent Arousal Symptoms: The person experiences increased anxiety, hypervigilance, irritability and anger, exaggerated startle response, difficulty sleeping, and/or impaired attention, concentration, and/or memory.

Onset of PTSD may be **acute** (duration less than 3 months), **chronic** (duration more than 3 months), or **delayed** (onset is 6 months or more following the traumatic stressor).

Anxiety. The subject describes a continual state of free-floating anxiety or nervousness. There is a constant gnawing apprehension that something terrible is about to happen. He or she maintains an intensive hypervigilance, scanning the environment for the least hint of impending threat or danger. Panic attacks may be occasional or frequent.

Physiological Arousal. The subject's autonomic nervous system is always on red alert. He or she experiences increased bodily tension in the form of muscle tightness, tremors, restlessness, fatigue, heart palpitations, breathing difficulties, dizziness, headaches, and gastrointestinal or urinary disturbances. About one-half of PTSD subjects show a classic startle reaction: surprised by an unexpected door slam, telephone ring, sneeze, or even just hearing their name called, the subject may literally "jump" out of his seat and then spend the next few minutes trembling with fear and anxiety.

Irritability. There is a pervasive chip-on-the-shoulder edginess, impatience, loss of humor, and quick anger over seemingly trivial matters. Friends get ticked off, coworkers shun the subject, and family members may be verbally abused and alienated. A particularly common complaint is the patient's increased sensitivity to children's noisiness or the family's bothering questions.

Avoidance and Denial. The subject tries to blot out the event from his or her mind. He avoids thinking about the traumatic event and shuns news articles, radio programs, or TV shows that remind him of the incident. "I just don't want to talk about it," is the standard response, and the individual may claim to have forgotten important aspects of the event. Some of this is a deliberate, conscious effort to avoid reminders of the trauma; part of it also involves an involuntary psychic numbing that blunts most incoming threatening stimuli. The emotional coloring of this denial may range from blasé indifference to nail-biting anxiety.

Intrusion. Despite the subject's best efforts to keep the traumatic event out of his or her mind, the horrifying incident pushes its way into consciousness, often rudely and abruptly, in the form of intrusive images of the event by day and frightening dreams at night. In the most extreme cases, the individual may experience dissociative flashbacks or reliving experiences in which he seems to be mentally transported back to the traumatic scene in all its sensory and emotional vividness, sometimes losing touch with current reality. More commonly, the intrusive recollection is described as a persistent psychological demon that "won't let me forget" the terrifying events surrounding the trauma.

Repetitive Nightmares. Even sleep offers little respite. Sometimes the subject's nightmares replay the actual traumatic event; more commonly, the dreams echo the general theme of the trauma, but miss the mark in terms of specific content. For example, an individual traumatized in an auto accident may dream of falling off a cliff or having a wall collapse on him. A sexual assault victim may dream of being attacked by vicious dogs or drowning in a muddy pool. The emotional intensity of the original traumatic experience is retained, but the dream partially disguises the event itself. This symbolic reconfiguration of dream material is, of course, one of the main pillars of Freudian psychoanalytic theory (Miller, 1991, 2012).

Impaired Concentration and Memory. The subject complains of having gotten "spacey," "fuzzy," or "ditsy." He or she has trouble remembering names, tends to misplace objects, loses the train of conversations, or can't keep his mind focused on work, reading material, family activities, or other matters. He may worry that he has brain damage or that "I'm losing my mind."

Sexual Inhibition. Over 90 percent of PTSD subjects report decreased sexual activity and interest; this may further strain an already stressed-out marital relationship. In some cases, complete impotence or frigidity may occur, especially in cases where the traumatic event involved sexual assault.

Withdrawal and Isolation. The subject shuns friends, neighbors, and family members and just wants to be left alone. He has no patience for the petty, trivial concerns of everyday life—bills, gossip, news events—and gets annoyed at being bothered with these piddles. The hurt feelings this engenders in those he rebuffs may spur retaliatory avoidance, leading to a vicious cycle of rejection and recrimination.

Impulsivity and Instability. More rarely, the trauma survivor may take sudden trips, move from place to place, walk off his job, disappear from his family for prolonged periods, uncharacteristically engage in drunken binges, gambling sprees, or romantic trysts, make excessive purchases, or take dangerous physical or legal risks. It is as if the trauma has goaded the subject into a "what-the-hell—life-is-short" attitude that overcomes his usual good judgment and common sense. Obviously, not every instance of irresponsible behavior can be blamed on trauma, but a connection may be suspected when this kind of activity is definitely out of character for that person and follows an identifiable traumatic event. Far from taking such walks on the wild side, however, the majority of trauma survivors continue to suffer in numbed and shattered silence.

Acute Stress Disorder

Acute stress disorder (ASD) was introduced as a diagnostic category into the DSM-IV (APA, 1994) primarily to help identify those at risk of developing later PTSD. ASD is defined as a reaction to the traumatic stress that occurs within four weeks after the index trauma. Although ASD focuses more on dissociative symptoms than PTSD, it also includes symptoms of reexperiencing, avoidance, and hyperarousal. Preliminary prospective studies suggest that between 60% and 80% of individuals meeting criteria for ASD following a traumatic event will meet criteria for PTSD up to two years later.

The ASD diagnosis has been contentious since its inception. It has been criticized on the grounds of being conceptually and empirically redundant with PTSD, as well as pathologizing common symptoms of psychological distress in the immediate aftermath of trauma (Koch et al., 2006). However, it recognizes that some patients may show traumatic reactions close in time to the injurious event and reinforces the importance of early treatment where this is clinically indicated.

Psychological Theories of the Trauma Response

As noted in the historical introduction, theorizing about traumatic disability syndromes has typically swung between mentalistic and physicalistic accounts. Kretschmer (1926) described two classes of behavioral response that organisms use to ward off attack. The first he characterized as the *violent motor reaction*, exemplified by the wild flailing response many animals show when trying to escape injury or confinement. The counterpart to this in human clinical conditions, he believed, would occur in the form of dissociative fugue states, convulsive paroxysms, and violent emotional attacks with subsequent amnesia and tremors.

Kretschmer's (1926) second kind of reaction was called the *sham death* or *immobilization reflex,* in which inaction and seemingly stuporous features predominate. Many animals "freeze" when confronted with a threat; this immobilization serves to obscure the identity or whereabouts of the threatened party or conveys a message of innocuous nonchallenge that will hopefully deflect the confrontation. Human analogs to this second pattern might include hypnoid states, hysterical sensory or motor impairment, speechlessness, or "spells" of many kinds, reminiscent of the posttraumatic reactions to threat and injury.

Ludwig (1972) revised and expanded Kretschmer's (1926) formulation by positing a pervasive natural tendency for animals and humans to react in progressively more primitive ways when confronted with potentially dangerous and inescapable situations. Under such conditions, organisms readily and automatically resort to behaviors appropriate at earlier stages of development, behaviors that appear regressive or "immature." These include babbling, rocking, crying, vivid fantasizing, mute withdrawal, incontinence, and so on—the kinds of reaction often associated with "shell shock" or other kinds of acute traumatic states.

Modlin (1983) has succinctly characterized the psychodynamic explanation of PTSD as follows. When faced with definable external danger, the human organism mobilizes for action. If, however, the protective fight-flight reaction is prevented or inhibited from operating, then the mind is suffused with an excessive amount of stimulation. On the psychological level, the alarm devices of the ego keep pace with the psychological alerting. The normal ego has stored energy available to bind or discharge excessive amounts of excitation, but if the discharge is blocked and homeostatic balance is disrupted, free-floating anxiety and continuing tension result.

In other cases, such as posttraumatic amnesia produced by a closed head injury (Miller, 1993), the victim may first become aware that the accident occurred when consciousness is later regained. Realistic external danger no longer exists to be met or handled in the present. The fight-flight mechanism is temporarily mobilized, but finds no substantial target to act against or from which to escape. Action, in these cases, is not actually blocked but is rather simply "too late" and therefore irrelevant. One immediate task the ego must accomplish in this kind of situation is to regain its suddenly disrupted contact with reality and to grasp and justify what has occurred. The bewildered ego is flooded

LIBRARY

with alarm and anxiety because it has failed in its self-preservative duty. When this psychological homeostatic task fails, panic may result.

The process of coping with traumatic stress through alternation between intrusive re-experiencing and denial is seen by some authorities (Brom & Kleber, 1989) as a normal, adaptive process. In effect, the individual is self-titrating the "dose" of the traumatic recollections so that he or she is not overwhelmed by the intensity of emotions and other reactions that the memories evoke. The intrusive re-experiencing may offer the opportunity to assimilate the experience —to mentally "digest" it—as well as to revise the expectations and general worldview of the individual.

Almost always, the response to significant trauma involves a strong existential component. Coping, virtually by definition, involves a search for meaning (Yalom, 1980). Brom & Kleber (1989) and Janoff-Bulman (1992) point out that people ordinarily prefer to perceive the world as organized, predictable, and comprehensible. A serious traumatic life event shatters one's assumptions and beliefs about the world and oneself, prompting the typical reaction of "Why me?" One way to overcome the perceived chaos and create some order in the situation is to attribute an active role to the self in circumstances where the victim was actually powerless; this is often referred to as *cognitive* or *interpretive control* (Thompson, 1981). In this way, the victim tries to preserve at least the illusion of control and thereby diminish the threat of recurrence. Many people would rather blame themselves than feel helpless because, if the tragic event was somehow my fault, at least there was *some* reason for it—and potentially something I can do differently if there is a "next time," which provides a sense of predictability and control.

Psychophysiology and Neuropsychology of Stress and Stress Syndromes

Psychophysiology of Adaptation to Stress

With the rise of the scientific method, clinicians began to see the workings of the body as interlocking sets of self-regulating systems (McEwen & Lasley, 2002; Southwick et al., 2008; Weiner, 1977, 1992). The modern study of the psychophysiology of stress is generally regarded as beginning with Claude Bernard's (1865) concept of the *milieu internal,* a term he used to describe the self-regulating mechanism that every healthy organism utilizes to maintain a constant physiological state. This equilibrium could be disrupted by stress or disease, but as long as the organism survived, it would endeavor to restore and maintain this optimal internal state.

In the early 20th century, Walter Cannon (1914, 1939) used the term *homeostasis* to refer also to a psychological state of equilibrium that could be derailed by stress but that the organism would attempt to re-regulate back into health. Cannon also urged physicians to consider the effects of psychological stress on physiological functioning, ushering in the modern study of psychosomatic illness (Alexander, 1950; Weiner, 1977, 1992).

Probably the most famous account of the stress response comes from the work of Hans Selye (1956, 1973, 1975) whose active research spanned the decades from the 1930s to the 1970s. Selye developed the concept of the *General Adaptation Syndrome,* or GAS, which he believed to define the physiological response to stressors of almost every type—from infections and toxins to social stress and interpersonal power struggles. The GAS was said to consist of three overlapping, but distinct stages.

In the *stage of alarm,* the organism marshals its physiological resources to cope with the stressor. For Selye, this involves activation of the hypothalamic-pituitary-adrenal axis, resulting in the increased production of cortisol by the adrenal cortex. This hormone has an anti-inflammatory effect on the body and also has neuroactive and psychoactive effects on the brain. The alarm-stage stress response also mobilizes the sympathetic nervous system and increases secretion of adrenalin from the adrenal medulla.

In the *stage of resistance,* the body goes into a kind of extended overdrive, as all systems stay on high alert while the organism is coping with the stressor, which may be anything from a bad flu to a bad divorce. In the best case, the organism rallies and the crisis is eventually passed, with the individual becoming more resilient in the process. In this case, Nietzsche (1969) is right: "Whatever doesn't kill me makes me stronger." Indeed, in some instances, adaptive responding to stress can lead to *transcendent coping* and *posttraumatic growth* (Calhoun & Tedeschi, 1999; Tedeschi & Calhoun, 1995, 2004; Tedeschi & Kilmer, 2005).

But no organism can stay on red alert forever. If the crisis is not resolved, at some point the organism reaches the *stage of exhaustion,* in which physiological reserves are finally depleted and the organism begins to deteriorate and may even die. Sorry, Nietzsche, but in this case, "Whatever doesn't kill me … can make me really, really sick."

More recent research has revealed that the stress response may be more graded and nuanced, depending on the individual. For example, Dienstbier (1989; 1991) has used the term *toughness* to refer to a distinct reaction pattern to stress—mental, emotional, or physiological—that characterizes animals and humans who cope effectively with stress (Miller, 1989, 1990). Two main physiological systems underlie the toughness response.

The first involves a pathway from the brain's hypothalamus to the sympathetic branch of the autonomic nervous system and from there to the adrenal medulla. The sympathetic nervous system, or SNS, is responsible for the heart-pounding, fight-or-flight response that mobilizes body and mind to deal with challenging situations. As part of this response, the adrenal gland releases its main hormone, adrenalin.

The second system involved in the toughness response also begins with the hypothalamus but acts through the pituitary gland, which in turn stimulates the adrenal cortex to release cortisol—the chief stress hormone involved in Selye's triphasic GAS response. Together, the pattern of SNS-adrenal medulla and pituitary-adrenal cortex responses to stressful challenges characterizes the nature of the toughness trait.

It is the flexibility and graded nature of the response of these two interrelated systems that define an individual's physiological resilience or toughness. In resiliently tough organisms — animal or human — the normal, everyday activity of the two systems is low and modulated; tough individuals are at relative ease under most ordinary circumstances, and their physiological responses reflect this relative quiescence. But when faced with a stressful challenge or threat, the SNS-adrenal medulla system springs into action quickly and efficiently, while the pituitary-adrenal cortex system remains relatively stable. As soon as the emergency is over, the adrenalin response returns quickly to normal, while the cortisol response stays low.

The smoothness and efficiency of the physiological arousal pattern are what characterize the psychophysiological toughness response—a response that has important aftereffects on the brain. Such a restrained reaction prevents depletion of catecholamines, important brain neurotransmitters that affect mood and motivation.

However, the physiological reactions of less resiliently tough individuals tend to be excessive and longer lasting, even in the face of everyday hassles. The result is more intense and disorganizing arousal, less effective coping, and faster depletion of brain catecholamines, which can lead to helplessness and depression. With each tribulation, major or minor, less resilient individuals tend to over-respond, unable to do much about the current situation and having little confidence in their future ability to cope.

That's where the real psychological significance of psychophysiological toughness comes in. Dienstbier (1989) points out that the toughness response—or its absence—interacts with a person's cognitive appraisal of his or her own ability to cope with challenge. This in turn contributes to the person's self-image as an effective master of adversity or a helpless reactor — a self-assessment that influences later psychophysiological reactions to stress.

Neuropsychology of PTSD and the Trauma Response

In recent years, several theoretical models have been proposed to more fully describe the brain mechanisms that may account for the trauma response and the symptoms of PTSD and other stress response syndromes (Miller, 1990, 1998a). Kolb's (1987) theory of PTSD takes as its starting point the concept, first articulated by Freud (1920), of a *cortical stimulus barrier* that serves to protect the individual from being overwhelmed by excessive stimulation. Massive psychic trauma may overcome this stimulus barrier and, according to this hypothesis, produce synaptic changes by way of neurophysiological sensitization. If continued at high intensity and repeated frequently over time, the neural processes mediating discriminative perception, learning, and memory may become impaired. High levels of cortisol appear to suppress neuronal functioning in the brain's hippocampus, which plays an important role in memory as well as an important feedback role in the modulation of the stress response. Oscillations in the brain's stress-memory system may thereby account for the cycles of intrusion and avoidance seen in PTSD. At high enough levels, cortisol may even result in death of neurons in the hippocampus (Parker, 1990; Sapolsky, 1984).

Kolb (1987) identifies another limbic structure, the amygdala, as interacting with the hippocampal system in mediating stress effects. Together with certain other structures, the hippocampus and the amygdala comprise the limbic system, which is the brain network involved in the functions of learning, memory, motivation, and emotion. For its part, the amygdala functions as a sort of rapid-decision, "good-or-bad" emotional evaluator of environmental stimuli. Stress overload in this system may force the individual into a state of hair-trigger hypersensitivity, in which a multitude of internal and external stimuli lead to continued heightened arousal. Recurrent intense emotional arousal further sensitizes and simultaneously disrupts those processes related to habituation and learning, leading to an exacerbation of PTSD symptoms.

With excessive limbic sensitization and diminished capacity for adaptive information-processing by the cortical stimulus barrier, subcortical and brain-stem structures escape from inhibitory cortical control and repeatedly reactivate the perceptual, cognitive, affective, and somatic clinical expressions related to the original trauma. These abnormally reactivated memory loops are projected into daytime consciousness as intrusive thoughts and images, and into sleep as traumatic nightmares.

Cortical neuronal changes are responsible for impairment of perceptual discrimination, reduced impulse control, and affective blunting. Excessive activation or release of subcortical systems results in conditioned startle reactions, irritability, hyperalertness, intrusive thoughts, repetitive fearful nightmares, and psychophysiological symptoms such as heart palpitations, panic attacks, musculoskeletal pain, headache, and gastrointestinal disturbances. The repeated reminders of the traumatic event associated with somatic symptoms disrupt the patient's body-image and self-concept and are responsible for numbing and avoidance behaviors such as social withdrawal, alcohol and drug abuse, and compulsive risk-taking, as well as emotional disturbances that include depression, survivor guilt, shame, and suicidality.

Deitz's neuropsychological theory (1992) attempts to extend Kolb's formulation (1987) by conceptualizing a dual pathway of traumatic information processing in the brain. The first system links perceptual evaluation and emotional tone with the cognitive and language regions of the brain, allowing the individual to "make sense" of the experience, no matter how frightening or painful. A second, independent limbic system pathway bypasses the conscious evaluative system and feeds directly into the emotion-memory complex of the hypothalamus, hippocampus, and amygdala.

For survival purposes, it is critical that the amygdala-processed positive/negative, good/bad discrimination be made as fast as possible to allow time for the appropriate fight-or-flight or approach-avoidance response to take place. However, in order to link the emotional tone to neocortical processing—the conscious feeling and meaning connected to language and abstract thought—the second, phylogenetically newer pathway is needed. Where these two systems are out of sync, as in the case of severe trauma, the conscious cognitive-linguistic memory of the trauma may be "repressed," while the emotional reaction persists in response to stimuli the patient may not even recognize. Thus, he or she may be further distressed by the "senselessness" of their reaction.

Charney et al. (1993) have elaborated a psychobiological model of PTSD that appears to characterize it as a *neurosensitization syndrome* (Miller, 1997). According to this model, sensitization by fear associated with traumatic stress results in a change in excitability of amygdalar neurons. This in turn influences the functioning of a variety of limbic and brainstem structures involved in the somatic and autonomic expression of fear and anxiety. For example, a reduced activation threshold of the emotionally reactive locus coeruleus results in increased levels of motivating and exciting neurotransmitters at several brain sites. Further, locus coeruleus activation of the amygdala enhances memory retrieval. By this mechanism, some of the acute neurobiological responses to trauma may facilitate the pathologically entrenched encoding of traumatic memories.

In patients with PTSD, specific sensory phenomena, such as sights, sounds, and smells circumstantially related to the traumatic event, persistently produce a recurrence of traumatic memories and flashbacks. The brain regions mediating these processes include the amygdala, locus coeruleus, hippocampus, and sensory cortex. Specifically, the amygdala functions to attach a fearful or anxious emotional tone to neutral stimuli associated with the trauma. The functional interchange between the amygdala and the sensory cortices, where memories of each sense are stored, may be critical for the ability of specific sensory to elicit traumatic memories. In addition, activation of the amygdala may also be responsible for the highly correlated set of behaviors associated with traumatic memories. Thus, the brain's response to trauma serves to heighten the fearfulness of traumatic memories at the same time as it impairs the overall ability of the individual to learn, remember, adapt, cope, and move on.

Risk and Resiliency Factors for Traumatic Factors for Traumatic Stress Responses

As noted above, not everyone who experiences a traumatic critical incident develops the same degree of psychological disability, and there is significant variability among individuals in terms of their degree of susceptibility and resilience to stressful events (McEwen & Lasley, 2002; Miller, 1998a, 1998b, 2008a; Waugh et al., 2008; Weiner, 1992; Westphal et al., 2008). While many individuals are able to resolve acute critical incident stress through the use of informal social support and other adaptive activities (Bowman, 1997, 1999; Carlier & Gersons, 1995; Carlier et al., 1997; Gentz, 1991), in other cases, critical incident stress that is not resolved adequately or treated appropriately in the first few days or weeks may evolve into a number of disabling psychological traumatic disability syndromes (Miller, 1997, 1998, 2008a, 2012).

Risk factors for PTSD or other traumatic disability syndromes in law enforcement officers (Paton et al., 2000) may be: (1) *biological,* including genetic predisposition and inborn heightened physiological reactivity to stimuli; (2) *historical,* such as prior exposure to trauma or other coexisting adverse life circumstances; (3) *psychological,* including poor coping and problem-solving skills, learned helplessness, and a history of dysfunctional interpersonal relationships; and (4) *environmental/contextual,* such as inadequate departmental or societal support.

Resiliency or *protective factors* are traits, characteristics, and circumstances that make some people more resistant to traumatic stress effects (Bowman, 1997, 1999; Hoge et al., 2007; Miller, 1990, 1998a, 1998b). As a general trait factor, features associated with resilience to adverse life events in both children and adults (Bifulco et al., 1987; Brewin et al., 2000; Garmezy, 1993; Garmezy et al., 1984; Luthar, 1991; Miller, 1990, 1998a, 1998b; Rubenstein et al., 1989; Rutter, 1985, 1987; Rutter et al., 1976; Werner, 1989; Werner & Smith, 1982; Zimrin, 1986) include: (1) good cognitive skills and intelligence, especially verbal intelligence, and good verbal communication skills; (2) self-mastery, an internal locus of control, good problem-solving skills, and the ability to plan and anticipate consequences; (3) an easy temperament, not overly reactive emotional style, good sociability, and positive response to and from others; and (4) a warm, close relationship with at least one caring adult or mentor, other types of family and community ties and support systems, and a sense of social cohesion as being part of a larger group or community. Indeed, on close inspection, these appear to be virtually the opposite of the traits of impulsivity, neuroticism, and poor social connection and support that characterize those most vulnerable to trauma.

Kobasa (1979a, 1979b; Kobasa et al., 1982) introduced the concept of *hardiness,* which has been defined as a stable personality resource consisting of three psychological attitudes and cognitions (Maddi & Khoshaba, 1994): (1) *commitment* = an ability to turn events into something meaningful and important, something worth working for and seeing through to completion; (2) *control* = the belief that, with appropriate effort, individuals can influence the course of events around them, that they are not helpless, but effective influencers of their fate and the responses of others; and (3) *challenge* = a belief that fulfillment in life results from the growth and wisdom gained from overcoming and managing difficult or challenging experiences, a realistically confident but not reckless "bring-'em-on" attitude.

Similarly, Antonovsky (1979, 1987, 1990) has proposed a stress/health-mediating personality construct termed *sense of coherence,* or SOC, which is expressed in the form of three component orientations or beliefs: (1) *comprehensibility* = events deriving from a person's internal and external environments in the course of living that are structured, predictable, and explicable. Things "make sense" and therefore seem less overwhelming; (2) *manageability* = the individual possesses the resources to meet the demands posed by the adverse events—the person feels realistically in control, not helpless; (3) *meaningfulness* = the person conceptualizes the adversity as a challenge worthy of his or her investment and engagement—there is an intellectual and emotional satisfaction in tackling a tough problem and seeing it through to conclusion. In this model, the higher a person's SOC, the better he or she will be able to clarify the nature of a particular stressor, select the resources appropriate to that specific situation, and be open to feedback that allows the adaptive modification of behavior when necessary.

Applying these concepts specifically to law enforcement personnel, Paton et al. (2000) have delineated a core set of resiliency factors that enable police officers to withstand and even prevail in the face of seemingly overwhelming trauma. These include: superior training and skill development, what I (Miller,

2006b) have characterized as the ITTS ("It's The Training, Stupid") principle; a learning attitude toward the profession, to which I (Miller, 2006b) have referred as building a "culture of knowledge"; higher intelligence and problem-solving ability; good verbal and interpersonal skills; adequate emotional control and adaptive coping mechanisms; a sense of realistic optimism; and the ability and willingness to seek help and support where necessary. Note that these characteristics closely track the core personality features associated with resilience to stress that have been identified in the more general studies cited earlier.

Psychological Treatment of Stress and Trauma Syndromes

The variety of PTSD syndromes described above, and the complex neuropsychodynamics that contribute to the unique manifestations in individual cases, necessarily demand that mental health and law enforcement professionals show some degree of practical flexibility in their treatment of traumatized individuals. The comprehensive treatment of patients with traumatic disability syndromes has been considered elsewhere (Miller, 1998a, 2006b, 2008a, 2008b), and other chapters of this book describe a range of specialized techniques for law enforcement stress management.

A treatment-oriented conceptualization that takes into account the neuropsychobiological bases of PTSD is Everly's (1990, 1993, 1995) two-factor model of PTSD treatment, consisting of (1) *neurobiological hypersensitivity* involving heightened nervous system and endocrine responsivity, and (2) *psychological hypersensitivity* involving disruptions and transfigurations in the individual's worldview and self-concept. Accordingly, the following is an outline of a recently developed comprehensive protocol for proactive and follow-up treatment of traumatic stress syndromes in law enforcement and emergency services personnel that has evolved out of this author's own work in stress management and crisis intervention in a wide variety of settings, including law enforcement and emergency services, schools and workplaces, and medical and mental health facilities (Miller, 1994, 1995, 1998a, 1999, 2000, 2005, 2006b, 2007c, 2008a, 2008b, 2008c).

The Best Form of Crisis Intervention Is Crisis Prevention

The best way to manage a crisis is to prevent it from occurring in the first place. Hardly a day goes by in police work that opportunities for staving off crises do not occur. In fact, police officers may actually have a special advantage over other emergency service professionals in this regard. Firefighters and paramedics are, by definition, responders to emergencies that have already begun or worsened—an explosion in a toxic chemical plant or an auto accident with injuries, for example. These professionals can react, but they usually can't predict, anticipate, or prevent; few communities have "fire patrols" or "medical patrols."

The patrol function of police officers, however, places them in a unique position to see trouble coming and to take action before it boils over to a critical level of harm. Of course, not every law enforcement crisis can be anticipated or averted, but—recalling the adaptive personality traits cited earlier—those officers who are particularly successful in their jobs seem to have a talent for keeping problems under control, yet being able to take assertive action when necessary.

All Successful Crisis Intervention Involves Crisis Prevention

This is the corollary to the above principle. No matter what point in the crisis, it is virtually never too late to intervene successfully and prevent further harm, disability, or trauma from occurring. For example, talking two intoxicated citizens out of a brawl prevents them from incurring physical injuries or legal charges. Quickly breaking up the fight once they have grabbed each other and tussled on the ground prevents them from racking up more serious arrestable charges and from incurring more than scrapes and bruises, while at the same time preventing bystanders from becoming involved and being arrested or injured themselves. Both of these proactive measures also prevent physical injury and stressful traumatization to the officers themselves.

If one combatant stabs the other or bashes him in the head with a bottle, restraining and arresting the assailant and calling for paramedic assistance and additional police backup prevents the victim from being killed by another blow or stab wound, while at the same time preventing injury to the officer from a now clearly violent subject. Finally, how the arrest was handled, and making sure one or more officers remaining on-scene after the melee is over to reassure frightened or angry citizens that the officers' actions were justifiable and in the interest of public safety, may prevent a potential civil disturbance or simply smoldering community animosity arising from the original brawl and the police action used to break it up.

Stress Management and Crisis Intervention Are Interrelated

It is a principle of my overall approach to law enforcement training (Miller, 2006b, 2008a) that stress management cannot be separated from crisis intervention, as each comprises an essential component of the other. Crises are most likely to arise under conditions of stress, and that stress is almost further exacerbated by the very crises they provoke. It's all about vicious cycles—and turning them into positive cycles. As reviewed in the earlier sections on psychophysiology and neuropsychology, stress provokes and exacerbates crises and crises elevate stress. Effective crisis intervention reduces stress, which in turn makes crisis management easier, which further increases resilience—psychophysiological "toughness"—and confidence for future crises. Officers who know how to manage their own stress are less likely to be goaded or baited into escalating a confrontation with a citizen into a crisis and will be better able to use clear thinking and effective action if a crisis unavoidably occurs.

Therefore, effective stress management *is* an important crisis intervention skill, a form of primary prevention. Whether the stresses involve citizens in a officer's patrol area or hassles and crises in the officer's own life, learning to deal constructively with life's challenges constitutes a primary layer of *psychological body armor* (Miller, 2008a) for deflecting the worst consequences of a stressful critical incident or life circumstance.

Stress Management and Crisis Intervention Principles Are Universal

The psychophysiological toughness training principles of stress management and crisis intervention should be seen as broad-purpose skills that can be applied to a wide range of critical situations. This does not mean that one size fits all: training and experience are still required to be effective in any particular domain of law enforcement action—vehicle stop, suspect search, building entry, and so on—since each domain contains distinct features and, indeed, each individual crisis will contain unique elements (Garner, 2005).

But just as emergency medical care for diverse injuries and illness (gunshot wound, heart attack, epileptic seizure) follows certain universal principles (assess vital signs, establish heart rhythm and airway, scan for internal injuries), so it is with emergency crisis intervention. This is all the more true inasmuch as one kind of crisis can easily transform into another: a domestic squabble turns into a hostage-barricade situation; a citizen dispute becomes a civil disturbance; a burglary investigation jumps over into an assault-of-officer or suicide-by-cop episode. Thus, understanding the phenomenon and mastering the stress management and crisis intervention skills in this book's subsequent chapters will enable current and future officers to handle a broad range of law enforcement crisis situations.

20/20 Hindsight = 20/20 Insight = 20/20 Foresight

20/20 hindsight has gotten a bum rap, as it is often equated with second-guessing, Monday-morning quarterbacking, or useless self-flagellation. But in reality, looking back on an unsuccessful action, analyzing it, and trying to learn from it is an absolutely essential process for developing any skill—*if* this analysis by *hindsight* leads to a certain degree of *insight* into what went wrong and how it happened. This insight into what happened last time can then be used to create a new set of options and action plans for next time—*foresight*. What we're talking about here is the whole concept of learning from experience and developing expertise and practical wisdom for future application.

In fact, this 20/20 principle is used all the time in law enforcement, emergency services, and the military, under the heading of *operational debriefing*. Within law enforcement, it is an essential component of hostage negotiation team training and undercover operations, to cite two examples. Indeed, all professionals engage in an ongoing process of continuing education and self-improvement—a *culture of knowledge* (Miller, 2006b). The present volume will continue to contribute to that knowledge in the field of law enforcement stress management.

Learning Never Stops, or "It's The Training, Stupid" (ITTS)

Nobody is born knowing anything. Consistent with the 20/20 principle, all the natural skill and talent in the world won't make you an expert in any subject, unless you develop and train that talent to the fullest extent possible. Consider the professional athlete, artist, or musician (Hays & Brown, 2004). Certainly, without a natural gift for his or her sport or skill, training alone won't take the individual past his upper limit of capability. But raw talent alone is insufficient: the athlete or performer has to work at developing that skill to its ultimate level in order to attain excellence and stay in that upper one-percent zone, to continue to push the envelope. Indeed, the best form of stress management is proper training and knowledge because the more automatic, flexible, and generalized a particular area of skill and expertise, the less surprised and overwhelmed an officer will be in any situation.

In fact, research shows that those individuals at the top of their fields never coast; if anything, they actually put in many times more effort than those with less innate talent. That is, they take what's great and devote extraordinary effort to making it greater (Briggs, 1988; Simonton, 1994). That's why for true professionals in any field, learning, training, and teaching never stop. In the *culture of knowledge*, we keep growing and, as we do so, we contribute to the growth of our colleagues, our organization, and our profession.

Conclusions

The fields of psychotraumatology and stress management have expanded to the point where no single professional can be an expert in every syndrome or technique. The positive flip side of this information expansion is that so much is now known and so many strategies are now available for identifying, preventing, responding to, and successfully treating stress syndromes that arise in law enforcement, emergency services, and other areas. But, despite this diversity, the basic principles of effective stress management and crisis intervention are remarkably consistent and generalizable. Thus, the mental health or law enforcement professional who acquires expertise in this field will be a vital asset is dealing with the critical challenges of our new century.

References

Alexander, F. (1950). *Psychosomatic medicine: Its principles and applications.* New York: Norton.

American Psychiatric Association (1980). *Diagnostic and statistical manual of mental disorders* (3rd ed.). Washington DC: American Psychiatric Association.

American Psychiatric Association (1987). *Diagnostic and statistical manual of mental disorders* (3rd ed.-rev.). Washington DC: American Psychiatric Association.

American Psychiatric Association (1994). *Diagnostic and statistical manual of mental disorders* (4th ed.). Washington DC: American Psychiatric Association.

American Psychiatric Association (2000). *Diagnostic and statistical manual of mental disorders* (4th ed., text revision). Washington DC: American Psychiatric Association.

Antonovsky, A. (1979). *Health, stress, and coping.* San Francisco: Jossey-Bass.

Antonovsky, A. (1987). *Unraveling the mystery of health: How people manage stress and stay well.* San Francisco: Jossey-Bass.

Antonovsky, A. (1990). Personality and health: Testing the sense of coherence model. In H.S. Friedman (Ed.), *Personality and disease* (pp. 155–177). New York: Wiley.

Bernard, C. (1865). *Introduction a l'etude de la medecine experimentale.* Paris: Bailliere et Fils.

Bifulco, A.T., Brown, G.W. & Harris, T.O. (1987). Childhood loss of parent, lack of adequate parental care and adult depression: A replication. *Journal of Affective Disorders, 12,* 115–128.

Bowman, M. (1997). *Individual differences in posttraumatic response: Problems with the adversity-distress connection.* Mahwah, NJ: Erlbaum.

Bowman, M.L. (1999). Individual differences in posttraumatic distress: Problems with the DSM-IV model. *Canadian Journal of Psychiatry, 44,* 21–33.

Brewin, C.R., Andrews, B., Valentine, J.D. (2000). Meta-analysis of risk factors for posttraumatic stress disorder in trauma-exposed adults. *Journal of Consulting and Clinical Psychology, 68,* 748–766.

Briggs, J. (1988). *Fire in the crucible: The alchemy of creative genius.* New York: St. Martin's Press.

Brom, D. & Kleber, R.J. (1989). Prevention of posttraumatic stress disorders. *Journal of Traumatic Stress, 2,* 335–351.

Calhoun, L.G. & Tedeschi, R.G. (1999). *Facilitating posttraumatic growth.* Mahwah, NJ: Erlbaum.

Cannon, W.B. (1914). The interrelations of emotions as suggested by recent physiological researchers. *American Journal of Psychology, 25,* 256–282.

Cannon, W.B. (1939). *The wisdom of the body.* Philadelphia: Norton.

Carlier, I.V.E. & Gersons, B.P.R. (1995). Partial PTSD: The issue of psychological scars and the occurrence of PTSD symptoms. *Journal of Nervous and Mental Disease, 183,* 107–109.

Carlier, I.V.E., Lamberts, R.D. & Gersons, B.P.R. (1997). Risk factors for posttraumatic stress symptomatology in police officers: A prospective analysis. *Journal of Nervous and Mental Disease, 185,* 498–506.

Charcot, J.M. (1887). *Lecons sur les maladies du system nerveux* (Vol. 3). Paris: Progress Medical.

Charney, D.S., Deutsch, A.Y., Krystal, J.H., Southwick, S.M. & Davis, M. (1993). Psychobiologic mechanisms of posttraumatic stress disorder. *Archives of General Psychiatry, 50,* 294–305.

Dienstbier, R. A. (1989). Arousal and physiological toughness: Implications for mental and physical health. *Psychological Review,* 96:84–100.

Dienstbier, R.A. (1991). Behavioral correlates of sympathoadrenal reactivity: The toughness model. *Medical Science of Sports and Exercise, 23,* 846–852.

Dietz, J. (1992). Self-psychological approach to posttraumatic stress disorder: Neurobiological aspects of transmuting internalization. *Journal of the American Academy of Psychoanalysis, 20,* 277–293.

Evans, R.W. (1992). The postconcussion syndrome and the sequelae of mild head injury. *Neurologic Clinics, 10,* 815–847.

Everly, G.S. (1990). PTSD as a disorder of arousal. *Psychology and Health: An International Journal, 4,* 135–145.

Everly, G.S. (1993). Psychotraumatology: A two-factor formulation of posttraumatic stress. *Integrative Physiological and Behavioral Science, 28,* 270–278.

Everly, G.S. (1995). The neurocognitive therapy of posttraumatic stress: A strategic metatherapeutic approach. In G.S. Everly & J.M. Lating (Eds.), *Psychotraumatology: Key papers and core concepts in post-traumatic stress* (pp. 159–169). New York: Plenum.

Ferenczi, S., Abraham, K. & Simmel, E. (1921). *Psychoanalysis and the war neuroses.* Vienna: International Psycho-Analysis Press.

Frazier, F. & Wilson, R.M. (1918). The sympathetic nervous system and the "irritable heart of soldiers." *British Medical Journal, 2,* 27–29.

Freud, S. (1920). Beyond the pleasure principle. In J. Strachey (Ed. & Transl.), *The standard edition of the complete psychological works of Sigmund Freud* (Vol. XVIII, pp. 7–64). New York: Norton.

Garmezy, N. (1993). Children in poverty: Resilience despite risk. *Psychiatry, 56,* 127–136.

Garmezy, N., Masten, A.S. & Tellegen, A. (1984). The study of stress and competence in children: A building block for developmental psychopathology. *Child Development, 55,* 97–111.

Garner, G.W. (2005). *Surviving the street: Officer safety and survival techniques* (2nd ed.). Springfield, IL: Charles C Thomas.

Gilliland, B.E. & James, R.K. (1993). *Crisis intervention strategies* (2nd ed.). Pacific Grove, CA: Brooks/Cole.

Hays, K.F. & Brown, C.H. (2004). *You're on! Consulting for peak performance.* Washington, DC: American Psychological Association.

Hoge, E.A., Austin, E.D. & Pollack, M.H. (2007). Resilience: Research evidence and conceptual considerations for posttraumatic stress disorder. *Depression and Anxiety, 24,* 139–152.

Hoge, E.A., Austin, E.D. & Pollack, M.H. (2007). Resilience: Research evidence and conceptual considerations for posttraumatic stress disorder. *Depression and Anxiety, 24,* 139–152.

Holbrook, J. (2011). Veterans' courts and criminal responsibility: A problem-solving history and approach to the liminality of combat trauma. In D.C.

Kelly, S. Howe-Barksdale & D. Gitelson (Eds.), *Treating young veterans: Promoting resilience through practice and advocacy* (pp. 259–300). New York: Springer.

Horowitz, M.J. (1986). *Stress response syndromes* (2nd ed.). New York: Jason Aronson.

Janoff-Bulman, R. (1992). *Shattered assumptions: Toward a new psychology of trauma.* New York: Free Press.

Kardiner, A. (1941). *The traumatic neuroses of war.* Washington DC: National Research Council.

Kobasa, S.C. (1979a). Personality and resistance to illness. *American Journal of Community Psychology, 7,* 413–423.

Kobasa, S.C. (1979b). Stressful life events, personality, and health: An inquiry into hardiness. *Journal of Personality and Social Psychology, 37,* 1–11.

Kobasa, S.C., Maddi, S. & Cahn, S. (1982). Hardiness and health: A prospective study. *Journal of Personality and Social Psychology, 42,* 168–177.

Koch, W.J., Douglas, K.S., Nicholls, T.L. & O'Neill, M.L. (2006). *Psychological injuries: Forensic assessment, treatment, and the law.* New York: Oxford University Press.

Kolb, L.C. (1987). A neuropsychological hypothesis explaining posttraumatic stress disorders. *American Journal of Psychiatry, 144,* 989–995.

Kretschmer, E. (1926). *Hysteria.* New York: Basic Books.

Ludwig, A.M. (1972). Hysteria: A neurobiological theory. *Archives of General Psychiatry, 27,* 771–777.

Luthar, S.S. (1991). Vulnerability and resilience: A study of high-risk adolescents. *Child Development, 62,* 600–616.

Maddi, S.R. & Khoshaba, D.M. (1994). Hardiness and mental health. *Journal of Personality Assessment, 63,* 265–274.

McEwen, B. & Lasley, E.N. (2002). *The end of stress as we know it.* Washington, DC: Dana Press.

Mearburg, J.C. & Wilson, R.M. (1918). The effect of certain sensory stimulations on respiratory and heart rate in cases of so-called "irritable heart." *Heart, 7,* 17–22.

Meek, C.L. (1990). Evaluation and assessment of post-traumatic and other stress-related disorders. In C.L. Meek (Ed.), *Post-traumatic stress disorder: Assessment, differential diagnosis, and forensic evaluation* (pp. 9–61). Sarasota, FL: Professional Resource Exchange.

Merskey, H. (1992). Psychiatric aspects of the neurology of trauma. *Neurologic Clinics, 10,* 895–905.

Miller, H.B., Miller, L. & Bjorklund, D. (2010). Helping military parents cope with parental deployment: Role of attachment theory and recommendations for mental health clinicians and counselors. *International Journal of Emergency Mental Health, 12,* 231–235.

Miller, L. (1989). To beat stress, don't relax: Get tough! *Psychology Today,* December, pp. 62–63.

Miller, L. (1990). *Inner natures: Brain, self, and personality.* New York: St. Martin.

Miller, L. (1991). *Freud's brain: Neuropsychodynamic foundations of psychoanalysis.* New York: Guilford.

Miller, L. (1993). *Psychotherapy of the brain-injured patient: Reclaiming the shattered self.* New York: Norton.

Miller, L. (1994). Civilian posttraumatic stress disorder: Clinical syndromes and psychotherapeutic strategies. *Psychotherapy, 31,* 655–664.

Miller, L. (1995). Tough guys: Psychotherapeutic strategies with law enforcement and emergency services personnel. *Psychotherapy, 32,* 592–600.

Miller, L. (1997). Neurosensitization: A pathophysiological model for traumatic disability syndromes. *Journal of Cognitive Rehabilitation, 15*(6), 12–23.

Miller, L. (1998a). *Shocks to the system: Psychotherapy of traumatic disability syndromes.* New York: Norton.

Miller, L. (1998b). Ego autonomy and the healthy personality: Psychodynamics, cognitive style, and clinical applications. *Psychoanalytic Review, 85,* 423–448.

Miller, L. (1999). Workplace violence: Prevention, response, and recovery. *Psychotherapy, 36,* 160–169.

Miller, L. (2000). Law enforcement traumatic stress: Clinical syndromes and intervention strategies. *Trauma Response, 6*(1), 15–20.

Miller, L. (2005). Psychotherapy for terrorism survivors: New directions in evaluation and treatment. *Directions in Clinical and Counseling Psychology, 17,* 59–74.

Miller, L. (2006a). Officer-involved shooting: Reaction patterns, response protocols, and psychological intervention strategies. *International Journal of Emergency Mental Health, 8,* 239–254.

Miller, L. (2006b). *Practical police psychology: Stress management and crisis intervention for law enforcement.* Springfield: Charles C Thomas.

Miller, L. (2007a). Police families: Stresses, syndromes, and solutions. *American Journal of Family Therapy, 35,* 1–20.

Miller, L. (2007b). Line-of-duty death: Psychological treatment of traumatic bereavement in law enforcement. *International Journal of Emergency Mental Health.*

Miller, L. (2007c). Traumatic stress disorders. In F.M. Dattilio & A. Freeman (Eds.), *Cognitive-Behavioral Strategies in Crisis Intervention* (3rd ed., pp. 494–527). New York: Guilford.

Miller, L. (2008a). *METTLE: Mental toughness training for law enforcement.*Flushing, NY: Looseleaf Law Press.

Miller, L. (2008b). *Counseling crime victims: Practical strategies for mental health professionals.* New York: Springer.

Miller, L. (2008c). *From difficult to disturbed: Understanding and managing dysfunctional employees.* New York: Amacom.

Miller, L. (2008d). Stress and resilience in law enforcement training and practice. *International Journal of Emergency Mental Health, 10,* 109–124.

Miller, L. (2012). *Criminal psychology: Nature, nurture, culture.* Springfield, IL: Charles C Thomas.

Modlin, H.C. (1983). Traumatic neurosis and other injuries. *Psychiatric Clinics of North America, 6,* 661–682.

Nietzsche, F. (1969). *Twilight of the gods.* London: Penguin.

Oppenheim, H. (1890). Tatsachliches und hypthothetisches uber das wesen der hysterie. *Berlin Klinik Wschr, 27,* 553.

Parker, R.S. (1990). *Traumatic brain injury and neuropsychological impairment: Sensorimotor, cognitive, emotional, and adaptive problems in children and adults.* New York: Springer-Verlag.

Paton, D., Smith, L., Violanti, J.M. & Eranen, L. (2000). Work-related traumatic stress: Risk, vulnerability, and resilience. In J. Violanti, D. Paton & C. Dunning (Eds.), *Posttraumatic stress intervention: Challenges, issues, and perspectives* (pp. 187–203). Springfield: Charles C. Thomas.

Pizarro, J., Silver, R.C. & Prouse, J. (2006). Physical and mental health costs of traumatic experiences among Civil War veterans. *Archives of General Psychiatry, 63,* 193–200.

Rosen, G. (1975). Nostalgia: A forgotten psychological disorder. *Psychosomatic Medicine, 5,* 342–347.

Rubenstein, J.L., Heeren, T., Houseman, D., Rubin, C. & Stechler, G. (1989). Suicidal behavior in "normal" adolescents: Risk and protective factors. *American Journal of Orthopsychiatry, 59,* 59–71.

Rutter, M. (1985). Resilience in the face of adversity: Protective factors and resistance to psychiatric disorder. *British Journal of Psychiatry, 147,* 598–611.

Rutter, M. (1987). Psychosocial resilience and protective mechanisms. *American Journal of Orthopsychiatry, 57,* 316–331.

Rutter, M., Tizard, J., Yule, W., Graham, P. & Whitmore, K. (1976). Research report: Isle of Wight studies, 1964–1974. *Psychological Medicine, 6,* 313–332.

Sapolsky, R.M., Krey, L.C. & McEwen, B.S. (1984). Glucocorticoid-sensitive hippocampal neurons are involved in terminating the adrenocortical stress response. *Proceedings of the National Academy of Sciences, 81,* 6174–6177.

Scanff, C.L. & Taugis, J. (2002). Stress management for police special forces. *Journal of Applied Sport Psychology, 14,* 330–343.

Selye, H. (1956). *The stress of life.* New York: McGraw-Hill.

Selye, H. (1973). The evolution of the stress concept. *American Scientist, 61,* 692–699.

Selye, H. (1975). *Stress without distress.* New York: Signet.

Sherman, N. (2005). *Stoic warriors: The ancient philosophy behind the military mind.* New York: Oxford University Press.

Simonton, D.K. (1994). *Greatness: Who makes history and why.* New York: Guilford.

Southard, E. (1919). *Shell-shock and other neuropsychiatric problems.* Boston: Leonard.

Southwick, S.M., Ozbay, F., Charney, D. & McEwen, B.S. (2008). Adaptation to stress and psychobiological mechanisms of resilience. In B.J. Lukey & V. Tepe (Eds.), *Biobehavioral resilience to stress* (pp. 91–116.). Boca Raton: CRC Press.

Tedeschi, R.G. & Calhoun, L.G. (1995). *Trauma and transformation: Growing in the aftermath of suffering.* Thousand Oaks, CA: Sage.

Tedeschi, R.G. & Calhoun, L.G. (2004). Posttraumatic growth: Conceptual foundations and empirical evidence. *Psychological Inquiry, 15,* 1–18.

Tedeschi, R.G. & Kilmer, R.P. (2005). Assessing strengths, resilience, and growth to guide clinical interventions. *Professional Psychology: Research and Practice, 36,* 230–237.

Thompson, S.C. (1981). Will it hurt less if I can control it? A complex answer to a simple question. *Psychological Bulletin, 90,* 89–101.

Trimble, M.R. (1981). *Post-traumatic neurosis: From railway spine to whiplash.* New York: Wiley.

Waugh, C., Tugade, M. & Fredrickson, B. (2008). Psychophysiology of resilience and stress. In B.J. Lukey & V. Tepe (Eds.), *Biobehavioral resilience to stress* (pp. 117–138). Boca Raton: CRC Press.

Weiner, H. (1977). *Psychobiology and human disease.* New York: Elsevier.

Weiner, H. (1992). *Perturbing the organism: The biology of stressful experience.* Chicago: University of Chicago Press.

Werner, E.E. (1989). High-risk children in young adulthood: A longitudinal study from birth to 32 years. *American Journal of Orthopsychiatry, 59,* 72–81.

Werner, E.E. & Smith, R.S. (1992). *Overcoming the odds: High risk children from birth to adulthood.* Ithaca, NY: Cornell University Press.

Westphal, M., Bonanno, G.A. & Bartone, P.T. (2008). Resilience and personality. In B.J. Lukey & V. Tepe (Eds.), *Biobehavioral resilience to stress* (pp. 219–257). Boca Raton: CRC Press.

Wilson, J.P. (1994). The historical evolution of PTSD diagnostic criteria: From Freud to DSM-IV. *Journal of Traumatic Stress, 7,* 681–698.

Yalom, I.D. (1980). *Existential psychotherapy.* New York: Basic Books.

Zimrin, H. (1986). A profile of survival. *Child Abuse and Neglect, 10,* 339–349.

Discussion Questions

1. As typically used by mental health professionals, to what two things does stress refer?
2. What changes started occurring in battlefield tactics in the American Civil War and World War I that exacerbated stress-related nervous ailments?
3. How is the term "syndrome" defined in the clinical classification?
4. What is the characteristic set of symptoms for *posttraumatic stress disorder*?
5. How is *acute stress disorder* defined?
6. Kretschmer describes two classes of behavioral responses that an organism uses to ward off attack. What are they?
7. How has Modlin characterized the psychodynamic explanation of PTSD?
8. How is the term *homeostasis* defined?
9. What are the three stages of the *General Adaptation Syndrome* developed by Hans Selye?
10. What does the term *toughness* refer to?
11. What are the two main physiological symptoms that underlie the toughness response?
12. As a general trait factor, features associated with resilience to adverse life events in both children and adults include which elements?
13. How is the concept of *hardiness* defined?
14. Paton has delineated a core set of resiliency factors that enable police officers to withstand and even prevail in the face of seemingly overwhelming trauma. What do these factors include?
15. What specific function in police work places its personnel in the unique position to see trouble coming and to take action before it boils over to a critical level of harm?
16. Why does 20/20 hindsight not deserve to be given the bum rap that it has been given?

2

Vicarious Traumatization: Potential Hazards and Interventions for Disaster and Trauma Workers[*]

Kathleen M. Palm, Melissa A. Polusny, and Victoria M. Follette

Introduction

Terrorism, natural disasters, war-related combat, and other large-scale traumatic events have led to an increased interest in identifying risk factors and developing effective treatment for post-traumatic stress reactions. While there has been a great deal of research on post-traumatic stress disorder (PTSD) among trauma survivors, few researchers have examined the effects that traumatic events have on people who are indirectly exposed. Although studies suggest that physical proximity to traumatic events is related to a greater likelihood of experiencing traumatic symptomology,[1,2] people who do not experience the event directly also may report stress reactions.[3–5] This phenomenon has been referred to in the trauma literature as "vicarious traumatization," "secondary traumatization," or "compassion fatigue." While there has been some debate about how these concepts differ,[6] for the purposes of this paper, the term "vicarious traumatization" is used to refer to post-traumatic stress reactions experienced by those who are indirectly exposed to traumatic events. Vicarious

* Reprinted with the permission of Cambridge University Press.

trauma reactions may include intrusive imagery and thoughts, avoidance and emotional numbing, hyper-arousal symptoms, somatization, and physical and alcohol use problems similar to those experienced by direct trauma survivors.[7,8] Further, working with trauma survivors may lead to changes in self-identity, world-view, spirituality, and general psychological functioning.[9] It has been suggested that trauma workers may experience a disruption in major beliefs regarding safety and personal vulnerability, benevolence of the world, and feelings of powerlessness.[10] Consequently, the way these individuals make sense of or find meaning in the world may be altered. People who may experience indirect effects of disasters include family, friends, neighbors, work colleagues, and professionals who assist the primary victims.[11] In addition, technological advancements that have allowed for extensive media coverage of disasters, war, and other potentially traumatic events also have exposed media specialists and large numbers of the general population repeatedly to vivid images of life-threatening and horrific events, potentially resulting in negative emotional consequences for many.

While there has been much discussion in the literature about vicarious traumatization, a great deal of this material has been anecdotal and based on few empirical studies.[12] The extent to which vicarious trauma reactions interfere with general functioning has not been determined, and the empirical evidence supporting the phenomenon of vicarious trauma has been inconsistent.[12] The findings are mixed in regard to the prevalence and severity of vicarious trauma reactions among disaster workers, the predictors of distress, and individual and organizational risk factors; hence, the implications for prevention and treatment also are unclear. In this paper, we review representative findings and present suggestions on how to limit the potential hazards of trauma work, based on the current state of the literature.

Impact of Indirect Trauma Exposure on Professionals

There are a number of occupations that may be particularly affected by vicarious or indirect trauma. Pearlman and Saakvitne suggested that indirect trauma reactions are more likely among those whose job duties require an empathic interaction with trauma survivors.[13] Some of these professionals include healthcare providers, emergency service personnel, journalists, and other media specialists involved in mass communication.

Disaster Professionals

Many people in different professional areas care for the immediate and long-term needs of disaster victims, including physicians, nurses, mental health-care providers, and emergency response personnel (i.e., police officers, firefighters, paramedics). While individuals in these occupations have focused a great deal of their attention on meeting the needs of trauma survivors, the personal psychological risks also are significant and should be addressed.

Healthcare Providers

Empirical research, while somewhat limited, suggests that adaptation to traumatic material depends on the interaction between the characteristics of the situation and the characteristics of the individual. The former includes listening to descriptions of graphic details of the event, personal event-related loss, and consecutive interactions with trauma survivors.[13–15] Some individual characteristics that influence adaptation include the efficacy of coping skills, current stress, and physical and mental health. This interaction is important to consider, given that in most disasters, many people have been directly affected by one event. Not only will professionals have to work with a greater number of traumatized individuals than before the current traumatic event, but they also may be involved in treating consecutive cases in which the same overall trauma content is dealt with.

The findings of research examining the relationship of healthcare providers' exposure to severe trauma cases and vicarious trauma reactions have been inconsistent. Some literature suggests that stressors related to disaster and trauma work (i.e., loss of friends or family and fear for personal safety) increase disaster professionals' vulnerability to psychological and emotional distress, which also may affect their professional work. Other research suggests that disaster workers, especially those who are involved in rescue work, are well-prepared and experienced, and may be quite resilient to indirect trauma effects.[16]

Other examples of inconsistencies in the literature include findings that indicate no significant relationship exists between psychological distress and the number of trauma survivors in individual professional's caseloads.[15,17] However, other studies have found the opposite—the number of trauma survivors treated is associated with increased reported distress by mental health professionals.[18–20]

Eidelson and colleagues surveyed 592 mental health professionals who have practices at varying distances from Ground Zero, the site of the 11 September 2001 World Trade Center (WTC) terrorist attacks.[21] Proximity to Ground Zero was associated with increased work demands, changes in personal life, and work-related stress. On the other hand, previous experience working with trauma survivors seems to have been a protective factor against developing vicarious trauma reactions. Mental health practitioners with fewer years of experience were more likely to report increased work-related stress. This latter finding is consistent with Pearlman and MacIan's research on vicarious traumatization that indicated that trauma therapists with less experience reported greater disruptions in self-trust, self-intimacy, self-esteem, and overall distress.[22] Interestingly, Eidelson and colleagues found that participation in volunteer activities was a significant predictor of positive feelings in working with disaster victims.[21] Anecdotal reports of respondents suggest that these positive attitudes were related to the therapists feeling a greater sense of purpose in their activities, perhaps similar to their motivations for engaging in volunteer work.

Emergency Service Personnel

Emergency services personnel often are directly and indirectly exposed to disasters. As might be expected, research has documented that the prevalence of post-disaster psychiatric disorders is lower among those indirectly exposed to disaster compared to those directly exposed to the same disaster.[23] Two years after the Oklahoma City bombing, Tucker and colleagues surveyed body handlers involved in the aftermath, including medical examiners, pathology residents, dental residents, and students.[23] They found higher rates of alcohol-use disorders among body handlers (25%) compared to direct trauma victims (10%). These relatively higher rates of alcohol abuse/dependence among disaster personnel do not appear to have been due to increased alcohol use following bombing-related work; rather, the data suggest that rescue workers may be more likely to cope with occupational stressors in general through alcohol use. Although most of these particular disaster workers showed emotional resiliency and reported low levels of symptoms two years after the disaster, increased alcohol use was associated with higher post-traumatic stress and depressive symptoms.[23] Other studies suggest that emergency workers are at risk for developing post-traumatic stress reactions and other psychiatric symptoms (i.e., depression), even if they have not directly experienced major disasters.[24, 25] Clohessy and Ehlers surveyed 56 paramedics and ambulance technicians regarding their exposure to traumatic events and post-traumatic stress reactions.[24] Although these individuals did not directly experience major events, 21% met symptom criteria for a diagnosis of post-traumatic stress disorder. Potentially traumatic incidents that were rated as most stressful by participants were dealing with cot (crib) death, dealing with incidents involving children, relatives of patients, and burn patients. The most frequently reported symptoms were intrusive thoughts about the event, irritability, sleep disturbance, and detachment from others. In addition, work conditions, such as shift work, false alarms, and unpredictability, contributed to the participants' reports of distress. In a similar study, Van der Ploeg and Kleber assessed psychological distress in ambulance workers.[25] Of the 187 participants who completed the questionnaires, 85% had responded to one or more traumatic incidents within the past five years; 12% of this subsample indicated experiencing clinical levels of post-traumatic stress symptoms. Further, compared to a reference group, the ambulance workers were more likely to report greater fatigue and risk factors associated with burnout.

Journalists

Anecdotal reports and surveys of journalists suggest that this group and other mass media personnel frequently experience distress following intense, trauma-related assignments.[26] Many correspondents, cameramen, and photojournalists become first-responders, like police and firefighters, when they venture into combat zones and disaster areas and witness or directly experience traumatic events. Journalists' exposure to traumatic material may be complicated further by conducting interviews with victims, witnessing the aftermath of horrific events, and the limited time they may have to process emotional reactions between the interviews and writing their news stories. Despite the inherent risks involved in this profession, there only have been two published studies that assessed the psychological effects of journalists' direct and indirect exposure to such traumatic events. Feinstein, Owen and Blair surveyed 140 war journalists and a comparison group of 107 journalists who never had covered war.[27] War journalists reported significantly greater levels of PTSD and depressive symptoms compared to their peers, and had lifetime prevalence rates of PTSD similar to PTSD rates found in combat veterans. In addition, war journalists reported drinking excessively, consuming nearly 2–3 times more alcohol weekly than did non-war journalists. However, they were no more likely to receive psychiatric help than were the non-war journalists. In a recently published study of 906 American newspaper journalists, Pyevich, Newman, and Daleiden found that greater work-related trauma exposure, such as witnessing or covering stories about traumatic events, was significantly associated with PTSD symptoms, even after accounting for personal exposure to other traumatic situations.[28] Moreover, journalists with more negative cognitive beliefs (e.g., beliefs regarding the benevolence of the world, meaningfulness of the world, perceived personal invulnerability) tended to experience more work-related PTSD symptoms.

Researchers have begun to study the impact of media coverage of disasters on vicarious traumatization in the general population. These findings suggest that television coverage of traumatic events can be a trigger of traumatic memories, reactivate PTSD symptoms in veterans, and elicit immediate physiological arousal among those who have experienced individual traumatic events such as motor vehicle accidents or assault.[3, 29] Therefore, it is reasonable to extrapolate that media specialists who report on the aftermath of disasters and mass trauma may be at significant risk of experiencing vicarious traumatization.

Suggestions for Limiting Vicarious Trauma Reactions

In order to ensure effective response to and care for disaster survivors, it is important to establish conditions that will enhance personal and occupational functioning among those who are indirectly exposed to trauma through their occupations. However, focusing exclusively on reducing an individual's trauma responses misses the greater scope of the problem.[30] Effective service delivery not only should include individual but also organizational considerations.

Disaster Professionals — Individual Considerations

Some disaster workers and healthcare professionals may be overwhelmed by their own personal responses to disaster in addition to the accounts reported by their clients and patients. When there is insufficient physical or psychological distance from the trauma, there also is increased risk for negative outcomes. However, there are naturally occurring strategies that individuals can use for themselves and others in order to cope more effectively; for example, spending time with other people, asking for support, and engaging in activities that provide a sense of purpose. Moreover, it is important that disaster workers and healthcare providers attend to their personal needs in order to have the physical and psychological energy to work more effectively with others. These significant personal factors include physical health, balance, social support, and acceptance.

Maintaining a balance between the professional, physical, and emotional aspects of living is important for everyone.[31, 32] This balance can be fostered by attending to the non-professional parts of one's life (i.e., role as parent, partner, student, gardener, hiker, runner, artist, etc.). Paying attention to these multiple dimensions may be beneficial in several ways, including the fostering of engagement in pleasant life activities, and connection with social support networks. The therapy outcome literature suggests that these two factors are important treatment components for alleviating depression,[33] and this may well generalize to treatment for trauma exposure.[34]

Maintaining balance as much as is possible in the work environment also is an important consideration.[15] For example, therapists working with disaster survivors should consider ways to provide more balance at work by developing a caseload of clients with different types of problems; working with populations other than trauma survivors; limiting caseloads; avoiding the scheduling of difficult clients one after another; scheduling breaks during the day, and finding opportunities to work with colleagues. Additional changes to consider include attending support groups, taking vacation time, identifying personal limits, and talking to co-workers. Disaster workers who are unable to communicate with co-workers about their reactions to various difficult situations may have more difficulty seeking support, and therefore, be at increased risk of experiencing feelings of isolation. Related findings by Van der Ploeg and Kleber indicated that poor communication with co-workers was predictive of ambulance worker's post-traumatic responses one year after the event.[25]

Despite efforts to manage stress at work, there are times when the demands of the emergency situation will not allow for any real balance at work. For example, immediately following the terrorist attacks of 11 September, all emergency care providers worked long shifts with little or no opportunity to escape from the Ground Zero site. Therefore, when there is a break in the work schedule, general care strategies are extremely important. Some suggestions that are provided to trauma survivors seem reasonable for disaster professionals as well. Adequate social support outside of the work environment is an important aspect of self-care for disaster professionals,[20, 35, 36] and feelings of connection in both professional and personal contexts may help them meet their own needs more effectively. Therefore, it seems advisable for therapists to spend time with family, friends, religious/spiritual groups, and/or other organizations in order to bolster and benefit from the natural support systems present in their environments.

Emotional distress is a natural and understandable outcome of working with those who have survived horrifying events. Accepting these responses as "normal" allows for the opportunity to explore these reactions without blame, shame, or pathologizing. However, feelings of shame, anger, and sadness are not necessarily problems. Rather, it is the struggle to deal with these experiences that may lead to personal complications.[37] Avoiding these issues may lead to further isolation, doubt, shame, and ineffective behaviors (e.g., substance use, aggression, self-harm). The literature suggests that the likelihood of experiencing high levels of PTSD symptoms decreases as a function of using acceptance as a coping strategy.[38]

People may differ in their resiliency and the extent to which indirect exposure to traumatic material leads to vicarious traumatic stress responses. However, a useful preventive strategy may be to limit unnecessary exposure to further traumatic material; for example, decreasing repeated television viewing of disastrous events. Some additional suggestions include limiting television viewing before sleeping, and reading news media that may not be as graphic in communications about the disaster (e.g., newspaper or journal articles).[39]

Disaster Professionals—Organizational Considerations

It often is possible to make structural changes at the organizational level such that the risk of vicarious traumatization reactions amongst individuals is decreased, in part by making resources for coping more readily available. Changes that can be made at this level include providing appropriate training, ensuring manageable caseloads, and having adequate consultation opportunities available for difficult cases the healthcare provider is treating. There are several organizational resources that decrease the likelihood of negative psychological responses from working with trauma survivors. Some examples include: access to continuing education; fostering a respectful and supportive environment; encouraging vacations; and offering community support networks for disaster workers and healthcare providers.[31]

Efforts to improve work environments can be made within organizations to limit the potential of indirect trauma reactions among disaster workers. According to reports by disaster workers, factors related to organizational setting, including lack of social support from co-workers, lack of support from supervisors, and poor communication, were important predictors of vicarious traumatization, burnout symptoms, and fatigue.[24]

Consistent supervision of cases and consultation should be a regular part of the healthcare provider's work.[18, 40] In our view, organizations have the responsibility to create an environment that supports the pursuit of on-going learning and consultation. Mental health professionals should be encouraged to seek training in empirically supported treatments for traumatic stress and related problems. An outside consultant may be invited to provide in-service training in the delivery of treatment services to trauma survivors, as well as discuss the indirect effects of working in trauma areas. In the wake of a large-scale disaster, it is possible that a significant percentage of staff may experience trauma symptoms, and therefore, outside resources may be better suited to provide needed case supervision. Professional, organizational, and personal strategies for self-care also can be discussed in the case-supervision context.

Journalists and Other Mass Communication Specialists—Individual Considerations

Similar to other personnel whose occupations require that they respond to disasters and care for trauma victims, journalists and other media specialists likely will benefit from the self-care strategies discussed above. However, unlike healthcare providers who often have received formalized education and training in the detection and treatment of traumatic stress, mass-media specialists may have little knowledge or understanding of the psychological impact of exposure to traumatic events. As a result, they may be less able to identify problematic coping strategies that may exacerbate their distress. Therefore, journalists and other mass communications professionals should be provided with information about traumatic stress reactions, effective coping, and possible interventions. Specifically, they should be provided with information that will help them to utilize their natural social support systems.

Mass-media specialists who develop work-related, posttraumatic stress disorder (PTSD) may benefit from empirically validated treatments for PTSD; however, further research is needed to explore how such interventions can be best modified to most effectively help this particular group. Brief interventions, such as critical incident stress debriefing (CISD), have been developed and applied with other first responders, i.e., firefighters, police. These interventions have been controversial and possibly may be more iatrogenic than beneficial. Given what we know about brief interventions with other first responders,[41] care should be taken to develop and test effective interventions for journalists.

Journalists and Other Mass Communication Specialists—Organizational Considerations

Emerging data on the psychological hazards experienced by journalists in covering traumatic events should be of serious concern to news organizations. Behaviors such as alcohol abuse, that may function to temporarily lessen stress responses, can significantly reduce one's quality of life and may result in chronic impairment. Most disaster professionals, especially mental health workers, have some knowledge and training related to traumatic stress. The extensive training of mental health professionals in diagnosis and treatment of psychological problems as well as the increased likelihood that mental health professionals have participated in their own personal therapy,[42] may better prepare these particular individuals for the psychological hazards of trauma-related work. Journalists, on the other hand, may enter into assignments to cover traumatic life events with little or no training or understanding of the hazards they face. Journalism and mass-communication programs should incorporate information about the growing evidence of the potential psychological hazards of certain types of journalistic work into their curricula, and should disseminate basic information about traumatic stress responses and preventive self-care.

It would be highly beneficial if news organizations worked to create an atmosphere in which mass-communication specialists can freely discuss their responses to work assignments without fear of being passed over for other assignments. Access to appropriate treatment of post-traumatic stress responses should be made available and encouraged, again, without negative consequences to those distressed. While some extended assignments may result in repeated indirect and direct exposure to traumatic situations, it may be useful for news organizations to consider ways in which work assignments can be varied to include correspondent work that does not involve traumatic situations.

Conclusions

At an individual and at a societal level, there has been a significant shift in our sense of safety in the world. While people always have been aware of the dangers inherent in life, through wars and natural disasters, several factors have enhanced our sense of vulnerability. Technology most certainly is at the core of this shift on many levels. Advances in our media technology allow for instantaneous coverage of terrifying events around the world. Beginning with coverage of the Vietnam War, horrific events involving war and other disasters were brought into our homes with the evening news. Over time, the intensity of this media coverage has escalated, with journalists reporting from the front, embedded with the troops they are covering. Not only is the reporting nearer in proximity to the event (both in time and space), images are repeated over and over in the television and print media. Individuals who lived through 11 September 2001 never will forget the image of the planes flying into the WTC towers. This intensity of media coverage combined with many other significant tragedies, for example, the Challenger and Columbia space shuttle catastrophes, multiple wars, Hurricane Andrew, and numerous other massive natural disasters, have increased individuals' contact with the fragility of life and a sense of increased vulnerability in the presence of so many dangers.

We have created a world in which trauma has become commonplace; however, we believe that there are positive actions that can be taken. We work within a number of imbedded systems, and there are several points of possible intervention. Many professionals will be brought into increased contact with traumatic material simply as a function of their jobs. Healthcare workers, rescue personnel, firefighters and police, mass-media specialists, and many others will be involved regularly in experiences that are painful and traumatic. For these professionals, there should be regular training on general strategies for dealing with trauma, including normalizing responses to these abnormal situations. Organizational structure should include appropriate supervision, case management, and opportunities for professional support. Equally importantly, we should not fail to emphasize that natural forms of support through friends, family, and spiritual groups have been found to provide protection from long-term trauma reactions.

Professional training that addresses the broader issues involved in working with trauma also is important. Additionally, we would argue that empowerment of trauma workers to advocate for survivors and work on relevant policy issues can have a positive impact. As a society, we need to move forward, identifying areas for both acceptance and change. Whatever our professional roles, we can live lives that affirm values of compassion, hope, and support. As Margaret Mead stated so eloquently, "Never doubt that a small group of committed people can change the world. It is the only thing that ever has."

References

1. Schlenger W.E., Caddell J.M., Ebert L., Jordan BK, Batts KR: Psychological reactions to terrorist attacks: Findings from the National Study of Americans' Reactions to September 11. *JAMA* 2002; 288:2684-2685.
2. Schuster MA, Stein BD, Jaycox LH, *et al.*: A national survey of stress reactions after the September 11, 2001 attacks. *New England Journal Med* 2001; 345:1507-1512.
3. Ahern J, Galea S, Resnick H, *et al.*: Television images and psychological symptoms after the September 11 terrorist attacks. *Psychiatry: Interpersonal & Biological Processes* 2002; 65:289-300.
4. Pfefferbaum B, Nixon SJ, Krug RS, *et al.*: Clinical needs assessment of middle and high school students following the 1995 Oklahoma City bombing. *American Journal of Psychiatry* 1999; 156:1069-1074.

5. Pfefferbaum B, Nixon SJ, Tivis RD, *et al.*: Television exposure in children after a terrorist incident. *Psychiatry: Interpersonal & Biological Processes* 2001; 64:202-211.

6. Jenkins, SR, Baird S: Secondary traumatic stress and vicarious trauma: A validational study. *Journal of Traumatic Stress* 2002; 15:423-432.

7. McCarroll JE, Ursano RJ, Wright KM, *et al.*: Handling bodies after violent death: Strategies for coping. *American Journal of Orthopsychiatry* 1993; 63:209-214.

8. Ursano RJ, Fullerton CS, Vance K, *et al.*: Post-traumatic stress disorder and identification in disaster workers. *American Journal of Psychiatry* 1999; 156:353-359.

9. McCann L, Pearlman LA: Vicarious traumatization: A framework for understanding the psychological effects of working with victims. *Journal of Traumatic Stress* 1990; 3:131-149.

10. Janoff-Bulman R: *Shattered Assumptions: Towards a New Psychology of Trauma.* New York: Free Press, 1992.

11. Figley CR: Compassion Fatigue as Secondary Traumatic Stress Disorder: An Overview. In: Figley CR (ed): *Compassion Fatigue: Coping with Secondary Traumatic Stress Disorder in Those Who Treat the Traumatized*: New York: Brunner/Mazel, 1995.

12. Sabin-Farrell R, Turpin G: Vicarious traumatization: Implications for the mental health of health workers? *Clinical Psychology Review* 2003; 23:449-480.

13. Pearlman, LA, Saakvitne KW: *Trauma and the Therapist: Countertransference and Vicarious Traumatization in Psychotherapy with Incest Survivors.* New York: Norton, 1995.

14. Durakovic-Belko E, Kulenovic A, Dapic R: Determinants of post-traumatic adjustment in adolescents from Sarajevo who experienced war. *Journal of Clinical Psychology* 2003; 59:27-40.

15. Follette VM: Survivors of Child Sexual Abuse: Treatment Using a Contextual Analysis. In: Hayes SC, Jacobson NS, Follette VM, Dougher MJ (eds), *Acceptance and Change: Content and Context in Psychotherapy.* Reno, NV: Context Press, 1994, pp 255-268.

16. North CS, Tivis L, McMillen JC, *et al.*: Psychiatric disorders in rescue workers after the Oklahoma City bombing. *American Journal of Psychiatry* 2002; 159:857-859.

17. Baird S, Jenkins SR: Vicarious traumatization, secondary traumatic stress, and burnout in sexual assault and domestic violence agency volunteer and paid staff. *Violence and Victims* 2003; 18:71-86.

18. Brady JL, Guy JD, Poelstra PL, *et al.*: Vicarious traumatization, spirituality, and the treatment of sexual abuse survivors: A national survey of

women psychotherapists. *Professional Psychology: Research and Practice* 1999; 30:386-393.

19. Kassam-Adams N: The Risks of Treating Sexual Trauma: Stress and Secondary Trauma in Psychotherapists. In: Stamm BH (ed): *Secondary Traumatic Stress: Self-care Issues for Clinicians, Researchers, and Educators.* Lutherville, MD: Sidran Press, 1995.

20. Schauben LJ, Frazier PA: Vicarious trauma: The effects on female counselors of working with sexual violence survivors. *Psychology of Women Quarterly* 1995; 19:49-54.

21. Eidelson RJ, D'Alessio GR, Eidelson JI: The impact of September 11 on psychologists. *Professional Psychology: Research and Practice* 2003; 34:144-150.

22. Pearlman LA, Mac Ian PS: Vicarious traumatization: An empirical study of the effects of trauma work on trauma therapists. *Professional Psychology: Research and Practice* 1995; 26:558-565.

23. Tucker P, Pfefferbaum B, Doughty DE, *et al.*: Body handlers after terrorism in Oklahoma City: Predictors of posttraumatic stress and other symptoms. *American Journal of Orthopsychiatry* 2002; 72:469-475.

24. Clohessy S, Ehlers A: PTSD symptoms, responses to intrusive memories and coping in ambulance service workers. *British Journal of Clinical Psychology* 1999; 38:251-265.

25. Van der Ploeg E, Kleber RJ: Acute and chronic job stressors among ambulance personnel: Predictors of health symptoms. *Occup Environ Med* 2003; 60:i40-i46.

26. Simpson R, Boggs J: An exploratory study of traumatic stress among newspaper journalists. *Journalism and Communication Monographs* 1999; Spring:1-24.

27. Feinstein A, Owen J, Blair N: A hazardous profession: War, journalists, and psychopathology. *American Journal of Psychiatry* 2002; 159:1570-1575.

28. Pyevich CM, Newman E, Daleiden E: The relationship among cognitive schemas, job-related traumatic exposure, and post-traumatic stress disorder in journalists. *Journal of Traumatic Stress* 2003; 16:325-328.

29. Long N, Chamberlain K, Vincent C: Effect of the Gulf War on reactivation of adverse combat-related memories in Vietnam veterans. *Journal of Clinical Psychology* 1994; 50:138-144.

30. Kirmayer LJ: Confusion of the senses: Implications of ethnocultural variations in somatoform and dissociative disorders for PTSD. In: Marsella AJ, Friedman MJ (eds): Ethnocultural Aspects of Post-traumatic Stress Disorder: Issues, Research, and Clinical Applications. Washington, DC: American Psychological Association, 1996, pp 131-163.

31. Clay R: Tapping their own resilience. *APA Monitor on Psychology* 2001; 32:36-37.

32. Pearlman LA, Saakvitne KW: Treating therapists with vicarious traumatization and secondary traumatic stress disorders. In: Figley CR (ed): *Compassion Fatigue: Coping with Secondary Traumatic Stress Disorder in Those Who Treat the Traumatized.* New York: Brunner/Mazel, 1995.

33. Martell CR, Addis ME, Jacobson NS: *Depression in Context: Strategies for Guided Action.* New York: WW Norton, 2001.

34. Mulick P, Naugle A: Behavioral activation in the treatment of comorbid PTSD and major depression. Paper presented at the annual meeting of the Association for the Advancement of Behavior Therapy, Reno, NV, 2002.

35. Shakespeare-Finch J, Smith S, Obst P: Trauma, coping resources, and family functioning in emergency services personnel: A comparative study. *Work & Stress* 2002; 16:275-282.

36. Polusny MA, Follette VM: Long-term correlates of child sexual abuse: Theory and review of the empirical literature. *Applied and Preventive Psychology* 1995; 4:143-166.

37. Hayes SC, Strosahl KD, Wilson KG: *Acceptance and Commitment Therapy: An Experiential Approach to Behavior Change.* New York: Guilford Press, 1999.

38. Silver RC, Holman EA, McIntosh DN, *et al.*: Nationwide longitudinal study of psychological responses to September 11. *JAMA* 2002; 288:1235-1244.

39. Palm KM, Smith AA, Follette VM: Trauma therapy and therapist self-care. *Behavior Therapist* 2002; 25:40-42.

40. Follette VM, Batten SV: The role of emotion in psychotherapy supervision: A contextual behavioral analysis. *Cognitive and Behavioral Practice* 2000; 7:306-312.

41. Litz B, Gray M, Bryant R, *et al.*: Early intervention for trauma: Current status and future directions. *Clinical Psychology: Science and Practice* 2002; 9:112-134.

42. Follette VM, Polusny MM, Milbeck K: Mental health and law enforcement professionals: Trauma history, psychological symptoms, and impact of providing services to sexual abuse survivors. *Professional Psychology: Research and Practice* 1994; 25:275-282.

Discussion Questions

1. How has vicarious traumatization been defined?
2. What are some examples of vicarious trauma reactions?

3. What are examples of the people who may experience the indirect effect of disasters?

4. There are a number of occupations that may be particularly affected by vicarious or indirect trauma. What are they?

5. Empirical research, while somewhat limited, suggests that adaptation to traumatic material depends on a number of factors. What are they?

6. The findings of research examining the relationship of healthcare providers' exposure to severe trauma cases and vicarious trauma reactions have been inconsistent. What was suggested by the authors?

7. What was discovered two years after the Oklahoma City bombing as it relates to alcohol-use disorders among emergency service personnel?

8. In what ways are journalists' exposure to traumatic events different from those of first responders?

9. What were the differences in the rate of alcohol consumption between war journalists and non-war journalists?

10. There are naturally occurring strategies that individuals can use for themselves and others in order to cope more effectively. What was suggested by the authors?

11. What types of organizational considerations were suggested to assist disaster professionals in reducing the risk of vicarious traumatization reactions?

12. What are some important differences in the preparation of mental health professionals as opposed to journalists when it comes to understanding the hazards of trauma-related work?

3

Who Says Stress Is Bad for You?

Mary Carmichael

*It can be, but it can be good for you, too—a fact
scientists tend to ignore and regular folks don't appreciate.*

If you aren't already paralyzed with stress from reading the financial news,
here's a sure way to achieve that grim state: read a medical-journal article that
examines what stress can do to your brain. Stress, you'll learn, is crippling
your neurons so that, a few years or decades from now, Alzheimer's or Parkinson's disease will have an easy time destroying what's left. That's assuming you
haven't already died by then of some other stress-related ailment such as heart
disease. As we enter what is sure to be a long period of uncertainty—a gant-
let of lost jobs, dwindling assets, home foreclosures and two continuing wars—
the downside of stress is certainly worth exploring. But what about the up-
side? It's not something we hear much about.

In the past several years, a lot of us have convinced ourselves that stress is
unequivocally negative for everyone, all the time. We've blamed stress for a
wide variety of problems, from slight memory lapses to full-on dementia—and
that's just in the brain. We've even come up with a derisive nickname for people who voluntarily plunge into stressful situations: they're "adrenaline junkies."

Sure, stress can be bad for you, especially if you react to it with anger or
depression or by downing five glasses of Scotch. But what's often overlooked
is a commonsense counterpoint: in some circumstances, it can be good for
you, too. It's right there in basic-psychology textbooks. As Spencer Rathus
puts it in "Psychology: Concepts and Connections," "some stress is healthy and
necessary to keep us alert and occupied." Yet that's not the theme that's been
coming out of science for the past few years. "The public has gotten such a
uniform message that stress is always harmful," says Janet DiPietro, a developmental psychologist at Johns Hopkins University. "And that's too bad, because most people do their best under mild to moderate stress."

The stress response—the body's hormonal reaction to danger, uncertainty or change—evolved to help us survive, and if we learn how to keep it from overrunning our lives, it still can. In the short term, it can energize us, "revving up our systems to handle what we have to handle," says Judith Orloff, a psychiatrist at UCLA. In the long term, stress can motivate us to do better at jobs we care about. A little of it can prepare us for a lot later on, making us more resilient. Even when it's extreme, stress may have some positive effects—which is why, in addition to posttraumatic stress disorder, some psychologists are starting to define a phenomenon called posttraumatic growth. "There's really a biochemical and scientific bias that stress is bad, but anecdotally and clinically, it's quite evident that it can work for some people," says Orloff. "We need a new wave of research with a more balanced approach to how stress can serve us." Otherwise, we're all going to spend far more time than we should stressing ourselves out about the fact that we're stressed out.

When I started asking researchers about "good stress," many of them said it essentially didn't exist. "We never tell people stress is good for them," one said. Another allowed that it might be, but only in small ways, in the short term, in rats. What about people who thrive on stress, I asked—people who become policemen or ER docs or air-traffic controllers because they like seeking out chaos and putting things back in order? Aren't they using stress to their advantage? No, the researchers said, those people are unhealthy. "This business of people saying they 'thrive on stress'? It's nuts," Bruce Rabin, a distinguished psychoneuroimmunologist, pathologist and psychiatrist at the University of Pittsburgh School of Medicine, told me. Some adults who seek out stress and believe they flourish under it may have been abused as children or permanently affected in the womb after exposure to high levels of adrenaline and cortisol, he said. Even if they weren't, he added, they're "trying to satisfy" some psychological need. Was he calling this a pathological state, I asked—saying that people who feel they perform best under pressure actually have a disease? He thought for a minute, and then: "You can absolutely say that. Yes, you can say that."

This kind of statement might well have the father of stress research lying awake worried in his grave. Hans Selye, who laid the foundation of stress science in the 1930s, believed so strongly in good stress that he coined a word, "eustress," for it. He saw stress as "the salt of life." Change was inevitable, and worrying about it was the flip side of thinking creatively and carefully about it, something that only a brain with a lot of prefrontal cortex can do well. Stress, then, was what made us human—a conclusion that Selye managed to reach by examining rats.

Selye had virtually no lab technique, and, as it turned out, that was fortunate. As a young researcher, he set out to study what happened when he injected rats with endocrine extracts. He was a klutz, dropping his animals and chasing them around the lab with a broom. Almost all his rats—even the ones he shot up with presumably harmless saline—developed ulcers, overgrown adrenal glands and immune dysfunction. To his credit, Selye didn't regard this finding as evidence he failed. Instead, he decided he was onto something.

Selye's rats weren't responding to the chemicals he was injecting. They were responding to his clumsiness with the needle. They didn't like being dropped and poked and bothered. He was stressing them out. Selye called the rats' condition "general adaptation syndrome," a telling term that reflected the reason the stress response had evolved in the first place: in life-or-death situations, it was helpful.

For a rat, there's no bigger stressor than an encounter with a lean and hungry cat. As soon as the rat's brain registers danger, it pumps itself up on hormones—first adrenaline, then cortisol. The surge helps mobilize energy to the muscles, and it also primes several parts of the brain, temporarily improving some types of memory and fine-tuning the senses. Thus armed, the rat makes its escape—assuming the cat, whose brain has also been flooded with stress hormones by the sight of a long-awaited potential meal, doesn't outrun or outwit it.

This cascade of chemicals is what we refer to as "stress." For rats, the triggers are largely limited to physical threats from the likes of cats and scientists. But in humans, almost anything can start the stress response. Battling traffic, planning a party, losing a job, even gaining a job—all may get the stress hormones flowing as freely as being attacked by a predator does. Even the prospect of future change can set off our alarms. We think, therefore we worry.

Herein lies a problem. A lot of us tend to flip the stress-hormone switch to "on" and leave it there. At some point, the neurons get tired of being primed, and positive effects become negative ones. The result is the same decline in health that Selye's rats suffered. Neurons shrivel and stop communicating with each other, and brain tissue shrinks in the hippocampus and prefrontal cortex, which play roles in learning, memory and rational thought. "Acutely, stress helps us remember some things better," says neuroendocrinologist Bruce McEwen of Rockefeller University. "Chronically, it makes us worse at remembering other things, and it impairs our mental flexibility."

These chronic effects may disappear when the stressor does. In medical students studying for exams, the medial prefrontal cortex shrinks during cram sessions but grows back after a month off. The bad news is that after a stressful event, we don't always get a month off. Even when we do, we may spend it worrying ("Sure, the test is over, but how did I do?"), and that's just as biochemically bad as the original stressor. This is why stress is linked to depression and Alzheimer's; neurons weakened by years of exposure to stress hormones are more susceptible to killers. It also suggests that those of us with constant stress in our lives should be reduced to depressed, forgetful wrecks. But most of us aren't. Why?

Step away from the lab, and you'll find the beginnings of an answer. In the 1970s and '80s, Salvatore Maddi, a psychologist at the University of California, Irvine, followed 430 employees at Illinois Bell during a companywide crisis. While most of the workers suffered as their company fell apart—performing poorly on the job, getting divorced and developing high rates of heart attacks, obesity and strokes—a third of them fared well. They stayed healthy, kept their jobs or found others quickly. It would be easy to assume these were the workers who'd grown up in peaceful, privileged circumstances. It would also be wrong. Many of those who did best as adults had had fairly tough childhoods. They had suffered no abuse or trauma but "maybe had fathers in the military and moved around a lot, or had parents who were alcoholics," says Maddi. "There was a lot of stress in their early lives, but their parents had convinced them that they were the hope of the family—that they would make everyone proud of them—and they had accepted that role. That led to their being very hardy people." Childhood stress, then, had been good for them—it had given them something to transcend.

More recently, Robert Sapolsky of Stanford University has studied a similar phenomenon in alpha males. He's seen plenty of "totally insane son of a bitch" types who respond to stress by lashing out, but he's also interested in another type that gets less press: the nice guy who finishes first. These alphas don't often get into fights; when they do, they pick battles they know they can win. They're just as dominant as their angry counterparts, and they're subject to the same stressors—power struggles, unsuccessful sexual overtures, the occasional need to slap down a subordinate—but their hormone levels never get out of whack for long, and they probably don't suffer much stress-induced brain dysfunction. Sapolsky likes to joke that they've all been relaxing in hot tubs in Big Sur, transforming themselves into "minimalist Zen masters." This is a joke because they've clearly come by their attitudes unconsciously: Sapolsky studies wild baboons.

Sapolsky's and Maddi's work points to a flaw with much of the neurobiological research: so far, it has done a poor job of accounting for differences in how individuals process stress. Researchers haven't identified the point at which the effects of stress tip over from positive to negative, and they know little about why that point differs from person to person. (That is why they don't like to tell people that a little stress can be good, says Rabin—because "we don't know how to judge for each individual what a 'little' stress is.") The research thus tends to paint stress as a universal phenomenon, even though we all experience it differently. "If there are rats or mice or cultured neurons in a dish that seem superresilient to stress, far too many lab scientists view this as a pain in the ass, something that just throws off patterns," says Sapolsky. "It's only people who are tuned into animal behavior or humans and the real world who are interested in how amazing the outliers are." Explaining these outliers' healthy attitudes, says Sapolsky, is now "the field's biggest challenge."

As Maddi's work makes clear, a lot of the explanation stems from early experiences. This may be true of Sapolsky's baboons as well. Sapolsky suspects that part of what makes an animal a dominant Zen master instead of an angry alpha lies in what sort of childhood he had. If an adult baboon picks up on conflict around him but keeps his cool, "quelling the anxiety and exercising impulse control," that may be behavior his mom modeled for him years earlier. The key? Factors such as how many steps the baby baboon could take away from his mother before she pulled him back—i.e., how much she allowed him to learn for himself, even if that meant a few bumps and bruises along the way. "I think the males who had mothers who were less anxious, who allowed them to be more exploratory in the absence of agitated maternal worry, are more likely to be the Zen ones who are calm enough to resist provocation," he says. A little properly handled stress, then, may be necessary to turn children into well-adjusted adults.

Part of the explanation will also be found in genes. Scientists have already identified one that helps control how the brain processes serotonin; some variants seem to protect people from depression, depending on whether they've suffered through previous traumas. This gene may not mediate everyday stress, but others are bound to be fingered eventually, and "once people have found scores of genes," says Sapolsky, "I'm willing to bet the farm that that's going to begin to explain who gets depressed after disastrous unrequited love and who just feels lousy for two weeks."

The X and Y chromosomes also play a role in how people respond to stress, though how much of one isn't clear. Men and women both experience stress as a rise in adrenaline and cortisol. What differs is their reaction. Women "are more likely to turn to their social networks, and that prompts the release of oxytocin, which mutes the stress systems," says Shelley Taylor, a psychologist at UCLA. If they're surrounded by loved ones when a stressor arises, she says, "there's some evidence they don't even show as much of the initial hormonal response." Without that response, there's less risk of long-term harm to the brain. It's a critical concept—yet it wasn't on stress physiologists' radar until the mid-'90s, when Taylor pointed out that most stress research in animals and humans had been conducted overwhelmingly on males.

Finally, there's that murky territory where genes and environment interact, with lifelong effects: the womb. It's not hard to find studies suggesting that maternal stress harms later child development. But what the evidence means, no one knows. "Project Ice Storm," a survey of nearly 150 expectant mothers who toughed out a 1998 squall in Quebec—some without power for up to 40 days—is one of the scariest studies. Late last year researchers reported that the women's children had lower-than-average IQs and language skills at age 5; they say the storm and its stress on the mothers had "significant effects [on the children] … in every area of development that we have examined." The study surveys many children in great detail, but it doesn't mean all pregnant women should panic about their stress levels (or panic about the fact that they've just panicked). An ice storm isn't the same kind of stressor that people encounter in everyday life, and the women in the ice-storm study don't necessarily represent all women. Those who were stuck in Quebec during the storm were likely some of the ones with the fewest resources. Their children may have been prone to low scores as five-year-olds simply because they were poor.

A lot of the research on stress and infant development can be picked apart this way, says DiPietro, of Johns Hopkins. Also, she notes, "nobody ever got funded by saying stress *doesn't* harm babies." DiPietro herself is a rare exception. Two years ago, she showed that women under moderate stress in mid-to-late pregnancy wound up with toddlers who were developmentally advanced, scoring highly on language and cognitive tests. In an upcoming paper, she confirms the trend: two-week-old babies whose mothers were under moderate stress show evidence of faster nerve transmission—and possibly more mature brain development—than those whose moms had stress-free pregnancies. It's hard to know what to make of the findings, but DiPietro has an intriguing theory. A stressed-out mother's "internal environment"—her heartbeat, blood pressure and other signals the fetus can perceive—is constantly in flux. Her restlessness may stimulate the fetus's brain, giving it something to think about. In this light, DiPietro thinks, the kind of mild to moderate stress that is pervasive in many women's hectic lives may be beneficial, perhaps even "essential," for fetal development. The idea is controversial—but if it's correct, it certainly complicates the theory that stress can permanently damage a child in utero.

When Stanford's Sapolsky gives lectures on stress, he cites the "depressing" research on failing neurons, some of which he has conducted. But his talks end optimistically, thanks to his observations in the wild. "If some baboons just happen to be good at seeing water holes as half full instead of half empty … we should be able to as well," he once told an audience. Even if we're not born well equipped to deal with stress, he said, "we can change," because as humans, we ought to be "wise enough to keep this stuff in perspective."

So how do we do that? One place to start is with the human equivalent of Zen baboons: Buddhist monks. Their mental stability and calmness isn't mystical; it's biological. The brain can grow new cells and reshape itself, and meditation appears to encourage this process. Monks who have trained for years in meditation have greater brain activity in regions linked to learning and happiness. "The mind is far more malleable than we previously assumed," says Saki Santorelli, executive director of the Center for Mindfulness in Medicine, Health Care, and Society at the University of Massachusetts Medical School. Studies at the center have shown that meditation can help people cope with stress. It may repair or compensate for damage already done to the brain.

Not all of us want to or can become monks; not all of us can spare even eight weeks for a course at the Center for Mindfulness. But there are quicker ways to learn to harness and handle stress. For this article, I tried one: the Williams LifeSkills program, a cognitive mini-makeover based on the research of Duke University psychiatrist Redford Williams. LifeSkills teaches adherents to approach life like a Zen baboon, picking the right battles—and it can be completed in a day and a half. "You won't achieve enlightenment, but it will help you," Williams told me before I embarked on the course, which gave me a formula for assessing conflicts (How important is this to me? Should I be mad? Can I do something about the problem? Would that be worth the trouble?). He was right. I did feel a bit calmer afterward. But then, I had willed myself to. I liked Williams; I was hoping his program would work.

This is the problem with all stress-management tactics: you have to want them to succeed and be willing to throw yourself into them, or they'll fail. If you force yourself to do them, you'll just stress yourself out more. This is why exercise relieves stress for some people and makes other miserable. It's also why Sapolsky says he's "totally frazzled" but doesn't bother with meditation: "If I had to do that for 30 minutes a day," he says, "I'm pretty sure I'd have a stroke."

For all of the science's shortfalls, there's animal research that suggests why something that should lower stress can actually *cause* stress if it's done in the wrong spirit. In a classic study, scientists put two rats in a cage, each of them locked in a running wheel. The first rat could exercise whenever he liked. The second was yoked to the first, forced to run when his counterpart did. Exercise, like meditation, usually tamps down stress and encourages neuron growth, and indeed, the first rat's brain bloomed with new cells. The second rat, however, lost brain cells. He was doing something that should have been good for his brain, but he lacked one crucial factor: control. He could not determine his own "workout" schedule, so he didn't perceive it as exercise. Instead, he experienced it as a literal rat race.

This experiment brings up a troubling point about stress. Psychologists have known for years that one of the biggest factors in how we process stressful events is how much control we have over our lives. As a rule, if we feel we're in control, we cope. If we don't, we collapse. And no amount of meditation or reframing our thinking can change certain facts of our lives. With the market languishing and jobs hemorrhaging and the world going to hell, too many of us probably feel like that rat in the second wheel: it's hard to convince ourselves we're in control of anything.

But stress science even provides a little hope here, if we go back to Selye. He first published his ideas during the Great Depression—a time of stress if ever there was one, and a time in which survival demanded creativity. That Depression ended. Now we're entering what may be a new one, and we'll need more creative thinking to get out of it. We're going to have to figure out what parts of our future we can control, and we'll need to engage with them thoughtfully. Fortunately, we have the kind of brain that permits that. Sure, it will be stressful. Maybe that isn't a bad thing.

Discussion Questions

1. What did the psychologists Spencer Rathus and Janet DiPietro have to say about stress?
2. How was posttraumatic growth defined?
3. What did Bruce Rabin, a distinguished psychoneuroimmunologist, pathologist and psychiatrist, have to say about people who seek out stress?
4. Who was Hans Selye and what did he have to say about stress?
5. What did neuroendocrinologist Bruce McEwen of Rockefeller University have to say about stress as it relates to learning, memory, and rational thought?
6. Men and women both experience stress as a rise in adrenalin and cortisol but there is a difference in their reactions. What is this difference?
7. What was learned as a result of the "Project Ice Storm" study as it relates to the 1998 squall in Quebec?
8. What did the developmental psychologist, Janet DiPietro, conclude as it relates to women who are under moderate stress in mid-to-late pregnancy and its impact on their unborn children?
9. What was discovered as a result of the classic study of scientists putting two rats in a cage, each of them locked in a running wheel?

4

The Usual Suspect

Anthony L. Komaroff, M.D.

Walter Bradford Cannon did not strike people as someone interested in black magic. A world-famous physiologist, Cannon often wore three-piece suits in his laboratory at Harvard Medical School. He spent his life making very precise measurements of bodily functions and drawing cautious conclusions from those measurements. That's why his colleagues were surprised by the paper that Cannon published in the *American Anthropologist* in 1942. In it he described well-documented examples of healthy young adults in South America, Africa, Australia, New Zealand, various islands of the South Pacific and Haiti who had been hexed by witch doctors. Once the word of their hexing was out, the victims were often abandoned by their tribe and even by their families. Within a few days, they were dead. These "voodoo deaths" just happened, without any discernable violence having been done to the victims. Black magic, it would seem. Cannon had an alternative explanation, however: he believed the victims had been scared to death.

Cannon was the first to describe the "fight or flight" reaction: when the brain perceives a serious threat, it sends chemical and electrical signals that prepare the heart, lungs, blood vessels and immune system for the battle or chase to come. Cannon pointed out that—in a world full of sudden physical threats—this stress reaction helped preserve the lives, and hence the reproductive capacity, of human beings; it thus had been fostered and preserved by evolution. In the case of the voodoo victims, however, Cannon argued that the stress reaction was harmful rather than protective. When the reaction remained activated for several days—sustained by fear and aggravated by a loss of social support—it led to a collapse of the circulation and death.

While there is much evidence linking stress to the heart and blood vessels, the relationship is not nearly as simple as a recounting of Cannon's voodoo paper might suggest. And despite some widely held and popular ideas, the link between stress and other diseases is even less clear. Surely, experiencing stress may worsen the symptoms of almost any condition. But there is little evidence that stress is the exclusive or even the principle cause of any disease.

For decades, we believed that stress led to an overproduction of stomach acid, which caused duodenal ulcers. Stress does increase the amount of acid produced in the stomach, and there's no doubt that, once a person has a duodenal ulcer, acid makes the ulcer hurt. But we now know that the ulcer's cause is not stress but a bacterial infection, curable with antibiotics. Doctors also once believed that the inflammatory bowel diseases—Crohn's disease and ulcerative colitis—were caused by stress. Today we know they are caused by inherited tendencies toward abnormal inflammation in response to gut bacteria. Treatments based on that theory do a lot more to relieve symptoms than does stress management. There also is little evidence that stress causes asthma, although some patients have flare-ups more often at times of stress. And despite much folklore, there is no proof that stress causes cancer or worsens its prognosis. Stress-reduction programs can be very helpful in easing the suffering of a victim of cancer, but there is no strong evidence that they lengthen life.

It's the role of stress in heart disease that has received the most attention over the years, and with good reason. Like our ancestors, we all occasionally face the single, sudden and extreme stressors that the stress response evolved to protect us from. For us, the acute stressor may not be an approaching pride of lions, or the knowledge that we have just been hexed and therefore soon will be dead. Rather, it may be a car that has run a red light and is hurtling toward us. Our response to such sudden and extreme stressors can protect us, but it also can have dire consequences if we already have heart disease.

Perhaps even more important is the drip-drip-drip of chronic, low-grade stressors—the traffic jam that means we'll be late for an appointment, worrying about how to pay the bills this month, or recurring tension with a spouse or child. These chronic stressors, like sudden and acute stressors, also can affect the most common and lethal form of heart disease we face—atherosclerosis (sometimes called "hardening") of the coronary arteries.

Coronary atherosclerosis deforms artery walls. Ultimately, it can block blood flow, starving the heart muscle of the nutrition it needs. Plaques of atherosclerosis cause symptoms two ways. If the plaques grow large enough to significantly obstruct the flow of blood, the heart won't get the blood supply it needs when it is forced to work harder—for example, by exercise or by anger. The heart is not actually damaged, but the pain can recur whenever the heart is again forced to work hard. Alternatively, a plaque can rupture, either when the heart is working hard or even when a person is at rest and at peace. Plaque rupture causes a blood clot to form that suddenly and often completely stops the flow of blood through the artery.

Chronic stressors can speed the development of atherosclerosis and enhance the dangers from it once it has developed. They can also contribute to heart disease indirectly if they lead us to overeat, under-exercise or smoke. Stress is a toxic emotional and physical response; anger, hostility, depression and anxiety are examples of such toxic responses. Anxiety, for instance, involves apprehension combined with palpitations, fatigue and shortness of breath. Some people respond to chronic stressors with remarkable equanimity. Others spend a substantial fraction of their day experiencing one or more of the toxic reactions. This is influenced in part by our genes, but is also controllable with stress-management techniques. And if these toxic reactions are not controlled, there is growing evidence that heart disease is more likely to occur and at an earlier age.

Sudden, major stressful life events can sometimes cause catastrophic results in people with underlying heart disease—including heart disease they didn't know they had because it had never before caused symptoms. The sudden outpouring of adrenaline in reaction to the event can cause the heart to work unusually hard, or can cause a plaque of atherosclerosis to rupture, which in turn can generate dangerous heart rhythms and sudden death.

In a paper published nearly 40 years ago in the *Annals of Internal Medicine*, internist and psychiatrist George Engel reconstructed the events in the hours before 170 people died suddenly. Particularly for women, Engel found that the most common trigger for sudden death was a major loss—of a spouse, of self-esteem. For men, sudden danger more often was a trigger. Subsequent evidence supports Engel's thesis. For example, sudden deaths increased immediately following the Northridge earthquake in southern California in 1994, and after September 11, 2001—and not just in New York City.

Interestingly, Engel found that sudden death also could follow a triumph or a happy ending to a long struggle. He reported the sudden death of a just-released prisoner upon returning home, a man who had just scored his first hole in one, an opera singer who was receiving a standing ovation. Even joy can rattle our silently diseased arteries. Mind you, we still should seek happiness. But Engel's study suggests that we seek it in frequent, small dollops rather than in rare surges of ecstasy.

Obviously, "voodoo death" is not a problem in developed nations. However, a recently described heart disease may be. A sudden, extremely stressful situation can flood the blood with adrenaline and cause a type of heart disease called stress-induced cardiomyopathy (it's called "takotsubo cardiomyopathy" in Japan, where it was first described). More than 80 percent of the victims of this disease are women. The flood of adrenaline causes millions of tiny arteries inside the heart muscle to clamp down. The apex of the heart is weakened, causing it to balloon out. Even though the large coronary arteries on the outside of the heart muscle are free of significant atherosclerosis, this condition can cause the same symptoms as the more typical heart disease—chest pain, shortness of breath, shock and even death. We don't yet know how common the condition is.

Despite the role of stress in some diseases, we physicians sometimes oversell stress as a medical problem. It's a doctor's job to make a diagnosis and figure out the causes of disease. When we can't, it's a problem—our problem. I'm afraid we sometimes protect our egos by invoking stress, which effectively says to our patients that their suffering really is their problem. I've seen many patients with difficult-to-diagnose diseases like multiple sclerosis or lupus who, before the diagnosis was finally made, spent months and even years going from doctor to doctor. Repeatedly, they were told, "It's just stress." As a result of this "diagnosis," the doctors felt a lot better—but not the patients. The facts are that stress can worsen the symptoms of any disease and stress management can offer relief. Stress, however, is rarely the sole, convenient explanation for a patient's suffering.

Discussion Questions

1. What explanation was provided by Walter Bradford Cannon as to why healthy young adults in South America, Africa, Australia, New Zealand, various islands of the South Pacific and Haiti who had been hexed by witch doctors died within a few days after they were hexed?
2. What is the "fight or flight" reaction?
3. What medical conditions were once well accepted as being caused by stress but have now been discounted as being stress-caused?
4. What is coronary atherosclerosis and how can it cause a heart attack?
5. How can chronic stressors indirectly contribute to heart disease?
6. How can sudden major stressful life events sometimes cause catastrophic results in people with underlying heart disease, including heart disease?
7. What did the psychologist George Engel discover about sudden deaths as it relates to women?
8. What did the psychologist George Engel discover about sudden deaths as it relates to men?

Part Two

What Does Stress Mean for Cops?

The readings in Part One clearly support the position that this phenomenon called stress is indeed a bodily reaction to specific sociocultural and environmental events. Selye included crowding, sensory deprivation, and urbanization as some of these key factors and identified a number of occupations as particularly susceptible to stress:

- Accountants
- Industrial occupations
- Physicians and dentists
- Lawyers
- Members of the armed forces
- Air traffic controllers
- Police officers

It is the impact on the latter that is, of course, the subject of this book. To the editors of this book and to numerous law enforcement administrators and academicians, it is apparent that the manifestations and effects of police stress can be dangerous to the individual officer, his or her family and department, and the community at large. As Burgin has summarized:

> From the perspective of the individual officer, stress manifests itself in physiological problems, such as heart disease, alcoholism, and other stress related disorders. Psychological disorders and emotional instability are also outcomes of stress, as are broken marriages, overt verbal and/or physical hostility toward the public, and in the extreme, suicide by the police officer.
>
> From the perspective of the police organization, stress takes its toll through (a) losses of police officer efficiency, (b) complaints from the public, (c) lawsuits resulting from police malpractice, (d) workmen's compensation claims, (e) disability retirements, and (f) from burnedout personnel in supervisory and management positions who create

still more stress in their subordinates, peers and commanding officers (Burgin, 53–54).

So what is police stress? What does the phenomenon mean for cops? As we explore the topic, can we easily identify means by which we can reduce and mitigate its impact? The authors in Part Two provide a comprehensive overview of the subject and its general impact on officers, setting the stage for subsequent chapters in this book.

Arter prepared his discussion on the application of general strain theory to law enforcement officer stress specifically for this volume. An academically challenging reading, it offers three specific benefits to the reader. First, it suggests one alternative framework for conceptualizing coping strategies utilized to deal with stress. Second, it supplies an extensive bibliography on both law enforcement stress and strain theory. Finally, it provides a qualitative analysis of stress experienced by specific groups of law enforcement officers.

Large-scale critical events, such as the attacks on the World Trade Centers, have served to emphasize the effect of traumatic incidents on law enforcement officers. Yet the on-going exposure to the routine events of the officer's job can cause even more potential long-term psychological and physiological damage. The combination of all these on-the-job factors, coupled with the stress normally associated with daily life, creates the high level of stress anticipated within this profession. In their chapter, Sheehan, a faculty member at the FBI Academy, and Van Hasselt discuss the Law Enforcement Officer Stress Survey, an instrument which can be used to identify major sources of stress, analyze the impact of such stress on officers, and develop a set of scenarios which can ultimately become an early screening tool for officers undergoing major stress reactions.

With their major metropolitan social problems, high crime rates, and violence committed against officers, police stress is often thought of as a phenomenon primarily occurring in big cities. Yet officers in small towns and rural communities have their own unique set of stressors which impact their professional and personal lives. Recognizing that life-changing critical incidents can occur in any geographic setting, Lindsey and Kelly focus on the special demands on such officers in areas where they are well known, where there are too few officers, and where there is little opportunity to decompress. Perhaps most important, they offer suggestions by which stress in such environments may be better handled.

In the final selection in Part Two, Patton discusses the impact of a constant exposure to danger, violence, and suffering on the coping capabilities and wellness of police officers. As part of his analysis, he examines the impact of "spiritual wellness" on the ability of law enforcement personnel to cope with the stress in their lives.

Further Reading

Band, Stephen R., and Manuele, Caroline A. (1987). "Stress and Police Officer Performance: An Examination of Effective Coping Behavior," *Journal of Police and Criminal Psychology*, 3(3), 30–42.

Brooks, Laure Weber, and Piquero, Nicole Leeper (1998). "Police Stress: Does Department Size Matter?" *Policing: An International Journal of Police Strategies and Management*, 21(4), 600–617.

Burgin, A. Lad (1978). "The Management of Stress in Policing." Police Chief, 45(4), 53–54.

Copes, Heith (2005). *Policing and Stress.* Upper Saddle River, NJ: Pearson Prentice Hall.

Ellison, Katherine (2004). *Stress and the Police Officer (2nd Edition).* Springfield, IL: Charles C Thomas.

Finn, Peter (2000). "On-the-job Stress in Policing: Reducing It, Preventing It," *National Institute of Justice Journal*, January 18–24.

Graves, Wallace (1996). "Police Cynicism: Causes and Cures," *FBI Law Enforcement Bulletin*, 65 (6), 16–20.

Hennessy, Stephen M. (1995). *Thinking Cop, Feeling Cop.* Scottsdale, AZ: Leadership, Inc.

Kroes, William H. (1976). *Society's Victim—The Policeman.* Springfield, IL: Charles C Thomas.

Miller, Laurence (2006). *Practical Police Psychology: Stress Management and Crisis Intervention for Law Enforcement.* Springfield, IL: Charles C Thomas.

Selye, H. (1967). *The Stress of Life* (Revised Edition). New York, NY: McGraw Hill.

Toch, Hans (2002). *Stress in Policing.* Washington, DC: American Psychological Association.

While this book focuses on stress affecting law enforcement officers in the United States, the reader should recognize that police stress is not just an American phenomenon. To review the impact of stress on officers outside this country, the authors recommend:

Ainsworth, Peter B., and Pease, Ken (1987). *Police Work.* London, England: British Psychological Association.

Alexander, David A., and Walker, Leslie G. (1996). "The Perceived Impact of Police Work on Police Officers' Spouses and Families," *Stress Medicine*, 12, 239–246.

Arendt, M., and Elklit, A. (2001). "Effectiveness of Psychological Debriefing," *Acta Psychiatrica Scandinavica*, 104: 423–437.

Hetherington, Angela (1993). "Traumatic Stress on the Roads," in R. Allen (Ed.), Handbook of Post-Disaster Interventions (Special Issue). *Journal of Social Behavior and Personality*, 8(5), 369–378.

Karlsson, Ingemar, and Christianson, Sven-Ake (2003). "The Phenomenology of Traumatic Experiences in Police Work," *Policing: An International Journal of Police Strategies and Management*, 26(3), 419–438.

Kop, Nicolien; Euwema, Martin; and Schaufeli, Wilmar (1999). "Burnout, Job Stress, and Violent Behaviour Among Dutch Police Officers," *Work & Stress*, 13(4), 326–340.

Key Terms in Part Two

Acute stress disorder (ASD): A short-term pattern of severe psychological reactions to stress. According to the American Psychological Association's Diagnostic and Statistical Manual of Mental Disorders (DSM), these symptoms normally occur within one month after exposure to an extreme traumatic stressor.

Alienation: The tendency of law enforcement officers to separate themselves or withdraw from non-law enforcement personnel.

Behavioral coping strategies: Acting out methods used by an individual to deal with strain; these may include efforts to minimize or eliminate the sources of strain or to retaliate against those perceived as responsible for the strain.

Cognitive coping strategies: Thought-based methods used by an individual to deal with strain; these may include mental rationalizations to justify their response.

Cynicism: Contemptuous distrust of human nature and motives, representing an attitude that expects nothing but the worst in human behavior.

Desacralization: Losing contact with the aspect of one's life that had previously been considered sacred and special.

Emotional coping strategies: Methods used by an individual to deal with strain. These may include destructive means, such as alcohol or drug abuse, or positive ones, such as meditation or physical exercise.

Employee Assistance Program (EAP): A program established in many public and private sector organizations which is available to provide employees with a number of services, including health assistance, financial advice, and psychological counseling.

Law Enforcement Officer Stress Survey (LEOSS): A tool developed by Supervisory Special Agent Donald Sheehan of the FBI and Dr. Vincent Van Hasselt to serve as a screening device in recognizing the impact of stress on police officers.

Post-traumatic stress disorder (PTSD): The APA's DSM-IV defines PSTD as the "development of characteristic symptoms following exposure to an extreme traumatic stressor involving direct personal experience of an event that involves actual or threatened death or serious injury or other threat to one's physical integrity; or witnessing an event that involves death, injury, or threat to the integrity of another person ... the person's response to the event must involve fear, helplessness or horror ... ."

Spirituality: the capacity of all people to possess—and know they possess— beliefs, values, and convictions that give meaning and purpose to life.

Strain theory: This theory holds that negative relationships and the desire to avoid negative situations are the primary motivations in an individual; negative affective states can lead to the desire for corrective action or deviant reactions to the stressors experienced.

Stress Management in Law Enforcement (SMILE): A stress management training course for law enforcement officers first developed at the FBI Academy by Supervisory Special Agent Donald Sheehan.

5

Applying General Strain Theory to Policing: Examining Police Stress

Michael L. Arter

Introduction

General strain theory focuses on the individual and the intimate environment as determinates of reactive behaviors to strain. Negative relationships and the desire to avoid negative situations are the primary motivations identified in general strain theory. Agnew's earliest work (1985, 1989, 1992) proposes that individuals react to aversive environments, particularly those in which they believe they are trapped or are unjust, in an aggressive and retaliatory nature. Negative affective states, primarily anger and related emotions that can result from negative relationships, lead to the desire for corrective action or deviant reactions to experiential stressors. Negative relationships can involve any situation in which the individual is not realizing expectations, or is not being treated in a desirable manner. Each of these principles has applicability in the policing profession.

General strain theory also posits that cognitive, behavioral, and emotional coping strategies are utilized by individuals in attempts to deal with strain (Agnew, 1992). Cognitive coping strategies include feats of mental rationalizations to justify individual responses in addressing the strain or adversity. Behavioral coping strategies can include efforts to minimize or eliminate the sources of strain, or retaliate against those perceived as responsible for the strain. Finally, emotional coping strategies can be destructive, in the form of self medication through alcohol and drug abuse, or positive, through meditation or physical and mental exercises. Police officers have been shown to employ each of these coping strategies routinely to minimize the impact of regular occupational stressors (Ballenger et al., 2010; Linsday & Shelley, 2009; Marmar, et al., 2006; Swatt, Gibson, & Piquero, 2007; Toch, 2002).

The propositions and central tenets of general strain theory have been empirically supported in terms of a significant relationship between negative affect and delinquency (Agnew, 1985, 1989; Agnew & White, 1992). Additionally, aversive environments (Agnew, 1985, 1989), repeated exposure to negative stimuli (Agnew, 1992; Agnew & White, 1992), the cumulative nature of strain (Agnew & White, 1992), and perceptions of inequity (Agnew, 1992) all have been found to be positively associated with delinquency and deviance.

Negative life events and negative relations with adults also have been shown to be positively related to delinquency (Brezina, 1999; Paternoster & Mazerrolle, 1994), as well as to a higher number of stressful life events (Hoffman & Cerbone, 1999). Additionally, there are findings that maltreatment is associated with increased anger and adherence to deviant beliefs (Brezina, 1998). Finally, delinquency has been found to function as an effective (although maladaptive) coping strategy for many youth (Brezina, 1996), and other illegitimate coping strategies are more likely in those who experience more anger, strain, and association with delinquent peers (Broidy, 2001; Capowich, Mazerolle, & Piquero, 2001; Piquero & Sealock, 2000), or for those who are high in negative emotionality and low in constraint (Agnew, Brezina, Wright, & Cullen, 2002; Ganem, 2010).

The present research sought to extend the empirical application of general strain theory from delinquency studies into the adult realm, focusing specifically on police officers and undercover operations. The basic principles of general strain theory were applied to adult participants in the same or similar manner as they have been applied to juveniles. The sources of strain examined included actual or anticipated failure to achieve positively valued goals, actual or anticipated removal of valued goals, and actual or anticipated presentation of negatively valued stimuli (Agnew, 1992). Each of these types of strain is focused at the social-psychological level and is extremely relevant to police officers in general and specifically to those involved in the undercover environment.

Additionally, the coping mechanisms employed by police officers in attempts to mediate the sources of strain were examined in the context of the general strain literature and the limited police stress literature. This study focused on the stressors that lead up to the utilization of these coping strategies, and the impact of inappropriate strategies on the personal, social, and professional lives of the officers involved. The scant undercover literature available points to the detrimental impact that such assignments and maladaptive coping can have for officers involved. The findings in the literature indicate that the length and duration of such assignments are correlated with individual responses to stress (Giordo, 1991). This research reinforces those findings to some degree.

The use by police officers of maladaptive coping strategies to mediate stress, and the psychological and emotional damage that can occur at the individual officer level, supports the need for current and valid empirical research. An officer's personal life can play a significant role in the ability to effectively and responsibly perform assigned duties. This would appear to be even more pertinent in the undercover environment, where a clear mental state is crucial. Officer safety, the legal accumulation of evidence, and the successful prosecution of targeted offenses are only a few of the "real world" implications that require a sound state of mind.

The purpose of this study was to apply the findings of research involving a high stressed adult population to the principles of general strain theory, which has been applied extensively to juveniles, and less frequently to adult populations. If this theory is truly a "general" theory, the principles and concepts should be applicable to all populations. This study sought to provide such a test for this theory.

Literature Review

Law enforcement has been identified as one of the most stressful occupations, both in the United States and worldwide (Anshel, 2000). The authority, responsibilities, and duties of police officers place a heavy burden on those public servants who have chosen the law enforcement profession. The demands of this profession, in conjunction with the expectations and scrutiny of the public being served, are often more than the body or spirit can handle. Consequently, police officers experience higher mortality rates, higher rates of coronary disease, and higher rates of alcohol abuse and clinical depression as compared to the general population (Toch, 2002). Stress in law enforcement can have a significant impact on the individual officer, the law enforcement profession as a whole, and on every citizen that is encountered during the performance of the police mission. Undercover stress, while not having as large of an impact on the same population as "routine" police duties, may impact dramatically on the officers involved in such assignments, on the families of those officers, on other officers within the same agency, and on the law enforcement profession in general. Furthermore, undercover assignments, and the "fallout" of undercover operations, can have a dramatic impact on the general population, the law enforcement agencies involved, and the criminal justice system in general.

Overall, the literature on police stress addresses a broad range of job related stressors, reactions to the stressors, and limitedly examines both adaptive and maladaptive coping strategies utilized by officers to mediate the effects of experienced stress. The use of alcohol is the most frequently cited and subculturally accepted maladaptive coping strategy found in the literature. While the use of alcohol also has been indicated to be a "successful" mediator of stress (Violanti, Marshall, & Howe, 1985), there is little empirical research that has focused specifically on alcohol as an adaptive coping mechanism. Additionally, several studies indicated that job assignments are related to levels of stress in police officers and to the use of alcohol as a means of mediating stress (Davey, Obst, & Sheehan, 2000; Violanti & Aaron, 1994, 1995). While police related stress, and the coping methods utilized in response to such stress, are serious concerns for all police officers, some assignments within the law enforcement profession are viewed as more stressful than others and subsequently may benefit more from further examination of these issues.

Undercover police assignments have been reported to be one of the most stressful of all duty assignments (Arter, 2008; Farkas, 1986; Giordo, 1985, 1991; Poegrebin & Poole, 1993). The nature of the requirements to achieve success in an undercover capacity, the inherent stressful conditions encountered in undercover duties, and the isolation that can result from the undercover role, each and cumulatively can create a major source of additional stress on the officer involved in such assignments. Accordingly, undercover assignments, and the stress involved in such assignments, warrant further examination.

To varying degrees, stress is a factor in everyone's life. Individuals differ in recognition and interpretation of experienced stimuli (Horowitz, 2001). Therefore, stress exists only when it is recognized by the individual as being stressful. Furthermore, individual life stressors can be mediated (or exacerbated) by an individual's social support network (or lack thereof), and by factors in the occupational setting (Payne, 1980).

Occupational stressors vary by the nature of the occupation and organizational/administrative management styles. Everyone (including police officers) attempts to achieve certain psychological rewards from the work environment (Bruhn & Wolf, 1986). Stress results when individuals do not realize psychological rewards in the workplace or when the rewards are removed (or threatened to be removed) from the worker's immediate enjoyment (Selye, 1974). Stress also can be mediated by a compensating social support network (Gibson, Swatt, & Jolicoeur, 2001; Kirschman, 2006; Marmar et al., 2006). Unfortunately, such social support networks often are not available to many police officers, and maladaptive behavioral responses may be implemented in attempts to mediate experiential stressors (Terry, 1981).

The literature indicates that there are unique stress producing aspects in policing that are not experienced by others within the same community or geographic location. Police experience a distinctive work environment that entails exposure to violence, the requirement to make split second decisions, threats to personal safety, the suffering of others, and the realization of the frailties of the human existence (Finn & Tornz, 2000; Kelly, 2002). Additionally, police officers may experience repeated abuse from those they serve (Anshel, 2000) and do not experience the support of the general public in many circumstances (Beehr, Johnson, & Nieva, 1995; Madonna & Kelly, 2002). This lack of public support negatively impacts on the attainment by police officers of the psychological rewards discussed above (Anshel, 2000; Finn & Tornz, 2000; Kelly, 2002). Continued frustration by police officers due to this perceived lack of public support (Anshel, 2000) and support from the criminal justice system in general (Band & Manuel, 1987), coupled with the accumulated experiences of critical incidents, can be overwhelming to many officers and result in a chronic stressful condition (Marmar et al., 2006; Toch, 2002; Weiss et al.,2010). This phenomenon appears unique to the policing profession, due to the nature of duty requirements, expectations of the public being served, the political powers overseeing the policing function, and the individual officers themselves.

Policing also provides a unique setting that prohibits responses that are available to others outside the policing profession. While the "fight or flight" option is available to the general population and utilized on a daily basis in numerous situations, such an option is not available to police officers. Flight cannot be considered when faced with a threatening situation. Control must be maintained, and the threat must be encountered. Additionally, police officers do not enjoy the rewards of acceptance in the occupational and social settings that those in other occupations may enjoy. Such recognition and acceptance is one of the highest-order workplace needs (Shostack, 1980). Policing in general does not provide such acceptance in many circumstances for the officers involved.

Both micro- and macro-level factors are involved in determining an individual's reaction to either experienced or perceived stress. The limited policing literature available indicates that micro-level factors may be more influential on such reactions than are macro-level factors (Horowitz, 2001; Storch & Panzarella, 1996; White & Marino, 1983). A better understanding of these factors can provide significant insight into the reactions to work related stress encountered by police officers in general and undercover officers specifically. Micro-level factors include individual personality structuring, defense mechanisms, coping mechanisms, behavioral patterns, and family and social relationships (Selye, 1974).

The police subculture may be viewed as both a macro-level and micro-level factor that must be considered when addressing individual reactions to experienced and perceived stressors. However, there is little rigorous research addressing this issue. The research that is available appears to recognize the two defining characteristics of the police subculture, social isolation and group loyalty, as aggravators of the stressors inherent in police duties (Paoline, 2001). Social isolation provides a defense mechanism whereby police officers can "justify" the cynicism and disdain held for members of the public, and crystallizes the "us" and "them" mindset that permeates many police departments and is subsequently adopted by individual officers (Blau, 1994). The police subculture also can play a dramatic role in formulating the individual officer's perceptions, expectations, and reactions to the experiential stressors encountered on a daily basis.

The police stress literature indicates that police officers in general, and undercover officers specifically, exhibit unique defense mechanisms and coping strategies. Some of the maladaptive coping strategies discussed include emotional detachment (Macleod, 1995), cynicism (Band & Manuele, 1987; Stearns & Moore, 1993), alcohol abuse (Ballenger et al., 2010; Davey et al., 2000; Lindsay & Shelley, 2009; Violanti et al., 1985), sexual promiscuity (Macleod, 1995), and high risk behavior (Band & Manuele, 1987; Giordo, 1985; Macleod, 1995). A strong marital relationship appears to be a protective factor against the maladaptive coping strategy of alcohol abuse, and operational officers seem more prone to the abuse of alcohol than are administrative officers (Davey et al., 2000; Kirschman, 2006; Marmar et al., 2006).

Specific police behavioral patterns have been limitedly identified in the policing literature, and some of the effects of police assignments have been documented. The sparse literature on undercover policing tends to indicate that those officers who have functioned in an undercover capacity have a greater risk of drug and alcohol abuse than those who have never been assigned to undercover duties (Anshel, 2000; Giordo, 1991; Marx, 1988). The lack of adequate support and supervision (Arter, 2008; Kapeler & VanHoose, 1995; Miller, 1987), role confusion and role ambiguity (Farkas, 1986; Pogrebin & Poole, 1993), and extreme pressure to succeed (Marx, 1988) each have been indicated to have a significant impact on the personal and professional lives of the officers involved. The impact of such assignments can be seen in dramatic changes in personal relationships (Farkas, 1986), in the abuse of alcohol both during and after assignments (Farkas, 1986; Terry, 1981; Violanti et al., 1985), and in exhibiting depression, anger, paranoia, and interpersonal insensitivity (Giordo, 1985). Along with these micro level effects, there are identified implications at the macro level, such as greater violations of due process rights (Stevens, 1999) and undercover related corruption (Giordo, 1991; General Accounting Office, 1998).

Toch (2002) explains that stress is a transitional process that incorporates characteristics of both the individual's environment and the individual's behavioral responses. The empirical research examined appears to support this by showing that both experiential and organizational stressors are significantly related to the level of stress reported by police officers and undercover officers (Violanti & Aron, 1994, 1995). Furthermore, overall happiness with life and general life satisfaction appear to mediate the likelihood of police burnout (Stearns & Moore, 1993). On the other hand, the stoic and manly persona adapted by those in policing and undercover assignments has been shown to be correlated with higher levels of stress (Giordo, 1985; Stearns & Moore, 1993).

The undercover literature tends to point to the detrimental impact that such assignments can have on the personal, professional, and social lives of the officers involved. The findings of this limited research indicate that the length and duration of undercover assignments can have an impact on individual responses to stress (Giordo, 1991). Moreover, undercover officers are influenced by both task related stressors and individual stressors, with an observed increase in individual stressors as task related stressors increase (Terry, 1981). The lack of adequate supervision in undercover assignments (Arter, 2008; Kappeler & VanHoose, 1995; Miller, 1987), coupled with heightened individual stressors (Giordo, 1985; Marx, 1988), often result in a deeper isolation and attempts to mediate the situation (Macleod, 1995). The disruption of interpersonal relationships (Arter, 2008; Farkas, 1986; Pogrebin & Poole, 1993) and the continuous fear of discovery and failure (Macleod, 1995) are several of the unique stressors that require more attention in studying undercover assignments.

Undercover officers seem to utilize coping strategies that are both similar and dissimilar to those employed by other police officers. Alcohol has been identified as both a mediator and aggravator of undercover related stress (Farkas, 1986; Giordo, 1991; General Accounting Office, 1998; Macleod, 1995), and the use of alcohol during and after undercover assignments appears to be the most prevalent coping strategy employed by undercover officers. In addition, there is a positive and significant correlation between undercover assignments and both drug and alcohol abuse and disciplinary problems (Giordo, 1991). Sexuality also has been identified as a common coping mechanism employed by undercover officers (Marx, 1988; Pogrebin & Poole, 1993). Additionally, undercover officers experience both lifestyle changes and personality changes as a means of insulating themselves from the stressors being experienced (Macleod, 1995; Pogrebin & Poole, 1993). These personality changes can include self-centeredness, narcissism, arrogance, and an extreme sense of machismo (Macleod, 1995).

A portion of the undercover literature indicates the eventual impact of undercover assignments can be seen in an erosion of the personal value systems of officers (Giordo, 1991), frequent displays of immorality and abuse of individual rights on the part of assigned officers (Lersch, 2002), and the abuse of both drugs and alcohol on the part of undercover officers (Giordo, 1991; Macleod, 1995). Related long-term outcomes of such assignments include personality disturbances, such as depression, anger, and paranoia (Giordo, 1985), difficulties in making the transition back to routine duties (Giordo, 1985; Macleod, 1995; Marx, 1988), and the disruption of interpersonal relationships (Farkas, 1986; Pogrebin & Poole, 1993; Macleod, 1995).

Considering the literature review in the context of the current research endeavor, it appears fairly intuitive that the policing profession in general, and those involved in undercover assignments specifically, could benefit from an examination of the factors which contribute to occupational stress in policing. Additionally, recognizing policing as an adult population which is subjected to and experiences higher levels of stress than the general population, allows this population to be utilized to test the principles and concepts of general strain theory.

General Strain Theory and Policing

General strain theory is focused at the social-psychological level, addressing the individual and the individual's intimate environment as determinants of reactive responses to strain. This perspective joins with and reinforces social control theory and differential association theory, but it also provides an alternative explanation (or motivation) for crime and delinquency. Where social control theory focuses on positive relationships with conventional sources as controlling individual behavior, and differential association focuses on positive relationships with unconventional sources as influencing individual behavior, general strain theory focuses on negative relationships and the effects of such relationships on influencing individual behavior.

General strain theory's focus on negative relationships makes it a unique theory, and provides strength and value to the explanation of crime and delinquency. From this perspective, negative affective states, primarily anger and related emotions that often result from negative relationships, lead to delinquent adaptations among many youth (Agnew, 1992). The same premise can be intuitively extended to adult populations as well, specifically adult populations that routinely experience negative situations that evoke strong emotional responses (e.g., fear, frustration, anger).

One of the continuing criticisms of strain theory, as with many other theories, is that many individuals experience the same or similar situations, conditions, and stimuli, but not all react with delinquency or deviancy. General strain theory seeks to explain this phenomenon through an examination of coping strategies employed to deal with strain at the individual level. Cognitive, behavioral, and emotional coping strategies are the three approaches identified as relevant to general strain theory (Agnew, 1992). Cognitive coping strategies involve mentally minimizing the impact of the adverse situation or condition. For example, espousing that a particular goal is unimportant (or not as important as other more attainable goals) allows an individual to minimize the impact of strain. Another cognitive coping strategy is to maximize the positive in a given situation and minimize the negative. Achieving lowered goals and raising the level for accepting adversity are examples of this strategy. The last cognitive coping strategy internalizes blame in the individual by stating that the adversity is deserved. Deserved strain is more acceptable than undeserved strain because it alleviates the perception of inequity (Agnew, 1992).

Behavioral coping strategies involve acting to minimize or reduce the source of strain (such as requesting transfer from a stressful assignment), or acts of revenge directed against those on whom the adversity is blamed. This strategy may involve either legitimate or illegitimate behavior. An individual may seek to attain a positively valued goal, seek to maintain or achieve a positively valued stimulus, or escape from or terminate a negative or aversive stimulus (Agnew, 1992). Additionally, another possible behavior occurs when an aversive stimulus or situation is blamed on another, and a subsequent desire for revenge is fostered. This desire for vengeance is separate and distinct from the desire to end the aversive condition (Agnew, 1992).

Emotional strategies include constructive methods, such as meditation, exercise, and other processes directed at relieving the negative emotions, and destructive methods, such as drug and alcohol abuse. These strategies involve intentional and direct acts to mediate or alleviate experienced negative emotions, instead of attempting to reinterpret experiences or altering the situation by behavioral responses (Agnew, 1992).

The type of coping strategy (if any) employed by the individual can intervene (or exacerbate) at any stage in this causal process. Beneficial coping strategies would mitigate the level of perceived aversion, and detrimental coping strategies would aggravate the level of aversion (see Figure 1).

Figure 1. General Strain Theory Applied to Policing

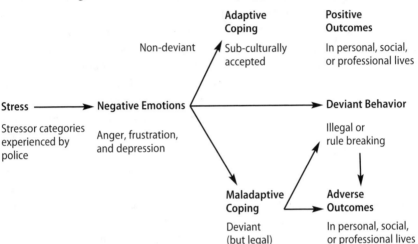

General strain theory is gaining wide respect and recognition in criminology as a dominant theory to explain crime and delinquency. This theory recognizes the value of supportive theories, and it acknowledges the impact of macro-level variables at the micro level. It is understood that the environment can affect individual sensitivity to strain and stressors, as well as the strategies that may be employed in attempts to cope with strain. The propositions and concepts of other prominent theories, such as social control theory and differential association, are accepted in general strain theory by acknowledging the importance of attachments and peer influence in reacting to strain.

With this in mind, the literature and empirical support for general strain theory provide a sound theoretical framework from which to examine the micro-level factors and characteristics associated with criminality and deviant behaviors. Although the social sciences have only considered general strain theory for several decades, the influence of this theory has been substantial in examining delinquency as both a response to strain and a mediator of strain. General strain theory has matured from a focus on the direct effect of negative stimuli to a consideration of the multi-dimensional micro-level factors that are taken into consideration at the individual level when faced with experienced, vicarious, and/or anticipated strain.

One weakness of the literature is seen in the limited number of studies utilizing adult populations. An adequate amount of research has been conducted to test general strain theory; however, the focus on juveniles reduces applicability. To date, there has been limited research utilizing adult populations (Anderson & Lo, 2011; Gibson, Swatt, & Jolicouer, 2001; Langton & Piquero, 2007; Slocum, 2010; Swatt, Gibson, & Piquero, 2007). Consequently, current research is reduced in scope and limitedly tests general strain theory as a true "general" theory. This theory can be utilized to explain adult criminal activity, and various types of both adult and juvenile deviance, as well as unique deviant reactions to stressors and strains in the social and occupational settings. Such an application would include situational crimes that are committed in response to a series of unique straining events, or one critically straining event. Agnew presents general strain theory as one link in the theoretical chain to support and strengthen other major theories in explaining crime and delinquency from a holistic and inclusive perspective. It is the only major theory to focus on negative relationships at the individual level as a cause of crime and delinquency. Therefore, the application of general strain theory has potential that has not yet been fully realized.

Adults engage in efforts of pain-avoidance and react to anger and frustration in similar manners as adolescents. Adults who find themselves in an aversive environment where they feel trapped, with no means of escape, may react with anger or frustration, especially if the aversive environment or situation is perceived as being unjust or unwarranted. In fact, adults may be even more susceptible to the effect of negative relationships than are juveniles. Both personal lives and the occupational setting provide continual situations in which the individual struggles in environments that may not be meeting expectations (Agnew, 1992, 2002). Such continuous strain can be cumulative in nature (Agnew, 2002) and have a cumulative impact at the individual level (Agnew & White, 1992). Continuing on this logical path from juvenile to adult populations, it would follow that general strain theory is applicable to understanding the behavior of adult populations that are experiencing higher levels of strain. Therefore, this project utilized general strain theory as the theoretical model for assessing the impact of undercover operations on police officers.

All individuals seek recognition and other psychological rewards from the occupational setting (Bruhn & Wolf, 1986). Although the work requirements, setting, and working conditions can be both unique and subject to inherent fears and dangers not found in most work environments, police officers, including those who work in undercover assignments, also seek (and require) these psychological rewards. Selye (1974) explained that strain in the workplace occurs when individuals are blocked from realizing these psychological rewards, or when these rewards are removed (or threatened to be removed) from the enjoyment of the individual involved. This is applicable to law enforcement officers and comports to the basic principles of strain identified in Agnew's (1992) general strain theory. Blocked goals (rewards), the removal of positive stimuli (rewards), and the introduction of negative stimuli (common in police/undercover work) are the three types of strain recognized in the presentations of general strain theory.

Agnew (1992) also discussed the impact that inequity plays in reactive responses to strain, in that those who perceive situations or events as undeserved or unjust are more likely to respond in a deviant manner than those who do not hold such a perception. Unjustness and undeserved criticism were identified by Terry (1981) as external stressors encountered in police work. Policing has been recognized as being highly frustrating to many officers, due to the unjust and undeserved perception by the media of highly publicized police work, and the general lack of public respect for the policing profession. Officers view this negativism as both unjust and undeserved (Kelly, 2002). Furthermore, anger and frustration in juvenile populations have been related both directly and indirectly to delinquency and deviant behavior (Brezina, 1998, 1999; Aseltine, Gore, & Gordon, 2000). The same process might be seen in the reactive responses to stressors in policing that create levels of anger and frustration. Such application even can be extended logically from experiential stressors to both vicarious and anticipated stressors (Agnew, 2002).

Furthermore, the specific application of general strain theory to undercover policing involves many of the areas of concern that were addressed in the literature on undercover police stress. The individual stressors identified are numerous, but the most prevalent include the lack of support during assignments (Farkas, 1986; Marx, 1988), isolation and secrecy (Blau, 1994; Giordo, 1985; Marx, 1988), feelings of self betrayal and self condemnation (Kappeler et al., 1998), and pressures to conform with the expectations (and demands) of the police subculture (Paoline, 2001). Pressures to meet these expectations, and the threat of removal of the positive stimuli of the assignment itself, are each compatible with the theoretical propositions of general strain theory.

The literature on occupational stress also indicates that an adequate social support network outside the occupational setting can provide a sense of satisfaction and accomplishment that may not be attained from the occupational environment (Payne, 1980). On the other hand, the police stress literature indicates that such a social support network outside the occupational setting may not be available to those in the policing profession (Farkas, 1986; Giordo, 1985, 1991; Marx, 1988). This lack of a supportive network to mediate the impact of work related stressors, coupled with repeated exposure to perceived and actual negative stimuli from the general public, can result in feelings of isolation and resentment on the part of many officers (Giordo, 1985, 1991; Macleod, 1995; Marx, 1988). Police, as public servants, may view this negativity as both unjust and undeserved, and often respond defensively or even retaliatively (Blau, 1994; Farkas, 1986; Macleod, 1995).

Undercover assignments expose officers to a vast array of psychological stressors that are consistent with the operationalization and conceptualization of strain incumbent in general strain theory. Stress can be cumulative, and continuous exposure can result in chronic stress (Selye, 1974; Toch, 2002). Undercover assignments appear to expose the officer to stressors that are continuous and cumulative, both from actual work experiences and related events in the personal, professional, and social lives of the officers involved. Applying the principles of general strain theory to better understand the factors involved in police undercover assignments, and responses that occur at the individual officer level, can provide valuable insight into the impact that such assignments have on the personal, social, and professional well-being of undercover officers and the law enforcement profession in general.

Methodology

Data were gathered through phenomenological inquiry to describe and analyze the perspectives of law enforcement officers regarding the effects of working undercover assignments. The initial research questions were investigated through a qualitative design that consisted of formal and informal interviews of an initial sample of both routine and undercover officers from two large metropolitan police departments in the South. The sampled officers were invited to function as co-researchers in this project, in order to provide added depth to the study and substantively improve the quality and nature of the data obtained. Employing respondents as co-researchers enhanced access within the agencies selected, as well as tapped into information rich sources in an effort to address the issues under examination.

Site Selection

The sites selected for this study were two large metropolitan police departments in the South that utilize undercover assignments routinely in targeting narcotics violations, vice activity, street crimes, and organized crime. The sites were chosen due to their routine use of undercover operations as investigative tools, as well as researcher familiarity with the agencies, which provided formal and informal contacts with informants and gatekeepers within the organizational settings. The nature of the operations that utilize undercover techniques in these agencies is believed to be characteristic and typical of operations conducted in law enforcement agencies in general, regardless of size or geographic location. The scale of undercover operations obviously varies across law enforcement agencies due to size, population of jurisdiction, resources available, and geographic location, but the operational characteristics are expected to be effectively the same.

Sample Selection

Sampling was conducted both to the point of saturation (at the primary site), and to the point of exhaustion of the sampling frame (at the pilot site). The sample involved three research categories (i.e., currently undercover, formerly undercover, and never been undercover) with a cumulative total of 32 officers. The sample by category included 12 undercover officers, 9 former undercover officers, and 11 officers who had never been assigned in an undercover capacity. Each officer category included participants from both collection sites. One fourth (n = 8) of the sample was recruited from the initial, smaller site, which served as the pilot site, with the remaining officers (n = 24) being recruited from the larger primary collection site.

The first sample category was composed of officers currently assigned in an undercover function and who had been so for a minimum of four months prior to selection. The second sample category included officers who had been assigned to undercover duties in the past for longer than a four-month period, but had returned to traditional duties not related to the undercover function. The last sample category included those officers who had never been assigned in an undercover capacity, but had completed probationary status (one year of sworn duty) within their specific agency. The exclusion of probationary personnel was implemented to negate the role of inexperience in any identified differences between sample categories.

Variables

The independent variables under examination included six broad stressor themes involving multiple categories within each area of stress that differ to varying degrees between respondent categories. The six independent variables were administrative stressors, criminal justice system stressors, experiential stressors, undercover stressors, family stressors, and social stressors. Consistent with the general strain theory model, there were two categories of mediating or intervening variables. The mediating variables included negative emotions and coping strategies. As recognized with the independent variables, the mediating variables included differing themes within each that followed the general strain theory model. Mediating variables can function as both dependent and independent variables within the theoretical model. For example, negative emotions are the dependent variable resultant from the independent variable of stress. Negative emotions would be the independent variable if these emotions caused or resulted in a deviant reactive response.

The primary dependent variable was acts of reported deviancy. Deviancy was conceptualized for these purposes by allowing the data to define what constituted both objective and subjective deviancy, and by following the guidance of Hindelang, Hirschi, and Weis (1981) to produce a definition that was "valid on its face" (p. 89). Individual, categorical, and group standards were considered during data analyses, along with prior literature, in order to further guide this conceptualization. Basically, deviancy was conceptualized as behavior or actions that would result in departmental sanctioning, were in violation of departmental policy or procedure, or were a violation of law. Examples include rude behavior toward citizens, excessive force, adultery, and acts of nonfeasance, malfeasance, or misfeasance.

The definition of deviancy also included behaviors that are (sub)culturally scorned by other members, or are inconsistent with the formal and/or informal policing code of conduct. This would include, but is not limited to, failure to assist a fellow officer, the exhibition of fear during assigned duties, insubordination, endangering self or others, and association with, or compassion for, those who violate the law. Deviancy also included actions or behaviors that are, as described by Hindelang et al., (1981), "on their face" considered as behavioral deviations from either expected or accepted social or cultural practices. Examples of this would include over-indulgence in alcohol, promiscuity, dishonesty, failure to enforce certain laws, selective enforcement of laws, and rude or insolent behavior.

Finally, the respondents assisted in defining deviancy by what was said, how it was said, and the rationalizations and justifications presented to explain specific actions and behaviors. Regardless of whether an act was viewed as deviant by policy, law, or cultural norm, if it was interpreted by the individual as deviant, it was identified as an act of deviance for these purposes. As this is a phenomenological study, it is imperative that subjective recognition of acts that are not consistent with individual values, norms, or expectations be recognized as deviance in order to better understand reactive responses to macro and micro level stressors. Individuals often rationalize or justify behaviors or actions as a means of attempting to validate past actions or responses to strain.

Reliability and Validity

Various methodological checks and balances were incorporated into this examination to ensure maximum reliability and validity in the findings. Member checks were conducted with half (n=16) of the participants to ensure complete and accurate interpretation was conducted during data analysis. A second reader was utilized to reassess data and coding schemes which resulted in an inter-coder rating of .92, adding strength to the reliability of the findings. The second reader also was utilized to counter-balance any possible researcher bias which may have been ingratiated into any level of data collection or analysis. Finally, data were collected in increments with the first collection site being used as a pilot study to identify any "weak" questions or any areas of concern that required modification, less attention, or greater emphasis.

Findings

The results of this study show an association between higher levels of stress and reported acts of deviance. Specifically, those officers who had never functioned in the undercover capacity ("never") reported the least amount of work related stress and, as a group, also reported the fewest acts of deviancy. Those who were currently serving in an undercover assignment ("current") reported both the highest levels of stress from duty assignments, as well as the greatest number of deviant acts, by a substantial margin. The officers who had been assigned to undercover duties, but had returned to a non-undercover assignment ("former") serve to highlight the impact undercover assignments have in terms of the relationship between strain and deviancy. When reporting on the present duty assignment, which did not involve undercover duties, only one third (n=3) of the "former" category reported experiencing high levels of stress from duty assignments. However, when reporting retrospectively to time spent in the undercover capacity, every officer in this category (n=9) stated they experienced high levels of stress that adversely affected their lives in various ways. Additionally, of the 12 reported acts of deviance by the "former" category, all but one were related to stressors encountered while functioning in the undercover role. To state this differently, when working in a more stressful assignment, more deviance took place; when removed from the more stressful environment, deviance decreased. This relationship appeared to hold across categories.

The findings also highlight other obvious and subtle differences among the three categories of respondents. The "never" category reported a more personal focus regarding stressors and reactive responses to job related stress. The "former" category was more concerned with family issues and career stability, and the "current" category placed more emphasis on duty performance, succeeding in the undercover capacity, and fulfilling personal and professional expectations of the job. The deviance reported categorically, in general, serves to emphasize these differences, as well as accentuate the correlation between job related stress and deviant reactive responses.

Strain and Deviance by Category

The "never" category is consistent with the premise of general strain theory that individuals are more likely to respond with deviancy when the strain they are exposed to affects core activities, core identity, and core values or goals, or are high in degree and seen as unjust (Agnew, 2001). As reported by this category, for the most part, these individual officers do not experience high levels of stress and do not routinely engage in deviant acts or behaviors. However, when a high degree and unjust situation is perceived by the officers in the "never" category, there is the potential for a response that may be either a subtle or a more blatant act of deviancy. An angry or verbally abusive tone or demeanor from a citizen contacted while the officer is performing assigned duties may be viewed by the officer as unjust, unwarranted, and affecting core activities. Threatening behaviors or retaliatory actions against that citizen is an example of this type of deviant response. Creating a pretext to stop a suspected "drug dealer," or stacking charges on an individual in hopes of eliciting more punishment for that individual, are each examples of deviant (although perhaps subculturally accepted) responses to the perception of an unjust criminal justice system that affects core activities, core identity, and core values or goals.

The deviance reported, for the most part, by this category of respondents was situationally responsive to stressors that were more immediate and viewed as high in degree in the context of the immediate situation. The other deviance reported by the "never" category involved issues that were subculturally deviant, but may have been viewed as appropriate responses by those outside the law enforcement profession. An example of this deviance involved the failure to take action according to proper departmental protocol when responding to a potential critical incident. This failure to respond appropriately was precipitated by a prior critical (and life threatening) incident in which the officer had been involved. The stress of reliving the earlier incident resulted in what may have been viewed by the department (and was viewed by the officer) as inappropriate.

Other examples involved officers receiving discounts for foods and services from local businesses, or being asked by the department to solicit goods and services for police-community functions. The officers' responses to these activities were seen by the officers themselves as not being in line with subcultural or personal expectations, and therefore subjectively deviant. Each of these examples was a result of strain that may be seen as being of long duration, frequent, and, for the individual, high in degree.

The "current" category was the most affected by work-related stress and reported, by a substantial margin, the most acts of deviance. Ten of the 12 officers in the "current" category stated they experienced significant levels of stress related to the undercover function. This category also was responsible for approximately 64% of the reported acts of deviance, indicating those who experience more stress are more likely to respond with deviance.

The focus of concern for the vast majority of officers in the "current" category was on duty performance and succeeding in the undercover capacity. The officers assigned to undercover duties reportedly enjoyed the assignment, and many stated they went out of their way to ensure they could remain in the duty assignment as long as possible. In other words, the undercover assignment was viewed as a positively valued stimulus by the officers within this category, and actions were taken to protect against the removal (or threatened removal) of this positively valued stimulus. In general, undercover officers seem to identify with the role of undercover duties, and such duties become a part of their core values and beliefs.

Functioning and being successful in the undercover role often became the core activity of concern for many in the "current" category. Officers in this category developed an undercover core identity, with the corresponding core goals, values, and needs for personal satisfaction and sense of accomplishment/achievement. So while the "never" category reacted to stressors that were high in degree or seen as unjust, the "current" category responded to stressors that affected core activities, identity and goals. Each of these types of strain was identified by Agnew (1992, 2001) as being likely to produce more deviant responses than is exhibited by those who do not experience these types of strain.

The "former" category is unique in this study and provides a quasi-replication of the phenomena described in the "never" and "current" categories. Concerning the previous two categories, the least stressed group reported the fewest number of deviant acts, and the most stressed group reported the most. The "former" category provides the opportunity for what would be considered in the experimental setting a "removed treatment" condition. The "former" category functioned in the undercover role and returned to routine duties. This allows for the examination of one group that was not subjected to the test stimulus, one group that has been, and one group that received it and then had it taken away. The results of this strategy provide for an explanation that is highly supportive of the general strain theory model.

The "former" category reported regarding the present duty assignment and also retrospectively to the time in the undercover function. Reports specific to each duty assignment serve to articulate the relationship in this study between levels of stress and deviant responses to that stress. Specifically, only three of the nine officers in this category reported being highly stressed in the present assignment, and only one act of reported deviance was related to present duties. All other acts of deviance were reported retrospectively to the time in undercover, when all nine of the officers stated they were highly stressed by undercover duties. However, as with the other categories, every officer did not respond to stress with deviance. This is consistent with the subjective nature of stress and reactive responses, and individual coping techniques.

Once again, an explanation for the deviant responses in this category can be understood from the general strain perspective. Strains that affect core activities, core identity, and core values or goals are more likely to result in deviant responses. When the officers in this category were faced with stressors from undercover duties, as reported by both the "current" and "former" categories, they subsequently reported more acts of deviance. When the stress of the undercover assignment was removed, the deviant responses all but disappeared.

Another difference that was reported by officers in this category involved the coping strategies employed to mediate job related stress. Officers in this category reported both adaptive and maladaptive coping strategies based upon the present assignment and time in undercover. Basically, officers in this category reported they utilized more maladaptive coping strategies during time in the undercover function and, when removed from that stressful assignment, utilized and employed more adaptive coping strategies. This serves to highlight the subjective nature of acute and cumulative stress and how the individual strives to reduce immediate stress as quickly and as "effectively" as possible, without considering the long term impact such coping strategies may entail.

In summary, categorical explanations for deviance appear rooted in both the nature of the duty assignments themselves, which can include expressed and perceived stressors, and the objective and subjective responses to those stressors. It seems apparent from this discussion that duty assignment can be a pertinent factor in determining both levels of stress and deviant responses to stress. The general strain model provides a theoretical foundation for explaining deviance at the group or categorical level. However, while strain can be addressed in this way, it must be acknowledged that, for the most part, deviance is a micro level response to subjective and objective stressors. Accordingly, deviant responses in this study also are examined at the individual level.

Explaining Deviance at the Individual Level

Overall, 67 acts of deviance were reported by 21 respondents across categories. Over a third of all respondents reported no acts of deviance (n = 12), a fourth reported just one or two acts of deviance (n = 8), and the remainder reported three or more acts. Having considered the nature and responses to stress categorically, it appears obvious that both stress and deviant reactive responses are highly subjective in nature. If this were not the case, it would be assumed that individuals would respond very similarly and there would be less distinction across groups and individuals. In other words, the 67 acts of deviance would be evenly distributed among the sample of 32 respondents, or, at a minimum, distributed evenly among the categories. This was not the case.

Stress and reactive responses to stress appear highly subjective and conditioned upon environmental, cultural, and individual factors. General strain theory is focused at the socio–psychological level and considers each of the above-mentioned factors, as well as the mediating strategies that are employed at the individual level. Tables 1, 2, and 3 provide a visual summary of each individual officer by respondent category. Specific cases from these tables can highlight how the immediate findings comport with the general strain theory model. Basically, those individuals who reported being under significant stress from the specific duty assignment, and experienced negative emotions or negative affective states as a result of such stress, but also employed adaptive coping strategies and/or had supportive factors available, were less likely to respond to stress with acts of deviance. In contrast, those who were stressed similarly, but who employed maladaptive coping strategies and did not have supportive personal factors, were more likely to respond to this stress in a deviant manner. These findings are consistent with the premise of general strain theory and provide support for this theory as a general theory applicable to adult populations as well as police.

Never Category

Table 1 provides a summary of the data provided by each individual officer in the "never" category. Respondents are arranged in order by the highest reported acts of deviance to the least reported acts of deviance. The patterns that emerge from this category comply with the expectations of the general strain theory model. Specifically, every officer who reported no significant stress, and no negative emotions associated with the duty assignment, also reported no acts of deviance. This held regardless of the coping strategies employed. Only two officers in this category reported high levels of stress associated with the performance of duties. One of these officers reported negative emotions associated with the assignment and one did not. Each of these officers reported the use of adaptive coping strategies, both were single, and each reported one act of deviance.

The two most experienced officers in this category reported three acts of deviance each. Both of these officers reported they were not significantly stressed by the duty assignment, yet they both experienced negative emotions associated with the performance of certain duties and one officer was involved in a critical incident. Each of these officers also reported the use of maladaptive coping (e.g., alcohol, detachment, cynicism) in attempts to mediate the duty-related stressors. These findings also are consistent with the general strain theory model. Although not chronically stressed, incidents of acute stress, or high-intensity situational stress, can result in a socially (or subculturally) un-acceptable reaction when ineffective or counter-productive coping strategies are employed.

Table 1
Never Category—Stress Summary

	Stress	Negative Emotions	Coping Style	Acts of Deviance
1.	No	Yes	Adaptive Maladaptive	3
2.	No	Yes	Maladaptive	3
3.	No	Yes	Adaptive	1
4.	No	Yes	Adaptive	1
5.	Yes	Yes	Adaptive	
6.	No	No	Adaptive	1
7.	Yes	No	Adaptive	1
8.	No	No	Adaptive	0
9.	No	No	Maladaptive	0
10.	No	No	Adaptive	0
11.	No	No	Adaptive	0

Former Category

Table 2 provides the summary details for the officers in the "former" category. Since all but one of the acts of deviance were reported during the time spent in undercover, this examination will focus on the retrospective reports of this category of officers. The patterns for this category are similar to those observed in the previous category. All officers reported significant stress associated with the time in undercover duties. Four officers responded with acts of deviance to the stress, and five did not.

Of the five officers who did not respond to duty-related stressors with acts of deviance, three experienced no associated negative emotions, while two did experience negative emotions. All of these officers reported the use of adaptive coping strategies (e.g., exercise, hobbies, family and friends, time for self), which seemed to effectively mediate duty-related stress and negative emotions to a manageable level. Additionally, all the officers in this category were married and used family support as a means of adaptive coping.

All of the officers who reported acts of deviance in response to duty-related stressors also reported negative emotions associated with duty functions. Additionally, each of these officers reported the use of maladaptive coping techniques (e.g., alcohol, detachment, cynicism) in attempts to mediate the stressors of the undercover function. While the acts of deviance in this category may have involved acts that would be classified as subculturally deviant and not illegal acts per se, the acts were identified by the respondents as inconsistent with the expectations, requirements, or ideals of policing, the duty assignment, or the individual. Once again the findings of the individuals within this category comport to the general strain theory model.

Table 2

Former Category—Stress Summary

	Stress	Negative Emotions	Coping Style	Acts of Deviance
12.	Yes	Yes	Adaptive Maladaptive	3
13.	Yes	Yes	Adaptive Maladaptive	3
14.	Yes	Yes	Adaptive Maladaptive	3
15.	Yes	Yes	Adaptive Maladaptive	3

16.	Yes	No	Adaptive	0
17.	Yes	No	Adaptive	0
18.	Yes	Yes	Adaptive	0
19.	Yes	No	Adaptive	0
20.	Yes	Yes	Adaptive	0

Current Category

The individual cases within the current category, presented in Table 3, provide further support for the general strain theory model. While the cases are
not as distinct as was seen in the two previous categories, and these officers
appear more susceptible to high-intensity situational stressors, the majority of
cases are consistent with the principles of general strain theory. Those individuals who reported the use of adaptive coping strategies (e.g., exercise, hobbies, friends and family, time for self) were less likely to respond to stress with
acts of deviance than were those who utilized maladaptive coping techniques.
Virtually all of the officers who reported higher amounts of deviance utilized
maladaptive coping (e.g., alcohol, detachment, rationalization, cynicism) in attempts to mediate duty-related stressors. The other pattern that emerged indicated the experience of negative emotions was associated with both the use
of maladaptive coping and subsequent acts of deviance. Those who did not
report the experience of negative emotions associated with the stressors of duty
assignment were less likely to report acts of deviance at the same level as those
who did report associated negative emotions.

Table 3

Current Category — Stress Summary

	Stress	Negative Emotions	Coping Style	Acts of Deviance
21.	No	Yes	Maladaptive	13
22.	Yes	Yes	Maladaptive	10
23.	Yes	Yes	Maladaptive	6
24.	Yes	Yes	Maladaptive	4
25.	Yes	No	Adaptive	4
26.	Yes	Yes	Maladaptive	3
27.	Yes	No	Adaptive	2
28.	Yes	No	Adaptive	1
29.	Yes	No	Adaptive	1

30.	Yes	No	Adaptive	0
31.	Yes	No	Adaptive	0
32.	No	No	Adaptive	0

Discussion

The findings of this study not only extend the utility of general strain theory through application to an adult population, but also extend this theory from delinquency and crime to the broader concept of deviance. While some may view this too encompassing to be of value, I would argue this extension provides greater application for general strain theory beyond the examination of acts only labeled delinquent or criminal. Further support for this theory is garnered from the assessment of coping strategies utilized in efforts to mediate strain. Additionally, this study provides insight into the nature of stress inherent within differing policing assignments and on the value of adaptive coping strategies to mediate such stress.

To summarize these findings, those officers who reported higher levels of job related stress also reported a greater number of deviant responses to that stress. Consistent with general strain theory, anger and frustration were seen as key negative emotions associated with many of those reporting higher levels of stress. Furthermore, and supporting later additions to general strain theory (Agnew, 2001), strain that was seen as unjust, high in magnitude, or created a pressure to engage in deviance resulted in more reported acts of deviance by the respondents describing those types of strain.

It must be noted that this study did not specifically distinguish the types of stress recognized by Agnew (1992) when founding this theory. However, this study does follow the concepts of Agnew's (2001) later work regarding equity, magnitude of strain, environmental influence, and pressure for deviant coping. As Agnew (2001) stated, in agreement with Selye (1974) and Horowitz (2001), subjective reactions to objective strain evolve over time due to specified coping strategies and individual and environmental conditioning. The reported findings are consistent with this premise. Not every officer who experienced the same objective strain reacted subjectively in the same manner. For example, those officers who returned to patrol after working undercover did not report the same stress in patrol that the officers who never worked undercover reported. Finally, across categories, those officers who reported adaptive coping strategies were less likely to report deviance than were the officers who employed maladaptive strategies.

Policy Implications

The primary purpose of this study was to add to the existing theoretical and empirical literature regarding police stress in general and undercover stress specifically. Stress was measured in the natural setting to assess the role of duty assignment in producing differing levels of stress. The policy implications for this research also are both theoretically and empirically based.

Practical implications hold relevance primarily for police agencies, police officers, and those interested in the mediation or resolution of job-related stressors in the law enforcement profession. The finding that administrative stressors are the primary source of stress for officers across duty assignments suggests that police agencies should initiate internal programs to measure, monitor, and address issues of concern at the individual officer and police sub-unit levels. The "top down" policing approach, which has been the mainstay of policing organizations for decades (Bennett, & Hess, 2001; Swanson, Territo, & Taylor, 2001), does not appear conducive to instilling a sense of appreciation and respect in those officers who function in the line capacity. A "bottom up" approach to supervision and management may go far to develop a more appreciative work environment within policing. Such an approach, and other innovative changes to the traditional and hierarchical policing structure, may make administrative requirements, reported by so many officers as so distasteful, seem more palatable.

Undercover officers also should be evaluated periodically in order to ascertain if the cumulative nature of experiential or other duty-related stressors is causing adverse consequences in the officers' personal, social, or professional lives. It became apparent during the course of the interviews that the officers in undercover units form very close ties with fellow officers. It could be possible that these officers become "too close" and may rationalize or overlook key signs that indicate cumulative or chronic stress in another officer. While an "outside" evaluator may not be accepted by undercover units and could cause more harm than good, the use of officers who previously had functioned in the undercover capacity as evaluators would seem a reasonable choice for such evaluations. Officers who have worked in the undercover capacity would be more readily accepted by their peers currently assigned, and also would be able to empathize with and understand the unique stressors inherent in the undercover capacity.

Finally, training on adaptive stress reduction techniques should be a required portion of annual re-certification training for all police officers. Departments should retain a qualified professional to implement and monitor stress reduction programs, and facilities to assist in adaptive stress-reducing techniques should be made available to every officer, either at departmental locations or through a civilian facility. Police departments should attack stress on the front end where it can be treated efficiently, before maladaptive strategies are employed and accompanying negative consequences occur.

In the immediate study, undercover assignments were reported as being the most stressful within policing, as well as one of the most professionally (and personally) rewarding. Future research should be directed toward identifying the specific characteristics of undercover assignments that make the function so rewarding, in spite of the higher levels of stress associated with such duties. Isolating these characteristics could lead to a better understanding of the inherent stressors in policing and result in application to increase job satisfaction and personal rewards across the policing spectrum.

In conjunction with the recommendations identified above, studies should be directed toward understanding why routine police duties lack expected intrinsic rewards. The immediate findings indicated that those assigned to routine duties were the least stressed, but also exhibited the highest levels of job dissatisfaction. Research should be directed toward identifying and understanding the individual characteristics and other factors that result in this lack of satisfaction with the routine police duty assignment.

One of the more subtle findings of this study is the realization that certain individual characteristics and qualities make the undercover assignment both more personally rewarding and professionally satisfying for some officers. Research in undercover assignments should be directed toward an understanding of the characteristics and qualities of those officers who are attracted to and successful in undercover assignments. Also, the individual characteristics of those officers who are not successful in the undercover function should be assessed to better determine individual qualities that are correlated with success in the undercover role.

Finally, the role of the undercover function has evolved in modern times, resulting in less use of media-publicized deep undercover operations. Local and state agencies are directing the undercover function more frequently toward the regulation and enforcement of "vice" crimes, such as prostitution, gambling, and street-level drug use and sales. Additionally, the undercover function has expanded into the area of "cyber crimes" in order to covertly investigate those who exploit or threaten children through interactive communications on the Internet. The impact these evolving undercover roles are having on those officers assigned have not yet been adequately assessed. As this appears to be the emerging trend in the use of undercover operatives, more research should be directed

Conclusion

Stress is a highly subjective and complex phenomenon that is influenced by multiple factors at many different levels. This study provides a theoretical and empirical examination of the association between stress, negative emotions, attitudes, and behaviors. Additionally, there appeared to be an association between the type of coping strategy employed to mediate or avoid stress, and the degree of stress experienced at the individual level. Negative emotions and maladaptive coping strategies each were associated with reported acts of deviance. Adaptive coping techniques and family support appear to be effective mediators of stress associated with duty assignments in policing. In this study, the findings from an adult population were successfully applied to the general strain theory model, adding support for it as a true general theory.

Prior literature does not focus (and often does not address) the beneficial value of undercover assignments for individual officers, nor does it provide evidence that such a phenomenon is a frequent occurrence in such duty assignments. However, it is necessary to recognize and acknowledge those officers who benefit both personally and professionally from the undercover experience. This was a key finding from this study. Although the undercover officer category reported the highest levels of duty related stress and highest levels of deviance in response to the stress, as a group they also reported the highest levels of job satisfaction and highest levels of personal and professional benefit from working the undercover function. This pattern held for both the currently undercover and for the formerly undercover category as they reported retrospectively to their time in undercover.

Additionally, in negotiating access to the agencies that participated, as well as agencies that chose not to be involved, one point became apparent. Many of the administrators and managers who were contacted to negotiate access stated they had worked undercover assignments during their careers. It follows that, at a minimum, the professional lives of these individuals did not suffer adversely from undercover duties. In fact, the opposite may be true. The successful completion of undercover duties may have been a factor in proving these officers capable of dealing with the stressors inherent in such assignments and law enforcement in general, and may have established their qualifications for supervisory and leadership positions. Accordingly, additional interest was focused on the benefits of such assignments, as well as the costs identified previously. Future studies should consider this phenomenon further.

This study found that policing is an inherently stressful occupation, with the undercover assignment being the most stressful of those examined. Although the undercover function created the most stress among policing duties, it also provided more intrinsic rewards than other assignments. The more personal nature of, and individual involvement in, proactive investigations appears to provide officers conducting such investigations with a deeper sense of achievement. Consequently, such officers attain job satisfaction at a higher rate than those officers who feel they are continuously pushing offenders through a revolving door of justice.

Individuals who choose to serve society as law enforcement officers are subjected to a unique and often stressful working environment. Violence, human suffering, loss of life, and negative and often disrespectful interactions with those being served each may contribute, individually and synergistically, to an erosion of individual identity and objectivity. Cynicism can emerge in those officers who experience the cumulative nature of these encounters, resulting in isolation from those being serviced and a rededication to family or issues that are more personally rewarding.

The impact of job-related stressors on the individual officer is one that cannot be identified and resolved through the findings of any one study, or series of studies. Stress is a highly subjective and individual phenomenon that requires broad examination at the theoretical level and specific application at the practical level. However, job-related stress in policing must be accorded the attention required in order to minimize the adverse consequences at the individual officer level and to help maintain the dignity and respect of the policing profession.

References

Agnew, R. (1985). A revised strain theory of delinquency. *Social Forces, 64*(1), 151–167.

Agnew, R. (1989). A longitudinal test of the revised strain theory. *Journal of Quantitative Criminology, 5*(4), 373–387.

Agnew, R. (1992). Foundation for a general strain theory of crime and delinquency. *Criminology, 30*(1), 47–87.

Agnew, R. (2001). Building on the foundation of general strain theory: Specifying the types of strain most likely to lead to crime and delinquency. *Journal of Research in Crime and Delinquency, 38*(4), 319–361.

Agnew, R. (2002). Experienced, vicarious, and anticipated strain: An exploratory study on physical victimization and delinquency. *Justice Quarterly, 19*(4), 603–632.

Agnew, R., Brezina, T., Wright, J.P., & Cullen, F.T. (2002). Strain, personality traits, and delinquency: Extending general strain theory. *Criminology, 40*(1), 43–71.

Agnew, R. & White, H.R. (1992). An empirical test of general strain theory. *Criminology, 30*(4), 475–499.

Anshel, M.H. (2000). A conceptual model and implications for coping with stressful events in police work. *Criminal Justice and Behavior, 27*(3), 375–4000.

Arter, M. L. (2008). Supervising the undercover function. In J. Ruiz and D. Hummer (eds) *Handbook of Police Administration* (pp. 249–259). Boca Raton, FL: CRC Press.

Aseltine Jr., R.H., Gore, S., & Gordon, J. (2000). Life stress, anger and anxiety, and delinquency: An empirical test of general strain theory. *Journal of Health and Social Behavior, 41*, 256–275.

Ballenger, J. F., Best, S.R., Metzler, T.J., Wasserman, D. A., Mohr, D.C., Liberman, A., Delucchi, K., Weiss, D.S., Fagan, J.A., Waldrop, A.E., & Marmar, C.R. (2010). Patterns and predictors of alcohol use in male and female urban police officers. *The American Journal on Addictions, 20*, 21–29.

Band, S.R., & Manuele, C.A. (1987). Stress and police officer performance: An examination of effective coping behavior. *Journal of Police and Criminal Psychology, 3*(3), 30–42.

Beehr, T.A., Johnson, L.B., & Nieva, R. (1995). Occupational stress: Coping of police and their spouses. *Journal of Organizational Behavior, 16*(1), 3–25.

Bennet, W.W. & Hess, K.M. (2001). *Management and Supervision in Law Enforcement.* Belmont, CA: Wadsworth/Thompson.

Blau, T.H. (1994). *Psychological services for law enforcement.* New York: Wiley.

Brezina, T. (1996). Adapting to strain: An examination of delinquent coping responses. *Criminology, 34*(1), 39–60.

Brezina, T. (1998). Adolescent maltreatment and delinquency: The question of intervening processes. *Journal of Research in Crime and Delinquency, 35*(1), 71–99.

Brezina, T. (1999). Teenage violence toward parents as an adaptation to family strain. *Youth & Society, 30*(4), 416–444.

Broidy, L. (2001). A test of general strain theory. *Criminology, 39*(1), 9–33.

Bruhn, J.G., & Wolf, S. (1986). Stress, satisfaction, and morale in relation to health and productivity. In S.G. Wolf, Jr. and A. J. Finestone (Eds.), *Occupational stress* (pp. 1–7). Littleton, MA: PSG Publishing.

Capowich, G.E., Mazerolle, P., & Piquero, A. (2001). General strain theory, situational anger, and social networks: An assessment of controlling influences. *Journal of Criminal Justice, 29*, 445–461.

Davey, J.D., Obst, P.L., & Sheehan, M.C. (2000). Work demographics and officers' perceptions of the work environment which add to the prediction of at risk alcohol consumption within an Australian police sample. *Policing: An International Journal of Police Strategies & Management, 23(1)*, 69–81).

Farkas, G.M. (1986). Stress in undercover policing. In J. Reese & H. Goldstein, (Eds.), *Psychological services for law enforcement* (pp. 433–440). Washington, DC: U.S. Government Printing Office.

Finn, P., & Tornz, J.E. (2000). On-the-job stress in policing—reducing it, preventing it. *National Institute of Justice Journal,* NIJ 180079, 18–24.

Ganem, N. M. (2010). The role of negative emotion in General Strain Theory. *Journal of Contemporary Criminal Justice, 26(2)*, 167–185.

General Accounting Office. (1998). *Drug-related police corruption* (GAO/GGD Publication No. 98-111). Washington, DC: Government Printing Office.

Gibson, C.L., Swatt, M.L., & Jolicoeur, J.R. (2001). Assessing the generality of general strain theory: The relationship among occupational stress experienced by male police officers and domestic forms of violence. *Journal of Crime and Justice, 24(2)*, 29–57.

Giordo, M. (1985). Health and legal issues in undercover narcotics investigation: Misrepresented evidence. *Behavioral Sciences & the Law, 3(3)*, 299–308.

Giordo, M. (1991). Drug corruption in undercover agents: Measuring the risk. *Behavioral Sciences and the Law, 9*, 361–370.

Hindelang, M.J., Hirschi, T., & Weiss, J. (1981). Measuring delinquency. Beverly Hills, CA: Sage.

Hoffmann, J.P., & Cerbone, F.G. (1999). Stressful life events and delinquency escalation in early adolescence. *Criminology, 37*, (2), 343–373.

Horowitz, M.J. (2001). *Stress Response Syndromes* (4th ed). Northvale, NJ: Aronson.

Kappeler, V.E., & VanHoose, D.D. (1995). Law enforcement; Illegal drug use by narcotics agents—retiring the addicted centurion. *Criminal Law Bulletin, 31(1)*, 61–70.

Kelly, P.A. (2002). Stress: The cop killer. In J.M. Madonna, Jr., and R.E. Kelly (Eds.) *Treating police stress: The work and the words of peer counselors,* Springfield, IL: Charles C. Thomas.

Kirschman, E. (2006). *I Love a Cop: What Police Families Need to Know*. New York: Guildford Press.

Lersch, K.M. (2002). All is fair in love and war. In K.M. Lersch, *Policing and misconduct* (pp. 55–84). Upper Saddle River, NJ: Prentice Hall.

Linsday, V. & Shelley, K. (2009). Social and stress-related influences of police officers' alcohol consumption. *Journal of Police Criminal Psychology*, 24, 87–92.

Macleod, A.D. (1995). Undercover policing: A psychiatrist's perspective. *International Journal of Law and Psychiatry*, 18(2), 239–247.

Madonna, Jr., J.M. & Kelly, R.E. (2002). *Treating police stress: The work and words of peer counselors*. Springfield: Thomas.

Marmar, C.R., McCaslin, S.E., Metzler, T.J., Best, S., Weiss, D.S., Fagan, J., Liberman, A., Pole, N., Otte, C., Yehuda, R., Mohr, D., & Neylan, T. (2006). Predictors of posttraumatic stress in police officers and other first responders. *Annals New York Academy of Sciences*, 1071, 1–18.

Marx, G.T. (1988). *Undercover: Police surveillance in America*. Berkeley, CA: University of California Press.

Miller, G.I. (1987). Observations on police undercover work. *Criminology*, 25(1), 27–45.

Paoline III, E.A. (2001). *Rethinking police culture: Officers' occupational attitude*. New York: LFB Scholarly.

Paternoster, R., & Mazerolle, P. (1994). General strain theory and delinquency: A replication and extension. *Journal of Research in Crime and Delinquency*, 31(3), 235–263.

Payne, R. (1980). Occupational stress and social support. In C.L. Cooper and R. Payne (Eds.), *Current concerns in occupational stress*, (269–298). New York: John Wiley & Sons.

Piquero, N.L., & Sealock, M.D. (2000). Generalizing general strain theory: An examination of an offending population. *Justice Quarterly*, 17(3), 449–484.

Pogrebin, M.R., & Poole, E.D (1993). Vice isn't nice: A look at the effects of working undercover. *Journal of Criminal Justice*, 21, 383–394.

Selye, H. (1974). *Stress without distress*. Philadelphia: Lippincott.

Shostak, A.B. (1980). *Blue-collar stress*. Reading, MA: Addison-Wesley.

Stearns, G.M., & Moore, R.J. (1993). The physical and psychological correlates of job burnout in the Royal Canadian Mounted Police. *Canadian Journal of Criminology*, April, 127–148.

Stevens, D.J. (1999). Corruption among narcotic officers: A study of innocence and integrity. *Journal of Police and Criminal Psychology*, 14(2), 1–10.

Storch, J.E., & Panzarella, R. (1996). Police stress: State-trait anxiety in relation to occupational and personal stressors. *Journal of Criminal Justice*, 24(2), 99–107.

Swanson, C.R., Territo, L., & Taylor, R.W. (2012). *Police Administration: Structures, Processes, and Behavior.* Upper Saddle River, NJ: Prentice Hall.

Swatt, M.L, Gibson, C.L. & Piquero, N.L. (2007). Exploring the utility of general strain theory in explaining problematic alcohol consumption by police officers. *Journal of Criminal Justice, 35,* 596–611.

Terry III, W.C. (1981). Police stress: The empirical evidence. *Journal of Police Science and Administration,* 9(1), 61–75.

Toch, H. (2002). *Stress in policing.* Washington, DC: American Psychological Association.

Violanti, J.M., & Aron, F. (1994). Ranking police stressors. *Psychological Reports, 75,* 824–826.

Violanti, J., & Aron, F. (1995). Police stressors: Variations in perception among police personnel. *Journal of Criminal Justice, 23,* 287–294.

Violanti, J.M., Marshall, J.R., & Howe, B. (1985). Stress, coping, and alcohol use. The police connection. *Journal of Police Science and Administration, 13,* 106–110.

Weiss, D.S., Brunet, A., Best, S.R., Metzler, T.J., Liberman, A., et al., (2010). Frequency and severity approaches to indexing exposure to trauma: The critical incident history questionnaire for police officers. *Journal of Traumatic Stress, 23,* 734–743.

White, S., & Marino, K. (1983). Job attitudes and police stress: An exploratory study of causation. *Journal of Police Science and Administration,* 11(3), 264–274.

Discussion Questions

1. What does General Strain Theory focus on?
2. What do cognitive coping strategies include?
3. What do behavioral coping strategies include?
4. In what ways can emotional coping strategies be destructive?
5. What was the purpose of this study?
6. What is there about undercover assignments that make them one of the most stressful of all police duty assignments?
7. The literature indicates that there are unique stress-producing aspects of policing that are not experienced by others within the same community or geographic location. What are they?
8. While the "fight or flight" option is available to the general population and utilized on a daily basis in numerous situations, such an option is not available to police officers. Why is this so?

9. Both micro- and macro-level factors are involved in determining an individual's reaction to either experienced or perceived stress. What are some examples of micro-level factors?
10. The police stress literature indicates that police officers in general, and undercover officers specifically, exhibit unique defense mechanisms and coping strategies. What are some of the maladaptive coping strategies they employ?
11. Undercover officers experience both lifestyle changes and personality changes as a means of insulating themselves from the stressors they experience. What do some of these personality changes include?
12. Cognitive, behavioral, and emotional coping strategies are the three approaches identified as relevant to general strain theory. What are the differences between these three strategies?
13. Undercover officers should be evaluated periodically in order to ascertain if the cumulative nature of experiential or other duty-related stressors is causing adverse consequences in the officers' personal, social, or professional lives. Who is it recommended should be doing the evaluation?

6

Identifying Law Enforcement Stress Reactions Early

Donald C. Sheehan and Vincent B. Van Hasselt

The collapse of the World Trade Center and the partial destruction of the Pentagon starkly and vividly showed the whole world the damage inflicted upon America by the Al Qaeda Terrorist Organization. These horrific acts harmed all Americans, including thousands of law enforcement officers. Clearly, large-scale critical incidents are stressful, but so are the numerous smaller scale events that so many law enforcement officers encounter on the job. Who can accurately measure the stress caused by being wounded in the line of duty, having a partner killed or injured, shooting another person, seeing abused or deceased children, and witnessing severe motor vehicle accidents? Who can calculate the effects of continued exposure to murders, suicides, kidnappings, hijackings, rapes, and other violent acts that assault the sensibilities of law enforcement officers? Too often, assistance is delayed until officers display maladaptive behaviors, such as excessive drinking, domestic violence, or even suicide. Predictably, adverse events take their toll, but, as yet, the extent of the stress reactions has not been fully assessed. The time has come to identify stress reactions early so that officers can receive meaningful help *before* problems emerge.[1]

---

1. For a complete examination of the authors' work on the Law Enforcement Stress Survey, see V.B. Van Hasselt, D.C. Sheehan, A.H. Sellers, M.T. Baker, and C. Feiner, "A Behavioral-Analytic Model for Assessing Stress in Police Officers: Phase I, Development of the Law Enforcement Officer Stress Survey (LEOSS)," *International Journal of Emergency Mental Health* 5, no. 2 (Spring 2003): 77–84.

Reviewing Causes

Critical incidents, both large and small, are not the only events that negatively impact law enforcement officers. Other more subtle, but no less devastating, factors interfere with the psychological equilibrium so necessary for the emotional welfare of law enforcement officers. For example, organizational stressors, such as inadequate training, poor supervision, lack of recognition for superior job performance, perceived nepotism in awarding promotions and financial incentives, inadequate pay, and insensitivity to family or personal needs, often cause discord.[2] Job stressors, such as long hours, "on call" status, and extended periods outside the home, can have adverse effects. Varied work schedules caused by rotating shifts, irregular days off, and court time frequently interfere with sleep patterns and family activities. Public scrutiny, media focus, and civil litigation can make inherently difficult situations even more stressful. Specialized duties, such as undercover assignments,[3] evidence recovery, crisis negotiation, and hostage rescue, also increase stress levels.

Moreover, law enforcement officers have personal problems just like everyone else. The normal physical changes associated with aging can be quite stressful for officers who rely on their ability to physically control situations. Natural changes to all of the body's systems (muscle, bone, cardiovascular, respiratory, nervous, immune, and neuroendocrine) have strong consequences.[4] Eventually, fading visual acuity, failing hearing, diminishing muscle mass, waning stamina, dwindling dexterity, and attenuating balance impose limitations on officers whose years of experience alone cannot always offset. Injuries and illness also play a part in this dynamic. Psychological factors, such as unfulfilled personal relationships, lack of spiritual meaning, loss of control over an important aspect of their lives, unrealized career goals, and interpersonal conflict, can prove incredibly stressful.

Summarizing Reactions

Critical incidents alone do not cause most law enforcement officers undue stress; neither do cumulative stressors, such as organizational and job factors,

---

2. J.M. Brown and E.A. Campbell, *Stress and Policing: Sources and Strategies* (New York, NY: Wiley, 1994).

3. S.R. Band and D.C. Sheehan, "Managing Undercover Stress: The Supervisor's Role," *FBI Law Enforcement Bulletin*, February 1999, 1–6.

4. H.L. Bee, *The Journey of Adulthood* (Upper Saddle River, NJ: Prentice Hall, 2000).

nor personal stressors, such as physical and psychological elements. Instead, the confluence of all of these different factors does. Proof of this exists everywhere. Cumulative stress contributes to high rates of gastrointestinal disorders, high blood pressure, and coronary heart disease in the law enforcement community. Alcohol and prescription drug abuse often occurs. High levels of domestic violence in law enforcement families have been related to stress on the job.[5] Critical incidents leave some officers with acute stress disorder (ASD) or post-traumatic stress disorder (PTSD) and many more with transitory symptoms, such as intrusive thoughts, sleeping difficulties, changed eating patterns, and muted emotional responses.

Since 1980, when the American Psychiatric Association introduced PTSD as a diagnosable condition, several developments have occurred. In 1994, the short-term pattern of some severe psychological reactions was acknowledged with the inclusion of ASD. Most discussions of these extreme reactions to stress revolve around core symptoms experienced after a life-threatening event and include—

- reexperiencing the trauma in the form of nightmares and intrusive thoughts;
- avoiding reminders of the event; and
- experiencing numbing to the point of not having loving feelings, increased arousal in the form of exaggerated startle response, hypervigilantism, and sleeping difficulties.

Many factors influence whether or not a particular incident results in ASD, PTSD, or its symptoms. Recent research[6] suggested that certain factors predict the likelihood of someone experiencing PTSD and its symptoms. Most predictive was a dissociative experience during or in the immediate aftermath of the traumatic event and high levels of emotion during or shortly after the traumatic event. Perceived life threat during the traumatic event and perceived social support following the event are helpful predictors. Other less strong predictors include prior trauma, psychological adjustment before the trauma, and a family history of mental illness. Prior exposure to a similar event probably is the most difficult to understand because it is counterintuitive. In most other aspects of life, experience helps. Unfortunately, many law enforcement offi-

---

5. D.C. Sheehan, ed., U.S. Department of Justice, Federal Bureau of Investigation, *Domestic Violence by Police Officers* (Washington, DC, 2000).

6. E.J. Ozer, S.R. Best, T.L. Lipsey, and D.S. Weiss, "Predictors of Post-traumatic Stress Disorder and Symptoms in Adults: A Meta-Analysis," *Psychological Bulletin* 129, no. 1 (2003): 52–73.

cers discover that repeated exposure to certain events can have seriously detrimental effects. The frequency, duration, and intensity of stressors represent determining factors as well. Stress reactions vary among individuals because perceptions of situations differ and reactions are subjective.

These debilitating symptoms are not the worst things that can happen. Sadly, among law enforcement officers, job-related stress frequently contributes to the ultimate maladaptive response to stress: suicide.[7]

Making Critical Distinctions

Discussing this topic requires making some distinctions. According to Dr. Han Selye, the generally acknowledged founding pioneer of stress research, stress is the nonspecific response of the body to any demand placed upon it.[8] A stressor is an external, environmental event that has the potential to cause a reaction. A stress reaction is an internal sequence of events that occurs as a result of a real or imagined threat. A negative stress reaction is called distress. However, not all law enforcement officers exposed to stressors become distressed.

On a positive note, stress management appears to help, and sound reasons for this exist. Because stressors are external events, individual law enforcement officers and their organizations cannot always control them. Sometimes, unfortunate events happen in spite of everyone's best efforts. Stress management focuses on the reactions that are internal and more subject to individual control. The reasoning for this states that officers cannot always control what somebody else does to them, but, at some point, they can choose to control their own reactions to the event.

Stress management, as practiced by the FBI,[9] involves three distinct steps: understanding, recognizing, and coping. The understanding and recognizing

---

7. D.C. Sheehan and J.I. Warren, eds., U.S. Department of Justice, Federal Bureau of Investigation, *Suicide and Law Enforcement* (Washington, DC, 2001).

8. H. Selye, *Stress Without Distress* (New York, NY: Signet, 1975).

9. D.C. Sheehan, "Stress Management in the Federal Bureau of Investigation: Principles for Program Development," *International Journal of Emergency Mental Health* 1 (1999): 39–42.

steps occur preincident, wherein administrators take great care to ensure personnel understand the nature of the stress response and learn to recognize the common symptoms experienced by those responding to stressful events. Coping constitutes the FBI's third stress management step that transpires after events happen and where administrators make every effort to support personnel through a variety of programs, such as employee assistance, chaplain support, critical incident seminars, and peer support. Although not all law enforcement agencies in the United States may have such a comprehensive program, the underlying principles are useful in moving effective law enforcement stress management forward.

Identifying the Pressing Issue

All of this information has been thoroughly studied, documented, and discussed. The potential ill effects of job-related stressors clearly are established for law enforcement officers. Researchers no longer need to focus on the stressors officers experience or all of their negative reactions. Now, the critical task is to identify, at the earliest stage possible, when particular law enforcement officers incur an excessive stress reaction to the numerous pressures confronting them. To this end, the authors present the Law Enforcement Officer Stress Survey (LEOSS) as a potential tool for agencies to employ in their efforts to help their officers cope with job-related stress.

Developing the Context

For 5 years (1995–1999), Special Agent Sheehan taught Stress Management in Law Enforcement (SMILE) at the FBI Academy. The purpose of the course was to reduce drinking, prescription drug abuse, domestic violence, divorce, suicide, and other maladaptive responses to stress among members of the FBI National Academy. These individuals, comprised of command-level law enforcement officers, attended a 10-week training program involving various criminal justice subjects. Chosen from local, state, and federal agencies throughout the United States and from several foreign countries, these veteran officers provided invaluable insight into job-related stress.

As part of the course, which had 50 officers per session, Special Agent Sheehan asked these highly successful officers what bothered them. The lists he compiled revealed a staggering assortment of human suffering. The problems—personal and professional, traumatic and cumulative, and large and small—all appeared. Class after class replicated the results. These observations buttressed what Special Agent Sheehan had observed year after year while working with the spouses, children, parents, siblings, and partners of slain officers during National Police Week under the auspices of Concerns of Police Survivors, Inc.[10] He realized that something was missing between stress management training and treatment for severe stress reactions.

Finding the Missing Link

Stress management training makes law enforcement officers more stress resistant, and various treatment modalities by mental health practitioners can help those who have extreme reactions. To date, what has been missing is an assessment tool that provides early detection of stress-related problems among law enforcement officers. To be useful, a law enforcement stress evaluation tool has to have several characteristics. It specifically must address the unique challenges and stressors that officers face. It also has to be brief in format to facilitate its use by a population that historically has resisted interaction with the mental health system.

Formulating the Answer

Special Agent Sheehan discussed the problem with Dr. Van Hasselt, who suggested using a behavioral analytic model[11] to construct a screening device. This is a sophisticated and highly effective means of identifying distress in law enforcement officers. It involved five basic steps: situational analysis, item development, response enumeration, response evaluation, and construction of the instrument. Simply put, the authors asked officers to identify major areas of stress. Then, based on these responses, the authors formulated the situations into scenarios.[12] They asked other officers to rate each scenario on two

---

10. For information, access the organization's Web site, *http://www.nationalcops.org.*

11. V.B. Van Hasselt, A.E. Kazdin, M. Hersen, J. Simon, and A.K. Mastantuono, "A Behavioral-Analytic Model for Assessing Social Skills in Blind Adolescents," *Behavior Research and Therapy* 23 (1985): 395–405.

12. The authors used the officers' own words in the scenarios to better describe how law enforcement officers refer to situations that they encounter in the performance of their duties.

different scales. One scale evaluated the likelihood that a law enforcement officer would encounter the situation described. The second scale rated how difficult each situation would be for the officer experiencing it. Thus, the resulting instrument became the Law Enforcement Officer Stress Survey.[13]

Taking the Next Step

The authors have completed the first phase of the development of LEOSS.[14] The next step will involve determining scoring strategies and developing norms. The objective is to develop a tool that can help all law enforcement officers. To this end, individual law enforcement officers exhibiting distress reactions can receive timely assistance. In addition, law enforcement managers can design training programs to show their officers effective strategies for dealing with stressful situations.

Conclusion

Granted, the law enforcement profession is inherently stressful for many reasons, and numerous officers experience distress in a variety of forms. But, officers are not destined to suffer as much as they have in the past. A valid and reliable early screening tool that effectively and efficiently measures stress reactions by officers can assist mental health practitioners in making timely, focused interventions and law enforcement supervisors in formulating useful training programs. The authors will continue to explore the possibilities of the Law Enforcement Stress Survey becoming that tool.

---

13. Supra note 1.

14. The authors gratefully acknowledge the cooperation and support of the FBI National Academy and Nova Southeastern University in gathering data for this project, but do not release any rights to the Law Enforcement Officer Stress Survey. The authors developed the LEOSS external to any institution and retain its sole intellectual property.

Law Enforcement Officer Stress Survey

First Rating Scale

For each scenario, please circle a number 1 (Not Common) to 7 (Common) that best reflects how common the situation is for you. For example, a 1 would mean you have not experienced the situation, whereas a 7 would mean the situation is extremely common.

1	2	3	4	5	6	7
Not Common					Common	

Second Rating Scale

For each scenario, please circle a number 1 (Not Difficult) to 7 (Difficult) that best reflects how difficult or problematic that situation is or has been for you. For example, a 1 would mean that the situation is not difficult or problematic for you at all, whereas a 7 would mean that the situation is extremely difficult or problematic for you.

1	2	3	4	5	6	7
Not Difficult					Extremely Difficult	

Scenarios

1. You are called to a burglary in progress. The assailant may be armed.

2. You are called to respond to a silent alarm from a bank.

3. You respond to a shooting in progress between two gangs.

4. You are executing an arrest and search warrant for a violent criminal and are unsure of his location.

5. You are executing an arrest warrant when the suspect barricades himself.

6. You respond to a major motor vehicle accident with multiple injuries and possible fatalities.

7. You are engaged in the promotional process.

8. You have been brought up on civil rights violations that are untrue.

9. You have plans with your family, but work demands interfere and you are unable to participate.

10. You are on a high-pursuit chase in icy conditions.

11. You are investigating an officer's death in which suicide is suspected.

12. You are responsible to notify the parents of a child killed by a hit-and-run driver.

13. You are called to contain a public rally that is becoming agitated.

14. You have been recruited to investigate a fellow officer.

15. You have been injured during an assault, and your backup is late responding.

16. You find that your subordinates did not complete the assignment you gave, for which you are responsible.

17. You must rely on employees you feel are not trustworthy or competent.

18. You are trying to solve a high-profile case while the public pressure for immediate results but continues to be uncooperative.

19. You have spent hours putting data into your computer, only to have it go down and lose your data.

20. You are making progress on a case when you are reassigned for political reasons.

21. You find that work is taking up more time and energy, leaving you with little left for family and recreation.

22. You are unable to complete a project because your supervisor keeps changing the direction or priorities.

23. You are on your way to a high-emergency call when the radio has interference and you are unable to get all of the information you need.

24. Changing shifts has interfered with your sleep patterns, causing you to experience increased fatigue.

25. You frequently argue with your spouse, but are unable to resolve anything because of scheduling conflicts.

Discussion Questions

1. Critical incidents, both large and small, are not the only events that negatively impact law enforcement officers. What were some others discussed in this article?
2. What are the effects of cumulative stress?
3. In 1994, the short term pattern of some severe psychological reactions was acknowledged with the inclusion of Acute Stress Disorder (ASD). Most discussions of these extreme reactions to stress evolved around core symptoms experienced after a life-threatening event. What do these include?
4. Stress management, as practiced by the FBI, involves three distinct steps. What are they?
5. What is the value of a valid and reliable early screening tool in measuring job stress?

7

Issues in Small Town Policing: Understanding Stress

Dennis Lindsey and Sean Kelly

"It is not socially acceptable for law enforcement officers to show emotion ... it is a sign of weakness ... a loss of control ... and we are trained and programmed to not lose control under any circumstances. It is inbred into us in the academy, probationary training, and all aspects of law enforcement that if we can't handle the stress, we need to get out."[1]

Between 1976 and 1999, more than 1,800 law enforcement officers were killed in the line of duty.[2] The average of 78 dead officers each year is devastating.[3] All law enforcement professionals would do anything to prevent a fellow officer from suffering a violent, premature death. And, yet, in 2000, approximately 400 police officers committed suicide.[4] Even sadder, those deaths

---

1. "Police Officers and Post Traumatic Stress Disorder"; retrieved May 10, 2004, from *http://www.home.social.rr.com/jpmock/ptsd/ptsd.htm.*

2. U.S. Department of Justice, Bureau of Justice Statistics; retrieved from *http://www.ojp.usdoj.gov.*

3. While assigned to the Leadership and Ethics Unit at the DEA Academy as part of a fellowship program for state and local police officers, Lieutenant Kelly discussed the impact of stress on the daily lives of law enforcement with Special Agent Lindsey. They shared what they knew about stress, suicide, and small police departments. As their interest grew, so did their research. This article presents a summary of work already published or available on the Internet. They hope that by bringing this information to the forefront, law enforcement administrators will take steps to recognize and reduce the effect of stress on their officers. Those interested in discussing the issue further may contact Special Agent Lindsey at 703-632-5163 or at *drlindsey2003@yahoo.com* and Lieutenant Kelly at 603-868-2324 or at *skelly@ci.durham.nh.us.*

4. National P.O.L.I.C.E. Suicide Foundation; retrieved May 10, 2004, from *http://www. psf.org.*

represent the ones *reported* as police officer suicides. How many other officers have died at their own hand due to the stress of "the job"?

To put this in sharper focus, 87 percent of police departments in the United States have 25 or fewer officers;[5] hence, the loss of those 400 represents *all* of the 25 sworn officers in 16 police departments. Moreover, suicide in law enforcement is three times greater than the national average.[6] Between 1950 and 1990, the number of police officer suicides doubled.[7] These grievous statistics reveal the tragic toll that stress takes on those in the law enforcement profession — a toll that officers themselves may not fully realize. After all, who protects the protectors? Who defends the defenders? Who cares for the caretakers?[8]

The Price of Policing

Today, many police departments engage in extraordinary efforts to select qualified officers. They measure candidate fitness through written examinations, oral interviews, physical fitness batteries, extensive background investigations, polygraph examinations, and psychological testing. By the time an agency selects a candidate, it has spent a great deal of money to determine if that new officer is physically, mentally, emotionally, morally, and ethically fit to do the job. In some cases, an agency may spend as much as $100,000 to recruit, select, and train *one* police officer in the first year.

For a small police department, $100,000 (or any amount) represents a substantial investment and an enormous portion of its budget. This investment is not trivial but one that often appears at risk of being squandered. For example, if it costs an agency $50,000 each year for the wages and benefits for one officer, then, for 10 years, the officer would cost the agency $500,000. That amount does not take into account increases in salary and benefits, tuition-based training costs, and other factors. An accurate figure may be closer to $600,000 over that 10-year period. If the agency has not

---

5. International Chiefs of Police (IACP) Research Center, *Big Ideas For Smaller Police Departments*, 2002.

6. T. Baker and J. Baker, "Preventing Police Suicide," *FBI Law Enforcement Bulletin*, October 1996, 24–27.

7. J.M. Violanti, "The Mystery Within: Understanding Police Suicide," *FBI Law Enforcement Bulletin*, February 1995, 19–23.

8. For a comprehensive overview of police officer suicide, see Donald C. Sheehan and Janet I. Warren, eds., U.S. Department of Justice, Federal Bureau of Investigation, *Suicide and Law Enforcement*(Washington, DC, 2001).

taken the steps to recognize and reduce stress for that officer and the worst case scenario—suicide—comes to fruition, the monetary cost to replace that officer with another of similar training and experience comes to $1.2 million. What community has that kind of money? But, more important, what about the emotional cost? No one can fix a dollar amount on the welling of emotion, the additional stress, and the devastation felt by the agency's officers, their families, and, most of all, the family of the officer stressed to the point of committing suicide.

The Physiology of Stress

Regardless of agency size or service area, all law enforcement officers are subject to gross amounts of stress from nearly the moment they enter the profession. Most have been trained to recognize the source of external stressors at work, such as police-involved shootings, violent crime investigations, and physical injury. But, what most law enforcement officers do not understand is the enormous destructive, if not deadly, physiological (internal) effect of stress on the human body.

Though humans have evolved socially over the last several thousand years, their biological system still is wired to either attack or run from danger (fight or flight). As police officers, this creates a physical and emotional conflict with the passing of each call for service. Under highly emotional circumstances, officers must exercise extreme restraint: when excited, they must remain calm; when nervous, they must demonstrate their command of the situation; when in a highly emotional state, they must remain stoic. This conflict between biology and societal expectations takes a physical toll on officers. Regardless of societal expectations of them and despite their outward appearances, officers respond biologically the same as the cave dweller: their bodies expect them to attack or to flee. As police officers, they are wired to attack; the hiring process and subsequent training support the risk-aggressive personality. But, in reality, society expects officers to withdraw or compromise on most issues, but also demands that when danger occurs, they must remain and fight.

This conflict results, for example, in officers effecting a search warrant at a location where they *know* armed adversaries await. Similarly, while others may flee, they must enter burning buildings to save lives. Officers take inordinate risks that ordinary citizens do not confront. In the end, their bodies pay the ultimate price. Human biology cannot be overcome; the emotional energy that officers hold in over a period of years on the job *will* take its toll.

How much does an officer's body deteriorate? The life expectancy in the United States is 74.4 years for men and 80.1 years for women.[9] In a 40-year study, police officers with 10 to 19 years of service had an average age of death of 66 years.[10] The research found a "significantly increased risk of digestive and hematopoietic cancers among police officers who have 10 to 19 years" on the job; these findings concurred with other studies that theorized a link between cancer and stress.[11] This same period of employment linked stress with maladaptive behaviors, such as alcohol and tobacco use, and findings indicated that officers have a significantly high mortality risk of esophageal cancer and significantly elevated risk of cirrhosis of the liver.[12] Cirrhosis of the liver was elevated in officers with only 9 years on the job. Officers with 30 years on the job increased their mortality rate more than three times.[13] Exposure to radar may lead to increased risk of testicle, breast, and prostate cancer.

Exposure to gun cleaning solvents, carbon monoxide, and other hazardous materials on the highway may promote heart and kidney diseases. Lead from firearms training and fingerprint powders is linked to cerebrovascular and other diseases.[14]

The Stress of Small Town Policing

Police officer suicide does not happen without warning signs. Some may be as overt as an officer being involved in a shooting. Agencies know that such officers (and their families) need intervention to assist them in coping with the taking of another human life. Often, however, no single traumatic incident leads to an officer committing suicide. More likely, it is cumulative stress that has impacted the human body over time that leads to the physical desperation that then leads to the mental and emotional desperation that ultimately results in suicide.[15]

---

9. *CIA World Fact Book*, "Interactive Table of World Nations" (July 1, 2002); retrieved on May 10, 2004, from *http://www.mrdowling. com*.

10. John M. Violanti, "Study Concludes Police Work Is a Health Hazard," *American Police Beat*, November 2002.

11. Ibid.

12. Ibid.

13. Ibid.

14. Ibid.

15. For additional information, see Donald C. Sheehan and Vincent B. Van Hasselt, "Identifying Law Enforcement Stress Reactions Early," *FBI Law Enforcement Bulletin*, September 2003, 12–17.

Each day, officers gird themselves for the dangers and rigors of the job. When they go off duty, the process of "coming down" begins to take effect on the body and mind. Having been hypervigilant for the duration of the shift, the body demands downtime to preserve itself. However, family life and the day-to-day activities of living require the body to continue pushing.

Demands by the body to relax and rejuvenate conflict with the needs of a healthy family life. Because of their line of work, officers often receive requests for legal advice while attending family functions. Or, when at a party with their spouses' friends, they must respond to questions about a police officer's conduct in an agency 3,000 miles away. An event that is supposed to be fun, that is supposed to invigorate them, and that is supposed to be enjoyable becomes another time when they suddenly must put on the shield and wear their "cop hat." Officers constantly face the inability to come down from a hypervigilant state, causing their bodies to deteriorate further and faster.

Stress Accumulation

About 15 years ago, I responded to a report of a suicide in progress. Though many years have passed, I can describe in graphic detail what that shotgun-in-the-mouth suicide looked like. It wasn't in progress. It had happened more than 8 hours earlier in the backyard of a trailer on a hot August day. Animals had scavenged.

Police officers who live and work in small towns almost never have an opportunity to decompress. Being well known to the residents, business owners, and others in the community, officers cannot separate on-duty and off-duty time. Essentially, small town police officers live in a fishbowl. Off duty trips to the store frequently become job related because everyone seems to know the officers and their family vehicles. Spouses often come under close observation because residents may think "that spouse" is driving fast because he or she is the spouse of a police officer and can get away with it. Taking their children to school becomes complicated when other parents wonder out loud why officers are not at work or when a school administrator asks for advice about an unruly child or parent. All of this "off-duty" interaction disallows decompression and contributes to stress and the deterioration of the small town police officer's body.

In addition to these daily stressors, small town police officers often find themselves in the unenviable position of being the only officer on duty. The nearest backup may be in a town or county many miles away. The level of stress that these officers feel as a result of calls for service may prove greater than that of officers in larger communities with backup at their immediate disposal. The obvious reason for this is that they could be facing danger *alone*. The less obvious reason, however, is that they have not shared the experience with another officer. Lone officers cannot verbalize their experiences, their emotions, or their reactions. Their first opportunity to express their anxiety could be at the shift change several hours later. The passage of time can have devastating long-term effects on an officer's ability to decompress from the incident and the accumulated stress that it produced.

Finally, officers in small police departments face the hazards of post-traumatic stress disorder (PTSD) as often as their fellow officers employed by large law enforcement agencies. Estimates indicate that "roughly 4 percent of all emergency workers will develop post-traumatic stress disorder."[16] In general, "examples of trauma that are likely to cause PTSD (in order of severity) include natural disasters; serious accidents; serious accidents where a person is at fault; intentional life-threatening violence by another person; life-threatening trauma caused by betrayal by a trusted individual; and life-threatening trauma caused by betrayal by someone you depend on for survival."[17] For police officers, a more specific list of stressors would include "killing someone in the line of duty; having your partner killed in the line of duty; lack of support by the department/ bosses; shift work and disruption of family time/family rituals; and the daily grind of dealing with the ... public."[18]

Applied to small town policing where every officer is expected to be the first responder to nearly every manner of human tragedy, PTSD readily exists. It may not result from a single incident, but, rather, from the accumulation of stress over a period of time, then triggered by a particular incident that falls within the recognized causes.

In small town policing, officers generally live and work in the community that they serve. In these tight-knit localities where officers know the residents and, in turn, where the residents know them, other contributing factors make the presence of PTSD even more likely. These include "personal identification with the event; knowing the victim; lack of preparation or lack of knowledge of the event ahead of time; the severity and intensity of the event; accumulative exposure to PTSD-causing events; preexisting PTSD; and helplessness"[19] (real or perceived). "No matter how experienced (cops) are or think (they) are,

---

16. Supra note 1.
17. Supra note 1.
18. "The Effects of Stress on Police Officers," text of speech by Dr. Daniel Goldfarb to union delegates; retrieved on May 10, 2004, from *http://www.heavy badge.com*.
19. Supra note 1.

there are incidents (they) may experience or witness that affect (them) deeply emotionally. Our reaction to these experiences is to do what we have always done and been trained to do. We set aside our feelings and deal with the incident. Our job, and sometimes survival, demands it. Afterwards, we don't make a conscious effort to deal or not deal with our feelings, we just move on to the next incident (regardless of whether the subsequent incident is today, tomorrow, or next month) without even thinking about it."[20]

In small towns where traumatic events often do not occur back-to-back, officers *should* have an opportunity to decompress after a stressful call for service or incident. However, because the community is small and because the tax dollars that support the agency come from the local residents, the police department usually remains under a magnifying glass. When citizens see police cars parked at the station, they may complain that the officers are not working. This scrutiny means that despite the greater *potential* of a small town officer to decompress by getting out of the public's eye after an incident, they remain on patrol, simmering their own fatal brew.

The Need to Intervene

Small agencies, as well as large ones, often risk squandering the investment in their officers by not taking steps to identify stress in its early stages and working to reduce or eliminate the culture that prevents officers from seeking assistance. Agencies must not ignore early warning signs of stress, such as citizen complaints, declining quantity and quality of the work product, decreasing scores on performance appraisals, failing personal relationships, and sudden changes in the personal appearance and grooming habits of affected officers. With regard to police suicides, the prelude symptoms include divorce, increased use of alcohol (not necessarily alcoholism), depression, and a failure to get help.[21] "Police officers going through a divorce are five times more likely to commit suicide than an officer in a stable marriage. The national divorce rate is 50 percent. All research shows police officers suffer a substantially higher (divorce) rate with estimates ranging between 60 and 75 percent."[22] Agencies must ensure that their officers address such problems and receive qualified assistance in solving them.

---

20. Supra note 1.
21. Supra note 18.
22. Supra note 18.

Agencies must encourage their officers to have outside interests and hobbies and to balance dedication to the department with an equal devotion to family, friends, and personal interests. Agencies must promote the importance of such a balance and ensure that their officers recognize the dangerous cycle that puts them at risk: by working longer and harder, they will be rewarded so that they will work longer and harder. This can result in divorce, estrangement from children, chemical dependency, and, ultimately, premature death.[23] Agencies must fight against such a mind-set even in today's challenging environment where they must do more with less ... and less ... and less. If not, in the end, their officers may pay a price far too high for the savings in a line-item budget.

The culture of police work also must change. While their recruitment methods must reflect the need to hire the finest people available, agencies must then prove their fidelity to these officers by supporting them at every moment of their career and home life. Police training academies must create an environment of nurturing support so that officers will be better able to police a community of *people*, not suspects. This does not mean, in any way, the lessening of physical and tactical training, but quite the contrary. Theorists indicate that people intensely trained to expect and react to stress-inducing incidents respond better physically and emotionally in both the short and long term.

Further, performance evaluations should reflect the needs of officers and their families in addition to the traditional ratings that reflect the ability to complete job tasks. After all, the two are inexorably linked. Police administrators need to look at the agency missions and ask themselves if they remain relevant. Are the tasks that officers must perform still relevant? Do they fit the needs of the community? Are their officers thought of as members of the community? Are their families included as part of the community? Do agency rules, regulations, policies, and procedures reflect the need for officers to decompress? Do their actions support their claims of "family first"? For example, instituting a simple regulation that requires all officers (and their families) to attend and successfully complete crisis counseling immediately following any type of traumatic incident can reduce the stigma of seeking help. Making such counseling commonplace will start an evolution of necessary change.

Finally, officers themselves can take simple steps to help their bodies resist the debilitating effects of stress. Among other things, they should—

---

23. For additional information, see Gerald J. Solan and Jean M. Casey, "Police Work Addiction: A Cautionary Tale," *FBI Law Enforcement Bulletin*, June 2003, 13–17.

- eat a carefully balanced diet;
- drink plenty of fluids (caffeine free);
- avoid the use of tobacco products;
- exercise aerobically on a daily basis;
- sleep a minimum of 8 hours in every 24 ("a person kept awake for 17 hours will perform at a standard comparable to that of someone with a blood alcohol concentration (BAC) of 0.05 percent. After 24 hours without sleep, a person will have capabilities similar to someone with a BAC of 0.10 percent"[24]);
- schedule time for themselves;
- take vacations, not just a day off, because the body requires at least 72 hours to adjust to the mind-set of not being at work;
- designate time for hobbies; and
- have a complete annual physical, including blood testing for cholesterol, lead, and all high-risk blood-borne diseases.

Conclusion

Today's world of terrorists and increasingly violent criminals presents highly stressful challenges to law enforcement officers in all American communities, whether large or small. Job-related stress does not limit itself to those officers in large, urban areas but impacts those in small, rural localities as well.

Clearly, 400 police officer suicides each year is not acceptable. The law enforcement community must not allow this to continue; society must not allow this to continue. Only by recognizing suicide as the ultimate indicator of the overwhelmingly stressful profession that law enforcement has become can efforts be found to help its members not only cope with the stress but to enjoy long, healthy lives. Those who have chosen the roles of protector, defender, and caretaker deserve no less.

Discussion Questions

1. Why is it not socially acceptable for law enforcement officers to show emotion?

---

24. Australian Transport Safety Bureau, *Driver Fatigue: An Accident Waiting to Happen*; retrieved on May 10, 2004, from *http://www.science.org.au/nova/074/074sit.htm*.

2. Today, many police departments engage in extraordinary efforts to select qualified officers. What do these efforts include?

3. How much might it cost an agency to recruit, select and train one police officer in the first year?

4. We humans have evolved socially over the last several thousand years, but our biological system is still wired to either attack or run from danger (fight or flight). What type of emotional conflict results from this?

5. How much does an officer's body deteriorate as a result of stress associated with emotional conflicts?

6. Why do police officers who live and work in small towns almost never have the opportunity to decompress?

7. Do police officers in small police departments face the same or different hazards of post-traumatic stress disorder (PTSD) as often is the case with officers employed by large law enforcement agencies?

8. What would a specific list of stressors for police officers include?

9. What does the research show regarding police officers' divorce rate?

10. What can agencies do to encourage officers to engage in conduct that will reduce on-the-job stress?

11. In what ways must the culture of police work change?

12. What simple steps can officers take to help their bodies resist the debilitating effects of stress?

8

Coping with the Career: A Review of Acquired Life Patterns of Veteran Officers

Gary L. Patton

Research and literature have helped to identify that police work can prove more emotionally dangerous than physically threatening.[1] "Police officers are susceptible to many job related stressors that have both immediate and long-term physiological and psychological consequences."[2] Officers certainly have experienced depression, anxiety disorders, chemical dependence, suicidal ideation, and burnout. In fact, data have indicated that officers who continue to experience stress following a critical incident were more likely to resign or to commit suicide.[3] Such findings have demonstrated the urgent need for a comprehensive approach to counseling law enforcement officers.

To this end, the author conducted a study to acquire new and additional understanding of the experience of being a law enforcement officer, with particular attention to personal wellness and spirituality. His research focused on gaining these insights from veteran officers about how their work, with all of the unique problems and challenges, affected their personal lives from a perspective of belief systems and sense of wellness.

---

1. P.S. Trompetter, "The Paradox of the Squad Room: Solitary Solidarity" in *Psychological Services for Law Enforcement*, eds. J.T. Reese and H.A. Goldstein (Washington, DC: U.S. Government Printing Office, 1986), 533–535.

2. A.D. Yarmey, *Understanding Police and Police Work: Psychological Issues* (New York, NY: New York University Press, 1990), 106.

3. M.D. Mashburn, "Critical Incident Counseling," *FBI Law Enforcement Bulletin*, September 1993, 5–8.

Two basic questions prompted this research. How is a law enforcement officer's spirituality and belief system affected by continuous exposure to crime, danger, violence, and suffering? And, does a state of spiritual wellness assist veteran officers in coping with the stress in their lives and, if so, how?

Methodology and Purpose

The author used a qualitative phenomenological methodology with participant observation. Nine sworn veteran law enforcement officers (with 6 or more years of service) participated in the research. The author spent approximately 35 to 40 hours with each officer over the course of 6 to 8 months, observing and discussing issues during ride-along patrols or at other meetings.[4] Three research questions generally guided these discussions and observations.

1. What does the continuous exposure to crime, danger, violence, and suffering do to the coping and wellness of law enforcement officers?
2. Does a state of spiritual wellness assist police officers in coping with the stress in their lives and, if so, how?
3. What interventions are suggested by an analysis of the data to provide a holistic approach to counseling officers?

For the purpose of his study, the author defined *spirituality* as "the capacity of all people to possess—and know that they possess—beliefs, values, and convictions that give meaning and purpose to life."[5] The literature on this topic has indicated that a body of knowledge relates spirituality as one component of overall wellness and a resource for coping with life issues. For example, Bollinger felt that spiritual needs were the deepest of all human needs and that when a person's spirituality is addressed, it can facilitate the development of a meaningful identity.[6] In addition, one officer reported in Meredith's work that

---

4. The author recorded the numerous issues as themes that he then coded into categories and classified according to patterns. Ultimately, nine life patterns emerged that conveyed the themes and categories that the officers had expressed. The patterns were analyzed by Blumer's theory of Symbolic Interactionism. At the completion of the study, the author returned the text to the participating officers to determine accuracy and validity in the selection of the themes and content. All participating officers concurred that the text accurately reflected their views and comments.

5. G.L. Patton, "A Qualitative Study of Spirituality with Veteran Law Enforcement Officers" (PhD diss., Ohio University, 1998).

6. A.T. Bollinger, *The Spiritual Needs of the Aging: In Need of a Specific Ministry* (New York, NY: Alfred Knopf, 1969).

often it is others who have been close to the officer who note that a change in behavior, disposition, and mental state has taken place.[7]

Law enforcement officers are known as a population that often exhibits some particular and debilitating physical and emotional symptoms, such as cynicism, alienation, and emotional numbing. Therefore, the relevant question is, Are some of the emotional and personal distress and effective coping demonstrated by veteran law enforcement officers related to spiritual issues?

Life Patterns

In his research, the author summarized some of the issues identified as both useful and distressful under nine life patterns: desacralization, alienation, affiliation, unique life experience, searching and yearning, search for excitement, preserving integrity, affirmation, and reformation and renewal. The participating officers identified and agreed that they demonstrated these patterns in their thinking, emotions, and behavior.

Desacralization

In the experience of desacralization, people lose contact with the aspects of their lives that they previously had considered sacred and special. In effect, their previously cherished and sacred dreams, hopes, and plans become common and questionable.[8] In the process of desacralization, people tend to lose their sense of wonder, and life becomes somewhat common and ordinary. The process can continue to a point where the person exhibits detrimental changes in previously cherished and honored beliefs and convictions.

Given the sense of disappointment and disillusionment that law enforcement officers frequently encounter in their work, it is reasonable to conclude that they seem to experience a loss of some of the special reasons and motivations that they had set out to fulfill and experience. For example, they routinely see human suffering and the effects of crime and human cruelty, and justice sometimes is not administered as immediately or thoroughly as they would have expected or hoped.

Certainly, officers encounter times of high drama and intense excitement, yet they do not spend a shift racing from one call to another as some people

---

7. N. Meredith, "Attacking the Roots of Police Violence," *Psychology Today* 5 (1984): 20–26.

8. A.H. Maslow, *The Farther Reaches of Human Nature*, 2nd ed. (New York, NY: D. Van Nostrand, 1971).

assume. When this repeated experience of waiting and watching is linked with the times of heightened adrenaline, officers feel like they ride an emotional roller coaster. While they can get excited and dismayed, they frequently deal with the events they encounter with a sense of apathy. The officers in the author's research indicated that they would not be able to cope if they "took their work too serious" or let themselves feel too much.

Another aspect of desacralization is the sense of futility that officers often feel. They deal with many of the same people on a frequent basis, which prevents them from realizing a sense of completion and finality in their work. Such numerous encounters with people who exhibit dysfunctional problems or criminal conduct have prompted some officers to express that they sometimes wonder whether they are part of the solution or part of the problem.

It appears that these officers have learned not to let themselves experience intense emotions, either pleasant or unpleasant, very often. Boredom and monotony are apparent in the officers' lives and can result in a sense of apathy that helps keep their feelings from going too high or too low as they learn not to care as much as they did.

As a result, officers live with frequent and prolonged exposure to situations that people outside of law enforcement do not encounter. Through these experiences and attempts to cope with them, it is understandable that officers acknowledge that their belief systems become altered to accommodate the world realities they see and respond to. Consequently, people and practices once highly valued and sacred to officers may become less so as a result of coping with a world where they regard few things as special. Further, even if officers try to keep people, places, and experiences maintained as sacred, given the losses that occur in the profession, they wonder whether they can retain them permanently. Because many of the participating officers indicated that being a police officer became their primary way of identifying themselves, the sense of desacralization was how they came to see themselves as well.

Alienation

Law enforcement officers believe that in all ways it is dangerous to trust people too much. The extent of danger certainly applies to their physical safety but also to what people will want from them. The officers in the author's study spoke about people wanting favors from them and to become acquainted with them to get some benefit by "knowing a policeman." It became evident that the officers expect people to take advantage of them or lie to them. In every aspect of relating to others, officers develop a suspicious nature.

One officer commented, "We are raised to believe that other people are telling us the truth until we discover otherwise. As police officers, we learn to believe that everybody is lying until we find a reason to believe otherwise." This pattern is consistent with the findings of Lockard and Niederhoffer as they addressed cynicism among law enforcement professionals.[9] They demonstrated through statistical analysis that police officers became increasingly cynical with length of service, but this cynicism eventually leveled off. This begs the question, Is this leveling off an improvement in their cynicism or the beginning of a sense of apathy and indifference?

Because officers experience a change in their perspective of other people, they also begin to respond to them in different ways. Some of these include being emotionally distant, cynical, and very reserved or cautions in their interactions.

Alienation is regarded as an issue of spiritual distress because it is related to the spiritual concept of belonging, as in the absence of belonging. Therefore, it is important to note that another pattern revealed in the author's study is the need for affiliation. His research identified that officers experience a substantial degree of loneliness. It is critical to discuss this in conjunction with the data that suggest officers also have a need for acceptance and a desire to reconnect with others. Not only did the officers recognize how much time they spent alone in their patrol cars but they also talked about how "most people do not like us very much." Obviously, officers recognize a definite disrespect from many citizens. Along with this lack of respect comes a vivid awareness that they often are not appreciated.

Affiliation

Human beings have innate needs for socialization and connection with other people. Indications from various stages in life reveal that healthy emotional, intellectual, and even physical functioning include aspects of relating to other individuals.

In 1989, the National Institute of Child Health and Human Development (NICHD) began to investigate the relationship between early child care experiences and children's developmental outcomes.[10] The researchers focused on measuring facets of children's development, including social, emotional, intellectual,

---

9. J.L. Lockard, *Survival Thinking for Police and Correction Officers* (Springfield, IL: Charles C Thomas, 1991); and A. Niederhoffer, *Behind the Shield: The Police in Urban Society* (Garden City, NY: Doubleday, 1967).

10. NICHD Early Child Care Research Network, "Effects of Early Childcare and Parenting in Adolescence: New Results of the NICHD Study of Early Child Care and Youth Develop-

language development, behavioral problems and adjustment, and physical health as related to how they were cared for. With data based on more than 1,300 children from various ethnicities, races, and socioeconomic backgrounds between 1991 and 2008, the researchers found academic and obedience problems among children who received the poorest child care during their first 4.5 years of life. These conditions were noted to continue into adolescence.

Because law enforcement officers have a sense of alienation from others, they find their belonging needs met among each other. Data from veteran officers reveal comments based on a sense of conviction about the "blue line," a demarcation between those who are police officers and those who are not. Officers are convinced that nobody can understand them as they understand themselves. Research has shown that officers demonstrated, both by behavior and comments, that part of their affiliation with each other was because they have shared unique experiences in life that few other people can appreciate fully.

Unfortunately, at times, the blue line can cause those people closely related to officers also to experience alienation. For example, officers commonly discussed times when they chose to spend substantial portions of their off-duty hours with other officers, rather than their immediate families.

Unique Life Experiences

Three consistent and recurring themes in the law enforcement profession involved concerns about compromise, threats, and enticements. People wanting and expecting favors or special treatment, having to make decisions that potentially violate their sense of integrity, and the possibility of reprisal constitute profound issues that officers must address on an ongoing basis.

Evidently, officers encounter experiences and events that civilians either never face or, at least, rarely do. A prevailing view in the literature holds that officers experience a high incidence of burnout.[11] However, Robinette proposed that instead of burnout, many officers demonstrate a complex state of unresponsiveness.[12] Data from the stories the officers told supported that their experiences are uncommon due either to the type, unpredictability, and chaos of the situation or the degree of damage or death. Rather than identifying the state of unresponsiveness demonstrated by the officers as burnout, the re-

---

ment" (paper presented at the biennial meeting of the Society for Research in Child Development, Denver, CO, April 2009).

11. A.D. Yarmey, *Understanding Police and Police Work: Psychological Issues.*

12. H.M. Robinette, *Burnout in Blue: Managing the Police Marginal Performer* (New York, NY: Praeger, 1987).

searcher concluded from the data that the needs they represent are related more to disruption in their spiritual lives and personal belief systems.

Law enforcement officers live in a world where death, while not a constant threat, is an ever-present possibility. Each of these participants told stories of dangerous situations that could have resulted in death due to either accident or assault. Living with the awareness and presence of danger creates stress that threatens the officer on and off duty. According to their explanation, officers are taught levels of readiness for action, ranging from a completely relaxed state—not often experienced unless they are outside the realm where they work—to being involved in a situation where injury or death is possible. Between these two extreme states are the positions of being ready for the possibility of danger and remaining alert to the realization of imminent danger. The participating officers shared that they seldom—if ever—live in a state of relaxation and complete sense of calmness. Certainly, such a unique life experience has profound and lasting effects on officers' bodies, minds, and spirits. These concerns are heightened by the fact of the frequency, intensity, and duration of the uncommon life experiences encountered in law enforcement.

Searching and Yearning

The human quest for meaning and purpose in life is expressed in the terms of a pattern of personal searching and yearning that the literature has identified as related to spirituality.[13] In different terms, researchers have addressed the tendency humans have to question their experiences and to wonder about how present situations fit into their destiny and desires. They concluded that it is an aspect of spirituality to have the ability and the urge to search for meaning and purpose in the events of life.

In the author's study with veteran law enforcement officers, themes emerged that appeared to be related to what Frankl referred to as "metaclinical problems," the distress that people feel when faced with experiences that force them to deal with questions about life and suffering.[14] They concluded that it is an aspect of spirituality to have the ability and the urge to search for meaning and purpose in the events of life. In addition, the author found that the consensus among the officers participating in his study was that if anything was going

---

13. V.E. Frankl, *Man's Search for Meaning* (New York, NY: Washington Square Press, 1959); J. Watson, *Nursing: Human Science and Human Care, A Theory of Nursing* (New York, NY: National League for Nursing Press, 1988); and J.B. Borysenko, *Fire in the Soul* (New York, NY: Warner, 1989).

14. V.E. Frankl, *Man's Search for Meaning.*

to continue to be disruptive to them professionally and personally, it would be situations involving the death and suffering of children.

Search for Excitement

While the need for excitement and to some degree a willingness to take risks is part of what attracts people to law enforcement, it also seems that these urges are what keeps officers going when they become veterans. This pattern is consistent with the work of Reiser who stated that law enforcement recruits have been noted to need action and recognition.[15]

In conversations with law enforcement officers, it is common to hear discussions of the need and desire for excitement. Officers in the author's research indicated that not only was it their duty but their desire to be involved in dangerous and risky situations. He heard the officers discuss their disappointment at missing an exciting event while off duty or on a particularly slow shift.

Preserving Integrity

The author's research revealed that the participating officers continued to maintain a strong conviction for justice well into veteran status. Both in conversation and behavior, the author noted that these veteran officers held to a strong sense of right and wrong. Accordingly, these participants would stir to action when they perceived something to be unfair or unjust. This is significant given that it could appear to be inconsistent with the other patterns previously noted.

An interesting observation of this sense of keeping their integrity occurred in situations where a "true victim" was at risk or actually harmed. Despite previously identified patterns of alienation and desacralization, the veteran officers in this study could easily relate to a sense of compassion for vulnerable people who experienced harm. The author particularly noted this in calls involving children and the elderly.

The pattern of preserving integrity also is specific to the honor of their badge and sense of duty. Even after prolonged exposure to crime, danger, suffering, and violence, these veteran officers strongly identified with the pride and honor of duty and service to maintain justice and a sense of order in society. The participants in this study, while having to relate to some people not regarded

---

15. M. Reiser, *The Police Department Psychologist* (Springfield, IL: Charles C Thomas, 1972).

as honorable, appeared to value a distinction between these individuals and the suspects and criminals they had to contend with.

Affirmation

Even with a realization that the exposure to crime, danger, suffering, and violence has predicated some losses and changes in their lives from a spiritual and belief perspective, the participating officers also affirmed that they viewed their role in law enforcement from a sense of calling. That is, they did not view it as just a job they chose but as a profession that requires a sense of purpose and conviction to do well. They often explained this by saying, "Some people are not cut out for this work." Despite long and sometimes irregular hours, low pay scales, and the scrutiny of the public on their decisions, these veteran officers believed that eventually their efforts would make a difference.

Reformation and Renewal

Finally, these veteran law enforcement officers recognized a need to find some fulfillment in the very environment that often caused them to experience profound disillusionment. This approach of finding fulfillment in life is easily associated with a spiritual quest for meaning and purpose in life. Some of the participants in this study discussed the need for peace and joy in life and to find some sense of contentment. Some officers talked about how the environment of law enforcement gave them time alone when they could think and reflect on their work, their future, and their relationships. The participants also stated that they found a sense of hope and renewal by realizing that their work may have prevented a tragedy or wrong from happening or possibly helped to correct something. In various terms, the law enforcement officers participating in this research conveyed the hope that at some point, they will have made a difference through their work. This proves consistent with the idea that law enforcement is a profession that people are called to and that in that calling, some transforming experience leads to work being fulfilling and meaningful. Again, these are aspects of living often associated with the spiritual dimension of life.

Conclusion

The patterns identified through the author's research may not be generalizable to all people in the law enforcement profession. However, they can provide a place to begin to understand the context of law enforcement careers and to supply some understanding about how continued exposure to crime, danger, suffering, and violence affect the lives of those who serve as sworn officers of the law.

The author offers two general recommendations. First, because some identifiable life patterns are named in relation to serving in a law enforcement capacity, it could be effective to begin to address these patterns in academies and training programs as people enter the field of law enforcement. Second, given that these patterns are created through a continued exposure to crime, danger, suffering, and violence, interventions for officers struggling with these life patterns can be more efficacious by relating assistance to these specific patterns. This contrasts with the concept of attempting to assist officers by simply letting them talk. While that also can be useful, sometimes the officers themselves may be talking without fully recognizing the specific issues troubling them. If identifiable patterns can be named in conversation, then officers and those helping them can be more intentional about the kind of assistance and training provided.

Overall, the information furnished by veteran law enforcement officers provides a new approach to assisting the entire profession of those sworn to serve the citizens of the United States. By identifying specific life processes, more research and innovation can be implemented to enhance healthy life patterns and to assist with those that confound wellness and spiritual vitality.

Discussion Questions

1.   How did Patton define spirituality?
2.   What happens to people during the experiences of desacralization?
3.   What were the findings of Lockard and Niederhoffer as they relate to cynicism in law enforcement professionals?
4.   What is the result of officers experiencing a change in their perspective of people?
5.   In 1989 the National Institute of Child Health and Human Development (NICHD) began to investigate the relationship between early child care experiences and children's developmental outcomes. What did the researchers focus on and what were their findings?
6.   What are "metaclinical problems"?
7.   Despite previously identified patterns of alienation and desacralization the veteran officers in Patton's study could easily relate to the sense of compassion for vulnerable people who experienced harm. What two categories of individuals were specifically noted?

Part Three

Are There Ways We Can Tell It Is There?

During the 1960s, Holmes and Rahe were able to identify 43 life events which have a major stressful impact on large segments of the population; attach a numerical weight to each event; and relate the cumulative effect of each stressor to the onset of disease. Since that early work, the Holmes-Rahe scale (or, as it frequently is called, the Social Readjustment Rating Scale or Schedule of Recent Events) has been replicated thousands of time, with literally millions of people in a variety of cultures having completed the instrument. It, perhaps more than any other tool, has been used to correlate the occurrence of stress with the onset of physiological and psychological illnesses.

As was the case in the study of stress within the general population prior to the work of Holmes and Rahe, the study of law enforcement stress has often been based upon descriptive or anecdotal information. While the causes and impact of stress on police officers can be quantitatively recognized, it is only within the last 20 or so years that we have been able to quantitatively assess its effects.

In an early attempt to quantify police stress and using an approach similar to that of Holmes and Rahe, Sewell (1983) identified 144 critical events in the working life of a police officer and, using a survey instrument, was able to give each a numerical value. In Sewell's Law Enforcement Critical Life Events Scale, these events ranged from the most stressful (violent death of a partner in the line of duty) to the least stressful (completion of a routine report).

In parallel research, Spielberger and his colleagues developed the Police Stress Survey, a 60 item self report instrument which also gauged the frequency and intensity of specific stressors in law enforcement. The results of that questionnaire allowed items to be grouped into two subscales: organizational stress, i.e., that which was administrative in nature, and operational stress, which included those factors inherent to police work.

Malloy and Mays (1984) provided a critical commentary on the issue of job related stress in law enforcement. They suggested that the basic assumptions underlying police stress have been ignored or accepted without empirical verification. Consequently, they attempted to identify the assumptions underlying the concept of police stress; reviewed the empirical evidence related to these assumptions; and offered an alternative paradigm, particularly focusing on the differential response to environmental stressors by officers, designed to guide future research on police stress. The conclusion of their work, which was similar in tone to an article by Sewell, Ellison, and Hurrell (1988), called for the use of more organized, quantitative research to understand stress in policing.

Since these early efforts at quantitative understanding of police stress, more studies, based on firm social scientific principles, have been generated. For Part Three, our questions become: Are there ways we can tell that this phenomenon of police stress is really there? By what means can we measure it? How can this empirical knowledge contribute to our ability to understand and reduce police stress?

There are, of course, a variety of issues to be discussed in quantitatively focusing on police stress. Pasillas, Follette, and Perumean-Chaney examined the use of avoidant coping in order to deal with emotions, thought, and memories of stressful events. Using a battery of questionnaires, including the Police Stress Survey, these researchers found that the use of avoidant techniques to deal with stress was associated with higher levels of organizational stress. While the sample size was small (N=48) and confined to one city, the usefulness upon replication and identification of successful intervention strategies could be important.

Maslach made her reputation in the early 1980's by identifying, defining, analyzing, and quantifying "burnout" in police officers and others in the helping professions. Using her Burnout Inventory, administered to 452 officers, Hawkins sought to replicate Maslach's work, and his findings, in fact, paralleled many of hers. Significantly, for instance, Hawkins found that emotional exhaustion, depersonalization, and lack of personal accomplishment were linked to officers under stress. The implications for the police organization are significant: with more knowledge in hand, the agency can better identify and respond to the needs of the individual officer, assure the health of the organization, and ensure enhanced citizen-officer contact.

It is critical that research onto law enforcement officer stress, its ramifications, and effective prevention and mitigation techniques continue. As is the case in other categories of human services, the development of evidence-based practices will afford future generations of officers protections that their predecessors never enjoyed. Barath's writing reviews two research studies at the Ontario Police College and suggests findings that may be useful in American law enforcement.

Further Reading

Bartol, Curt R.; Bergen, George T.; Volckens, Julie Seager; and Knoras, Kathleen M. (1992). Women in Small-town Policing: Job Performance and Stress," *Criminal Justice and Behavior*, 19(3), 240–259.

Bradway, Jacquelyn Hodges (2007). "Gender Stress: Differences in Critical Life Events among Law Enforcement Officers," in Territo, Leonard, and Sewell, James D., *Stress Management in Law Enforcement*, 141–155.

Burke, Ronald J. (1989). "Career Stages, Satisfaction, and Well-Being Among Police Officers," *Psychological Reports*, 65, 3–12.

Davey, Jeremy D.; Obst, Patricia L.; and Sheehan, Mary C. (2001). "Demographic and Workplace Characteristics Which Add to the Prediction of Stress and Job Satisfaction Within the Police Workplace," *Journal of Police and Criminal Psychology*, 16(1), 29–39.

Franke, Warren D.; Ramey, Sandra L.; and Shelley, II, Mack C. (2002). "Relationship Between Cardiovascular Disease Morbidity, Risk Factors, and Stress in a Law Enforcement Cohort," *Journal of Occupational and Environmental Medicine*, 44(12), 1182–11889.

Holmes, Thomas H., and Rahe, Richard H. (1967). "The Social Readjustment Rating Scale," *Journal of Psychosomatic Research*, 11, 213–218.

Liberman, Akiva et al. (2002). "Routine Occupational Stress and Psychological Distress in Police," *Policing: An International Journal of Police Strategies and Management*, 25(2), 421–441.

Malloy, Thomas E., and Mays, G. Larry (1984). "The Police Stress Hypothesis: A Critical Evaluation," *Criminal Justice and Behavior*, 11(2), 197–224.

Moran, Meredith M. (2007). "Stress and the Female Officer," in Territo, Leonard, and Sewell, James D., *Stress Management in Law Enforcement*, 131–139.

Ozer, Emily J., Best, Suzanne R.; Lipsey, Tami L.; and Weiss, Daniel S. (2003). "Predictors of Posttraumatic Stress Disorder and Symptoms in Adults: A Meta-Analysis," *Psychological Bulletin*, 129(1), 52–73.

Pole, Nnamdi; Neylan, Thomas C.; Best, Suzanne R.; Orr, Scott P.; and Marmar, Charles R. (2003). "Fear-Potentiated Startle and Posttraumatic Stress Symptoms in Urban Police Officers," *Journal of Traumatic Stress*, 16(5), 471–479.

Quire, Donald S., and Blount, William R. (1990). "A Coronary Risk Profile Study of Male Police Officers: Focus on Cholesterol," *Journal of Police Science and Administration*, 17(2), 89–94.

Sewell, James D. (1983). "The Development of a Critical Life Events Scale for Law Enforcement," *Journal of Police Science and Administration*, 11(1), 109–116.

Sewell, James D.; Ellison, Katherine W.; and Hurrell, Joseph J. (1988). "Stress Management in Law Enforcement: Where Do We Go from Here?" *The Police Chief*, 55(10), 94–98.

Spielberger, Charles D.; Westberry, L.G.; Grier, K.S.; and Greenfield, G. (1981). *The Police Stress Survey: Sources of Stress in Law Enforcement*. Tampa, FL: University of South Florida Human Resources Institute.

Storch, Jerome E., and Panzarella, Robert (1996). "Police Stress: State-Trait Anxiety in Relation to Occupational and Personal Stressors," *Journal of Criminal Justice*, 24(2), 99–107.

Violanti, John M. and Aron, Fred (1994). "Ranking Police Stressors," *Psychological Reports*, 4(3), 343–360.

Violanti, John M. and Aron, Fred (1995). "Police Stressors: Variations in Perception among Police Personnel," *Journal of Criminal Justice*, 23(3), 287–294.

Key Terms/Names in Part Three

Avoidance: Techniques which allow an individual under stress to reduce the contact with specific stressors. Examples include withdrawal (e.g., use of sick leave, isolation from one's peers, or call avoidance) or escaping behaviors (e.g., increased use of alcohol or drugs).

Burnout: A feeling of emotional exhaustion and disillusionment experienced by persons within helping professions. Researchers have found that it is often accompanied by cynicism and negative attitudes toward those with whom the worker has contact; verbal and non-verbal techniques which depersonalize the client and allow the worker to emotionally distance him or herself; and with reduced personal accomplishment by the worker.

Critical Incident Exposure: An officer's exposure to the dangerous or traumatic aspects of police work. Generally, the routine aspects, similar to those found in other professions, are not included in this definition.

Depersonalization: In the helping professions, including law enforcement, the development of negative or cynical attitudes and feelings toward those who are the recipients of one's services.

Emotional exhaustion: The feeling by those in "people work" of being emotionally overextended and exhausted by one's work.

Ineffective coping strategies: Techniques used by police officer to deal with stress which either exacerbate the impact or create new and additional sources of stress. Examples would including increased use of alcohol and/or drugs, gambling, overeating, extramarital affairs, and family conflict.

Law Enforcement Critical Life Events Survey (LECLES): First published by Dr. James D. Sewell in 1980, this scale identified 144 specific stressors in the occupational life of a police officer and, based on a quantitative analysis as a result of a survey of law enforcement officers, assigned numeric values to the impact of each.

Maslach Burnout Inventory-Human Services Inventory (MBI-HSS): An instrument designed to assess three aspects of the burnout syndrome: emotional exhaustion, depersonalization, and lack of personal accomplishment.

Police Stress Survey: Developed by Dr. Charles Spielberger and his colleagues, this scale, first published in 1981, tracked the Holmes-Rahe scale in identifying and quantifying 60 stressors which directly contributed to stress on the job.

Psychological distress: Selye used two words to describe the effects of stress. *Eustress* described its beneficial effects: physical and psychological actions which prepare the body and mind to successfully handle a stressor. *Distress* focused on its negative manifestations: the toll stress takes on one's body and mind.

Reliability: In social research, the accuracy or precision of a measuring instrument. Synonyms for reliability generally include dependability, consistency, and accuracy.

Thomas Holmes and Richard Rahe: Dr. Holmes, later the Emeritus Professor of Psychiatry and Behavioral Sciences at the University of Washington School of Medicine, and Dr. Rahe, at that time a medical student, co-authored the research that resulted in the Social Readjustment Rating Scale, first published in 1967. The scale, replicated thousands of time in the past 40 years, is one of the most widely used instruments which correlates the impact of a variety of significant life events with the onset of medical and psychological illnesses. Dr. Holmes died in 1988; Dr. Rahe retired after 20 years as a psychiatrist in the United States Navy and remains active in the medical field.

Validity: In determining the validity of research measures, the question generally asked is "are we measuring what we think we are measuring?"

9

Occupational Stress and Psychological Functioning in Law Enforcement Officers

Rebecca M. Pasillas, Victoria M. Follette, and Suzanne E. Perumean-Chaney

There is considerable interest in the issue of occupational stress and its impact on law enforcement officers' overall well-being (see Abdollahi, 2002, for a review). Unlike most professions, law enforcement officers experience a variety of negative psychological and physical experiences. They are commonly and frequently exposed to traumatic experiences such as physical injury, working with child abuse, domestic violence, and rape cases (Martin, McKean, & Veltkamp, 1986; Martelli, Waters, & Martelli, 1989; Rallings, 2002; Violanti, 1996). These types of experiences make them susceptible to possible psychological problems. They are also exposed to a variety of organizational stressors such as assignment of disagreeable duties, fellow officers not doing their job, or inadequate or poor quality equipment. Organizational stressors are commonly cited as the main contributors to police stress (Biggam, Power, Macdonald, Carcary, & Moodie, 1997; Brandt, 1993; Evans & Coman, 1993; Davey, Obst, & Sheehan, 2001; Laufersweiler-Dwyer & Dwyer, 2000; Martelli, Waters, & Martelli, 1989; Zhao, He, & Lovrich, 2002).

When comparing the work of law enforcement officers to other emergency personnel, police work tends to have more of a negative impact on the mental well-being of police officers. For example, Brough (2004) compared the traumatic and organizational stressors within police officers, firefighters, and paramedics due to their similar job characteristics using a structural equation model. The author found that police work predicted psychological strain (i.e. anxiety/depression and social dysfunction) differently from firefighter and paramedics. It appears that police work puts more additional distress on the individual than the work of fire and emergency medical services. Results also indicated that despite these differences, operational stressors (i.e., responding to calls, being out on the field, etc.) were found to predict trauma symptomatology and psychological strain for all emergency personnel.

Most of the literature examining occupational stress and its relationship to officers' psychological distress is anecdotal. There is descriptive data research on the psychological functioning of law enforcement officers but not in the context of occupational stress (Biggam, Power, & Macdonald, 1997; Biggam, Power, Macdonald, Carcary, & Moodie, 1997; Neylan, Metzler, Best, Weiss, Faggan, Liberman, Rogers, Vedantham, Brunet, Lipsey, & Marmar, 2002; Violanti, 1992). A limited amount of empirical data that examines the relationship of occupational stress on psychological functioning exists. This research indicates that higher levels of occupational stress are associated with greater psychological distress in law enforcement professionals (Brown, Fielding, & Grover, 1999; Collins & Gibbs, 2003; Mearns & Mauch, 1998; Violanti & Aron, 1993).

Given that law enforcement officers with higher levels of occupational stress appear to have more psychological distress, it may be that officers are utilizing ineffective coping strategies. Law enforcement officers use a variety of coping strategies but a high percentage (73%) think they utilize ineffective coping strategies, especially when dealing with occupational stress (Alexander & Walker, 1994). Research on the over reliance on avoidant, suppressing, and disengaging coping shows these strategies to be ineffective, and they may be associated with poor psychological functioning (Coffey, Leitenberg, Henning, Turner, & Bennett, 1996; Leitenberg, Greenwald, & Cado, 1992; Runtz & Schallow, 1997). Contrary to what might be expected, using more avoidant coping strategies may result in experiencing events as more stressful, thus leading to an increase of general psychological distress (Hayes, Wilson, Gifford, Follette, & Strosahl, 1996).

The construct of experiential avoidance proposed by Hayes and colleagues (1996) is "the phenomenon whereby one is unwilling to remain in contact with particular private experiences (e.g., bodily sensations, emotions, thoughts, memories, behavioral predispositions) and takes steps to alter the form or frequency of these events and the contexts that occasion them (p. 1154)." This phenomenon may explain how psychological problems develop. Law enforcement officers experiencing reoccurring stressful and/or traumatic incidents may avoid contacting negative private events (e.g., distressing thoughts and feelings about their work) by engaging in behaviors such as dissociation, substance abuse, and isolation. For example, Hart and Cotton (2003) found that police officers reporting negative work experiences were directly predicted to engage in withdrawal behaviors (i.e., sick leave, stress leave, and turnover behaviors). Burke (1998) reported that those officers indicating more work stressors were more likely to use escapist coping, which increased work-family conflict and psychosomatic symptoms. Escapist-coping was described as avoidant, withdrawal, and use of alcohol and drugs. Similarly, Kohan and O'Connor (2002) found that occupational stress was associated with negative affect and alcohol consumption in law enforcement officers. Negative affect was described as similar to behavioral inhibition and withdrawal. With older police officers (i.e., 50 years and older), perceived work stress was significantly correlated with avoidant coping strategies, which included "hanging out in bars, yelling at others, smoking, gambling, and passive withdrawal" (Gershon, Lin, & Li, 2002). Although a link has been established between higher levels of occupational stress and the greater use of avoidant coping strategies, research focusing on this link and its relationship with psychological distress in law enforcement professionals is still very limited.

Brough (2004) suggested that employers need to provide prevention and treatment efforts for the mental well-being of emergency personnel, which includes law enforcement officers. Yet, the law enforcement culture might inhibit individuals from seeking professional psychological services. Because men typically dominate the law enforcement profession and are less likely to seek psychological services than women (e.g., Addis & Mahalik, 2003), the culture of law enforcement officers will likely reflect the stigmatized attitudes toward seeking professional psychological services. Specifically, it is the stigma received from others that may impact mental health utilization. For example, the police subculture involves the maintenance of tough, macho images and being distrustful of outsiders (Toch, 2002). If law enforcement officers do seek assistance for their psychological difficulties, then the inference that they are "weak," "cowards," or unable to perform their work effectively is implied by their co-workers (Miller, 1995). Studies have indicated that police officers tend not to seek mental health services when experiencing psychological difficulties (Terry, 1981; Fell, Richard, & Wallace, 1980; Graf, 1986; Greenstone, 2000). Loo (1984) suggested that police officers might fear being stigmatized as "crazy" or "weak" for seeking help, which in turn may impact their performance evaluations and opportunities for transfer or promotion. This phenomenon has been found in the way police officers disclose their emotions. Howard and colleagues (2000) found that officers want to disclose their emotions about traumatic events because it is a healthy human experience. However, they will only do this when describing the expectations of their peers. At the same time, officers will avoid discussing their emotions about a traumatic event because they fear that it will damage their work performance. This emotion-avoidance talk was found to occur whenever it was related to their reactions and the demands placed by the police organization. Therefore, developing an intervention that overcomes stigmatizing attitudes towards seeking psychological services in law enforcement is needed. However, preliminary data must be gathered in order to inform the types of resources needed for an intervention.

The purpose of this exploratory study was twofold. The first purpose was to expand the current empirical literature by assessing the relationship of avoidant coping strategies on occupational stress and psychological distress in law enforcement officers. It is hypothesized that officers using more avoidant coping strategies will report high levels of occupational stress and psychological distress. It is also hypothesized that avoidance coping and occupational stress, respectively, will predict the experience of psychological distress. A second purpose was to gather preliminary data to understand what factors are important to target in developing an intervention that will contribute to the mental and occupational health of law enforcement professionals.

Method

Participants

Participants were sworn police officers from a western police department serving a city of about 75,000 people. At the time of the study, this police department had 97 officers assigned to different divisions (i.e., 66 patrol officers and supervisors, 17 detectives, and 14 administrators or community outreach officers). Because the goal of this study was to assess officers in the field, administrators and community outreach officers were not recruited for participation. Of 83 remaining potential participants, a total of 48 officers participated in this study yielding a response rate of 58%. Some officers were not on active duty at the time of the data collection and, therefore, did not participate in this study.

The majority of the participants were men, Caucasian, married, and assigned to patrol work (see Table 1). On average, participants had 12.4 years of law enforcement experience (SD = 8.2) and 31% (n = 15) had a Bachelor's degree. Their mean age was 38.9 years (SD = 9.6). This sample was representative of the police department's patrol division.

Materials

Demographics

Demographic information was collected using a brief 15-item questionnaire designed to gather basic data such as gender, age, education level, marital status, ethnicity, years of experience in law enforcement, military experience, rank, and domestic violence training.

Coping Styles

The Ways of Coping (WOC) (Folkman & Lazarus, 1988) is a 66-item self-report instrument with eight coping subscales. It is designed to measure behavioral and cognitive coping strategies in response to stressful events. The WOC has been used in studies of police officers with alpha reliabilities for the eight subscales ranging from .42 to .79 (Patterson 2000; Violanti, 1992). Because the focus of this research was on avoidant coping, the Relative Escape-Avoidance subscale from the WOC was used.

Psychological Distress

The Brief Symptom Inventory (BSI) (Derogatis & Melisaratos, 1983) is a 53-item self-report instrument designed to assess general psychological distress. The BSI is a shortened version of the Symptom Checklist-90 Revised Scale. It consists of nine domains (i.e., Somatization, Obsessive-Compulsiveness, Interpersonal Sensitivity, Depression, Anxiety, Hostility, Phobia, Paranoid Ideation, and Psychoticism), plus three global indices (i.e., General Severity Index, Positive Symptom Total, and Positive Symptom Distress Index). For this study, the General Severity Index (GSI) was used to assess a more general level of psychological well-being. The test-retest reliability for the GSI is .90.

Occupational Stress

The Police Stress Survey (PSS) (Spielberger, Westberry, Grier, & Greenfield, 1981) is a 60-item self-report instrument that assesses the intensity and frequency of occurrence of specific stressors in law enforcement. The questionnaire includes two subscales: Organizational (administrative) stress and Operational (inherent police work factors) stress. Both scales have been found to be reliable (alpha = .90 and .92, respectively) (Violanti & Aron, 1993). For this study, modifications to the PSS were made. First, in order to explore the relationships between organizational and operational stressors, plus assess field events that occurred during the work shift, the PSS was separated into two questionnaires based on the subscales: PSS-Organizational and PSS-Operational. Secondly, the original PSS had participants rate how stressful an event was from 0–100 with the larger the number indicating the more stressful the event. This format was changed to a 5-point Likert type scale (e.g. *0 = not stressful at all, 1 = a little bit stressful, 2 = somewhat stressful, 3 = very stressful,* and *4 = extremely stressful*) on both the PSS-Operational and PSS-Organizational questionnaires as suggested by Wellbrock (2000). Additionally, the PSS-Operational questionnaire response options were changed for the second assessment phase in order to assess whether an event occurred during the previous shift (e.g., *Yes* or *No* responses). Finally, six items that asked about stress associated with responding to domestic violence calls (e.g., handling family disputes where adult(s) involved have been physically harmed or handling family disputes where children are present and/or involved) were added to the end of the PSS-Operational questionnaire. These items were added because domestic violence calls tend to be the most frequent and dangerous type of field event and were of particular interest to us as investigators (Biggam, Power, Macdonald, Carcary, & Moodie, 1997; Brown, Fielding, & Grover, 1999; Dolon, Hendricks, & Meagher, 1986).

Procedures

Permission was granted from the police department's administration to conduct this study. Consent to conduct this study at the police department was needed in order to maximize the number of participants and assess officers immediately after completion of their work shift. Participants were recruited at the beginning of each shift meeting. Those who volunteered to participate were asked to complete questionnaires before and after one work shift.

A token method of identifying the pre- and post-assessments from the same participant was utilized. Each pre-questionnaire packet was assigned a randomized number that was recorded onto a token, which was given to participants after they had completed their pre-questionnaire packets. Participants were told to keep their token until the end of their shift. At the end of the shift, they presented their token. The randomized number on the token was recorded onto the post-questionnaire packet. The token method provided the officers with complete confidentiality and anonymity.

All participants completed the following six questionnaires before their shift: demographics, WOC, BSI, PSS-Operational, and PSS-Organizational. At the end of the participants' shift, participants completed the PSS-Operational.

After completing the questionnaire, participants were given a referral list of psychological services. The receipt of the referral list was required from the Institutional Review Board. Snacks were provided to all law enforcement officers regardless of participation in the study.

Results

Data Analyses

Data were examined for accuracy of data entry and missing values. Mean scores were calculated to replace missing values in the data, which is the most conservative procedure for estimating missing values (Tabachnick & Fidell, 1996). One participant appeared to have misunderstood the instructions on the post-shift PSS-Operational questionnaire and, therefore, the participant's data on that specific questionnaire were omitted. One participant was missing the pre-shift PSS-Operational questionnaire in the first assessment packet due to a collating error. Two participants did not complete the post-shift PSS-Operational questionnaire in the second assessment packet because of work shift conflicts. These participants' data were included in the analyses when possible.

Exposure to Work Shift Events

To understand the types of field events this sample was exposed to, participants were asked what field events occurred during their work shift. Approximately 51% (n = 23) reported handling family disputes and crisis situations and 51% (n = 23) reported making critical on-the-spot decisions during their work shift. Based on officers' ratings of the stressfulness of field events, making critical on-the-spot decisions was rated the most stressful type of event ($M = .73$, $SD = 1.03$). Table 2 summarizes the top five field events experienced based on frequency and stress ratings.

Occupational Stress and Psychological Functioning

The mean GSI score assessing psychological distress for this sample was .57 ($SD = .49$), which is more than double the score seen in adult male nonpatient samples ($M = .25$, $SD = .24$) (Derogatis & Melisaratos, 1983).

Spearman correlations were conducted to assess the relationship between avoidant coping, operational stress, organizational stress, and psychological distress. Table 3 summarizes these results. As predicted, avoidant coping is associated with higher levels of psychological distress ($rs = .55$, $p < .01$) and organizational stress ($rs = .39$, $p < .01$). Additionally, higher levels of operational and organizational stress, respectively, were related to higher levels of psychological distress ($rss = .51, .53$, respectively, $p < .01$).

In order to evaluate the hypothesis that avoidance based coping and occupational stress predict psychological distress, a hierarchical regression was employed. Because of a high correlation between organizational and operational stress ($rs = .76$, $p < .01$), the variables were combined to form an occupational stress variable. One participant had a missing value on the PSS-Operational and that score was replaced with the mean score from all PSS-Operational values as suggested by Tabachnick and Fidell (1996). Residual plots were examined with respect to the fit between their distributions and the assumptions of multivariate analysis. Based on the residual analyses, the distributions indicated normality. To identify multivariate outliers, Malhalanobis distance was computed using $p < .001$ as a probability estimate for a case being an outlier (Tabachnick & Fidell, 1996). No cases were identified as significant multivariate outliers. Avoidant coping was entered on Step 1 and occupational stress was entered on Step 2. The regression after Step 2 with all the hypothesized variables yielded a multiple R of .71, $F = 22.48$, $p = .000$, accounting for 50% of the variance in psychological distress. Significant main effects were found for both avoidance coping and occupational stress. The results of this analysis are summarized in Table 4. Findings indicate that avoidant coping and occupational stress, respectively, are significantly predictive of psychological distress.

Discussion

This study expands the existing literature by focusing on the relationship between avoidant coping with occupational stress and psychological distress in law enforcement officers. Results indicate that officers reported higher levels of psychological distress than seen in the general population. The hypothesis that officers who report using avoidant coping strategies would experience high levels of occupational stress and psychological distress was supported. It was also hypothesized that avoidance based coping and occupational stress, respectively, would predict psychological distress and this was also supported. In brief, these findings suggest that individuals who report avoidant coping when experiencing stressful events such as police work are likely to experience more distress.

Although not the main focus of this study but interesting to note, this study also found that the top five frequent field events experienced during a work shift were rated as *slightly stressful* operational events. There are two possibilities for these findings. One might be social desirability. Officers may have rated the frequent field events as slightly stressful due to their adherence to the police culture's view that police officers should be "tough" (Toch, 2002). A second possibility may be that because many of these field events happen frequently, officers may have become habituated to these types of calls. It is likely that the field events experienced are stressful to most people and may influence a person's mental well-being. These types of calls may impact officers to a degree where they begin to build tolerance stress levels towards these field events. As a result, officers may not report these events as stressful because of their higher stress baselines.

The second purpose of this current study was to gather data to understand what factors are important to target in developing an intervention that will contribute to the mental and occupational health of law enforcement professionals. Based on this study's findings, the standardized betas indicate that occupational stress is a more important predictor of psychological distress than avoidant coping, although both are significant. Therefore, interventions aimed at decreasing occupational stress that, in turn, decreases avoidant behaviors may be useful in increasing the mental well-being of law enforcement officers. Such an intervention that focuses on workplace strategies to deal with organizational stress has been documented in promoting mental and occupational health (Bond & Bunce, 2000, 2003). For example, Bond and Bunce (2000) compared an emotion-focused stress management intervention (SMI) to a problem-focused intervention that teaches workers to identify and decrease workplace stressors that cause strain (Innovation Promotion Program; IPP; Bunce & West, 1996). The emotion-focused SMI taught workers to increase their ability to cope with workplace stressors by accepting their unwanted thoughts and feelings, while still pursuing their objectives that they wished to achieve (i.e., acceptance coping style). Workers were assessed after implementation of the intervention at week 3 and week 27. Bond and Bunce found that the general mental health of workers significantly improved in the emotion-focused SMI compared with the IPP. Additionally, Bond and Bunce (2003) have found that workers with higher levels of the acceptance coping style significantly predicted better mental health and job performance. Therefore, an intervention that enhances acceptance coping styles of workplace stressors and increases behavioral changes to help the law enforcement officers pursue their work objectives that they wish to achieve may be useful.

There are several limitations of this study. One limitation is that the study's sample was predominantly male and Caucasian. Having a sample with more women and minorities may result in more variance in the use of coping strategies. However, officers may be strongly influenced by the police culture to behave in ways consistent with these values and more diversity may not impact the results. Second, the type and frequency of operational and organizational events experienced by this study's officers may differ from other departments. The third limitation is that most of the findings are correlational and, therefore, one cannot make inferences of causality. Despite these limitations, the present study is representative of the population that was surveyed and expands the current literature on the issue of avoidant coping and its association with occupational stress and psychological distress in law enforcement professionals.

As recent events have demonstrated, law enforcement professionals often work under extreme stress. Indeed, when problems concerning their mental well-being are expressed, the underlying view of the police culture is that of stigmatization and pathology (Biggam, Power, MacDonald, Carcary, & Moodie, 1997). Unfortunately, this may result in the culture indirectly encouraging more avoidance by those who actually need to find alternate ways to improve their mental and occupational health. Therefore, the next step would be to focus on creating a supportive work environment in which supervisors and fellow law enforcement colleagues are able to acknowledge and deal with work stressors and mental health concerns in an accepting way. It is the hope that future research will concentrate on an intervention that minimizes the impact of occupational stress and enhances the personal lives of those who protect and serve the public.

Table 1
Law Enforcement Officers' Demographics (N = 48)

Descriptive	Percentage (%)	n
Gender		
Male	95.8	46
Female	4.2	2
Ethnicity		
White non-Hispanic	81.3	39
Hispanic	10.4	5
African-American	6.3	3
Native-American	2.1	1
Marital Status		
Single (never married)	6.3	3
Married	70.8	34
Separated	6.3	3
Divorced	16.7	8
Current Rank		
Patrol	77.1	37
Sergeant	8.3	4
Detective	8.3	4
Lieutenant	6.3	3

Table 2
Percentages of Field Events Experienced During Work Shift (N = 45)

Type of Field Event	Percent of Sample
Handling family disputes and crisis situations	51%
Making critical on-the-spot decisions	51%
Responding to family disputes	42%
Frequent changes from boring to demanding activities	38%
Responding to a felony in progress	27%

Most Stressful Field Event During Work Shift (N = 45)[a]

Type of Field Event	Mean (SD)
Making critical on-the-spot decisions.	.73 (1.03)
Handling family disputes and crisis situations	.54 (.86)
Responding to family disputes	.48 (.78)
Responding to a felony in progress	.44 (.97)
Frequent changes from boring to demanding activities	.42 (.72)

[a] The items were ranked on a scale ranging from 0 (*not stressful at all*) to 4 (*extremely stressful*).

Table 3
Correlation Table of Variables

	1	2	3	4	5
1. Psychological Distress (GSI)	–	.55**	.51**	.26	.53**
2. Avoidance (WOC)		–	.21	.21	.39**
3. Pre-Operational Stress[a]			–	.30*	.76**
4. Post-Operational Stress[b]				–	.25
5. Pre-Organizational Stress					–

*p < .05. **p < .01.
[a]n = 47. [b]n = 45.

Table 4
Hierarchical Regression for Variables Predicting Psychological Distress (N = 48)

Variable	B	SE B	B
Step 1			
Escape-Avoidance	.07	.02	.48**
Step 2			
Escape-Avoidance	.03	.02	.27*
Occupational Stress	.00	.00	.56**

*p < .05. **p .01.

References

Abdollahi, M. K. (2002). Understanding police stress research. *Journal of Forensic Psychology Practice, 2*(2), 1–24.

Addis, M. E., & Mahalik, J. R. (2003). Men, masculinity, and the contexts of help seeking. *American Psychologist, 58,* 5–14.

Alexander, D. A. & Walker, L. G. (1994). A study of methods used by Scottish police officers to cope with work-induced stress. *Stress Medicine, 10,* 131–138.

Biggam, F. H., Power, K. G., & Macdonald, R. R. (1997). Coping with the occupational stressors of police work: a study of Scottish officers. *Stress Medicine, 13,* 109–115.

Biggam, F. H., Power, K. G., Macdonald, R. R., Carcary, W. B., & Moodie, E. (1997). Self-perceived occupational stress and distress in a Scottish police force. *Work & Stress, 11*(2), 118–133.

Bond, F. W. & Bunce, D. (2000). Outcomes and mediators of change in emotion-focused and problem-focused worksite stress management interventions. *Journal of Occupational Health Psychology, 5,* 156–163.

Bond, F. W. & Bunce, D. (2003). The role of acceptance and job control in mental health, job satisfaction, and work performance. *Journal of Applied Psychology, 88* (6), 1057–1067.

Brandt, D. E. (1993). Social distress and the police. *Journal of Social Distress and the Homeless, 2* (4), 305–313.

Brough, P. (2004). Comparing the influence of traumatic and organizational stressors on the psychological health of police, fire, and ambulance officers. *International Journal of Stress Management, 11(3)*, 227–244.

Brown, J., Fielding, J., & Grover, J. (1999). Distinguishing traumatic, vicarious and routine operational stressor exposure and attendant adverse consequences in a sample of police officers. *Work & Stress, 13* (4) 312–325.

Bunce, D., & West, M. A. (1996). Stress management and innovation at work. *Human Relations, 49*, 209–232.

Burke, R. J. (1998). Work and non-work stressors and well-being among police officers: the role of coping. *Anxiety, Stress, and Coping, 11*, 345–362.

Coffey, P., Leitenberg, H., Henning, K., Turner, T., & Bennett, R. T. (1996). Mediators of the long-term impact of child sexual abuse: Perceived stigma, betrayal, powerlessness, and self-blame. *Child Abuse and Neglect, 20(5)*, 447–455.

Collins, P. A., & Gibbs, A. C. C. (2003). Stress in police officers: a study of the origins, prevalence and severity of stress-related symptoms within a county police force. *Occupational Medicine, 53*(4), 256–264.

Davey, J. D., Obst, P. L., & Sheehan, M. C. (2001). Demographic and workplace characteristics which add to the prediction of stress and job satisfaction within the police workplace. *Journal of Police and Criminal Psychology, 16*, 29–39.

Derogatis, L. R., & Melisaratos, N. (1983). The Brief Symptom Inventory: An introductory report. *Psychological Medicine, 13*, 595–605.

Dolon, R., Hendricks, J., & Meagher, M. S. (1986). Police practices and attitudes toward domestic violence. *Journal of Police Administration, 14* (3), 187–192.

Evans, B. J., & Coman, G. J. (1993). General versus specific measure of occupational stress: an Australian police survey. *Stress Medicine, 9*, 11–20.

Fell, R. D., Richard, W. C., & Wallace, W. L. (1980). Psychological job stress and the police officer. *Journal of Police Science and Administration, 8*, 139–144.

Folkman, S., & Lazarus, R. S. (1988). *Ways of Coping Questionnaire Manual.* Palo Alto, CA: Mind Garden/Consulting Psychologists Press.

Gershon, R. R. M., Lin, S., & Li, X. (2002). Work stress in aging police officers. *Journal of Occupational and Environmental Medicine, 44* (2), 160–167.

Graf, F. A. (1986). The relationship between social support and occupational stress among police officers. *Journal of Police Science and Administration, 14*, 178–186.

Greenstone, J. L. (2000). Peer support in a municipal police department. *The Forensic Examiner, 9*, 33–36.

Hart, P. M. & Cotton, P. (2003). Conventional wisdom is often misleading: police stress within an organisational health framework. In M. F. Dollard, A. H. Winefield, & H. R. Winefield (Eds.), *Occupational stress in the service professions*(pp. 103–141). London: Taylor & Francis.

Hayes, S. C., Wilson, K. G., Gifford, E. V., Follette, V. M., & Strosahl, K. (1996). Experiential avoidance and behavioral disorders: a functional dimensional approach to diagnosis and treatment. *Journal of Consulting and Clinical Psychology, 64,* 1152–1168.

Howard, C., Tuffin, K., & Stephens, C. (2000). Unspeakable emotion: a discursive analysis of police talk about reactions to trauma. *Journal of Language and Social Psychology, 19,* 295–314.

Kohan, A. & O'Connor, B. P. (2002). Police officer job satisfaction in relation to mood, well-being, and alcohol consumption. *The Journal of Psychology, 136* (3), 30–318.

Laufersweiler-Dwyer, D. L. & Dwyer, R. G. (2000). Profiling those impacted by organizational stressors at the macro, intermediate and micro levels of several police agencies. *The Justice Professional, 12,* 443–469.

Leitenberg, H., Greenwald, E., & Cado, S. (1992). A retrospective study of long-term methods of coping with having been sexually abused during childhood. *Child Abuse and Neglect, 16,* 399–407.

Loo, R. (1984). Occupational stress in the law enforcement profession. *Canada's Mental Health, 32,* 10–13.

Martelli, T. A., Waters, L. K., & Martelli, J. (1989). The police stress survey: reliability and relation to job satisfaction and organizational commitment. *Psychological Reports, 64,* 267–273.

Martin, C. A., McKean, H. E., & Veltkamp, L. J. (1986). Post-traumatic stress disorder in police and working with victims: A pilot study. *Journal of Police Science and Administration, 14(2),* 98–101.

Mearns, J. & Mauch, T. G. (1998). Negative mood regulation expectancies predict anger among police officers and buffer the effects of job stress. *The Journal of Nervous and Mental Disease, 186* (2), 120–125.

Miller, L. (1995). Tough guys: psychotherapeutic strategies with law enforcement and emergency services personnel. *Psychotherapy, 32,* 592–600.

Neylan, T. C., Metzler, T. J., Best, S. R., Weiss, D. S., Faggan, J. A., Liberman, A., Rogers, C., Vedantham, K., Brunet,A., Lipsey, T. L., & Marmar, C. R. (2002). Critical incident exposure and sleep quality in police officers. *Psychosomatic Medicine, 64,* 345–352.

Patterson, G. T. (2000). Demographic factors as predictors of coping strategies among police officers. *Psychological Reports, 87,* 275–283.

Rallings, M. (2002). The impact of offending in police officers. *Issues in Forensic Psychology, 3*, 20–40.

Runtz, M. G., & Schallow, J. R. (1997). Social support and coping strategies as mediators of adult adjustment following childhood maltreatment. *Child Abuse and Neglect, 21(2)*, 211–226.

Spielberger, C. D., Westberry, L. G., Grier, K. S., & Greenfield, G. (1981). *The Police Stress Survey: Sources of Stress in Law Enforcement* (Human Resources Institute Monograph Series Three: No. 6). Tampa, FL: University of South Florida, College of Social and Behavioral Sciences.

Tabachnick, B. G., & Fidell, L. S. (1996). *Using Multivariate Statistics (3rd ed.)*. New York, NY: HarperCollins College Publishers.

Terry, W. C. (1981). Police stress: the empirical evidence. *Journal of Police Science and Administration, 9*, 61–75.

Toch, H. (2002). *Stress in policing*. Washington, D.C: American Psychological Association.

Violanti, J. M. (1992). Coping strategies among police recruits in a high-stress training environment. *Journal of Social Psychology, 132*, 717–729.

Violanti, J. M. (1996). Trauma, stress, and police work. In Paton, D. & Violanti, J. M. (Eds.), *Traumatic Stress in Critical Occupations: Recognition, consequences, and treatment* (pp. 87–112). Springfield, IL: Charles C. Thomas.

Violanti, J. M., & Aron, F. (1993). Sources of police stressors, job attitudes, and psychological distress. *Psychological Reports, 72*, 899–904.

Wellbrock, K. D. (2000). Stress, Hardiness, Social Support Network Orientation, and Trauma-Related Symptoms in Police Officers. (Doctoral dissertation, California School of Professional Psychology, Los Angeles).

Zhao, J. S., He, N., & Lovrich, N. (2002). Predicting five dimensions of police officer stress: looking more deeply into organizational settings for sources of police stress. *Police Quarterly, 5* (1), 43–62.

Discussion Questions

1. Unlike most professions, law enforcement officers undergo a variety of negative psychological and physical experiences. What are some of the most common ones that could result in occupational stress?

2. Research has found that police work predicted psychological strain (i.e. anxiety, depression, and social dysfunction) differently from fire fighters and paramedics. What were their findings?

3. Law enforcement officers experiencing recurring stressful and/or traumatic incidents may avoid dealing with negative private events (e.g., distressing thoughts and feelings about their work) by engaging in certain types of behaviors. What are these behaviors?

4. What is there about the police culture that would discourage officers from seeking assistance when they are having psychological difficulties?

5. What was the purpose of the study conducted by the authors?

10

Police Officer Burnout:
A Partial Replication of
Maslach's Burnout Inventory

Homer C. Hawkins

Cherniss (1980) noted that burnout is a syndrome of emotional exhaustion, depersonalization, and reduced personal accomplishment that takes place among individuals who work with people in various capacities. An important aspect of the burnout syndrome is increased feelings of emotional exhaustion. As emotional resources are depleted, workers feel that they are no longer able to give of themselves at a psychological level. Another aspect of the burnout syndrome is the development of depersonalization, that is, negative, cynical attitudes and feelings about one's clients. This callous or even dehumanized perception of others can lead the individual to view their clients as somehow deserving of their troubles (Ryan, 1971). The development of depersonalization appears to be linked to the experience of emotional exhaustion. The burnout syndrome leads to reduced personal accomplishment, which refers to the tendency to evaluate oneself negatively, particularly with regard to one's work with clients (Maslach, Jackson, & Leiter, 1996).

Stressful situations that occur in the workplace have a significant effect on worker productivity (Maslach & Pines, 1977; Pines & Kafry, 1978). As a result, burnout has become a significant issue in various organizations. In society today, public service professionals constantly interact with people who have numerous problems and needs. Such interactions are becoming increasingly demanding, both at the physiological and psychological levels. The issue of burnout is addressed in secondary education (Byrne, 1994), social services (Maslach, 1978a), medicine (Maslach & Jackson, 1984), mental health (Figley, 1995), and law enforcement (Jespersen, 1988). Workers in all of these professions interact with people in stressful situations, some more than others. The question is, what happens to the individual over time when these interactions continue as a part of the job? Because of the nature of the work, the level of stress does not change over time. Some days are more stressful than others, and there are often long periods of intense circumstances that are very stressful. The following basic questions then arise: What do we do to cope? How do we adjust?

The purpose of this study is to examine burnout among sworn police officers in four departments in the Midwest. In this report, the reader will be reacquainted with some of the literature on the effects of burnout as it relates to job performance and organizational stress. Following the review of previous research, the method utilized in this study to measure burnout is explained and the results of the study are discussed.

Related Research

In viewing some of the important research in the area, several salient issues relating to police officer stress emerged and are discussed in this section. What happens to the individual officer in his or her personal life as well as on the job constitutes a significant portion of the related research in the area.

Burnout and Job Performance

Jackson and Maslach (1982) examined 142 police officers and their wives. Police officers experiencing burnout were more likely than those not experiencing burnout to report that they got angry at their wives and their children. Individuals who scored high on emotional exhaustion were more likely to report that they wanted to be alone rather than spend time with their families. They perceived that their children were more emotionally distant from them if they were experiencing feelings of depersonalization. Officers scoring high on depersonalization also were more likely to be absent from family celebrations. Reports of fewer friends were correlated with frequent feelings of depersonalization and the officers' wives also were more likely to state that they and their husbands did not share the same friends. Officers scoring high on emotional exhaustion were rated by their wives as having more frequent problems with insomnia. These officers were more likely to report having a drink to cope with stress if they had high scores on emotional exhaustion and to report taking tranquilizers when they scored low on personal accomplishment. The use of tranquilizers was corroborated by their wives who also were more likely to report that their husbands used medications if they scored low on personal accomplishment or high on emotional exhaustion.

The central issue is that emotional exhaustion, depersonalization, and personal accomplishment are linked (Maslach & Jackson, 1981). From this standpoint, one can focus on the effect of burnout on the job. When burnout exists, this has certain implications for the life of the police officer away from the job. The burned-out police officer responds differently to his or her spouse and children. In addition, there is the issue of insomnia and use of alcohol and tranquilizers. This has inherent consequences in their functioning as police officers and in their role as spouses and parents. When confronting this issue it is important to attempt to prevent burnout from taking place. In other words, how can this problem be remedied? Preventing burnout makes for a more productive, happier individual on the job and at home.

In their study focusing on burnout, Maslach and Jackson (1979) pointed to the emotional exhaustion, depersonalization, and reduced personal accomplishment that take place among individuals who work with people in some capacity. They further suggested that burnout can lead to a deterioration in the quality of service provided. Burnout appears to be correlated with various self-reported indicators of personal dysfunction, including physical exhaustion, insomnia, increased use of alcohol and drugs, and marital and family problems. Reese (1982), in support of this research, noted that burnout correlates with other indicators of human stress, such as alcoholism, mental illness, marital conflict, and suicide. Thus, burnout has a far-reaching effect, on the job and on one's family situation.

Schaufeli, Leiter, and Kalinmo (1995) found that emotional exhaustion was associated with mental and physical strain, work overload, and role conflict at work. Professional efficacy was related to satisfaction, organizational commitment, and job involvement. In studies of public contact workers, Maslach and Jackson (1984b) and Jackson, Schwab, and Schuter (1986) noted that high burnout scores were correlated with the expressed intention to leave one's job. Another outcome of burnout is the impairment of one's relationship with people in general, both on and off the job (Maslach, 1978b). In line with this thought, Maslach noted that physicians scoring high on emotional exhaustion were more likely to report that they wanted to get away from people. Mental health staff who scored high on emotional exhaustion were rated by coworkers as evaluating their clients more negatively over time.

A study of 43 physicians in a California health maintenance organization found that those who spent all or most of their working time in direct contact with patients scored high on emotional exhaustion. Emotional exhaustion scores were lower for those physicians who spent some portion of their time in teaching or administration. Support for this hypothesis is also noted in a survey of 142 police officers. The officers' Maslach Burnout Inventory-Human Services Inventory (MBI-HSS) scores were highly predictive of the intention to quit the police department (Jackson & Maslach, 1982; Maslach & Jackson, 1986). In line with this issue, Maslach (1976) found that burnout is related to the desire to leave one's job.

Organizational Stress

Concerning the issue of stress on the job, several aspects tend to surface. They include length of time on the job, job difficulty, organizational concerns, injury on the job, and line-of-duty shooting resulting in the death of an assailant.

Stotland, Pendleton, and Swartz (1989) suggested that being stressed on the job is not inevitable with time but that over time patrol officers' perceived ability to cope with their jobs becomes more significant with respect to their physical, mental, and behavioral health. They suggested that variations in the officers' perceptions of the difficulty of their jobs may be a function of a whole host of factors, including differences in assignment, talent, supervision, peer and family support, and performance evaluations. They went on to suggest that only supervisors showed less stress and strain with time and assignment or rank. Perhaps time had special consequences for this group. They pointed out that these supervisors obviously were successful and they may have expected to continue being successful. In none of the other groups of officers was there as much of a basis for expectation of increasing success. The issue of time here seems to concern whether individuals believe they are being successful on the job rather than how much time they have spent on the job. In this case, success may be the barometer relating to levels of stress.

Violanti and Aron (1995) suggested that time on the job is a factor related to feelings of stress. They noted that officers with 6 to 10 years of service had significantly higher mean stressor scores than those with 1 to 5 years of service. They suggested that this might be due, in part, to "reality shock"—the realization among more experienced officers that police work is more stressful and frustrating than they first perceived. Violanti and Aron went on to suggest that in their first 5 years on the job, officers have a feeling of idealism that tends to suppress feelings of stress and frustration.

Organizational factors causing stress are often discussed in the literature. Violanti and Aron (1995) mentioned four factors within organizations that cause stress: (a) an authoritarian structure, (b) lack of participation in decisions affecting daily work tasks, (c) lack of administrative support, and (d) unfair discipline. Storch and Panzarella (1996) stated that administrative matters are critical in causing stress on the job for police officers. Organizational factors rather than the danger of the work or encounters with human misery are what appear to produce stress. Such factors include work conditions, conflict with supervisors, and relationships with nonpolice. Sigler and Wilson (1988) and Sigler, Wilson, and Allen (1991) also found support for these issues. Crank and Caldero (1991) suggested that organizationally based issues were most likely to be mentioned as sources of stress, with problems relating to superiors emerging as the most frequently cited stressor. Shift changes were the second most frequently selected stressor.

Killing someone on the job or experiencing a fellow officer's being killed must rank as the most stressful factor in any police department (Gist & Taylor, 1996; Johnson & Nowack, 1996). The pervasive effects of these kinds of situations must be addressed by the organization. The means to address these situations must be in place; they should not have to be developed when the need arises.

Maslach's work has centered on depersonalization and emotional exhaustion as they relate to personal accomplishment on the job. In this study, the writer sought to replicate Maslach's research; in addition, this researcher explored whether sex, age, religion, marital status, education, length of time in law enforcement, length of time on a particular job, and race are related to emotional exhaustion, depersonalization, and personal accomplishment.

Method

Sample

The MBI-HSS was distributed to all officers in four police departments at their lineups before the beginning of their shifts. The first department had 66 officers who policed a city with a population of about 53,000. The second department had 49 officers who policed a city of about 65,000. The third department had 269 officers policing a city of approximately 110,000. The fourth department had 360 officers who policed a city of approximately 240,000. The total number of sworn officers in the four departments was 844, of whom 452 or 53.5% filled out questionnaires. There were a few questionnaires that were not completed and were excluded. This meant that the N for the various variables showed slight variations. The number of totally completed questionnaires was 442.

The survey consisted of distributing the questionnaires to every shift on a designated day. The day that was designated was the one in which the department would have the most individuals available. On any given day there were some officers not present because of vacations, illnesses, or normal days off. The individuals who filled out the questionnaires were those who were present for duty the day that this researcher conducted the survey. Of the total number of individuals who were asked to fill out a questionnaire, only 2 declined. The filling out of the questionnaire was voluntary and no compensation was offered. The questionnaire was filled out by just over half of the total. This represented a sample of the total number of officers in the four departments.

Instrumentation

The MBI-HSS is designed to assess three aspects of the burnout syndrome: (a) emotional exhaustion, (b) depersonalization, and (c) lack of personal accomplishment. In administering this survey, a human services demographic data sheet was included in the testing procedure. The data sheet was designed to elicit information such as sex, age, race, religion, marital status, number of children, highest level of school completed, highest degree received, primary work area, primary position, length of time spent per week on the job, length of time in law enforcement, and length of time on the present assignment (Maslach et al., 1996).

The emotional exhaustion (EE) subscale assesses feelings of being emotionally overextended and exhausted by one's work. The depersonalization (DP) subscale measures an unfeeling and impersonal response toward recipients of one's services, care, treatment, or instruction. The personal accomplishment (PA) subscale assesses feelings of competence and successful achievement in one's work with people. The frequency with which the respondent experiences feelings on each subscale is assessed using a six-point, fully anchored response format ranging from *never*(0) to *every day*(6).

Burnout is viewed as a continuous variable ranging from low to moderate to high degrees of burnout. A high degree of burnout is reflected by high scores on the EE and DP subscales and in low scores on the PA subscale. A PA score categorized as low is equal to or greater than 39, whereas a score that is equal to or less than 31 is in the high category. A low score is in the high category and is linked to burnout. A high burnout score will result in a low PA score that will result in a negative correlation. An average degree of burnout is reflected in average scores on the three subscales. A low degree of burnout is reflected in low scores on the EE and DP subscales and in high scores on the PA subscale (see Table 1).

Table 1
Categorization of Questions in the Maslach Burnout Inventory

| | | Frequency | |
Categorization	High	Moderate	Low
Emotional Exhaustion	27 or higher	17 to 26	0 to 16
Depersonalization	13 or higher	7 to 12	0 to 6
Personal Accomplishment	0 to 31	32 to 38	39 or higher

Reliability

Maslach focused on several studies that dealt with data on test and retest reliability of the MBI-HSS. For a sample of graduate students in social welfare and administrators in a health agency ($n = 53$), the two test sessions were separated by an interval of 2 to 4 weeks. The test-retest reliability coefficients of .82 for emotional exhaustion, .60 for depersonalization, and .80 for personal accomplishment were significant (Jackson et al., 1986). In another study, Leiter (1990) found test-retest correlations for the subscales that also were significant across a six-month interval.

Validity

Evidence of the validity of the MBI-HSS was obtained by distinguishing it from measures of other psychological constructs that might be presumed to be confounded with burnout. For example, it is possible that the experience of burnout may be nothing more than the experience of dissatisfaction with one's job. Although one would expect the experience of burnout to have some relationship to lowered feelings of job satisfaction, it was predicted that they would not be so highly correlated as to suggest that they were actually the same thing. A comparison of the participants scores on the MBI-HHS and the Measure of General Job Satisfaction (JDS) ($n = 91$ social and mental health workers) provided support for this reasoning. In viewing the correlations, job satisfaction had a moderate negative correlation with emotional exhaustion ($r = -.23$, $p < .05$) and depersonalization ($r = -.22$, $p < .02$), as well as a slightly positive correlation with personal accomplishment (r .17, $p < .06$) (Maslach et al., 1996). Support for this hypothesis is also noted in a study of 142 officers. The officers MBI-HHS scores were highly predictive of intentions to quit the police department (Jackson & Maslach, 1982).

Procedure

It took the respondents approximately 15 minutes to fill out the MBI-HSS. The author instructed the participants on the filling out of the questionnaire and distributed it. Respondents completed the survey in a group session in which privacy was ensured. They were not allowed to take the survey home because their answers might have been influenced by the people to whom they talked, such as spouses, friends, or coworkers. The questions concerned sensitive topics, and it was important that the respondents felt comfortable about expressing their feelings. Thus, anonymity was guaranteed. Finally, it is important to realize that there are widely varying beliefs about burnout. To reduce the possibility of a reactive effect concerning participants' personal beliefs or expectations about burnout, the respondents were unaware that they were filling out a burnout survey; rather, they were informed they were responding to a human services survey. The scale was presented as a survey of job-related attitudes and was not linked to the concept of burnout. This precaution is important if the MBI-HSS is to be administered effectively.

Results

Frequencies

The questionnaire was completed by 442 sworn police officers. Of that number, 134 (30.5%) scored low on emotional exhaustion, 143 (32.5%) scored in the moderate range, and 163 (37.2%) scored in the high range. For depersonalization, 68 (15.4%) scored low, 126 (28.5%) scored in the moderate range, and 248 (56.1%) scored in the high range. For personal accomplishment, 159 (36%) scored in the low range, 134 (30.3%) scored in the moderate range, and 148 (33.6%) scored in the high range (see Table 2). It is important to reiterate that being placed in category 3 is the high level, whereas the actual score is low.

Mean Differences

A one-way ANOVA was used to examine the independent variables that were not continuous. This included the following: sex, religious intensity, marital status, educational level, workjob (for individuals who had been in law enforcement for 10 years or more and had been in their present job for fewer than 5 years, as compared with those individuals who had been in law enforcement for 10 years or more and had been in their present position for more than 5 years), workjob1 (a comparison of the less-than-5-years group with 10 years or more in law enforcement and between 5 and 10 years in their present position), and race (see Tables 3 and 4). With regard to sex, female officers had significantly lower depersonalization scores. Married officers' mean scores for emotional exhaustion were significantly higher than for officers who were not married. For workjob, individuals who had been in law enforcement for 10 years and had been in their present position for fewer than 5 years, when compared with those who had been in law enforcement for 10 years or more and had been in their present position for more than 5 years, had significantly higher mean depersonalization scores. For workjob1, individuals who had 10 years or more in law enforcement and between 5 and 10 years on the job had significantly higher mean scores for emotional exhaustion and depersonalization. With regard to race, White officers' mean scores were significantly higher for emotional exhaustion and depersonalization.

Table 2
Frequencies for Sworn Officers

	Frequency	Percentage
Emotional Exhaustion		
Valid		
1 = low	134	30.5
2 = moderate	143	32.5
3 = high	164	37.2
Total	440	100.0
Depersonalization		
Valid		
1 = low	68	15.4
2 = moderate	126	28.5
3 = high	248	56.1
Total		
Personal Accomplishment		
Valid		
1 = low	159	36.0
2 = moderate	134	30.3
3 = high	148	33.6
Total	441	100.0

Correlations

According to a Pearson correlation, emotional exhaustion was significantly correlated with personal accomplishment ($p < .01$). The same was true when emotional exhaustion was correlated with depersonalization. Depersonalization, when correlated with personal accomplishment was also significant (p < .01) (see Table 5).

Correlations were also computed for age, years at the present job, and type of employment (how long the individual had been in law enforcement) (see Table 6).

With regard to age, the older the individual, the more likely he or she was to have low depersonalization scores. Furthermore, individuals had a higher probability of being emotionally exhausted the longer they were on a particular job. For type of employment, the longer an individual had been in law enforcement, the more likely he or she would be emotionally exhausted and to have low depersonalization scores.

Multiple Regression

In utilizing the multiple-regression statistical technique, the two independent variables, depersonalization and emotion exhaustion, were regressed with personal accomplishment (see Table 7). The R-squared change was .072, and the F change was significant at the .001 level. There was a strong relationship between high emotional exhaustion and depersonalization scores and low personal accomplishment.

The author felt that further exploration was needed concerning the racial effect with regard to depersonalization and emotional exhaustion. To see if race was a factor, it was necessary to include the personal profile variables, which were sex, age, religious intensity, marital status, education, length of time in law enforcement, and length of time on a particular job. These variables were entered into the multiple regression model first, followed by race and regressed with depersonalization and emotional exhaustion. For depersonalization, the R-squared was .143; R-squared change for the first set of variables was .083, and the F change was significant at the .001 level. The R-squared change for race was .060, and the F change was significant at the .001 level (see Table 8). For emotional exhaustion, the same set of variables were entered in the same sequence. The R-squared was .05 1; the R-squared change for the first set of variables was .016, and the F change was .512, which was not significant. The R-squared change was .035 for race, and the F change was significant at the .001 level (see Table 9). When controlling for race, White officers had higher emotional exhaustion and depersonalization scores.

Table 3
One-Way ANOVA by Demographic Characteristics, Emotional Exhaustion

	F *Ratio*	M	SD	n
Sex				
Male		18.73	11.29	373
Female		19.76	10.87	58
	.817			
Marital status				
Not married		17.33	10.26	132
Married		19.61	11.65	286
	3.730*			
Workjob				
Category 1		19.28	10.28	54
Category 2		20.95	12.21	177
	.831			
Workjob 1				
Category 1		19.28	10.28	54
Category 2		26.98	11.15	24
	8.801**			
Religious intensity				
1 = *very religious*		18.89	13.90	38
2		20.34	11.01	71
3		17.73	10.68	99
4		19.38	11.13	116
5		19.62	11.15	55
6		18.00	10.67	40
7 = *not at all religious*		12.29	10.39	7
	.972			
Educational level				
High school		22.46	14.04	28
Some college		18.75	11.53	207
4-year college		17.93	10.58	138
Postgraduate or degree		19.69	10.50	45
Other		21.20	7.50	10
	11.26			
Race				
Black		14.07	9.37	68
White		20.37	11.36	316
	18.225**			

*p < .05. **p < .01.

Table 4
One-Way ANOVA by Demographic Characteristics, Depersonalization

	F *Ratio*	M	SD	n
Sex				
Male		13.69	7.11	375
Female		11.26	5.91	57
	3.037*			
Marital status				
Not married		13.19	6.78	133
Married		13.51	7.10	286
	.193			
Workjob				
Category 1		10.89	6.17	54
Category 2		13.38	6.96	180
	5.583*			
Workjob 1				
Category 1		10.89	6.17	54
Category 2		15.96	7.47	24
	9.839**			
Religious intensity				
1 = *very religious*		11.05	7.25	38
2		14.75	7.41	71
3		12.64	7.25	101
4		13.34	5.81	116
5		15.20	7.19	56
6		13.50	7.40	40
7 = *not at all religious*		12.63	7.29	8
	2.020			
Educational level				
High school		14.00	7.85	28
Some college		13.02	6.73	207
4-year college		13.83	6.99	140
Postgraduate or degree		13.66	8.16	44
Other		12.80	4.42	10
	.309			
Race				
Black		9.14	5.77	66
White		14.31	6.89	317
	32.45**			

*$p < .05$. **$p < .01$.

Table 5
Pearson Correlations for Emotional Exhaustion (EE), Depersonalization (DP), and Personal Accomplishment (PA)

Variable	EE	DP	PA
EE			
Pearson correlation	1.000	.546**	−.227**
Significant (two-tailed)		.000	.002
N	441	435	435
DP			
Pearson correlation	.546**	1.000	−.251 **
Significant (two-tailed)	.000		
N	435	442	436
PA			
Pearson correlation	−.227**	−.251**	1.000
Significant (two-tailed)	.000	.000	
N	435	436	441

$**p < .01$, two-tailed.

Table 6
Pearson Correlations for Sworn Officers

Variable	EE	DP	PA
Age			
Pearson correlation	.070	−.151**	.029
Significant (two-tailed)	.149	.002	.559
N 421 423	421		
Years at present position			
Pearson correlation	.112*	−.065	−.028
Significant (two-tailed)	.022	.187	.557
N 417 419	427		
Type of employment			
Pearson correlation	.130*	−.127**	.060
Significant (two-tailed)	.007	.009	.222
N 423 425	423		

Note: EE = emotional exhaustion, DP = depersonalization, and PA = personal accomplishment. $*p < .05$. $**p < .01$.

Table 7

Multiple Regression of Depersonalization (DP) and Emotional
Exhaustion (EE) With Personal Accomplishment (PA)

						Change Statistics			
Model	R	R-Squared	Adjusted R-Squared	Standard Error of the Estimate	R-Squared Change	F Change	df1	df2	Significant F Change
PAa									
DP/EEb	.268	.072	.068	7.79	.072	16.546	2	427	.000*

a. Dependent variable.
b. Independent variables.
***p < .001.

Table 8

Multiple Regression Controlling for Race With Depersonalization

						Change Statistics			
Model	R	R-Squared	Adjusted R-Squared	Standard Error of the Estimate	R-Squared Change	F Change	df1	df2	Significant F Change
1	.287a	.083	.066	6.72	.083	4.974	7	387	.000*
2	.378b	.143	.125	6.51	.060	27.094	1	386	.000* * *

a. Personal Profile Variables.
b. Race.
* * *p < .001.

Table 9

Multiple Regression Controlling for Race With Emotional Exhaustion

						Change Statistics			
Model	R	R-Squared	Adjusted R-Squared	Standard Error of the Estimate	R-Squared Change	F Change	df1	df2	Significant F Change
1	.127a	.016	−.002	11.30	.016	.892	7	382	.512
2	.225b	.051	.031	11.11	.035	13.946	1	381	.000* * *

a. Personal Profile Variables.
b. Race.
< .001.

Discussion

In viewing sworn officers' scores on the MBI-HSS, there were some interesting findings. More than one third of the officers scored high on emotional exhaustion. In addition, 56.1% scored high on depersonalization. In looking at personal accomplishment, one third of the officers were in the high category (meaning that they had low scores on the personal accomplishment subscale). As indicated earlier, a high category level for personal accomplishment is a low score that is negative.

There was a strong correlation when emotional exhaustion and depersonalization were correlated individually with personal accomplishment. In addition, these variables in tandem were highly significant when regressed with personal accomplishment via the multiple-regression statistical technique. High emotional exhaustion and depersonalization scores meant low personal accomplishment scores. There was a strong relationship between high emotional exhaustion and depersonalization scores and low personal accomplishment scores. These results offer strong support for the findings of Maslach.

In turning to the responses on the personal profile segment of the questionnaire, female officers appeared to be more sensitive and married officers more prone to emotional exhaustion. The older officers seemed to be more sensitive with regard to the clientele they served although individuals who had been on a particular job for a long period of time seemed to be more prone to emotional exhaustion. For type of employment, the data suggested that the longer an individual had been in law enforcement, the greater the likelihood that this individual would be emotionally exhausted. By the same token, this individual would be more sensitive.

An intriguing finding concerns the variables workjob and workjob1. The data suggested an incidence of high depersonalization scores with workjob and high emotional exhaustion scores and depersonalization scores when looking at workjob1. This suggests the need for departments to consider moving individuals into different jobs whenever possible to reduce the possibility of emotional exhaustion and insensitivity to the people with whom the officers may be coming in contact in the course of their duties. A racial effect also was apparent. White officers seemed to be more prone to emotional exhaustion and to have higher depersonalization scores. This was made more apparent after controlling for race via the multiple regression statistical technique.

Depersonalization can be interpreted as functional and adaptive for the police officer in dealing with traumatic events. This definition of depersonalization points to the ability to take oneself out of a situation and to view it in an impersonal manner. This provides psychological protection for the officer. Depersonalization as defined by Maslach, is the treatment of the recipients of one's services in an uncaring manner; this differs from depersonalization as a defense mechanism used to deal with a traumatic event.

Implications

Emotional exhaustion, depersonalization, and personal accomplishment have important implications for police agencies, supervisors, and employee assistance programs. Police agencies need to be aware of the makeup of their police force. Police chiefs and high-ranking officials in police agencies need to be more aware of the makeup of their departments. Marital status, age, and length of one's work assignment are important factors. Being able to move individuals around in the workplace is also quite significant. Admittedly, smaller departments may be at more of a disadvantage when addressing this issue. However, this is very important and should be a focal point.

Supervisors who are in close touch with the rank-and-file police officer must be sensitive to these kinds of issues and ready to act to alleviate the emotional exhaustion and depersonalization syndromes. Oftentimes, a supervisor can act early on so that small problems do not develop into a serious issues. Being aware of the ongoing effects of police work and looking for early signs of difficulty can lead to a smoother running department.

Employee assistance programs are also very important. The police officer needs to be able to feel that he or she has a place to go if he or she has a problem. Whether the kind of help offered by a department is an internal program or an external program is an issue that can be addressed by future research in the area. The key is that an agency has some form of assistance in place for an officer to seek help. In addition, it is important that the officer feel that in seeking help the process of doing so will be kept confidential. It is important for police officers to have some place they can go when they feel they need help, and the seeking of help should not have repercussions.

References

Byrne, B. M. (1994). Burnout: Testing for the validity, replication, and the invariance of casual structure across elementary, intermediate and secondary teachers. *American Educational Research Journal, 31*, 645–673.

Cherniss, C, (1980). *Professional burnout in human service organizations.* New York: Praeger.

Crank, J. P., & Caldero, M. (1991). The production of occupational stress in medium-sized police agencies: A survey of line officers in eight municipal departments. *Journal of Criminal Justice, 19,* 339–439.

Figley, C. F (1995). *Compassion fatigue: Coping with secondary traumatic stress disorders in those who treat the traumatized.* New York: Brunner/Mazel.

Gist, R. M., & Taylor, V. H. (1996, May). Line of duty deaths and their effects on co-workers and their families. *Police Chief,* pp. 34–37.

Jackson, S. E., & Maslach, C. (1982). After effects of job related stress: Families as victims. *Journal of Occupational Behaviour, 3,* 63–77.

Jackson, S. E., Schwab, R. L., & Schuter, R. S. (1986). Towards understanding of the burnout phenomenon. *Journal of Applied Psychology, 71,* 630–650.

Jespersen, A. (1988, February). New approaches to stress. *Police Review,* pp. 436–437.

Johnson, B. R., & Nowak, P. (1996, September). Stress and officer involved shootings: The agency's responsibility. *Police Chief,* pp. 42–44.

Leiter, M. P. (1990). The impact of family and organizational resources on the development of burnout: A longitudinal study. *Human Relations, 43,* 1067–1283.

Maslach, C. (1976). Burned-out. *Human Behavior, 5*(a), 16–22.

Maslach, C. (1978a). The client role in staff burn-out. *Journal of Social Issues, 34,* 111–124.

Maslach, C. (1978b, Spring). How people cope. *Public Welfare,* 56–58.

Maslach, C. (1979, May). Burned out cops and their families. *Psychology Today,* 59–62.

Maslach, C., & Jackson, S. E. (1981). The measurement of experienced burnout. *Journal of Occupational Behavior, 2,* 99–113.

Maslach, C., & Jackson. S. E. (1984a). Burnout in health professionals: A psychological analysis. In E. Sanders & J. Suls (Eds.), *Social psychology of health and illness.* Hillsdale, NJ: Lawrence Erlbaum.

Maslach, C., & Jackson, S. E. (1984b). Patterns of burnout among a national sample of public contact workers. *Journal of Health and Human Resources Administration, 7,* 189–212.

Maslach, C., & Jackson, S. E. (1986). *Maslach burnout inventory manual*(2nd ed.). Palo Alto, CA: Consulting Psychological Press.

Maslach, C., Jackson, S. E., & Leiter, M. (1996). *Maslach burnout inventory manual*(3rd ed.). Palo Alto, CA: Consulting Psychological Press.

Maslach, C., & Pines, A. (1977). The burnout syndrome in the day care setting. *Child Care Quarterly, 6,* 100–113.

Pines, A., & Kafry, D. (1978). Occupational tedium in the social services. *Social Work, 23,* 499–507.

Reese, J. T. (1982, June). Life in the high-speed lane: Managing police burnout. *The Police Chief,* pp. 49–53.

Ryan, W. (1971). *Blaming the victim.* New York: Pantheon.

Schaufeli, W. B, Leiter, M. P., & Kalinmo, R. (1995). The Maslach Burnout Inventory—General survey. In M. P. Leiter *Extending the burnout construct.* Proceedings of the APA/NIOSH Conference, Work, Stress and Health 1995, Creating a Healthier Workplace, Washington, DC.

Sigler, R. T., & Wilson, C. N. (1988). Stress in the workplace: Comparing police stress with teacher stress. *Journal of Police Science Administration, 16,* 151–162.

Sigler, R. T., Wilson, C. N., & Allen, Z. (1991). Police and teacher stress at work and at home. *Journal of Criminal Justice, 19,* 361–370.

Storch, J. E., & Panzarella. R. (1996). Police stress: State-trait anxiety in relation to occupational and personal stressors. *Journal of Criminal Justice, 24*(2), 99–107.

Stotland, E., Pendleton, M., & Swartz, R. (1989). Police stress, time on the job and strain. *Journal of Criminal Justice, 17,* 55–60.

Violanti, J. M., & Aron, F. (1995). Police stressors: Variations in perceptions among police personnel. *Journal of Criminal Justice, 13,* 287–294.

Discussion Questions

1. What was the purpose of this study?
2. How is burnout defined by the author?
3. What were the manifestations of the behaviors of police officers who were experiencing burnout as it related to their wives and children?
4. What is the relationship between time on the job and feelings of stress?
5. It is suggested by some researchers that organizational factors cause stress? Which organizational factors were discussed briefly in this article?
6. What were some of the major findings of this study?

11

Stress Management Research at the Ontario Police College

Irene Barath

Historically, research about stress in policing has traversed two very different paths. The first path has investigated the effects of physical and psychological stressors on police officers in dynamic critical incidents that occur primarily in use-of-force situations. The findings of this research have been used to develop simulation training techniques to improve officers' survival skills and change the face of police training.[1] The determination of success in these situations is based on a multidisciplinary analysis of physical, psychological, and legal survival.

The second path has examined why some police officers enjoy their profession and others do not. This research has looked at internal and external stressors attached to the job of policing to identify what causes police officers the most stress and in some cases how officers manage their stress in both appropriate and inappropriate ways.[2] Research has looked at the long-term health

---

1. See Bruce K. Siddle, *PPCT Defensive Tactics Student Manual* (Belleview, Illinois: PPCT Management Systems, 1998); Alexis Artwohl and Loren W. Christensen, *Deadly Force Encounters: What Cops Need to Know to Mentally and Physically to Prepare for and Survive a Gunfight* (Boulder, Colorado: Paladin Press, 1997); and Dave Grossman and Loren W. Christensen, *On Combat: The Psychology and Physiology of Deadly Conflict in War and in Peace* (Belleview, Illinois: PPCT Management Systems, 2004).

2. See Artwohl and Christensen, *Deadly Force Encounters*; Kevin M. Gilmartin, *Emotional Survival for Law Enforcement: A Guide for Police Officers and Their Families* (Tucson, Arizona: E-S Press, 2002); Allen R. Kates, *CopShock: Surviving Posttraumatic Stress Disorder (PTSD)* (Tucson, Arizona: Holbrook Street Press, 1999); Katherine W. Ellison, *Stress and the Police Officer* (Springfield, Illinois: Charles C Thomas, 2004); and John M. Violanti et al., *Posttraumatic Stress Intervention: Challenges, Issues and Perspectives* (Springfield, Illinois: Charles C Thomas, 2000).

effects as well as the psychological toll the profession takes on some officers and does not take on others.

Police officers are often reminded that in many ways, perception is reality, and during a dynamic event every officer may perceive events differently, affecting the decisions made and the actions taken. But perceptions of an event are only the first step in what can be a long psychological process in an operational setting. Physiological responses to stress, such as tunnel vision, auditory exclusion, or a higher pain threshold, can be confusing to officers who experience them for the first time in confrontational situations.[3] After on-duty police officers resolve incidents where they are required to use force, they may be subjected to parallel investigations, Special Investigations Unit (SIU) scrutiny,[4] survivor guilt, and the self-doubt that can creep into the psyche after the incident is over.[5]

Officers involved in the same incident may be concerned that any differences between how they relate the incident to third parties will be perceived as deceptive. Officers should be comfortable and confident relating their own experiences if they understand what stress does to the physical and cognitive processes. If these critical incidents are not understood in their complexity, officers may not seek out the support systems available to them through their agency and their peers while facing the psychological and legal ramifications of their actions.

There have been many books and articles written about the manifestations of stress as it relates to police work when officers face life-threatening situations. The literature concerns preparatory information, pre-event strategies as well as intervention strategies for after the incident has occurred.[6] Sports psychology also has a specific application for police work.[7] For example, visuali-

---

3. See Artwohl and Christensen, *Deadly Force Encounters*; and Siddle, *PPCT Defensive Tactics Student Manual*.

4. The SIU (www.siu.on.ca) is an independent investigative body that is mandated to maintain confidence in Ontario police services by assuring the public that police actions resulting in serious injury or death are subjected to rigorous, independent investigations.

5. See Artwohl and Christensen, *Deadly Force Encounters*; Kates, *CopShock*; Grossman and Christensen, *On Combat*; and Violanti et al., *Posttraumatic Stress Intervention*.

6. For pre-event strategies, see Artwohl and Christensen, *Deadly Force Encounters*; and Grossman and Christensen, *On Combat*. For intervention strategies, see George S. Everly and Jeffrey T. Mitchell, *Critical Incident Stress Management: A New Era and Standard of Care in Crisis Intervention*, vol. 2, *Innovations in Disaster and Trauma Psychology* (Ellicott City, Maryland: Chevron, 1997); Jeffrey T. Mitchell and George S. Everly, *CISM: The Basic Course Workbook* (Ellicott City, Maryland: International CIS Foundation, 1998); Violanti et al., *Posttraumatic Stress Intervention*; and Kates, *Copshock*.

7. See Terry Orlick, *In Pursuit of Excellence: How to Win in Sport and Life through Mental Training*, 3rd ed. (Champaign, Illinois: Human Kinetics, 2000); Judy M. McDonald,

zation is only one of many techniques that can assist officers in maximizing their physical and mental performance when confronted with a dangerous situation. These resources are available to assist officers in educating themselves about some of the potential physical and psychological costs of doing their jobs, but educators must lay the foundation on which individual officers can build their awareness of job stress.

It is paramount for police officers involved in critical incidents to understand how they process information and that individuals will prioritize input during the incident at different speeds and points of focus based on their training, their previous life experience, and the degree to which they are experienced with such events. These issues are of particular concern to new police officers and to those assigned to dynamic, specialized operational areas such as weapon and drug investigations.

This article provides a review of two research studies at the Ontario Police College. The first study focused on stress and the implications for performance in an operational setting. The second study, completed in November 2007, focused on the strategies experienced police officers use to handle self-identified stressors in their lives both at work and at home. In addition, the study identified how experienced police officers identify success in their personal and professional lives.[8]

First Study: Stress during Critical Incidents

It is with an understanding of the issues described in the previous section that members of the Ontario Police College undertook a research project in

---

Gold Medal Policing: Mental Readiness for Performance Excellence (New York: Sloan Associate Press, 2006); and Shane Murphy, ed., *The Sport Psych Handbook* (Champaign, Illinois: Human Kinetics, 2005).

8. The research partnership consisted of the following members: Cheryl Regehr, Ph.D., professor and dean of the Faculty of Social Work and Sandra Rotman Chair, University of Toronto; Vicki LeBlanc, Ph.D., assistant professor in the Faculty of Medicine and scientist at the Wilson Centre for Research in Education, both in the Faculty of Medicine, University of Toronto; R. Blake Jelley, Ph.D., formerly of the Ontario Police College Research and Evaluations Unit and currently professor at the School of Business Administration at the University of Prince Edward Island; and the author. In addition to the four primary coordinators, numerous students and staff from both the University of Toronto and the Ontario Police College volunteered their time and expertise to assist with this study. This groundbreaking research collaboration led to a presentation in 2006 at the Annual Conference for the American Academy of Psychiatry and the Law. In addition, articles by the four members of the research team have been accepted for publication in three psychology journals.

partnership with members of the University of Toronto's Faculty of Social Work and Faculty of Medicine. The project was designed to investigate the relationships among psychological and physiological measures of stress and the performance of new police recruits.

Method: Recruits completed self-report questionnaires and provided physiological information in a study designed to induce acute stress. A Firearms Training Simulator (FATS) was used to put 84 police recruit volunteers through a specially designed simulation intended to mirror a realistic, operational situation.

The recruits who volunteered for this study had all been hired by their various police services and were in their third week of a 12-week on-site police training program, called Basic Constable Training, at the Ontario Police College. Approximately 400 recruits were registered in the Basic Constable Training program at the time volunteers were solicited. Study participants were videotaped during the simulation exercise, and their performances were assessed independently by three police college instructors after the training program was completed. Before and after the simulation, the participants completed surveys, answered self-assessment questionnaires, and responded to questions posed by researchers.

Demographic information was obtained through a brief questionnaire. Next, the Impact of Events Scale—Revised (IES-R), the Critical Incident History Questionnaire (CIHQ), the Social Provisions Scale (SPS), and the State-Trait Anxiety Inventory (STAI) were administered. In addition to baseline testing, the STAI was also administered immediately after the simulation and at 20- and 30-minute intervals following the simulation. Stress levels of the participants were assessed using saliva samples for cortisol levels at several times throughout the study session,[9] and participants' heart rates were continuously monitored by way of a mobile heart rate monitor strapped to the chest. Participants were assigned a number to protect their identities. None of the information gathered was used in any way to assess the capabilities of the students as it related to their participation in the Basic Constable Training program.

Due to the inexperience of the volunteers and the early stage of their training in the law, the session started with participants being briefed on the legal authorities of police officers when responding to 9-1-1 calls for service from

---

9. Cortisol, often identified as the "stress hormone," is secreted by the adrenal gland in response to stressful stimuli perceived either physically or psychologically. Small increases in cortisol can have some limited positive effects, such as decreasing pain sensitivity while increasing memory and immune system function. The long-term effects of sustained cortisol infusion, however, have produced some negative results, such as impaired cognitive performance, decreased bone density and muscle tissue, and increased body fat retention.

the public. The ensuing FATS scenario involved participants responding to an unknown 9-1-1 emergency call, with a female complainant requesting assistance. Upon arrival, the participants, each acting alone, were confronted by an aggressive male, who initially refused them entry to the apartment. Access to the confined apartment hallway was obtained when some attempts at communication were demonstrated and/or statements were made about the legal authority to enter. Each participant entering the main room of the apartment saw an unresponsive female victim on the floor, while the male provided inculpatory statements about having struck the female. Participants were forced to prioritize and handle several issues, including providing medical attention for the victim, ensuring their own safety, calling for assistance, and detaining or arresting the male suspect.

At a later date, assessors independently observed and rated the videotaped performances on participants' ability to gain entry to the premises in a lawful manner, officer and victim safety issues, the officers' knowledge of their legal authorities to act, and their ability to communicate with the persons in the scenario and with the dispatcher. Recruits' performances were also assessed on a relative percentage rating scale measuring the ability to obtain and maintain control of the situation, communication skills, judgment, and overall performance.

Study Results: Cortisol levels were correlated with heart rates, participants' self-assessments, and the assessments of the performance assessors. The level of physiological stress experienced by participants did not affect their performance, despite the results showing that the simulation was stressful enough to cause significant elevations in heart rate and cortisol levels. The students were, for the most part, able to complete the assignment with a reasonable level of competence based on their experience and training, but there were participants at both ends of the effectiveness spectrum. An interesting element that factored into the participants' vulnerability to psychological stress was the level of social support—for example, stable and caring relationships with family, friends, and coworkers—they had available. From this research, it is reasonable to conclude that the lower the level of social support available, the more difficulty an officer has in dealing with critical events that occur on the job.

One year after the study was completed, a follow-up survey was conducted with the original participants. Results from the follow-up indicate that support systems available to officers serve as important moderators of posttraumatic distress, and the best predictor of posttraumatic distress is how much stress participants felt during the training.

Finally, by way of physiological and psychological links to stress, it appears those who self-reported having previous critical incident experience had higher sustained levels of cortisol in their system for a longer period of time after the simulation event. This may have implications for officers' abilities to decompress after a critical incident when they have previous life experiences that have caused them significant psychological and physiological stress through trauma. For example, it is reasonable to expect that as officers continue in their careers, they will accumulate an increasing number of stressful experiences. The research suggests that experienced officers may have more difficulty decompressing from stressful incidents, which could have long-term effects. Although there is already a significant amount of research on the effects of stress related to policing,[10] this is another area for future study.

Second Study: Job Satisfaction

Policing is a dynamic profession that attracts people who seek out challenging and interesting work. Mortality statistics from Statistics Canada suggest the current average lifespan of Canadian men is 78 years. According to Ontario Provincial Police Association statistics, for police officers, that number has shot up from 54 years in 1985 to 74 years in 2005. Police officers who are contented in their lives at home and at work have a better chance to live life to its fullest. But when officers are dissatisfied, the first step in improving the situation is to acknowledge a problem exists, then try to understand why, and finally ask what can be done to solve it. The Ontario Police College recognizes that people can be more productive at work when they are successfully managing job stress and enjoying both their careers and their lives outside of policing.

This second path of stress research has examined cognitive and behavioral aspects of job satisfaction and the day-to-day business of police work, professionalism, attitude, and lifestyle. The literature identifies sources of stress for police officers, the strategies used to handle the stress, and the fact that stress can sometimes create cognitive distortions that affect officers' ability to make decisions.[11] Other research in this area has focused on the distinctions made

---

10. Gilmartin, *Emotional Survival for Law Enforcement*; Lawrence N. Blum, *Force under Pressure: How Cops Live and Why They Die* (New York: Lantern Books, 2000); and Violanti et al., *Posttraumatic Stress Intervention*.

11. Edward Delattre, *Character and Cops: Ethics in Policing* (Washington, D.C.: AEI Press, 2006); Gilmartin, *Emotional Survival for Law Enforcement*; Stephen Covey, *Seven Habits of Highly Effective Police Officers* (Salt Lake City, Utah: FranklinCovey, 2005); Blum, *Force Under Pressure*; and Patricia M. Fisher, *The Manager's Guide to Stress, Burnout and Trauma in Law Enforcement* (Victoria, British Columbia: Spectrum Press, 2001).

between stressors that are internal (such as administrative and organizational factors) and external (media scrutiny and public review) to the policing profession.[12] Much of the research in this area depends on anecdotal evidence and survey results.

Purpose of the Study: In the area of stress management and job satisfaction, the Ontario Police College has undertaken a survey of experienced police officers in all areas of policing and from police services of all sizes.[13] The purpose of this survey was to help identify how these officers define success inside and outside of their profession, how they feel about their current assignments, what areas of their work create the largest source of stress, and what strategies they are currently using to manage that stress.

Currently, recruits receive training on critical incident stress identification and management techniques related to their new profession. Officers taking some senior courses (for example, Drug Investigation and Sexual Assault Investigation courses) receive information on the physical and psychological impact of stress in dynamic and cumulative situations. Given feedback from these courses and in-class discussions, the research survey was designed and undertaken as a long-term analysis. The purpose of the survey is twofold. First, the survey tested the idea that the majority of occupational stress in policing comes from internal (organizational) and not from external sources. Second, the responses assisted in identifying job satisfaction factors and stress management techniques that could be transferred to others for their use.

Results: The study, conducted online at the Ontario Police College from November 2005 to November 2007, included input from 218 experienced police officers. Respondents included 171 men and 46 women. Of the respondent group, 51.8 percent were constables; 41.8 percent were detectives or sergeants; and the remaining participants held the rank of inspector or above. As for experience, 48.2 percent had served 3 to 9 years; 22 percent had served 10 to 16 years; and the remaining respondents had 17 years or more of experience. More than one in four respondents—26.6 percent—indicated that they had changed police services at least once.

The survey's results (N=218; November, 2007) suggest several interesting trends. In other research studies, contented police officers identify their families as being the priority in their lives. This suggests they have a strong sup-

12.   Fisher, *Manager's Guide to Stress in Law Enforcement*; Violanti et al., *Posttraumatic Stress Intervention*; and Susan Cartwright and Cary Cooper, *Managing Workplace Stress* (Thousand Oaks, California: Sage Publications, 1997).

13.   The study was undertaken with the assistance of Instructor Ramona Morris of the Research and Evaluation Unit at the Ontario Police College.

port system in place. This finding is in line with the findings from the present survey of experienced police officers from Ontario police services.

The survey results reveal that experienced officers are still passionate about the work they do, having retained the noble purposes of serving their communities and protecting vulnerable members. They love their work but are sometimes frustrated by perceived inequities in the administrative processes of their police agencies. Officers who identify themselves as having a high level of job satisfaction appear to handle the day-to-day cumulative stressors of police work by being involved with their families and their communities, pursuing self-development, and following a healthy lifestyle.

Career success is identified as receiving systemic acknowledgment through promotion for most officers who are at the first two levels of the rank structure. For most officers, this involves a promotion to the rank of sergeant. This is potentially problematic because the higher a person progresses in rank, the greater the competition for a limited number of positions becomes, which can lead to frustration on the part of those who are passed over.

In the current study, experienced police officers also consistently identified internal stressors and the administrative aspects of the job (such as paperwork, scheduling time off, court schedules, lack of available equipment, and unfair promotional practices) as creating the most significant distress for them. The manifestations of this distress range from minor irritation to self-destructive behavior such as substance abuse or engagement in unethical behavior. The interesting aspect of the available research is how significant the difference is between the amounts of stress officers attribute to organizational stressors versus external stressors.

Analysis of those officers who have changed police services indicates that most were looking for something intangibly better or an administrative system that has more equity built in, whereas others have moved to improve the quality of their family lives. This research has contributed to the development of career and performance management training. Strategies officers are using to deal positively with job stress have been identified, and researchers are examining if some of those skills are transferable to officers who are struggling. This way, all officers would have a chance to make good lifestyle and attitudinal decisions. In addition, if recruits are taught how to identify stress in themselves and their coworkers and are provided with stress management strategies, problems might be stopped before they start. Finally, police leaders could identify those areas of their administrative processes that are causing the most stress for their personnel and make adjustments where possible and appropriate.

With the final analysis complete, the research partnership has identified a list of specific sources of stress for officers and the strategies they use to deal with stress in positive ways as a first step toward improving the level of job satisfaction for every officer. All police officers should have the opportunity to enjoy their careers while providing a good life for their families until they move into a productive, successful retirement.

Discussion Questions

1. This article provided a view of two research studies at the Ontario Police College. What did the first study focus on?
2. What relationship was found between a participant's vulnerability to psychological stress and the level of social support?
3. What was determined to be the relationship between physiological and psychological stress and those who suffer from it having previous critical incident experience?
4. What was found by police officers who are content in their lives at home?
5. What are examples of internal stressors and external stressors?
6. What were the results of the survey taken by the Ontario Police College from November, 2005 to November 2007?

Part Four

What Are Some of the Bad Effects of Stress on Cops?

As the authors thus far have indicated, stress can severely impact individuals, especially in certain stress prone professions. We can identify a number of physical or physiological, psychological or emotional, or sociocultural manifestations of stress, which can affect an individual in a negative manner. From a physiological perspective, police officers frequently suffer from cardiovascular disease, kidney disease, hypertension, diabetes, ulcers, and digestive disturbances, all linked to the stress "on the job." From a psychological perspective, law enforcement officers have been known to show signs of short-term and clinical depression, of anxiety clusters manifesting themselves as nightmares, bad dreams, and insomnia, of paranoid patterns of behavior, and of post-traumatic stress disorder.

There are three primary sociocultural manifestations of stress which will be the focus of Parts Four and Five of this book. In Part Four, we will examine two of these negative effects in police officers: addictive behaviors and suicide. In Part Five, we will turn our attention to the impact of stress on the police family and the other serious effect: divorce and domestic violence.

One of the negative consequences of police stress is the common use of alcohol and, to a lesser degree, other substances to dull the impact of experiences and emotions on the job. Especially in the past, officers resorted to informal "choir practices," a gathering of shift members or law enforcement friends which, with the prodigious application of alcohol, allowed officer to defuse and decompress following the workday (or work night). Yet, the regular use of this legal substance as a coping mechanism frequently led to its abuse, and many departments have had to turn to their own version of Alcoholics Anonymous to deal with the issue. Too frequently, however, police administrators have ignored the extent of the problem until a particular problem or set of circumstances brought the issue to public light.

Adams and Walsh, reporters for the Minneapolis/St. Paul *StarTribune*, deal with just such a public and publicized problem in their chapter and place the problem of alcohol abuse in a proper perspective. In Minneapolis and St. Paul over the last several years, a number of alcohol-related incidents have occurred; the result has been the arrests of a number of officers for alcohol-related offenses, the disciplining of others for actions which violated departmental policy, and the death of at least one officer.

As is the case with other police stress issues, research on the problem is frequently descriptive and qualitative, rather than quantitative. It is important to also recognize that such negative manifestations of stress are not solely the province of American police officers. In their empirical work, Obst, Davey, and Sheehan found that entering the police service was associated with increased risk of harmful drinking and that, as recruits progressed through training and through their first year on the job, so did their risk of dependency. Such research is both necessary and appropriate as police agencies attempt to control alcohol abuse and dependency within their ranks.

Cross and Ashley recognize that the abuse of alcohol and other drugs are maladaptive behaviors associated with stress and trauma. The impact of such abuse is severe, with significant costs on and off the job to the individual and the agency. Breaking the cycle of abuse requires an agency to act decisively, offering specific intervention strategies for individual officers and an integrated treatment approach which includes both support services and training and research.

While we have frequently focused on the use by police officers of such illegal drugs such as cocaine and marijuana, others also pose significant dangers. The misuse of pain medications, widespread in many communities, also has found its way into the law enforcement community. Perhaps just as critically, as Humphrey and his colleagues note, is the proliferation of anabolic steroids and other performance enhancing drugs, abuse which cries out for effective policy and prevention by law enforcement administrators.

Traditionally in discussing addictive behaviors in law enforcement, we most frequently focus on alcohol and drug abuse. It is important to recognize, however, that stress can manifest itself in a variety of addictions: gambling, Internet use, pornography, and other risky behaviors. In a work prepared just for this volume, Allen Kates, the author of *Copshock: Surviving Posttraumatic Stress Disorder,* turns his attention to a rarely researched, but frequently discussed in law enforcement circles, addictive behavior: sex addiction in police officers,

Suicide is, of course, the most negative, inward-directed result of stress. According to classic stress lore, with some empirical support, the most suicide-prone professionals are psychologists, dentists, and law enforcement officers.

The concern about officer suicide is not new, and administrators and academicians alike have recognized the problem for decades. Between 1934 and 1940, for instance, 93 New York City police officers killed themselves, and that agency's suicide rate from 1950 to 1967 exceeded the suicide rate for all males in the United States during that time period.

The critical questions in any discussion of police suicide are two-fold: Is police suicide statistically a major or unique problem in American policing? If so, how can it be prevented? Consequently, Hamilton paints an introductory picture of the reasons for and extent of the problem of police suicide. For many officers who contemplate this ultimate action, the emotional wear and tear have taken a toll, and their heroic self-image is in conflict with the realities of the job. The "fraternity of pain" discourages talking about issues, and, upon reaching a certain psychological point, many officers see no other available option.

In 2008, recognizing the magnitude of the problem within his state, New Jersey Governor Jon S. Corzine established a Task Force on Police Suicide. Their in-depth analysis of the issue led to the promulgation of a report focusing on four key elements aimed at reducing such law enforcement officer deaths:

- Providing more suicide awareness training
- Improving access to and increasing the effectiveness of existing resources
- Recommending the adoption of best practices
- Combating the reluctance of officers to seek help

Further Reading

Baker, Thomas, and Baker, Jane P. (1996). "Preventing Police Suicide," *FBI Law Enforcement Bulletin*, 65(10), 24–27.

Green, James J. (1995). "Officer Needs Assistance: Suicide in the New York City Police Department," *CJ Update*, 23(2), 2.

Hem, Erlend; Berg, Anne Marie; and Ekeberg, Oivind (2001). "Suicide in Police—A Critical Review," *Suicide and Life-Threatening Behavior*, 31(2), 224–233.

Honig, Audrey, and White, Elizabeth K. (2000). "By Their Own Hand: Suicide among Law Enforcement Personnel," *The Police Chief*, LXVII (10), 156 and 159–160.

Josephson, Rosa Lee, and Reiser, Martin (1990). "Officer Suicide in the Los Angeles Police Department: A Twelve-Year Follow-up," *Journal of Police Science and Administration*, 17(3), 227–229.

Marzuk, Peter M.; Nock, Matthew, K.; Leon, Andrew, C.; Portera, Laura; and Tardiff, Kenneth (2002). "Suicide Among New York Police Officers, 1977–1996," *American Journal of Psychiatry*, 159(12), 2069–2071.

McCafferty, Francis L.; McCafferty, Erin; and McCafferty, Margaret A. (1992). "Stress and Suicide in Police Officers: Paradigm of Occupational Stress," *Southern Medical Journal*, 85(3), 233–243.

Paton, Douglas, and Violanti, John M. (2006). "Policing in the Context of Terrorism: Managing Traumatic Stress Risk," *Traumatology*, 12(3), 236–247.

Sheehan, Donald C., and Warren, Janet I. (2001). *Suicide and Law Enforcement*. Washington, DC: U.S. Department of Justice.

Stack, Steven, and Kelley, Thomas (1994). "Police Suicide: An Analysis," *American Journal of Police*, 13(4), 73–90.

Violanti, John M. (1995). "The Mystery Within: Understanding Police Suicide," *FBI Law Enforcement Bulletin*, 64(2), 19–23.

Violanti, John M. (1996). *Police Suicide: Epidemic in Blue*. Springfield, IL: Charles C Thomas.

Violanti, John M. (1999). "Alcohol Abuse in Policing: Prevention Strategies," *FBI Law Enforcement Bulletin*, 68(1), 16–18.

Violanti, John M.; O'Hara, Andrew F.; and Tate, Teresa T. (2011). *On the Edge: Recent Perspectives on Police Suicide*. Springfield, IL: Charles C Thomas.

Key Terms in Part Four

Anabolic-androgenic steroid (AAS): A type of performance-enhancing drug that includes the physiological human male hormone testosterone; these are controlled substances falling within the Anabolic Steroid Control Act.

At risk: As the result of changes in their personal or professional lives, officers who are "at risk" have a greater possibility for stress to negatively impact them. Such changes could include marital separation or divorce, child custody issues, being the subject of an internal affairs investigation, or involvement in a shooting incident.

Behavioral symptoms: Behavioral symptoms of stress include withdrawal, acting out, or substance abuse.

Cognitive symptoms: Such symptoms of stress, especially after a critical incident, include confusion, difficulty concentrating, or intrusive thoughts.

Emotional symptoms: Emotional symptoms of stress include anxiety or fear, depression, anger or guilt, or feelings of helplessness.

High risk/high stress job assignment: Those assignments within a police department, e.g. SWAT, child abuse investigations, or undercover investigations, in which there is a high level of stress and assigned personnel are at a higher risk of physical and psychological injury.

Human Growth Hormone (HGH): A type of performance-enhancing drug; these are not controlled by the Anabolic Steroid Control Act.

Integrated treatment approach: A model to intervention in officer stress situations, especially following a critical incident, which includes mental health consultation and intervention, mental health support services, training for all levels of personnel, and on-going research into agency issues.

Intervention strategies: Organized methods by which the effects of an officer's stress are dealt with, most normally under the guidance or with the involvement of trained mental health professionals.

Physical symptoms: Physical symptoms of stress can include fatigue, headaches, or changes in appetite or sleep patterns.

Substance abuse: Defined by the APA's Diagnostic and Statistical Manual as "a maladaptive pattern of substance use leading to clinically significant impairment or distress," it includes recurrent substance use which regularly impairs one's ability to do one's job; in situations which are physically hazardous (e.g., driving while intoxicated or impaired); or recurring substance-related legal or, the case of law enforcement officers, disciplinary problems.

Suicide: The act of taking one's life.

Suicide Rate: The number of suicides per a given population level, normally computed at the number of incidents per 100,000 population.

12

Cops under Pressure: Driven to Drink

Jim Adams and James Walsh

Some cops call it choir practice, those back-room hours after work when they try to escape the stress of life on the beat.

It's a time to gripe about bosses and bureaucracy, to commiserate about criminals—and to knock down a few drinks.

"During my career, there were many, many choir practices after work," said St. Paul Police Sgt C.R. Nelson, who joined the department in 1979 after getting alcoholism treatment and who just retired this month. "A lot of people unwind very appropriately. Unfortunately, some people don't."

Alcohol has long been a part of police culture; some studies suggest that nearly 25 percent of officers are dependent on it. But a rash of recent incidents around the region involving officers caught drinking too much is prompting police officials and counselors to take a hard new look at the culture, and either crack down on alcohol abuse or reach out to those needing help.

Drinking-related offenses are "a much bigger problem than any of us would like to see," said Interim Minneapolis Police Chief Tim Dolan.

St. Paul Police Chief John Harrington said drinking on his 560-member force tends to increase after a traumatic event, such as the death of an officer on duty. His department experienced that last year after Sgt. Gerald Vick was shot and killed while working undercover.

In the past year, seven Minneapolis officers have been arrested for drinking related offenses. Two officers, engaged to each other, were arrested this spring after an alcohol-related traffic accident in Columbia Heights. The woman threw a leg-kicking fit while detained in a squad car.

Her hefty fiancé had to be shot twice with a stun gun before cops could subdue and handcuff him.

In St. Paul, 25 officers were recently reprimanded after admitting to drinking together after work at a headquarters building last year.

Meanwhile, a state trooper who was a driver for Gov. Arne Carlson in the 1990s had a second drunken-driving incident last month and has resigned.

New Demands, More Duress

Even as they tighten their policies on drinking, police leaders in the Twin Cities and several suburbs say they do not see a crisis in their ranks.

In St. Paul, Harrington said that excessive drinking was "out of control" when he joined the force in the 1970s and that the number of officers needing treatment for alcoholism has declined since then.

Dolan agreed. He suggested that one reason more officers may be getting arrested for alcohol offenses is increased DWI enforcement and because flashing their badges when they are pulled over by another officer usually no longer means a free pass.

"Cops don't get byes on traffic stops or DWIs, where they might have in the past," Dolan said.

Since the death of Vick, who was killed while working undercover as he left a bar and had a 0.20 percent blood alcohol level, St. Paul police officials have limited how much undercover officers can drink and require a non-drinking partner to drive.

In Minneapolis, where two officers were arrested last year in domestic-abuse cases involving alcohol and six others were disciplined for drunken driving in 2004, Dolan said he is seeking tougher penalties for officers caught driving under the influence.

One possibility: placing officers whose licenses have been revoked—which can occur after a drunken-driving arrest—on unpaid leave, instead of desk duty, until their license is restored.

"Alcohol is a real challenge [for police] going into the 21st century," said Robert Douglas, who speaks at police-training seminars on the issue and was an officer and police chaplain in Baltimore for about 20 years.

Douglas said he fears that alcohol or drug abuse could get worse because heightened concerns over terrorism and security are putting more demands on police officers. He also noted that alcohol is often a factor in officer suicides—which appear to be increasing nationally—and domestic assaults.

Police suicides outnumber officers who get killed on duty, Douglas said. He leads the National Police Suicide Foundation, which documented about 450 officer suicides across the country last year. Other officials who have examined the issue say the number is closer to 300. Harlan Johnson, executive director of the Minnesota Chiefs of Police Association, said he has heard of two such suicides in the state in the past two years.

The Burdens of Stress

In Minneapolis, some officers drink too much because of family stress or heredity as well as job pressures, said Sgt. Steve Wickelgren, a psychologist and former patrol officer who coordinates the department's employee-assistance program. Sometimes, he said, it's not so much the stress from street duty or violence that officers talk most about; it's office politics or policies they feel interfere with their work.

"Officers fear change," he said. "They had no input into the decision-making, yet the front-line officers are the ones most affected."

John Delmonico, president of the Police Officers Federation of Minneapolis, the police union, said work stress on the Minneapolis force may have increased in recent years because the number of sworn officers has declined. Police officials said the city has about 130 fewer officers than its high of 923 in 1998.

But John Violanti, a research professor at the State University of New York at Buffalo, said the daily rigors that officers face on the streets are a big reason some of them turn to alcohol.

"They use [drinking] as a coping mechanism to deal with work trauma, not just shootings, but the everyday drudgery of dealing with abused kids and human misery," said Violanti, a former New York state trooper. "It has cultural acceptance: You have to be able to drink to be a good cop. It's a macho thing, a stress reliever."

Wickelgren said Minneapolis officers are trained about stress and family life before they get sworn onto the force. Last month, he spoke to recruits at a gathering that included officers' spouses and touched on the effects of stress on their personal lives.

After a day of high-speed chases or dealing with unruly suspects, officers may say, " 'I need to relax, leave me alone,' and distance themselves from everyone, which is negative for family life," Wickelgren said.

Helping Cops Cope

C.R. Nelson, who joined the St. Paul force after coming to Minnesota for chemical-dependency treatment and who has been sober for nearly 30 years, said that for most officers, after-hours drinking meant a few beers before heading home.

"But there were always those couple of guys who drank until dawn," he said.

Nelson said that since he had refused to participate in drinking sessions over the years—for fear of losing his sobriety—some fellow officers distrusted him.

"There's that old adage that you can't trust a man who doesn't drink," he said.

But over time, he said, troubled officers began seeking his help. He has mentored cops battling alcohol dependency.

Minneapolis and St. Paul have special programs for police employees. Other jurisdictions, including Dakota and Anoka counties, refer officers with drinking problems to counselors available to all employees.

"Counseling can be required as part of disciplinary action," said Anoka County Sheriff Bruce Andersohn. "There is no excuse for [drinking offenses], but if it is an issue, you try to help them so they can straighten themselves out or it will probably end in termination."

Boston's police department, with 2,300 officers, has a stress-support unit that addresses drinking problems, said Sgt. Herbert White Jr., its director.

He said he was a heavy drinker until a fellow officer arrested him for drunken driving after he hit a truck 17 years ago. He got treatment, recovered, remarried his wife and now supervises others who counsel officers.

White said that, before his arrest, he drank to numb his feelings and relax.

"A few drinks with the boys after work, some laughs and jokes and you are ready to go home," he said. "But how well do you sleep? Or do you just pass out?"

He said officers get in tense situations and sometimes develop "pre-anxiety," preparing themselves for what their shift may bring.

"You expect it, and you get it screaming down the road to a domestic violence call and then the dispatcher says a gun is involved," White said. "You get an adrenaline high. You get there, and you know the battle could be on. Sometimes it's nothing, but your body shakes when the adrenaline subsides."

Discussion Questions

1. What does the term "choir practice" mean as it relates to police work?
2. What are the estimated percentages of police officers who may be alcoholics?
3. What has happened in the past several years to make the Minneapolis Police Department focus attention on the problems of officers who drink to excess?

4. What has been suggested by one official as to why more police officers are being arrested for alcohol-related driving offenses?
5. What was suggested by John Violanti as to why some police officers may turn to alcohol?

13

Does Joining the Police Service Drive You to Drink? A Longitudinal Study of the Drinking Habits of Police Recruits

Patricia L. Obst, Jeremy D. Davey, and Mary C. Sheehan*

Introduction

The detrimental effects of alcohol on general well-being and performance are now well documented. In an organizational environment the negative consequences of alcohol can be a major problem. Industry can pay a high price for alcohol misuse through lowered productivity, increased absenteeism, accidents, and health and welfare costs (National Health and Medical Research Council, 1997). Within the context of policing, the potential for serious consequences of alcohol abuse are obvious. Policing is an occupation with high levels of public authority, accountability and responsibility. Police are also often in situations which are dangerous or hazardous to themselves and members of the public (Fenlon *et al.*, 1997). Policing can require fast reflexes and quick thinking. Excessive alcohol consumption or even just hangover effects can impede reaction time, can cause thinking and co-ordination to become sluggish and may lead to aggressive behaviour, particularly in the presence of threat (Lemon *et al.*, 1993; Taylor *et al.*, 1976). Hence the presence of alcohol, even

* Correspondence to: Jeremy D. Davey, Deputy Director Centre for Accident Research and Road Safety, School of Psychology and Counselling, Queensland University of Technology, Beams Road Carseldine, Qld, 4034, Australia. Tel: + 617 38644574. Fax: + 61 7 38644640. E-mail: j.davey@qut.edu.au.

low levels of residual alcohol, can impact greatly on police work. This may lead to the police officer themselves or members of the public unnecessarily being put at risk.

Much anecdotal evidence has suggested that as members of a high-stress oc-cupation police are at an increased risk of excessive alcohol consumption (McNeil & Wilson, 1993). In this light there has been a move to research alcohol con-sumption and the policing occupation. The research that has been done has come primarily from three sources: studies comparing police to other groups, studies comparing police to the general community and internal investigations. Such studies have suggested that around 25% of the police force show alcohol-related problems (Kroes, 1976); many drink on duty (Van Raalte, 1979) and have higher rates of consumption than the general population (Violanti et al., 1985). Unfor-tunately, many studies into alcohol consumption within police organizations have been conducted on very small samples, have relied on internal information or anecdotal evidence or have lacked adequate comparison data. Several authors have questioned the validity of such studies (e.g., McNeill & Wilson, 1993).

More recently a number of studies have been undertaken to examine the oc-cupation of policing in Australia. This work has begun to develop a small body of information on the nature and prevalence of drinking and aspects of the po-lice work environment that may contribute to drinking by some of its members. A recent survey of 4,193 Australian state police personnel revealed that while 65% were at low risk of hazardous alcohol consumption, 32% were at risk of harm-ful alcohol consumption and a further 3% showed a risk of alcohol dependence (Davey et al., 2000). A more in-depth study of 749 officers from an Australian state police service also found that over 35% of the sample reported drinking at lev-els which indicated a risk of harmful consequence (Davey et al., 2001). In the same study 23% of the sample reported being affected by co-workers' drinking in some way during the previous year and 14% stated that drinking outside work hours had affected their work performance at least once in the last year.

A survey of 852 New South Wales (NSW) police found that 48% of police-men and 40% of policewomen drank alcohol excessively through both prob-lematic drinking and by binge drinking (Richmond et al., 1998). These latest figures are considerably higher than for the general population, with recent Australian Bureau of Statistics (ABS) data showing 10.5% of men and 7% of women drink excessively (National Drug Strategy, 1996).

Elliott and Shanahan Research Australia (1994) found, in a survey of 555 ser-geants and senior sergeants in the Victorian Police Service, that 41% reported drinking on working days. McNeill & Wilson (1993) undertook a nation-wide survey of 895 police officers and found that although police reported drink-ing less frequently than the general Australian population when they did drink, they drank significantly more in a session. Binge drinking was also found to be more prevalent within the police sample than in the general population.

A study of 400 Northern Territory Police officers (Daulby, 1991) found 28% consumed alcohol at levels rated as moderate risk by the National Health and Medical Research Council. A further 12% drank at levels placing them at high risk of alcohol dependence. O'Brien & Reznik (1988) sampled 1066 NSW police officers and found 37% of male police were at-risk drinkers. They also found 31% of NSW officers of both sexes were classified as binge drinkers.

A study examining alcohol consumption across organizational environments (transport, health, metal fabrication, hospitality, emergency services) was conducted by the Victorian Occupational Health and Safety Commission (1992). The 137 police surveyed drank at rates above the survey group average, with 24% reporting drinking at hazardous or harmful levels.

Findings such as these suggest that police do drink at levels above the general population. Is this due to the kind of individuals who enter the police service, or is there something about the organization that encourages officers to drink? Research into police drinking has highlighted the impact of the workplace culture on drinking behaviour (Davey et al., 2001; Dietrich & Smith, 1986; Shanahan, 1992). Culture has been defined as the learned and shared norms of behaviour. Cultures are not universal; they emerge at different workplaces for different reasons and take distinct forms. Reference has been made by both researchers and police themselves of a culture conducive to a high level of alcohol consumption (Dietrich & Smith, 1986; Fenlon et al., 1997; OHSC, 1992). Drinking subcultures are more likely when there is high teamwork, and peer pressure (Fillmore, 1990); where alcohol use is more closely integrated with the job and there is a more permissive attitude to drinking at lunch or on the job (Whitehead & Simpkins, 1983); and where the nature of the work leads to drinking after work with colleagues as a means of relaxing, unwinding and debriefing (Shanahan, 1992). Fillmore (1990) also states that occupational identity (through camaraderie and/or mutual dependence) has implications for leisure-time activities and drinking styles and attitudes. High co-worker accessibility and high teamwork occurs in police and it could therefore be argued that an organizational drinking subculture is quite likely. This has been supported by research (e.g. Shanahan, 1992).

The current study was designed to examine the influence of the police workplace on individuals' drinking behaviours. The researchers endeavoured to overcome, some of the methodological flaws associated with previous police research by tracking new recruits over a 12-month period. Baseline data of drinking levels prior to entering the police academy for training were obtained and allowed a comparison to be made with drinking levels after induction into the service. This study therefore attempts to explore the impact of joining the police service on individual drinking behaviour.

Method

Participants

Two groups of police recruits in training formed the basis of the sample (n = 177). Group A consisted of new recruits, surveyed on their first day in the academy (n = 100, 64 males and 36 females), and group B consisted of trainee officers (n = 77) who had been in the academy for 6 months (49 males and 28 females). Both groups were surveyed on the same day. Group A was surveyed again after 6 months in the academy (n = 97) and again 12 months after the first survey, after a further 6 months of field placement (n = 92). Group B was surveyed again after 6 months of field placement (n = 72). Table I shows that the groups were comparable in terms of sex and age.

Measures

AUDIT. The international version of the AUDIT (Saunders *et al.*, 1993) was employed to assess the level of risk of harmful alcohol consumption within the police recruits. There are 10 items in the AUDIT which are classified into three domains, capturing a range of harms. The first domain (Q1–3) measures the quantity and frequency of alcohol consumption and screens for possible risk of hazardous consumption. The second domain (Q4–6) examines abnormal drinking behaviour, which may indicate early or established alcohol dependence. The third domain (Q7–10) probes for negative consequences related to alcohol consumption.

Table 1
Breakdown of Sample by Sex and Age

Group	Sex	18–25 years	26–30 years	31+ years	Total
A: New recruits					
	Male	40 (40%)	16 (16%)	8 (8%)	64 (64%)
	Female	31 (31%)	3 (3%)	2 (2%)	36 (36%)
	Total	71 (71%)	19 (19%)	10 (10%)	100 (100%)
B: Six months at academy					
	Male	36 (45%)	6 (8%)	7 (9%)	49 (64%)
	Female	22 (8%)	3 (4%)	3 (4%)	28 (36%)
	Total	58 (75%)	9 (12%)	10 (13%)	77 (100%)
Total *n*		129	28	20	177

Percentages are % of each group.

Each question is scored from 0 to 4 with a cumulative range of 0–40. A total score of 8–12 indicates a risk of harmful consumption, a score of 13 or more indicates risk of dependence. A score of four or more for females and five or more for males in Domain 1 indicates risk of a hazardous level of drinking. A score of four or more in Domain 2 indicates risk of psychological or physical dependence; and a score of four or more in Domain 3 indicates risk of significant life problems due to excessive alcohol consumption. These cut-offs were based on the AUDIT development study (Saunders *et al.*, 1993) and Centre for Drug and Alcohol Studies (1993).

Two additional questions were included in the questionnaire to indicate awareness of having a drinking problem. The first question asks the degree to which a person believes they have a drinking problem. The second question asks the degree of difficulty involved in cutting down or stopping alcohol consumption. These questions have been used in previous studies and were shown to be good brief indicators of awareness of possible problem drinking (e.g. Davey *et al.*, 2000; Lennings *et al.*, 1997).

Procedure

On entering the police service new recruits spend the first 6 months living and training at a police academy. In developing the questionnaire to assess the drinking habits of recruits and their experiences at the academy, focus groups were arranged with 40 police recruits who had been at the academy for 6 months. These officers were not part of either of the groups of recruits surveyed. Following the meeting and subsequent discussions, a questionnaire was developed that related specifically to the experiences of recruits.

The 10 AUDIT questions and two awareness questions comprised the body of the questionnaire. Participants' demographic details (age and gender) and various other academy-related issues which will be examined in future papers were also included in the questionnaire. The questionnaire was administered to recruits during class time. All recruits in attendance that day were invited to participate. Participants were informed that completion of the questionnaire was voluntary and that their responses were completely confidential and that no identifying marks would be made on their response sheets. Both groups completed the survey on the same day. Group A recruits were given the questionnaire on their first day at the academy, a follow-up questionnaire was given after 6 months of training and a final follow-up questionnaire 12 months after the initial survey (i.e. after 6 months of field placement). The questionnaire was given to Group B recruits after 6 months of training in the academy and a follow-up questionnaire after they had done 6 months of field placement.

Although these data are repeated measures data, owing to confidentiality issues the questionnaires could not contain identification markings and as a result could not be matched over time. The data obtained from this procedure are therefore treated as between-group data. While the authors acknowledge a loss in power by treating the data in this way, it would not increase the probability of Type I errors. The authors feel that guaranteeing complete confidentiality to recruits allowed for more open and honed answers, enhancing validity and in turn offsetting the loss of power.

Results

Table 2 shows the proportion of recruits at each survey time, falling into each AUDIT category. As can be seen, risk of problem drinking and dependency increased with time in training.

To examine if length of time in police service had a significant effect on drinking behaviour, as measured by AUDIT scores, a four-way ANOVA was run. Examination of the data via Levene's test of homogeneity of variance and normal probability plots revealed that all assumptions of ANOVA were met. Due to their proven impact on drinking behaviour, age and gender were also entered into the analysis as possible moderator variables. To ensure any possible differences between recruit groups did not impact on results, recruit group was also entered as a factor. Results showed that although a significant main effect of age emerged on total AUDIT scores ($F(2,404)$ 6.12, $p < 0.01$), with 18–25-year-olds ($M = 7.05$) scoring higher on AUDIT than 26–30-year-olds ($M = 6.01$) or 31–40-year-olds ($M = 4.2$), it did not significantly interact with any other variables. This indicates that age did not moderate the relationship between time in police service and AUDIT scores. The patterns of results were similar for both men and women, with no significant gender main effects or interactions emerging. Finally, no main effect or interaction involving recruit group emerged, indicating that no differences between recruit groups on the AUDIT scores emerged. Thus length of time in police service main effects are interpreted alone. Table 3 shows the mean scores on the AUDIT for both recruit groups.

Length of time in service did significantly effect AUDIT scores ($F(2,404) = 3.72$, $p < 0.05$). Post hoc examination via pairwise comparisons (familywise $c < 0.05$) shows that recruits' mean AUDIT scores on the first day in the academy ($M = 5.48$, $SE = 0.38$) were significantly less than the mean scores after 6 months of training ($M = 6.77$, $SE = 0.36$) or 12 months of training (M 6.90, $SE = 0.42$). The difference between 6 and 12 months of training did not emerge as significant. Figure 1 shows the mean AUDIT scores for each time category.

A MANOVA was utilized to examine the effect of length of time in the police service on the separate AUDIT domains. Again age and sex were entered as possible moderator variables and recruit group as a possible extraneous variable. Examination of the data showed that although scores on Domains 2 and 3 were somewhat positively skewed, assumptions for this procedure were met or considered robust. Multivariate results were the same as those detailed above. A main effect of age emerged (Wilks' $F(6,808) = 7.23$, $p < 0.001$), but it did not significantly interact with sex or time in service. No sex or recruit group main effects or interactions emerged. Length in service did have a significant multivariate effect on AUDIT domain scores (Wilks' $F(6,804) = 4.41$, $p < 0.001$). Univariately these results showed a similar pattern as seen in Table 2. As recruit group, sex and age did not interact with time in service and therefore did not moderate its relationship with AUDIT domain scores, again the time main effects are explored alone. Table 3 shows the mean scores on the AUDIT for both recruit groups and Table 4 shows the univariate results.

Post hoc analysis of the time main effect via pairwise comparisons (familywise ? < 0.05) revealed that in Domain 1 (drinking quantity and frequency) recruits on their first day at the academy scored lower (M = 4.45, SE = 0.28) than at 6 months (M = 5.33, SE = 0.24) or 12 months into training (M = 4.83, SE = 0.26). However, recruits at 12 months scored lower than at 6 months into training. In Domain 2 (abnormal drinking behaviour) recruits on their first day at the academy scored lower (M 0.78, SE = 0.15) than at 6 months (M = 1.10, SE = 0.13) or 12 months into training (M 1.45, SE = 0.16). In Domain 3 (negative life consequence recruits at 12 months (M = 0.61, SE = 0.005) scored higher than at 6 months into training (M = 0.35, SE = 0.006) or on their first day at the academy (M = 0.25, SE = 0.008) (see Figure 2).

Awareness of Problem Drinking

To assess differences between length of service on the awareness of problem drinking questions, two one-way ANOVAs were conducted with post hoc tests via Tukey's HSD with familywise error rate held at a < 0.05. Examination of the data showed that although scores were somewhat positively skewed, assumptions for this procedure were met or considered robust. Results showed a significant time of service effect for both acknowledgement of a drinking problem ($F(2, 433) = 5.54$, $p < 0.01$) and the ability to stop drinking ($F(2, 433) = 17.93$, $p < 0.001$). The recruits after 12 months of training were more likely to report having a drinking problem (M = 1.38, SE = 0.003) than on their first day at the academy (M = 1.05, SE = 0.002) or 6 months into training (M = 1.09, SE = 0.004). The same pattern was seen for the ability to stop drinking in the next three months. The recruits after 12 months of training were more likely to report not being able to stop drinking CM = 1.91, SE = 0.007) than on their first day at the academy (M 1.15, SE = 0.006) or 6 months into training (M = 1.26, SE = 0.009).

Table 2

Percentage of New Recruits
in Each AUDIT Risk Category

Time in Police Service	AUDIT Category		
	Low Risk	Risk of Problem	Risk Dependency
First day (n = 100)	73% (n = 73)	21% (n = 21)	6% (n = 6)
Six months of training (n = 171)	62% (n = 106)	25% (n = 42)	13% (n = 23)
Twelve months of training (n = 154)	58% (n = 89)	26% (n = 40)	16% (n = 25)

Table 3

Mean Scores for Each Recruit Group
on the AUDIT and AUDIT Domains

Recruit group	Time	Mean AUDIT Total (SD)	Mean AUDIT Domain 1 (SD)	Mean AUDIT Domain 2 (SD)	Mean AUDIT Domain 3 (SD)
A	First day (n = 100)	5.48 (3.4)	4.45 (2.7)	0.78 (1.5)	0.25 (0.59)
A	Six months of training (n = 97)	6.59 (4.8)	5.16 (3.1)	1.09 (1.7)	0.32 (0.84)
B	Six months of training (n = 77)	6.97 (5.2)	5.50 (3.2)	1.11 (1.6)	0.38 (0.70)
Total	Six months of training (n = 174)	6.78 (4.6)	5.33 (3.1)	1.10 (1.7)	0.35 (0.78)
A	Twelve months of training (n =92)	6.69 (4.4)	4.67 (3.1)	1.40 (2.0)	0.60 (0.95)
B	Twelve months of training (n = 72)	7.10 (5.2)	4.99 (3.3)	1.50 (2.1)	0.62 (0.98)
Total	Twelve months of training (n = 164)	6.90 (4.7)	4.83 (3.2)	1.45 (2.1)	0.61 (0.82)

Figure 1
Mean AUDIT Score of Recruits by Length of Time in Service
Error Bars Represent 1 SE above and below the Mean

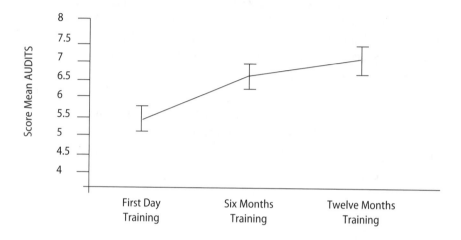

Table 4
Results of Univariate F Tests for AUDIT Domains

Variable	Domain	F	Eta2
Time (2, 406)	Domain 1	2.58a	0.015
	Domain 2	5.08b	0.034
	Domain 3	3.24a	0.023
Sex (1, 406)	Domain 1	1.34	0.018
	Domain 2	0.54	0.003
	Domain 3	0.44	0.002
Age (2, 406)	Domain 1	3.61a	0.034
	Domain 2	4.41a	0.032
	Domain 3	5,01a	0.030

a p < 0.05. b p < 0.01.

Discussion

Results show that entering the police service was associated with increased risk of harmful drinking. Six per cent of new recruits displayed a risk of serious dependency when assessed on their first day at the academy, this increased to 13% after 6 months and 16% after 12 months in the police service.

Due to their proven impact on drinking behaviour, age and gender were entered into all analyses as possible moderator variables. As expected, results indicated that age did impact on drinking behaviour with younger recruits displaying higher levels of risky drinking.

Figure 2
Time Main Effects on Domain 1, 2 and 3 AUDIT Scores
Error Bars Represent I SE above and below the Mean

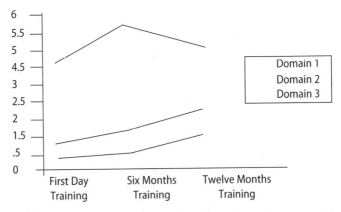

Interestingly, sex did not, with males and females displaying similar drinking behaviour. Neither age nor sex moderated the influence of length of time in service on drinking, with the time effect being similar across age groups and sex.

Length of time in service did significantly affect recruits' drinking behaviour. When surveyed on their first day at the academy, recruits showed significantly lower levels of at-risk drinking behaviour than the subsequent 6- and 12-month follow-up surveys. Considering the same recruits were followed through their police training, these results indicate that induction into the police service is a contributing factor to increased risky drinking behaviour. A major aspect of this induction process is the enculturation into the police service. This enculturation is possibly intensified by the fact the new recruits train and live at the academy during this initial 6-month period. These results indicate that this enculturation may encourage alcohol consumption.

The authors acknowledge that apart from the transition into the police service, other factors, such as changes in job status, income and family issues may have been operating. However, it is unlikely that all recruits were experiencing such changes in their lives. Thus, while some of the variance may be explained by other factors, the authors feel confident in suggesting that induction into the police service is a contributing factor to the increased levels of alcohol consumption seen in this study.

This overall pattern differed slightly when the domains assessed by the AUDIT were examined separately. In Domain 1, which examines drinking quantity and frequency, recruits surveyed on their first day at the academy reported drinking less frequently and in less quantities than when surveyed either 6 or 12 months into their training. This suggests that joining the police service did raise the frequency and amount of alcohol consumption of individual recruits. Interestingly, those surveyed at 12 months reported drinking with less frequency and in less quantity than those only 6 months into training. This shows that individual recruits' drinking habits increased quite quickly during their residential time at the academy (i.e. the first 6 months of training). This suggests that the academy itself, through its enculturation process, may lay the foundation for higher levels of drinking. Twelve months after entry, when recruits had worked in the field for 6 months, there was a reduction in recruits' drinking. Over this period recruits also leave the confines of living in the academy and move back into the community. However, drinking levels over this time remained significantly higher than on entry to the police service. Research into what occurs in the academy to produce these initial changes could have major implications for early intervention programmes.

Results in Domain 2, which examines abnormal drinking behaviours and the risk of alcohol dependency, revealed that as recruits progressed through training so did their risk of dependency. This increased risk is despite the reduction in frequency' noted between 6 months in the academy and the following 6 months in the field. In Domain 3, which examines negative consequences associated with risky drinking behaviour, the impact was not seen until 12 months into training. Those surveyed after 12 months reported more negative consequences than on intake or 6 months in the academy. This suggests that the negative consequences associated with risky drinking are not evident for some time after drinking levels have increased. The increase in risk of both dependency and negative consequences after 12 months, despite the drop in frequency while recruits are on field placement, may indicate a change in the nature of drinking. Perhaps drinking becomes similar to that of operational recruits who report high rates of binge drinking (McNeill & Wilson, 1993). Further research is needed to shed light on such changes in drinking patterns.

In line with these results, which highlight the increased risk of dependency and negative consequences, recruits after 12 months were more likely to report having a drinking problem than they were on their first day at the academy. The same pattern was seen for the self-reported ability to stop drinking. Recruits 12 months into training were more likely to report not being able to stop drinking than on their first day at the academy. This indicates a potential for further intervention as research has shown that awareness of the problem is the first step to recovery (Centre for Drug and Alcohol Studies, 1993).

In terms of the study's methodology, there are several limitations which the authors have attempted to address. The first concerns the pooling of the results from two groups of recruits. The recruit groups analysed were randomly selected. Analyses were conducted to check for differences in the groups in terms of age, gender and AUDIT scores and no significant differences emerged. Further, all analyses were run on the groups separately and the results showed the same patterns in both groups. In this light the authors felt, in the interest of clarity and parsimony, presenting the combined results was the most acceptable solution. Also the fact that the surveys were given to both groups at the same time controls for any secular trends. The second issue is to do with dropouts over time. Group A originally contained 100 recruits, 97 filled out the second survey and 90 the third. Group B reduced from 77 recruits to 72 at the second survey. Due to the nature of the methodology it was impossible to identify who the dropouts were. To ensure the dropouts were not unduly influencing the results, a worst case scenario approach was taken which presumed the dropouts were those with the lowest AUDIT scores. The pattern of the results remained the same, thus the authors presented the original analysis. Finally, a comparison control group was not included in the methodology. The authors acknowledge that this places limitations on the interpretation of results. However, the collection of pre-police service baseline data provides strong evidence on which to base future research. Through the use of longitudinal methodology these results offer strong evidence of how induction and enculturation into the police service impact on individuals' drinking behaviour. Research into what aspects of the enculturation process aid in this increase in risky drinking behaviour will shed further light on this area.

Acknowledgments

The authors would like to thank the Adjunct Professor of CARSQ, Dr Vic Siskind for his valuable comments on this paper, in particular on the statistical analysis.

References

Centre for Drug and Alcohol Studies (1993). *Early Intervention Unit, Information Sheet* No. 1/93. Camperdown, NSW: Royal Prince Alfred Hospital and University of Sydney.

Daulby, J. (1991). *Research and Assessment of Alcohol Problems in the NT Police*. Darwin: Northern Territory Police.

Davey, J., Obst, P. & Sheehan, M. (2000). The use of AUDIT as a screening tool in the police workplace. *Drug and Alcohol Review*, 19(1), pp. 49–54.

Davey, J., Obst, P. & Sheehan, M.C. (2001). It goes with the Job; officers insights into the impact of stress and culture on alcohol consumption within the policing occupation. *Drugs: education, prevention and policy*, 8(2), pp. 141–149.

Dietrich, J. & Smith, J. (1986). The nonmedical use of drugs including alcohol among police personnel a critical literature review. *Journal of Police Science and Administration*, 14, pp. 300–06.

Elliott and Shanahan Research Australia (1994). *Alcohol and Other Drugs in the Workplace: a benchmark survey comparing two Victorian organisations*. Melbourne: Elliott & Shanahan Research Australia.

Fenlon, T., Davey, J. & Mann, K. (1997). *National Guidelines for Police Workplace Alcohol Policy*. Canberra: Commonwealth Department of Health and Family Services.

Fillmore, K.M. (1990). Occupational drinking subcultures: an exploratory epidemiological study. In P.M. Roman (Ed.), *Alcohol Problem Intervention in the Workplace: Employee Assistance Programs and strategic alternatives* (pp. 77–94). New York: Quorum Books.

Kroes, W. (1976) *Society's Victim—the policeman: an analysis of job stress in policing*. Springfield: Charles C. Thomas.

Lemon, J., Chesher, G., Fox, A., Greeley, J. & Nakbe, C. (1993). Investigation of the hangover effects of an acute dose of alcohol on psychomotor performance. *Alcoholism Clinical Experimental Research*, 17, pp. 665–8.

Lennings, C., Feeney, G., Sheehan, M., Young, R., McPherson A. & Tucker, J. (1997). Workplace screening of mine employees using the alcohol use disorders identification test (AUDIT) and alcohol breathalyzation. *Drug and Alcohol Review*, 16, pp. 357–63.

McNeill, M. & Wilson, C. (1993). *Alcohol and the Police Workplace*. Adelaide: National Police Research Unit.

National Drug Strategy (1996). *National Drug Strategy Household Survey: survey report* 1995. Canberra: Australian Government Publishing Service.

National Health and Medical Research Council, Working Party of the Health Advancement Standing Committee (1997). *Workplace Injury and Alcohol.* Canberra: National Health and Medical Research Council.

O'Brien, L. & Reznik, K. (1968). *The Prevalence of Self Reported Risk Factors for Ischaemic Heart Disease, Problem Drinking and Emotional Stress Among NSW Police: summary of finding.* Sydney. Royal Prince Alfred Hospital.

Occupational Health and Safety Commission (1992). *Drugs and the Workplace: research report.* Melbourne: Victorian Occupational Health and Safety Commission.

Richmond, K., Wodak, A., Kehoe, L. & Heather, N. (1998). How healthy are the police? A survey of life style factors. *Addiction*, 93, pp. 1729–37.

Saunders, J., Aaslans, O., Amundsen, A. & Grant M. (1993). Alcohol consumption and related problems among primary health care patients. WHO collaborative project on early detection of persons with harmful alcohol consumption. *Addiction*, 88, pp. 349–62.

Shanahan, P. (1992). *A Study of Attitudes and Behaviours: working in the police force today and the role of alcohol.* Sydney Elliott and Shanahan Research Australia.

Taylor, S., Gammon, D. & Capaso, D. (1976) Aggression as a function of alcohol and threat. *Journal of Personality and Social Psychology*, 34, pp. 938–41.

Van Raalte, R. (1979). Alcohol as a problem among officers. *Police Chief.* 46, pp. 36–39.

Violanti, J., Marshall, J. & Howe, C. (1985). Stress, coping and alcohol use: the police connection. *Journal of Police Science and Administration*, 13, pp. 106–10.

Whitehead, P. & Simpkins, J. (1983). Occupational factors in alcoholism. In R. Kisin & H. Begleiter (Eds), *The Pathogenesis of Alcoholism; psychosocial factors.* New York: Plenum Press.

Discussion Questions

1. What statistical evidence was provided to show that entering the police service was associated with an increased risk of harmful drinking?

2. Is there any evidence to indicate that the age of the recruit impacted drinking behavior?

3. Did the authors find any relationship between the length of time in the police service and the recruit's drinking behavior?

14

Police Trauma and Addiction: Coping with the Dangers of the Job

Chad L. Cross and Larry Ashley

Law enforcement officers face traumatic incidents daily. These events, typically unexpected and sudden, fall well beyond the bounds of normal experience;[1] hence, they can have profound physical, emotional, and psychological impacts—even for the best-trained, experienced, and seasoned officers.

The ability to cope with stressful incidents is a personal journey that depends on an officer's past experiences with trauma; appropriate development of coping strategies for stress; availability of support networks (e.g., family, friends, and colleagues); and recognition of the dangers of ignoring signs and symptoms of post-incident stress, which is a normal response to abnormal circumstances.[2] Regardless of an officer's personal experiences with traumatic incidents, avoiding, ignoring, or burying the emotional aftermath of a traumatic event can lead to serious short- and long-term consequences. Sadly, however, some officers believe that substance use and abuse may offer the best way to cope with their otherwise unbearable feelings.

Certainly, not every officer deals with stress and trauma by abusing chemicals, and not every officer who chooses to abuse chemicals does so to numb the effects of trauma. However, overwhelming evidence suggests that the two factors often *are* linked, particularly in the high-stress environment of police work. Therefore, law enforcement administrators need to understand the re-

---

1. J.T. Mitchell and G.S. Everly, Jr., *The Basic Critical Incident Stress Management Course: Basic Group Crisis Intervention*, 3rd ed. (Baltimore, MD: International Critical Incident Stress Foundation, Inc., 2001).
2. Ibid.

sponses to trauma and stress, the link between trauma and substance abuse, and the strategies for intervention and treatment needed to help their officers survive the rigors of their chosen profession.

Understanding Trauma and Stress Responses

Critical incidents experienced by law enforcement officers are broad and far-ranging. A retired officer turned counselor, who survived a serious assault early in his career, has suggested that "any situation in which an officer's expectations of personal infallibility suddenly become tempered by imperfection and crude reality can be a critical incident."[3] Examples could include an officer-involved shooting, the death of a coworker, serious injury while on duty, life-threatening incidents, hostage situations or negotiations, exposure to intense crime scenes, a police suicide, or any situation that falls outside the realm of normal experience.

Stress responses and the symptoms resulting from such incidents can be cognitive (confusion, difficulty concentrating, or intrusive thoughts), physical (fatigue, headaches, or changes in appetite or sleep patterns), behavioral (withdrawal, acting out, or substance use), or emotional (anxiety or fear, depression, anger or guilt, or feelings of helplessness).[4] Most often, a combination of these symptoms emerges—frequently worsening and compounding as multiple traumas occur over time. If officers do not develop or take advantage of avenues for coping with stress appropriately, physical, mental, and emotional exhaustion ("burnout") can result.

Diagnosis of Psychological Stress Responses

Similar to military combat veterans, law enforcement officers experience a plethora of treacherous, violent stresses on a daily basis.[5] The psychological aftermath of such experiences can be either acute or chronic and can

---

3. A.W. Kureczka, "Critical Incident Stress in Law Enforcement," *FBI Law Enforcement Bulletin*, February/March 1996, 10–16; and A.W. Kureczka, "Surviving Assaults: After the Physical Battle Ends, the Psychological Battle Begins," *FBI Law Enforcement Bulletin*, January 2002, 18–21.

4. Ibid. and supra note 1.

5. J.M. Violanti, "Residuals of Police Occupational Trauma," *The Australian Journal of Disaster and Trauma Studies* 3 (1997); and J.M. Violanti and D. Paton, *Police Trauma: Psychological Aftermath of Civilian Combat* (Springfield, IL: Charles C Thomas, 1999).

emerge or reoccur across broad temporal scales. While on active duty and upon returning to civilian life, military personnel—and, likewise, law enforcement officers—carry this stress-laden emotional baggage, which can produce multitudinous residual effects that, all too often, lead to substance use and abuse.

Post-traumatic stress disorder (PTSD) is associated most often with critical incidents experienced by law enforcement officers,[6] but many other diagnostic criteria could be linked to stressful incidents, including such disorders as adjustment, mood, anxiety, impulse-control, and substance abuse/dependence. PTSD includes symptoms that develop owing to experiencing intense fear, helplessness, or horror, which, in turn, often can lead to re-experiencing the traumatic event, avoiding situations associated with it (even if not experienced at the time the event occurred), and "numbing" of the arousal response. These symptoms cause impairment or distress in social or occupational functioning. If the symptoms persist for more than 1 month or appear for the first time 6 months after the event, then possible PTSD would need to be investigated. If the symptoms appear and subsequently disappear within a one-month time frame, then acute stress disorder should be investigated.[7] Of note, subclinical individuals may chronically develop PTSD symptoms indistinguishable from those formally diagnosed with the disorder if they remain untreated.[8]

Impacts of Trauma

The impact of traumatic experiences differs for every individual; however, beginning with the studies of combat fatigue after World War II, similarities across individuals have led to a generalized conceptualization of expected stress reactions, particularly those that might lead to career burnout. If or when this occurs, law enforcement organizations and other first-responder public safety agencies may find themselves understaffed, unable to perform expected duties, and faced with increased apathy, suicide rates, and substance abuse.[9]

---

6. J.M. Violanti, *Police Psychological Trauma*, Law Enforcement Wellness Association, Inc.; retrieved on August 5, 2003, from *http://www.cophealth.com/articles/articles_psych trauma.html*.

7. *Diagnostic and Statistical Manual of Mental Disorders*, 4th ed., text revision (Washington, DC: American Psychiatric Association, 2000).

8. D.S. Weiss, C.R. Marmar, W.E. Schlenger, J.A. Fairbank, K. Jordan, R.L. Hough, and R.A. Kulka, "The Prevalence of Lifetime and Partial Post-Traumatic Stress Disorder in Vietnam Veterans," *Journal of Traumatic Stress* 5 (1992): 365–376.

9. J.M. Violanti, *Police Suicide: Epidemic in Blue* (Springfield, IL: Charles C Thomas, 1996); and supra note 5.

Generally speaking, stress responses begin with anxiety and panic reactions, which often lead to difficulties in concentration and feelings of being overwhelmed or out of control. This can progress to physical symptoms, such as tachycardia, gastrointestinal distress, and hypertension. If intervention does not occur, then worker apathy tends to increase, leading to absenteeism, lateness, procrastination, and increased use of chemical substances (e.g., tobacco, caffeine, alcohol, pain killers, or sleeping pills). If officers continue along this path, then major depressive symptoms begin to increase, feelings of hopelessness and helplessness abound, suicidal ideation and rates increase, and, all too often, substance abuse to dull these feelings leads to addiction and dependence.[10]

Linking Trauma and Substance Abuse

Substance use and abuse among law enforcement officers represent widespread, albeit somewhat underreported, phenomena. Alcohol and other drug abuse are maladaptive behaviors associated with stress and trauma, and when these behaviors emerge in law enforcement, the profession must afford them special attention.[11]

Alcohol Use and Abuse

Studies have indicated that nearly one-quarter of law enforcement officers are alcohol dependent as a result of on-the-job stress; however, researchers believe that this estimate falls well below the true number due to incomplete reporting.[12] A study of 852 police officers in New South Wales, Australia, for example, found that nearly 50 percent of male and 40 percent of female officers consumed excessive amounts of alcohol (defined as more than 8 drinks per week at least twice a month or over 28 drinks a month for males and more than 6 drinks per week at least twice a month or 14 drinks a month for females) and that nearly 90 percent of all officers consumed alcohol to some degree.[13]

---

10. Supra note 1.

11. B.A. Arrigo and K. Garsky, "Police Suicide: A Glimpse Behind the Badge," in *Critical Issues in Policing: Contemporary Readings*, 3rd ed., eds. R.G. Dunham and G.P. Alpert (Prospect Heights, IL: Waveland Press, 1997), 609–626.

12. J.M. Violanti, *Dying from the Job: The Mortality Risk for Police Officers*, Law Enforcement Wellness Association, Inc.; retrieved on August 5, 2003, from *http://www.cophealth. com/articles/articles_dying_a.html*.

13. R.L. Richmond, A.K. Wodak, and L. Heather, "Research Report: How Healthy Are the Police? A Survey of Lifestyle Factors," *Addiction* 93 (1998): 1729–1737.

The unique subculture of the law enforcement profession often makes alcohol use appear as an accepted practice to promote camaraderie and social interaction among officers.[14] What starts as an occasional socializing activity, however, later can become a dangerous addiction as alcohol use evolves into a coping mechanism to camouflage the stress and trauma experienced by officers on a daily basis.[15] When the effects of the alcohol wear off, however, the stress or trauma that led to the drinking episode still exists.

In addition, researchers have identified four occupational demands that can trigger alcohol use by law enforcement officers, namely depersonalization (reacting unemotionally to the everyday stresses of the job), authoritarianism (officers' behavior governed by a set of regulations, making them feel as if they are not in control), organizational protection (the structure in place to protect law enforcement agencies from criticism), and danger preparation (the stress related to officers knowing that their lives potentially are in constant danger).[16] Some may argue, then, that alcohol use among officers serves both as a personal coping mechanism related to socialization and presumed stress/trauma reduction and also as a reaction to the internal stresses created by law enforcement agencies themselves.

Drug Use and Abuse

Other drug use also is on the rise in law enforcement agencies.[17] This increasing problem has led to the establishment and maintenance of drug-testing programs. Though this has caused numerous challenges within the legal system, an ever-growing movement toward maintaining a drug-free workplace exists throughout law enforcement agencies.[18]

Sadly, those officers, clinically diagnosed or not, facing the aftermath of traumatic experiences may feel that drugs can help numb their pain, if only temporarily. Additionally, law enforcement officers maintain a role that may make them more susceptible to abusing drugs. For example, they have ample op-

14. Supra note 11; and H.W. Stege, "Drug Abuse by Police Officers," *Police Chief* 53(1986): 53–83.

15. Supra note 11.

16. J. Dietrich and J. Smith, "Nonmedical Use of Drugs and Alcohol by Police," *Journal of Police Science and Administration* 14 (1987): 300–306.

17. R.G. Dunham, L. Lewis, and G.P. Alpert, "Testing the Police for Drugs," *Criminal Law Bulletin* 24 (1998): 155–166.

18. T.J. Hickey and S.T. Reid, "Testing Police and Corrections Officers for Drug Use After Skinner and Von Raab," *Public Administration Quarterly* 19 (1995): 26–41.

portunities to obtain drugs because they often come in close contact with il-legal substances and the individuals who use or deal in them; they learn how, why, when, and where to obtain and use drugs and the rationalizations for such use from drug offenders; and they may find that drugs offer a way to help them cope with the constant stress on the job and the ever-present traumatic incidents that they encounter.[19]

Impacts of Substance Use and Abuse

Both the acute and chronic impacts of substance use and abuse often lead to profound negative consequences. Not limited to the individual user, these consequences can extend to loved ones, colleagues, the employing agency, and the citizens who depend on law enforcement personnel. In other words, sub-stance abuse by law enforcement officers is not a personal journey because they *always* must be prepared to conscientiously and continually react, respond, serve, and protect. Such high expectations can prove difficult to meet when sober, let alone when impaired by alcohol and other drugs or while recover-ing from using such substances.

Alcohol and other drug use and abuse have both overt and covert social and economic costs, including lost productivity and wages; increased family prob-lems, including risks of domestic violence; and rising costs to the criminal jus-tice system to respond to, house, or adjudicate substance abusers.[20] When substance abusers are members of the public safety sector, the problems mul-tiply—employees can become unable to perform their sworn duties, admin-istrators can find themselves increasingly overburdened trying to deal with a problem that can result in negative perceptions of their agencies, and the pub-lic can lose faith and trust in the system.

Substance use may lead to a number of problems for law enforcement of-ficers and their agencies. When officers deal with stress or trauma using alco-hol and other drugs, they may find that they simply cannot perform their duties adequately. They often become agitated, hypervigilant, and aggressive. They feel tired and overwhelmed and have difficulty concentrating on their work. Family problems mount, and officers become isolated. Accelerated sub-stance use leads to occasional and then progressive lateness and absenteeism. Continued use may result in the inability to perform the job at all and inten-

19. Supra note 17, 155.

20. *Alcohol and Drug Services: Impacts of Alcohol,* Health Services, San Diego County Web site; retrieved on August 12, 2003, from *http://www.co/san-diego.ca.us/cnty/cntydepts/ health/services/ads/aclimpct105.html.*

sified feelings of worthlessness and apathy, causing officers to become more and more depressed and confused. Ultimately, the end result is a tremendous increase in the risk of suicidal ideation, which studies have linked strongly to alcohol and other drug use among law enforcement officers.[21]

Breaking the Cycle of Trauma and Substance Abuse

Substance use often begins with the best intentions—a means of social interaction. However, when the mind-numbing qualities of alcohol and other drugs become a means of coping, albeit a shortsighted one, substance use then may progress into abuse and dependence because officers see no other avenue of reducing stress. More stress often means more chemical use, and, before long, officers may find themselves in a dangerous cycle. Unfortunately, however, this means that the officers never dealt with the real problem or issue in a satisfactory way; it remains an open wound that often cannot heal on its own, despite the best efforts of self-medication.

Where and when, then, does the cycle of trauma/stress and substance use/abuse end? If appropriate intervention does not occur, tragedy may result. But, agencies do not have to wait for tragedy to occur; they can act *beforehand* to save their officers.

Intervention Strategies

Traditional trauma/stress intervention involves some type or form of critical incident stress management or debriefing;[22] however, recent researchers have questioned the ability of these techniques to reduce the symptoms stemming from trauma.[23] These techniques may prove useful for some, but reactions to traumatic events and the stresses inherent in police work make a more individualized model more appropriate in many circumstances.[24] Situations may indicate individual and group mental health treatment, along with professional or peer

---

21. M. Wagner and R.J. Brzeczek, "Alcoholism and Suicide: A Fatal Connection," *FBI Law Enforcement Bulletin*, August 1983, 8–15; and supra notes 9 and 11, 620.

22. Supra note 1.

23. I.V.E. Carlier and B.P.R. Gersons, "Brief Prevention Programs After Trauma" and R. Gist and J. Woodall, "There Are No Simple Solutions to Complex Problems," in *Post-Traumatic Stress Intervention: Challenges, Issues, and Perspectives*, eds. J.M. Violanti, D. Paton, and C. Dunning (Springfield, IL: Charles C Thomas, 2000), 65–80 and 81–96.

24. J.M. Violanti, D. Paton, and C. Dunning, eds. *Post-Traumatic Stress Intervention: Challenges, Issues, and Perspectives* (Springfield, IL: Charles C Thomas, 2000).

counselors, as a necessary part of the intervention. However, treating law enforcement officers can pose some challenges to mental health personnel.

Traditionally, law enforcement officers have viewed the mental health profession with some skepticism because they often did not feel that counselors understood what it meant to do police work. To combat this mind-set and deal effectively with officers, counselors must receive some unique training. They also must have—

- a grounding in policing;
- a localized knowledge of the agency and administrations within which their clients reside;
- a unique comprehension of the trauma and stresses inherent in police work;
- an understanding of the dark humor often used by officers to vent stress-induced anger and frustration; and
- an ability to build rapport by establishing a trusting, respectful atmosphere wherein they can assure officers of complete confidentiality.[25]

A unique field, substance abuse counseling requires specialized training to appropriately and legally administer assessments and treatments. The first intervention for substance abuse should occur at the earliest possible time—*before* recruits become law enforcement officers. Police academies should contain didactic training in substance use and abuse and the inappropriateness of such behavior in police work. Increasing awareness at this stage of professional development not only puts useful and necessary information into the hands of future officers but also raises their awareness of the many potential problems, both personally and professionally, that substance use can cause. Additionally, training at this stage reaffirms that the law enforcement agency administration understands the pressures inherent in police work that may lead to substance use and abuse. Further, instruction by senior officers during the training phase provides appropriate models of behavior and sends the message to young recruits that they need not resort to substance use as a means of coping with the trauma and stress of the law enforcement profession.

Many brief interventions exist for initial stages of substance abuse, and most have focused on group interventions where members discuss the pros and cons of binge drinking and alcoholism. These discussions often focus on the health effects of alcohol and other drug use, an understanding of societal norms as a baseline to compare an individual's personal consumption, and the cognitive-

---

25. Supra note 3.

behavioral interventions to change the thinking patterns associated with substance use.[26] Long-term, heavy drinkers, on the other hand, may need detoxification and a period of recovery before introducing psychoeducational intervention.[27] Providing a supportive intradepartmental atmosphere for officers in need of this level of intervention is a necessary component.

Integrated Treatment Approach

It seems clear that treating trauma/stress and substance use/ abuse should occur in complement. After all, police trauma and stress will not disappear nor will substance use and abuse within the ranks. What can change, however, is the atmosphere within those law enforcement administrations that may tend to downplay, rationalize, or deny addictions. To help effect this change and to save time, money, and, most important, lives, law enforcement agencies can invest in an integrated model of awareness and treatment. To help agencies, the authors offer some considerations in developing such a model.

Support Services

- Law enforcement agencies should have mental health professionals trained and certified in addictions counseling on staff for consultations, interventions, and referrals. They should offer police counselors trained in policing who have knowledge of police infrastructure, programming, and administration.
- Agencies should have trauma teams that include mental health professionals on call for consultations and interventions when needed.
- They should make employee assistance professionals available to provide confidential services outside the agency.
- Agencies should institute peer counseling programs.[28] Ideally, these peer counselors would have experiences in both trauma and addictions or would work in teams to develop integrated programs. Officers are more likely to respect the experiences of fellow officers over outside professionals, and the models of positive behavior that such peer support groups offer may be a key component of successful intervention.

---

26. R.L. Richmond, L.H. Kehoe, S. Wodak, and A. Uebel-Yan, "Quantitative and Qualitative Evaluations of Brief Interventions to Change Excessive Drinking, Smoking, and Stress in the Police Force," *Addiction* 94 (1999): 1509–2140.

27. Psychological education designed to help clients access the facts about a particular mental health issue.

28. J.M. Madonna, Jr. and R.E. Kelly, eds. *Treating Police Stress: The Work and the Words of Peer Counselors* (Springfield, IL: Charles C Thomas, 2002).

Training and Research

- Young recruits should receive training in recognizing stress, dealing with traumatic incidents, and understanding the negative effects of substance use and abuse.
- Law enforcement agencies should make critical incident trauma management training available to all officers on an ongoing basis. Officers often receive training in such programs for the treatment of the citizens they protect. But, a strong effort also needs to focus internally within law enforcement agencies, specifically aimed at the traumatic incidents most often encountered in police work.
- Agencies should provide ongoing training to continually educate their officers on the effects of alcohol and other drug use. Agencies frequently serve their communities by supporting alcohol and other drug prevention programs, yet, all too often, they neglect the problems of their own personnel.
- Law enforcement agencies need to learn the value of early intervention programs over treatment programs and how to provide a supportive atmosphere that acknowledges trauma and addiction intervention efforts within their organizations. Further, upper-level officers and administrators need to exhibit empathy toward their officers, provide services when necessary, and encourage open communication about addiction problems in their ranks.
- Researchers, mental health professionals, and law enforcement experts need to further examine the role that trauma, stress, and addiction plays in the lives of all first-responding public safety personnel and find new methods of intervention and treatment to help these dedicated men and women deal with the tremendous pressure of their profession.

Conclusion

All members of the law enforcement community have an important role to play when it comes to evaluating, intervening, and treating trauma and addiction. When officers suffer the aftermath of trauma, they are not alone. Many may tout their "tough guy" image, see themselves as weak or abnormal if they seek help, and believe that admitting psychological or emotional pain will result in disciplinary action and, perhaps, job dismissal. Unfortunately, however, severe anxiety reactions, workplace apathy, absenteeism, and depressive symptoms have far-reaching impacts, not only on the officers suffering the trauma but, importantly, on their colleagues, the families they love, and the public they have sworn to protect and serve. Adding substance abuse to this already tragic scenario tremendously increases the potentially harmful impact—for when chemical substances enter the picture, *everyone* loses.

References

R.G. Dunham and G.P. Alpert, eds., *Critical Issues in Policing: Contemporary Readings,* 3rd ed. (Prospect Heights, IL: Waveland Press, 1997).

J.M. Violanti, *Police Suicide: Epidemic in Blue* (Springfield, IL: Charles C Thomas, 1996).

J.M. Violanti, D. Paton, and C. Dunning, eds., *Post-Traumatic Stress Intervention: Challenges, Issues, and Perspectives* (Springfield, IL: Charles C Thomas, 2000).

The Web site *http://www.cophealth.com* provides a wealth of information, including articles, books, and psychological material.

Discussion Questions

1. How do stress responses begin?
2. What can happen if intervention does not occur?
3. What is the link between trauma and substance abuse?
4. What were the results of studies done on police officers in New South Wales, Australia, related to alcohol consumption?
5. Researchers have identified four occupational demands that can trigger alcohol use by police officers? What are they?
6. Alcohol and other drug use and abuse have both overt and covert social and economic costs. What do these include?
7. Law enforcement officers frequently feel that counselors do not understand what it means to do police work. What should counselors do in order to make them more effective in counseling police officers?
8. Where should the first interventions for substance abuse in law enforcement officers occur?
9. It has been suggested by the authors that law enforcement agencies must invest in an integrated model of awareness and treatment. To help agencies, the authors offered some considerations in developing such a model. What were they?

15

Anabolic Steroid Use and Abuse by Police Officers: Policy and Prevention

Kim R. Humphrey, Kathleen P. Decker, M.D.,
Linn Goldberg, M.D., Harrison G. Pope Jr., M.D.,
Joseph Gutman, M.D., and Gary Green, M.D.

An officer crashes a police car and seriously injures an innocent bystander. The investigation reveals that the officer was acting erratically, had bloodshot eyes, and slurred his speech. The officer's supervisor is called, and the decision is made to test for alcohol consumption. The test results determine that the officer was in fact intoxicated. Disciplinary action is taken, resulting in the officer's termination for drinking alcohol while driving on duty. Though exposed to liability, the department recognizes the dangers of alcohol abuse and appropriately responds when a dangerous situation presents itself.

Another officer, involved in several shootings and use-of-force incidents, garners significant attention within his agency and the media. Investigations reveal that the unrelated incidents were questionable but lawful and, according to the officer, justified based on perceived threats. The agency's use-of-force review reluctantly finds the officer within policy but awaits the next incident. How many police leaders would recognize that this officer could have a problem similar to the one in the first example? If the officer's appearance indicated he was exceptionally muscular, would they consider the possible abuse of anabolic steroids? What would prompt them to believe that excessive use of force could be associated with "roid rage," a hyperaggressive, violent state of mind supposedly brought on by steroid use? When and how would they confirm that their suspicions are true? What if a defense or civil attorney proposed that an officer was a steroid abuser based on the officer's appearance and witnessed behaviors? Compared with alcohol and other illicit drugs, anabolic steroids (also known as anabolic-androgenic steroids, or AASs) are not easily detected. Supervisors typically are trained to look for inappropriate behaviors that might justify a "just cause" drug screen; however, with AASs the behaviors and other indicators might not be as easily recognized.

Recently, accounts of major league baseball's steroid era have come to light, Olympic athletes have admitted use, and many other major sporting icons have been stripped of their titles after being caught using performance-enhancing drugs such as AASs and human growth hormone (HGH). Unfortunately, growing evidence suggests a similar abuse of AASs and other performance-enhancing drugs by law enforcement professionals. Across the United States, several investigations associated with Internet pharmacies and "antiaging" clinics in association with unscrupulous physicians have revealed officers caught up in this web of illicit drug use.

Although the traditional reason for the use of AASs is to improve athletic performance, AASs also appeal to officers wanting a tactical edge or an intimidating appearance. Unlike with other forms of drug abuse, steroid users do not take their drug recreationally; on the contrary, some state they need these drugs in order to do their job effectively or improve their "job performance." From street officers who consider themselves vulnerable to bigger, more aggressive criminals to special-assignment officers who are regularly tested for their physical abilities, officers are turning to performance-enhancing drugs such as AASs and HGH as a shortcut to improved performance. This article will not delve into the abuse of HGH, which is not a controlled substance but is obtained by prescription only and has very limited use—none for normal adults.

In addition to the normal health concerns, there is one further issue when discussing abuse of steroids by those in the law enforcement profession. Officers carry weapons, are authorized to use lethal force, and are often involved in physically controlling or restraining people. If the stories of 'roid rage are true, how often are the officers who use anabolic steroids involved in unnecessary use-of-force incidents that could become a major liability for their agencies? Considering the legal issues, health effects, and commensurate costs associated with inappropriate use, agencies should proactively address this issue. Rather than look back on what could be an embarrassing "steroid era" of law enforcement—one in which the profession might be riddled with lawsuits, corruption, and claims of heavy-handedness—it is critical to address the current and future impact of this issue head-on.

Over the past few decades, several stories have surfaced regarding law enforcement personnel involved with anabolic steroids. The U.S. Drug Enforcement Administration (DEA) recently led Operation Raw Deal, considered the largest international steroid investigation to date. The operation discovered several links to current or former law enforcement officers. This was predicted almost 20 years ago by an article in the *FBI Law Enforcement Bulletin* that stated, "Anabolic steroid abuse by police officers is a serious problem that merits greater awareness by departments across the country."[1] In addition, a story on the television program *60 Minutes* in 1989 titled "Beefing up the Force" featured three police officers who admitted steroid use and claimed that their resulting aggression got them in serious trouble.

In the past year, a book titled *Falling Off the Thin Blue Line* was written and published by former Texas police officer David Johnson, who describes his addiction to steroids and speaks about the prevalence of steroid abuse in the law enforcement community.[2] Recently, investigations into illegal steroid purchases revealed the names of several officers on pharmacy distribution lists, garnering national media attention.

Unfortunately, agencies looking for methods to confront steroid abuse find few examples of effective policies and practices. This article summarizes the Phoenix, Arizona, Police Department's experience in this area over the past several years and suggests policy and testing considerations for anabolic steroids in the law enforcement community.

Problems with Testing

In 2005, the Phoenix Police Department (PPD) investigated several incidents either directly or indirectly involving officers accused of abusing anabolic steroids. As a result, the city formed a committee to determine policy changes and address the issue with public safety agencies (that is, police and fire departments) as well as all other city employees. Due to the demands of the law enforcement profession and the legal precedent supporting random drug testing, policies are naturally more stringent for police than for other city departments. The police department, with support from its labor organization, added anabolic steroids to the random testing process for all officers and the preemployment screen. Research is clear that significant health risks result

---

1. Charles Swanson, Larry Gaines, and Barbara Gore, "Abuse of Anabolic Steroids," *FBI Law Enforcement Bulletin* 60, no. 8 (August 1991): 19.

2. David Johnson, *Falling Off the Thin Blue Line: A Badge, a Syringe, and a Struggle with Steroid Addiction* (iUniverse, 2007).

from nontherapeutic uses of anabolic steroids.[3] For this reason, the PPD's focus on prevention revolved around a prevention video with questions and answers from a local endocrinologist who specializes in steroid abuse treatment.

Regarding testing, the task seemed simple enough: contact a local laboratory and test officers for performance-enhancing substances. However, implementation proved less than simple. First, adding AASs to the PPD's random test tripled its drug testing costs. Additionally, local laboratories were able to provide only an initial urine screen that tested for a handful of the growing number of AASs. Furthermore, compounding the difficulty of the task, testing for anabolic steroids goes beyond looking for the specific synthetic AAS; it also needs to detect compounds naturally created by the human body, such as testosterone. This entails an analysis of an individual's ratio of testosterone to epitestosterone (abbreviated T/E); when this value is found to be out of normal range, it may indicate the use of illegal substances. Additionally, as noted previously, HGH does not fall under the Anabolic Steroid Control Act, and currently there is no reliable test to detect it in the human body.

Testing for performance-enhancing substances presents a myriad of challenges:

- How can an agency test for "all" illegal AASs, and what does it do if a T/E ratio is not normal?
- How can an agency prove that someone is illegally or inappropriately using anabolic steroids?
- What if an officer who tests positive provides a prescription, and the prescribing physician indicates that the officer has a condition that necessitates the use of these drugs? Additionally, what constitutes abuse of prescribed drugs?
- Do 'roid rage and other psychiatric disturbances claimed to result from steroid abuse actually exist, and do they present a liability to an abuser's organization?

Jumping into a testing policy before answering these questions will lead agencies to the realization that testing for these substances is not as straightforward as, say, discovering heroin in a drug screen. Officers might present a prescription or might have ordered something over the Internet in what they believe is a legal transaction. The DEA works regularly to shut down numer-

---

3. See Kirk J. Brower, "Anabolic Steroid Abuse and Dependence," *Current Psychiatry Reports* 4, no. 5 (October 2002): 377–87; and Harrison G. Pope Jr. and Kirk J. Brower, "Anabolic-Androgenic Steroid Abuse," in *Kaplan and Sadock's Comprehensive Textbook of Psychiatry*, 8th ed., eds. Benjamin J. Sadock and Virginia A. Sadock (Philadelphia: Lippincott, Williams, and Wilkins, 2004), 1318–28.

ous unscrupulous doctors who seek to make money by connecting with pharmacies and engaging in illegal distribution, using the few very specific legitimate uses for AASs as cover for their operation. In these cases, ignorance is a common excuse from officers, who typically state that a doctor prescribed the drug, so it must be "okay."

The PPD sought out answers to these and other questions. Below is a description of the issue and some policy considerations.

What Are Steroids?

Steroids are a group of chemical substances that have certain structural similarities. AASs constitute a subgroup of this category that includes the physiological (normal) human male hormone testosterone as well as related compounds with similar functions. These compounds have legitimate medical uses but are frequently abused for illegitimate, recreational uses (bodybuilding, weightlifting, or "bulking up," as well as athletic performance enhancement). AASs should not be confused with other types of "steroids," such as corticosteroids. This latter group of drugs, including hydrocortisone and prednisone, is prescribed widely for legitimate medical purposes (for example, skin creams to treat rashes, in asthma inhalers, and so on). Corticosteroids do not cause increases in muscle mass, have almost no abuse potential, and are almost never sold on the illicit market. Therefore, for the purposes of this article, references to steroids mean specifically AASs, which are the type of steroids that are used illicitly.

AASs are controlled substances. They are prescribed by physicians for certain specific, legitimate medical reasons, such as treatment of a condition known as hypogonadism (abnormally low testosterone production in men), cancer (to suppress certain kinds of tumors), a rare genetic condition called angioneurotic edema, AIDS wasting syndrome, and some forms of anemia (low red blood cell counts). The U.S. Food and Drug Administration (FDA) lists specific allowable "indications," or uses, for all regulated drugs. The legitimate uses of AASs are minimal as noted; for example, an officer who states that a physician provided them for "elbow pain" would be using them inappropriately.

Medical investigators also perform research studies on human volunteers to better understand the benefits and risks of AASs. To be considered legitimate, such a study must be approved by an institutional review board operated according to the standards of the U.S. National Institutes of Health (NIH), Office for Human Research Protections, and registered with the FDA and/or the NIH Clinical Trials Registry (clinicaltrials.gov).

Illicit "Benefits" of AASs

AASs can be taken orally, by injection, as a skin patch or cream, or some-times by placing them between the cheek and gum. When combined with a high-protein diet and vigorous weightlifting, AASs "work." That means that they stimulate the formation of muscle tissue and are known to cause en-largement of muscle fibers. It is widely understood that testosterone (the major natural male AAS hormone in normal, healthy men) stimulates an increase in fat-free muscle mass while at the same time decreasing fat. Doses of AASs that exceed the normal production rate of testosterone can amplify this effect, re-sulting in supernormal gains in lean muscle mass and strength.

Patterns of Illegitimate Use

Abusers of AASs often follow a particular pattern of use, as discovered in one study of AAS users:[4]

- Many users reported taking a weekly dose in excess of (the equivalent of) 1,000 mg of testosterone. For comparison, adult human testicles normally produce 5–10 mg of testosterone per day—generally less than 100 mg/week.
- Most AAS users reported self-administering by injecting the drug di-rectly into their muscles.
- Some studies reveal that approximately 25 percent of those who inject AASs share needles or vials, increasing the risk of HIV infection, viral hepatitis, or other infections.
- Over 95 percent of AAS users reported self-administering multiple substances, with 25 percent taking growth hormone and/or insulin in addition to AASs.
- Users have been found to move on to illegal drugs other than athletic performance enhancers.
- Nearly 100 percent of AAS users reported noticeable side effects— but most users claim that these effects are mild and do not deter them from continuing to use AASs.
- Users often become fixated on their muscularity and are reluctant to stop using AASs for fear that they will get smaller again.

---

4. Andrew B. Parkinson and Nick A. Evans, "Anabolic Androgenic Steroids: A Survey of 500 Users," *Medicine and Science in Sports Exercise* 38, no. 4 (2006): 644–51.

General Medical Effects of Use

Anabolic steroids can cause temporary or permanent medical problems. Some known medical problems associated with AAS use follow:

- Decreased sperm production
- Abscess at the site of injection
- Increased or even severe acne
- Increased blood pressure
- Increased "bad" (LDL) and lower "good" (HDL) cholesterol, with attendant increased risk of heart attack
- Thickening of the wall of the heart (especially in the left ventricle)
- Increase or decreased sex drive (libido)
- Increased appetite
- Liver disease, especially with AASs taken orally (infrequent)
- Death from several causes, including suicide, atherosclerosis (hardening of the arteries leading to heart attacks or strokes), and cardiac complications
- HIV and similar risk issues associated with the sharing of needles or the use of nonsterile needles

Researchers still do not know a great deal about the long-term dangers of AAS use in individuals, but the evidence of potential dangers has been steadily increasing with new scientific publications in recent years. For example, one study of older champion power lifters (most or all of whom had likely used AASs) found that their death rate was almost five times as great as that of a comparison group of men of the same age in the general population. The reasons for death in the older power lifters included both medical problems such as heart disease and psychiatric problems such as suicide.[5]

Psychological Effects

Users of AASs can experience psychiatric symptoms during use, abuse, or withdrawal. Symptoms differ depending on the drug's absence or presence in the body. Symptoms tend to correlate with the size of the weekly dose and can worsen with long-term use. Importantly, the psychiatric symptoms are idio-

---

5. M. Parssinen et al., "Increased Premature Mortality of Competitive Powerlifters Suspected to Have Used Anabolic Agents," *International Journal of Sports Medicine* 21, no. 3 (April 2000): 225–27.

syncratic; some men taking a given dose of AASs may show no psychiatric effects at all, whereas a few men taking an identical dose might show extreme effects.[6] The reasons for this variability are not known, but it is clear that reactions to AASs cannot be predicted on the basis of an individual's baseline personality. In other words, even if a man has a mild-mannered, gentle personality when not taking AASs, there is still a risk that he might develop a sudden personality change and become uncharacteristically aggressive and violent while taking AASs.[7]

Symptoms Associated with Use or Abuse

- Aggression and violence (both general physical and sexual)
- Mania or hypomania (high energy levels associated with increased self-confidence, increased activity, impaired judgment, and reckless behavior)
- Psychosis—loss of touch with reality (for example, paranoia or delusions of grandeur; infrequent)
- Personality changes

Symptoms Associated with Withdrawal

- Long-term AAS abusers can develop symptoms of dependence and withdrawal on discontinuation.
- Withdrawal sometimes leads to severe depression and thoughts of suicide, in addition to medical effects, especially in individuals who have taken AASs for months or years.

Laws and Regulations Associated with AASs

The use of AASs for performance enhancement is banned by all major sports bodies, including the International Olympic Committee, the National Basketball Association, the National Hockey League, the National Football League,

---

6. See Ryan C.W. Hall et al., "Psychiatric Complications of Anabolic Steroid Abuse," *Psychosomatics* 46, no. 4 (July–August 2005): 285–90; and Harrison G. Pope Jr. and David L. Katz, "Psychiatric Effects of Exogenous Anabolic-Androgenic Steroids," in *Psychoneuroendocrinology: The Scientific Basis of Clinical Practice*, eds. Owen M. Wolkowitz and Anthony J. Rothschild (Washington, DC: American Psychiatric Publishing, 2003), 331–58.

7. Women can suffer from the same effects. However, because AASs are known to have noticeable masculinizing effects in women (such as increased body hair and a deepening of the voice), they are considerably less likely to take excessive doses and therefore also less likely to demonstrate overly aggressive behaviors.

Major League Baseball, the Union of European Football Associations, and Fédération Internationale de Football Association.

In the late 1980s, the U.S. Congress considered listing AASs in the Controlled Substances Act. Based on evidence of widespread abuse, AASs are now classified by the FDA and DEA as Schedule III controlled substances. The Crime Control Act of 1990, approved on November 29, 1990, includes provisions for control of these drugs and penalties for inappropriate trafficking in them. The Anabolic Steroid Control Act of 2004 further amended this law to increase the number of AASs that were included and make it easier to add additional drugs. A Schedule III substance is defined as follows:

- The drug or other substance has a potential for abuse that is less than the drugs or other substances in Schedules I and II.
- The drug or other substance has a currently accepted medical use in treatment in the United States.
- Abuse of the drug or other substance may lead to moderate or low physical dependence or high psychological dependence.

Schedule III drugs are available only by prescription, although control of wholesale distribution is somewhat less stringent than that of Schedule II drugs. Prescriptions for Schedule III drugs may be refilled up to five times within a six-month period.

The Controlled Substances Act defines AASs as any drug or hormonal substance chemically and pharmacologically related to testosterone other than estrogens, progestins, and corticosteroids.[8] This means that federal and most state laws dictate that the sale of steroids, possession of steroids, and possession of steroids with intent to sell are all classified as felonies. Any individual who is convicted of the sale of steroids or possesses steroids unlawfully with intent to sell may under federal law be penalized by up to five years in prison. That same individual may face more than five years of punishment depending on the applicable state law. Almost every state has sanctioned various laws placing AASs in the controlled-substance category, in addition to the federal law.

Due to users' sharing and redistribution habits, one can easily be charged with possession with the intent to sell or deliver AASs based simply on the quantity involved. Physicians dispensing such substances without an appropriate medical diagnosis, a treatment plan, or indications are subject to criminal penalties as well as disciplinary action by the appropriate medical licensing board, including the possible loss of their license.

---

8. More information on drug schedules and related issues is available at http://www.usdoj.gov/dea/pubs/csa/812.htm (accessed May 8, 2008).

In addition to the illegal use of these substances, in the last decade a significant number of cases involved counterfeit AAS preparations. These preparations can be simply useless (such as vegetable oil), or they can be dangerous if they are used for injection and turn out to be not sterile.

Policy Rationale

Negligent Retention: Agencies have a duty and a right to maintain fit officers and to protect the public from impaired officers. They must exercise reasonable means at their disposal to ensure that officers are fit. Both national and local standards regarding the use of AASs support the idea that officers abusing such substances could be at risk for impairment and could even be involved in criminal activity related to the use of these substances.

Employees' Rights: *National Treasury Employees* v. *Von Raab* is a landmark U.S. Supreme Court case in which employees carrying firearms were required to submit to drug testing.[9] The Court approved the testing program due to the extraordinary hazards of drug use in these officers. No specific guidelines for testing were put forth, but purely random testing is constitutional according to various courts. However, in the mid-1980s the Boston Police Department adopted a random drug-testing program that was struck down in 1991 by the Massachusetts Supreme Judicial Court.[10] Therefore, the acceptability of random drug testing is highly variable in different jurisdictions and likely depends on union and/or employment contracts.

Detection: To act against an officer, an agency must have reasonable suspicion that the officer is abusing substances or must have an agency-wide random drug-testing schedule. Agencies may not single out an officer for "random" drug testing in the absence of information to suggest use, dealing, and/or impairment.

Testing: Virtually all testing for AASs is on urine specimens. Courts have accepted gas chromatography/mass spectrometry (GC-MS) urine test results. Levels of most AASs in the blood are generally too low to be easily tested. Detection of AASs in hair samples appears possible but is still in an experimental stage of development.

Collection: Although most of the focus of drug testing is on sample analysis, proper collection and chain-of-custody procedures are also of paramount importance. It does not make sense to employ high-quality, expensive laboratories to analyze samples that have been improperly collected. In drug testing appeal

---

9. *National Treasury Employees Union* v. *Von Raab*, 489 U.S. 656 (1989).
10. *Guiney* v. *Police Comm'r of Boston*, 411 Mass. 328 (1991).

cases, the first challenge is usually to the collection process. Collection procedures should be thorough enough to withstand legal scrutiny and accurate enough to ensure that drug-using officers are properly identified.

Determination of Legitimate Use: If an individual is found using an illicit substance and cannot provide evidence of a legitimate prescription for a medically necessary condition, a fitness-for-duty evaluation is likely needed to ascertain whether the officer is using or abusing the substance in such a way as to jeopardize public safety. The most likely legitimate uses in which a working officer might be prescribed AASs would be for treating hypogonadism. The standard treatment of hypogonadism is the use of a testosterone patch or gel, both of which are highly unlikely to be abused. Injectable and sometimes oral preparations are the common choices of AAS abusers.

Research suggests that individuals taking AASs in excess of 100—200 mg of testosterone per week are outside the bounds of therapeutic use. Upon reaching a dose of 300 mg of testosterone per week, they are somewhat more likely to exhibit aggressive behaviors, which start to take place more frequently.[11] Determining the amount taken may be difficult; therefore, it might be necessary to establish a policy that disallows any level of use above therapeutic levels, since it would be difficult to predict aggressive, inappropriate behaviors.

Policy Considerations

The following key points should be included in policy statements for law enforcement personnel:

- Use of illegal substances or improperly prescribed controlled substances represents both legal and disciplinary issues for officers and can pose threats to the officer and public safety.
- If the agency has reasonable cause to suspect illegitimate drug use, it may require substance use testing, including but not limited to random urinalysis (for alcohol and drugs), blood work for a toxicology panel, and/or hair analysis.
- Where feasible, supervisors should consult with internal affairs/professional standards and/or the appropriate personnel department before acting on a suspicion of abuse of anabolic steroids.
- Employees found to be using illegal substances will be immediately placed on administrative leave (if not already on such leave) pending further investigation and/or an independent medical review or fitness-for-duty evaluation, and they will hand in their weapons.

---

11. Hall et al., "Psychiatric Complications of Steroid Abuse," 285–86.

- Employees found to have controlled substances that are not illegal but can impair performance, such as (but not limited to) opiate analgesics, controlled substances used as sleep aids or muscle relaxants, or anabolic steroids, may be required to submit to an independent medical review or fitness-for-duty evaluation by the appropriate medical specialist (whether an internist, cardiologist, endocrinologist, or psychiatrist, or a combination thereof) to ascertain whether these officers are using such substances appropriately and/or whether their use of such substances is impairing performance.
- If an employee is found to be possibly illegally using controlled substances and/or medications prescribed by a health-care provider, the agency shall report the case (representing potential illegal activity) to an outside agency for investigation of the officer (by a federal or separate state agency) for misconduct, wherever possible. The agency must also follow the required federal and state reporting procedures for legal proceedings against the health-care professional and the officer, if appropriate.

Reasonable Cause: Several symptoms can indicate that someone is abusing AASs. Symptoms may include the following:

- Visible increase in body mass over a short period of time (usually months)
- Fluid retention (bloating)
- Noticeable acne and/or oily skin
- Mood swings, particularly if aggressive
- Unreasonable emotional responses to situations
- Voice changes (such as deepening voices in women)
- Facial hair growth in women
- Multiple incidents of "use of force" or complaints of improper outbursts and attitude

Testing Process: Anabolic steroid testing is expensive compared to other illicit drug testing. There are literally hundreds of variations of AASs. Local laboratories used for an initial urine screen can test for a small number of typical steroids and can also screen the T/E ratio.[12] An elevated T/E ratio signifies possible abuse, as it is affected by the intake of AASs.

---

12. Christophe Saudan et al., "Testosterone and Doping Control," *British Journal of Sports Medicine* 40, Supplement 1 (2006): i21–i24.

Proper collection and chain-of-custody procedures are critical. Agencies hiring a specimen collection service, using their healthcare providers, or collecting samples using their department personnel should ensure that sample collection procedures are standardized. Immediate testing after notification and observed collection provide the strongest assurance against tampering. Examples of collection procedures can be obtained from the National Center for Drug Free Sport as well as other agencies.

If working with a local laboratory, an agency should consider a dual notification procedure in its laboratory contract. With dual notification, the laboratory will notify the agency as well as a medical review officer (MRO) of the results. If an individual who tests positive has a seemingly valid prescription, the MRO may consider the test negative; however, the agency might want to follow through with an independent medical review or fitness testing as noted earlier and would need to know that the initial test was positive.

Additionally, using an MRO who has expertise in performance-enhancing drug testing should be considered. If follow-up on a positive initial screen test is needed, the sample can be sent to a laboratory certified by the World Anti-Doping Agency for further analysis. Currently, the University of Utah and the University of California at Los Angeles are the only certified laboratories in the United States. Their analysis consists of a full panel for AASs and, if possible, can determine specifically what types and levels are present. In addition, certified laboratories have further testing capabilities that can determine if substances in the sample are naturally occurring or synthetic drug substitutes. The expense is significant, and these tests should be used for increased scrutiny, particularly when results are disputed or can be disputed by an individual.

Conclusion

The PPD is currently working with the Arizona Peace Officer Standards and Training organization to consider a state rule disallowing the use of AASs by police officers unless a medical exception is granted.

Preventing anabolic steroid abuse requires a multifaceted approach. After understanding the challenges associated with testing and deciding on appropriate discipline, it is critical for agencies to educate their officers and provide alternatives for health and fitness. The challenges are many, but failure to act now could cause significant suffering for law enforcement agencies in the future and mandates for action. For the safety of the community and the health of an agency's employees, it is essential to act to prevent the abuse of these drugs.

Discussion Questions

1. Compared with alcohol and other illicit drugs, anabolic steroids (also known as anabolic-androgenic steroids, or AASs) are not easily detected. Why?
2. Why do officers use anabolic steroids?
3. What did the Phoenix Police Department (PPD) do in 2005 after it investigated several incidents directly or indirectly involving officers accused of abusing anabolic steroids?
4. What were the results of the Phoenix Police Department adding anabolic steroids to its random test protocol for officers?
5. Testing for performance-enhancing substances presents a myriad of challenges. What are they?
6. What are steroids?
7. Anabolic-androgenic steroids are prescribed by physicians for certain specific and legitimate reasons. What are these?
8. In what ways can anabolic-androgenic steroids be administered?
9. Abusers of anabolic-androgenic steroids often follow a particular pattern of use, as discovered in one study of AAS users. What are some of these patterns?
10. What are some of the general medical effects of the use of anabolic-androgenic steroids?
11. What are the psychological effects of the use of anabolic-androgenic steroids?
12. What are the symptoms of the use or abuse of anabolic-androgenic steroids?
13. What are the symptoms of the withdrawal of anabolic-androgenic steroids?
14. What is a Schedule III substance?
15. What are Employee Rights under the *National Treasury Employees v. Von Raab*?
16. Certain key points should be included in policy statements for law enforcement personnel as they relate to the use of illegal substances. What are these considerations?

16

Sex Addiction in Police Officers as a Result of Stress and Trauma

Allen R. Kates

The purpose of this paper is to throw a spotlight on sex addiction in police officers which occurs as a result of overwhelming stress and the inability to cope with traumatic incidents. As this is a relatively new area of study, this exploration lays the groundwork for further study, screening and treatment.

Sex addiction has been in the news on a regular basis ever since former President Gerald Ford called former President Bill Clinton a sick sex addict in a 2007 book published after Ford's death.

Ford, whose wife started the ultra-chic Betty Ford Center that treats alcoholism and other addictions, including sex addiction, said Bill Clinton's, "... got a sex sickness ... . He's got an addiction. He needs treatment."[1]

Many other politicians, actors and athletes have admitted to sex addiction or have been "outed" in the press. Among the well-known alleged sex addicts are golf phenomenon Tiger Woods,[2] actor and former California Governor Arnold Schwarzenegger,[3] Major League baseball player Wade Boggs,[4] and pres-

1. DeFrank, Thomas M. (2007) *Write It When I'm Gone: Remarkable Off-the-Record Conversations with Gerald R. Ford*, p. 138. New York: Berkley Books.

2. James, Susan Donaldson. (2010, November 29) Tiger Woods Effect: More Sex Addicts Seek Help. *ABCNews.com*. Retrieved October 14, 2011, from http://abcnews.go.com/Health/MindMoodResourcesCenter/sex-addicts-seeking-treatment-jumps-50-percent-tiger/story?id=12237598.

3. Weiss, R. (2011). Sex Addiction, Schwarzenegger and Strauss-Kahn: Understanding Men in Power Who Sexually Act Out. Psych Central. Retrieved October 26, 2011, from http://blogs.psychcentral.com/sex/2011/05/sex-addiction-schwarzenegger-andstrauss-kahn-understanding-men-in-power-who-sexually-act-out/.

4. Boston Globe Staff. (2005, July 31) Wade Boggs: 2005 Hall of Fame Inductee, Nothing average about five-time batting champ. *Boston.com*. Retrieved October 28, 2011, from

idential hopeful John Edwards.[5] Still, we must view the accusations with a degree of skepticism. The evidence of their sex addiction is sensational but flimsy, even that of self-described sex addict Tiger Woods. Is he really a sex addict or a spoiled brat who locked himself away in a sex recovery treatment center in an attempt to save his marriage?

Before the term "sex addiction" was coined, people who compulsively switched sexual partners with abandon were often condemned as promiscuous, immoral, oversexed, aberrant and whorish. Sometimes they were also admiringly called rakish, bawdy, ribald, raunchy and profligate—as if irresponsible and reckless behavior was condoned as just boys sowing their wild oats or being young and stupid. They acted like frat boys who would soon grow out of their wacky ways and join the world of serious thinkers and doers.

Whatever you wish to call it, indiscriminate sexual activity with no concern for hurting their sexual partners, having unprotected sex, spreading sexually transmitted diseases, or making unwanted children, has serious consequences.

Definition and Symptoms of Sex Addiction

Not many studies have been written about sex addiction in general and almost nothing about how it affects law enforcement officers. The American Psychiatric Association, in developing the newest version of its diagnostic bible called the Diagnostic and Statistical Manual of Mental Disorders (DSM), is struggling to come up with a workable definition of sex addiction and may ultimately decide to ignore it.[6]

However, a handful of mental health researchers have developed what they believe are practical definitions.

- **Failure to control sexual behavior**
- **Significant harmful consequences**

---

http://articles.boston.com/2005-07-31/sports/29213277_1_red-sox-hall-of-fame-today-jdrry-remy.

5. Doane, Seth. (2010, June 3 Update). The Stories Behind Sex Addiction. *CBS News.* Retrieved October 24, 2011, from http://www.cbsnews.com/stories/2010/01/24/sunday/main 6136039.shtml.

6. Peele, Stanton. (2009, December 13) Will Sex Addiction Be in DSM-V? *Psychology Today.* Retrieved October 28, 2011 from http://www.psychologytoday.com/blog/addiction-in-society/200912/will-sex-addiction-be-in-dsm-v.

In a thorough study described in *Psychiatric Times*, Dr. Aviel Goodman, director of the Minnesota Institute of Psychiatry, says that sex addiction may be "characterized by recurrent failure to control … sexual behavior" which continues "despite significant harmful consequences."[7]

- **Tolerance over time**
- **Withdrawal when deprived**

In an insightful ABC News story titled, "The Tiger Woods Effect," the definition of sex addiction may include symptoms usually attributed to drug or alcohol addiction, such as a "building up of a tolerance over time" (leading to more frequent sexual encounters) and "going through withdrawal when deprived."[8]

- **Compulsive behavior which interferes with normal living**
- **Causes severe stress on family, friends, peers**

Dr. Patrick Carnes, the most prominent voice in the field of sex addiction, author of *Out of the Shadows: Understanding Sexual Addiction* (1983), the first book to help sex addicts, more broadly defines sex addiction as "any sexually related, compulsive behavior which interferes with normal living and causes severe stress on family, friends, loved ones and one's work environment."[9] That definition describes situations many police officers find themselves in.

- Heart racing, adrenaline pumping
- Intense, emotional arousal
- Self-soothing, emotional calm

To further depict how police officers experience sex addiction, (although police officers were not the focus), Robert Weiss, LCSW, CSATS, Director of Sexual Disorders Services for Elements Behavioral Health and founding director of the Sexual Recovery Institute in Los Angeles, says that:

"(Sex addicts) are going in with an intense fantasy—his heart is racing, his adrenaline is pumping. They are in it for the intense, emotional arousal that provides them with a self-soothing, emotional calm. If

---

7. Goodman, MD, Aviel. (2009, May 26) Sexual Addiction Update, Assessment, Diagnosis and Treatment. *Psychiatric Times*, Vol. 26 No. 6.

8. James, Susan Donaldson. (2010, November 29) Tiger Woods Effect: More Sex Addicts Seek Help.

9. Carnes, Ph.D., Patrick. Definition of sex addiction, retrieved October 27, 2011, from www.sexhelp.com/addiction_definitions.cfm.

you put yourself in a situation of danger, the response would be distracting, but it's soothing to them ... . It's like being in a trance. ..."[10]

• Vicious cycle of stress, release, shame, anxiety

Mr. Weiss states that "the compulsive behavior is triggered by anxiety, and continues in a vicious cycle of stress, release and then shame, which ignites the anxiety again ... ."[11]

• Obsessive
• Loss of control
• Excessive effort in pursuit

He adds that "(Sex addiction) has an obsessive quality. Like any addiction there is a loss of control." He says that a sex addict will spend an inordinate amount of time "looking and in pursuit" of his (uncommonly, *her*) sex object, but the least amount of time in the actual sex act.[12]

Statistics

Until more in-depth research is conducted, the small amount of data available suggests that sex addiction is a genuine problem. The Society for the Advancement of Sexual Health (SASH) estimates that 3 to 5 percent of Americans, most of them men, are sex addicts. Based only on people who seek treatment, the estimate is considered low.[13]

Why Sex Addiction is Not Described Yet in *CopShock*

I began researching the first edition of *CopShock, Surviving Posttraumatic Stress Disorder (PTSD)* in 1993, and for six years interviewed hundreds of police officers about their traumatic experiences, addictions, PTSD diagnoses, regrets, and successes. Many spoke of acting out sexually. No one talked of sex addiction then.

For instance, LAPD Detective Bill Martin doesn't talk of sex addiction in *CopShock* when he describes his broken marriage, PTSD symptoms and irresponsible sexual behavior. Bill was addicted to prescription drugs and alcohol

---

10. James, Susan Donaldson (2010, November 29) Tiger Woods Effect: More Sex Addicts Seek Help.

11. Ibid.

12. Ibid.

13. The Society for the Advancement of Sexual Health (SASH). Information retrieved October 26, 2011, from http://www.sash.net. See also: Sex Addiction Statistics and Facts, retrieved October 26, 2011, from www.myaddiction.com/education/articles/sex_statistics.html.

throughout his 33-year police career. He used drugs and booze to dampen flashbacks of bloody crime scenes and images of dead bodies.

He was always involved with groupies he picked up at cop bars. As he says, "All I wanted to do was get screwed up and loaded. When my dick was hard I didn't give a damn. I fucked anyone, anytime, anyplace and I gave no thought to sexually transmitted diseases."[14]

During and after his first marriage, he had a long-term relationship with a prostitute. One night at a police academy party, he had sex with the woman while they were dancing—in plain view of other officers and their dance partners. He admitted it was very risky behavior, but he couldn't stop himself.

As a child, Bill was severely beaten by his father for years, and when he was a teenager, he was raped by a man he thought was his friend. According to definitions of sex addiction, childhood physical, sexual or emotional abuse can set someone up for indiscriminate sexual encounters in the future.[15]

Even while I was researching the second edition of *CopShock* a few years ago, sex addiction, although emerging as a contested psychological field, had not become the darling of tabloid media and pop news, hammered relentlessly into our heads. It wasn't until Tiger Woods's 2009 revelations of sordid sexual exploits and a bout in a sex addiction treatment center that the term began to capture our collective imaginations.

Most Police Officers Cope Well with Stress and Trauma

So there's no misunderstanding, I am not branding all police officers as sex addicts. Most police officers handle stress and trauma just fine. They demonstrate healthy coping skills and do not attempt to manage their problems by self-medicating through alcohol, drugs, gambling or sex. They do not become cynical or hopeless, but approach each day with renewed energy and optimism. Even so, some do not know what to do after being shattered by a traumatic incident.

After all, police officers are human beings just like everybody else, and yet they see more horror in one year than most human beings see ever. It is no surprise that, when overwrought, some may engage in harmful coping mechanisms that make them feel better, but put their lives and the lives of innocent people in jeopardy.

---

14. Kates, Allen R. (2008) *CopShock: Second Edition, Surviving Posttraumatic Stress Disorder (PTSD)*, p. 209. Tucson, AZ: Holbrook Street Press. www.CopShock.com.

15. Ewald, Roschbeth. (2003, May 13) Sexual addiction. *AllPsych Journal*, retrieved October 28, 2011, from http://allpsych.com/journal/sexaddiction.html.

Case History of a Sex Addicted Police Officer

This case history[16] describes the life and law enforcement career of Alex Salazar. He worked for the Los Angeles Police Department for nine years, from 1990 to 1998. He started in Rampart Division as a rookie, went to Wilshire Division after about a year, and about three years later moved on to Southeast Division, Watts, where he became an undercover officer on the South Bureau Narcotics Undercover Buy Team. He worked undercover narcotics for about four years, a long time for anyone that fears he could be found out and killed.

Family upbringing

Alex was born in Hollywood, California, and grew up primarily in Azusa in LA County. After graduating high school, in 1986 he joined the U.S. Air Force, where he became a security specialist in Central America and then England. In 1989, he attended the police academy.

He grew up in a zealous Catholic household. He said that his family was like the "Mexican Brady Bunch" where his parents were good role models. "My mother was into whipping our asses and was a very strong disciplinarian."

Saw many dead bodies

After attending the police academy, in May 1990, Alex started work as a rookie in the LAPD's Rampart Division. About a year later, he married his high school sweetheart, a woman with whom he had a long, loving relationship.

Rampart was a busy division. From the moment Alex arrived and logged onto the MDT, mobile digital terminal, "our calls would light up. There would be a Code 2 urgent call, assault in progress, man with a gun shooting." He investigated multiple homicides, beatings, rapes and robberies, going from one to another without processing emotionally what he had seen or done. He saw more bodies in one night than a mortician saw in a week. But the work was exciting and Alex didn't feel that he needed counseling. Nobody else did, so why should he?

He saw other cops involved in risky sexual behavior

Although he liked to have fun, he was dedicated to his wife and their marriage. Everyday he saw police officers who were single or married having affairs and engaging in heavy drinking and risky sexual behavior. Alex didn't like drinking, but attended *Choir Practice* in local police bars with other cops

---

16. Salazar, Alex. Case history of former LAPD police officer Alex Salazar. Information gathered from audio interviews, discussions and emails conducted by Allen R. Kates, MFAW, BCECR, during October, 2011.

as a way to decompress and have a few laughs after a tour of mayhem and madness. He sipped one drink the whole night, shared war stories and listened to tales of sexual derring-do. He watched other cops dancing, petting, and groping.

Groupies at clubs

On and off duty, he and his partner cruised the clubs and dropped in to see if any illegal activities were going on. At *Club Vertigo*, "women would surround us and give us their phone numbers. I said 'I don't need this. I got a wife, I'm happily married.'" According to Alex, his partners were not so averse.

Work hard, party hard

Alex said "the ethos was: You work hard, you party hard. That meant arresting gangbangers, going to bars, getting drunk off your ass." He said that some officers shot out streetlights after a night of drinking and carousing.

Although he thought he was like any other cop, Alex did not engage in promiscuity or wild behavior. That is, until he had what he calls his "incident."

Alex attacked, injured. No one helped

On September 28, 1991, after he had recently moved to Wilshire Division, Alex was out shopping and witnessed a woman struggling with a man attempting to rob her at Broadway and 8th Street. Alex got out of his car, chased the man down, identified himself as a police officer and grabbed him by the arm. As the man was not resisting, Alex didn't pull his backup .38. He instructed the woman to call 911 for help.

After she left to find a phone, a crowd, including a number of gang members, gathered around Alex and his prisoner, and shouted at him to let the guy go. Someone pushed Alex from behind and the suspect took off. Then about six men threatened to beat him. Some swung belt buckles. Alex stepped off the curb, pulled his .38, and told them to back off. The gun had no effect and they continued to advance on him.

Suddenly, a passing car hit him and ran over his ankle, breaking it. Although badly injured, lying in the street, nobody helped him. The gangbangers then looted his car, smashed out the windows and kicked in the doors. A few minutes later, several black-and-whites roared onto the scene and ended the attack.

Alex was rushed to the hospital and underwent surgery where a metal plate and screws were inserted to support his ankle. He was off work for about four months.[17]

---

17. Dillow, Gordon. (1991, October 7). Alex Salazar: A cop doing his duty. *Downtown News: Los Angeles, CA.*

Turning point: nightmares, flashbacks, anger, suicidal thoughts

This was a turning point for Alex. He was 25 years old, but no longer the happy, carefree man he once was. His previous unresolved traumas infected his dreams, and gave more power to his nightmares and flashbacks of the attack. In his mind, he kept replaying being run over, a common response to a traumatic incident.

"I was helpless, lying in the middle of the street, no one coming to my aid," he said. He was angry all the time and felt that the department didn't care. He had suicidal thoughts and went to see the department's psychologist on a regular basis, but felt he wasn't getting anywhere.

He didn't care anymore

A few months after Alex's traumatic incident, he felt that he didn't care about anything or anybody any longer. "I didn't give a fuck anymore," he said. "Up until then I had always done everything right."

Development of sex addiction

The stress and disillusionment pushed him toward looking for new ways to cope. He didn't have to look far for role models. Many of his fellow officers were engaged in dangerous sexual encounters and, before long, Alex became involved in them, too.

It seemed that the more stress he was under, the more he pursued strange women for sex. The more women he had, the more he wanted, and his thoughts and conversations with other officers were habitually consumed with the acquiring and bedding of multiple partners.

Drinking heavily

Within months after his traumatic incident, Alex was drinking heavily and carried a small metal flask. Although he hated the taste of liquor, he needed something to relax him and dampen the traumatic images running around in his mind.

He especially liked to add Bacardi 151 rum, a high proof liquor nearly 76 percent alcohol, to an extra large Coke.[18] Although he would grimace at the taste, he knew it would give him the high he wanted.

"I was more of an alcohol abuser than an alcoholic," he said. "I didn't like the feeling of being drunk and throwing up. My whole goal was to get relaxed, go to bars, to the clubs, and not be so tense and hypervigilant. That loosened me up for all the sex antics."

---

18. Bacardi 151 rum. Retrieved October 26, 2011, from http://www.drinksmixer.com/desc 185.html.

Hypervigilance

When police officers are hypervigilant, they are aware of threats around them. That can save their lives. But when hypervigilance goes to an extreme, officers become hyperaware of everyone. Instead of determining who is a threat and who isn't, everyone, good person and bad, is perceived as a threat. As a result of his traumatic incident, Alex had become hyperaware, overly hypervigilant, a PTSD symptom that causes continuous adrenaline rushes and leads to exhaustion. Alex sought to reduce his hypervigilance through sex.[19]

Badge bunnies

Despite loving his wife, Alex began sleeping with other women indiscriminately. He said his wife wouldn't listen to him when he tried to explain the turmoil inside himself. Consequently, he went looking for "badge bunnies," groupies that hung out at police bars.

Impregnated wife and groupie, got gonorrhea

After about three years on the force, Alex was out of control, searching for one conquest after another. Half the time, he did not use protection when he was out with women he had picked up "because I had that *I-don't-care* attitude. After I got my ass run over and almost killed, my whole decision making processes were bad. I was led by my emotions, by my anger. I wasn't rational," he said.

"I got my wife pregnant and at the same time got another woman pregnant and she gave me gonorrhea."

Alex asked the woman to have an abortion, but she refused. He did not give gonorrhea to his wife, but, after a while, she found out what he'd been up to. He didn't care.

"I had become selfish, self-centered," he said. "It was all about *ME* now. I was no longer going to be Mr. Perfect. I was not going to do everything everybody wanted me to do. It was all about me fulfilling my selfish desires."

Children, divorced, sleeping with numerous women

His wife and the woman he got pregnant gave birth at almost the same time. Then, after nearly two years of marriage, he and his high school sweetheart divorced. Despite now being responsible for supporting two children, Alex

---

19. Gilmartin, K.M. (1986) Hypervigilance: a learned perceptual set and its consequences on police stress. In J.T. Reese & H.A. Goldstein, (Eds.) *Psychological services for law enforcement* (pp. 445-448). Washington, DC: U.S. Government Printing Office. See also: Kates, Allen R. (2008) *CopShock: Second Edition, Surviving Posttraumatic Stress Disorder (PTSD)*, p 112.

continued to engage in irresponsible behavior, often having unprotected sex with numerous women.

During his Wilshire stint, he frequented a bar called the *Short Stop*, a famous police hangout decked out in LAPD memorabilia. He recounts one night that he and his partner picked up two girls and took them to a hotel and "tagged teamed" them. He didn't want to share because he was not attracted to his partner's "date," but he "did it anyway because he was my partner."

One night he took a girlfriend up to the Hollywood sign. He said, "It was exciting up there by the lights, the crackling of the police radio in the background. I whipped it out and hit her on the hood of the car."

After he dropped her off, he returned to the police station and the Sergeant yelled at him. Apparently, he had a white stain on his pants around his fly. Alex made up a story about spilling ice cream on himself, and "I got the hell out of there."

Crash pads for sex

Alex said that the officers had "crash pads" around the division. On occasion, property managers put the word out that they had break-ins and wanted to give officers a free apartment or discount if they would watch the place and keep the peace.

He said that he often had sex with groupies in his car, but would have multiple women visit the crash pad, one right after another. "We set up appointments, even the married guys."

Code X, on duty booty

The on-and-off-the-job sex was often condoned and covered up by officers at the station. The desk officer kept track of "Code X" calls, an official sounding 10-Code that did not exist. It was made up to fend off wives, girlfriends and superiors trying to reach officers who were supposed to be on duty.

According to Alex, Code X actually meant "Hey, I'm out getting some *on duty booty*." The desk officer would make up a story saying the unreachable officer was on a homicide, on a call or otherwise unreachable. Then the desk officer called the wayward officer or sent a computer message that his wife or girlfriend was looking for him. It was a professional courtesy recognized by most officers.

All about partying, sex gave him a high, striptease

Alex feels that sex addiction is a cultural thing, police culture, that is. "It seems everybody was doing it. It was pretty rampant. We thought we were powerful. We became very narcissistic wearing the LAPD uniform. It was all about partying, getting your nut off as a way of stress relief."

He said that police parties were "wild drunken bashes" with lots of sexual activities, especially the Christmas parties. He said he was addicted to having sex with different women because "I felt there was a void within my soul. Having sex, getting drunk, took away the pain and anxiety. I would be angry, depressed and sad. Sex gave me a high."

To further describe the sex-drenched culture, Alex told me that his training officer once brought his girlfriend down to the station at midnight during morning watch to do a striptease for the guys. "She was a professional stripper and she took everything off. We cheered and yelled, of course. Everybody thought my training officer was the coolest guy."

Predatory sexual behavior

"We were like junkies," he said. "We had to have it and went out on the prowl." Alex said they cruised the bars looking for girls standing outside. They would talk to the girls and persuade them to hook up for sex back at the crash pad after the shift was over.

He went out on calls with a cop who took advantage of female victims of domestic violence. They arrested the husband, and when nobody was looking, the cop stole the husband's or wife's ID card. After they booked the husband at the jail, his partner returned to the home to drop off the card, saying he found it. The woman was inevitably in an emotional state. He consoled her, "she was crying and they hugged, and the next thing you know they were having sex."

In looking back on his actions, Alex said that he didn't view himself as a predator then. "But I do now because we would go out on the hunt. That's what a predator does."

He said the women "came in all shapes and sizes, Hispanic, white, black, Asian, everything. They were young and older, mostly women with low self-esteem. It was women who wanted to hook up with someone or find a husband, someone with a stable job. For predators like us, they were just a piece of meat. It was like putting a steak in front of a dog's mouth. What's he gonna do?"

Constant fear as undercover officer, sex as stress reliever

After Alex joined the South Bureau Narcotics Undercover Buy Team, he endured constant adrenaline rushes because of overwhelming stress. He said he would do about three buys a day, working with other undercovers doing more buys. Sometimes guns were put to his head or "I got my ass kicked because gangbangers thought I was from another gang." He said that he got into shootouts and "I was supposed to come home and act normal?"

He lived in a state of constant fear. Would they find out who he was? Would someone he busted previously suddenly appear? Would the bad guy try to rip him off and shoot him?

Alex learned to lie because if his lies were not believable, he could end up dead. "The stress is so great, your lies must be believable not only to the drug dealer, but also to yourself."

After a while, Alex began to think and act like the criminals he was trying to put behind bars. "When you look in the mirror, are you the good guy or the bad guy?" he said. "Do I tell my supervisor all the mixed emotions I'm experiencing?" Alex could not reconcile the moral and spiritual conflict warring inside himself, and that clash of opposing attitudes increased his stress. But tell his supervisor? No way. It would make Alex look like he couldn't handle the job.

He got so good at undercover work that he was promoted to leading the undercover investigators, directing a team of officers. At the end of a day, sometimes they would haul 40 or so people to jail. The increased status and workload contributed to his anxiety, but he did the job for four years, an exceptionally long period of time under extreme stress.

Police officers are sometimes described as adrenaline junkies and Alex lived off the adrenaline high. He said, "I was highly energized and just wanted to screw to get out my frustrations. After you have sex, you feel better. Sometimes we would have sex with two, three, four different women a day."

Department will use and abuse you

When Alex started in undercover, he was warned by a friend in narcotics that the supervisors and department would "use and abuse you," and to take measures to protect himself. Alex ignored the advice and the workload kept increasing, along with his stress.

When doing drug buys, his day started at 6 AM when his alarm clock went off. By 7 AM, he was out the door fighting Los Angeles traffic. By 8, he had picked up narcotics evidence and was on his way to court for an 8:30 hearing, sometimes having to testify in the morning and afternoon in different court houses. In late afternoon, he went out on dangerous and often life-threatening drug buys that sometimes lasted until one or two in the morning. Then, with only a few hours of sleep, he'd start his day again. And the next day was the same, and the day after that.

He was pushed to exhaustion, but was afraid to take a stand and say *No*. He was also warned that those in managerial positions would take credit for his arrests. They did, and that increased his cynicism about the department and perception that it was not supporting him.

Six suicides in four years

After Alex's traumatic incident, he felt that he was riding a train down a track to self-destruction, but could not stop it. His sex addiction, drinking and carousing were out of control. The few hours he had for sleep were often restless, and he would wake exhausted, facing a day of relentless stress and anxiety about being found out and killed. To add to his cynicism, despair and fear, during a period of just four years, two of his partners committed suicide and four other cops he knew killed themselves.

Alex's first partner commits suicide

Alex said that, prior to becoming a cop, he had never known anyone who had committed suicide, even in the military. His first partner was named Frank. "We bonded when we were rookies in Rampart Division. We were good friends."

They first met on a brutal shooting of a man near MacArthur Park. The victim was carjacked and shot in the face. Both Alex and Frank were with their training officers when they found the man. What Alex remembered most is the enormous amount of blood flowing from the man's mouth, an image he could not erase no matter how much booze he consumed or sex he engaged in. They pursued the killers on a 100-mile-an-hour chase, with Alex and Frank in the lead cars. The driver bailed out of the car and they chased him down, beat him and arrested him.

Alex and Frank talked about the incident whenever they met for drinks. Eventually, Frank moved on to Foothill Division and Alex went to Wilshire. As partners, they had shared a lot about their hopes and dreams. When Alex was about five years on the force, he was told that Frank shot himself in the mouth with his 9mm. "I was in disbelief because this was a guy I had ridden with, and we had spent a lot of time talking and laughing and joking around."

Alex said that Frank had shot someone during a confrontation and he was being investigated for possible unjustifiable homicide. Then his wife said she was going to leave him and "that's what caused him to eat his gun."

Alex blamed himself. "Maybe I could have talked to him. I was out drinking at *Club Fantasia* when I heard the news from one of the academy instructors who was working the door. I called my mom, crying, babbling, 'Mom, Frank is dead, *Frank is dead*.' His mother was frightened because she knew he was drinking and feared he might do something foolish."

Alex could not come to grips with Frank's suicide. If Frank, a cop Alex considered stable, could kill himself, then anybody could.

Another partner commits suicide

In a short time, another police partner committed suicide. Alex was told that the cop who brought his girlfriend down to the station to strip for the other men had killed himself, and Alex was devastated with grief. "He hooked up with this woman and ended up killing her and then himself in a murder-suicide. It wasn't a normal relationship. What guy is going to have his girlfriend strip in front of his friends? She wanted to leave him and he could not take the rejection."

Four more friends kill themselves

The suicides of his partners affected Alex profoundly, but four more officers he knew killed themselves. One killed himself on the day his ex-fiancé got married. Another killed himself over a woman who left him. The fifth suicide was one of his academy instructors. He had testified against the officers involved in the Rodney King affair and said they had used excessive force. He was called a *betrayer,* and this depressed him. The sixth suicide was a gang officer who killed himself in his garage with carbon monoxide over a love relationship gone bad.

Most of the suicides were over relationships. "When a police officer loses a relationship, they feel like they are helpless, losing control over everything," said Alex. "If nobody loves me, what good am I?"

Suicides as modeling behavior

For Alex, the suicides were modeling behavior. They demonstrated that if things got too tough, suicide was always an option. His partners did it. His friends did it. Many victims he had investigated did it. Why not him?

Alex felt that the department wanted "to throw me away after I had almost gotten killed trying to stop a robbery, doing the right thing. I thought, Wow, I'm a loser, I cheated on my wife, I cheated on my whole family, I'm fucked up, I have all these multiple relationships. My life is chaos. I always thought that I would lose it at some point. I could blow up or snap at any moment."

Remarried, arrested for domestic violence

During his undercover period at South Bureau Narcotics, Alex slept with many women, but dated one particular woman whom he married in 1997. Six months after the wedding, they had an argument about a video camera locked in her car. Alex tried to take her car keys, but she resisted and he bit her hand. He said there was no blood, but her sister-in-law called the police and Alex was charged with domestic violence.

The incident made him realize he was losing control of his personal life and acting irrationally. He was exhausted, depressed, suffering from PTSD symptoms and self-medicating on alcohol and sex. The domestic violence charge was a black mark on his police record. Now he would never be promoted and he saw his life spiraling down. He thought, "Shit, my career is over. What am I gonna do? What am I gonna be?"

The charge was dropped as baseless, but a few days later, he was told that his wife was cheating on him. He was cheating on her, but he was too enraged to see the irony, and he became jealous and obsessive.

He began following her to find out who she was sleeping with. She reported to the police that he was stalking her. "And I was—because I wanted to know if it was true. I finally caught her with the enemy, a Los Angeles

County Sheriff's Deputy." Today he laughs at that last statement, but he wasn't laughing then.

"That pushed me over the edge. Forget that I was cheating on her, the manly macho double standard. Oh, hell no," he said. "I saw myself as the victim and I smashed the windows of this poor guy's car."

Second arrest—for making terrorist threats

That destructive act, along with the stalking charge filed by his wife, caused the LAPD Internal Affairs Department to open an investigation and they started surveilling him. "From being a stalker, I became the stalked by my own department."

When Alex was working an off duty security job at Cedars-Sinai Medical Center, he noticed an unmarked car drive by several times and realized he was being watched. "So I went up to the unmarked car and asked the detective what his fucking problem was."

The officer called for backup. Five or six units arrived and officers from the Special Operations Section (SOS) of Internal Affairs "surrounded me with orders to get on the ground. Pissed off, I gave them the finger and told them, 'Fuck you! Take me down motherfuckers.' And they did."

Alex was arrested for making terrorist threats and held on $1 million bail. He spent four days in jail before the charge was dropped and he was freed.

After the incident, Alex was mortified. He told the LAPD therapist that he was suicidal. He thought the department saw him as a psycho cop and his career was over.

Alex resigned, not knowing what he would do or who he was anymore. His second marriage of about six months was annulled.

Diagnosed with Posttraumatic Stress Disorder

It was fortuitous that Alex left the department when he did. If he had tried to tough it out as a police officer, he may have ended up committing suicide over unresolved issues. He was seeing an outside therapist, and it was at this point he was diagnosed with Posttraumatic Stress Disorder (PTSD).

Suddenly, all his incomprehensible actions made sense. Seeing his drinking and sex addiction through the lens of PTSD, he understood how the traumatic incident where he was attacked and nearly killed, inflamed by memories of previous traumas as an undercover agent and patrol officer, combined to make his life a living hell of obsession, self-medication and reckless bravado.

Wasn't told he had PTSD

Several years after Alex had left the department, he had a discussion with the department's psychologist who had treated him for five years. The psychologist admitted that he knew Alex had Posttraumatic Stress Disorder as a result of the traumatic incident and because of a buildup of incidents throughout his career, but was not allowed to tell him because of liability issues.

If I hadn't heard this claim before, I would be shocked. But ever since I started my research on *CopShock* in 1993, I've heard the same condemnation from dozens of traumatized officers around the country. Usually the complaint was about small departments that refuse to recognize PTSD to prevent paying out pensions. This is the first time I've heard it about the LAPD. "They would rather have me act out and think I was losing my mind and maybe commit suicide than to tell me," Alex said.

Knowing the PTSD diagnosis early on would have helped Alex understand his behavior and suicidal thinking. It would have stopped his descent into sex addiction as a self-medication tool.

How Alex dealt with his sex addiction

In due course, the outside therapist who diagnosed Alex with PTSD also identified his sex addiction and helped Alex address the issues.

In addition, Alex researched other sources to help himself better understand what he was experiencing so he could manage his symptoms. He read psychology books like Carnes's *Out of the Shadows*, researched sex addition websites and tried to identify his compulsive and self-destructive patterns.

"Dealing with my sex addiction has been a lifelong process," he said. "There is no magical cure, and you are not miraculously healed. What helped me is introspection, being honest about my life, and understanding the path of how I got here. Getting rid of the shame and guilt has been difficult because of the people I have hurt."

There is little doubt that Alex suffered from sex addiction as it is currently and hesitantly defined, and he cannot say for certain that he has overcome it.

He displayed the typical symptoms: an inability to control his sexual behavior, an unwillingness to face the harmful consequences of his actions, a need to have more frequent indiscriminate sex with more and more women, and a feeling of deprivation when he couldn't have sex.

His compulsive behavior interfered with his personal and work life, and his sexual activities caused his loved ones and friends to experience severe stress. He lived for the intense emotional arousal and adrenaline rush that sex gave him and the soothing calm afterwards. He was constantly looking for someone to have sex with and spent many hours of his day in pursuit of that goal. He was engaged in the vicious cycle of stress, release, shame, anxiety—and the need to do it all over again.

About a year after Alex left the LAPD, he opened *All American Investigations*, a Los Angeles private investigation and security firm, which is highly successful (www.cops4hire.com). He has started a website to help police officers with issues such as sex addiction, PTSD, alcohol abuse, and to provide current news stories affecting law enforcement (See www.RenegadePoPo.com). He was willing to talk about his sex addiction for this article as a way of helping officers who are struggling and too embarrassed to reveal their compulsive and harmful behaviors.

Conclusions

We can't say with certainty that sex addiction is a symptom of PTSD or that it could lead to suicide. However, it appears to be an outcome of severe unresolved psychological, emotional, physical or sexual trauma. Perhaps the American Psychiatric Association may wish to examine sex addiction more closely for future editions of the DSM.

A disturbing part of this discussion is the seemingly predatory behavior of some police officers toward women. According to Alex, they were constantly on the prowl at clubs, bars and even in the homes of victims of domestic violence. Most officers are men with male urges, but this is beyond being young, stupid and libidinous. Predatory behavior crosses the line for professional police officers, even if women are making themselves readily available. It shows not only disrespect for women, but also disrespect for themselves, their families, and the badge they honor.

Treating sex addiction seems to require therapies beyond the usual treatment for standard addictions. For instance, the usual treatment program for alcohol and drug dependencies begins with total withdrawal, something that cannot be done with sex. Perhaps that is why sex addiction has a high relapse rate.[20]

However, there are many addiction clinics that offer treatment programs designed for the sex addict. Among the finest are:

Sexual Recovery Institute (SRI), Los Angeles, California

The Sexual Recovery Institute offers a number of specific programs for sex addiction sufferers such as a 12-Step Program, a two-week residential pro-

---

20. James, Susan Donaldson. (2010, November 29) Tiger Woods Effect: More Sex Addicts Seek Help.

gram, individual treatment, and telephone and online webcam services, as well as online support group meetings and weekly sexual recovery chats (www.sexualrecovery.com). On its website, the SRI provides a confidential Sexual Screening Addiction Test for both men and women at www.sexualrecovery.com/resources/self-test/gsast.php.

Sierra Tucson, Tucson, Arizona

Among other things, the Sierra Tucson treatment center treats sexual addiction, as well as PTSD and the effects of abuse and trauma. At the same time, it treats chemically dependent individuals. Patients are offered educational and therapeutic groups specific to their situation. For example, the Sexual Compulsivity Group provides therapy for people with sexual addiction/compulsivity and sex and love addiction. One of the therapies used is called EMDR or Eye Movement Desensitization and Reprocessing, as well as other successful therapies. Many police officers I've talked to who have undergone EMDR therapy speak very highly of its effectiveness. In addition, Sierra Tucson provides 12-Step meetings, individual attention and several grief and therapy groups. You can see more at www.www.SierraTucson.com.

Pine Grove Health and Addiction Services, Hattiesburg, Mississippi

Under the direction of Dr. Patrick Carnes, Pine Grove's *Gentle Path* program helps those suffering from sexual addiction, among other things. The *Gentle Push* program provides diagnostic assessment as well as a six-week intensive program to treat sex addiction. At the same time, residents are treated for anxiety, past traumas and other addictions such as chemical dependency. As at other treatment centers, Pine Grove offers EMDR therapy. For more about this exceptional program, please go to www.pinegrovetreatment.com/gentle-path.html.

The Sexual Recovery Institute, Sierra Tucson and Pine Grove Health and Addiction Services are only three of many good treatment centers that provide therapy and services for people who are sex addicts. Please check them out thoroughly before committing to a program to make sure that center is right for you.

Sex addiction in stressed-out police officers is a relatively new field that requires a great deal more study. At the moment, we don't know how widespread it is. It is my hope that this article will inspire mental health professionals to conduct further research.

Further Reading

Cross, Chad L. Ph.D., Aschley, Larry, Ed.S., LADC (2004, October 28) Police trauma and addiction: coping with the dangers of the job. *FBI Law Enforcement Bulletin*, Vol. 73, Issue 10, pp. 24 to 32. Retrieved October 28, 2011 at http://www.ncjrs.gov/App/Publications/abstract.aspx?ID=207385.

This article describes responses to trauma and stress, the link between trauma and substance abuse, and strategies for breaking the cycle of trauma and substance abuse.

Discussion Questions

1. How has sex addition been defined by psychiatrists and other mental health specialists?
2. What is a "badge bunny"?
3. What is meant by Kates's reference to "suicides as modeling behavior"?
4. Why was it fortuitous that Officer Alex Salazar left the department when he did?
5. What did Officer Alex Salazar finally do professionally when he left the LA Police Department?
6. What types of programs are offered by The Sexual Recovery Institute in Los Angeles, California?
7. What services are offered by the Sierra Tucson treatment center in Tucson, Arizona, for sexual addiction?
8. What services are provided by the Pine Grove Health and Addiction Services in Hattiesburg, Mississippi?

17

Special Report on Police Suicide: Cop Killer

Melanie Hamilton

> *Officer John Jones sets down his glass of scotch on the bedside table. He has been drinking more lately. Having a few at the end of his shift has always been his way to unwind. But now it's more than a few.*
>
> *Everything has just gone to hell since the internal affairs investigation. And nothing makes sense anymore. So John takes out his off-duty piece, an old wheel gun. He sits down on the bed, puts one in the cylinder, snaps it shut, and stares down at the blued metal machinery in his hand. The world around him is very quiet as he starts to raise the weapon to his head.*
>
> *Then the door opens. His four-year-old son walks in. He doesn't speak. He's just looking for Dad because he senses something is wrong. John quickly lays the gun aside and covers it with a pillow. Then he lifts the boy onto his lap and holds him tight. He's found a reason to keep living. At least for tonight.*

Officer John Jones and his private hell are a composite. But there are many officers each year who face similar moments of despair and choose to take their own lives. And they don't always find a reason not to pull the trigger.

Numbers are hard to come by because so many police suicides go unreported and there is no central source of information. But according to statistics collected by the National Police Suicide Foundation, a police officer takes his or her life every 22 hours. If that estimate is accurate, then nearly 400 cops kill themselves each year.

Suicide is a fact of life in law enforcement. If it hasn't touched your life in some way already, chances are it will.

This is not to say that every police officer is a walking time bomb waiting to kill himself. But the stresses of the job and the long hours spent away from family can take a toll.

Risk Factors

The reasons someone commits suicide can be very complicated, but there are several major causes.

Many of these risk factors are as applicable to the public as they are to law enforcement personnel. For example, people experiencing marital problems are 4.8 times more likely to take their own lives than people who are happily married. And any failing relationship that is meaningful to a person can be a precursor to suicide.

Substance abuse, including drugs or alcohol, is another common factor in suicide. It is not unusual for officers to take their lives while drunk. Part of the reason could be that, as well as being a depressant, alcohol tends to remove inhibitions.

Finally, even someone else's moment of despair can lead to your own. According to Rev. Robert Douglas of the National Police Suicide Foundation, children of police officers often kill themselves in the first five years after their parent completes the act.

Other risk factors are part of cop culture. It's been documented that suspended police officers and those under investigation are 6.7 times more likely to kill themselves. Many police officers feel that their lives are over if they can no longer be cops. This is especially true when they haven't reached retirement and their career is terminated because of a disciplinary matter.

Then there's the job itself.

Police officers are under a great deal of pressure to perform under traumatic circumstances. But they don't always feel they can allow themselves to be affected by the situations they encounter on the job. And oftentimes they can't while they're in the situation or they wouldn't be able to do their jobs. That leads to a lot of pent-up emotion, particularly dark emotion.

Emotional Wear and Tear

Chaplain Herb Smith, who works with the San Diego Police Department and the San Diego County Sheriff's Office, believes that the expectations of administration as well as the public wear on an officer, especially when his or her actions in an officer-involved shooting or other critical incident come under scrutiny.

"With law enforcement, there is a larger measure of the kinds of adversities and stressors that come into one's life," Smith says. "Officers get a lot of contradictory messages administratively and publicly. They're expected to enforce the law in an almost impossible way. [Then they are judged] by managers who are able to spend time developing a political assessment, deliberating what they would have done in the same situation, scrutinizing the decisions a police officer must make in a second or two."

The "Perfect" Trap

Smith also believes that the type of people who become police officers might be more susceptible to suicide because of the high expectations they put on themselves. A prime example of this is a recent well-publicized case of a Nebraska state trooper.

Mark Zach, 35, of the Nebraska State Patrol shot himself with his sidearm because he apparently believed he hadn't done all he could do to prevent a massacre at a Norfolk, Neb., bank. Four people were killed in that bank holdup, and reports say Zach blamed himself. He stopped one of the robbery suspects a week before the incident and found a concealed weapon.

The suspect was arrested for a concealed weapon charge and the gun was confiscated, but he posted bond. After the robbery, Zach learned that he made a mistake when checking the serial number. He transposed two digits when feeding the number into a police computer. If he'd input the right information, the gun wouldn't have come up clean and the suspect could have been arrested for having a stolen gun, and that might have stopped the holdup, which took the lives of three bank employees and a customer.

For armchair psychologists, the easy conclusion is that Trooper Zach couldn't live with the consequences of his mistake. He's not alone. An all-encompassing sense of responsibility is part of many cops' psyches.

Heroic Self Image

Another common denominator in many a cop's psyche is that he sees himself as a hero. Unfortunately, the public doesn't always agree and the disconnect can lead to depression and rage.

Police psychologist Carolyn M. Tenerowicz, who works for the Cleveland (Ohio) Police Department, says the new generation of cops is ill equipped to deal with the pressures of police work because they have different expectations than previous generations. "Years ago, police officers would commit suicide as a result of burnout and the tragedy of having given their life and all they had to give with very little in return," says Tenerowicz. "It was a really helpless exhaustion. Today, they're not able to tolerate the lack of appreciation that's presented to police officers. These suicides are a result of anger, not frustration, because they're not getting outside praise for their efforts."

But Smith takes a more sympathetic view of the reasons officers commit suicide. He feels that because they want to continue to do their job, police officers ignore difficulties in their professional or personal lives for fear that acknowledging them could lead to their dismissals.

"Often, police officers feel all they can do is police work. If they're having problems, they just force it and keep going," he says.

In addition to all the other difficulties of the job, an officer's proximity to traumatic experiences can magnify already existent problems, according to John Violanti, a professor at The University of Buffalo Department of Social and Preventative Medicine and a retired New York State trooper.

"Officers have many of the same problems that other people who commit suicide have, but the context of their job exacerbates those conditions and it makes it worse," Violanti explains. "In that sense they're more likely to commit suicide than someone in the general working population."

Fraternity of Pain

But what about other public safety officers? Are they as prone to suicide as cops and for the same reasons?

Again because suicide is such a touchy subject, the numbers are hard to come by. Comparative statistics for police officers, firefighters, and rescue workers are difficult to find, but it's well known that other public safety workers commit suicide as well.

Robert O'Donnell, the paramedic who rescued "Baby Jessica" McClure from an abandoned well in Midland, Texas, in 1987, killed himself in 1995. He is said to have suffered from post-traumatic stress disorder, a condition that also afflicts many police officers.

"Police officers see a lot of things that other people who are not officers would never see: human misery, traumatic events such as 9/11," says Violanti.

"The exposure that first responders get to these sorts of events are generally very close so that has an impact on their psychological well-being."

Talking It Out

In Violanti's research, he has found that law enforcement officers exposed to traumatic events think about suicide much more often than those who are not. But it doesn't always take a traumatic event to drive someone to the breaking point.

Daniel W. Clark, department psychologist for the Washington State Patrol, believes frequently talking about day-to-day problems can help someone cope better with life in general. "What leads to life-and-death issues," he says, "is when all the small stuff stacks up on us."

Unfortunately, law enforcement culture, which puts emphasis on physical and emotional strength, can make it difficult for cops to talk about the small events that cause stress in their lives.

For a cop, even divulging perceived weaknesses to friends can be difficult. Admitting vulnerabilities to a psychologist is even more daunting, and police officers' mistrust of anyone not in law enforcement makes speaking to mental health professionals even more difficult.

"Police officers are great help-givers, but they're pretty poor help-seekers," Clark says.

"You have to fight against cops' fears that something awful is going to happen if they do come forward," adds Dr. Elizabeth K. White, psychologist with the Los Angeles County Sheriff's Department.

White says this can be true of law enforcement officers seeking help for their friends, as well. "A colleague might blow it off, and tell himself his friend is just joking or will be OK in the morning, because he's afraid of the consequences, that he might destroy someone's career," she explains. "They don't want to step in so they hope it's nothing and pray that they're right. And then they feel awful if it turns out that it was something."

Because officers are so reluctant to seek out professional help, some agencies have established peer counseling programs. Fellow police officers are volunteering to take training classes in listening to their colleagues' concerns and recognizing warning signs so they can refer them to mental health professionals if necessary. Experts say peer counseling is very effective because it's a way to talk to someone who understands your feelings and concerns as a police officer and won't tell anyone else what you have said.

Unfortunately, not all police officers are convinced that talking to anyone, not even a peer, is safe. They've heard too many stories about officers seeking help and then being passed over for promotions or even being fired for perceived mental instability.

Fighting the Stigma

They have good reason to be concerned. The stigma associated with seeking emotional help is not completely unfounded, and there is a tradition of cutting an agency's losses by removing an officer from sensitive positions if he or she might possibly be a liability.

But agencies are making an effort to remove these obstacles to counseling, and it seems that the changes are working.

White says there is now less of a stigma attached to seeking help than there used to be. Part of this is generational. "Younger cops are more comfortable asking for assistance," White says.

Older cops are more skeptical when it comes to counseling. But Sgt. Garry Collins, whose unit deals with suicide prevention at the San Diego Police Department, believes veteran cops who have seen too many of their friends kill themselves over the years are starting to appreciate the psychological services that are now available to them.

But even if an at-risk police officer is willing to go see a psychologist, he or she doesn't want to publicize the visit. For this reason, department psychologists are often placed far from department headquarters to protect confidentiality.

Case in point. When the Houston Police Department required employees to visit the department psychologist at an office in the police headquarters building, they were too scared to seek help. But once Houston PD moved its psychological services back to a separate building in another part of town, more officers decided to avail themselves of its services.

Not only are law enforcement officers afraid management might find out they're seeking help, they don't want their friends and colleagues to know about it either. And usually they don't.

"It's only when a peer counselor or psychologist feels drastic measures need to be taken to ensure an officer's safety that the department needs to be brought in on what's going on," says White.

Clark likens a department's view of officers seeking help for suicidal thoughts or depression to seeking help for alcoholism. "If you don't seek help and you get tapped for a DUI early one morning, you're toast. In all likelihood, they're going to terminate you or severely reprimand you," he says. "But if you come forward and say, 'I have an alcohol problem; I need some help,' I believe most agencies are going to say, 'OK, we'll get you some treatment that will square you away.'"

With suicide, an officer who seeks treatment can often be successfully treated for depression and be back on the job. But you have to seek help to receive help, and an agency has to provide services that an officer feels comfortable using to make a suicide awareness program work.

Still, despite a growing movement among agencies to offer counseling services to officers and educate them on the warning signs and the adverse effects of suicide on everyone involved, officers are still killing themselves. And that leaves everyone they knew with one overriding and ultimately unanswerable question: Why?

What Can You Do?

- Know the warning signs of suicide.
- Attend classes on depression and suicide if they are offered at your agency to help you identify risks and know how to deal with suicide in case it ever happens at your agency.
- Don't be afraid to suggest that friends seek help if you are concerned they may attempt suicide. There are many places where you can receive help anonymously if your friend doesn't want to go through the department.
- If your agency doesn't already offer a suicide awareness program, suggest that one be started. Contact local departments and ask them for advice and help in starting your agency's own program. Or talk to other smaller departments about creating a joint program to raise suicide awareness and offer shared psychological services.

Suicide Prevention Resources

American Foundation for Suicide Prevention
1-888-333-2377
www.afsp.org

National Hopeline Network
1-800-SUICIDE
www.SuicideHotlines.com

National Police Suicide Foundation
(410) 437-3343
www.psf.org

Top 10 Reasons for Police Suicide

1. Death of a child or spouse
2. Loss of a child or spouse through divorce
3. Terminal illness
4. Responsibility for partner's death
5. Killing someone out of anger
6. Indictment
7. Feeling all alone
8. Sexual accusation
9. Loss of job due to conviction of a crime
10. Being locked up

Suicides Committed Each Year

General population	12 per 100,000
Military	13 per 100,000 (average of all branches)
Law enforcement	18 per 100,000

Survivor Stories

The real victims of suicide are the people left behind.

Judith Gentry's husband Tom killed himself six years ago in their bedroom. A trained ICU nurse, Gentry's no stranger to the stress and trauma of emergencies, but when she heard a gunshot and found her husband dead from a self-inflicted gunshot wound to the head, she called a girlfriend instead of dialing 911.

"It's really a horrible shock," says Gentry. "It feels like this just can't be real, that this is just a horrible nightmare and it'll end."

But her husband's death was a reality that she had to deal with. It's a reality that many police families have to deal with. And it's not easy.

Dying at Home

Families often have a hard time getting on with their lives after a suicide because they have so many reminders of what happened around them all the time.

"A line-of-duty death usually occurs in the field, whereas, unfortunately, a lot of our suicides occur at home. So a family member is often the one who finds the person," says Dr. Elizabeth K. White, psychologist with the Los Angeles County Sheriff's Department.

After finding her husband's body in their bedroom after he shot himself, Judith Gentry suffered from post-traumatic stress disorder herself. So this was another obstacle for her to face in dealing with her husband's suicide.

"If anybody would come up behind me and speak too loudly, I'd just jump," she says. "And that was bad. I live in the country so I had to hear guns going off during hunting season. It would just be a flashback, and that was real hard. You never really get over it."

White says that if an officer has killed himself in the home, a family often feels like their house is "violated." In fact, the homes are so "tainted" that some people end up selling them to avoid the memory of the event.

It took Maria Holcomb a year to be able to sleep in the bedroom she had shared with her husband, which was where he died. She preferred to sleep on the couch.

"The cleanup involved in something like this is nasty," says White. "I hate to be graphic, but blood is very hard to get out of things."

It's been more than six years since her husband died, and Gentry can now talk about him and the event of his death, but it took her a long time to get to that point.

"I think I've learned to live with it," Gentry says. "I think that it probably takes about three years to go all the way to the bottom and come back up. Your grief is just so multiplied when it's a suicide. It's just so much more difficult."

Sorrow and Pity

One of the most difficult things that the families of suicide must deal with is the attitudes and ignorance of others. People often view officers' surviving family members with pity if not outright disgust. In either case, it is not helpful to the survivors.

Holcomb received a call from her children's school telling her that other kids had been making fun of her son and daughter because their father had committed suicide. In fact, she says people still stop and point when they see her on the street, especially because she lives in a small town.

Sometimes even well-meaning people can be the most hurtful. One woman actually told the surviving spouse of a police suicide that she was praying for her husband because he was burning in hell for having committed the sin of suicide.

More often than not, people choose to avoid survivors of suicide and say nothing to them at all.

Losing Friends

Gentry kept in contact with a representative from the U.S. Marshal Service, where her husband worked, for more than a year. But when it came to friends, after the funeral they stopped coming.

"People tend not to call you after the initial funeral. I understand they don't know what to say," Gentry says, "but it was very painful." She believes her husband's friends don't want to see her because she reminds them of Tom and brings back their pain.

Maria Holcomb lost friends after her husband's death, as did her children. "Suicide is such a stigma," she says, "that even friends we knew don't know what to say to me and my kids so they say nothing. You're still real normal people and you need to have friends and you know life is going to go on. Just because this happened doesn't mean every time they call you you're going to sit there crying. People need to be educated."

Eileen Bowery had a hard time dealing with her husband Charlie's suicide, especially because his friends wouldn't speak with her. But one sergeant came by her house to express his sadness at Charlie's death and his concern for Bowery and her family. "That really helped," she remembers.

Bowery, whose husband was a Chicago cop who committed suicide in 2000, feels people might not be so afraid to talk to her if they were more educated about suicide and its aftermath.

"It's important to get the word out about police suicide because it is a fact of life, and it's such a stigma that even friends that we had don't know what to say to us so they say nothing. I've got family that just don't know what to do with us so they just ignore us."

Left Behind

The widows contacted for this story say they appreciate the time they got to spend with their husbands, but they feel cheated of the years they could have spent together had the officers' lives not ended.

And these women are not alone. A suicide affects everyone that person knew. That includes family, friends, and colleagues.

Gentry wants officers to understand the devastation to those they would leave behind by committing suicide, whatever the circumstances. "I think if police officers realized just how horrible it is for the survivors, maybe they would stop and get help rather than pull that trigger."

Resources for Survivors of Suicide

SOLES (Survivors of Law Enforcement Suicides)
(941) 541-1150
AskT8@aol.com

SOLOS (Survivors of Loved Ones' Suicides)
www.solos.org
(703) 426-1320

SPAN USA (Suicide Prevention Advocacy Network)
www.spanusa.org
1-888-649-1366

Tears of a Cop
www.tearsofacop.com

Death and Dishonor

Suicide is now the seventh-leading cause of death in the United States. That's for the general population. For police officers, the numbers are much more startling. More officers die by their own hand than in the line of duty.

But despite this terrible fact, many agencies don't have policies for how to handle the aftermath of a suicide. It's a complicated issue because in the eyes of many cops, suicide is a coward's way out and it invalidates an officer's years of service.

Nowhere is this more evident than in the difference between the treatment of the families of officers who commit suicide and those who die in the line of duty.

A line-of-duty death is seen as honorable, and the survivors receive support—both emotional and financial. Their loved one is buried as a hero and is remembered every year on a memorial wall.

But because suicide violates the unspoken code of honor that is sacred to many cops, there is often a battle over whether to grant a police suicide a police funeral. Such an intra-agency debate can cause irrevocable damage to the survivors and to the agency's morale.

Rev. Robert Douglas of the National Police Suicide Foundation believes that attending a funeral is important for all involved. "Having the other officers there to grieve and go through this hurt and this pain with the family makes the healing process much better for the family and much better for the officers," he says.

Eating a Gun

Why do police officers kill themselves with their sidearms? Because they can.

Eileen Bowery thinks her husband, Charlie, a Chicago cop, might not have killed himself had the department taken his gun when he was stripped of his badge and his gun-carry privileges as part of an internal affairs investigation.

Bowery says her husband was distraught because of the humiliation of having his badge taken at his home in front of his family and that the investigation put him under such strain that he became a different person, one who should not have even had possession of a gun.

But others say that taking his or her gun is not going to stop a cop from committing suicide. In fact, taking away those privileges can possibly cause a police officer to reach the despair that will lead to suicide. Such may have been the case with Charlie Bowery.

Why do cops almost always choose guns as the way to take their lives? There are several theories on the matter, all of which have to do with cop culture.

Some even argue that ready access to a firearm makes law enforcement officers more prone to committing suicide, but Daniel W. Clark, department psychologist for the Washington State Patrol, is not convinced.

"I've got studies in my files on construction workers who killed themselves with nail guns," Clark says. "That's what they're familiar with. Doctors, psychiatrists, tend to kill themselves with medication. That's what they're familiar with. Cops are familiar with guns."

Rev. Robert Douglas, a police chaplain who has experienced coming back from the brink of suicide himself, believes a gun is more than familiar. It becomes an officer's trusted friend.

"I think the weapon takes on a personality—more than just a piece of metal and more than just something that protects them. I had a bout with depression and a lot of other things in my life. And in the Marines and when I was in law enforcement, that weapon became my survival. And who's always there? Who's always available? That gun is there."

Douglas, who established the National Police Suicide Foundation, attributes this personification of a duty weapon to law enforcement culture. And perhaps the proof of his argument is that it's not just male officers who "eat their guns."

Women traditionally use less violent means such as poison or sleeping pills to end their own lives. But female police officers tend to kill themselves in the same way as their male counterparts. They shoot themselves in the head. This can be attributed to having been fully assimilated into the cop culture.

Law enforcement officers, Douglas says, learn to think and act like warriors, whether at work or at home. So when they plan to commit suicide, they choose a warrior's method, and they finish the job because they are taught to carry through with their plans.

A gun is "quick, it's aggressive, it's violent, and warriors kill themselves like that," Douglas says.

Losing Yourself

Some officers take their own lives because they can't imagine not being a cop.

One of the major reasons cops murder themselves is because they are under investigation. While many see the suicide as an admission of guilt, experts say it's more likely caused by an officer's fear of losing his or her badge, his or her identity as a cop.

According to Elizabeth K. White, a psychologist with the Los Angeles Sheriff's Department, putting an officer under investigation is a double-edged sword. "We find that suicide often is connected to being under investigation. It's a betrayal if they're innocent. And if they did do it, then they're facing incredible humiliation," she says. "So either way it's going to have a great impact on them."

Being put under investigation can start a ball rolling that is difficult to stop. The prospect of being drummed off the force is worse to some officers than death.

The San Diego Police Department, which began a full-scale suicide awareness and prevention program in December, lost an officer to suicide in January. The officer was waiting for a fitness-for-duty evaluation, following an alcohol-related offense. As soon as he was released on bail, he rented a motel room and shot himself in the head.

Sgt. Garry Collins, assigned to the San Diego PD's medical assistance unit and the newly established member assistance program (MAP), says the department has "tweaked the program since then. Now we respond to [officers under investigation] so the individual knows that they're looking at possibly some discipline, but it's not the end of the world and we're there for them to help them answer some questions."

Terry Holcomb, chief of the Dale Police Department in Johnstown, Penn., was under investigation for payroll fraud when he committed suicide in 2000. Following his death, his wife Maria felt she got no support from the department. "I had to get counseling for my children and me," she says. "I did that on my own. We got nothing."

But often it's difficult for a police department to know how to deal with a grieving spouse who has so much anger for them.

Eileen Bowery's husband, Charlie, a Chicago police officer, committed suicide three months after coming under investigation for allegedly shaking down Polish immigrants on the Northwest side of Chicago.

Bowery believes the whole situation should have been dealt with differently. When the department came to his home and took his badge away from him in front of his family, it was difficult for the family to deal with as well.

Rev. Robert Douglas of the National Police Suicide Foundation agrees that this was not the way to handle the situation. "Having that happen in front of your whole family has got to be the most embarrassing situation in the whole world," he says. "At some departments I've seen them come into the station house and remove the guy right from roll call or pull an officer's car over and arrest him right there. These are all very embarrassing."

Bowery still blames the Chicago PD for Charlie's death. And immediately afterward, she was so angry that she allowed no visible police presence at his funeral except for one car. She also had him buried in a simple suit instead of his uniform.

Discussion Questions

1. What evidence is there to suggest that someone else's moment of despair can lead to your own?
2. Why are suspended police officers or those under investigation 6.7 times more likely to kill themselves?
3. According to police psychologist Carolyn M. Tenerowicz, the reasons that police officers commit suicide today are different than they were in the previous generation. In what ways are they different?
4. Is there any evidence to support the assertion that there is a perceived stigma associated with a police officer seeking emotional help?
5. What are the top ten reasons for police suicide?

18

New Jersey Police Suicide Task Force Report

Introduction

Suicide is a very real problem for law enforcement officers and their families. Most studies have shown that the number of officer lives lost to suicide exceeds those killed in the line of duty. A number of potential risk factors are unique to law enforcement. Law enforcement officers are regularly exposed to traumatic and stressful events. Additionally, they work long and irregular hours, which can lead to isolation from family members. Negative perceptions of law enforcement officers and discontent with the criminal justice system also play a role in engendering cynicism and a sense of despair among some officers. A culture that emphasizes strength and control can dissuade officers from acknowledging their need for help. Excessive use of alcohol may also be a factor, as it is for the population in general.

Access to firearms is a critical factor in law enforcement officer suicides, since most officers are required to maintain their firearms on and off duty. One study of New York City police officers showed that 94% of police suicides involved the use of a service weapon. Suicide prevention research has overwhelmingly demonstrated that access to lethal means has an independent effect on increasing suicide risk.

New Jersey

New Jersey is one of 17 states funded by the Centers for Disease Control to participate in the National Violent Death Reporting System (NVDRS), a unique source of information on violent fatalities including suicide. This richly detailed surveillance system, maintained by the New Jersey Department of Health and Senior Services, collects information on the circumstances surrounding violent deaths in New Jersey, using information from police and medical examiner reports, death certificates, and newspapers. NVDRS also collects information on the occupations of suicide decedents and thus permits the comparison of law enforcement officer suicides with other suicides.

Using the definition of a law enforcement officer adopted by this Task Force, there were 55 suicides among this population between 2003 and 2007. Of these, 18 or nearly one third involved law enforcement officers who were retired or on disability, and 16, or nearly 30 percent, were current or retired corrections officers. Three of the 55 suicides were part of "murder-suicide" incidents. All but two suicides were committed by males. There was no time trend, so it does not appear that law enforcement suicides increased or decreased during this five-year period.

Statistics on law enforcement employment published annually in the Uniform Crime Reports (UCR) were used as denominators to estimate suicide rates for law enforcement officers. The UCR law enforcement employment data are divided into several categories, allowing the comparison of corrections officers with other law enforcement officers. Because population estimates for retired officers and officers on disability are not available, suicide rates can only be calculated for current law enforcement officers.

As Table 1 shows, the ratio of suicide rates among all active law enforcement officers as compared to all males aged 25 to 64 years is 1.3, meaning rates among law enforcement officers are thirty percent greater than similarly aged males. The ratio is 2.5 for active corrections officers and 1.1 among active non-corrections law enforcement officers.

Table 1. Suicide Rates of Law Enforcement Officers versus
Males 25–64 years, New Jersey, 2003–2007

Crude rates	Annual Suicides*	Population **	Crude Rate (per 100,000)	Ratio LE: Male
Current LE	7.4	40,000	18.5	1.3
Corrections only	2.4	6,900	34.8	2.5
Police only	5	33,200	15.1	1.1
New Jersey				
Total population	536	8,700,000	6.2	
Males 25–64 years	322	2,300,770	14.0	

* Average 2003–2007; excludes retired officers and officers on disability.
** Law enforcement population data from 2006 UCR

Risk Factors for Suicide among Law Enforcement Officers Compared to the Overall Population

In the overall population, the most common risk factor for suicide is a mental illness, particularly depression or bipolar disorder. Another important risk factor is access to lethal means, chiefly firearms. Relationship problems, mainly with intimate partners, are also significant, as are acute crises such as job, legal, or financial problems. Particularly among the elderly population, physical health problems, or the illness or death of a spouse, can trigger suicidal behavior. Substance abuse is another risk factor. As compared with males, females are more likely to have longstanding mental health problems, and are less likely to commit suicide in response to an acute event such as an incarceration or a break-up in a relationship.

To address the elevated suicide rates among law enforcement officers, the Task Force sought to determine what risk factors may be particularly important for this population. Experts cite three common issues in law enforcement officer suicide. The first is greater access to a lethal means, because law enforcement officers in general possess firearms on and off duty. In comparison, only eleven percent of households in New Jersey report gun ownership. Second, stress stemming from upsetting or critical incidents present a unique occupational hazard for law enforcement officers. Finally, factors related to shift work and the consequences of law enforcement officer schedules for family relationships are also significant.

Data from the New Jersey Violent Death Reporting System were used to compare the circumstances of law enforcement officer suicides with suicides of similarly aged males in New Jersey. One striking and not unexpected difference is in the use of firearms. More than eighty percent of suicides among law enforcement officers were committed with firearms, compared to approximately one third of suicides among similarly aged males in New Jersey. Additionally, law enforcement officer suicides were significantly less likely than others to be accompanied by documented mental health illnesses, prior suicidal behavior, or previous disclosure of an intent to commit suicide.

Law enforcement officer suicides were more likely than others to have circumstances related to a physical health problem, and to have had a problem with an intimate partner. But these findings are consistent with a general pattern of differences between firearm and non-firearm suicides. When law enforcement firearm suicides are compared with firearm suicides among similarly aged males, there are fewer significant differences in circumstances, except that law enforcement officers are less likely than others to have sought mental health treatment, had a "depressed mood" prior to death, and had previously disclosed an intention to commit suicide. These results show that the circumstances in law enforcement suicides are broadly similar to those in other firearm suicides, in that they are more likely to take place as a result of short-term acute situations rather than long-standing mental health issues. These findings are consistent with the fact that access to lethal means is a risk factor for suicide among law enforcement officers.

Table 2. Reported Circumstances of Law Enforcement and Other Suicides Males, New Jersey, 2003–2007

| | Percent with circumstance reported | | | | | |
| | All suicides | | | Gun suicides | | |
	Total	Law Enforcement	p	Total	Law Enforcement	p
Crisis in last two weeks	24.9	32.6		27.8	38.5	
Depressed mood	35.8	28.3		42.4	25.6	0.04
Death of family or friend	5.7	10.9		7.2	10.3	
Financial problem	9.2	13.0		8.2	10.3	
Physical health problem	21.8	34.8	0.03	31.2	38.5	
History of mental health treatment	32.1	13.0	0.01	21.4	10.3	0.09
Intimate partner problem	25.2	39.1	0.03	27.9	35.9	
Job problem	11.5	8.7		10.5	7.9	
Legal problem	3.4	2.2		2.8	2.6	
Mental health problem	37.6	19.6	0.01	26.1	18.0	
Perpetrator of intimate partner violence	5.2	10.9	0.09	9.7	12.8	
Left a suicide note	32.1	34.88		33.3	30.1	
Substance abuse	16.1	6.5	0.07	10.5	5.1	
History of attempts	16.5	6.5	0.07	7.7	5.1	
Disclosed intent	20.1	8.7	0.06	24.1	5.1	0.009
Current mental health treatment	26.8	13.0	0.04	18.2	10.3	
Alcohol problem	16.87	6.5	0.06	14.6	5.1	

Source: New Jersey Violent Death Reporting System, New Jersey Department of Health and Senior Services

Note: p-value shown when less than .10; indicates significant difference at 90% or greater.

Existing Resources and Barriers to Seeking Treatment

Resources for law enforcement officers who are in need of counseling include employee assistance programs, private practitioners, peer to peer counseling, and crisis intervention services. Law enforcement officers in general have health insurance benefits allowing them access to mental health treatment.

Employee Assistance Programs

Employee Assistance Programs (EAPs) are available to most, but not all, law enforcement officers in New Jersey. These services may be provided by a municipality, a county or the state. The functions of EAPs vary considerably, with some operating primarily as sources of referrals to private practitioners, while others provide short-term counseling on their own. Supervisors also refer officers to their EAPs when an officer is having performance problems such as absenteeism.

Cop 2 Cop

New Jersey has a nationally recognized statewide confidential peer counseling program called Cop 2 Cop, legislatively established in 1998 and operating under the auspices of the University Behavioral Healthcare at the University of Medicine and Dentistry of New Jersey. Cop 2 Cop is a crisis intervention hotline service operating 24 hours a day, seven days a week. It is staffed by volunteer retired members of federal, state, and local law enforcement departments, and mental health professionals who have received law enforcement specific training. Fielding over 23,000 calls for service since 2000, the Cop 2 Cop peer counselors are trained to listen to distressed officers and make appropriate referrals to mental health providers or other services.

Cop 2 Cop provides clinical assessment for officers and their families, maintains a referral network of clinical providers and offers Cop 2 Cop teams for statewide critical incident stress management services with expertise in suicide response. In addition, Cop 2 Cop deploys and provides mutual aid to all New Jersey critical incident stress management teams throughout the state. Cop 2 Cop provides peer counseling training and a variety of stress management training available to law enforcement departments. In the area of suicide prevention, Cop 2 Cop staff are certified trainers for a best practice law enforcement training program called Question, Persuade and Refer (QPR) and have provided QPR training to over 3,000 officers.

The "Blue Heart Law Enforcement Assistance Program" was enacted in 2007 and expanded Cop 2 Cop to ensure that officers wounded or involved in traumatic incidents received counseling, care and support. It gives Cop 2 Cop the authority to refer wounded participants to group therapy, peer counseling and/or debriefing. Cop 2 Cop runs the New Jersey Wounded Officers Support Group Program and the group meets monthly.

Critical Incident Stress Management (CISM) Services

In the course of their jobs, law enforcement officers may encounter traumatic incidents that may result in varying degrees of emotional distress that might ultimately undermine an officer's psychological well-being and put him/her at risk for suicidal behavior.[1] Critical Incident Stress Management (CISM) is a comprehensive system specifically designed to prevent and mitigate adverse psychological reactions to a traumatic event. The approach includes assessment, strategic planning, preparation, pre-incident education, demobilizations, crisis management debriefings, individual, family, small group, organizational and pastoral interventions.

A defusing, which should typically occur within 24 hours after the incident, is an informal procedure to provide information to responders. Debriefing is a structured group discussion and occurs several days after the incident. Discussion centers on the incident and officers' reactions, but also includes a psychological education component that teaches officers positive ways to deal with stress. Providing mental health and peer counseling can be a critical stress reducer after a critical incident. New Jersey has two CISM systems that provide similar services at no cost to all first responders including law enforcement, emergency medical services and fire fighters.

New Jersey Critical Incident Stress Management Team (NJCISM) is a statewide system that delivers peer support to any member of emergency services. Headed by a Chairman, its 225 members include: 134 law enforcement, 21 emergency medical services, 4 firefighters, 3 dispatchers, 9 ER nurses, 9 law enforcement chaplains, 6 family members/survivors, 3 law enforcement spouses, and 22 mental health personnel. The deployed team consists of a peer counselor and a mental health provider when the situation dictates.

---

1. The New Jersey State Police S.O.P. C37 defines "critical incident" as any event that can cause an enlisted or civilian employee to experience an unusually strong psychological and/or emotional reaction, including the use of deadly force by or against an enlisted employee, accidental discharge of a weapon, or any additional unusual circumstance.

New Jersey Crisis Intervention Response Network (CIRN) is another statewide system that adheres to the 'Mitchell Model' in delivering a multi-component crisis intervention program for all first responders. Headed by a statewide clinical director, CIRN has 87 members, 11 of whom are mental health professionals. This team is deployed by a call from a first responder, supervisor, or department who contacts the CIRN 24/7 hotline number. The deployed team consists of a peer and mental health professional.

In addition to these statewide networks, the New Jersey State Police, Cop 2 Cop and several other organizations maintain critical incident stress management teams as additional resources. The Critical Incident Stress Guidebook for New Jersey provides resource and contact information for state, county and local providers of critical incident stress management services and resources related to traumatic loss and disaster response.

Psychological First Aid

Psychological first aid is an evidence-based approach and intervention to assist survivors and responders in the immediate aftermath of a traumatic event. The approach is based on the concept of human resiliency, enhancing short and long term adaptability, coping and self-efficacy skills. Psychological First Aid for First Responders and First Receivers training was developed for NJLearn, the New Jersey Homeland Security Emergency Responder (online) Training Center. This free online program will help First Responders and Receivers of all types, understand the emotional impact of such events, and introduce strategies and skills for managing the emotional consequences of disasters and terrorism. The program will soon be posted on the New Jersey Office of Homeland Security and Preparedness website.

Barriers to Seeking Treatment

Despite the existence of resources, Task Force members and presenters frequently noted that, for a variety of reasons, many at-risk officers do not seek help. The primary barriers are a law enforcement culture that emphasizes strength and control, perceptions and distrust of mental health providers, the stigma associated with seeking help, general concerns about loss of privacy that may adversely affect their careers, and embarrassment or shame. Some officers may not feel comfortable with mental health providers who do not have specific experience with law enforcement populations. Officers often worry that seeking help may result in the loss of their firearm, job and health benefits. Additionally, peer to peer counselors who are current members of law enforcement agencies may not be as effective as they could be due to concerns about confidentiality.

Survey of Law Enforcement Supervisors

To learn more about officers' use of resources, and gather suggestions for improvements, an online survey was administered to law enforcement supervisors, including police chiefs, supervisors of sheriffs, state and county corrections supervisors, and parole supervisors. The survey asked about:

- the types of services used when referring officers for assistance with psychological and substance abuse related problems,
- the types of services supervisors thought their officers used if they sought assistance on their own,
- whether their officers received training about coping with stress, and
- whether their officers received training about how to interact with mentally ill civilians.

Respondents were also asked their opinion about how to improve the effectiveness of their EAPs, and ways to improve the mental health and well-being of officers.

1. Services Used

Overall, survey results suggested that supervisors tend to rely on their EAPs as their primary referral for officers under their command. The second most frequently used service was Cop 2 Cop. Results varied by size of department. For example, among smaller departments (fewer than 20 officers), only 25 percent of supervisors reported that an EAP was their first choice in making a referral. More than 35 percent of these supervisors reported that they "rarely or never" made such a referral to services. In departments with more than one hundred officers, more than eighty percent of supervisors listed the EAP as their most likely referral, and none reported that they rarely or never made such a referral. When officers sought help on their own, supervisors thought they were most likely to seek a private practitioner, followed by Cop 2 Cop. This did not vary by size, as approximately half of all supervisors selected private practitioners as the most likely service used by officers seeking help on their own.

As noted above, a common suggestion among the responders about how to improve services to officers was to address the stigma among law enforcement officers about seeking assistance.

2. *Availability of Training*

Approximately half of all supervisors interviewed reported having stress or psychological wellbeing training available to officers under their command. The percent with such training was highest among sheriffs and county corrections, and lowest among parole supervisors. This percent varied moderately by size, with about 48 percent of the smallest agencies, and 55 percent of the largest agencies reported having such training. Three quarters of respondents reported that training related to working with the mentally ill was available to their officers. This percent was highest among county corrections supervisors (88.9%) and lowest among parole supervisors (38.0%). There was no consistent variation by agency size.

The most common suggestion on how to improve services for officers in the areas of stress reduction, mental health and substance abuse services was a call for additional training. These comments were equally likely to be made across agency types, and by size of agency.

3. *Employee Assistance Programs*

The most common response to how to improve EAPs was an expression of a positive view of these programs; with thirty percent of responders providing this response. This view was most common among sheriff and parole supervisors, and least common among state and county corrections. A concern about lack of confidentiality or a stigma associated with seeking assistance from EAPs was next often cited, with approximately twenty five percent providing this response. More often than not, this was a perception ascribed to officers and apparently not shared by the survey respondent. This view was most common in state and county corrections, and least common among parole supervisors.

Summary

1. The Cop 2 Cop program is an important asset for law enforcement officers in crisis, and is used by many officers. Additional services include EAPs, peer to peer counseling within the NJSP, and crisis intervention units who provide counseling in the event of critical incidents.

2. The survey results suggest a fairly high but uneven level of comfort with EAPs.

3. Supervisors expressed a desire for increased training in the areas of suicide prevention and mental health awareness, and ways to combat the stigma associated with seeking help.

Recommendations

While researchers and advocates may disagree on law enforcement officer suicide rates, and the relative importance of different risk factors, there is broad consensus on the most constructive avenues for preventing law enforcement officer suicide: 1) increase suicide awareness training, 2) improve access to resources, and 3) identify best practices to emulate. The Task Force recommendations focus on these three areas.

Increase Training

Suicide prevention experts widely recommend training in suicide awareness and prevention for officers and supervisors, and survey results suggest a strong demand for this training among law enforcement supervisors. Yet there are relatively few examples of suicide prevention training programs in law enforcement agencies. The International Association of Chiefs of Police recently compiled resources and best practices in this area and those materials were considered in developing these recommendations. According to the National Police Suicide Foundation, fewer than two percent of law enforcement agencies have suicide prevention programs. Those that do provide this training include New York City, Los Angeles, the California Highway Patrol, Chicago, Miami, and the Washington State Patrol. There is evidence that awareness training can have a positive effect. The Air Force Academy program was found to reduce suicide among its officers.

The Task Force recommends the following related to training:

1. Suicide prevention awareness training should be provided to all recruits in basic training.

The Task Force recommends that the Attorney General issue a directive requiring that a suicide prevention component be included in the Police Training Commission's Basic Training curriculum. As part of this, the Office of the Attorney General and the Department of Human Services will produce a training video that will be shown during Basic Training. The video will address officers, peers, and supervisors, and will thus serve multiple training purposes. The Department of Corrections will produce a training video with corrections-specific scenarios, with a consistent core message to the video produced for local and municipal law enforcement officers. The training videos will be placed on the websites of the Office of the Attorney General and other law enforcement agencies.

2. Suicide prevention training should be provided to active law enforcement officers and supervisors.

The Task Force recommends that the Attorney General send a letter to all law enforcement supervisors strongly recommending that all officers and supervisors receive suicide prevention training and information on a regular basis, including but not limited to viewing the suicide prevention video within six months of its release, and every three years thereafter.

Improve Access

Suicide awareness training provides officers and supervisors with information about risk factors for suicide and warning signs of suicidality, therefore, it is imperative that resources be available for officers in need of counseling services. While a number of excellent resources are available in New Jersey, including EAPs, Cop 2 Cop, and health insurance benefits, a number of steps can be taken to improve access to services for officers both by providing them more information about available resources, and by taking specific steps to increase the effectiveness of existing resources.

Peer to peer counselors are an important resource to address some officers' reluctance to access services from mental health professionals. But concerns about confidentiality may inhibit some officers from using peer counselors. The retired federal, state, and local officers who staff the phone lines at Cop 2 Cop have confidential status because of their training and because they are no longer active officers. Peer counselors who are also active law enforcement officers under New Jersey law do not have confidential status, and may be required to testify if there is an investigation of an incident. This may have a chilling effect on officers, and reduce the effectiveness of peer counseling for that reason. States including Colorado, Washington, Oregon and Arizona have peer confidentiality legislation outlining criteria under which confidentiality is granted.

The Task Force makes the following recommendations about improving access to services:

1. Consider legislation affording confidentiality to peer counselors in narrow circumstances, provided that they are clearly serving as peer counselors.

The Task Force recommends consideration of legislation affording confidentiality to first responder peer counselors when they are serving as part of an official peer counseling program. The Task Force recommends that, at a minimum, peers be required to take three core courses based on the International Critical Incident Stress Foundation (ICISF) guidelines including training on group crisis intervention, individual crisis intervention and peer support, and advanced group crisis intervention, as well as ongoing training. This limited privilege would be unavailable to witnesses to an event leading to the need for a peer counselor or to anyone reporting harm to themselves or others, or to the commission of illegal acts.

Peer counseling services would be voluntary among departments and those choosing to become peer counselors would be required to complete the minimum initial and ongoing training requirements.

2. Provide contact information for resources able to supply callers with information on mental health providers in the locality of their choice.

More readily available sources of information on mental health providers in the State will improve law enforcement officers and their families' access to these services. The Task Force recommends that the State make available information on mental health providers. Examples of such contacts include Cop 2 Cop, New Jersey Mental Health Cares (Mental Health Association of NJ warmline), and 211. The information should be made available through State websites, mass emails, and information disseminated to all law enforcement agencies. The Attorney General and the Commissioner of Human Services websites should be used, among others, to disseminate this information.

3. Move Cop 2 Cop to the Department of Human Services to increase the effectiveness and visibility of the services it provides.

To best align the mission of Cop 2 Cop services with a contracting state agency, the Task Force recommends that the legislature modify proposed legislation A2803/S1979 transitioning the contract for the toll-free information "Law Enforcement Officer Crisis Intervention Services" telephone hotline from the Department of Health and Senior Services to the Department of Human Services. This recommendation requires that the legislation provide accompanying staff resource or salary coverage for contract oversight.

4. Improve effectiveness of EAPs so that they are better able to meet the needs of law enforcement officers.

While law enforcement officers surveyed by this Task Force most often had praise for the services provided by county, municipal and state EAPs, the next most frequent feedback regarding EAPs was that law enforcement officers are reluctant to use them. To address this issue, the Task Force recommends that the Attorney General and the Commissioner of the Department of Human Services reach out to EAP Directors and encourage them to advertise themselves to the law enforcement communities they serve. The Attorney General, the Commissioner of Human Services, and Cop 2 Cop will offer EAP Directors copies of the training and anti-stigma materials and other materials appropriate for law enforcement personnel.

5. Increase awareness of existing resources.

The Task Force recommends that in the letter from the Attorney General and the Commissioner of Human Services, law enforcement supervisors be reminded to use the existing resources described above and to publicize their availability to officers under their command.

The New York City Police Department in particular, has developed such a policy through its Early Intervention Unit and Psychological Services Unit that allows an officer to temporarily relinquish his or her firearms in a confidential and non-disciplinary manner when an officer is in need of counseling. The Task Force recommends that law enforcement agencies consider the appropriateness of these or similar policies for their departments.

6. Create an anti-stigma poster campaign for law enforcement.

The Task Force recommends that the Department of Human Services, together with the Office of the Attorney General and the Governor's Task Force on Mental Health Stigma, design an anti-stigma poster campaign. Posters will be made available by DHS for all law enforcement agencies to post in locker rooms and other common areas. The Police Benevolent Association, the Fraternal Order of Police, and the State Trooper Fraternal Association will assist with initiatives to reduce stigma among their membership.

7. Target messaging to retired law enforcement officers and officers on disability.

The Task Force recommends that the Department of Personnel periodically provide information in the retirement and disability checks of retired law enforcement officers and officers on disability, informing them of the availability of resources such as Cop 2 Cop if they are feeling depressed or in need of mental health services. The Task Force also recommends that information materials regarding suicide prevention resources be included in the initial retirement packages sent to law enforcement officers.

8. Monitor suicide rates among law enforcement.

The Task Force recommends that available data on law enforcement suicides continue to be monitored through the New Jersey Violent Death Reporting System.

9. Reconvene the Task Force.

The Task Force recommends that the Governor reconvene the Task Force in one year's time, or earlier if needed, to review the progress of the recommendations set forth in this report.

Best Practices

The Task Force recommends that law enforcement agencies consider adopting some or all of the following examples of "best practices" that address the barriers to seeking treatment.

1. Comprehensive Law Enforcement EAP.

The New Jersey State Police, Office of Employee and Organizational Development (OEOD), provides comprehensive, confidential services to employees and members of their immediate families who are experiencing organizational, behavioral, or personal difficulties, which can adversely affect their ability to function on the job effectively, efficiently, and safely. Since 1981, the OEOD has provided services to the state troopers and their families, and those services have been expanded to five other areas: Management & Organizational Services; Critical Incident Stress Management; Chaplain Services; Peer Advocate Services Unit; and Wellness.

The Peer Advocate Services Unit provides confidential assistance and services to enlisted members and their families. This unit educates members on services and resources available during a personal or professional crisis. Providing preventative education minimizes risk management for the member and the Division of State Police. These services may be initiated voluntarily by the requesting member, a co-worker or supervisor referral, or in conjunction with the medical services unit.

The Task Force recommends that law enforcement agencies consider the OEOD as a model employee assistance program that provides services tailored to law enforcement officers' mental health needs.

2. Cop 2 Cop.

The Cop 2 Cop statewide program is the only Certified Police Helpline in the country accredited by the American Association of Suicidology. The Task Force recommends that law enforcement supervisors encourage their officers to avail themselves of this resource and that they contact Cop 2 Cop if they have specific training or outreach needs.

3. Policies mandating counseling after traumatic events.

The Task Force recommends that law enforcement agencies consider implementing policies mandating counseling after traumatic incidents. The Collingswood Police Department in New Jersey currently mandates counseling for all officers involved in critical incidents, a policy designed in part to reduce the stigma associated with seeking help. The New Jersey State Police has a similar policy. Such referrals ensure officers have an opportunity to receive assistance and help to eliminate the stigma associated with seeking help.

4. Non-Disciplinary Firearm Removal.

Concerns about the career consequences of the involuntary removal of an officer's department issued firearm may deter distressed officers from seeking help, which only compounds the risk. Some jurisdictions have designed "non-disciplinary" firearm removal policies in attempt to reduce this barrier to seeking help.

5. Align Department Policies and Procedures with CALEA and NJACP
   Standards.

The Commission on the Accreditation for Law Enforcement Agencies, Inc. (CALEA) and the New Jersey Association of Chiefs of Police (NJACP), have developed standards to improve the delivery of public safety services and promote officer wellness. While accreditation can be an ultimate goal, adopting some of the CALEA standards related to employee support services may help to foster an environment where mental health and stress related issues can be dealt with efficiently and effectively. The Task Force recommends that law enforcement agencies consider compliance with relevant CALEA and NJACP standards as an avenue they may want to pursue as part of an overall suicide prevention initiative.

Conclusion

The Task Force report identifies the key risk factors for law enforcement suicide and recommends ways to address the barriers to officers seeking treatment. The recommendations reflect the Task Force findings that the most constructive avenues for preventing law enforcement suicides are increasing suicide awareness training, improving access to resources and identifying best practices that law enforcement agencies can emulate.

Discussion Questions

1. A number of potential risk factors are unique to law enforcement according to the New Jersey Task Force Report. What are they?
2. What type of counseling was recommended as resources for law enforcement officers who are in need of these services?
3. What is the Cop 2 Cop program? What type of services does the Cop 2 Cop program provide?
4. When was the "Blue Heart Law Enforcement Assistance Program" enacted? What was it intended to accomplish?
5. What is Critical Incident Stress Management (CISM)?
6. What is the New Jersey Critical Incident Stress Management Team (NJCISM)?
7. What is the New Jersey Crisis Intervention Response Network (CIRN)?
8. What is psychological first aid?
9. What barriers to seeking treatment are commonly found in the law enforcement culture?
10. The New Jersey Task Force conducted an on-line survey of law enforcement and corrections supervisors. What were its results as they relate to the services supervisors seek for personnel in need of counseling?
11. While researchers and advocates may disagree on law enforcement officer suicide rates and the relative importance of different risk factors, there is a broad consensus on the most constructive avenues for preventing law enforcement officer suicide. What are the three that are set forth in the New Jersey Task Force Report?

Part Five

How Does Stress Impact the Cop's Family Life?

The negative effects of stress cannot be focused solely on the individual officer and his or her life at work. Most officers are part of a family—with spouses, children, and parents—who experience the impact of police stress on the personal life of that officer and on their own lives. As one NYPD officer explained his reaction under stress:

> You change when you become a cop—you become tough and cynical. You have to condition yourself to be that way in order to survive this job. And sometimes without realizing it, you act that way all the time, even with your wife and kids. But it's something you have to do because if you start getting emotionally involved with what happens at work, you'll wind up in Bellevue [psychiatric hospital] (Maslach and Jackson, 59).

It is generally accepted that problems can result when law enforcement officers, who are taught to behave in certain controlling and authoritarian ways on the job, continue to interact with their families in the same manner when at home. Transferring professional dispositions to personal situations can and often does cause conflict, fear, and resentment with an officer's spouse and children. Certain specific behaviors—professionalism, detachment, and suspicion—when, even unintentionally, exhibited at home by police officers can cause significant interpersonal problems.

It is an unfortunate fact that, in some cases, law enforcement seems to have institutionalized marital and family turmoil into the profession. The worst manifestation of such turmoil is domestic violence. Historically, police families must manage many difficult stresses and are left to their own devices to provide the necessary resources to meet these stresses. Consequently, many police marriages end in failure.

Recognition of the vicarious victimization of police families is critical to our understanding of the complexity and comprehensiveness of the issue of police stress. It is toward this understanding that the authors in Part Five turn their attention.

While Part Four provided detailed discussions of addictive behaviors that frequently result from an inability to handle the stress of the job, one such addictive behavior is best discussed here: addiction to police work. It is the work-addicted lifestyle that adds tremendous pressures on a police marriage, with results that can be devastating. As Solan and Casey explain, "the only ethic involved is the certainty that the job must be done," and workaholics are a key contributor to unhealthy family patterns.

Torres, Maggard, and Torres recognize that a missing ingredient in many police stress management and employee assistance programs is the orientation and preparation of spouses and families early in an officer's career. To their point of view, the transition of an officer from civilian to sworn is also paralleled by the transition of the family into the law enforcement culture. To this end, the Irvine, CA, Police Department has developed a program of awareness, which includes a formal orientation for family and friends that occurs at the same time the officer is undergoing his or her own initial orientation following graduation from academy. As a result of this effort, the Irvine Police Department seeks to assure that the entire family understands the problems associated with policing, is able to recognize warning signs of stress, and understands the resources available to the family during times of crisis.

Violanti, one of the country's major researchers into both alcohol abuse and suicide in law enforcement, has long focused on the importance of early intervention as a necessary part of an agency's response to the impact of stress on law enforcement personnel. In this section, he deals with the direst ramification of an organization's failure to deal with the stress of their personnel: murder of family members by an officer who then commits suicide. In this particular work, he discusses the antecedents and demographics of such cases, attempting to stimulate further research on the topic and foster enhanced action by agency administrators.

In the Second Edition of *Stress Management in Law Enforcement*, Prabhu and Turner discussed the development of the Model Policy on Police Officer Domestic Violence by the International Association of Chiefs of Police. In this edition, we turn to Oehme, Donnelly, and Summerlin to present Florida's Model Policy on Officer-Involved Domestic Violence, included as the appendix to this article. As they note, a formal policy sets the tone for the agency's response to a domestic violence situation, as well as providing a starting point for agency efforts at developing and implementing prevention and wellness initiatives. Key to success within any agency will be the leadership asserted by the agency's administration, the involvement of family members, and effective community relationships and resources.

Further Reading

Alexander, David A., and Walker, Leslie G. (1996). "The Perceived Impact of Police Work on Police Officers' Spouses and Families," *Stress Medicine*, 12, 239–246.

Borum, Randy, and Philpot, Carol (1993). "Therapy with Law Enforcement Couples: Clinical Management of the 'High-Risk' Lifestyle," *The American Journal of Family Therapy*, 21(2), 122–135.

Finn, Peter, and Tomz, Julie Esselman (1997). *Developing a Law Enforcement Stress Program for Officers and Their Families*. Washington, DC: National Institute of Justice.

Kannady, Grace (1993). "Developing Stress-Resistant Police Families," *The Police Chief*, LX (10), 92–95.

Kirschman, Ellen (1997). *I Love a Cop: What Police Families Need to Know*. New York, NY: The Guilford Press.

Lott, Lonald D. (1995). "Deadly Secrets: Violence in the Police Family," *FBI Law Enforcement Bulletin*, 64(11), 12–16.

Maslach, Christina, and Jackson, Susan E. (1979). "Burned-out Cops and Their Families." *Psychology Today*, 12(12), 58–62.

Means, Mark S. (1986). "Family Therapy Issues in Law Enforcement Families," in James T. Reese and Harvey A. Goldstein (eds.), *Psychological Services for Law Enforcement*. Washington, DC: U.S. Government Printing Office.

Prabhu, Sandy, and Turner, Nancy (2000). "Rising to the Challenge: Preventing Police Officer Domestic Violence," *The Police Chief*, LXVII(11), 43–55.

Ryan, Joseph F. (1990). "A Law Enforcement Dilemma: Family Violence in Police Families," *Law Enforcement Journal*, 1(1), 27–30.

Sheehan, Donald C. (2000). *Domestic Violence by Police Officers*. Washington, DC: U.S. Government Printing Office.

Southworth, Richard N. (1990). "Taking the Job Home," *FBI Law Enforcement Bulletin*, 59(11), 19–23.

Key Terms in Part Five

Domestic violence: As defined in the IACP Model Policy on Domestic Violence by Police Officers, domestic violence refers to "an act or pattern of violence perpetrated by a police officer upon his or her intimate partner not done in defense of self or others, including bodily injury or threat of bodily injury, sexual battery, physical restraint, stalking, violation of a court order or injunction for protection, or death threats or death."

Field Training Officer (FTO) Program: An organized program of training for rookie police officers in which their performance is guided, directly supervised, and evaluated by specially trained Field Training Officers.

IACP Model Policy on Police Officer Domestic Violence: Developed following a series of four national summits in 1997, this model policy for individual agencies defines the issues in domestic violence within a law enforcement agency; identifies strategies for prevention, education, and training; establishes a process for early warning and intervention; defines an incident response protocol for the agency; provides for victim safety and protection; and identifies the administrative and criminal investigative protocols which should be followed in the aftermath of an incident of domestic violence.

Incident Response Protocol: Within Florida's Model Policy on Officer-Involved Domestic Violence, the incident response protocol defines the specific responsibilities of the communications officer, patrol officer, and on-scene supervisor when responding to emergency calls involving police domestic violence.

Intimate Partner of a Law Enforcement Officer: As defined in Florida's Model Policy on Officer-Involved Domestic Violence and Florida statute, an intimate partner of a police officer includes spouses, former spouses, persons related by blood or marriage, persons who are presently residing together as if a family or who have resided together in the past as if a family, and persons who are parents of a child in common regardless of whether they have been married. It also includes individuals who have or have had a continuing and significant relationship of a romantic or intimate nature.

Lautenberg Amendment to the Gun Control Act: As a result of the passage of this amendment in 1996, any person, including a law enforcement officer, convicted of a federal or state misdemeanor charge of domestic violence is no longer allowed to possess or purchase a firearm.

19

Police Work Addiction:
A Cautionary Tale

Gerard J. Solan and Jean M. Casey

Great leaders lead by example, and Police Chief William Smith was no exception. He was totally selfless and always available, arriving at his command each morning before eight o'clock and not leaving until everyone else had gone home. It was not uncommon to find him working on Saturday or Sunday. The deputy chief told those assembled at the church that he actually was reluctant to leave each night before the chief. Everyone felt sad that Chief Smith left a young family and even sadder that he should pass away in the prime of his life.

Certainly, police officers are expected to put aside all other needs when duty calls, and, without question, duty does call. Commanders and officers alike must sustain an endless capacity to meet this demand. Communities hold fast to the expectation that the police will do all that can be humanly done and, at times, much more than should be expected of mere humans. Therein lies the great challenge for law enforcement officers and supervisors, maintaining a healthy balance in meeting reasonable responsibilities to the job, to themselves, and to their families.

The Old Covenant

Some in public safety view the aphorism "work ethic," surely a curious juxtaposition of words, as representative of the old covenant. This paradigm celebrates the job above all else. Team players count the most; the job comes first; no sacrifice is too great.

Police supervisors, socialized within this old covenant, operate in a world that expects human carnage as a by-product. Work ethic represents a "code" for doing whatever it takes, and, perhaps, the only ethic involved is the certainty that the job must be done. Lost in this reasoning is the moral responsibility that supervisors hold for the fair and ethical treatment of officers and their families. As a practical matter, getting the job done through people requires consideration of, and for, those very people.

The Price of Work Addiction

Perhaps, Chief Smith represents an extreme example of the dangers inherent in the work-addicted lifestyle. However, literature on work addiction asserts that work constitutes the drug of choice for some 30 percent of the population, for whom working is so vital to their emotional well-being that in fact, they have become addicted to it.[1] While the actual mortality rate for work addiction may be low, the social lethality of this behavior proves overwhelming. These unfortunate individuals are predisposed to involve themselves—and their families—in a life not unlike that of Chief Smith. Clearly, work addicts (or workaholics, the more common descriptor) cannot assess what is important in healthy lifestyle choices and, thus, experience a diminished quality of life.

Regrettably, they do not suffer alone. They unwittingly share this pain with their families and colleagues alike.

Workaholics are married to their work. Their vows to love and honor their spouses above all "others" no longer hold meaning or possibility. No spouse and no family can compete with this all-consuming obsession.

Workaholics themselves are a key contributor to the unhealthy family patterns resulting from work addiction for a number of reasons. First, they may have grown up in a dysfunctional family system where role models taught unhealthy patterns of relating to others. Research indicates that the family of origin contributes greatly to the development of the workaholic, and the roots of the workaholic's perfectionism often lie in childhood experiences.[2] In these dysfunctional homes, families reward children for good performance, not for who they are. They give praise and conditional love only whenever children perform a certain way or meet certain high expectations. In adulthood, this same need for perfection is the basis for the obsession for work—everything must be done properly and always at a very high level of competence and perfection.

Second, the need for workaholics to feel dominant and "in control" may make them less able to relate to peers. They may interact more easily with older

---

1. B.E. Robinson. *Chained to the Desk* (New York, NY: New York University Press, 1998), 3.

2. B. Killinger, *Workaholics: The Respectable Addicts* (Buffalo, NY: Firefly Books, 1991).

and younger people or those of a lower status or socioeconomic level than themselves. This need for continually being in control of themselves and in charge creates tension in family relationships. The one constant involved in this work mind-set devalues the quality of social interactions. Loved ones have a reasonable expectation that time spent together is time well spent and, therefore, should not be made to feel that such time comes at the expense of personal productivity. Loved ones can sense "just going through the motions." The same holds true for relationships with peer groups and clients. People have a strong sense for those who are too busy to make time to properly address issues. Conflict becomes inevitable, and everyone "gets drawn into the act by waltzing around the workaholic's schedule, moods, and actions."[3]

Chief Smith was the proud father of two sons, ages 10 and 14. His wife of 18 years, a stay-at-home mother, formed a close relationship with the children, having adjusted to the irregular and long hours of the chief's workday. After his death, Mrs. Smith explained that her husband lived on the periphery of the family's life. She said that whenever he spent time with her and their children, he seemed to do so grudgingly, as though they were depriving him of valuable time away from his office. She noted that sometimes when he was home, he only slept and never interacted with the family. She also spoke about going to family gatherings, such as birthday parties, with only the children and finding it hard to explain to friends and family that her husband was either sleeping or working on his day off, rather than celebrating a special occasion. She thought that he ignored his family, and she felt taken for granted and unwanted. Other times, he came home and treated the three of them like the police officers he supervised. He was demanding, controlling, and very jealous of her close relationship with their children. She never knew which personality he would exhibit.

The self-imposed behavior of work addiction also causes physical symptoms. Excessive pumping of adrenaline resulting in abnormal blood pressure, heart trouble, stomach sensitivity, nervousness, and the inability to relax under any circumstances are commonplace. Workaholics report feeling pressure in their chests, dizziness, and light-headedness.[4] Obviously, any longterm stress that manifests such symptoms as these can result in dangerous health consequences of many types. Chief Smith's protracted work addiction led to serious illness and his ultimate, untimely death.

Those people obsessed with work share the traits of others with such addictions as substance abuse, food dependencies, or sexual compulsions. A clas-

---

3. Supra note 1, 75.
4. Supra note 2.

sic definition of a workaholic describes "a person whose need for work has become so excessive that it creates noticeable disturbance or interference with his bodily health, personal happiness, and interpersonal relations, and with his smooth social functioning."[5] The unique difference between work addiction and other addictions, however, is that supervisors often sanction work addiction. Supervisors and peers admire this so-called work ethic, and it can be both financially and professionally rewarding.

Without question, healthy work can provide a sense of accomplishment and greatly enhance an individual's well-being. Employees who work hard, with great energy and dedication, are not necessarily addicted to their work. Most of the time, they thoroughly enjoy their work. However, the key is their ability to maintain a balance in their lives so that their work does not consume them.

Workaholics, on the other hand, become gradually more emotionally crippled as they become embroiled with the demands and expectations of the workplace. They are "addicted to control and power in a compulsive drive to gain approval and success."[6] The obsession with work grows out of the workaholic's perfectionism and competitive nature. As with other addictions, work is the "fix," the drug that frees the workaholic from experiencing the emotional pain of the anger, hurt, guilt, and fear in the other areas of the workaholic's life. Workaholics constantly focus on work, seeking to meet their personal emotional needs through their professions.

With this information in mind, law enforcement supervisors must understand the dangers that work addiction presents. These supervisors also must remember that they have an ethical responsibility to intervene when they observe the telltale signs of the work-addicted personality.

A New Covenant

Perhaps, the poet Robert Frost had Chief Smith in mind when he observed, "By working faithfully 8 hours a day, you may eventually get to be boss and work 12 hours a day." Certainly, expectations run high in the law enforcement profession. Establishing and maintaining relationships creates tremendous demands on time, resources, and energy; life balance easily becomes lost. The wise boss must understand and accept this reality.

Twenty-first century police management has embraced a sea of change. Police supervisors now routinely use technology to gather and analyze data across the full spectrum of police performance measures, and, more important, they

---

5. W.E. Oates, *Confessions of a Workaholic* (New York, NY: Abingdon Press, 1971), 4.
6. Supra note 2, 6.

hold officers accountable for results. Today, supervisors acknowledge a new covenant, which demands that they set out quantifiable work standards to measure work performance.

Prudent and ethical supervisors must measure subordinate productivity in many ways. They must consider the relative limits of what can be reasonably achieved by different officers, with diverse skills and abilities, across the spectrum of assignments and work shifts, as well as family and personal situations. Supervisors must understand that officers have different tolerance levels to manage the personal, as well as the professional, issues that they encounter. Most important, commanders must realize that the quickest route to supervisory negligence is a shortsighted focus on results, not people.

Conclusion

While law enforcement professionals should possess a strong sense of duty and responsibility for the public's welfare, they must not forget the well-being of their families, friends, and, most important, themselves. The sad lesson of Chief William Smith demonstrates the need for officers to take the long-term view, beyond the crisis of the moment. Thomas Merton, a Trappist monk and prominent author, said, "We cannot be happy if we expect to live all the time at the highest peak of intensity. Happiness is not a matter of intensity, but of balance and order and rhythm and harmony." The real challenge for law enforcement professionals rests with at least seeking, if not achieving, that balance for their families, their peers, their communities, and, most of all, themselves. In so doing, they will become better spouses, friends, coworkers, and officers who value their work, but do not let it overwhelm their lives.

Discussion Questions

1. The term *work ethic* represents a "code" for what type of behavior?
2. What does the literature on work addiction assert?
3. What evidence was provided to support the assertion that workaholics do not suffer alone?
4. What physical symptoms are caused by the self-imposed behavior of work addiction?
5. What are the unique differences between work addiction and other addictions?
6. In what ways can prudent and ethical supervisors measure subordinate productivity?

Table 1
Work-Addiction Risk Test

To find out if you are a workaholic, rate yourself on each of the statements below, using a rating scale of 1 (never true), 2 (sometimes true), 3 (often true), or 4 (always true). Put the number that best describes your work habits in the blank beside each statement. After you have responded to all 25 statements, add up the numbers for your total score. The higher your score, the more likely that you are a workaholic, whereas the lower your score, the less likely that you are a workaholic.

___ 1. I prefer to do most things myself, rather than ask for help.

___ 2. I get impatient when I have to wait for someone else or when something takes too long.

___ 3. I seem to be in a hurry and racing against the clock.

___ 4. I get irritated when I am interrupted while I am in the middle of something.

___ 5. I stay busy and keep many irons in the fire.

___ 6. I find myself doing two or three things at one time, such as eating lunch, writing a memo, and talking on the telephone.

___ 7. I overcommit myself by accepting more work than I can finish.

___ 8. I feel guilty when I am not working on something.

___ 9. It is more important that I see the concrete results of what I do.

___10. I am more interested in the final result of my work than in the process.

___11. Things just never seem to move fast enough or get done fast enough for me.

___12. I lose my temper when things do not go my way or work out to suit me.

___13. I ask the same question again, without realizing it, after I already have received the answer.

___14. I spend a lot of time mentally planning and thinking about future events while tuning out the here and now.

___15. I find myself continuing to work after my coworkers have stopped.

___16. I get angry when people do not meet my standards of perfection.

___17. I get upset when I am in situations where I cannot be in control.

___18. I tend to put myself under pressure from self-imposed deadlines.

___19. It is hard for me to relax when I am not working.

___20. I spend more time working than socializing with friends or on hobbies or leisure activities.

___21. I dive into projects to get a head start before all of the phases have been finalized.

___22. I get upset with myself for making even the smallest mistake.

___23. I put more thought, time, and energy into my work than I do into my relationships with loved ones and friends.

___24. I forget, ignore, or minimize celebrations, such as birthdays, reunions, anniversaries, or holidays.

___25. I make important decisions before I have all of the facts and a chance to think them through.

For clinical use, scores on the test are divided into three ranges. Those scoring in the upper third (67–100) are considered highly workaholic. If you scored in this range, it could mean that you are on your way to burnout, and new research suggests that family members may be experiencing emotional repercussions as well. Those scoring in the middle range (57–66) are considered mildly workaholic. If you scored in this range, there is hope. With acceptance and modifications, you and your loved ones can prevent negative long-term effects. Those scoring in the lowest range (25–56) are considered not workaholic. If you scored in this range, you are probably an efficient worker instead of a workaholic and have no need to worry that your work style will negatively affect yourself or others.

Source: B.E. Robinson, *Chained to the Desk* (New York, NY: New York University Press, 1998), 52–54. Minor editorial revisions have been made to several test items.

20

Preparing Families for the Hazards of Police Work

Sam Torres, David L. Maggard Jr., and Christine Torres

That stress is endemic in police work and a hazard of the job is well known to police chiefs and law enforcement administrators. This aspect of policing has major implications for police chiefs because police officer stress may manifest in ways that can hurt officers, their loved ones, their department, and the public: burnout, lower tolerance levels, poor judgment, substance abuse, health problems, deteriorating relationships with family and friends, low productivity, high turnover, use of excessive force, citizen complaints, and increased rates of workers' compensation claims, to name just a few.

It is essential that police administrators recognize the negative consequences associated with work-related stress and implement proactive strategies to help the officers and the department. By providing employee assistance programs and services to police officers and their families, departments can help reduce the negative consequences of officer stress for officers, families, the department, and the community. Many police executives who understand the problems of job-induced stress have implemented stress management programs for their officers. Usually these programs are only used reactively after a critical incident or when the stressors of police work build up to a point where they are creating difficulties.

The Irvine Police Department recognized that an ingredient missing from its employee assistance programs was the orientation and preparation of family and friends for the new officer's transition into the police culture. In fact, this is the entire family's transition into the law enforcement culture. By providing family members and friends with this knowledge and insight, the department hopes to help families and friends of new officers come to (1) understand the potential pitfalls of policing, (2) acquire insight into the potential attitudinal and behavioral changes in the new officer, (3) be alert to

personality and behavioral changes that may require action, and (4) be familiar with resources available for intervention before the situation deteriorates too
far and family relationships are irreparably damaged.

Orientation Program for Family and Friends

Once a person is hired as a new officer by the Irvine Police Department, a
complete and total commitment is made to provide support to assure success
through the academy, including the field training officer (FTO) program, and
the 18-month probationary period. Prior to commencing their academy training, officers complete a pre-academy program that places an emphasis on physical conditioning in order to prepare the recruits for the rigorous training that
will occur in the 24-week academy.

The Irvine Police Department conducts the orientation program on the first
day on the job with the agency for the new officer after completion of the academy. The orientation takes about two hours and includes the following phases:

- A swearing-in ceremony conducted by the chief and including the
  badge-pinning ceremony and reception line
- A reception for new officers, all sworn and nonsworn personnel, family, and friends
- An FTO program orientation for new officers
- An orientation for family and friends of new officers, complete with
  an orientation packet for those in attendance

Family and friends attend their own orientation while the new officers receive their FTO program orientation. The family orientation features four
phases. In the initial phase of the orientation, the lieutenant responsible for
professional development services welcomes the new officer's family and friends,
and briefly explains the objectives of the orientation. One of the major goals
of the orientation is to help family and friends understand the attitude and
culture of policing and to prepare them to understand and address problems
that inevitably will occur as a result of their loved one's new career in policing.

Orientation Packet

During the second phase of the orientation for family and friends, the department's human resource specialist explains the content of the packet that is
provided family needs to know what the new officer will be experiencing on

the job. Communication is emphasized repeatedly as a major method of minimizing stress-related problems. Other issues presented include the need to be aware of the various resources and support available, and the need to be aware of behavioral cues indicating potential problems. At all phases of the presentation, family and friends are encouraged to ask questions.

At a recent orientation, the new officers were slightly older than most recruits. Many were making a transition into law enforcement after having careers elsewhere, and several had children. The orientation was of particular importance to them and their families.

A Tour of the Police Department

In the fourth and last phase of the orientation, the participating lieutenant takes the spouses, parents, friends, and children on a tour of the police department. The tour includes an examination of the police vehicle that their loved one would be driving. Needless to say, the presentation of the police vehicle was particularly enjoyable to the children who participated. At each point in the tour, the lieutenant took care to describe what each area would mean to the new officer. He said of the patrol car, for example, "This is where dad will write his reports." There were many informal questions during the tour.

The general feeling of family and friends was one of appreciation that the department cared enough about the new officers and their families to take the time to introduce them to police work and the potential pitfalls of the job. The orientation program appears to be most beneficial to the spouses and intimate partners of new officers, since it is they who will be exposed to any attitudinal and behavioral changes of the officer. It is precisely these families that will quickly experience the stressors when their officer-parent begins to miss holidays, school events, and children's soccer or baseball games. The families of this group of officers, it is felt, need to be educated and to understand, at the outset, the potential stressors of the law enforcement career and the constructive coping mechanisms and resources for dealing with problems.

Issues to Consider for the Next Orientation

One challenge of the program was to prevent a police spouses club from developing. While this was not necessarily viewed as undesirable, it was concluded that it would not serve the best interests of the new officer or the department at this stage, because it is likely that several new officers will not be successful during the FTO program or their probationary period. It is distressing when a new officer is not successful, and the formation of a strong bond to peers and the department in the form of a spouses club makes the separation more difficult. The goal is to be supportive of new officers and their loved ones while avoiding the development of a strong bond, at least during the FTO and probationary period.

Administrators and staff identified two ways to improve the orientation for family and friends. The first way is to modify each orientation to serve the particular needs of that officer group, as one group may be composed largely of older-than-average officers who are married and have children while another group may be younger, single, and have no children. The second way is to present a more balanced perspective of police work by discussing the benefits and satisfaction that frequently come with a career in law enforcement, even as we prepare friends and family to understand and respond to the stresses of police life.

A letter from the wife of one new police officer provides a snapshot of Irvine's family orientation program. She writes: "The reception, the tour, the time you took to put the package together with the book, the time for questions, and the way everyone extended themselves to the families was truly meaningful. As we look forward to our future entwined with this organization, know that I am truly grateful for the generous support and reassurance you have shown us all."

Discussion Questions

1. The Irvine Police Department recognized there was a certain ingredient missing from their employee assistance program. What was the missing ingredient and what did they do to compensate for it?

2. Why did the Irvine Police Department conclude that it would not serve the best interests of the new officers of the department to start a police spouses club?

21

Homicide-Suicide in Police Families: Aggression Full Circle

John M. Violanti

"Suicidal individuals are profoundly aggressive"
(Buie & Maltsberger, 1989)

Palermo (1994) suggested that homicide-suicide should be considered as an extension of aggression first turned inward in the form of suicide. He contends that the perpetrator acts primarily out of a realistic sense of loss, which might be, at times, compounded by psychological and sociological factors. In his view, the perpetrator is unable to accept the failure of what he thought was a satisfactory relationship. The perpetrator is viewed as an aggressive individual who hides behind a façade of self-assertion, is unable to withstand the reality of an unexpected rejection, and possibly a drastic life change. He commits suicide after killing his extended self.

This paper describes some of the possible antecedents of homicide-suicide in police families. Police officers themselves are considered to be at increased risk for suicide, and such self-aggression may be easily extended to others (Violanti, in press). There are certain factors in policing that increase the risk of homicide-suicide, including aggression, domestic violence, violence exposure, the availability of lethal weaponry, and work-related attributes of police officers. Additionally, this paper will provide a description of police homicide-suicide cases.

Background: Homicide-Suicide

Although homicide-suicide has a low rate of occurrence nationwide, it has a profound impact on the police officer's children, extended family, community, and department (Morton, Runyan, Moracco, et al., 2003). Past studies of homicide-suicide have estimated rates of occurrence in the United States to be between 0.2 and 0.38 per 100,000 persons annually (Bossarte, Simon, & Barker, 2006; Marzuk, Tardiff, & Hirsch, 1992; Barraclough & Harris, 2002). Homicide-suicide incidents usually include one victim and one perpetrator. In a majority of incidents the perpetrator is male, older than the victim, and is likely to be Caucasian (Bossarte et al., 2006). A history of depression and/or mental illness is also common among perpetrators (Rosenbaum, 1990).

Victims of these incidents are more likely to be women who have separated or are divorced from their partners. In previous studies of homicide-suicides, more than 95% of the perpetrators were known to the victims. Most often, the perpetrator was a former or current husband or other intimate partner with the homicide taking place in the home of the victim (Bossarte et al., 2006; Chan, Beh, & Broadhurst, 2004). The perpetrator is more likely to die by suicide when the motive is related to possessiveness/jealousy, sickness, or stress and these incidents are more likely to be premeditated rather than a homicide alone (Dawson, 2005). The majority of deaths associated with homicide-suicides in the United States involve a firearm, with handguns being used most frequently. Other weapons associated with homicide-suicide incidents include knives, blunt objects, and motor vehicles; other methods of homicide have included strangling/asphyxiation, poisoning, and physical assault (Violence Policy Center, 2002).

An interesting study recently conducted by Bossarte et al., 2006 provided important information on homicide-suicide in the United States. Sixty-five incidents were identified for the year 2003; 144 incidents for the year 2004. In 2003, with seven states reporting, there were 65 homicide-suicide incidents, including 84 homicide victims (homicide rate = 0.230/100,000 persons) and 65 suicides (suicide rate = 0.177/100,000 persons). In 2004, with 13 states participating, there were 144 homicide/suicide incidents, including 164 homicides (homicide rate = 0.238/100,000 persons) and 144 suicides (suicide rate = 0.205/100,000). Among male perpetrators, nearly one third (30.6%) of those who killed their intimate partner ($n = 438$) also ended their own lives, while only 1.7% of those who killed a non-intimate ($n = 3459$) also killed themselves.

Homicide-Suicide in Police Families

The Police Occupation: Exposure to Aggression and Violence

Police officers work in an occupational culture premised on violence. They also have firearms available, a lethal method for both suicide and homicide. Police officers may be more prone to violence at home due to their exposure at work. Studies have shown that the estimated incidence of domestic violence among police officers (25-40%) is significantly higher than in the general population (16%; Pam, 2001). Because of job-related factors, police officers appear to be disproportionately at risk for homicide-suicide. They have access to guns, which some use as instruments of violence against others or themselves, usually with lethal results. Domestic violence appears to be heavily implicated in police homicide-suicide. The police culture encourages control, aggression, authoritarianism, domination, a strong sense of entitlement, and other conduct that correlates with aggressive behavior at home (Pam, 2001).

Exposure of police officers to violence and aggression may increase the risk of homicide-suicide. Several studies have suggested associations of suicide and aggression (Romanov et al., 1994). Farberow and colleagues (1990) compared suicide completers with accident victims, and concluded that suicide completers were more likely to have histories of angry outbursts. Other associations noted in relation to suicide are hostility and irritability. Officers considering suicide may be more likely to have a history of violence and act violently in a greater variety of relationships, especially spousal (D'Angelo, 2000).

One of the major determinants of police suicide is relationship problems (Violanti, 1997). The aggression and rage developed from bad relationships in police families can provide a direct route to homicide-suicide as well. A link between severe domestic violence, partner estrangement, and suicide has been firmly established in studies of homicide-suicide (Felthous & Hempel, 1995; Marzuk et al., 1992) and homicide alone (Wilson & Daly, 1993). Partner relationship disruptions preceding completed suicide such as divorce, separation due to arguments, breakup of steady dating, and serious arguments with a romantic partner leading to a change in the relationship have previously received attention (Heikkinen & Lonnqvist, 1995; Rich, Warsradt, Nemiroff, Fowler, & Young, 1991). Murphy and colleagues (1992) concluded that disruptions in partner relationships were the most prevalent type of disruption preceding homicide-suicide. Similarly, spousal separations were judged to be the primary precipitants for suicide more often in younger than older men and more often in men than women (Heikkinen et al., 1992).

Police Domestic Violence: A Precursor to Homicide-Suicide?

The escalation of violence from street to home is reflected in domestic violence in police families. If not stopped, violence in the home can continue to escalate to the level of deadly consequences. Two studies on police domestic violence present a detailed analysis. In the first study, Neidig and colleagues (1992a) surveyed 385 male officers, 40 female officers, and 115 female spouses attending in-service training and police conferences. This study included measures on demographics, work-related factors, and a Conflict Tactics Scale. Results indicated 25% of male and 27% of female officers reported minor assaults on their spouses. Only 3% of the male and none of the female officers reported severe assaults on their spouses. The overall rates of violence remained consistent across respondents, ranging from 37% to 41%. When compared to civilian and military populations, police rated higher in all aggressive acts except those involving severe violence (Straus, Gelles, & Steinmetz, 1980).

Neidig et al. (1992a) also focused on work-related variables. The highest rate of domestic violence existed among narcotics and patrol officers, officers working night shifts, officers working more than 50 hours a week, and officers who used more than 19 sick days a year. A second study by Neidig and colleagues (1992b) yielded similar results. Surveying a sample of 1,042 police and auxiliary officers at a national Federation of Police (FOP) conference, they found approximately 24% of male and 22% of female officers reported relationship violence. Police officers also had a higher annual incidence of marital aggression when compared to civilian populations.

A study by the Southwestern Law Enforcement Institute (1995) stands among the first to survey police agencies about the problem of police domestic violence. Of the 123 departments responding, approximately 29% reported that domestic violence cases had increased. A large percentage of departments (79%) attributed such an increase to an increase in reporting due to changing social attitudes and values. Roughly 45% stated they have no specific policy for dealing with domestic violence and generally handled them on a case-by-case basis. When asked about discipline following a first-sustained offense, approximately 52% imposed counseling upon the offending officer. After a second sustained offense, approximately 48% replied that suspension and days off without pay served as proper discipline.

An investigation by the Los Angeles Board of Police Commissioners, Domestic Violence Task Force, Office of the Inspector General (1997), provided a comprehensive view of domestic violence in the Los Angeles Police Department (LAPD) from 1990 to 1997. Overall, the LAPD findings indicated the department sustained 40% of the 227 reported cases of domestic violence from 1990 to 1997. Discipline imposed appeared extremely light upon examination of the facts of each case. Alcohol abuse appeared a prominent factor in many of the cases. Additionally, the study found approximately 31% of all allegations involved repeat offenders. Only 6% of all reported incidents concluded with an arrest within the city limits of Los Angeles, while 16% resulted in arrest by jurisdictions outside the city limits.

Kirschman (1997) suggested a correlation with violence in police families: type of work assignment, sleep deprivation due to long hours and shift work, burnout, job dissatisfaction, poor coping skills, and excessive sick leave. The legitimate use of aggression often becomes necessary in policing, but such aggression may spill over into the officer's home life. Officers can become desensitized to verbal, physical, and emotional violence because they have become second nature due to work exposures (D'Angelo, 2000). D'Angelo suggests that police officers can actually become addicted to violence which involves the inability to control the amount, frequency, or duration of violence. The expression of anger and rage progresses over time with increases in amount and severity. Such interactions can ultimately result in homicide-suicide.

Police Alcohol Use and Homicide-Suicide

Alcohol use has long been characterized as a problem among police officers (Richmond, Wodak, Kehoe, & Heather, 1998; McNeill, 1996, McNeill & Wilson, 1993; Violanti, Marshall, & Howe, 1985). Davey, Obst, and Sheehan (2000) utilized the Alcohol Use Disorders Identification Test (AUDIT) on a large sample of police officers and found that 32% scored at risk for harmful alcohol consumption range. Richmond, Kehoe, Hailstone, and colleagues (1999) found that 48% of their male and 40% of their female police sample were drinking alcohol to an excess. Alcohol use was even higher among younger police officers.

It is not uncommon to find a synergistic effect of alcohol use and suicide. Violanti (2004) suggested that certain traumatic police work exposures increased the risk of high level posttraumatic stress disorder (PTSD) symptoms, which subsequently increased the risk of high alcohol use and suicide ideation. The combined impact of PTSD and increased alcohol use led to a ten-fold increase risk for suicide ideation.

Alcohol use is a common risk factor in homicide-suicides (Bossarte et al., 2006). In a review of factors associated with perpetration of a homicide followed by suicide where toxicological information was available, 34% of the perpetrators had detectible blood alcohol content during postmortem exams and other substances were identifiable in 18% of that same group (Morton, Runyan, Moracco, et al., 2003).

Methods

Data on police homicide-suicides were collected from police_dv@yahoogroups.com, a website devoted to topics concerning domestic violence and related problems in police families. Accounts of police homicide-suicide cases were extracted from newspaper accounts of the incidents described on the website. A sample of 29 homicide-suicide cases were collected, ranging from January 1, 2003 to February 28, 2007. There were several newspaper articles on each incident, providing increased robustness of information for the present study. While some may question the validity of newspaper reports, Rainey and Runyan (1992) point out that newspapers are a viable source of information for intentional injury surveillance. They found that newspaper reports were decidedly more complete for variables of interest than reports filed with governmental officials in the area of the event, and have potential value in raising public awareness.

Results

Table 1 provides a descriptive analysis of characteristics of the police homicide-suicide incident.

Table 1.
Descriptive Characteristics of the Police Homicide-Suicide Sample

Homicide Victim		
Year of occurrence	n	(%)**
2003	1	3.4
2005	7	24.1
2006	15	51.7
2007*	3	10.3
Age of victim	n	(%)**
7-30 yrs	8	38%
31-40 yrs	9	42%
41-56 yrs.	4	15%
Gender of victim	n	(%)
Male	5	17
Female	24	83
Relationship to perpetrator	n	(%)
Wife/ex-wife	16	55
Girlfriend/ex-girlfriend	8	28
Child	3	11
Husband	2	6
Homicide-Suicide Perpetrator		
Age of perpetrator	n	(%)**
24-35 yrs	6	35
36-40 yrs	6	35
41-57 yrs	5	30
Gender of perpetrator	n	(%)
Male	27	93
Female	2	7

Weapon used	*n*	(%)
Service Firearm	26	90
Other	2	10
Rank level	*n*	(%)
Patrol officer	15	52
Higher rank	14	48
Type of department	*n*	(%)
Local	22	76
State	6	21
Federal	1	3
Circumstances		
Motivation for act	*n*	(%)**
Divorce/estrangement	10	35
Domestic violence	12	42
Marital problems	2	7
Other	1	4
Presence of domestic violence	*n*	(%)
Yes	18	62
No	11	38
Past domestic violence	*n*	(%)
Yes	20	70
No	9	30

N = 29
*—as of February, 2007
**—% do not add up to 100% due to missing cases

Based on reporting frequency, Table 1 suggests that police homicide-suicides are increasing yearly. There were approximately twice as many cases reported in 2006 as in the two previous years. The mean age of the homicide victim was approximately 33 years of age ($SD = 10.2$); approximately 39 years ($SD = 8.3$) was the mean age for the perpetrator. The majority of homicide victims were women ($n = 24$; 83%), however five of the victims were men killed by women police officer perpetrators. The primary weapon employed was police service firearm (90%). Most incidents occurred on the local police departmental level (76%) as opposed to state and federal level departments. The use of alcohol before or during the incident could not be determined from the data available. However, Comstock, Mallonee, Kruger, et al. (2003) reported that it is common to find alcohol use in the majority of homicide-suicide cases. Similar to the majority of nationwide homicide-suicides, the homicide victim was primarily a spouse or female acquaintance. In three cases, a child was also killed by the perpetrator.

A Description of Police Homicide-Suicide Cases

The following case descriptions are presented to further enhance an understanding of the police homicide-suicides in this sample.

Case 1

A county deputy jailer was fatally shot inside her home early Sunday in what police are calling a domestic-violence killing. The woman, 42 years of age, was shot in the chest in her home shortly after midnight Sunday. She died several hours later. The killing marks the third time in less than a week that domestic violence turned deadly. As authorities searched for the man Sunday in Tennessee and Arkansas, her car, which was stolen after the shooting, was found about 12:40 p.m. The body of a man was inside the car, dead from a gunshot. Police were working to identify the man. Before the woman died, she identified the man who shot her as a corrections officer. Police have identified a corrections officer as the man they say killed his ex-girlfriend, and then himself in a domestic violence incident that turned deadly.

Case 2

A birthday argument between a guard and his wife escalated into a homicide-suicide last Wednesday night. Both were found dead on the second floor of their home just before 11 p.m. According to police, he shot his wife with a 9 mm pistol and then turned the gun on himself. Neighbors reportedly saw the couple arguing outside their home both earlier in the week and in the hours before the shooting. The husband believed his wife was having an affair with a co-worker. She had threatened a month earlier to leave him, friends said.

Case 3

A 33-year-old Police Deputy Inspector shot his 28-year-old wife several times, killing her. It happened on Friday night during an argument the couple had in their car. The officer had earlier approached his wife in a cafeteria and ordered her into the car. He later committed suicide. During the month prior to the homicide, the wife told friends she felt threatened and afraid. However she never filed any claims or notified the police. He was well-known as a campaigner against domestic violence, only weeks earlier receiving praise for his efforts in the protection of women.

Case 4

A county Sheriff's Office jailer shot his 4-year-old son, his wife, and then himself. The jailer called 911 and informed the dispatcher of the situation prior to turning the weapon on himself. Shortly after the killings, the Sheriff said that the jailer had been in good spirits and had not exhibited signs of depression or agitation at any time prior to the homicides. Last week, the Sheriff investigated allegations made by the jailer's wife, accusing the sheriff's office of not acting on information regarding abuse at the hands of her husband. The wife's father said Friday that he had contacted County officials multiple times to report domestic abuse, but officials did not act. He alleges his daughter was the victim of physical abuse, and said he had witnessed his daughter with black eyes.

Case 5

Sheriff kills wife, then himself—Two people are dead after an apparent homicide-suicide Saturday evening, the first violent deaths in the county this year. The county Sheriff said the wife died of multiple gunshot wounds at the hands of her estranged husband, 34, moments before he turned the gun on himself. The incident happened just before 5 p.m. at the residence of her brother. Evidently they had been having troubles. She died the same day she had left her husband and had gone to stay with her brother. Just before 5 p.m., the wife was sitting in her car in a relative's driveway just when the husband, 34, walked up to the vehicle and shot her several times. The family had three children, a grown child, a teenaged son who was at the residence when the incident occurred, and a seven-year-old daughter.

Case 6

A detective was stabbed and shot to death by her estranged husband yesterday—in front of their three children—before he turned the gun on himself, police said. About 2 p.m., the husband took a large kitchen knife and stabbed his wife several times in the back and torso, the police said, then took her semiautomatic handgun and shot her in the head. He then went outside and fatally shot himself—all while their three young children were home. Almost 18 months before she died, cops were called to their house when her husband threw a block of knives at her and then picked up one of them to threaten her. She declined to press charges. A major obstacle to a successful prosecution is that often the victim, because of fear or other concerns, will make a complaint, then later recant.

Case 7

Officers arrived at the home where an officer lived with his 29-year-old wife. The two were found dead inside the home. Information from family and friends indicate they were having some problems. The fatal gunshot wound to the officer appeared to have been self-inflicted, the chief said. Relatives and neighbors have told investigators the couple was having marital problems. They believe the wife was suffocated.

Case 8

The bodies of officer, 52, and his wife, 50, were found inside their home about 7:30 p.m. Monday, after neighbors saw the couple argue in the front yard and heard shots fired in the home a short time later, police said. The wife filed for divorce last week, police said. Officer worked for the police force for 17 years, police said.

Conclusion

Data from the present sample suggest that homicide-suicide in police families appears to be increasing. However, the present results should be interpreted with caution due to the small sample size and possible reporting bias to the website. It is likely, however, that the number of homicide-suicide cases reported is much lower than the actual number. In this sense our sample estimate is quite conservative and should serve only as a first look at this tragic topic.

The present results suggest that domestic violence coupled with exposure to violence and aggression which police officers encounter may be common triggers for homicide-suicide in police families. While exposure to violence at work cannot be changed, the extension of such violence into the police family can be reduced. The key to prevention of homicide-suicide may thus lie with reduction of domestic violence. Many departments are now considering a formal policy to deal with this problem. The Los Angeles Police Domestic Violence Task Force (1997, p. 39), for example, provided recommendations:

- Create specialized unit within Internal Affairs Division with the primary responsibility of conducting investigations of officers involved in domestic violence situations.
- Treat offending police officers no differently than any other citizen. A crime report should be taken in every instance where a crime is alleged or there exists evidence that a crime occurred. Make an arrest in every legally mandated instance.
- Refer every domestic violence investigation with prima facie evidence of criminal misconduct to the appropriate prosecuting agency in a timely manner.
- Do not discontinue domestic violence investigations merely because the victim recants or indicates unwillingness to testify in disciplinary hearings.
- Mandate termination of employees in serious cases of domestic violence where officers demonstrate by a convincing pattern that they cannot control their abusive conduct.

- Increase suspensions for sustained acts of domestic violence in length and severity. Mete out long-term suspensions or terminations to those who have repeated instances of sustained allegations.
- Document sustained allegations of misconduct and consider them in performance reviews and promotions.
- Develop a Batterers Program under the direction of the Behavioral Science Services Section. Require contracts to include mandatory counseling in all sustained complaints involving domestic violence.

Difficulty in the internal detection of police domestic violence exists for other reasons. Many victims will not report domestic violence incidents to authorities because of shame, guilt, or fear of reprisal. As one police spouse stated, "You don't anger your husband when he carries a gun." In reported incidents, police administrators may not take complaints seriously. They may not fully understand the dynamics of domestic violence and thus may fail to take proper action. Other supervisors may believe ignored domestic violence problems will solve themselves (Violanti, 2001).

Recent passage of the federal Domestic Violence Gun Ban Law prohibits persons convicted of domestic violence offenses from owning or using firearms. While the law intends to decrease the risk of injury or death, it may also add to obstructing detection of police domestic violence. Officers will increasingly hesitate to report other officers for domestic violence because such officers will have their firearms taken away and will likely lose their jobs. Chief John W. Lamb, head of the Denver Police Department's Civil Liability Bureau, succinctly stated, "The police department has no unarmed positions, so if this law is not changed, it will be career ending for those affected by it. If you can't carry a gun, you can't do your job" (cited in Clark, 1997).

We hope that this first attempt to categorize possible antecedents and demographics of police homicide-suicides will help to stimulate further research on this issue. Many national databases such as the National Violent Death Reporting System (NVDRS) are in the process of providing linkages of homicide-suicide incidents. With the addition of occupational linkages, such databases will allow a more comprehensive picture of this tragedy in police families.

References

Barraclough, B., & Harris, C. (2002). Suicide preceded by homicide: the epidemiology of homicide-suicide in England and Wales 1988-1992. *Psychological Medicine, 32,* 577-584.

Bossarte, R.M., Simon, T.R., Barker, L. (2006). Characteristics of homicide followed by suicide incidents in multiple states, 2003-04. *Injury Prevention, 12* (Suppl. II): ii33-ii38.

Buie, D.H., & Maltsberger, J.T. (1989). The psychological vulnerability to suicide. In D. Jacobs & H.N. Brown (Eds.), *Suicide: Understanding and responding* (pp. 59-72). Madison, CT: International Universities Press.

Chan, C.Y., Beh, S.L., & Broadhurst, R.G. (1998). Homicide-suicide in Hong Kong 1989-1998. *Forensic Science International, 140,* 261-267.

Clark, J.R. (1997). Police careers may take a beating from fed domestic violence law. *Law Enforcement News, XXIII,* 1-3.

Comstock, R.D., Mallonee, S., Kruger, E., et al. (2003). Epidemiology of homicide-suicide events: Oklahoma, 1994-2001. *American Journal of Forensic Medicine Pathology, 26,* 229-235.

D'Angelo, J. (2000). Addicted to violence: The cycle of domestic abuse committed by police officers. In D.C. Sheehan (Ed.), *Domestic violence by police officers* (pp 149-161). Washington, DC: U.S. Government Printing Office.

Davey, J.D., Obst, P.L., & Sheehan, M.C. (2000). The use of AUDIT as a screening tool in the police workplace. *Drug and Alcohol Review, 19,* 49-54.

Dawson, M. (2005). Intimate femicide followed by suicide: Examining the role of premeditation. *Suicide & Life-Threatening Behavior, 35,* 76-90.

Farberow, N.L., Kang, H.K., & Bullman, T.A. (1990). Combat experience and postservice psychosocial status as predictors of suicide in Vietnam veterans. *Journal of Nervous and Mental Disease, 178,* 32-37.

Felthous, A.R., & Hempel, A. (1995). Combined homicide-suicides: A review. *Journal of Forensic Sciences, 40,* 846-857.

Heikkinen, M.E., & Lonnqvist, J.K. (1995). Recent life events in elderly suicide: A nationwide study in Finland. *International Psychogeriatrics, 7,* 287-300.

Kirschman, E. (1997). *I love a cop: What police families need to know.* New York: Guilford Press.

Los Angeles Board of Police Commissioners (1997). Domestic violence in the Los Angeles Police Department: How well does the Los Angeles Police Department police its own? Report of the Domestic Violence Task Force. Office of Inspector General. Los Angeles, CA.

Marzuk, P.M., Tardiff, K., & Hirsch, C.S. (1992). The epidemiology of homicide-suicide. *Journal of the American Medical Association, 267*(3), 3179-3183.

McNeill, M. (1996). Alcohol and the police workplace factors associated with excessive intake. Research Unit. Report series 119. South Australia: Nation Police Research Unit.

McNeill, M., & Wilson, C. (1993). Alcohol and the police workplace. National Police Research Unit. Report series 119. South Australia: Nation Police Research Unit.

Morton, E., Runyan, C.W., Moracco, K.E., et al. (2003). Partner homicide-suicide involving female homicide victims: a population-based study in North Carolina, 1988-1992. *Violence Victims, 13*, 91-106.

Murphy, G.E., Wetzel, R.D., Robins, E., & McEvoy, L. (1992). Multiple risk factors predict suicide in alcoholism. *Archives of General Psychiatry, 49*, 459-463.

Neidig, P.H., Russell, H.E., & Seng, A.F. (1992a). Interspousal aggression in law enforcement families: A preliminary investigation. *Police Studies, 15*, 30-38.

Neidig, P.H., Russell, H.E., & Seng, A.F. (1992b). FOP marital aggression survey. *National FOP Journal*, Fall/Winter, 10-15.

Palermo, G.B. (1994). Homicide-suicide—an extended suicide. *International Journal of Offender Therapy and Comparative Criminology, 38*, 205-216.

Pam, E. (2001). Police homicide-suicide in relation to domestic violence. In D.C. Sheehan & J.I. Warren (eds.), *Suicide and law enforcement*. Washington, DC: US Government Printing Office.

Police domestic violence forum—Reports on police homicide-suicides (2007). Police_dv@yahoogroups.com.

Rainey, D.Y., & Runyan, C.W. (1992). Newspapers: A source for injury surveillance? *American Journal of Public Health, 82*, 745-746.

Rich, C.L., Warsradt, G.M., Nemiroff, R.A., Fowler, R.C., & Young, D. (1991). Suicide, stressors, and the life cycle. *American Journal of Psychiatry, 148*(4), 524-527.

Richmond, R.L., Kehoe, L., Hailstone, S., Wodak, A., & Uebel-Yan, M. (1999). Quantitative and qualitative evaluations of brief interventions to change excessive drinking, smoking and stress in the police force. *Addiction, 94*, 1509-1521.

Richmond, R.L., Wodak, A., Kehoe, L. & Heather, N. (1998). How healthy are the police? A survey of lifestyle factors. *Addiction, 93*, 1729-1737.

Romanov, K., Hatakka, M., Keskinen, E., Laaksonen, H., Kaprio, J., Rose, R.J., & Koskenvuo, M. (1994). Self-reported hostility and suicidal acts, accidents, and accidental deaths: A prospective study of 21,443 adults aged 25-59. *Psychosomatic Medicine, 56*, 328-336.

Rosenbaum, M. (1990). The role of depression in couple involved in murder-suicide and homicide. *American Journal of Psychiatry, 147*, 1036-1039.

Southwestern Law Enforcement Institute (1995). *Domestic assault among police: A survey of internal affairs policies*. Richardson, Texas: Southwestern Law Enforcement Institute.

Straus, M.A., Gelles, R.J., & Steinmetz, S.K. (1980). *Behind closed doors: A survey of family violence in America.* New York: Doubleday.

Violanti, J.M. (1997). Suicide and the police role: A psychosocial model. *Policing: An International Journal of Police Strategy and Management, 20,* 698-715.

Violanti, J.M. (2001). A Partnership against Police Domestic Violence: The Police and Health Care Systems. In D.C. Sheehan (Ed.), *Domestic violence by police officers* (pp 353-364). Washington, DC: U.S. Government Printing Office.

Violanti, J.M. (2004). Predictors of police suicide ideation. *Suicide and Life-Threatening Behavior, 4,* 277-283.

Violanti, J.M. (in press). *Police suicide: Epidemic in blue,* 2nd Ed. Springfield, IL: Charles Thomas.

Violanti, J.M., Marshall, J.R., & Howe, B. (1985). Stress, coping and alcohol use: The police connection. *Journal of Police Science and Administration, 13,* 106-110.

Violence Policy Center (2002). American roulette: the untold story of homicide-suicide in the United States. 2002. Available at http://www.vpc.org.

Wilson, M., & Daly, M. (1993). Spousal homicide risk and estrangement. *Violence & Victims, 8,* 3-16.

Discussion Questions

1. What assertion was made by Palermo of the way homicide-suicide should be considered?
2. Briefly describe the backgrounds of the victims and perpetrators in homicides-suicides.
3. What was the majority of weapons used in homicides-suicides?
4. What are the job-related factors that appear to make police officers disproportionately at risk for homicide-suicide?
5. How did the author explain his assertion that one of the major determinants of police suicide is relationship problems?
6. Which group of officers had the highest rate of domestic violence?
7. What is the relationship between posttraumatic stress disorder and increased alcohol use?
8. What recommendation were made by the Los Angeles Police Domestic Violence Task Force to reduce the incidence of domestic violence in police families?
9. What are the implications of the passage of the federal Domestic Violence Gun Ban Law for police officers?

22

Agency Innovation to Promote Change: A Model Policy on Officer-Involved Domestic Violence Provides a Starting Point to Foster Healthy Police Families

Karen Oehme, Elizabeth A. Donnelly, and Zachary Summerlin

Domestic violence committed by criminal justice officers is a crime that concerns every law enforcement agency; frighteningly, it occurs at least as frequently among police families as it does in the civilian population (International Association of Chiefs of Police [IACP], 1999; Klein and Klein, 2000; Johnson, Todd and Subramanian, 2005; Waters and Ussery, 2007). In 2008, the Board of Directors of the Florida Police Chiefs Association (FPCA) reviewed a list of newspaper accounts of allegations against officers, including the choking, beating, and raping of officers' family members. The chiefs took note when researchers at Florida State University proposed developing new materials such as an online prevention curriculum, a Florida model policy about officer-involved domestic violence, and a host of other resources that would launch a statewide effort to highlight the problem and begin broad-based prevention efforts. The chiefs were enthusiastic about the program and eager for its speedy implementation. Thus, the Law Enforcement Families Partnership (LEFP)* was born, with the chiefs themselves signing on the FPCA as the pro-

---

* *Florida State University and The Verizon Foundation provide major funding for The Law Enforcement Families Partnership.*

ject's first major partner, to be followed by every statewide criminal justice agency and organization in the state (Oehme, Siebert, Siebert, Stern, Valentine, and Donnelly, 2011). The motto of the project became "Preventing Violence Begins at Home."

Later in 2009, a large LEFP stakeholder committee gathered to create Florida's Model Policy on Officer-Involved Domestic Violence, using the IACP policy and the comprehensive policies of three other states—Washington, North Dakota, and New Jersey—as a starting point (Oehme and Martin, 2011; LEFP, 2010). The purpose of the policy, included as the appendix to this article, was to provide clear procedures and protocols for preventing, investigating, reporting, and responding to domestic violence involving law enforcement officers (LEFP, 2010). Over time, the members of the committee realized that, although a statewide prevention curriculum was helpful and a model policy was crucial, much of the change necessary to prevent the problem of violence would require an ongoing effort at the individual agency level. Thus, the Florida model policy strongly emphasized the importance of agency action to take "concrete steps to prevent the crime" of officer-involved domestic violence while also guiding proper agency intervention once violence occurs. (LEFP, 2010). With the provisions of the Model Policy as a starting point, this Chapter now provides individual agencies with an additional framework and specific, innovative steps to promote prevention of officer-involved domestic violence, wellness in the law enforcement community, and safety among the families of officers.

Formal Policy Sets the Tone

For those agencies that do not have formal, written policies for responding to officer-committed domestic violence, these can be created through a review of existing policies and with the input of a local or statewide stakeholder task force. The development of and adherence to a new agency policy (or adoption of an existing policy) for addressing officer-involved domestic violence increases the likelihood that future prevention work will be strong and effective. Effective prevention can also reduce agency liability. Florida's LEFP committee notes and templates, along with an extensive compilation of LEFP recommended policies, are available online. Much of the groundwork for developing policies can be credited to the efforts of the IACP and the states that followed its blueprint. Earlier researchers also compiled policies and created a helpful checklist of important provisions for agencies to follow, but warned that the resulting policies must be utilized consistently to be effective (Lonsway, 2006).

Guiding Principles Help Shape New Agency Prevention Efforts

Once an agency has a solid intervention policy in place and follows it consistently, the agency can embark on (or enhance) agency-wide *prevention* and wellness efforts to avert domestic violence. Such work should be guided by four overarching principles that are true to the purpose of the prevention recommendations of the Florida model policy:

- safety of vulnerable family members is the highest priority;
- both the prevention of violence and officer wellness are part of the agency's commitment to its members and their families, as well as the broader community;
- diversity of the agency should be acknowledged and respected in all prevention and wellness efforts; and
- only a zero tolerance policy for officer-involved domestic violence can properly reinforce the agency's denunciation of such violence.

These principles can assist in steering the development and administration of new agency initiatives and help agency representatives structure and plan the implementation of new or revised policies. Any efforts to launch an agency-wide prevention and wellness effort should incorporate these core principles, although individual agencies may decide to expand this list.

It is worth expanding upon these basic principles to provide a complete picture of an appropriate framework for agency efforts to prevent officer-involved domestic violence. The linear nature of such an issue-driven strategic plan is likely to work well for many law enforcement agencies. First, and perhaps most crucially, the highest priority of the agency in a new prevention and wellness plan must be the safety of the vulnerable family members. Every new effort implemented by the agency to help officers should be critically examined to ensure that vulnerable family members are not inadvertently harmed by the activity. The "family" of any particular officer should be considered an expansive term, one that can incorporate spouses, children, non-married intimate partners, former spouses/partners, other family relationships, and lesbian, gay, bisexual and transgender (LGBT) relationships. Prevention efforts, then, should include consideration of the impact of officers' actions on a broadly-defined and inclusive notion of family. Agencies will likely require assistance to meet this principle; consultation with local domestic violence victim advocates and experts when planning new training or wellness efforts is almost certainly the best way to ensure that agency efforts do not unintentionally endanger family members. This principle also acknowledges that it may be the officer himself or herself who is the victim of domestic violence. The agency is best guided through such complex dynamics by a collaborative training effort with experienced community advocates.

Second, prevention and wellness training and initiatives should be considered part of the agency's commitment to employing healthy officers and its obligation to the community, which has placed an enormous amount of trust in agency authority. Agency efforts should be incorporated as a shift in the agency structure and culture, not simply considered an add-on that has a defined duration. Significant shifts in agency culture to build prevention efforts may take time; thus, such efforts should be periodic and ongoing, with reinforcing common messages and themes. Because the changes are intended to be long-term, agencies should emphasize sustainable local efforts—as opposed to, for example, a single, sizable, budget-straining meeting once a year. The agency's wellness efforts should always encourage help-seeking before serious problems occur. The model policy lists nearly two dozen topics for officer training related to domestic violence, but encourages agencies to reach out into the community to explore the full range of training resources.

The range of relevant wellness considerations for officers is broad and extends beyond domestic violence to include problems such as alcohol abuse, substance abuse, post-traumatic stress disorder (PTSD), and depression, all of which have been associated with domestic violence. (Beckham, Moore, and Reynolds, 2000; Murphy and Ting, 2010; Leonard and Blane, 1992; Gortner, Gollan, and Jacobson, 1997.) However, it is important to note that alcohol, substance abuse, and other problems do not *cause* an officer to commit domestic violence; still, incorporating help-seeking strategies for these issues into the agency's strategic planning can have long-term benefits to officers, families, and the agency itself.

Third, the consideration and valuing of multiculturalism and diversity in the rank and file—including (but not limited to) gender, race, ethnicity, and sexual orientation—should be a part of all new prevention and wellness efforts. Individuals experience and interact with their cultures differently; acknowledging and valuing diversity is an important and effective way to demonstrate respect for individuals (St. Onge, Cole and Petty, 2003). This principle requires that agencies develop multicultural partnerships through outreach and create inclusive strategies for officer wellness efforts. Agencies should also make inquiries of local organizations that offer culturally specific services so that officers may feel that their life experiences and culture are respected and validated.

Finally, while the agency should incorporate prevention into its structure and help-seeking into its core mission to keep officers healthy, a zero-tolerance policy for domestic violence once it has occurred is the only way to ensure that the entire force understands the seriousness of the crime and the agency's response to it. The Florida Model Policy enumerates the responsibilities of supervisors, individual officers, and the agency itself with regard to an appropriate response to domestic violence committed by a criminal justice officer. Once an officer has committed domestic violence, prevention efforts have failed, and the officer must be held accountable. The legitimacy of the agency is at stake after such a violation occurs.

There are many ways in which an agency can embark on a prevention and wellness efforts. Listed below are several recommended practices.

Wellness Begins at the Top

The head of each agency sets the tone for the entire department. Thus, a newly announced initiative embracing healthy law enforcement families will only be taken seriously if the head of the agency him/herself is sincere about the new mission. As suggested in the tragedy in which a police chief murdered his wife and then committed suicide ("Tacoma Police Chief," 2003), other people in the community and agency know whether the head of the agency follows his own agency's rules. The LEFP included a "Readiness to Lead" tool which asks department heads to consider and address their own specific behavior before embarking on an agency-wide anti-domestic violence initiative (LEFP, 2009). The same principle should apply to issues such as alcohol abuse, PTSD, and healthy relationship training. A leader's hypocrisy will doom the effort before it starts. Similarly, administrators and supervisors should address their own private and public behavior before leading the agency effort.

Pre-Employment Screening Can Keep Troubled Candidates off the Force

As discussed in the Model Policy, agencies should screen applicants for any history of violence or aggression, including elder abuse, child abuse, domestic violence, animal abuse, substance abuse, dating violence, or stalking. Although the Model Policy does not prohibit an agency from hiring an officer with a background of any of these problems, it is certainly safer, more efficient, and more cost-effective to prevent possible offenders from joining the force in the first place than to discipline or discharge an officer already on the force.

An Individual or Team Should Be Created to Build Agency Wellness and Prevention Efforts

A person or group of people (depending on the size of the agency) should be selected within the agency and tasked with coordinating the agency's strategic plan for prevention and wellness. Such a team should identify a set of goals, then create a proposed plan of action informed in consultation with the agency head, other officers, and appropriate community members, such as local health and mental health professionals and domestic violence experts. The team should plan events and regularly submit progress reports to the agency head and officers, listing trainings, speakers, and other results of team efforts. Trainings should be considered mandatory and conducted during work hours so as to maximize officer attendance and reinforce the significance of the trainings.

Family Members Should Be Included in Specific Events and Efforts

Florida's Model Policy specifically recommends that agencies reach out to intimate partners/family members about the agency's policy on officer-involved domestic violence and provide those family members with a point of contact within the agency about local support services. Sending family members informational brochures about local services, including domestic violence resources, may also be appropriate. Involving family members in specific trainings on domestic violence can communicate the agency's condemnation of the crime. These issues should be discussed with local domestic violence advocates to ensure that vulnerable parties are not put at further risk. (For example, sending an agency mailing to a spouse of an officer who has exhibited warning signs of domestic violence could endanger that spouse.)

The Agency Should Build Community Relationships

One of the key lessons of the LEFP was that many officers were not aware whether their agency had an existing relationship with the established local domestic violence agency (Oehme and Martin, 2011). This is disconcerting, as one of the most crucial partnerships that a law enforcement agency can make is with the local domestic violence organization. These groups are active in every state (National Coalition Against Domestic Violence [NCADV], 2011), and in many communities they have been part of a collaborative group of agencies tasked with responding to domestic violence and child abuse (Lowry and Trujillo, 2008; Jackson and Garvin, 2003). Thus, they are usually well-informed about a wide spectrum of existing community services, including health care providers, mental health and substance abuse agencies, and community organizations (Goldman, Salus, and Wolcott, 2003). Such groups are also likely to have already accomplished much of the work of identifying gaps in the spectrum of community services and to have had training on the importance of collaboration.

Local Resources Can Create the Core Training

Sustained local efforts to prevent domestic violence can only succeed if agencies tap into their local resources. Training on domestic violence, PTSD, alcohol abuse, depression, job stress, workplace violence and a variety of other problems can be accomplished in conjunction with local health and mental health professionals with expertise on these issues; such professionals may be invited to the agency to speak at trainings, roll call, and special events. If the agency is in a community that has a university or community college, there may also be faculty members with relevant expertise available for training.

Speakers can draw from their own materials or use trainings in the public domain, such as those created or funded by U.S. government agencies. For example, the National Center for PTSD (NCPTSD) Training (2011) and the International Society for Traumatic Stress Studies (ISTSS) (2011) both have free online training that local professionals can use as a foundation for their own trainings. The Substance Abuse and Mental Health Services Administration (SAMHSA) also has an online alcohol abuse course (2009), and the LEFP has two free trainings on the web, one for alcohol abuse, and the other on PTSD (2010). Many materials on workplace violence are available on the Minnesota Center against Violence and Abuse (MINCAVA) website, including a Desk Reference for Recognizing and Responding to Domestic Violence in the Workplace (2011).

There are also many self-tests that officers may be encouraged to use privately which involve topics such as depression, anxiety, alcohol use, and other mental health issues. These may be tools that local experts incorporate into their trainings to help officers consider whether they should seek additional private help in the community or through the agency's Employee Assistance Program (EAP).

Employee Assistance Personnel Should Have Expertise

Before contracting with them, agencies should ensure that EAPs have expertise on the dynamics of domestic violence, as well as on the complex issues of co-occurring substance abuse and domestic violence. EAPs should also have experience in working with diverse clients on important issues such as stress reduction, PTSD, and counseling on healthy family functioning. However, if violence by any particular officer is suspected, investigation and accountability for that officer (under the dictates of the agency's policy) is appropriate— not family counseling, which can further endanger the victim.

Reinforcing Professionalism Builds Ethical Behavior

Leadership should also create opportunities to emphasize and explain to officers the professional ethics of the agency, including mandatory reporting requirements. Training opportunities can be used to remind officers that they have a duty to report crimes and serious misconduct, including domestic violence, committed by their colleagues. Although officers may be hesitant to break a "code of silence" and disclose misconduct by their colleagues (Chin and Wells, 1998, Westmarland, 2005), leadership should work toward a culture shift that instills in officers the importance of abiding by agency disclosure policies. Officers should also be provided options and clear steps for reporting major violations by others, including confidential and anonymous reporting procedures. Because officers' attitudes toward professional ethics are the strongest predictors of reporting major policy violations (Kargin, 2009), agency leaders should take the time to present training on professional conduct and reinforce with officers the mandates of their profession. Training can emphasize that the duty to report a fellow officer's domestic violence is as much of an obligation as responding quickly to a civilian crime in progress.

National Trainings Can Provide Unique Opportunities

If agencies have funds for national speakers, they may contact national organizations with the mission of ending domestic violence. "A Call to Men," for example, is an organization that conducts regional trainings with the specific mission of making men leaders in the battle against domestic violence. In 2010, the LEFP paid for scholarships to send area officers to such a conference. These trainings may not be affordable for individual agencies in the current economic environment, but several agencies might be able to join together to bring such conferences to the community. Any individual or group brought in for training should be directed to speak explicitly about officer-committed violence as well as civilian violence.

The Example of a Plan

Below is an example of how an agency might begin to frame its prevention and wellness plan.

Title: The Community Law Enforcement Agency's
Prevention and Wellness Plan

Goals:

1. To provide extensive educational opportunities for officers about the dynamics and consequences of officer-involved domestic violence, including red flags that indicate that an officer might be at a heightened risk of committing the crime.

2. To thoroughly explore resources in the community that can be utilized to help promote safe, healthy officers and law-enforcement families.

3. To provide officers with comprehensive information about community prevention and wellness resources, as well as how to access them.

4. To communicate clearly to the entire force that officers should get help when they need it, and to teach officers how to access that help.

5. To educate officers about the impact of alcohol abuse on their bodies, their families, and the force as a whole.

6. To educate officers about the dangers of job stress and provide them with advice and suggestions from (and referrals to) local mental health professionals to reduce such stress.

7. To educate officers about the signs and symptoms of PTSD and discuss local resources for treatment.

8. To communicate the agency's zero-tolerance policy on domestic violence, and emphasize the requirement of mandatory reporting of crimes and major policy violations of other officers.

9. To create an agency contact for the family members of officers.

Timeline: 24 months for the initial development, with quarterly status reviews.

Action Plan designating responsible personnel: The set of tasks designed to help each group meet the above goals. Tasks will vary by agency, and will be assigned to specific personnel to initiate and follow up.

Conclusion

There is much that individual law enforcement agencies–even small ones–can do to prevent officer-involved domestic violence and to encourage wellness among their officers. By taking advantage of community resources and pre-existing (or newly created) policies, agencies can communicate a message that they do not condone domestic violence committed by officers, and can create comprehensive strategies to meet the goal of preventing such violence. Moreover, by reaching out and maximizing existing resources, law enforcement agencies can train and educate officers to take better care of their bodies, minds, and families. The process begins with an agency policy on officer-involved domestic violence, continues through each agency's adaptation and expansion of the aforementioned strategies, and ends–with persistence, time, and effort–with an agency's success at preventing violence in the homes of its rank and file.

References

A Call to Men. (n.d.). Available at their Web site: http://www.acalltomen.org/.

Beckham, J.C., Moore, S.D., and Reynolds, V. (2000). Interpersonal hostility and violence in Vietnam combat veterans with chronic posttraumatic stress disorder: A review of theoretical models and empirical evidence. *Aggression and Violence Behavior, 5*(5), 451–466.

Chin, G. J. and Wells, S.C. (1998). The "Blue Wall of Silence" as evidence of bias and motive to lie: A new approach to police perjury. *University of Pittsburgh Law Review, 5*, 233–299.

Goldman, J., Salus, M. K., Wolcott, D., and Kennedy, K. Y. (2003). A coordinated response to child abuse and neglect: The foundation for practice. U.S. Department of Health and Human Services, Administration for Children and Families, Office on Child Abuse and Neglect. Retrieved 12-6-

2011, from http://www.childwelfare.gov/pubs/usermanuals/foundation/foundation.pdf.

Gortner, E. T., Gollan, J. K., and Jacobson, N. S. (1997). Psychological aspects of perpetrators of domestic violence and their relationships with the victims. *Psychiatric Clinics of North America, 20*(2), 337–352.

International Association of Chiefs of Police. (1999). *Police Officer Domestic Violence: Concepts and Issues Paper.* Retrieved 12-6-2011, from http://www.ncjrs.gov/ PDFFILES1/NIJ/GRANTS/181409.PDF.

International Society for Traumatic Stress Studies. (2011). *Online Continuing Education.* Available at http://www.istss.org/source/ContinuingEd/index.cfm?section=OnlineContinuingEducation.

Jackson, M., and Garvin, D. (2003). Coordinated Community Action Model. Retrieved December 8, 2011, from Minnesota Center Against Violence and Abuse (MINCAVA) Web site: http://www.mincava.umn.edu/documents/ccam/ccam.html.

Johnson, L., Todd, M., and Subramanian, G. (2005). Violence in police families: Work-family spillover. *Journal of Family Violence, 20*(1), 3–12.

Kargin, V. (2009). An investigation of factors proposed to influence police officers' peer reporting intentions. Retrieved from ProQuest Digital Dissertations. (AAT 3369984.)

Klein, R., and Klein, C. (2000). The extent of domestic violence within law enforcement: An empirical study. In D.C. Sheehan (Ed.), *Domestic violence by police officers* (pp. 225–232). Washington, D.C.: U.S. Department of Justice.

Law Enforcement Families Partnership. (n.d.) *Members, Meetings, and Minutes of the Committee on Florida's Model Policy on Officer-Involved Domestic Violence.* Committee notes available at http://familyvio.csw.fsu.edu/LEF/lef_mem.html.

Law Enforcement Families Partnership. (2009). *Readiness to Lead.* Available at: http://lefp.files.wordpress.com/2010/09/readiness_to_lead_assessment. pdf.

Law Enforcement Families Partnership. (2010). *Florida's Model Policy on Officer-Involved Domestic Violence.* Available at http://training.familyvio.csw.fsu.edu/content/docs/ FloridaModelPolicyonOfficerDV2010.pdf.

Law Enforcement Families Partnership. (2010). *Alcohol and PTSD Training.* Available at http://hpr.familyvio.csw.fsu.edu/.

Leonard, K. E., and Blane, H. T. (1992). Alcohol and marital aggression in a national sample of young men. *Journal of Interpersonal Violence, 7*(1), 19–30.

Lonsway, K. (2006). Policies on police officer domestic violence: Prevalence and specific provisions within large police agencies. *Police Quarterly, 9*(4), 397–422.

Lowry, S. M., and Trujillo, O. (2008). Cross-system dialogue: An effective strategy to promote communication between the domestic violence community, child welfare system, and the courts. Retrieved December 8, 2011, from The Greenbook Initiative Web site: http:// www. thegreenbook.info/ documents/crosssystemdialogue.pdf.

Minnesota Center Against Violence and Abuse. (2011). *Domestic violence— interventions—articles.* Available MINCAVA electronic clearinghouse Web site: http://www. mincava.umn.edu/categories/889.

Murphy, C.M., and Ting, L. (2010). The effects of treatment for substance use problems on intimate partner violence: A review of empirical data. *Aggression and Violent Behavior, 15*(5), 325–333.

National Center for Post-Traumatic Stress Disorder Training. (2011). *Course Modules.* Retrieved December 8, 2011, from http://www.ptsd.va.gov/professional/ptsd101/course-modules/course-modules.asp.

National Coalition Against Domestic Violence. (n.d). *State Coalition List.* Retrieved December 8, 2011, from Web site: http://www.ncadv.org/resources/StateCoalitionList.php.

Oehme, K., and Martin, A. (2011) A practical plan for prevention and intervention: Florida's new model policy on officer-involved domestic violence. *Criminal Justice Studies, 24*(4), 395–408.

Oehme, K., Siebert, D. C., Siebert, C. F., Stern, N., Valentine, C., and Donnelly, E. (2011). Protecting lives, careers, and public confidence: Florida's efforts to prevent officer-involved domestic violence. *Family Court Review, 49*(1), 84–106.

St. Onge, P., Cole, B., and Petty, S. (2003). *Through the Lens of Culture.* Retrieved December 8, 2011, from The National Community Development Institute Web site: http://www. ncdinet.org/media/docs/7058_ThroughtheLensofCulture.pdf.

Substance Abuse and Mental Health Services Administration. (2009). *Center for Substance Abuse Prevention's (CSAP's) Prevention Pathways.* Available at http://pathwayscourses. samhsa.gov/.

Tacoma Police Chief Shoots Wife Before Killing Himself, Authorities Say. (2003, April 23). *N.Y. Times,* Retrieved December 8, 2011, from http://www.ny-times.com/2003/04/28/ us/tacoma-police-chief-shoots-wife-before-killing-himself-authorities-say.html.

Waters, J. A., and Ussery, W. (2007). Police stress: History, contributing factors, symptoms, and interventions. *Policing: International Journal of Police Strategies and Management, 30*(2), 169–170.

Westmarland, L. (2005). Police ethics and integrity: Breaking the blue code of silence. *Policing and Society, 15,* 145–165. doi: 10.1080/104394605000 71721.

Appendix

I. Statement of Purpose

The purpose of this model policy is to establish uniform statewide guidelines that provide clear procedures and protocols for preventing, investigating, reporting, and responding to domestic violence involving officers. Officers include sworn law enforcement officers, sworn correctional officers, and sworn correctional probation officers.

II. Policy Statement

Public confidence in officers is important to agencies' ability to maintain public safety. The public must trust that officers are held to the standards of the law regarding domestic violence. Therefore agencies should:

A. Employ administrative prevention strategies to prevent domestic violence by officers.

B. Promptly respond to allegations of domestic violence by officers according to this policy and all applicable laws.

C. Give primary consideration to protection of the victim of domestic violence and enforcement of the laws.

D. Respect the due process rights of all officers, according to applicable legal precedent and collective bargaining agreements.

E. Expeditiously report and conduct thorough investigations into any allegation of an officer involved in domestic violence.

F. Train officers and seek to educate their families about domestic violence and avenues for assistance.

III. Definitions

A. Agencies—refers to Criminal Justice Agencies that employ sworn law enforcement officers, sworn correctional officers, and sworn correctional probation officers.

B. Domestic violence—as defined by F.S. 741.

C. Domestic Violence/Rape Crisis Advocacy Organization or Provider— refers to a domestic violence center or rape crisis center as defined by F.S. 39.

D. Employee—as defined by F.S. 440.02(15).

E. Family or Household Member—as defined by F.S. 741.

F. Intimate Partner of a Law Enforcement Officer—refers to a family or household member or dating relationship as defined by F.S. 741.

G. Law Enforcement Officer—as defined by F.S. 943.10.

H. Protection Order—as defined by F.S. 741.

I. Stalking—as defined by F.S. 784.048 (2).

J. Sworn Employee—includes law enforcement or correctional officer, correctional probation officer, part-time law enforcement officer, part-time correctional officer, auxiliary correctional officer, auxiliary correctional probation officer, and part-time correctional probation officer as defined in F.S. 943.10.

K. Victim—as defined by F.S. 741.

IV. Prevention through Collaboration with Domestic and Sexual Violence Advocacy Organizations.

A. Agencies should, whenever possible, collaborate with local certified domestic violence centers for mutual benefit. These centers are a valuable resource to agencies, and can offer a wide range of assistance for cross-training, victim assistance, and help in identifying ways to reduce domestic violence and sexual violence in the community. Local certified domestic violence programs may be able to assist supervisory and administrative staff with issues relating to the following:

   1. Training on warning signs of officer-involved domestic violence.
   2. Development of domestic violence training curricula.
   3. In-service training.
   4. Identification of well-known local, state, and national experts for trainings, meetings, and/or conferences.

B. Agencies should provide training, when requested, to local domestic and sexual violence victim advocacy organizations on the agencies' domestic violence policies, procedures, and protocols.

C. Agencies should identify and collaborate with other local advocacy groups that regularly assist victims. When these agencies are aware of and work with community resources and advocacy organizations, they can help connect victims, families, and children with appropriate services. Whenever possible, agencies should establish and maintain ongoing relationships with the following:

   1. Domestic and sexual violence organization advocates;
   2. Shelter staff;
   3. Hotline crisis workers;

4. Social service providers (such as homeless coalitions, emergency shelter food banks, and hospitals or other emergency medical providers);
5. Victim/witness personnel;
6. Coordinating councils/coalitions; and
7. Others knowledgeable about the challenges facing domestic violence victims.

V. Training and Education

A. Agencies should ensure that all their officers have training in the following topics related to domestic violence:
   1. The duties and responsibilities of law enforcement in response to domestic violence calls, enforcement of injunctions, and data collection.
   2. The legal duties imposed on law enforcement officers to make arrests and offer protection and assistance, including guidelines for making felony and misdemeanor arrests.
   3. Techniques for handling incidents of domestic violence that minimize the likelihood of injury to the officer and that promote safety of the victim.
   4. The dynamics of domestic violence and the magnitude of the problem.
   5. The legal rights of, and remedies available to, victims of domestic violence.
   6. Documentation, report writing, and evidence collection.
   7. Tenancy issues and domestic violence.
   8. The impact of law enforcement intervention in preventing future violence.
   9. pecial needs of children at the scene of domestic violence and the subsequent impact on their lives.
   10. The services and facilities available to victims and batterers.
   11. The use and application of sections of the Florida Statutes as they relate to domestic violence situations.
   12. Verification, enforcement, and service of injunctions for protection when the suspect is present and when the suspect has fled.
   13. Emergency assistance to victims and how to assist victims in pursuing criminal justice options.
   14. Working with uncooperative victims, when the officer becomes the complainant.

B. Training Specific to Officer-Involved Domestic Violence:
In addition to the above training, agencies should ensure that all officers take prevention training that is specific to the issues of officer-involved domestic violence.

There is free online training available through Florida State University, at http://familyvio.csw.fsu.edu, that agencies are encouraged to use. Agencies may also use training from other sources, including, but not limited to, local certified domestic violence centers, local, state, or national researchers, victim advocates, mental health professionals, or other professionals who have expertise in the issues specific to officer-involved domestic violence. Such training should include:

1. The dynamics of officer-involved domestic violence, including misuse of authority, power and control, and surveillance techniques.
2. Information about available employee-assistance programs or local resources that can help officers before violence escalates.
3. How to recognize potential indicators of domestic violence behavior by law enforcement officers.
4. How to investigate or document information on indicators of potential abusive officer behavior.
5. How to notify the immediate ranking supervisor who will inform the agency head in accordance with the agency's chain of command.
6. The consequences of officer-involved domestic violence.
7. Special considerations of victim safety and confidentiality.
8. Information about programs for victims and batterers.
9. Understanding why a victim's fear of a perpetrator may make the victim (whether civilian or officer) afraid to cooperate with responding officers. This includes, but is not limited to, a victim's fear that a perpetrator's status as an officer may mean that the officer will not be held accountable for his/her actions.

C. Informational and Resource Materials for Officer Family Outreach
Agencies are also encouraged to make available information and resources related to domestic violence to the families/spouses/partners of officers. Below are a few ways to disseminate such information, but agencies retain the discretion to use methods they deem are the most safe and appropriate:

1. Posting the domestic violence hotline number on the agency website.
2. Posting the phone number of the local domestic violence and sexual assault hotline number on the agency website.

3. Designating a specific supervisor as the officer whom family members can contact with concerns about escalating violence or other dynamics of abuse.

4. Disseminating written information (for example, in new employee packets or agency-wide with other general mailings).

VI.   Screening and Intervention

A.   Pre-Hire Screening and Investigation

While it is recognized that all agencies are required to and do perform a background check of all new lateral and entry-level applicants, agencies should make reasonable inquiries to determine whether or not the applicant has been criminally investigated, arrested or convicted of elder abuse, child abuse, domestic violence, animal abuse, dating violence, stalking and/or sexual assault-related incidents. Additionally, inquiries should be made as to whether or not the applicant has ever been the subject of an injunction proceeding or administrative action for elder abuse, child abuse, domestic violence, animal abuse, dating violence, stalking and/or sexual assault-related incidents.

In light of the significant stressors involved in the performance of the duties of an officer and the risks of hiring a person with a history of violence/aggression, agencies should exercise caution in an employment determination if the background check of an applicant reveals incidents of violence or abuse. Such incidents should warrant further review and examination of the applicant's qualification for an officer position with the agency.

B.   Post-Conditional Offer of Employment

Agencies are not required under Florida law or Florida Administrative Code to conduct psychological evaluations of candidate officers; however, if an agency does conduct such evaluations, the screening should include a focus on any indications of abusive or violent background or tendencies.

If a psychological evaluation reveals concern about violence or abuse, such concerns should warrant close examination of the applicant's qualifications, especially in light of the significant stressors that accompany officers' responsibilities.

C.   Post-Hire Intervention

1. When new officers are hired, the agency should reach out to their intimate partners/family members to introduce this policy and other relevant agency policies.

2. Agencies should engage in periodic outreach to officers and their intimate partners/family members with information on this policy, the point of contact within the agency and referrals for local support services.

VII. Responsibilities of the Officer, Supervisors, and Agency

A. Officer Responsibilities:
   1. Officers are encouraged to take personal responsibility in seeking confidential referrals and assistance from the agency to prevent a problem from escalating to the level of criminal conduct against an intimate partner.
   2. Officers who engage in the following actions may be subject to investigation and disciplinary action:
      a. Failure to report first hand or well-founded knowledge of abuse or violence committed by a fellow officer to a supervisor.
      b. Failure to cooperate with the investigation of a law enforcement officer domestic violence case (except in the case where that officer is the victim).
      c. Interference with cases involving themselves or fellow officers.
      d. Intimidation/coercion of witnesses or victims (i.e., surveillance, harassment, stalking, threatening, or falsely reporting).
   3. Officers who learn they are the subject of any criminal investigation, regardless of jurisdiction, are required to make a report to their supervisors and provide notice of the court dates, times, appearances, and proceedings in a timely fashion as determined by the agency. Failure to do so may result in investigation and disciplinary action.
   4. Officers who learn they are the subject of any protective order proceeding, whether or not the order is issued and regardless of jurisdiction, should immediately notify their supervisor and provide a copy of the order, if issued. Subject to a qualifying protection order, the officer should surrender all firearms unless the order allows for possession of the primary service weapon. Failure to do so may result in investigation and disciplinary action.

B. Supervisor Responsibilities:
   1. Supervisors should be aware and, when appropriate, document any pattern of abusive behavior potentially indicative of an officer's possible domestic violence including but not limited to the following:

a. Aggressiveness
   (1) Excessive and/or increased use of force on the job
   (2) Unusually high incidences of physical altercations and verbal disputes
   (3) Citizen and fellow officer complaints of unwarranted aggression and verbal abuse
   (4) Inappropriate treatment of animals
   (5) Unexplained increased frequency of on- or off-duty officer injuries
b. Domestic violence-related issues
   (1) Monitoring and controlling any family member or intimate partner through such means as excessive phone calling
   (2) Stalking or inappropriate surveillance of any intimate partner or family member
   (3) Frequent or repeated incidents of discrediting and/or disparaging an intimate partner or family member
c. Deteriorating work performance
   (1) Tardiness
   (2) Excessive Absences
   (3) Alcohol and drug abuse
2. When the supervisor notes a pattern of problematic behavior (as detailed above), the supervisor should:
   a. Address the behaviors through a review or other contact with the officer and document all contacts.
   b. Forward written reports capturing the behaviors to the appropriate agency official through the chain of command in a timely manner.
   c. Prepare and submit to the appropriate agency official a written request for a psychological exam/counseling by a psychologist/psychiatrist/licensed mental health professional who is knowledgeable about domestic violence or a request that the agency official direct the officer to seek assistance via the Employee Assistance Program (EAP) to access a certified program for batterers, and if such a program is not available, a counselor knowledgeable about domestic violence.
C. Agency Responsibilities
   1. The agency should inform all civilian and sworn employees of the type and extent of services offered by the contracted Employee Assistance Program (EAP) for employee-initiated counseling and

other similar assistance. This information should include relevant services for preventing and ending victimization and perpetration of domestic violence.

2. Agencies are encouraged to contract with EAPs that include professionals trained in domestic violence dynamics who are equipped
to make appropriate referrals in domestic violence cases. At a minimum, the EAP should be able to provide the employee and/or
family member with referrals to the local domestic or sexual violence advocacy organizations or providers (including certified
domestic violence center, certified rape crisis center, and Batterer's
Intervention program providers).

3. If the agency administrators or supervisors suspect that an officer is a victim of domestic or sexual violence, the agency may
offer support and inform the officer about all existing EAPs and
available services for counseling, including services offered by a
domestic violence or sexual assault advocacy organization, and
that if the officer seeks such assistance it is confidential. However, the agency should not compel a victim to acknowledge that
he/she is a victim, to seek assistance or to cooperate in any investigation against his/her abuser, and a victim's employment
should not be impacted in any way by his or her decision to seek
or decline assistance.

4. In response to observed escalating, threatening, or other problematic behaviors, or at the request of the employee or family member of an employee, the agency should provide specific information
about confidential counseling or assistance programs and may offer
or recommend intervention services to employees before an act of
domestic violence occurs. If domestic violence is suspected, referral to a domestic violence or sexual assault advocacy organization
or provider as described above in 2c above is critical.

5. A disclosure on the part of any officer, intimate partner or family member to any member of the agency that an officer has personally committed domestic violence will be treated as an admission
or report of a crime and should be investigated both administratively and criminally.

6. Agencies should anticipate that an investigation of a sworn employee may be necessary for a domestic violence crime. Thus,
agencies should develop a plan to have an agency point of contact
to assist victims, both for internal and for criminal investigations.
For internal investigations, agencies should be able to provide vic-

tims with a description of the internal affairs process, including how long it may take, the victim's role in the investigation, and what the victim can expect to occur during the process.

7. As required by F.S. 741.29 for all victims of domestic violence, the agency shall provide victims of domestic violence by agency employees contact information about public and private non-profit domestic violence services and information regarding relevant confidentiality policies related to the victim's information.

8. The agency should provide for an impartial administrative investigation and appropriate criminal investigation of all acts of domestic violence allegedly committed by a sworn employee. Administrative investigations may be conducted by the employing agency or through agreements with other law enforcement agencies.

9. Whenever any agency becomes aware that it has made a domestic violence-related arrest of an officer from another agency, the arresting agency should notify the employing agency of the arrest, the specific charge, and the time of the arrest as soon as practically possible.

VIII. Incident Response Protocol

A. Agency-Wide Response
1. All reports of possible criminal activity implicating officers as alleged perpetrators in domestic violence should be documented and forwarded to the local certified domestic violence center in accordance with F.S. 741.29(2), and the investigating agency's policies governing the handling of all reports of domestic violence by citizens.
2. The on-scene supervisor should forward a copy of the report alleging domestic violence by the officer to the agency head through the chain of command. In the event the report of domestic violence is alleged to have been committed by the agency head, prompt notification should be made to the office that appointed the agency head or to the State Attorney's Office as appropriate.
3. Follow up contact with the victim should be initiated by the victim advocate unit or a ranking officer of the investigating agency in a timely manner during the initial investigation. As permitted by law, contact should be maintained throughout the criminal and administrative investigation for the purposes of:
   a. providing information regarding safety planning and local domestic violence victim services

       b. providing copies of all incident reports at no cost

       c. advising the victim of all case developments

       d. advising the victim that if there is any violation of an injunction, harassment, violence or the threat of future violence, such behavior should immediately be reported to the law enforcement agency in the jurisdiction where it occurred, and it should also be reported to the agency's follow up contact designee.

  B. Communications Response

     1. Communications officers/dispatchers should be instructed to assign a high priority to all domestic violence calls, including those that involve or appear to involve an officer from any agency.

     2. Communications officers/dispatchers should immediately notify the supervisor on duty and the dispatch supervisor of any domestic violence call received that involves, or appears to involve, an officer, regardless of the involved officer's jurisdiction.

     3. Communications officers/dispatchers should prepare and preserve documentation of the facts and circumstances of the call, including the 911 tape, for use in potential administrative or criminal investigations.

     4. Communications officers/dispatchers should make contact with local domestic violence victim advocacy organizations, if necessary, to facilitate immediate delivery of services if requested by the victim.

  C. On-Scene Patrol Officer Response

     1. Upon arrival on the scene of a domestic violence call or incident involving an officer, the primary responding officer should immediately notify dispatch and request that a supervisor report to the scene, regardless of the involved officer's jurisdiction.

     2. Responding officers shall perform the following actions in accordance with F.S. 741.29, Florida Statutes:

       a. Obtain needed medical assistance

       b. Address the immediate safety of all parties involved

       c. Secure the scene and preserve evidence

       d. Make an arrest if probable cause exists

       e. Provide the victim with a copy of the legal rights and remedies notice

       f. Assist the victim if immediate access is requested to local domestic violence victim advocacy organizations

       g. Document the incident in a written report, whether or not an arrest is made, which includes

(1) a description of physical injuries observed, if any

(2) the grounds for not making an arrest or for making more than one arrest

(3) the fact that a copy of the legal rights and remedies notice was given to the victim

3. The written incident report should be submitted to the reporting officer's supervisor prior to the end of the officer's shift.

D. On-Scene Supervisor Response and Additional Critical Considerations

1. A patrol supervisor should respond to the scene of any domestic violence incident investigated within the agency's jurisdiction that involves an officer (regardless of whether the officer is a victim or a suspect), even if the officer is from another jurisdiction.

2. If the accused is employed by the investigating agency, the on-scene supervisor should make appropriate notifications consistent with agency policy for an employee suspected of or arrested for criminal activity.

3. If the victim is employed by the investigating agency, the on-scene supervisor should notify the victim's supervisor as soon as possible. This involvement of a supervisor is intended to be supportive, and not punitive. It is also offered to help prevent further personal and workplace violence. The agency supervisor should offer the victim all available services, including EAP information, and the contact information for the local certified domestic violence center. However, no supervisor should compel any victim to utilize such services.

4. If the involved party is an officer from another agency, the on-scene supervisor should ensure that the officer's employer is notified as soon as possible following review of the incident or arrest report.

IX. Weapons Policy

Agency policy regarding an officer's possession of weapons while under a temporary or final order of injunction or following his/her conviction for domestic violence should be consistent with state and federal laws and applicable court orders.

X. Victim Safety and Protection

A. Agencies should establish relationships with certified domestic violence centers, advocacy groups/organizations, and other resources in their community to enable them to refer victims and their children to appropriate services, including linguistically and culturally appropriate services.

B. Each agency should designate a principal contact person for the victim whose responsibility should be to inform the victim of the agency's confidentiality policies and their limitations, and ensure that victim confidentiality, including the location of the victim if the victim has moved to a "safe place," is maintained throughout the case. The designated principal contact should advise the victim of the availability of the Statewide Domestic Violence Hotline, local certified domestic violence center or other domestic violence advocacy groups/organizations to receive safety planning, shelter, legal advocacy, children's services, and identify other needs.

C. All officers should understand the potential for victim/witness intimidation or coercion by the perpetrator, and the increased danger when the victim reports the domestic violence and/or leaves an abusive partner.

D. If an officer suspects or the victim reports perpetrator intimidation or coercion, the officer should prepare a written report and submit it immediately to the investigator in charge of the case through the chain of command. The investigator in charge should seek out secondary sources of information and supplemental evidence to confirm intimidation or coercion.

E. The agency should develop a policy for instances when an officer is arrested for domestic violence. Where appropriate, the policy should provide for the relief of the accused officer's agency-issued firearms and weapons. Additionally, the policy should recommend that an inquiry be made of the victim as to whether he or she would like any other weapons removed from the home for safekeeping by the agency.

F. To the extent permitted by law, the officer(s) conducting the administrative and criminal investigations should keep the victim informed about the progress of the investigations in an effort to address the victim's needs and safety concerns during disposition of the case.

XI. Post Incident Administrative Investigation Process and Criminal Decisions

A. The agency should observe all other appropriate policies and procedures generally applicable to investigation of alleged misconduct. The agency should respect the rights of the accused employee under applicable collective bargaining agreements and law.

B. Administrative investigations should be conducted through the agency professional standards function or by an outside agency as directed by the agency head.

C. Where sufficient information exists, the agency should make appropriate restrictions to assignments, law enforcement powers, building and records access and consider administrative reassignment and/or leave.

D. In determining the proper course of administrative action, the agency may consider consulting with treatment professionals and reviewing such factors as the employee's past conduct and history of complying with agency rules.

E. Agency personnel may be ordered to undergo fitness for duty evaluation or assessment prior to any disposition, depending on circumstances and in accordance with agency policy, applicable collective bargaining agreements, and civil service standards.

Discussion Questions

1. What evidence was presented to suggest that domestic violence by police officers is as common as it is among civilians?

2. What is the motto of the Law Enforcement Families Partnership (LEFP)?

3. What is the purpose of the Florida's Model Policy on Officer-Involved Domestic Violence?

4. Who was given the credit for much of the groundwork for developing policies dealing with police domestic violence?

5. What are the four overriding principles of the Florida Model Policy on Officer-Involved Domestic Violence?

6. What do the authors mean when they write: "the 'family' of any particular officer should be considered an expansive term"?

7. As the authors note, the range of relevant wellness considerations for officers is broad and extends beyond domestic violence. What other issues were recommended to be included?

8. What did the authors recommend regarding the pre-employment screening of applicants in order to prevent future police domestic violence?

9. The authors recommended that an individual or a team should be created to build agency wellness and prevention efforts. What

specific recommendation was made regarding the goals of such a team?

10. What recommendations were made regarding involving family members in specific events and efforts as they relate to police domestic violence?

11. How can local resources be used in the core training on domestic violence prevention among police officers?

Part Six

How Does the Worst
of the Worst Affect Cops?

No discussion of police stress can occur without a full acknowledgement that the stress of law enforcement significantly differs from the stress of other occupations. While the magnitude and manifestations may parallel those experienced in other occupations, the source of the stress sets law enforcement apart. Unlike all but other crisis professions, e.g., fire and emergency medicine, only law enforcement deals on a daily basis with stress that results from the violent act of one person toward another. Only law enforcement must deal directly with the sights, sounds, smells, and emotions associated with violence, whether caused by a human being or "Mother Nature." Only law enforcement must handle the impact caused by "people pain," the vicarious stress one feels because another is going through trauma.

Maslach recognized that one response of emergency workers who are required to give "too much, too often, to other people in need" was burnout. As she observed:

> Hour after hour, day after day, health and social service professionals are intimately involved with troubled human beings. What happens to people who work intensely with others, learning about their psychological social or physical problems? Ideally, the helpers retain objectivity ... without losing their concern for the person they are working with. Instead, our research indicates, they are often unable to cope with this continual emotional stress and burnout occurs. They lose all concern, all emotional feeling for the person they work with and come to treat them in a detached or even dehumanized ways (Maslach, 16).

By its nature, police work often involves highly complex skills, considerable emotional strain and little recognition. Human suffering and death are often an intrinsic part of the work, and the often traumatic nature of police work has been found to render the police officer vulnerable to those more severe stress reactions characteristic of Post Traumatic Stress Disorder (PTSD).

So what exactly is this trauma related stress? In what kind of circumstances is it likely to occur? How does the worst of the worst affect cops? Perhaps more important, how can we begin to mitigate it? Here in Part Six, our authors will address these questions.

Earlier in this book, authors such as Miller and Palm and her colleagues have discussed the issue of vicarious traumatization, the stress that officers feel because others are experiencing tragedy and crisis. In her writing, Tovar discusses the results of a research project in which she examined the way in which officers were able to reconcile disruptions to their core beliefs and successfully manage the ramifications of vicarious trauma. As a result of her findings, she suggests methods that a law enforcement agency may take to assist its personnel in dealing with the negative effects of their occupational stress and vicarious victimization.

Research has indicated the extremely stressful impact of dealing with criminal cases involving children as victims (See, for instance, Sewell (1983) and Violanti and Aron (1995) cited in Part Three of this book). Nowhere is that stress more pronounced than in child exploitation and pornography investigations. Law enforcement personnel, both sworn and civilian, assigned to internet crimes against children units spend hours each day viewing videos and photographs of acts that, to most civilians, would be considered unimaginable. Krause suggests that the high-risk nature of these investigations require agency administrators to be especially aware of the susceptibility of their personnel to stress and capable of recognizing common signs of stress among law enforcement personnel. She calls attention to efforts at both the FBI and the South Carolina Law Enforcement Assistance Program to enhance the protection of their personnel and identifies nine procedural and organizational safeguards appropriate for agencies to use in mitigating the stress experienced by those involved in such investigations.

Historically, much of the attention of stress researchers has been on the effects of individual traumatic incidents on police personnel. Yet, more recently, others have focused on the long-term effects of being routinely exposed to many traumatic events over a period of time, such as during the career of a police officer. To Marshall, the concept of Cumulative Career Traumatic Stress (CCTS) explains many of those sporadic symptoms that are similar to those resulting from Post Traumatic Stress Disorder (PTSD), but do not completely fulfill the duration criteria of the DSM-IV. Significantly, Marshall's research found that, among the long-term effects of CCTS, a high percentage of respondents reported a negative change in their outlook toward others, a lack of trust in others as a direct result of the job, and a change in religious beliefs since becoming a police officer.

On April 16, 2007, in two separate attacks on the campus of Virginia Polytechnic Institute and State College ("Virginia Tech") in Blacksburg, Virginia, a mentally disturbed senior-level student, Seung-Hui Cho, killed 32 people and wounded 25 others before committing suicide. On that day, McDearis, police chaplain for the Blacksburg Police Department and pastor of the Blacksburg Baptist Church, was called upon to fill roles he had never assumed he would. With the tragedy of this massacre as a backdrop, his writing addresses those invisible wounds carried by America's law enforcement warriors as they deal with incomprehensible scenes of violence.

Further Reading

Andrews, Bernice; Brewin, Chris R.; Philpott, Rosanna; and Stewart, Lorna (2007). "Delayed-Onset Posttraumatic Stress Disorder: A Systematic Review of the Evidence," *American Journal of Psychiatry, 164(9):1319–1326.*

Blum, Lawrence N. (2000). *Force Under Pressure: How Cops Live and Why They Die.* New York, NY: Lantern Books.

Bohrer, Shannon (2005). "After Firing the Shots, What Happens?" *FBI Law Enforcement Bulletin,* 74(9), 8–13.

Burns, Carolyn M.; Morley, Jeff; Bradshaw, Richard; and Domene, Jose (2008). "The Emotional Impact on and Coping Strategies Employed by Police Teams Investigating Internet Child Exploitation," *Traumatology,* 14(2), 20–31.

Dick, Penny (2000). "The Social Construction of the Meaning of Acute Stressors: A Qualitative Study of the Personal Accounts of Police Officers Using a Stress Counseling Service," *Work & Stress,* 14(3), 226–245.

Henry, V.E, (1995). "The Police Officer as Survivor: Death Confrontations and the Police Subculture," *Behavioral Sciences and the Law,* 13, 93–112.

Hetherington, Angela (1993), "Traumatic Stress on the Roads," in R. Allen (ed.), Handbook of Post-Disaster Interventions (Special Issue), *Journal of Social Behavior and Personality,* 8(5), 369–378.

Kates, Allen R. (1999). *CopShock: Surviving Posttraumatic Stress Disorder.* Tucson, AZ: Holbrook Street Press.

Kates, Allen R. (2009). "PTSD Can Attack Years Later," *Sheriff Magazine,* 61(4), 34–37.

Lerner, Mark D., and Shelton, Raymond D. (2001). *Acute Traumatic Stress Management: Addressing Emergent Psychological Needs During Traumatic Events.* Commack, NY: American Academy of Experts in Traumatic Stress.

Loo, R. (1986). "Post-shooting Stress Reactions among Police Officers," *Journal of Human Stress,* 12(1), 27–31.

Maslach, Christina (1976). "Burned-out," *Human Behavior*, 5(9), 16–22.

McCann, I. Lisa, and Pearlmann, Laurie Anne (1990). "Vicarious Traumatization: A Framework for Understanding the Psychological Effects of Working with Victims," *Journal of Traumatic Stress*, 3(1), 131–149.

Miller, Laurence (1998). *Shocks to the System: Psychotherapy of Traumatic Disability Syndromes*. New York, NY: W.W. Norton and Company.

Miller, Laurence (2011). "Psychological Interventions for Terroristic Trauma: Prevention, Crisis Management, and Clinical Treatment Strategies," *International Journal of Emergency Mental Health*, 13(2), 95–120.

Paton, Douglas, and Violanti, John M. (2006). "Policing in the Context of Terrorism: Managing Traumatic Stress Risk," *Traumatology*, 12(3), 236–247.

Parkinson, Frank 1993). *Post-Trauma Stress*. Tucson, AZ: Fisher Books.

Plant, Barbara (2001). "Psychological Trauma in the Police Service," *International Journal of Police Science and Management*, 3(4), 327–349.

Pranzo, Peter J., and Pranzo, Rachela (1999). *Stress Management for Law Enforcement (Behind the Shield: Combating Trauma)*. Longwood, FL: Gould Publications.

Reese, James T.; Horn, James M.; and Dunning, Christine (1990). *Critical Incidents in Policing*. Washington, DC: U.S. Department of Justice.

Sewell, James D. (1993). "Traumatic Stress of Multiple Murder Investigations," *Journal of Traumatic Stress*, 6(1), 103–118.

Sewell, James D. (1994). "The Stress of Homicide Investigations," *Death Studies*, 18(6), 565–582.

Key Terms/Names in Part Six

Acute stress: Stress derived from sudden events that may be of relative short duration and which provoke an almost immediate psychological reaction. Examples would include dealing with violent individuals, responding to the scene of a violent death, and dealing with multiple fatalities.

Chronic stress: Stress derived from the on-going nature of police work and whose effect accumulates within an officer. It would include routine events such as shiftwork, court appearances, and routine citizen contacts.

Critical incident stress debriefing (CISD): A group process of psychological crisis intervention specifically designed for emergency service personnel. It is recommended to take place within 24 and 48 hours after an event and promotes emotional processing of traumatic events through ventilation and normalization of reactions and through recognition of and preparation for recurrence of symptoms in the future.

Critical incident stress management: A structured, comprehensive process for emergency workers which includes pre-crisis preparation, crisis intervention, and post-crisis follow-up.

Cumulative Career Traumatic Stress (CCTS): This approach to understanding police stress holds that officers may experience trauma symptoms sporadically throughout a career as a result of being routinely exposed to many traumatic events over a period of time.

Defusing: Normally, a one-on-one supportive intervention by a supervisor immediately after a traumatic event. Its goal is to assess and respond to the immediate needs of an individual and to evaluate the need for further professional intervention.

Jeffery T. Mitchell: The developer of the process of critical incident stress management in 1983, Dr. Mitchell has been recognized as an international leader in trauma intervention.

Post-trauma intervention: Includes a variety of psychological techniques used to deal with trauma within a short period of time after its occurrence.

Symptomatology: The pattern of symptoms exhibited by an individual as a result of exposure to traumatic events or to chronic stress.

23

Vicarious Traumatization and Spirituality in Law Enforcement

Lynn A. Tovar

It is no secret that police work causes many law enforcement officers to feel stressed. Patrol officers face the risk of violence on a daily basis, leading many people to consider law enforcement an inherently stressful occupation.[1] Also, specific duties within police departments, such as child abuse investigations, may cause more anguish than others.

Yet, the mental toll of these positions often is overlooked, and, generally, the source of this anguish is examined anecdotally rather than empirically. Law enforcement administrators need to take a closer look at how traumatic events can alter their employees' worldviews and senses of spirituality, which ultimately affects the well-being of both personnel and organizations.

A positive spirit can help police officers reduce work-related stress by allowing them to minimize the impact of traumatic experiences. Therefore, managers and training coordinators need to acknowledge their critical role in

---

1. Cary A. Friedman, *Spiritual Survival for Law Enforcement* (Linden, NJ: Compass Books, 2005); Pamela A. Collins and A.C. Gibbs, "Stress in Police Officers: A Study of the Origins, Prevalence and Severity of Stress-Related Symptoms Within A County Police Force," *Occupational Medicine* (Exeter, UK: BMI Health Services, 2003); Theodore H. Blau, *Psychological Services for Law Enforcement* (New York: John Wiley & Sons, Inc., 1994); Dawn B. Fain and George M. McCormick, "Use of Coping Mechanisms As a Means of Stress Reduction in North Louisiana," *Journal of Police Science and Administration* 16, no. 1 (1988): 21–28; S.J. Hallet, *Trauma and Coping in Homicide and Child Sexual Abuse Detectives* (San Diego, CA: California School of Professional Psychology, 1996); M. Reiser and S.P. Greiger, "Police Officers as Victims," *Professional Psychology: Research and Practice* 15, no. 3 (1984): 315–323; and Terry A. Beehr, Leonor B. Johnson, and Ronie Nieva, "Occupational Stress: Coping of Police and their Spouses," *Journal of Organizational Behavior* 16 (January 1995): 3–25.

changing the behaviors and attitudes related to workplace stress by developing wellness and spirituality programs for their agencies. Understanding this stress, its sources and effects, and various ways to combat it will enrich officers' quality of life. Effective training programs and a culture of spirituality help officers manage stress, respond to trauma, and lead a more satisfying life.[2]

People-Oriented Occupational Stress

Stress is an inevitable component of life. In our fast-paced society, individuals must respond to a barrage of problems and changes in a timely manner, take on greater responsibilities, and become increasingly more efficient at their jobs.[3] However, in addition to this common, unavoidable stress, law enforcement work presents more challenges by frequently exposing personnel to traumatic events. As a result, police work meets the definition of a "critical occupation." Personnel in critical occupations, such as firefighters, paramedics, ambulance drivers, rescue workers, and emergency medical response teams, deal with traumatic events and their consequences. Officers, along with these emergency services professionals, play a critical role to protect the community, a weighty responsibility that brings significant pressure.[4] Those who do not learn to cope with this anguish progress to a more severe stage of stress known as burnout.[5]

Vicarious Traumatization

The concept of vicarious traumatization, as introduced by McCann and Pearlman, provides a theoretical framework to understand the complicated and often painful effects of trauma on crisis workers.[6] By definition, "the ef-

2. Leslie H. McLean and R. Wilburn Clouse, *Stress and Burnout: An Organizational Synthesis* (Nashville, TN: Vanderbilt University, 1991).

3. Ava J. Senkfor and Jean M. Williams, "The Moderating Effects of Aerobic Fitness and Mental Training on Stress Reactivity," *Journal of Sport Behavior* 18 (1995): 130–57.

4. Douglas Paton and John M. Violanti, *Traumatic Stress in Critical Occupations* (Springfield, IL: Charles C Thomas Publishing, 1996).

5. Ronald J. Burke and Astrid M. Richardsen, "Stress, Burnout, and Health," in *Handbook of Stress, Medicine, and Health*, ed. Cary L. Cooper (Boca Raton, FL: CRC Press, 1991).

6. Lisa McCann and Laurie A. Pearlman, "Vicarious Traumatization: A Framework for Understanding the Psychological Effects of Working with Victims," *Journal of Traumatic Stress* 3, no. 1 (January 1990); and B.H. Stamm, ed., *Secondary Traumatic Stress: Self-Care Issues for Clinicians, Researchers and Educators* (Lutherville, MD: Sidran Press, 1989).

fects of vicarious traumatization on an individual resemble those of traumatic experiences. They include significant disruptions in one's affect tolerance, psychological needs, beliefs about self and others, interpersonal relationships, and sensory memory, including imagery."[7]

Vicarious traumatization results from empathetic engagement with traumatic experiences.[8] Tragic events that harm innocent victims are, unfortunately, an inevitable part of our larger world and society. Because law enforcement officers hold the responsibility of responding to these incidents, they repeatedly witness human beings' intentional cruelty to one another. As investigators listen to graphic accounts of victims' experiences and participate in reenactments of tragic events, these encounters stir powerful emotions as officers engage with victims' pain and suffering. Officers can become painfully aware of the potential for trauma in their own lives, and this empathetic engagement leaves them vulnerable to the emotional and spiritual effects of vicarious traumatization.

Officers who fall victim to vicarious traumatization may demonstrate changes in their core sense of self or psychological foundation. These alterations include shifts in the officers' identities and worldviews; their ability to manage strong feelings, maintain a positive sense of self, and connect with others; their spirituality or sense of meaning, expectation, awareness, and connection with others; their spirituality or sense of meaning, expectation, awareness, and connection; and their basic needs for safety, self-esteem, trust, dependency, control, and intimacy.[9] These effects, which disrupt officers' professional and personal lives, are cumulative and potentially permanent.

A Study of Vicarious Trauma

Focused Research

To investigate how vicarious trauma manifests in law enforcement agencies, the author studied the ways that officers deal with these painful and horrific experiences that completely contradict their previously held conceptions about how the world should be. The study examined how law enforcement officers reconcile these disruptions to their core beliefs (e.g., good versus evil, hope versus despair, safety versus vulnerability) and manage the physical, psycho-

---

7. Ibid.
8. Ibid.
9. Ibid.

logical, and social ramifications of vicarious trauma. The study analyzed the sources and effects of these stresses, as well as the ways in which the participants reconstructed their lives to regain their psychological and physical health. Also, the author presents suggestions on how organizations can assist police officers in their struggles, particularly by encouraging them to learn wellness and spirituality-based coping mechanisms.

To gather this information, the author interviewed 15 law enforcement investigators from the Chicago area who worked on juvenile sexual abuse cases. She asked questions to determine how, if at all, the interviewees were influenced or changed by their professional experiences. Face-to-face interviews afforded her the opportunity to observe the participant's body language, such as eye rolls, long pauses between responses, or voice inflections that indicated contempt, concern, frustration, or sorrow. Narrative interviews illustrated to the author how various episodes, experiences, or events in officers' lives impacted their feelings, emotions, coping mechanisms, and interactions with peers and victims.

Lessons Learned

The study's results indicated that participants exhibited numerous signs of vicarious traumatization, including hypervigilance, symptomatic reactions, relationship problems, lack of communication, denial, repression, isolation and disassociation, change in worldviews, and a loss of sense of meaning. Participants' statements clearly demonstrated the impacts of juvenile sexual assault investigations in their lives. The first interviewee stated, "I think that is a part of what this job has done to me. You look at society or you look at people with a jaundiced-eye, cynical perspective. We don't always see the best, we see the worst, or we have suspicion about someone." One interviewee described the physical effects of psychological trauma, such as "headaches, the general tightness in the shoulders. I don't sleep well. I haven't slept well in a very long time. When I wake up in the morning, I never feel refreshed."

Also, as is common of vicarious traumatization victims, some subjects demonstrated significant changes to their previously held values. Another interviewee stated, "I think before I got on the job and people would ask, 'Do you believe in God?' I would say, 'Yeah, I believe in Him, but I just don't go to church.' Now when people ask if I believe, I will say, 'If you saw what I saw—and I spent 2 hours in Children's Memorial Hospital—and if you saw what I saw ... there is no God.' Yeah, I would say it has had an impact on my belief." The investigators demonstrated that their experiences permanently transformed their lives, both professionally and personally; as a result, new perspectives, new beliefs, and coping strategies emerged. Also, investigators who felt most distant from traumatic experiences were more open in their acknowledgement of their effects and more able to critically reflect on them.[10]

Positive Steps to Action

These results demonstrate that law enforcement agencies must take measures to help their personnel combat the negative effects of occupational stress and vicarious traumatization. Two important methods to improve the well-being of officers include facilitating spirituality in the workplace and implementing training programs to teach coping mechanisms.

Spirituality in the Workplace

What is spirituality in the workplace? In this study, the author ascribes to a broad definition of the term. "Spirituality" does not denote religious practices, God, or theology but rather an inherent human awareness of the elusive impact of experience. It attributes meaning to one's life through hope and idealism, connection with others, and awareness of experience. More specifically, "workplace spirituality recognizes that people have an inner life that nourishes and is nourished by meaningful work in the context of community."[11]

The organization should remain concerned about how officers' work affects their inner lives and emotions and, thus, foster a culture that welcomes spirituality as a coping mechanism. The four cultural characteristics of a spiritual organization include a strong sense of purpose, trust and respect among coworkers, humanistic work practices, and the toleration of employee expression in the workplace.[12] An awareness of spirituality can shed a great deal of light on the officers' behavior in the workplace; as a result, the organizational culture that accepts spirituality can better help employees develop to their full potential.[13]

Because many individuals desire to embrace spirituality in their personal life and in their workplace, organizations can promote a spiritual culture by em-

10. Lynn A. Tovar, "Transformation of Self: Portrait of Youth Investigators and Forensic Interviewers Exposed to Repeated Trauma," (diss., Northern Illinois University, 2002).

11. Stephen Robbins and Timothy A. Judge, *Organizational Behavior* (Boston, MA: Prentice Hall Publishers, 2009).

12. Ibid.

13. Ibid.

phasizing the value of community in a productive work environment.[14] Similarly, law enforcement agencies need to recognize that their employees have both a mind and a spirit, and they seek to find meaning in their duties and the community they serve. Many police officers feel the desire and commitment to connect with other humans, whether inside the workplace or externally, including the citizens and victims they help. A strong sense of spirituality in the workplace promotes positive attitudes, health, happiness, empowerment, inner peace, truth, and healthy relationships.

Wellness Training

Once law enforcement administrators recognize the link between wellness and overall personnel development, they should provide training opportunities to teach officers how to cope with stress on the job. These educational programs will function as both professional and personal development for officers who suffer from vicarious traumatization.

Before administrators develop wellness programs for their departments, they should perform a two-part training needs assessment. First, managers should analyze the current state of wellness training in their agencies. Then, they must understand the severity of occupational stress among their officers. They should ask questions, such as, How has your work affected your personal identity, spirituality, sexuality, relationships, and emotional responsiveness? Does your work lead to feelings of frustration and hopelessness or to joy and accomplishment? What programs does the organization have in place to help officers deal with these changes?

After agencies gain a better understanding of their needs, they can develop educational programs to remedy these issues. Trainers should instruct officers about the causes and effects of stress, as well as constructive ways to combat it. A well-rounded stress reduction/spirituality curriculum should provide information about stress indicators, the benefits of physical exercise and proper nutrition, and effective interpersonal communication methods.[15]

Departments should implement prevention measures by immediately educating new recruits on stress and wellness. However, continuing instruction becomes even more important for officers later in their careers; these experienced officers more likely will suffer from the effects of stress already.

---

14. Len Tischler, "The Growing Interest in Spirituality in Business," *Journal of Organizational Change Management* 12, no. 4 (1999): 273–279.

15. John M. Violanti, "Residuals of Police Occupational Trauma," *The Australasian Journal of Disaster and Trauma Studies* 3 (1996).

As a result, agencies must provide support for their personnel, which can come in many forms. Support from the officer's agency and family is a critical factor in a troubled person's decision to seek help. Many administrators institute employee assistance programs to provide 24-hour help lines and confidential counseling.

In addition, psychological debriefings comprise an important technique to help personnel cope with traumatic events. Conducting debriefings soon after incidents allows police officers to express their feelings and discuss the occurrence in a supportive group setting.[16] Also, peer support groups allow officers who have been affected by trauma to talk to fellow law enforcement professionals who will listen to them and provide assistance. Trainers and administrators must understand, however, that many law enforcement officers fear that acknowledging such stress impacts their work and, thus, may not seek help on their own.

Last, administrators must acknowledge that each law enforcement agency is unique and has its own set of stress-related problems. It, therefore, is necessary to conduct ongoing assessments into the causes and minimization of stress among their officers.

Conclusion

Law enforcement officials should seek a greater understanding of the toll that work-related stress has on police officers. Organizations have begun to recognize that occupational stress and vicarious traumatization pose serious hazards for their workers' mental health; as such, they need to consider facilitating wellness and spirituality programs in the workplace.[17] These programs are positive, proactive ways to address the deeper impact of police work on officers' lives.

Training coordinators and administrators need to understand the day-to-day events of the patrol officers, specialized investigators, and other personnel who struggle with repeated exposure to trauma in their lives. Then, they can pro-

---

16. Jeffrey T. Mitchell and Grady P. Bray, *Emergency Services Stress: Guidelines for Preserving the Health and Careers of Emergency Services Personnel* (Englewood Cliffs, NJ: Prentice Hall, 1990).

17. Sukumarakurup Krishnakumar and Christopher P. Neck, "The 'What,' 'Why,' and 'How'" of Spirituality in the Workplace," *Journal of Managerial Psychology* 17, no. 3 (2002): 153–164; and Jean-Claude Garcia-Zamor, "Workplace Spirituality and Organizational Performance," *Public Administration Review* 63, no. 3 (May–June 2003): 353–363.

vide their employees with appropriate professional development and training opportunities to remedy these issues. This training will help officers overcome stress and constructively respond to vicarious traumatization by showing them methods to incorporate wellness and spirituality into their lives.[18]

As many law enforcement agencies across the country downsize due to budget cuts, layoffs, or attrition, it remains critical to focus on retraining effective, hardworking officers. Therefore, organizations should consider the above philosophies and approach training in a holistic manner. In a workplace where training and development foster a culture of wellness and spirituality, employees will individually and collectively begin to create, relate, and experience a richer, dynamic, and more meaningful life, both professionally and personally.

Discussion Questions

1. How is vicarious traumatization defined?
2. What are the elements of vicarious traumatization?
3. From what does vicarious traumatization result?
4. Officers who fall victim to vicarious traumatization may demonstrate changes in their core sense of self or psychological foundation. What are the behavioral manifestations of such changes?
5. The author of this article interviewed 15 law enforcement investigators from the Chicago area who worked on juvenile sexual abuse cases. She asked questions to determine how, if at all, the interviewees were influenced or changed by their professional experiences. What were the results?
6. Tovar's study resulted in identifying numerous signs of vicarious traumatization. What were the specific signs?
7. What is spirituality in the workplace?
8. Once law enforcement administrators recognize the link between wellness and overall personnel development, what course of action should they take to assist police officers coping with on-the-job stress?

---

18. Roger E. Herman, Joyce L. Gioira, and T. Chalky, "Making Work Meaningful: Secrets of the Future-Focused Corporation," *Futurist* 32, no. 9 (1998): 24–29.

24

In Harm's Way: Duty of Care for Child Exploitation and Pornography Investigators

Meredith Krause

Since the 1990s, law enforcement agencies have witnessed rampant growth in the computer-facilitated possession, production, and distribution of child pornography due in large part to technological advances that have eased the exchange of large caches of this material. These changes, together with the emergence of social-networking Web sites, Listserv systems, and newsgroups, have provided online forums for the international criminal community of child predators and facilitated unfettered cyber access to potential child victims. In response to this clear and present danger, federal, state, and local law enforcement agencies have developed and deployed enhanced and targeted initiatives.[1]

With the emergence and growth of these programs, law enforcement personnel have been drafted and reassigned to engage in the full range of activities essential to the investigation of computer-facilitated, often online, child exploitation and pornography. While many of these investigators are selected on the basis of their previous experience working juvenile sex crimes, child abuse, or domestic violence, others are chosen by virtue of their technological savvy, their willingness to volunteer for the work, or other reasons unrelated to their professional suitability for this high-risk duty (e.g., resource and staffing issues). Once assigned to this activity, these employees face numerous personal and professional risks, often without adequate understanding, guid-

---

1. U.S. Department of Justice, Office of Juvenile Justice and Delinquency Prevention, *Fact Sheet: Internet Crimes Against Children (ICAC) Task Forces*. (Washington, D.C., 2008); and Project Safe Childhood, 2008; *http://www.projectsafechildhood.gov/guide.htm.*

ance, or support from their peers, supervisors, local prosecutors and judges, or family members.

Understanding the Risk

Because of the nature and relative novelty of this investigative activity, "cyber cops" face a wide range of personal and professional challenges often overlooked and minimized by both managers and investigators themselves. Unique to the cyberspace battlefield, these stressors are compounded by those typically encountered by all law enforcement personnel. Chief among these, the repeated exposure to obscene, toxic, and exceptionally disturbing pictures and videos of child victims is routinely ranked among the top four stressors in the law enforcement profession, following only a fatal line-of-duty shooting, the line-of-duty death of a fellow officer, and the survival of a physical attack.[2]

Given the compelling nature of the child victims, investigators frequently experience great internal and external pressure to cover the overwhelming number of leads that they receive, make cases, and save lives. The corrosive effects of these demands often are exacerbated by the relatively recent emergence of this investigative technique, the problems associated with investigative dependence on computer hardware and software, and the lack of reliable access to technologically knowledgeable support personnel. These frustrations are compounded by the ever-changing cyber landscape that offers offenders new illicit opportunities and renders established crime-fighting techniques and tools cumbersome and often obsolete.

These practical problems become further complicated by the need for personal, technological, and organizational resources sufficient to establish and sustain a credible online persona that interacts with targets in a way that does not raise suspicion or allow for traceability. Oftentimes, the need to interact with suspects when they are available online also presents a logistical and scheduling challenge, requiring investigators to work odd hours to maintain continuity of contact or to remain at their posts in the search for a known, live victim. In turn, this may lead to accumulated overtime, interference with family and social responsibilities, and isolation from colleagues. Such personal hardships can be compounded by the difficulties associated with establishing and maintaining a secure connection to the Internet that cannot be traced back

---

2. J.M. Violanti and F. Aron, "Police Stressors: Variations in Perception Among Police Personnel," *Journal of Criminal Justice* 23, no. 3 (1995): 287–294.

to a law enforcement agency and providing appropriate technology and computer analysis response team support to investigators as evidence accumulates. Moreover, these investigations often push the limits of existing practice, policy, and legislation or case law and may proceed with insufficient guidance regarding investigative techniques, evidentiary requirements, legal standards, and punitive responses. Similarly, the investigative and geographic scope of these cases can demand unparalleled levels of cross-jurisdictional coordination and cooperation, a source of clear strain to investigators, police managers, and prosecutors alike.[3]

Over time, many investigators develop an extraordinary commitment to this meaningful and satisfying work. In most instances, this dedication fosters great success for the investigators, as well as their agencies, and buoys them during times of personal or professional challenge (e.g., when cases lag or during major life changes). Sometimes, however, this commitment can have deleterious effects on personal, emotional, or family functioning and may interfere with the ability to detect these negative consequences. Even when faced with evidence of them, investigators may feel that they do not have the option of transferring to a new assignment, believing that they are turning their backs on child victims, creating a void in their agency, or facing few suitable alternative assignments. This relentless dedication also may result in the emergence of a false sense of security, causing investigators to underestimate the personal risks associated with online work. This self-deception may translate into face-to-face interactions with subjects and render investigators vulnerable to the unpredictable and often dangerous actions of perpetrators during interviews or arrests.

Table 1. Stressors Unique to Child Exploitation and Pornography Investigations

- Repeated exposure to obscene content
- Pressure to cover leads, make cases, save live victims
- Relative novelty of investigative approach and techniques
- Dependence on technology and support personnel
- Need for encryption and defensible online persona
- Constantly changing cyber landscape
- Shortage of computer forensic examiners
- Unusual time demands of online chat
- Interjurisdictional cooperation and coordination
- Potential for developing a false sense of safety or security

---

3. Y. Jewkes and C. Andrews, "Policing the Filth: The Problems of Investigating Online Child Pornography in England and Wales," *Policing and Society* 15, no. 1 (2005): 42–62.

Calculating and Mitigating the Peril

The stressors unique to child exploitation and pornography cases add to the long list of acute and chronic organizational, personal, and interpersonal demands commonly associated with policing.[4] In much the same way that employees in high-risk assignments, such as undercover work or SWAT, warrant unique managerial and organizational support (e.g., in the form of recruiting, selecting, monitoring, and training), child exploitation and pornography investigators also need special "care and feeding" to optimize their personal and professional functioning.[5]

As Figure 1 illustrates, the risk for negative personal and professional outcomes is determined by the frequency, duration, type, and intensity of exposure to disturbing images or stressors; the perceived control over the source of the stress or distress; and the coping strategies an individual possesses.[6] Investigators commonly report that the type of exposure often proves critical in determining their response. Live-action, webcam feeds represent the most disturbing content, followed by video with audio, video without audio, and still pictures.[7] The age of the victim also plays a key part, with younger victims (i.e., those under the age of 3) posing the greatest risk.

---

4. Violanti and Aron; J.M. Violanti, "Operationalizing Police Stress Management: A Model," in *Police Psychology: Operational Assistance*, ed. J.T. Reese and J.M. Horn (Washington, DC: U.S. Department of Justice, 1988), 423–435; and E.K. Marshall, "Cumulative Career Traumatic Stress (CCTS): A Pilot Study of Traumatic Stress in Law Enforcement," *Journal of Police and Criminal Psychology* 21, no. 1 (2006): 62–71.

5. S.R. Band and D.C. Sheehan, "Managing Undercover Stress: The Supervisor's Role," *FBI Law Enforcement Bulletin*, February 1999, 1–6; N.S. Hibler, "The Care and Feeding of Undercover Agents," in *Police Psychology into the 21st Century*, ed. Neil S. Hibler, I. Kurke Martin, and Ellen M. Scrivner, (Hillsdale, NJ: Lawrence Erlbaum Associates, Inc., 1995), 299–317; L. Miller, "Undercover Policing: A Psychological and Operational Guide," *Journal of Police and Criminal Psychology* 21, no. 2 (2006): 1–24; and I.J. Vasquez and S.A. Kelly, "Management's Commitment to the Undercover Operative: A Contemporary View," *FBI Law Enforcement Bulletin*, February 1989, 3–12.

6. Although not included, factors related to temperament or personality also could shape an investigator's susceptibility to adverse outcomes. The five factors highlighted in figure 1, however, are recognized as proximal risk determinants that may be reasonably addressed through programmatic and organizational initiatives.

7. Personnel engaged in Innocent Images National Initiative (IINI) and Internet Crimes Against Children (ICAC) task forces provided this anecdotal input to the author during in-

Figure 1. Susceptibility to Stress Factors

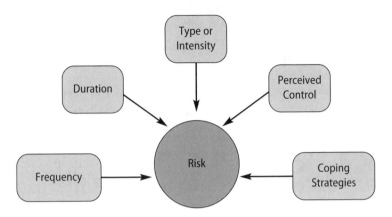

The application of adaptive, proactive coping strategies that enhance the sense of perceived control over the exposure can help mitigate these risks.[8] For instance, many investigators report that they scan pictures by focusing on the extent to which these meet evidentiary standards, not on the face or feelings of the victim. Some limit the length of time each day or the number of consecutive days that they spend viewing images. Imposing emotional distance and compartmentalizing their response to such disturbing content can prove effective in buffering investigators against adverse outcomes associated with "caring too much." Although both healthy and warranted, these strategies, however, often fall victim to the demands of obtaining and executing search warrants and preparing for trial. As such, agencies should view these periods as times of heightened risk and afford investigators all available resources and support (material and moral) to shield them against adverse outcomes.

Implementing organizational safeguards also may mitigate the hazards posed to high-risk investigators. Research on police trauma, together with informal surveys of personnel engaged in child pornography investigations, has suggested that membership in a cohesive and supportive investigative team constitutes the single best buffer against work-related stress. The existence of such a team depends on widespread organizational support for the activity and the assignment of supervisors who grasp the complexity of the work and provide consistent and meaningful case or file review. Selecting experienced volunteers

---

dividual conversations and training sessions devoted to the issue of child exploitation and pornography.

8. M.H. Anshel, "A Conceptual Model and Implications for Coping with Stressful Events in Police Work," *Criminal Justice and Behavior* 27, no. 3 (2000): 375–400.

who have the benefit of a realistic preview of their duties, including exposure to some sample images, prior to their assignment can maximize the effectiveness of the investigative team. Many agencies require this job preview before or during specialized training devoted to the practical, technical, and legal intricacies inherent in this high-risk assignment. Enhancing this initial, basic training with ongoing mentorship, advanced instruction, and conference attendance can prove critical to building competence and resilience in new investigators. Finally, all investigators must have the option of transferring to an alternative assignment without penalty as the need arises. Although this organizational safeguard presents a clear staffing challenge and requires delicate handling by managers, it represents a critical step in reducing psychological or professional casualties.

Observing Common Stress Reactions

Even with diligent application of these coping strategies, child exploitation and pornography investigators may experience signs and symptoms of stress, burnout, vicarious trauma, or compassion fatigue at some point in their careers.[9] Given that many feel called to the work, voice a firm unwillingness to "abandon" the victims by changing assignments, and grow numb to the strains inherent in this unique activity, their families, colleagues, chaplains, and managers emerge as crucial sources of support, monitoring, and feedback. In many instances, investigators fail to recognize the emotional, attitudinal, behavioral, physical, and spiritual changes that have overtaken them or may feel helpless or ashamed to admit these effects. In such cases, external supports are critical to identifying and averting the chronic, negative outcomes (e.g., divorce, estrangement from family and friends, job turnover, or health crises) that may result from prolonged stress reaction.

While Table 2 summarizes many of the common signs,[10] stress reactions are unique, and individual responses simply represent a deviation from what is normal, or typical, for that person. All of these warning signs constitute nor-

---

9. Marshall; C.R. Figley, "Police Compassion Fatigue (PCF): Theory, Research, Assessment, Treatment, and Prevention," in *Police Trauma: Psychological Aftermath of Civilian Combat*, ed. J.M. Violanti and D. Paton (Springfield, IL: Charles C Thomas, 1999), 37–64; I.T. VanPatten and T.W. Burke, "Critical Incident Stress and the Child Homicide Investigator," *Homicide Studies* 5, no. 2 (2001): 131–152; and J.M. Violanti and A. Gehrke, "Police Trauma Encounters: Precursors of Compassion Fatigue," *International Journal of Emergency Mental Health* 6, no. 2 (2004): 75–80.

10. Figley.

Table 2. Common Signs of Stress Among Law Enforcement Personnel

Emotions	Thoughts	Behaviors	Work	Relation-ships	Health	Spirituality
Powerless-ness	Decreased concentra-tion	Impatience	Decreased morale	With-drawal	Shock	Loss of purpose
Anxiety	Decreased self-esteem	Irritability	Decreased motivation	Decreased intimacy	Sweating	Decreased self-satis-faction
Guilt	Apathy	With-drawal	Task avoid-ance	Mistrust	Increased heartbeat	Hopeless-ness
Anger/rage	Rigidity	Moodiness	Overly focused on detail	Isolation	Breathing problems	Question-ing mean-ing of life
Survivor guilt	Disorienta-tion	Regression	Apathy	Misplaced anger	Aches/pains	Anger at God
Shutdown	Perfection-ism	Sleep changes	Negativity	Misplaced blame	Dizziness	Question-ing beliefs
Numbness	Minimiza-tion	Night-mares	Decreased apprecia-tion	Intolerance	Decreased immunity	Question-ing God
Fear	Preoccu-pation	Appetite changes	Staff con-flict	Increased conflict	Increased medical problems	Loss of faith
Helpless-ness	Thoughts of harm	Hyper-vigilance	Absen-teeism	Over-protective		Increased skepticism
Sadness	Thoughts of harm	Accident proneness	Exhaustion			
Depletion			Change in communi-cation			
Sensitivity						

Source: C.R. Figley, "Police Compassion Fatigue (PCF): Theory, Research, Assessment, Treatment, and Prevention," in Police Trauma: Psychological Aftermath of Civilian Combat, *ed. J.M. Violanti and D. Paton (Springfield, IL: Charles C Thomas, 1999).*

mal reactions to the abnormal experiences that all law enforcement officers routinely encounter and should be sources of concern only when they linger or begin to interfere with an individual's daily functioning, relationships, or health.

As Table 2 illustrates, law enforcement personnel may experience a range of reactions in response to short- and long-term exposure to stress and strain in the course of their professional and personal lives. These signs and symptoms may reflect the adverse impact of transient, short-lived stressors or of more serious and long-standing issues, such as burnout, vicarious traumatization, or compassion fatigue.

In the case of burnout, investigators experience exhaustion of body, mind, and motivation due to exposure to prolonged and unresolved work stress or frustration. Burnout is particularly common among police and other types of employees who face work overload and who perceive a lack of control over organizational issues, insufficient rewards, unfairness, decreased sense of camaraderie, or value conflict due to their job situation.[11]

By contrast, vicarious traumatization involves internal changes in core beliefs, identity, needs and wants, relationships, and view of others as a result of repeated exposure to traumatic material.[12] Whether temporary or permanent, these changes are intrinsically linked to trauma exposure and not to any organizational or personal failure. For child exploitation and pornography investigators, vicarious traumatization may significantly impact their parenting practices or style due to shifts in their beliefs about the trustworthiness of others (e.g., coaches or babysitters) or the level of perceived threat in the world.

Finally, compassion fatigue, sometimes referred to as secondary traumatic stress, entails a state of significant tension and preoccupation with victims' suffering that mirrors the symptoms commonly associated with post-traumatic stress disorder (PTSD). This clinically significant stress reaction, commonly referred to as the cost of caring, can be seen in disaster workers, sexual assault and crisis counselors, mental health employees, and emergency services personnel. All frequently tend to the needs of severely traumatized and sympathetic

---

11. C. Alexander, "Police Psychological Burnout and Trauma," in *Police Trauma: Psychological Aftermath of Civilian Combat*, ed. J.M. Violanti and D. Paton (Springfield, IL: Charles C. Thomas, 1999), 54–64.

12. K.M. Palm, M.A. Polusny, and V.M. Follette, "Vicarious Traumatization: Potential Hazards and Interventions for Disaster and Trauma Workers," *Prehospital and Disaster Medicine* 19, no. 1 (2004): 73–78; and R.B. Thomas and J.P. Wilson, "Issues and Controversies in the Understanding and Diagnosis of Compassion Fatigue, Vicarious Traumatization, and Secondary Traumatic Stress Disorder," *International Journal of Emergency Mental Health* 6, no. 2 (2004): 81–92.

victims and, in so doing, learn the intimate details of their suffering. Repeated exposure to the trauma of the victims, in turn, results in physical, emotional, and behavioral changes that mirror PTSD but fail to reach formal diagnostic thresholds due to the indirect nature of the trauma exposure.[13]

Over time and in combination with other line-of-duty stressors, this secondary trauma exposure may result in the gradual onset of a cluster of anxiety symptoms and personal changes often described as cumulative career traumatic stress,[14] police and public safety complex posttraumatic stress disorder,[15] or cop shock.[16] While the incidence and prevalence of these anxiety disorders among child exploitation and pornography investigators remain unknown, repetitive and prolonged exposure to extremely graphic and disturbing images of child abuse and trauma clearly places them at elevated risk and warrants enhanced attention and support.

Research on stress reactions among police and public safety personnel has suggested that a range of factors may increase individual susceptibility to stress reactions.[17] Specifically, the risk of adverse outcomes appears heightened in those with prior trauma exposure, positive histories of unresolved personal issues, limited access to social support, minimal case consultation or file review opportunities, inadequate preparation and training, and ongoing personal life stressors (e.g., chronically ill family members or financial worries).

Accepting a Duty of Care

Due to the rapid growth in the number of employees engaged in child exploitation and pornography investigations,[18] law enforcement agencies have

---

13. P.J. Morrissette, *The Pain of Helping: Psychological Injury of Helping Professionals* (New York, NY: Bruner Routledge, 2004).

14. Marshall.

15. D. Rudofossi, *Working with Traumatized Police-Officer Patients* (Amityville, NY: Baywood Publishing Company, Inc., 2007).

16. A.R. Kates, *Cop Shock: Surviving Post-traumatic Stress Disorder* (Tucson, AZ: Holbrook Street Press, 1999).

17. VanPatten and Burke; Palm, Polusny, and Follette; and C. Stephens, N. Long, and R. Flett, "Vulnerability to Psychological Disorder: Previous Trauma in Police Recruits," in *Police Trauma: Psychological Aftermath of Civilian Combat*, ed. J.M. Violanti and D. Paton (Springfield, IL: Charles C Thomas, 1999), 65–77.

18. U.S. Department of Justice, *Fact Sheet: Internet Crimes Against Children (ICAC) Task Forces*. For example, since the inception of the Internet Crimes Against Children Task Force Program in 1998, the number of ICAC task forces has grown to 59, including 1,800 affiliate agencies and the full-time equivalent involvement of nearly 300 police personnel. Their

witnessed tragic personal, professional, and familial outcomes among a small group who emerged from the cyberspace battlefield as wounded warriors. These anecdotal experiences, together with a growing willingness among investigators to acknowledge the stressors and strains unique to their work, have led law enforcement organizations to consider their duty of care and the necessity of tailored responses to the needs of these high-risk employees.

Within the FBI, investigators and support personnel engaged in child exploitation and pornography investigations as part of the Innocent Images National Initiative (IINI) participate in the Undercover Safeguard Unit's compulsory assessment process.[19] While initially developed to select, assess, monitor, and support traditional undercover agents, the process was expanded in the late 1990s to include IINI personnel due to their involvement in online undercover activities (i.e., online chat) and their status as high-risk investigators facing a unique set of stressors and strains. Currently, IINI personnel participate in the safeguard process prior to entry into their assignment and at yearly intervals thereafter. All are reminded of the voluntary nature of the assignments and are queried at length regarding their motivation for volunteering, suitability for the job, presence of potentially troubling stressors or habits, personal abuse or trauma histories, support systems, and other factors relevant to their suitability.

On the basis of this information, safeguard personnel render a final decision regarding suitability and placement, which they communicate to the candidate's home office and consider at each subsequent assessment. Although involvement is compulsory, compliance rates are high, and participants frequently report it as a valuable experience that allows them to ventilate their emotions, express their frustrations, and seek feedback from an objective third party not involved in their chain of command and who truly understands the nature of their work. This positive valence is likely due to clearly established limits of confidentiality that govern these interactions; the sole focus of safeguard personnel on the wellness of their undercover flock; and the individualized nature of the feedback, support, and coaching (intended to optimize both personal and professional functioning) that each employee receives. In addition, the willingness to staunchly advocate for the needs of struggling IINI personnel, con-

---

combined efforts resulted in 2,400 arrests and more than 10,500 forensic examinations of seized computers in fiscal year 2007. Per M.A. Mason's statement before the House Judiciary Committee, October 17, 2007, approximately 240 FBI agents participate in investigations under the Innocent Images National Initiative, a program that has resulted in over 15,000 investigations and 4,800 convictions since its inception in 1996.

19. M.S. Krause, "Addressing the Needs of Undercover Employees: A Practical Approach," *FBI Law Enforcement Bulletin*, August 2008, 1–8.

front recalcitrant supervisors, and facilitate transfer and reassignment as each employee's needs dictate has cemented the credibility of the safeguard process.

While the program's strength resides in its proactive selection, assessment, and monitoring orientation, it is resource intensive and difficult to replicate in financially strapped law enforcement agencies. Such organizations have attempted to identify alternative prevention and intervention approaches that meet the needs and wants of their high-risk personnel. In some cases, these efforts have resulted in the referral of struggling investigators to employee assistance programs or departmental psychologists or psychiatrists. This method has received several criticisms, including that it—

- lacks a proactive focus on primary prevention of work-related stress reactions;
- adds to the multiple roles that departmental psychologists and psychiatrists play;
- relies on a mental health-based response that may be unpalatable to some; and
- relegates high-risk investigators to a one-size-fits-all support program that may or may not recognize or understand the unique demands placed on them.[20]

In response to these concerns, the South Carolina Law Enforcement Assistance Program (SCLEAP) has adapted the peer support framework[21] to meet the needs of state and local law enforcement personnel engaged in the state's Internet Crimes Against Children (ICAC) Task Force. While this initiative currently is in its infancy, SCLEAP has assembled an initial team of 12 investigators, solicitors, and attorneys who possess considerable credibility among their task force peers by virtue of their personal attributes and their professional experience in the arena of child exploitation and pornography. Highly knowledgeable about the challenges and stressors unique to ICAC investigations, the team will receive ongoing training on the peer support method, complemented by administrative and clinical support from SCLEAP members.

Operating much like other peer-based assistance programs, the team can offer confidential and voluntary nondepartmental assistance to personnel strug-

---

20. F.G. Dowling, B. Genet, and G. Moynihan, "A Confidential Peer-Based Assistance Program for Police Officers," *Psychiatric Services* 56 (2005): 870–871.

21. Dowling, Genet, and Moynihan; International Association of Chiefs of Police/IACP, *Peer Support Guidelines* (2006); *http://www.iacp.org*; and L.A. Morris, J.M. Morgan, and R.M. Easton, *Development of Peer Support Programs in Native American and Campus Police* (Washington, DC: National Institute of Justice, 2001).

gling with personal or job-related stressors.[22] The support will be informed by the recognition that ICAC investigators face a cascade of cumulative stressors common to policing and unique to their assignment, exacerbated by repetitive exposure to disturbing images of child victims. In addition, the composition of the team, wherein all members possess unique personal and professional experience with and insight into their shared battles and strains, will maximize its effectiveness with and relevance to ICAC personnel. The team will engage in proactive outreach efforts (e.g., task force meetings and informal social gatherings) designed to enhance awareness of the high-risk nature of ICAC investigations, erode resistance to seeking help, and build camaraderie and cohesion among ICAC members who work across the state and sometimes bear the sole responsibility for these investigations in their agencies.

Together, these programs represent the two ends of the continuum of services appropriate for personnel engaged in child exploitation and pornography investigations. Given the unique demands placed upon these employees and the undeniable challenges and strains that they face as a result of their work, these efforts offer the special care and handling that high-risk investigators deserve. These programs also reflect a proactive commitment to primary prevention conceptually anchored in the extant knowledge base regarding police stress, traumatoid states, and the challenges inherent in high-risk investigations.

Box 1. Procedural and Organizational Safeguards

- Cultivate organizational support for and value of investigative activity
- Use experienced volunteers
- Offer realistic job preview
- Provide adequate training and support
- Conduct consistent and productive case review and supervision
- Form a cohesive investigative team with adequate material and personnel resources
- Encourage discussion of work-related strains and stressors with a trusted confidant
- Proactively manage amount of time spent online or viewing images
- Facilitate the transfer to a new assignment when needed without penalty

---

Conclusion

The rapid growth in the investigation of online child exploitation and pornography cases over the past decade has placed a new group of material, tech-

---

22. Dowling, Genet, and Moynihan; and Morris, Morgan, and Easton.

nological, legal, and personnel burdens on local, state, and federal law enforcement agencies. While the creation of regional and federal task forces designed to pool knowledge, resources, and personnel have dispersed these responsibilities, individual investigators continue to face undeniable pressures, strains, and stressors.

Unique among their law enforcement colleagues, child exploitation and pornography investigators knowingly and repeatedly expose themselves to some of the most disturbing and heinous images of child victims to collect evidence, close investigations, and prepare for trial. These challenges add to the well-established list of demands that law enforcement employees regularly encounter and pose a significant risk for psychological casualties and occupational dysfunction in the absence of adequate policy, procedural safeguards, training, supervisory support, and crisis prevention and intervention programs.

Discussion Questions

1. According to the author, what are the top four stressors in law enforcement?
2. What stressors are unique to child exploitation and pornography investigations?
3. What elements will affect the investigator's response to working with child pornography?
4. The application of adaptive, proactive coping strategies that enhance the sense of perceived control over the exposure to stress can help mitigate these risks. What suggestions were made to mitigate these risks?
5. Even with the diligent application of coping strategies, child exploitation and pornography investigators may experience certain psychological negative effects. What are these?
6. Even though the various warning signs officers experience constitute normal reactions, there are certain guidelines that should be followed once they have the potential for becoming even greater problems. What are they?
7. What does vicarious traumatization involve?
8. What is compassion fatigue?
9. What procedural and organizational safeguards have been recommended to protect employees against the psychological effects of constant exposure of child pornography?

25

Cumulative Career Traumatic Stress (CCTS): A Pilot Study of Traumatic Stress in Law Enforcement

Ellen K. Marshall

During the past twenty years there has been a surge of public and professional attention that has focused on the psychological and physical effects of continuous exposure to traumatic stressors. Typically, individuals exposed to chronic traumatic stress are either victims of abuse for a period of time in their lives or those who are exposed to traumatic experiences or events as a part of their occupation (Dunning, 1995; Everly, 1995; Stephens, Long, & Miller, 1997). Individuals who serve as emergency personnel are often continually exposed to high levels of traumatic stress and intense emotional experiences resulting from exposure to traumatic and critical events (Blak, 1991; Sewell, 1999; Hetherington, 1999; Violanti, 1996b). Chronic exposure to these experiences has the potential to severely impair the law enforcement officer's ability to provide emergency services to the community that he or she serves (Carlier, 1999; Spielberger, Westberry, Grier, & Greenfield, 1981).

It is understood that the law enforcement profession demands long hours, unusual and fluctuating work hours, exposure to bad weather, continual stress, poor diet, frustration, separation from family, poor physical exercise, exhaustion, the threat of serious physical injury or death, alienation from community, alcohol and drug abuse, sleeping problems, little time off, and more (Alexander, 1999; Bohl, 1990; Blau, 1974; Spielberger et al.,1981). All of these may undermine the officer's physical, mental, and emotional health over the period of a career while at the same time jeopardizing the officer's work performance and personal life.

The *Diagnostic and Statistical Manual IV (DSM-IV)* (1994), defines a traumatic event as "an event that an individual has experienced, witnessed, or is confronted with that involves death or the threat of death or serious physical injury to the self or others and causes the individual to experience intense fear, helplessness, or horror" (p. 427). In contrast to the condition of Posttraumatic Stress brought about by a single event, this author believes that officers may experience trauma symptoms sporadically throughout a career as a result of being routinely exposed to many traumatic events over a period of time. I refer to this experience as Cumulative Career Traumatic Stress (CCTS).

The symptoms of CCTS are similar to Posttraumatic Stress Disorder (PTSD), but rather than presenting suddenly as a result of a single traumatic event directly experienced by the officer, such as a shooting, the officer may experience one or a combination of symptoms sporadically throughout a career as he or she is exposed to a myriad of traumatic events over a period of years. The trauma symptoms that are experienced fail to fit the duration criteria of PTSD, but are none-the-less frequently experienced and left unacknowledged. This in turn creates the potential to cause a slow and subtle deterioration of the officer's psychological and emotional stability. For example, an officer who has responded to a fatal motor vehicle collision may experience nightmares or flashbacks of the scene for a few days after the incident. Several months later, the officer may respond to another motor vehicle fatality or similar scene that brings back memories of the collision.

Many times throughout a career, an officer may be involved in incidents that threaten his or her physical safety or which directly threaten the officer's life (Alexander, 1999; Bonifacio, 1991; Fennel, 1981). These events are typically quickly forgotten and are often viewed as a "part of the job." This cycle repeats itself throughout the officer's career. As past events are hopefully forgotten, new events trigger additional trauma symptoms and may exhume old memories (Blau, 1974; Davidson, Fleming, & Baum, 1986; Dunning, 1999).

CCTS involves the sporadic experience of trauma symptoms such as intrusive thoughts and memories of troubling incidents (via flashbacks or nightmares), emotional numbing, moodiness, anxiety, avoiding reminders of an incident/s, loss of hope, hyper-vigilance, memory and/or concentration problems, sleeping and/or eating problems, disconnection from family and friends, and hyperarousal (e.g. jumpiness, easily startled), among others. These symptoms typically will not last for more than a few days to a week, but may be re-experienced at a later time either alone or in conjunction with other trauma symptoms.

There are a number of ways in which CCTS might adversely affect the officer. These include psychological problems, impaired job performance, marital/family problems, and diminished physical health to name a few. Implicit in the process of understanding why an officer may be experiencing the adverse reactions of CCTS is the understanding that these symptoms are normal reactions to the abnormal and unique demands of policing.

The theory of Cumulative Career Traumatic Stress explains that although most law enforcement officers will not develop PTSD, they may suffer from some, if not all, of the symptoms of PTSD, with varying intensities and occurrences throughout their career as a result of continual exposure to traumatic and horrific experiences. This author asserts that the culmination of these trauma reactions causes the officer to experience traumatic symptoms sporadically throughout a career. Compared to soldiers who experience combat for a tour of six months to a year, police officers are likely to see many years of street combat where the enemy is not easily identified (Gentz, 1991; Follette, Polusny, & Milbeck, 1994; Spielberger et al. 1981; Sewell, 1999).

The cluster of trauma and stress symptoms experienced by many police officers is a direct result of the occupation. An officer may be exposed to more trauma in one week than most people would experience in a lifetime. However, an officer has been trained and conditioned to dissociate from or suppress emotions in order to perform his or her duties as a first responder. This by no means indicates that officers adjust to the traumatic stress. The emotions they may experience at a scene are suppressed or denied, not forgotten.

This preliminary study clearly demonstrates: (1) that officers are frequently exposed to traumatic events, (2) that officers sporadically experience traumatic symptoms after just one year of service, and (3) that these experiences alter the officer's worldview.

Method

The 55-item questionnaire was administered to a sample of Delaware police officers. Two agencies responded with permission to submit the request for participation, the Newark Police Department in Newark, DE and the Delaware State Police. The sample was defined by sending the request for participation to officers in each agency via interdepartmental email. Participation was strictly voluntary.

The questionnaire, based in part on the author's experience as a law enforcement officer and trauma therapist, was divided into four parts. Part one consisted of a series of questions designed to collect demographic information such as: gender, race, marital status, children, education level, years of service, rank, assignment, and shift schedule. Part two listed 20 items reflecting traumatic events that may be experienced by an officer at least once during a career such as: involvement in a shooting, high speed pursuit, serious assault, motor vehicle accidents, child-involved incidents, and more. Part three measured the frequency of experienced posttraumatic symptoms based on a Likert Scale of: Never, Seldom, Occasionally, and Frequently. The posttraumatic symptoms were divided into three categories: (1) re-experiencing, (2) avoidance, and (3) arousal. There were five questions in each category that were designed to reflect PTSD criteria such as flashbacks, sleep problems, recurring memories, difficulty concentrating, and restlessness. Part four consisted of 20 questions that were designed to assess personality and behavior changes such as: use of alcohol, relationship difficulties, change of worldview, and changes in religious beliefs.

Participants

The sample was predominately Caucasian (92 percent) and male (88 percent). Patrol officers represented 45 percent of the sample. Of this sample, just over 80 percent have a college education with 6 percent holding a graduate degree. The majority of the respondents reported having 5 years or less on the job (29 percent), 23 percent have 6–10 years of job experience, 21 percent have 11–15 years, a little over 13 percent have 16–20 years, and almost 12 percent have over 21 years of experience.

The present findings provide some descriptive evidence that police officers experience trauma symptoms over the course of a career. With the majority of respondents having less than five years of job experience, it can be posited that the effects of continual traumatic exposure are quick to manifest. The majority of respondents indicated experiencing trauma symptoms, although the questionnaire did not address how many of the symptoms may have been experienced by an individual respondent nor did the questionnaire address how many of each type of incident the officer had responded to during his or her career.

The study proved beneficial in that it provided some preliminary evidence for the effects of exposure to trauma on police officers. This evidence is reflected in the reported rates of exposure to traumatic events and the experiencing of traumatic stress symptoms as a result of the traumatic event exposure. In addition, the results also supported the hypothesis that officers experience a change in worldview as compared to prior police experience.

Repeated Exposure to Traumatic Incidents

The CCTS questionnaire measured the number of traumatic incidents the respondents had been exposed to since being in law enforcement. Twenty different incidents were questioned. The incidents that were included in this study were drawn from Spielberger's (1981) study of the most stressful incidents in law enforcement. The respondents were asked to answer either yes or no to each exposure question.

The highest-ranking exposure to a traumatic incident involved respondents having confronted a person with a weapon. All of the respondents (100 percent) reported having confronted a person in possession of a weapon. In this type of situation, the conclusion can be made that the officer's life or physical safety is directly threatened at that moment, meeting the *DSM IV* criteria for a traumatic event.

The second highest-ranking exposure was responding to a domestic incident where a violent act was committed. Ninety-eight percent of the respondents reported being exposed to this type of incident.

The third ranking incident involved the respondent drawing his or her weapon on a person. Again, 98 percent of the respondents reported having to draw their weapon on a person. Typically, this is only done when the officer's life or another's life or physical safety is directly threatened. In addition, 98 percent of the respondents reported having to use force on another person.

Confronting an aggressive crowd and responding to a serious or fatal motor vehicle accident both ranked fourth in exposure at 94 percent. Only three officers reported that they had never responded to either type of incident.

Seventy-eight percent of the respondents reported they had confronted a person possessing a gun, making this type of incident the fifth highest traumatic incident reported. Again, this type of incident would most likely involve the officer's life or physical safety being directly threatened, meeting the *DSM-IV* criteria defining a traumatic event.

The moderate rates of traumatic incident exposure involved responding to a complaint that involved child abuse or neglect that the officer found disturbing. Seventy-six percent of the respondents reported having been exposed to this type of event and found it to be disturbing. Seventy-six of the respondents also reported having been involved in a high speed pursuit.

A surprisingly high number of respondents, 62 percent, reported having had to respond to homicide complaints and 62 percent of the respondents also have conducted death notifications. Typically, officers are asked to provide death notifications with no prior crisis management training and without mental health professional support.

Over half of the officers, 56 percent, reported responding to an incident involving the death of a child. According to prior research (Spielberger, Westberry, Grier, & Greenfield; 1981), this type of incident is ranked in the top ten of the most stressful incidents an officer may handle. Fifty percent of the respondents reported having been assaulted at least once during their career.

Included in the low response ratings is the officer relating an incident to his or her personal life. Forty-three percent of the officers reported having experienced relating an incident to their personal life. Considered a traumatic event in policing with the potential to cause PTSD (Spielberger et al., 1981; Bohl, 1990; Dunning, 1999; Everly, 1995; Gentz, 1991; Solomon, 1995), 35 percent of the respondents reported having had a co-worker shot or killed in the line of duty.

Meeting PTSD traumatic event criteria, 31 percent of the respondents have experienced someone attempting to seriously kill or injure the respondent while on duty. Also considered one of the most severe traumatic events in law enforcement (Sewell, 1999), 19 percent of the officer respondents reported having shot and/or killed a person while in the line of duty.

Fifteen percent of the respondents reported being injured in a duty-related motor vehicle accident. Thirteen percent reported being involved in a shooting and 11 percent reported being seriously injured while on duty.

Experiencing of Traumatic Stress Symptomatology

The majority of the top rated experienced symptomatologies, as reported by the respondents, fall under the arousal and re-experiencing criteria of traumatic stress (see Table 1). These reported symptoms include recurring memories of an incident, easily losing temper, recurring images or thoughts, sleeping difficulty, jumpiness or restlessness, and difficulty concentrating.

The most experienced traumatic symptom as reported in this study was recurring memories of an incident with a 74 percent response rate and 62 percent reporting experiencing recurring images or thoughts. Sixty-six percent of the respondents reported that they lose their temper easily since being on the job. Sixty-two percent of the officers reported that they have experienced trouble sleeping since being on the job and 56 percent experience jumpiness or restlessness while 51 percent reported having difficulty concentrating as compared to pre-policing experiences. Forty-seven percent of the respondents experience flashbacks of an incident and 43 percent experience nightmares as a result of an incident while 45 percent of the officers reported being easily startled.

The lower response rates primarily reflected the numbing criteria of traumatic stress symptomatology including feeling detached from others (41 percent), having numbed emotions (47 percent), being unable to enjoy emotions (25 percent), and feeling as if there is no hope for the future (17 percent).

Table 1
Repeated Experiencing of Traumatic Symptoms

Variable	Percent
Nightmares resulting from an incident	43
Flashbacks of an incident	47
Recurring memories of an incident	74
Re-experiencing of physical reactions	33
Recurring images or thoughts	62
Avoid reminders of an incident	54
Feeling detached from others	41
Unable to experience enjoyable emotions	25
Feel as if there is no hope for the future	17
Numbed emotions	47
Difficulty concentrating	51
Jumpiness or restlessness	56
Easily startled	45
Trouble sleeping	62
Lose temper easily	66

Changes in Worldview

One of the most surprising and important factors to be addressed in this study are the changes in worldview as experienced by the respondents since being in law enforcement (see Table 2). A striking 96 percent of the respondents reported that their opinions of others have changed since being on the job. Based on this author's experience in law enforcement, this opinion change is not positive, but a negative outlook toward others, as reflected in 88 percent of the respondents experiencing prejudices. Running a very close second, 92 percent of the respondents reported that they no longer trust others as a result of the job, which may have an influence on the reported 82 percent who now feel the world is an unsafe place.

Fifty-four percent reported that job stress affects their relationships and 53 percent reported that their faith or religious beliefs have changed. Fifty-one percent experienced appetite changes and 47 percent have lost interest in pleasurable activities. Thirty-one percent experience intense fear, helplessness, or horror and 35 percent use alcohol to relax. Lastly, but most importantly, 11 percent have experienced suicidal ideation as a result of the job.

Table 2
Changes in Worldview

Variable	Percent
Opinion of others has changed	96
No longer trust others	92
Experience prejudices	88
Faith/religious beliefs have changed	53
Feel world is an unsafe place	82
Changes in appetite	51
Experience intense fear, helplessness, horror	31
Relationships affected by job stress	54
Use of alcohol to relax	35
Lost interest in pleasurable activities	47
Thought of suicide	11

Summary

The effects of CCTS are also delayed and closely resemble the symptoms of PTSD or burnout. However, the symptoms are more trauma-related than stress-based. The symptoms may appear "out of the blue" in officers who have not previously manifested stress symptoms. In addition, the stress reactions may vary due to personality characteristics, ego strength, available social support, life experiences, prior trauma, years of service, education level, effective coping strategies, the intensity of the event, the number of exposures to traumatic events, and available support in the police organization.

Officers operating under severe, chronic, and traumatic stress may be at risk of error, accidents, and over-reaction that can compromise their performance, jeopardize the public, and pose significant liability costs to the organization. However, officers are very rarely provided with effective stress management strategies to help alleviate these problems.

The operational duties of police work may at times place officers in life-threatening situations in which the decisions they make can mean the difference between life and death for themselves and others (Gentz, 1991; Terry, 1981; Violanti, 2001 & 1996b; Yarney, 1990). Many of these situations fall under the category of a traumatic event. Many incidents are intensely stressful and emotionally charged, yet the emotions and stress are denied and carried silently by the officer. The unusually stringent demands for self-control are compounded by continual exposure to traumatic events and stress (Reiser, 1974; Sherman, 1980; Violanti & Paton, 1999).

Despite the obvious negatives, unrealistic expectations are imposed by this occupational culture which discourages officers from admitting to experiencing stress and from openly expressing negative emotions (Bonifacio, 1991; Brown & Campbell, 1994; Dunning, 1999; Ellison & Genz, 1978). Organizational policy may even punish those who admit to or are found to be suffering from excessive stress. Most officers receive little to no training in self-management skills needed to help them regain psychological and physiological equilibrium.

The continuing rise of violent and horrific crime in our communities demands an increasing workload for police (Spielberger et al., 1981; Follette, Polusny, & Milbeck, 1994). The need for officers to learn stress recognition and management skills will only increase over time. The integration of stress management and critical incident management programs must occur for effective self-management and greater effectiveness in serving the community (Bohl, 1990; Horn, 1991; Mitchell & Bray, 1990).

While law enforcement administrations have no control over the types of demands placed upon the police, they do have the ability to help protect their officers from excessive and traumatic stress and consequently support the officers' physical, psychological, and emotional health (Reiser, 1974; Sherman; 1980). Although the primary purpose of this study was to address excessive and traumatic stress in policing, the need of organizational involvement in the preventive efforts of traumatic stress should be addressed in future research. Often viewed as the officer's responsibility, police administrations must realize and accept their part in this context (Anson & Bloom, 1988; Solomon, 1995; Stratton, 1983; Violanti, 1993). If left unchecked and ignored, intolerable work experiences from which an officer sees no escape often leads to psychological breakdown and in extreme cases, suicide (Solomon, 1995; Stephens, 1997; Violanti, 1996a).

References

Alexander, C. (1999). Police psychological burnout and trauma. In J. M Violanti & D. Paton (Eds.), *Police trauma: Psychological aftermath of civilian combat.* (pp. 54–64). Springfield, Ill: Charles C Thomas.

American Psychiatric Association. (1994). *Diagnostic and Statistical Manual of Mental Disorders-IV.* Washington, DC: American Psychiatric Association.

Anson, R. & Bloom, M. (1988). Police stress in an occupational context. *Journal of Police Science and Administration, 16,* 229–235.

Blak, R. A. (1991). Critical incident debriefing for law enforcement personnel: A model. In J. T. Reese, J. M. Horn, & C. Dunning (Eds.), *Critical incidents in policing.* (pp. 23–30). Washington, DC: Government Printing Office.

Blau, T.H. (1974). *Psychological services for law enforcement.* New York: John Wiley & Sons.

Bohl, N. (1990). The effectiveness of brief psychological interventions in police officers after critical incidents. In J. T. Reese, J. M. Horn, & C. Dunning (Eds.), *Critical incidents in policing.*(pp. 51–61). Washington, DC: Government Printing Office.

Bonifacio, P. (1991). *The psychological effect of police work.* New York: Plenum Press.

Brown, J. M., & Campbell, E. A. (1994). *Stress and policing: Sources and strategies.* New York: John Wiley & Sons.

Carlier, I. V. (1999). Finding meaning in police traumas. In J. M Violanti & D. Paton (Eds.), *Police trauma: Psychological aftermath of civilian combat.* (pp. 227–240). Springfield, Ill: Charles C Thomas.

Davidson, C. M., Fleming, I., & Baum, A. (1986). Post-traumatic stress as a function of chronic stress and toxic exposure. In C. E. Figley (Ed.), *Trauma and its wake: Traumatic stress, theory, research, and intervention.* New York: Brunner/Mazel.

Dunning, C. M. (1995). Fostering resiliency in rescue workers. In A. S. Kalayjian (Ed.), *Disaster and mass trauma.* Long Branch, NJ: Vista Press.

Dunning, C. M. (1999). Postintervention strategies to reduce police trauma: a paradigm shift. In J. M. Violanti & D. Paton (Eds.), *Police trauma: Psychological aftermath of civilian combat.*(pp. 269–289). Springfield, Ill: Charles C Thomas.

Ellison, K.W. & Genz, J.S. (1978). Police officer as burned-out Samaritan. *FBI Law Enforcement Bulletin, 47,* 1–7.

Everly, G.S. (1995). *Innovations in disaster and trauma psychology: Applications in emergency services and disaster response.* Ellicott City, MD: Chevron Publishing.

Fennel, J.T. (1981). Psychological stress and the peace officer, or stress—a cop killer. In G. Henderson (Ed.), *Police human relations.* Springfield, IL: Charles C Thomas.

Finn, P., & Tomz, J. E. (1997). *Developing a law enforcement stress program for officers and their families.* Washington, DC: U.S. Department of Justice, Office of Justice Programs, National Institute of Justice.

Follette, V.M., Polusny, M.M., & Milbeck, K. (1994). Mental health and law enforcement professionals: trauma history, psychological symptoms, and impact of providing services to child sexual abuse survivors. *Professional Psychology: Research and Practice, 25,* 275–282.

Gentz, D. (1991). The psychological impact of critical incidents on police officers. In J. T. Reese, J. M. Horn, & C. Dunning (Eds.), *Critical incidents in policing.* (pp. 119–121). Washington, DC: Government Printing Office.

Hetherington, A. (1999). Traumatic stress on the roads. In L. Territo & J.D. Sewell (Eds.), *Stress management in law enforcement,* (pp. 146–154). Durham, NC: Carolina Academic Press.

Horn, J.M (1991). Critical incidents for law enforcement officers. In J. T. Reese, J. M. Horn, & C. Dunning (Eds.), *Critical incidents in policing.* (pp. 143–148). Washington, DC: Government Printing Office.

Mitchell, J. & Bray, G. (1990). *Emergency services stress: Guidelines for preserving the health and careers of emergency services personnel.* Englewood Cliffs, NJ: Prentice Hall.

Reiser, M. (1974). Some organizational stresses on policemen. *Journal of Police Science and Administration, 2,* 156–159.

Sherman, L. (1980). The causes of police behavior: The current state of quantitative research. *Journal of Research in Crime and Delinquency, 17,* 69–100.

Sewell, J.D. (1999). The stress of homicide investigations. In Territo, L. & Sewell, J.D. (Eds.). *Stress management in law enforcement.* Durham, NC: Carolina Academic Press.

Solomon, R. M. (1995). Critical incident stress in law enforcement. In G. Everly & J. Mitchell (Eds.) *Innovations in disaster and trauma psychology.* (pp. 123–157). Ellicott City, MD Chevron Publishing.

Spielberger, C. D., Westberry, L. G., Grier, K. S., & Greenfield, G. (1981). *The Police Stress Survey: Sources of stress in law enforcement.* Tampa, FL: Human Resources Institute.

Stephens, C., Long, N., & Miller, I. (1997). The impact of trauma and social support on posttraumatic stress disorder: A study of New Zealand Police Officers. *Journal of Criminal Justice, 25,* 303–313.

Stratton, J. G. (1983). Traumatic incidents and the police. *Police Stress, 6,* 4–7.

Terry, W.C. (1981). Police stress: The empirical evidence. *Journal of Police Science and Administration, 9,* 61–75.

Violanti, J.M. (1993). What does high stress training teach recruits? An analysis of coping. *Journal of Criminal Justice, 21,* 411–417.

Violanti, J.M.(1996a). *Police suicide: Epidemic in blue.* Springfield, IL: Charles C Thomas.

Violanti, J. M. (1996b). Trauma stress and police work. In D. Paton & J.M. Violanti (Eds.) *Traumatic Stress in Critical Occupations:Recognition,Consequences and Treatment.* Springfield, IL: Charles C Thomas Publishers.

Violanti, J.M. (2001). Post traumatic stress disorder intervention in law enforcement: Differing perspectives. *The Australian Journal of Disaster and*

Trauma Studies, 2, retrieved September 10, 2002 from http://www.massey.ac. nz.html.

Violanti, J.M., & Aron, F. (1994). Ranking police stressors. *Psychological Reports, 75,* 824–826.

Violanti, J. M., & Paton, D. (Eds.). (1999). *Police trauma: Psychological aftermath of civilian combat.* Springfield, Ill: Charles C Thomas.

Yarney, D.A. (1990). *Understanding police and police work: Psychosocial issues.* New York: University Press.

Author's Note: Communications may be addressed to Ellen K. Marshall, Ph.D., Delaware Technical & Community College, Criminal Justice Department, P.O. Box 610, Georgetown, Delaware 19947.

Discussion Questions

1. What types of individuals are typically exposed to chronic traumatic stress?
2. How does the Diagnostic and Statistical Manual IV (DSM-IV) define a traumatic event?
3. How does Cumulative Career Traumatic Stress (CCTS) differ from Post Traumatic Stress Disorder (PTSD)?
4. What are the behavioral manifestations of CCTS?
5. How may CCTS adversely affect the officer?
6. In this study, a CCTS questionnaire was administered. What were the three highest ranking traumatic incidents identified by the respondents?
7. What were some of the top rated experience symptomologies reported by the respondents experiencing traumatic stress?
8. In what ways have the officers under study changed their world view since becoming police officers?

26

Wounded Warriors and the Virginia Tech Tragedy

Thomas R. McDearis

Introduction

April 16, 2007, was already a strange day in Blacksburg, Virginia. Nestled in the Blue Ridge Mountains, Blacksburg is accustomed to unusual weather patterns. However, 35 degrees, snow flurries, and wind gusts of 60 miles per hour are quite odd for spring, even in a town where the joke is, "If you don't like our weather, wait an hour, and it'll be something else."

I was taking the day off that Monday. As ridiculous as it now seems, I thought I had a problem. My printer had gone out, and I was complaining, in my mind, that I had to go out in that wretched weather to buy a new one. Moving slowly, having no urgency to be anywhere, I had just stepped to another room when I heard my cell phone ringing. Unable to reach it, I thought that they could leave a message, and I would call them back. Seconds later, it rang again. Experience told me that this call was important.

Upon answering the phone, I heard a member of the local rescue squad say, "Do you know what's going on? There's shooting, lots of it. Somebody's inside Norris Hall, and they're shooting the place up. You better get over there fast." Having once been a deputy sheriff, I knew the gravity and danger of such a call.

I currently serve as a chaplain of the Blacksburg Police Department and as the senior pastor of the Blacksburg Baptist Church. Sensing that the day was about to thrust me into places where instant identification would be crucial, I grabbed my badge and my police uniform from the closet. But, before I could get dressed, the phone rang again and again. Lieutenant Bruce Bradbery, now a captain, of the Blacksburg Police Department yelled, "Pray! Pray hard! Don't stop. Go to the hospital as fast as you can." Another call came from an unidentified number. Although I still am unsure who it was, I never will forget the voice saying, "It's terrible. Come quick. We need your help."

The Unthinkable Attack

At the time, I had no way of knowing that the first chapter of this tragedy had begun over 2 hours earlier when the same assailant shot and wounded a young woman in her dorm on the Virginia Tech campus. She would die 2 hours later. Upon hearing either the gunshot or the girl's cry for help, the floor's resident assistant went to her aid. He was shot in the head upon entering her room and died instantly.

Although it is not known why this first assault was made, this tragic event revealed itself to be a mistake toward the assailant completing his ultimate plan. Had that event not occurred only those officers on patrol and the command staffs of the Virginia Tech and Blacksburg police departments would have been available to respond to the shootings in Norris Hall. However, following the first shootings, a student in a neighboring room reported what she thought was someone who had fallen from a bunk bed in the room next door. Virginia Tech Rescue was dispatched, and a Virginia Tech police officer responded as well. Upon arrival, the officer found two bodies and called for assistance. As time passed, that initial call brought a contingent of officers from the Virginia Tech and Blacksburg police departments, including the emergency response (SWAT) teams from both, to the campus. Also, the Blacksburg police requested patrol assistance from the Montgomery County Sheriff's Office, a call that made still more officers available when the shootings began in Norris Hall.

At 9:42 a.m., the first call was received from Norris Hall; others would follow. An active shooter was on the second floor of the classroom building. Officers from both Virginia Tech and Blacksburg responded. Although the assailant had chained the doors of Norris Hall from the inside, the police made entry within 8 minutes of the first call. Breaching doors with gunfire and bolt cutters, they made an attack on the second floor of Norris Hall where they could hear shots being fired in rapid succession. They immediately announced their presence upon reaching the second-floor hallway. At that time, one more shot was heard, that of the assailant taking his own life. The building then became utterly silent. No screams or calls for help were heard. A room-to-room search was conducted. Once the suspect was identified and the floor was secured, the medical evacuation began.

The Terrible Toll

As I raced to the local hospital, I could tell something truly terrible was unfolding. Law enforcement units and ambulances from across a 40-mile region were streaming toward Virginia Tech. En route to the hospital, I called Lieutenant Bradbery for an update. I had no idea that he was loading injured and dying students from the classroom building into his police SUV and speeding them two blocks away to the staging area where dozens of ambulances were now lining up to transport the wounded. I asked where he was, and he replied, "I can't talk now. Get to the hospital. This is bad. I've never seen anything like it."

Tragedy is not new to me. While in college, I not only served with the sheriff's office but also worked part time for a funeral home and with the local ambulance service. Later, while serving my first rural church, I was a captain with the county's fire and rescue service. I have seen my share of death and injury, but not like this.

Arriving before I could hear the wail of the first sirens from approaching ambulances, I thought the emergency department of Montgomery Regional Hospital looked surreal, like an episode of "ER." Doctors, nurses, and technicians suited in their sterile gowns; the entire hospital abuzz with the trauma alert; four surgical suites cleared for trauma surgery. It was eerie and, oddly, quite reassuring.

Several police officers arrived at the hospital almost in tandem with me. As they began setting up security and a media area, I was summoned to a trauma room to minister to a young student who had been gravely wounded in the first attack at Ambler-Johnson Hall and whose eyes now portrayed the close of life. I offered a prayer of benediction. Minutes later, she was evacuated to the region's level-one trauma center where neurosurgeons awaited her arrival. Sadly, shortly after leaving our hospital, the young woman died.

As I emerged from the room, Lieutenant Bradbery called me and said, "I've just put eight students in an ambulance and they're on their way. Tell the ER to be ready." After passing the message, a number of us went to the ambulance bay to await the incoming victims. Within minutes, the first sirens blared into the hospital driveway as we stood ready to unload the broken students. Yelling "red," meaning the students were critical and a top priority, we grabbed the stretchers and pushed them to waiting medical teams. One girl, shot several times, grabbed my hand and said, "Hold me. I'm gonna die." I held her as long as I could, and, thankfully, she did not die.

In less than 10 minutes, the driveway was filled with ambulances bringing 18 of the 25 wounded victims to our hospital. Many were badly injured and some less so, but all were stunned and shocked that such a thing could happen. They mirrored the feelings of the entire community.

As the first line of ambulances unloaded their shattered cargo, we all become annoyed that we could not hear any other sirens approaching. What was the hold up? What was taking so long? As we stood in the ambulance bay awaiting more victims, a nurse came to me with tears in her eyes. "That's all of them," she said, "but they say they have at least 12 dead, maybe more." Only then did it hit us. We would hear no more sirens. A silence had befallen Norris Hall. A silence no siren could awaken.

Fifteen minutes later, I called Lieutenant Bradbery. Asking how many victims were dead and hoping that he could correct the number I had been told earlier, I never will forget his answer, "I don't know for sure, but it's like a war zone. I'd say between 30 and 40. At least that many." My mind could not comprehend 12 dead, much less between 30 and 40. For me, however, even worse was to come.

The Inner Turmoil

Less than 10 minutes after speaking with Lieutenant Bradbery, I received a call from my church staff regarding a missing student who had been in room 211 of Norris Hall. By this time, I knew that some of the worst carnage in Norris Hall had occurred in room 211. Yet, I had no way to confirm this student's whereabouts. I immediately canvassed the hospital to ascertain if she had been brought in without my noticing. She was not there. I then called the other hospitals in the region, spoke with police officers on the scene, and gave them her name and description. There was no sign of her. I knew this left only one place for her to be, but I tried to tell myself that several victims had yet to be identified at other hospitals. Surely, she was one of them.

For the next three hours, I cared for the less severely wounded students, letting them talk and helping them with phone calls to their parents and friends. We set up a hospitality room for the friends of the wounded. Dozens of them arrived seeking information and support, and we did the best we could to keep them calm and informed. I made my rounds to the many police officers from several agencies surrounding the hospital. How were they doing? What were they thinking? What did they need? How could I help? Questions any chaplain would ask in the aftermath of a major tragedy.

By 1 p.m., the worst of the crisis at the hospital had subsided, so I left to go to Norris Hall. Another chaplain and I arrived just as the process of removing bodies began. To me, the Virginia Tech campus is one of the most beautiful state university campuses in America. Most of the buildings are constructed of magnificent stone known locally as Hokie Stone, named for the Virginia Tech mascot. As we entered the archway of this grand 1920s-era classroom building, a door suddenly burst open, and through it came a stretcher carrying a stark black, sadly occupied, body bag. It was the epitome of paradox.

Over the next two hours, we chaplains paced the area talking with stunned and sometimes angry police officers. I found one officer standing behind a bush with tears in his eyes, clearly wanting no one to see him. However, most were doing better than I had expected. Having shifted early into "cop mode," they performed their arduous tasks with poise and professionalism. Most had placed the bulk of their emotions in neutral. They all knew that they had important work to do that could not be hampered by tears or rage.

Sometime after our arrival at Norris Hall, I received another call informing me that no one had found the missing student from our church. I called the police command post to see if she was listed among the wounded. She was not. I decided to go to room 211 to see if she was there. However, as I started toward Norris Hall, I received a phone call from Blacksburg's police chief. The Inn at Virginia Tech had been designated as the receiving point for the families of the deceased. The chief asked me and the other chaplain to join a lieutenant at the Inn to establish a command post and to begin the process of notifying the families of their losses. I told the chief that I was about to go search for the missing student, but she asked me to avoid doing so. She told me that even if I found her, I could not tell her parents until the police had positively identified her. Understanding the situation, I followed the chief's instructions. However, this was hard for me. I was functioning in two roles on April 16, 2007. I was a representative of the Blacksburg Police Department, but I also was the pastor of the Blacksburg Baptist Church. These roles rarely are in conflict, but, occasionally, the lines between them can become blurred. This day was one of those times.

Upon arriving at the Inn, the first people I saw were the missing student's parents. There was anguish on their faces. Suddenly, I felt like I should have gone to Norris Hall to find their daughter. That is what I would have wanted someone to do for me. I quickly called to ask if the victims of room 211 were still in the classroom, but the bodies had been cleared. A wave of guilt swept over me. As a police chaplain, it is not my job to seek out and identify murder victims, but, as this family's pastor, I felt an obligation to try to find their daughter. Yet, I knew this was not my choice to make. The final choice lay with the chief of police. My job as a chaplain was to inform the many families of their losses and then minister to their needs. But, those two parents right in front of me were *my* church members. I felt so torn inside. However, my great respect for our chief and the knowledge of my role in this tragedy led me to follow the chief's instructions. To be effective, a police chaplain must understand this role, and, if you cannot fulfill the requirements of the job, you should step out of it. I chose to try to fulfill the requirements of the position, even though it left me feeling guilt-ridden.

From the early evening of April 16 until the early afternoon of April 17, we informed families of their tragic losses. It was a slow process. Most of the students were not carrying identification, so nearly all had to be identified by other means. As the families received the grim news, a few were calm and almost stoic. Most, however, were not. If I live 100 years, I never will forget those screams, one after the other for 2 consecutive days. It was months before I stopped hearing those screams in my dreams. And, oh, how desperately those families clung to hope. Those poor people grasped to every ounce of hope they could for as long as they could. They were so desperate for the truth. But, until the truth was finally spoken, in their minds, their children, husbands, and wives were still with them. Again, it was such a paradox: families desperately wanting to know while, simultaneously, never wanting to know.

On the evening of April 16, a second personal blow came my way. Having been called to make another notification, I asked the name of the victim. The chief turned and handed it to me. I was shocked when I saw the name of another student who also attended our church. A girl who always seemed to sparkle with joy; I rarely saw her without a smile on her face. She had big dreams for the future, she had the drive and the intelligence to make them come true, and all of her dreams included God and the greater good of humankind.

The Invisible Wounds

The following days were a blur. President Bush and Governor Kaine arrived on April 17 for the joint memorial service on campus. I helped escort the families to the coliseum while dozens of police officers provided security. Then came the funerals. I led three of them and assisted the police at the funeral home and at the sites of several others. Between the services, we conducted critical incident debriefings with the police officers. Many were held at my church. But, regardless of the setting, the response was usually the same. Some officers were annoyed because they were required to be present. Some were talkative. There were tears. Often, there was silence coupled with a deep sense of mutual compassion. Everyone understood how the others were feeling, so support and respect permeated the various police departments.

Like most of Blacksburg, I spent the following days trying to make sense of the senseless act that so shattered our town and our university. I wanted to think that, until the morning of April 16, a broken printer and a day of blustery weather were among our more significant crises, but such was not true. Less than a year earlier, in August 2006, two local officers were killed in the line of duty, shot by an escaped prisoner. The police officers and sheriff's deputies of the region still were grieving when the Virginia Tech tragedy unfolded, thus making April 16 even more heart wrenching and stressful.

In the days that followed, many spoke honest words to me that were hard to hear, "It feels like God took a day off that Monday." How do you care for people amidst such doubt and suffering? It was a dilemma being faced by all of the police chaplains from every department involved. What do you say when you know, all too personally, the frustration that everyone feels?

Having been a cop, I know the culture. I knew from experience that this was no place for spouting scripture or offering unwanted religious platitudes. Yet, even among these strong, determined warriors, support was needed. What should we do next? At least a partial answer soon came, something different from what I had previously witnessed.

In the aftermath of the Virginia Tech tragedy, officers from five area agencies began making contact. Most did not want the others to know that they were talking to the "cop's parsons," so they would call at night or find some reason to drop by our churches. Some called to ask if I wanted to join them for lunch. Some just needed to let off steam. Some did nothing more than tell the latest joke. Some sent e-mails or text messages. But, in the months following the tragedy, seldom a week went by without calls from officers, their spouses, or their significant others.

Officers would stop us in the halls of the police headquarters "to chat." More police officers and sheriff's deputies passed through the back door of my church in April, May, and June 2007 than had been inside that building in 50 years. Most were not there to "find God," although a few did so in the weeks after the shootings. But, most did not come for overt religion. Some came sincerely asking, "Tommy, how are *you* doing?" Others just wanted to share their story with another who was there. But, the point is that many came, and all were welcomed because *they* were the wounded warriors. They had walked in the blood of children and in that of heroic professors who tried to bar classroom doors with their bodies in an effort to save their students. These warriors in blue and brown were indeed strong and professional, but they were wounded nonetheless. They had seen a huge chunk of hell that day, as well as another on that earlier August day when their comrades had fallen. Their spirits were heavy. They were spiritually drained. They needed someone to understand and to offer them encouragement. Some needed assurance that the bad guy had not won. Others just needed assurance, period. So, they came to their chaplains. It has been my experience that not a lot of officers do that. It was one of the great affirmations of my life that so many of them did. Somewhere along the way, a bond of trust had apparently formed, and, for that trust, we chaplains were extremely grateful.

The Need for Care

How do you care for the spirits of the wounded warriors when so many run for cover upon hearing the word *spiritual*? It is indeed a dilemma. For us, the chance to do so came only after having spent many years walking in the shadows of these warriors. Rather than being the "cop's preachers," we have tried to simply be a presence. We never get worked up if a cop cusses. So what? We are not in the judgment business. We are in the helping business. We have tried to be there when death or sickness came calling or when marriages or relationships were coming apart. When a word from God was appropriate, helpful, and desired, we have tried to offer it. But, we always have extended support, friendship, humor, and a presence—a spiritual presence—for wounded spirits. Is that enough? No, but it is a start. And, with all my heart and soul, I believe God moves through those who will make their lives an avenue upon which the gifts of hope and healing can travel. And, I *know* even the strongest and the bravest warriors have wounds that *must* be healed if those warriors are to remain strong and fit for battle.

Too many of our warriors in blue give in to cynicism, alcoholism, and depression without ever reaching out for another's help. Some give up completely. When they do, we all lose. One officer who commits suicide is not only one too many but is one less warrior to respond when evil descends upon our streets or our classrooms.

How do we repair these wounded spirits? Much work needs to be done before we can fully answer that question. But, the work *must* be done. Virginia Tech was not and will not be the last place where law enforcement officers will walk amidst the wounds. Every time they do, a part of the spirit cracks. And, after all, even the hardest stone can crumble if the cracks become too deep.

Discussion Questions

1. What is the background of the author?
2. Where did this incident occur?
3. What was meant by the expression that most of the officers had shifted their emotions into "cop mode"?
4. What did the author see as his responsibility as a police chaplain?

Part Seven

What Is the Impact of Foreign Wars on Our Cops?

America's protracted wars in Afghanistan and Iraq, coupled with military responses to other worldwide hot spots, have taken their toll on American law enforcement. Police personnel serving in military reserve and National Guard units have been activated for service, and agencies throughout the country have found themselves short of staff for extended periods of time.

As these wars come to an end, the impact on policing in this country will continue. First, for law enforcement personnel returning to their agency from combat service, post-traumatic stress disorder, with its associated physical and psychological manifestations, poses a real threat to the emotional well-being of these officers and their agencies. Similarly, deactivated military personnel seeking initial employment in law enforcement face the same danger.

Second, as we saw in the years following the conclusion of the Vietnam conflict, veterans suffering from PTSD, traumatic brain injuries, and other combat injuries frequently will become a law enforcement issue. Sadly, we can expect our combat veterans to experience increased joblessness, homelessness, substance abuse, and mental health issues, as well as conflict within their families. As these individuals act out as a result of their traumatic experiences and the related problems with returning to civilian life, their behavior is often called to the attention of law enforcement, which must initiate an appropriate response, even when, as is commonly the case, not knowing the circumstances underlying the individual's immediate actions. Too frequently, the criminal justice system is forced to be the source of resolution for problems which are not of its making or, in reality, within its expertise.

Third, the cost of dealing with the physical and psychological damage to our armed forces personnel will be tremendous in future years. Estimated at upwards of $59 billion over the next decade (Bilmes and Stiglitz, 2009:35), the appropriation of funds to provide medical care and disability payments resulting from these wars may ultimately impact the funding of the nation's law enforcement agencies, particularly in the Federal grants upon which many entities have come to rely.

So what are the considerations we need to examine in assessing the impact of foreign wars on our cops and our law enforcement agencies? What are the most common psychological dangers our personnel will encounter as they re-enter the world of civilian policing? What steps should agencies take to ensure the readjustment, proper treatment, and appropriate training of returning veterans? What commonalities do military and law enforcement have and how can they learn from one another?

Territo sets the stage for Part Seven in his discussion of military combat veterans and their impact on a law enforcement agency. As he notes, law enforcement officers returning from a combat deployment and combat veterans seeking first-time employment as police officers both face the potential impact of psychological issues resulting from their combat experiences. A critical distinction in adapting to either role is an understanding and acceptance that differing rules of engagement govern combat and civilian police work, neither of which would be easily translated into the other environment. The adjustment of combat personnel to the civilian law enforcement environment has significant implications for the employment, psychological screening, training, supervision, and performance monitoring of such personnel.

Recent research indicates an increased risk of suicide among returning combat veterans and among police officers. When police officers are deployed into military combat situations, the risk for suicide may therefore increase substantially. In a chapter written specifically for this book, Violanti discusses research on suicide rates, the potential impact of the trauma of war and police work on police suicide, and the development of a resilient police organization for the prevention of suicide. He emphasizes the importance of the role of the agency's leadership in creating a climate of trust within the organization and identifies areas demanding future research efforts.

Funded by a grant from the Office of Community Oriented Policing Services within the U.S. Department of Justice, Webster and her colleagues at the Institute for Law and Justice focus on issues relating to the reintegration of police officers who have been deployed into military combat zones. This work discusses the psychological effects of combat and natural disasters, particularly post-traumatic stress disorder (PTSD), and explains efforts to reduce the risk of PTSD through primary and secondary prevention techniques and tertiary interventions. Of particular import is the chapter's review of strategies being used by four separate law enforcement agencies (Los Angeles Police Department, Los Angeles Sheriff's Department, Kansas City, Missouri, Police Department, and Richland County, South Carolina, Sheriff's Department) to assist their personnel in making the transition back into the agency and their civilian police role.

In the concluding article, also written specifically for this edition of *Stress Management in Law Enforcement*, Miller reflects that, "like siblings separated at birth, military psychology and law enforcement psychology have, for decades, each independently addressed the cognitive, perceptual, emotional, and behavioral challenges facing the men and women who perform extreme service in defense of their communities." Drawing on parallels in the response to combat and critical incident stress, he discusses the basic principles of psychotherapy and psychotherapeutic techniques used to effectively intervene with the "wounded warrior," whether soldier or cop. His work is a call for a comprehensive system of clinical and operational psychology focused on personnel in high-danger, high-demand professions, such as law enforcement and the military.

Further Reading

Bilmes, Linda J., and Stiglitz, Joseph E. (2009). "Report: The $10 Trillion Hangover: Paying the Price for Eight Years of Bush," *Harper's Magazine*, 318(1904): 31–35.

Bremner, J. Douglas (2002). *Does Stress Damage the Brain? Understanding Trauma-related Disorders from a Mind–body Perspective*. New York, NY: Norton.

Figley, Charles R. (Ed.). (1978). *Stress Disorders among Vietnam Veterans: Theory, Research, and Treatment*. New York, NY: Brunner/Mazel.

Figley, Charles R., & Leventman, Seymour (Eds.). (1980). *Strangers at Home: Vietnam Veterans since the War*. New York, NY: Brunner/Mazel.

Figley, Charles R., and Nash, William P., Eds. (2007). *Combat Stress Injury: Theory, Research, and Management*. New York: Routledge.

International Association of Chiefs of Police (2009). *Employing Returning Combat Veterans as Law Enforcement Officers*. Alexandria, VA: The International Association of Chiefs of Police.

Shay, Jonathan (1994). *Achilles in Vietnam: Combat Trauma and the Undoing of Character*. New York, NY: Scribner.

Shay, Jonathan (2002). *Odysseus in America: Combat Trauma and the Trials of Homecoming*. New York, NY: Scribner.

Key Terms in Part Seven

Defense mechanisms: The mental stratagems the mind uses to protect itself from unpleasant thoughts, feelings, impulses, and memories.

Operation Enduring Freedom: The military effort in Afghanistan.

Operation Iraqi Freedom: The military effort in Iraq.

Organizational climate: Officers' perceptions of how their organization functions; it serves as the best single predictor of job satisfaction.

Police resiliency: The capacity of agencies and officers to draw upon individual, collective, and institutional resources to cope with demands, challenges, and changes encountered during and after critical incidents.

27

Military Combat Veterans: What They Mean for Your Department

Leonard Territo

Introduction

According to data from the Law Enforcement Management and Administrative Statistics survey compiled by the Bureau of Justice Statistics in 2003, 23 percent of the approximately 18,000 law enforcement agencies in the U. S. had military reservist officers in their ranks that have been called to active duty, many having served in Iraq and Afghanistan. An estimated 11,380 full-time sworn police officers were called up as full-time military reservists in a 12-month period. Most of these, about two-thirds, were officers from local police departments. As a portion of all sworn officers in these agencies, these 11,380 officers constitute about 2 percent of the available law enforcement workforce.[1] However, at the time of this writing all American military personnel have been pulled out of Iraq and a significant draw down of our troops in Afghanistan is already underway, thus suggesting that most of these law enforcement officers/reservists will soon be returning to their agencies. Undoubtedly many of them have served in combat assignments.

Two Different Categories

There are two different categories of returning combat veterans: combat veterans returning to their law enforcement agencies and combat veterans who

---

1. "Employing Returning Combat Veterans as Police Officers," *International Association of Chiefs of Police*, June 25, 2007, p. 9.

have no previous law enforcement service experience but will be entering that service for the first time.

Before starting this discussion it is important to first examine how the Iraq war differs from the last few wars American troops have fought.

Urban Combat in Iraq

The battles in Iraq were fought not in deserts or jungles, but in the streets of Baghdad and other Iraqi cities. Military operations on urban terrain pose a great challenge. Among other problems, opposition forces blend in with the population throughout the city. The urban-warfare environment is similar to U.S. urban policing environments, except urban-warfare environments are far more dangerous and the rules of engagement are quite different.

For example, veterans returning from the Vietnam War could easily distinguish their combat environment—mostly jungle, farms, or open terrain—from their urban or suburban policing environment. In the case of returning Iraq veterans, their combat environment and their policing environments may appear surprisingly similar to the urban areas they police back home. It is this similarity that may raise performance issues as veterans return to or start their policing duty.[2]

Sustained operations under combat circumstances could cause returning officers to mistakenly blur the lines between military combat situations and civilian crime situations, possibly resulting in inappropriate decisions and actions—particularly related to use of lethal force.

Former Law Enforcement Officers Returning from Combat Assignments

Returning veterans who have been directly involved in deadly combat situations have often witnessed and participated in combat operations in which they have been exposed to potentially traumatic and stressful situations typically well outside the range of normal everyday experience.

Even if these individuals were experienced law enforcement officers, it is highly unlikely that while serving as such, they would have actually witnessed their comrades being killed, blown to pieces or receiving devastatingly serious

---

2. *Ibid*, pp. 9 and 10.

injuries. These types of military combat experiences do not always cause long term psychological problems, but unfortunately, in too many cases they do.

Psychological Issues Facing Combat Veterans

One of the more common negative psychological issues resulting from combat is post-traumatic stress disorder (PTSD), which has been defined by the American Psychological Association's Diagnostic and Statistical Manual:

> *A development of characteristic symptoms following exposure to an extreme traumatic stressor involving direct personal experience of an event that involves actual or threatened death or serious injury or other threat to one's physical integrity; or witnessing an event that involves death, injury, or threat to the integrity of another person ... the person's response to the event must involve fear, helplessness or horror ... .[3]*

Characteristic Symptoms of PTSD

Anxiety. The subject describes a continual state of free-floating anxiety or nervousness. There is a constant gnawing apprehension that something terrible is about to happen. He or she maintains an intensive hypervigilance, scanning the environment for the least hint of impending threat or danger. Panic attacks may be either occasional or frequent.

Physiological Arousal. The subject's autonomic nervous system is always on "red alert." He or she experiences increased bodily tension in the form of muscle tightness, tremors, restlessness, fatigue, heart palpitations, breathing difficulties, dizziness, headaches, and gastrointestinal or urinary disturbances. About one-half of PTSD subjects show a classic startle reaction: surprised by an unexpected door slam, telephone ring, sneeze, or even just hear their name called, the subject may literally "jump" out of his or her seat and then spend the next few minutes trembling with fear and anxiety.

Irritability. There is a pervasive chip-on-the-shoulder edginess, impatience, loss of humor, and quick anger over seemingly trivial matters. Friends get ticked off, coworkers shun the subject, and family members may be verbally

---

3. Leonard Territo and James D. Sewell (eds.), *Stress Management in Law Enforcement*, Durham, NC: Carolina Academic Press, 2007, p. 44.

abused and alienated. A particularly common complaint is the individual's increased sensitivity to children's noisiness or the family's bothering questions.

Avoidance and Denial. The subject tries to blot out the event from his or her mind and avoids thinking about the traumatic event and shuns news articles, radio programs, or TV shows that remind him or her of the incident. "I just don't want to talk about it," is the standard response, and the individual may claim to have forgotten important aspects of the event. Some of this is a deliberate, conscious effort to avoid reminders of the trauma; part of it also involves an involuntary psychic numbing that blunts most incoming threatening stimuli. The emotional coloring of this denial may range from blasé indifference to nail-biting anxiety.

Intrusion. Despite the subject's best efforts to keep the traumatic event out of his or her mind, the horrifying incident pushes its way into consciousness, often rudely and abruptly, in the form of frightening dreams at night. In the most extreme cases, the individual may experience flashbacks or relive experiences in which he or she seems to be mentally transported back to the traumatic scene in all its sensory and emotional vividness, sometimes losing touch with current reality. More commonly, the intrusive recollection is described as a persistent psychological demon that "won't let me forget" the terrifying events surrounding the trauma.

Repetitive Nightmares. Even sleep offers little respite. Sometimes the subject's nightmares replay the actual traumatic event; more commonly, the dreams echo the general theme of the trauma, but miss the mark in terms of specific content. For example, an individual traumatized in an auto accident may dream of falling off a cliff or having a wall collapse on him or her. A sexual assault victim may dream of being attacked by vicious dogs or drowning in a muddy pool. The emotional intensity of the original traumatic experience is retained, but the dream partially disguises the event itself. This symbolic reconfiguration of dream material is, of course, one of the main pillars of Freudian psychoanalytic theory.

Impaired Concentration and Memory. The subject complains of having gotten "spacey," "fuzzy," or "ditsy." He or she has trouble remembering names, tends to misplace objects, loses the train of thought during conversations, or can't keep his or her mind focused on work, reading material, family activities, or other matters. The subject may worry that he or she has brain damage or that "I'm losing my mind."

Sexual Inhibition. Over 90 percent of PTSD subjects report decreased sexual activity and interest; this may further strain an already stressed marital relationship. In some cases, complete impotence or frigidity may occur, especially in cases where the traumatic event involved sexual assault.

Withdrawal and Isolation. The subject shuns friends, neighbors, and family members and just wants to be left alone. He/she has no patience for the petty, trivial concerns of everyday life—bills, gossip, news events—and gets annoyed at being bothered with these piddles. The hurt feelings this engenders in those who are rebuffed may spur retaliatory avoidance, leading to a vicious cycle of rejection and recrimination.

Impulsivity and Instability. More rarely, the trauma survivor may take sudden trips, move from place to place, walk off the job, disappear from his or her family for prolonged periods, uncharacteristically engage in drunken binges, gambling sprees, or romantic trysts, make excessive purchases, or take dangerous physical or legal risks. It is as if the trauma has goaded the subject into a "what-the-hell–life-is-short" attitude that overcomes good judgment and common sense. Obviously, not every instance of irresponsible behavior can be blamed on trauma, but a connection may be suspected when this kind of activity is definitely out of character for that person and follows an identifiable traumatic event. Far from taking such walks on the wild side, however, the majority of trauma survivors continue to suffer in numbed and shattered silence.[4]

Other Psychological Issues

In addition to PTSD there are other psychological difficulties that may emerge. These may be manifested in:

- Frequent use of sick leave
- Difficulty passing fitness-for-duty tests
- Depression
- Suicidal thoughts/behavior
- Substance abuse
- Domestic disturbances/violence
- Other relationship issues
- Inappropriate use of force[5]

---

4. Laurence Miller, "Stress Traumatic-Stress and Post-Traumatic Stress Syndromes," in Leonard Territo and James D. Sewell (eds.), *Stress Management in Law Enforcement*, 2nd Edition, Durham, NC: Carolina Academic Press, 2007, pp. 19–21.

5. "Employing Returning Combat Veterans as Police Officers," *op cit.* p. 11.

Re-Entry Psychological Evaluation
of Returning Police Veterans

What should police administrators do to be relatively certain that a returning veteran is not experiencing any of the psychological issues just set forth which may not have conspicuously manifested themselves while on active military duty?

First, if the returning police veteran was involved in violent and deadly combat situations while serving in the military, the agency should seriously consider having the returning officer interviewed by the clinical psychologist who either administers the agency's pre-employment psychological screening of police applicants and/or provides psychological counseling for its officers.

Second, it must be made clear to all returning officers that the agency is not trying to make re-entry into the agency difficult but rather to assist them in making a smooth and uneventful transition.

Third, even if the department cannot because of legal or contractual reasons require returning veterans to participate in a re-entry psychological screening process, the immediate supervisors of these officers should be alerted to any behaviors which suggest PTSD, as well as other psychological problems previously listed.

Agency leaders should make certain that supervisors are sensitive to and familiar with these conditions. If the behavioral indicators emerge, the supervisors should understand their obligations to refer these officers to agency mental health specialists.

The following actual example describes what happened to a combat veteran when he returned home to America after serving in a combat zone in Iraq where his experience had been conditioned him to be hyper-vigilant to certain types of potentially deadly situations.

> A combat veteran was driving on an interstate highway in his civilian car with his wife and small children. As he approached an overpass without warning he maneuvered his car erratically from one lane to the other, frightening his family and motorists in adjoining lanes. Fortunately, there was no accident occurred.
>
> Afterward the veteran acknowledged what he had done as he approached the overpass was to instantaneously flashback to the time when he was driving a Humvee in Iraq where it was not at all uncommon for rocket-propelled grenades (RPGs) to be fired at U.S. military vehicles or shot at by snipers as they approached an overpass. The

erratic maneuver he employed on the Interstate was one of the evasive tactics he commonly took in Iraq to avoid being struck by RPG's.[6]

It is likely this behavior would be diminished over time but in the short run it is obvious that such behaviors can be quite dangerous and may manifest themselves in ways which can be dangerous and deadly.

Initial Re-Assignment of Experienced Law Enforcement Officers Returning to Duty

If a law enforcement agency serves a large urban area with multiple patrol districts invariably there will be some districts that have a higher rate of violent crimes than others and would therefore have a greater potential for the returning officer to be exposed to violence. Every police administrator and police officer knows which districts these are. Thus it would be advisable for these returning combat veterans to be initially assigned to areas as well as to shifts which are less prone to these types of events thereby facilitating a smooth and uneventful transition back into their law enforcement agencies.

Newly Employed Officers

Employing combat veterans who have not previously been police officers presents both similar as well as new problems to law enforcement agencies. They may come home to civilian life suffering from the same types of psychological problems as our first group, but fortunately, there are no administrative or legal restrictions regarding psychological testing for these applicants. Pre-employment psychological testing is now fairly common for police applicants and such tests, along with a comprehensive interview by a clinical psychologist, should be able to identify applicants with any serious psychological problems.[7]

---

6. A news broadcast on National Public Radio NPR radio station, WUSF, Tampa, Florida, 2008.

7. According to the 2005 COPPS questionnaire data tabulated by John Super in a poll of 478 agencies (federal, state, and local) offering a pre-employment psychological evaluation, the most popular tests in order of their preference and percentage of use) were the following: Inwald Personality Inventory (69%), California Psychological Inventory (66%), Minnesota Multiphasic Personality Inventory (51%), the Wonderlic Personnel Test (49%) and Personality Assessment Inventory (42%). Each of these tests has varying degrees of validity and no single test should be relied upon. Rather, a multitude of tests must be utilized in order to assess the candidate's aptitude for police officer selection. For further discus-

Difference between Military Combat and Civilian Community

There is growing concern that current police academy training curricula do not contain course material specific to the needs of returning combat veterans. For example, current curricula do not address the cultivated reactions service members developed in response to enemy threats in domestic environments.

Specialized training and transition assistance that address these specific needs is required but has not yet been developed.[8] It is important that police academy instructors be aware of the significant differences between the *military* rules of engagement and *civilian* rules of engagement relating to the use of deadly force.

Military Rules of Engagement

The following were the rules of engagement for U.S. military forces in Iraq and are presently the U.S. rules of military engagement for military personnel in Afghanistan:

1. On order, enemy military and paramilitary forces are declared hostile and may be attacked subject to the following instructions:

    (a) Positive identification (PID) is required prior to engagement. PID is a reasonable certainty that the proposed target is a legitimate military target. If no PID, contact your next higher commander for decision.

    (b) Do not engage anyone who has surrendered or is out of battle due to sickness or wounds.

    (c) Do not target or strike any of the following except in self-defense to protect yourself, your unit, friendly forces, and designated persons or property under your control: civilians, hospitals, mosques, national monuments and any other historical and cultural sites.

    (d) Do not fire into civilian populated areas or buildings unless the enemy is using them for military purposes or if necessary for your self-defense. Minimize collateral damage.

    (e) Do not target enemy infrastructure (public works, commercial communication facilities, dams), lines of communication (roads, high-

---

sion of this topic see Charles R. Swanson, Leonard Territo and Robert W. Taylor, *Police Administration: Structures, Processes and Behavior*, Upper Saddle River, NJ: Pearson Prentice Hall, 2008, pp. 407 and 408.

8. "Employing Returning Combat Veterans as Police Officers," *op cit.* pp. 10 and 11.

ways, tunnels, bridges, railways) and economic objects (commercial storage facilities, pipelines) unless necessary for self-defense or if ordered by your commander. If you must fire on these objects to engage a hostile force, disable and disrupt but avoid destruction of these objects, if possible.

(f) The use of force, including deadly force is authorized to protect the following:
  • Yourself, your unit, and friendly force.
  • Enemy prisoners of war
  • Civilians from crimes that are likely to cause death or serious bodily harm, such as murder or rape
  • Designated civilians and/or property, such as personnel of the Red Cross/Crescent, UN, and US/UN supported organizations

(g) Treat all civilians and their property with respect and dignity. Do not seize civilian property, including vehicles, unless you have the permission of a company level commander and you give a receipt to the property's owner.

(h) Detain civilians if they interfere with mission accomplishment or if required for self-defense.

CENTCOM General Order No. 1A remains in effect. Looting and the taking of war trophies are prohibited.

Remember:

  • Attack enemy forces and military targets.
  • Spare civilians and civilian property, if possible.
  • Conduct yourself with dignity and honor.
  • Comply with the Law of War. If you see a violation, report it.[9]

Civilian Rules of Engagement

Civilian rules of engagement on the other hand are quite different from those set forth by the military. For example state laws and departmental policies still remain fairly diverse even after *Garner* v. *Tennessee* although with narrower bounds. Firearms policies will range from the Defense of Life Regulations, which permit shooting only to defeat an eminent threat to an officer's or another person's life to other extremes which require a minimal compliance with

---

9. Appendix E: Rules of Engagement for U.S. Military Forces in Iraq, accessed at: http://www.hrw.org/reports/2003/usal203/11.htm,12/07/2007/.

the Garner Rule and permit shooting at currently non-violent fleeing suspects who the officer reasonably believes committed a felony involving the threat but not the use of violence.

Many large police agencies use both approaches. The defense of life approach significantly reduces the possibility of wrongful death allegations. There are of course many other facets of a civil deadly force policy which are, not surprisingly, quite different than the ones employed by the military. For example, some of the following are elements typically found in police use of deadly force policies:

- rules regarding the shooting at juveniles
- shooting at or from vehicles
- warning shots
- shooting to destroy animals
- secondary guns
- off-duty weapons
- registration of weapons

Resistance to Training in Police Academies

Interestingly, but alarmingly, it is not at all uncommon for police academy instructors who teach the unit of instruction on deadly force or less lethal force to encounter combat veterans in their classes who question the limitations imposed upon them under civil law regarding rules of engagement. As a matter of fact, it has been reported that it is not at all uncommon for some recruits, who are returning combat veterans, to argue with a police academy instructor and take strong exception to the limitations imposed upon them by these civilian rules of engagement.

In reality military personnel involved in combat situations, as a rule, do face much greater dangers from a different kind of enemy and different types of weaponry than do police officers in civilian life. Therefore, in military combat situations these veterans would have been able to employ legally and justifiable deadly force that would not be permitted in civilian life. This is not to suggest that recruit officers attending a police academy cannot differentiate between the two types of rules of engagement. However, as earlier suggested, previous exposure to military combat training and military rules of engagement for an extended period of time can result in some resistance to this reorientation on the part of the recruits because of what they perceive to be unnecessary restrictions which endanger their lives. In addition, the old adage that "we fight like we train" can be potentially dangerous and deadly, especially if the combat veteran reverts reflexively back to the combat training received while serving in the military.

If a police academy instructor encounters an unreasonably high level of resistance from a recruit to this reorientation, it would be advisable to notify the police academy director immediately. Additional private instruction or counseling may be necessary. It is important to remember that the police academy instructors can serve either officially or unofficially as gatekeepers and can identify those individuals who may not be suited for law enforcement work.

Post Academy Assignment

The law enforcement agency should be absolutely certain that, upon graduation from the police academy, these recruits are assigned to professionally mature and highly experienced supervisors and field training officers who have been alerted to all of the potential problems related to their situation.

Summary

- Returning combat veterans who were former law enforcement officers should be interviewed by the clinical psychologists who administer the agency's pre-employment screening or provide counseling to its police officers. This is to be certain that returning veterans are not experiencing post-traumatic stress disorder or an equally serious psychological problem.
- The immediate supervisor of the returning combat veterans should be made aware of the symptoms of post-traumatic stress disorder and other psychological problems and if necessary be prepared to refer these officers to the agency's mental health specialist.
- If it is at all possible, the returning law enforcement officer's initial assignment should not be in an area or on a shift that has a large amount of violent crimes.
- All police applicants should be given a comprehensive pre-employment psychological screening whether or not they have been combat veterans.
- Instructors who are teaching combat veterans in the police academy should be prepared to deal with resistance from combat veterans who may fail to appreciate why civilian rules of engagement must take precedent over the military rules of engagement. Instructional personnel should

also be familiar with the military rules of engagement to which combat veterans would have been exposed.

- It is important that police academy instructors who teach deadly and less lethal force are experienced, articulate, patient and persuasive. The police academy instructor should notify the police academy director of any recruit who appears to be highly resistant to the reorientation of acceptance of civilian rules of engagement over the military rules of engagement.

- Upon graduation, recruit officers should be assigned to professionally mature and highly experienced supervisors and field training officers who are familiar with the potential problems related to the situation.

Discussion Questions

1. What two categories of veterans are discussed in this article?
2. In what ways does the Iraq war differ from the last few wars American troops have fought?
3. What are the characteristic symptoms of post-traumatic stress disorder (PTSD)?
4. In addition to PTSD, what other psychological difficulties might emerge?
5. How do the rules of engagement differ between the military and civilian law enforcement?
6. What course of action should be taken by a police academy instructor who encounters an unreasonably high level of resistance from a recruit (former combat veteran) to the re-orientation of shifting from the military rules of engagement to the civilian rules of engagement?

28

Double-Dose Trauma: Suicide Risk among Deployed Police Officers

John M. Violanti

Introduction

Since October 2001, approximately 1.64 million U.S. troops have been deployed for Operations Enduring Freedom and Iraqi Freedom (OEF/OIF) in Afghanistan and Iraq (Tanielan & Jaycox, 2008). Of these deployments, an estimated 11,380 full-time sworn officers were called up as full-time military reservists. Most of these, about two-thirds, were officers from local police departments. About one quarter were from sheriffs' offices, and 9 percent were officers from the primary state agencies. As a proportion of all sworn officers in these agencies, these 11,380 officers constitute about 2 percent of the available workforce (Hickman, 2006).

Tanielan and Jaycox (2008) estimated that approximately 300,000 individuals currently suffer from posttraumatic stress disorder (PTSD) or major depression during deployment. PTSD is a specific type of severe stress brought about by exposure to an event during which the individual experiences life endangerment, death, or serious injury or threat to self or others; and responds to the experience with feelings of intense fear, horror, or helplessness. Symptoms may include intrusive recollections of the event; distressing dreams; flashbacks; dissociative phenomenon; and psychological and physical distress with reminders of the event. (American Psychiatric Association, DSM-IV-TR, 2000.)

PTSD and Suicide

PTSD is often associated with increased suicidal ideation. Marshall, Olfson, Hellman, Blanco, et al. (2001) found that persons diagnosed with PTSD had a three-fold risk of suicide ideation compared to those without PTSD. The high risk of ideation remained even when depression was controlled. Freeman, Roca, and Moore (2000) found that combat veterans with PTSD had significantly more suicide attempts and self destructive behaviors.

Studies of veterans with PTSD have reported an increased risk of suicidal behavior, 82.6% of veterans in outpatient treatment reporting symptoms of suicidal ideation (Davidson, Hughes, Blazer, & George, 1991; Hendin & Haas, 1991). Moreover, a high preponderance of anxiety disorders, particularly PTSD, has been found in veterans with completed suicide, relative to the general population of completed suicides (Lehmann, McCormick, & McCracken, 1995). The incidence of PTSD was higher among Vietnam veterans who killed themselves than among those killed in motor vehicle accidents (Farberow, Kang, & Bullman, 1990). These results found the incidence of suicide to be higher in victims who met diagnostic criteria for PTSD than among victims who did not. In a study of refugees, suicidal behavior was significantly greater among victims with a diagnosis of PTSD than among non PTSD victims (Ferrada-Noli, Asberg, Ormstad, Lundin, and Sundbom, 1998).

Many persons diagnosed with PTSD have comorbid difficulties (Green, Lindy, & Grace, 1989). For example, in a study of Vietnam veterans with PTSD, Roszell, McFall, and Malas (1991) found that nearly 50% indicated a current sense or belief of foreshortened future, and over 64% had a current coexisting diagnosis of major depression (93% were currently diagnosed with some form of mood disorder).

Military or Civilian Combat: The War Is the Same

In my view, police work may be considered "civilian combat" (Violanti, 1999). Much of current research suggests that suicide rates are high both in the military and in police work. The police officer involved in both military and civilian combat can experience the "double-barreled" effect of such traumatic incidents.

Many work related exposures of police officers are often characterized as traumatic compared to other occupations (Paton, Violanti & Smith, 2003). Exposures perceived as "disturbing" or "traumatic" are generally ranked by police officers as the most stressful. Law enforcement officers are confronted daily with the reality of trauma. Faced with responding to fatal accidents, crime, child abuse, homicide, suicide, and rape, police officers are exposed to all the potential factors that can precipitate a traumatic response (Carlier, Fouwels, Lamberts & Gersons, 1996). There is also an increased risk of trauma due to frequent exposure to death and the threat of death (Sugimoto & Oltjenbruns, 2001).

Posttraumatic symptomatology can produce many negative consequences, including increased alcohol use and suicide among police officers. Being the target of, exposed to, as well as witness to events that can precipitate a sense of horror, helplessness, and hopelessness, it is not surprising that police officers have been empirically found to suffer the mental injuries associated with traumatic stress (Dunning, 1999). The ways that trauma can affect the police are wide-ranging. To begin with, there are the effects on the traumatized officers themselves. Immediately after a traumatic experience, they tend to exhibit a cluster of characteristic reactions: shock, nightmares, irritability, concentration problems, emotional instability and physical symptoms. With support from those around them, most officers manage to come to terms with the traumatic event and get on with their lives and careers (Carlier et al. 1996, Carlier, Lambert & Gersons 1997; Carlier, Lambert & Gersons 2000).

For those who cannot cope adequately with traumatic events, symptoms of PTSD may become overwhelming. They may become more fearful, aggressive, indifferent, depressed, distracted or self-absorbed than they were before the traumatic event. Clearly these changes affect the quality of their lives. In extreme cases, officers might even conclude that life is no longer worth living (Violanti, 2003; Carlier & Gersons, 1996). The reality of psychological wounds due to workplace trauma has also been one of effects that resulted from 911 terrorist attacks and the recent war in Iraq. Since these events, the police and others have been put under additional strain due to personnel shortages in many emergency first responder occupations as a result of military deployment and homeland security measures (Violanti, 2003). The above studies suggest associations between exposure to traumatic work events, PTSD symptomatology and suicide. We posit in the present study that these factors increase the risk of suicide ideation in police officers which, in turn, may increase the risk of completed suicide.

The Risk of Suicide among Deployed Veterans

Exposure to combat has been described as one of the most intense stressors that a person can experience (Grinker & Spiegel, 1945) and, for many people who experience combat, it is the most traumatic experience of their life (Kulka, Schleger, Fairbank, et al., 1990). Previous research conducted after other military conflicts has shown that deployment and exposure to combat result in increased risk of posttraumatic stress disorder (PTSD), major depression, substance abuse, functional impairment in social and employment settings, and the increased use of health care services (Centers for Disease Control Vietnam Experience Study Group, 1988; Prigerson, Maciejewski, & Rosenheck, 2002; Rona, Hyams & Wessely, 2005). A recent study showed that 17% of soldiers and Marines who returned from Iraq screened positive for PTSD, generalized anxiety, or depression, a prevalence nearly twice that observed among soldiers surveyed before deployment (Rona et al., 2005).

Combat is not the only stressor endured by deployed military personnel. The Department of Defense (DoD) Mental Health Advisory Team (MHAT) surveys of both active-duty troops and reserve and National Guard soldiers deployed to Iraq during Operation Enduring Freedom in 2005 and 2006 found that the most important noncombat stressors were deployment length and family separation; deployment length was of even higher concern to soldiers who had been deployed more than once (Mental Health Advisory Team, Operation Iraqi Freedom, 2006). The team also noted that the length of deployment of active-duty Army personnel in Iraq was extended from 12 to 15 months and that 13,000 National Guard troops were expecting to be called up for second tours of Iraq.

Of the more than 180,000 Operation Iraqi Freedom (OIF) and Operation Enduring Freedom (OEF) veterans who have accessed VA healthcare services since 2002, 38% have been diagnosed with mental health disorders (MHAT, 2006). Rates of co-occurring mental and substance use disorders in veterans are especially high, with 44% of VA inpatients treated in 2001 for having a co-occurring disorder (MHAT, 2005). Many of these disorders are precipitants for suicidal thinking. According to the MHAT (2005), the prevalence of significant depressive symptoms among veterans is 31%, 2 to 5 times higher than among the general US population. Veterans with co-occurring disorders, such as depression and alcohol abuse or depression and posttraumatic stress disorder (PTSD), have been reported to be at much higher risk for suicide. Other risk factors for suicide common in VA patients include the male gender, the elderly, those with diminished social support, medical and psychiatric conditions associated with suicide, and the availability and knowledge of firearms (MHAT, 2005).

Veteran studies specific to suicide have yielded additional evidence. Milliken, Auchterlonie and Hoge (2007) examined demographic factors associated with veterans' suicide using longitudinal, nationally representative data (1999-2004). Of 807, 694 veterans meeting study criteria, 1683 (0.21%) committed suicide during follow-up. Increased suicide risks were observed among male, younger, and non-Hispanic White patients. Veterans without service-connected disabilities and with comorbid substance use were also at higher risk. Younger depressed veterans with PTSD had a higher suicide rate than did older depressed veterans with PTSD (Zavin, Kim, McCarthy, Austin, et al., 2007).

Kang and Bullman (2008) examined a cohort of 490,346 veterans who served in OIF/OEF and were separated from active duty between October 2001 and December 2005. The overall risk for suicide was elevated (Standardized Mortality Ratio (SMR) = 1.15; 95% CI, 0.97-1.35). The suicide risk was increased for former active duty veterans (SMR = 1.33; 95% CI, 1.03-1.69) and for veterans diagnosed with a selected mental disorder (SMR = 1.77; 95% CI, 1.01-2.87). Kang et al. (2008) comment that the rates of suicide among military personnel have historically been lower than those of the U.S. general population; thus, an SMR of 1.15 represents an increase in the risk of suicide among combat exposed personnel in comparison with prewar rates. Kaplan, Huguet, McFarland and Newsom (2007) conducted a prospective follow-up study on 320,890 male veterans with data obtained from the US National Health Interview Surveys 1986-94 linked to the Multiple Cause of Death file (1986-97) through the National Death Index. Veterans were at an increased risk of suicide in the general US. population, whether or not they were affiliated with the Department of Veterans Affairs.

The Risk of Suicide among Police Officers

One would expect that the police suicide rates should be lower than they are, given that they are an employed, healthy and psychologically tested group (McMichael, 1976). Certainly, they should be lower than the U.S. general population, since this reference group includes the institutionalized, mentally ill, and unemployed.

A good amount of epidemiological evidence suggests that there is an elevated rate of suicide within law enforcement. An early national occupational study by Guralnick (1963) found the suicide ratio of male police to be 1.8 times that of the Caucasian male general population. Suicides accounted for 13.8% of police deaths compared to 3% of deaths in all other occupations, and more officers died as a result of suicide than homicide. Milham (1979) found Washington State male police officers from 1950-1971 to have a suicide mortality rate higher than normally expected in the general male population.

Vena, Violanti, Marshall, and Fiedler (1986) found male officers to have an age-adjusted mortality ratio for suicide of approximately three times that of male municipal workers in the same cohort. Lester (1992) found that 7 of 26 countries for the decade of 1980-1989 had police suicide rates above the general population. A mortality study of police officers in Rome, Italy found the suicide ratio among male police officers to be 1.97 times as high as the general male Italian population (Forastiere, et al., 1994). Violanti, Vena, and Marshall (1996) found that male police officers had a suicide rate of 8.3 times that of homicide and 3.1 times that of work accidents. Compared to male municipal workers, male police officers had a 53% increased rate of suicide over homicide, a three-fold rate of suicide over accidents, and a 2.65-fold rate of suicide over homicide and accidents combined.

Darragh (1991) conducted an epidemiological analysis on factors based on 558 consecutive cases of self-inflicted death in the United Kingdom, which revealed a dramatic increase in suicide among security force personnel. Helmkamp (1996), in a study of suicide among males in the US Armed Forces, found military security and law enforcement specialists had a significant increased rate ratio for suicide. Hartwig and Violanti (1999) found that the frequency of police suicide occurrence in Westphalia, Germany, has increased over the past seven years, particularly in the 21-30 and 51 60 years of age categories. Most of suicides were male officers (92%). Cantor, Tyman and Slatter (1999) found the high rate of suicide among Australian police attributable to stress, health, and domestic difficulties. Occupational problems were more intense than personal ones.

Charbonneau (2000), in a study in Quebec, Canada, found police suicide rates to be almost twice that of the general population. Rates were elevated mostly among young officers (20-39 years of age). Gershon, Lin, and Li (2002) provided recent evidence of job-related problems among police officers related to suicide. Officers had an approximate four-fold risk of being exposed to traumatic work events, a 3-fold risk of exhibiting PTSD symptoms, a 4-fold risk of alcohol abuse, and a 4-fold risk of aggressive behavior.

Other factors associated with police work have been examined that could influence increased rates of suicide. Rothmann and Strijdom (2002) found suicide ideation in South African Police to be associated with a sense of incoherence. Officers were unable to perceive traumatic police work exposures as manageable. They did not feel that they had the resources available, either personally or organizationally, to meet the demands imposed upon them by their difficult work. Berg, Hem, Lau, Loeb, and Ekeberg (2003), in a nationwide study on suicide ideation and attempts among 3272 Norwegian police, found that 25% felt that life was not worth living, 6.4% seriously considered suicide, and 0.7% attempted suicide. Serious suicide ideation was mainly attributed to personal and family problems. Violanti (2004) found that certain traumatic police work exposures increased the risk of having a high level of posttraumatic stress disorder (PTSD) symptoms, which subsequently increased the risk of alcohol use and suicide ideation. The combined impact of PTSD and increased alcohol use led to a ten-fold increased risk of suicide ideation.

Depression possibly associated with work stress and suicide ideation may be possible precipitants of increased police suicide risk. Violanti, Fekedulegn, Andrew, Hartley, Manatskanova, and Burchfiel (2008) examined the association between depressive symptoms and suicide ideation in a sample of police officers. Prevalence of depression was higher among women than men officers (12.5% vs. 6.2%). For each standard deviation increase in depression symptoms, the prevalence ratio (PR) of suicide ideation increased 73% in women officers (PR = 1.73, 95% CI = 1.32-2.27) and 67% in men officers (PR = 1.67, 95% CI = 1.21-2.30).

Summary

This research evidence suggests that both veterans and police officers are at increased risk for suicide. A proportion of this risk has been attributed to exposure to traumatic events and PTSD. The deployed police officer may therefore be subjected to an even higher risk of suicide due to a double-dose trauma effect through exposure on the street and combat.

Suicide Prevention: What Can Be Done?

Changing Resistance to Treatment

A major obstacle to preventing suicide is lack of treatment. Both military personnel and police officers are resistant to seek help when confronted with mental discomfort. According to Tanielan and Jaycox (2008) only about half (53 percent) of those who met the criteria for current PTSD or major depression had sought help from a physician or mental health provider for a mental health problem in the past year.

The reasons for this resistance are similar across both groups. Hoge, Castro & Messer (2004), for example, found that approximately 65% of deployed service veterans did not want to be seen as "weak," 50% thought that it would hurt their career, and 38% did not trust mental health professionals. Police officers often view themselves as people who solve problems, not people who have problems. This police cultural aspect often prevents troubled officers from seeking help. It is necessary to educate future generation officers concerning these factors and to reduce the stigma associated with getting help.

Resiliency: A Protective Factor against Suicide?

Are there protective factors which may help officers to cope with the stresses, strains, and the trauma of war and police work? Increasing resiliency may provide the necessary prevention mechanism required to psychologically survive the trauma of war. Following Antonovsky's (1990) definition, resilience reflects the extent to which individuals and groups can call upon their psychological and physical resources and competencies in ways that allow them to render challenging events coherent, manageable and meaningful. In this sense, resiliency refers not only to personality factors but also to the police social milieu, including the organization. We term this combination the "police stress shield" (Paton, Violanti, Johnston, Burke, Clarke & Keenan, 2008).

It is also important to consider the common meaning of resiliency. Resilience is often used to imply an ability to "bounce back." Being able to bounce back is an important capability. However, because police officers are called upon *repeatedly* to deal with increasingly complex and threatening incidents, it is appropriate to expand the scope of this definition to include the development of one's capacity to deal with *future* events (Paton, Smith, Violanti & Eranen, 2000). Therefore, resilience can not only provide support in the here and now but also in the future. This is the notion of 'adaptive capacity' (Klein, Nicholls & Thomalla, 2003). Police resiliency therefore includes the capacity of agencies and officers to draw upon individual, collective, and institutional resources to cope with demands, challenges and changes encountered *during and after* critical incidents.

Police Organizational Resiliency

An effective application of resilience must integrate organizational perspectives, with the police organization perhaps exerting a greater influence in this process. The police organization defines the context within which officers experience and interpret critical incidents and their sequelae and within which future capabilities are nurtured or restricted (Paton, 2006). There are three characteristics of a resilient organization to consider: (1) organizational climate; (2) trust; and (3) leadership.

Organizational Climate
Hart and Cooper (2001) proposed a conceptual model of organizational climate that predicts salutary outcomes. Organizational climate describes of-

ficers' perceptions of how their organization functions, and these perceptions influence both their well-being and their performance in their organizational role (Hart & Cooper, 2001). Burke and Paton (2006) tested the ability of this model to predict satisfaction in the context of emergency responders experience of critical incidents. Organizational climate was the best single predictor of job satisfaction and represents a significant influence on officers' ability to render their critical incident experiences meaningful and manageable. Organizational climate had a direct positive influence on coping, resulting in an increase in positive work experiences. Organizational climate also demonstrated a direct negative influence on negative work experiences. The important role played by organizational climate indicates that police agencies have a key role in facilitating officer adaptability and resilience.

Trust

Police officers are noted for not trusting. This may be a result of occupational socialization which emphasizes that trusting can put one in danger on the street. Instead it is "safe" to be suspicious of everyone. Unfortunately, this lack of trust may impede the officer's ability to seek help in stressful situations. Trust is a prominent determinant of the effectiveness of interpersonal relationships, group processes and organizational relationships (Barker & Camarata, 1998; Herriot, Hirch & Reilly, 1998), and plays a crucial role in empowering officers (Spreitzer & Mishra, 1999). People functioning in trusting, reciprocal relationships are left feeling empowered, and more likely to experience meaning in their work. Trust has been identified as a predictor of people's ability to deal with complex, high risk events (Siegrist & Cvetkovich, 2000), particularly when relying on others to provide information or assistance.

An officer contemplating suicide does not trust. This is especially true regarding the organization. The resilient organization is one where the officer can go to for help without reprise or hesitation. An officer is more willing to commit to acting cooperatively in high risk situations when they believe those with whom they must collaborate or work under are competent, dependable, likely to act with integrity and to care for their interests (Dirks, 1999). Organizations functioning with cultures that value openness and trust create opportunities for officers to engage in learning and growth, contributing to the development of officers' adaptive capacity (Barker & Camarata, 1998; Siegrist & Cvetkovich, 2000).

Leadership

Resilient police organizations have leaders who care about their people. For the suicidal officer, a leader can be the first step to getting help. Leaders play a central role in developing and sustaining empowering environments (Liden,

Wayne, & Sparrow, 2000; Paton & Stephens, 1996). They have a major role to play in creating and sustaining a climate of trust as a result of their being responsible for translating organizational culture into the day-to-day values and procedures that sustain officers. Leadership practices such as positive reinforcement help create an empowering the work environment (Paton, 1994).

Leaders are in a unique position to shape how members of the group understand stressful experiences. The leader who, through example and discussion, communicates a positive construction or re-construction of shared stressful experiences, may exert an influence on the entire group in the direction of his/her interpretation of experience. Thus, leaders who are high in hardiness will likely have a greater impact on their groups under high-stress conditions, when by their example as well as explanations they articulate to group members (including interpretive stories and parables), they encourage an interpretation of stressful events as interesting challenges which they are capable of meeting, and in any event can learn and benefit from. This process itself, as well as the positive result of the process (a shared understanding of the event as something worthwhile and beneficial) could be expected to also generate an increased sense of shared values, mutual respect and cohesion. (Bartone & Snook, 1999.)

Supportive supervision is a crucial factor (Liden, et al., 2000) because it enhances resiliency necessary for the feelings of competence. Support enables officers to find increased meaning in their work and perhaps their lives. In times of crisis, supervisory support can make the difference between life and death. Focusing on constructive discussion of work related problems and how they can be resolved draws away from one's personal and psychological weaknesses in difficult situations and replaces it with an active approach to anticipating how to exercise control (Paton & Stephens, 1996). This can be valuable for suicide prevention efforts.

Police managers need to communicate to the worker a reaction and assessment that reinforces comprehensibility, manageability, and meaningfulness regarding their performance in the event within the context of the organization. They need to be especially cognizant of the profound effect their words and actions can have on workers. Unintended negative consequences can be harder to address and more long-lasting and devastating than the traumatic event itself. Cohen and Welch (2000) underscore the ability of the attitudes, beliefs, values, and culture of the organization and its members to mediate the effects of stress and trauma. Administrators must be aware of the messages they send that undercut workers' beliefs regarding their role in prevention, protection, intervention, mitigation, remediation, investigation, and resolution. Coworkers and peers, supervisors, and mental health caregivers must no longer ignore the importance of socio-cultural context and group norms (Dunning, 2003).

Resilient police organizational climates can help to reduce the psychological strain on officers as well as provide a "place to go to" in crisis situations, especially in cases of potential suicide. The police stress shield model describes resilience as resulting from the interaction between person organizational factors. However, the benefit of any model is a function of it being theoretically rigorous and capable of informing the design practical programs in police organizations. Guidelines for changing hardiness, peer support, supervisor support, and organizational trust are available in the literature (Cogliser & Schriesheim, 2000; Hart et al., 1993; Herriot et al., 1998; Perry, 1997; Quinn & Spreitzer, 1997).

The International Association of Chiefs of Police (IACP) Veteran Re-Integration Study

The IACP conducted a study of returning combat veterans which addressed providing support for the re-integration of military personnel into law enforcement (IACP, 2009). They made the following recommendations:

Within 30-60 Days:

- Publicly acknowledge veteran officers for their service on their return to their agency/community
- Create within-agency focus groups to learn more about veteran officers' needs
- Develop communication methods with veteran officers and their families throughout the deployment cycle
- Offer veteran officers a flexible timetable to meet a range of transitional needs
- Create a specialized Field Training Officer (FTO) type program structured to assist veteran officers
- Allow the veteran officer to ride-along or job-shadow with a peer
- Address the confidentiality policies of the services offered and clarify misconceptions
- Update veteran officers on new policies, procedures, laws, and changes in equipment and technology

Within 6-9 Months:

- Establish peer and family support groups
- Incorporate training that addresses equipment differences and the re-programming of muscle memory
- Develop a comprehensive family care plan checklist

- Structure training for each veteran officer's specific needs
- Review rules of engagement and standard operating procedures
- Establish a comprehensive driver training program
- Develop a comprehensive web-based communications system
- Update returning officers on new policies, procedures, laws, equipment, and technology
- Develop an ethics and language review to ease the transition back to a civilian culture

Within 1-2 Years:

- Develop core training (e.g., firearms, in-service, specialized training)
- Create scenario-based training to identify transitional issues and to practice tactics
- Address the unique training needs of federal agencies
- Develop strategies to employ disabled combat veterans
- Gauge the effectiveness of military and civilian law enforcement partnerships

(IACP, 2009, pp. 46-47)

These suggestions are very good in the sense that they provide necessary support to help returning veterans to assimilate back into their role as civilian officers. Such support is essential to help ameliorate the impact of the trauma of war and to normalize officers.

Conclusions

In this chapter, we have outlined research and some ideas regarding the tragedy of suicide and war, both on the civilian and military fronts. Entangled within the nexus of war is the police officer, who on both fronts is exposed to the trauma of daily work. We hope that this chapter will in some small way will bring a sense of awareness to this problem. The trauma of combat coupled with that of police work can produce a devastating impact on deployed police officers. As noted in this chapter, suicide is a worst case outcome to such exposures. Efforts by police departments to support returning officers are essential if we are to prevent such tragedies.

What happens in a police department after a suicide can be devastating. Quite often, entire departments succumb to a depressed mood and productivity falls. There is often a grief wave in the department when an officer suicides. Police administrators have commented that somehow their officers do not seem the same after a suicide; supervisors notice an effect on morale, happiness and work. Suicide postvention involves a designed plan to help reduce the negative impact on departments and family. Postvention is essential because it allows for the proper grieving of survivors and departments and shows that someone cares enough to be concerned about those who survive suicide. Police leaders should arrange for psychological debriefings after the suicide of an officer that will help individual survivors and the department deal with the crisis.

Future Research Considerations

There is a limited extent of research on returning combat veterans who are police officers. Although similar in many exposures, war and the street are contextually different and operate under different circumstances and rules. What little research evidence we have tells us that the trauma of war coupled with the trauma of the street requires an extra effort of readjustment for the returning officer. What are not known are the parameters of that adjustment, and we need to explore this further in research.

An additional neglected area of suicide research concerns women police officers deployed to combat. According to McFarland (2009), women veterans are 2-3 times more likely to commit suicide than nonveteran women. Furthermore, female veterans are more likely to be young and use firearms to commit suicide compared with their civilian counterparts. The study results revealed that, from 2003 to 2006, there were 171 female veteran suicide cases vs. 5174 nonveteran female suicides. A total of 75 (44%) women veterans shot themselves, and 96 (56%) died by other methods. In contrast, 33% of nonveteran women died by firearms. The odds ratio for suicide for female veterans vs. other women was 1.79:1.

The issues highlighted in this chapter deserve further consideration in order to advance police suicide prevention among returning veterans. Suicide is a clear indication of the intolerable strain placed on the police officer's work and life roles. At this time in history, officers are now faced with the additional strain of war. In the least, we should adequately address this problem and provide methods and means to prevent future tragedies, for fear that more officers may fall from the edge.

References

American Psychiatric Association. (1994). *Diagnostic and Statistical Manual-IV*. Washington, D.C.: American Psychological Association.

Antonovsky, A. (1990). Personality and health: Testing the sense of coherence model. In H.S. Friedman (Ed). *Personality and disease* (pp. 155-177). New York: John Wiley & Sons.

Barker, R.T. & Camarata, M.R. (1998). The role of communication in creating and maintaining a learning organization: Preconditions, indicators, and disciplines. *The Journal of Business Communication, 35,* 443-467.

Berg, A.M., Hem, E., Lau, B., Loeb, M., & Ekeberg, O. (2003). Suicidal ideation and attempts in Norwegian police. *Suicide and Life Threatening Behavior, 33,* 302-312.

Burke, K. & Paton, D. (2006). Well-being in Protective Services Personnel: Organizational Influences. *Australasian Journal of Disaster and Trauma Studies, 2006-2.* http://trauma.massey.ac.nz/issues/2006-2/burke.htm.

Cantor, C.H., Tyman, R., & Slater, P.J. (1995). A historical survey of police in Queensland, Australia, 1843-1992. *Suicide and Life Threatening Behavior, 25,* 499-507.

Carlier, I.V.E., Lamberts, R.D., & Gersons, B.P.R. (1997). Risk factors for post-traumatic stress in police officers: A prospective analysis. *Journal of Nervous and Mental Disease, 185,* 498-506.

Carlier, I.V.E., Lamberts, R.D., & Gersons, B.P.R. (2000). The dimensionality of trauma: A multidimensional scaling comparison of police officers with and without posttraumatic stress disorder. *Psychiatry Research, 97,* 29-39.

Carlier, I.V.E., A.J. Fouwels, R.D. Lamberts, & B.P.R. Gersons (1996). Post-Traumatic Stress Disorder and Dissociation in Traumatized Police Officers. *The American Journal of Psychiatry, 153,* 1325-1328.

Centers for Disease Control Vietnam Experience Study Group (1988). Health status of Vietnam veterans, 1: Psychosocial characteristics. *Journal of the American Medical Association, 259,* 2701-2707.

Charbonneau, F. (2000). Suicide among the police in Quebec. *Population, 55,* 367-378.

Cogliser, C.C. & Schriesheim, C.A. (2000) Exploring work unit context and leader-member exchange: A multi-level perspective. *Journal of Organizational Behavior, 21,* 487-511.

Cohen, J. & Welch, L. (2000). Attitudes, beliefs, values, cultures as mediators of stress. In V. Rice (Ed) *Handbook of stress, coping and health.* Thousand Oaks, CA: Sage.

Darragh, P.M. (1991). Epidemiology of suicide in Northern Ireland. *Irish Journal of Medical Science, 160,* 354-357.

Davidson, J., Hughes, D., Blazer, D., & George, L. (1991). Post-traumatic stress disorder in the community: An epidemiological study. *Psychological Medicine, 21,* 713-721.

Dirks, K.T. (1999). The effects of interpersonal trust on work group performance. *Journal of Applied Psychology, 84*, 445-455.

Dunning, C. (1999). Post intervention strategies to reduce police trauma: A paradigm shift. In J.M. Violanti & D. Paton (Eds.) *Police trauma: Psychological aftermath of civilian combat.* Springfield, Illinois: Charles C. Thomas.

Dunning, C. (2003). Sense of coherence in managing trauma workers. In D. Paton, J.M. Violanti & L.M. Smith (Eds). *Promoting capabilities to manage posttraumatic stress: Perspectives on resilience.* Springfield, ILL: Charles C. Thomas.

Farberow, N.L., Kang, H.K., & Bullman, T. (1990). Combat experience and post service psychosocial status as predictors of suicide in Vietnam veterans. *Journal of Nervous and Mental Disease, 178*, 32-37.

Ferrada-Noli, M., Asberg, M., Ormstad, K., Lundin, T., & Sundborn, E. (1998). Suicidal behavior after severe trauma, part one: PTSD diagnosis, psychiatric comorbidity, and assessments of suicidal behavior. *Journal of Traumatic Stress, 11*, 103-112.

Forastiere, F., Perucci, C.A., DiPietro, A., Miceli, M., Rapiti, E., Bargagli, A., & Borgia, P. (1994). Mortality among urban policemen on Rome. *American Journal of Industrial Medicine, 26*, 785-798.

Freeman, T.W., Roca, V., & Moore, W.M. (2000). A comparison of combat related posttraumatic stress disorder patients with and without a history of suicide attempt. *The Journal of Nervous and Mental Disease, 188*, 460-463.

Gershon, R.R., Lin, S., & Li, X. (2002). Work stress in aging police officers. *Journal of Occupational and Environmental Medicine, 44*, 160-167.

Green, B.L., Lindy, J.D., & Grace, M.C. (1989). Multiple diagnosis in posttraumatic stress disorder: The role of war survivors. *Journal of Nervous and Mental Disease, 177*, 329-335.

Grinker, R.R., & Spiegel, J.P. (1945). *Men under stress.* Philadelphia, PA: Blakiston.

Guralnick, L. (1963). Mortality by occupation and cause of death among men 20-64 years of age. *Vital Statistics Special Reports, 53*, Bethesda, Maryland: DHEW.

Hart, P.M., & Cooper, C.L. (2001). Occupational Stress: Toward a more integrated framework. In N. Anderson, D.S. Ones, H.K. Sinangil, & C. Viswesvaren (Eds) *International handbook of work and organizational psychology, vol. 2: Organizational psychology.* London: Sage Publications.

Hartwig, D. & Violanti, J.M. (1999). Suicide by police officials in North Rhine-Westphalia. An evaluation of 58 suicide between 1992-1998. *Archives of Kriminologie, 204*, 129-142.

Helmkamp, J.C. (1996). Occupation and suicide among males in the US Armed Forces. *Annals of Epidemiology, 6*, 83-88.

Hendin, H. & Haas, A. (1991). Suicide and guilt as manifestations of PTSD in Vietnam combat veterans. *American Journal of Psychiatry, 148*, 586-591.

Herriot, P., Hirsh, W., & Reilly, P. (1998). *Trust and Transition: Managing today's employment relationship.* New York: John Wiley & Sons.

Hickman, M.J. (2006). Impact of the military reserve activation on police staffing. *Police Chief, 73*, October, 15-23.

Hoge, C.W., Castro, C.A., & Messer, S.C. (2004). Combat duty in Iraq and Afghanistan, mental health problems, and barriers to care. *New England Journal of Medicine, 351*, 13-22.

International Association of Chiefs of Police (2009). *Employing returning combat veterans as law enforcement officers.* Alexandria, VA: IACP.

Kang, H.K., & Bullman, T.A. (2008). Risk of suicide among US veterans after returning from the Iraq or Afghanistan war zones. *Journal of the American Medical Association, 300*, 652-653.

Kaplan, M.S., Huguet, N., Mcfaraland, B.H., & Newsom, J.T. (2007). Suicide among male veterans: A Prospective population based study. *Journal of Epidemiology and Community Health, 61*, 619-624.

Klein, R., Nicholls, R., & Thomalla, F. (2003). Resilience to natural hazards: How useful is this concept? *Environmental Hazards, 5*, 35-45.

Kulka, R.A., Schlenger, W.E., Fairbank, J.A., Hough, R.L., Jordan, B.K., Marmar, C.R., & Weiss, D.S. (1990). *Trauma and the Vietnam War Generation: Report of Findings from the National Vietnam Veterans Readjustment Study.* New York: Brunner/Mazel Publishers.

Lehmann, L., McCormick, R., & McCracken, L. (1995). Suicidal behavior among patients in the VA health care system. *Psychiatric Services, 46*, 1069-1071.

Lester, D. (1992). Suicide in police officers: a survey of nations. *Police Studies, 15*, 146-148.

Liden, R.C., Wayne, S.J., & Sparrow, R.T. (2000). An examination of the mediating role of psychological empowerment on the relations between the job, interpersonal relationships, and work outcomes. *Journal of Applied Psychology, 85*, 407-416.

Marshall, R.D., Olfson, M., Hellman, F., Blanco, C., & Struening, E.L. (2001). Comorbidity, impairment, and suicidality in subthreshold PTSD. *American Journal of Psychiatry, 158*, 1467-1473.

McFarland (2009). *Women veterans at risk for suicide.* American Psychiatric Association 162nd Annual Meeting: Abstract SCR 21-61. Presented May 20, 2009.

McMichael, A.J. (1976). Standardized mortality ratios and the healthy worker effect: scratching beneath the surface. *Journal of Occupational Medicine, 18*, 165-168.

Mental Health Advisory Team (MHAT) (2006). *IV Operation Iraqi Freedom 05-07: Final Report.* Washington, DC: Office of the Surgeon Multinational Force—Iraq and the Office of the Surgeon General United States Army Medical Command. Available: http://www.armymedicine.army.mil/news/mhat/mhat_iv/MHAT_IV_Report_17NOVO6.pdf.

Milham, S. (1979). *Occupational mortality in Washington state.* U.S. Dept. of Health, Education, and Welfare, 1-3. Washington, DC: US Government Printing Office.

Milliken, C.S., Auchterlonie, J.L., & Hoge, C.W. (2007). Longitudinal Assessment of Mental Health Problems Among Active and Reserve Component Soldiers Returning From the Iraq War. *Journal of the American Medical Association, 298,* 2141-2148.

Paton, D. & Stephens, C. (1996). Training and support for emergency responders. In Paton, D. & Violanti, J. (Eds.) *Traumatic Stress in Critical Occupations: Recognition, consequences and treatment.* Springfield, ILL: Charles C. Thomas.

Paton, D. (1994). Disaster Relief Work: An assessment of training effectiveness. *Journal of Traumatic Stress, 7,* 275-288.

Paton, D. (2006). Posttraumatic growth in emergency professionals. In L. Calhoun and R. Tedeschi (eds) *Handbook of Posttraumatic Growth: Research and Practice.* Mahwah, NJ: Lawrence Erlbaum Assoc.

Paton, D., Violanti, J.M., & Smith, L.M. (2003). *Promoting capabilities to manage posttraumatic stress: Perspectives on resilience.* Springfield, Illinois: Charles C. Thomas.

Paton, D., Violanti, J.M., Johnston, P., Burke, K., Clarke, J. & Keenan, D. (2008). Stress shield: A model of police resiliency. *International Journal of Emergency Mental Health, 10,* 95-107.

Perry, I. (1997). Creating and empowering effective work teams. *Management Services, 41,* 8-11.

Prigerson, H.G., Maciejewski, P.K., & Rosenheck, R.A. (2002). Population attributable fractions of psychiatric disorders and behavioral outcomes associated with combat exposures among U.S. men. *American Journal of Public Health, 92,* 59-63.

Quinn, R.E., & Spreitzer, G.M. (1997). The road to empowerment: Seven questions every leader should consider. *Organizational Dynamics, Autumn,* 37-49.

Rona, R.J., Hyams, K.C., & Wessely, S. (2005). Screening for psychological illness in military personnel. *Journal of the American Medical Association, 293,* 1257-1260.

Roszell, D.K., McFall, M.E., & Malas, K.L. (1991). Frequency of symptoms and concurrent psychiatric disorder in Vietnam veterans with chronic PTSD. *Hospital and Community Psychiatry, 42*, 293-296.

Rothman, S. & Strijdom, S. (2002). Suicide ideation in the South African Police Services in the Northwest province. *South African Journal of Industrial psychology, 28*, 44-48.

Siegrist, M. & Cvetkovich, G. (2000). Perception of hazards: The role of social trust and knowledge. *Risk Analysis, 20*, 713-719.

Spreitzer, G.M. & Mishra, A.K. (1999). Giving up control without losing control: Trust and its substitutes' effect on managers involving employees in decision making. *Group & Organization Management, 24*, 155-187.

Sugimoto, J.D., & Oltjenbruns, K.A. (2001). The environment of death and its influence on police officers in the United States. *Omega, 43*, 145-156.

Tanielan, T., & Jaycox, H. (2008). Invisible wounds of war psychological and cognitive injuries, their consequences, and services to assist recovery. Santa Monica, CA: Rand corporation.

Vena, J.E., Violanti, J.M., Marshall, J.R., & Feidler, F. (1986). Mortality of a municipal worker cohort III: police officers. *Journal of Industrial Medicine, 10*, 383-397.

Violanti, J.M. (2004). Predictors of police suicide ideation. *Suicide and Life Threatening Behavior, 4*, 277-283.

Violanti, J.M. & Paton, D. (Eds.) (1999). *Police Trauma: Psychological Aftermath of Civilian Combat.* Springfield, ILL: Charles C. Thomas.

Violanti, J.M. (2003). Suicide and the police culture. In Hackett, D. & Violanti, J.M. (Eds.) *Police Suicide: Tactics for prevention.* Springfield, ILL: Charles C. Thomas.

Violanti, J.M., Fekedulegn, D., Charles, L.E., Andrew, M.E., Hartley, T.A., Mnatsakanova, A., & Burchfiel, C.M. (2008). *Depression and suicidal ideation among police officers.* Presentation. Work, Stress, and Health Conference, March, 2008, Washington.

Violanti, J.M., Vena, J.E. & Marshall, J.R. (1996). Suicides, homicides, and accidental deaths: A comparative risk assessment of police officers and municipal workers. *American Journal of Industrial Medicine, 30*, 99-104.

Zivin, K., Kim, M., McCarthy, J.F., Austin, K.L., Hoggatt, K.J., Walters, H. & Valenstien, M. (2007). Suicide mortality among individuals receiving treatment for depression in the veteran's affairs health system: Associations with patient and treatment setting characteristics. *American Journal of Public Health, 97*, 2193-2198.

Discussion Questions

1. How many law enforcement officers have been called up to active military duty since October 2001? By what types of law enforcement agencies were they originally employed?
2. According to estimates by Tanielan and Jaycox, how many individuals currently suffer post-traumatic stress disorder (PTSD)?
3. According to Tanielan and Jaycox, what is posttraumatic stress disorder?
4. What is the relationship between posttraumatic stress disorder and suicide?
5. Many work-related exposures of police officers are often characterized as traumatic compared to other occupations. What specific examples were provided by the author?
6. The ways that trauma can affect police officers is wide ranging. What specific examples were provided?
7. What were reported as the most important non-combat stressors?
8. What did the mental health specialists working for the VA look for when they assessed Operation Iraqi Freedom and Operation Enduring Freedom veterans?
9. Veteran studies specific to suicide have yielded additional evidence. What is some of this evidence?
10. What does the epidemiological evidence suggest relating to elevated rates of suicide within American law enforcement?
11. What can be done to prevent suicides?
12. What is meant by organizational climate?
13. What are the implications of police officers not being very trusting?
14. Why is the quality of leadership so important in suicide prevention?
15. What recommendations were made by the International Association of Chiefs of Police regarding the reintegration of military personnel into law enforcement?

29

Combat Deployment and the Returning Police Officer

Barbara Webster

Introduction

About 100,000 members of National Guard and Reserve units were on active duty in any given month in 2006,[1,2] some serving in Iraq or Afghanistan for the second or third time. A portion of these men and women are police officers, with a recent report indicating that public safety professionals comprise 10 percent of National Guard and Reservists deployed to Iraq (Ritchie and Curran, 2006). In addition, future police recruits will include some of the military service members who are active in combat now. Some who conduct psychological screenings have identified this as a serious issue (Best, 2006).

What does this mean for police departments? As one Iraq war veteran explains, "Not everyone [returning from war] is damaged, but everyone is changed."[3] In sponsoring this report, the Office of Community Oriented Policing Services

---

1. Barbara Webster, "Combat Deployment and the Returning Police Officer," U.S. Department of Justice, Office of Community Oriented Policing Services, (2005), pp. 1–2, 5–23.

2. More than 101,000 Guard and Reserve personnel were reported as mobilized in May 2006 compared to approximately 98,500 in October 2006. The total includes Guard and Reserve personnel from all branches of military service; about 80 percent are Army National Guard and Army Reserves. Updates are published regularly in U.S. Department of Defense press releases published at www.defenselink.mil/releases.

3. Paul Reickhoff, founder and executive director, Iraq and Afghanistan Veterans of America, "Penguin Podcast 10: Paul Reickhoff on the Iraq War," http://us.penguingroup.com/static/html/podcast/ archive.html.

(the COPS Office) wanted to better understand how police officers' lives are changed by their combat experiences, and to explore police departments' efforts to help their members make successful transitions back to work.

Overall, people who experience or witness combat show an incredible capacity to move on with their lives after their return home. The danger lies in acting as if this will happen automatically. Almost 35 percent of U.S. military personnel who serve in Iraq seek help for mental health concerns through military programs (Hoge et al., 2006). Some are diagnosed with Post Traumatic Stress Disorder (PTSD)—essentially, a disorder of physical and emotional arousal brought on by the experience of traumatic events.[4]

Combat zone deployment does not always mean engaging in direct combat or witnessing others being killed or injured, experiences that greatly increase the risk for developing PTSD. Exposure to traumatic events is possible regardless of the military unit's assignment in Iraq or Afghanistan; and depression, substance abuse, anxiety, and sleep disorders are also problems for some who have served there.

In addition to service members who request or are referred to military resources for assistance with PTSD or other mental health concerns, unknown numbers of others have problems but do not seek help, or turn to private service providers not affiliated with the military health care system.[5] Some will not need or will not ask for professional help until years after their return, with recent research showing the likelihood of delays in the development of symptoms (Grieger et al., 2006). Although much remains to be learned about the effects of combat zone deployment on police officers specifically, clearly some officers and their families will need professional services to deal successfully with the changes in their lives, and all will need some form of support, including support from the workplace.

Psychological Effects of Combat and Natural Disasters

Back home, a veteran "drives as close to the middle of the road as he can. Over on the side, in a plastic bag or stuffed in the carcass of a dead dog,

---

4. Although the focus of this report is on combat stress, PTSD can also result from such life-threatening events as natural disasters, terrorist acts, serious accidents, and rape and other violent personal assaults.

5. For example, see "Stressed-Out Soldiers: Men at One Base Say the Army Is Ignoring PTSD Cases," CBS Evening News, July 12, 2006. www.cbsnews.com/stories/2006/07/12/eveningnews/main1798343. shtml.

that's where he knows the enemy intent on killing him hides bombs.....
[He] left Iraq more than 16 months ago ..."[6]

Within the first few days after exposure to a lifethreatening event, it is common for people to experience nightmares, flashbacks, insomnia, feelings of detachment or emotional numbness, and a range of other reactions— both physical and emotional—that may interfere with their ability to function as before. This initial set of reactions is not the same as PTSD, which is a medically recognized anxiety disorder that may be diagnosed about a month or later after the trauma.[7]

PTSD and Other Consequences of Service in Combat Zones

It was not until 1980, several years after the Vietnam War, that PTSD was first included in the American Psychiatric Association's *Diagnostic and Statistical Manual of Mental Disorders* (DSM).[8] But as Vietnam veteran Steve Bentley explains, "PTSD is a new name for an old story—war has always had a severe psychological impact on people in immediate and lasting ways."[9] Bentley's article on the history of PTSD drives this point home, beginning with an Egyptian warrior who described how he felt when facing battle 3,000 years ago: "Shuddering seizes you, the hair on your head stands on end, your soul lies in your hand."

People have given the psychological effects of war many labels, including "soldier's heart" in the American Civil War; "shell shock" in World War I, which some attributed to concussions resulting from exploding shells; and "battle fa-

6. Babwin, D. "Vets Get Help for Post-Traumatic Stress Syndrome," Associated Press, April 10, 2006.

7. See "National Center for PTSD Fact Sheet: What Is Posttraumatic Stress Disorder (PTSD)?" www.ncptsd.va.gov/ncmain/ncdocs/fact_shts/fs_what_is_ptsd.html.

8. The *Diagnostic and Statistical Manual of Mental Disorders*, published by the American Psychiatric Association, categorizes mental disorders and guides U.S. mental health professionals in making diagnoses. See www.psych.org/MainMenu/Research/DSM-IV.aspx.

9. Bentley, Steve, "A Short History of PTSD: From Thermopylae to Hue Soldiers Have Always Had a Disturbing Reaction to War," 1991. Reprinted in *The VVA Veteran*, Vietnam Veterans of America, March 2005, p. 1. ww.archive.vva.org/TheVeteran/2005_03/feature_HistoryPTSD.htm. Bentley served two tours of duty in Vietnam and later worked as a Vet Center counselor.

tigue" in World War II.[10] Currently, making a formal diagnosis of PTSD involves assessing three clusters of symptoms and behaviors:

- Intrusion, in the form of intrusive thoughts, nightmares, or flashbacks, "when sudden, vivid memories, accompanied by painful emotions, take over the person's attention."[11] The person may feel like he or she is actually reliving the traumatic experience.
- Avoidance of close emotional relationships with family, friends, and colleagues and of activities and situations that remind the person of the traumatic event. Also included in this category is the inability to feel or express emotions at all; depression; and feelings of guilt over having survived while others did not.
- Hyperarousal, which includes being easily startled and constantly feeling that danger is near. Other reactions in this category include anger and irritability, loss of concentration, and disturbed sleep.

Flashbacks and startle reactions can be prompted by the sound of gunshots or a truck backfiring, or by any of the sights, sounds, smells, and tastes that an individual closely associates with a particular traumatic event. As in the example above, returned Iraq veterans often mention the sight of objects lying by the roadside. The smell of wet drywall became unbearable for one first responder who pulled bodies from the Pentagon following the September 11 terrorist attacks.[12]

Although PTSD may develop soon after a traumatic experience, it may not occur, or may not be reported, until months or years later (Grieger et al., 2006; Price, 2006; Hoge, 2006). Effective treatments are available, but left untreated, PTSD may take on a chronic course, waxing and waning throughout the person's lifetime. Findings from the National Vietnam Veterans Readjustment Study indicated that nearly one-half million Vietnam veterans—15 percent of the men and 8 percent of the women who served—suffered from PTSD 15 or more years later (Price, 2006).

Research related to PTSD has been extensive during the past 25 years; for example, Tolin and Foa (2006) identified 2,477 articles on PTSD (i.e., books, book chapters, and journal articles) published in English between 1980 and

---

10. Also see "The Soldier's Heart," Public Broadcasting Service, March 2005. This documentary and a transcript are available for viewing at www.pbs.org/wgbh/pages/frontline/shows/heart.

11. American Psychiatric Association, *Let's Talk Facts About Post Traumatic Stress Disorder*. 2005. www.healthyminds.org.

12. Jenkins, C. L. "For Lifesavers, Stress of Rescue Still Hits Home," *The Washington Post*, Alexandria Arlington Extra, September 5, 2002, 9–10.

2005. Recent research, much of which has been conducted with police officers, includes studies of biological markers and symptoms associated with
PTSD, as well as prospective studies[13] of public safety professionals, which
allow for an improved understanding of risk and resilience factors of PTSD
development (Neylan et al., 2005; Otte et al., 2005; Pole et al., 2005).

In addition, diagnostic criteria for PTSD have changed since 1980. Originally, for example, PTSD was defined as a "normal response to an abnormal
event," but this was deleted from the *DSM-IV* (currently in use) because studies showed that most people experience at least one traumatic event during their
lifetimes and a majority do not develop PTSD as a result (Kessler, 2000). The *DSM-
IV* also introduced two additional diagnostic criteria: the related event must involve actual or threatened death or injury, and the person's response must involve
either "intense fear, helplessness, or horror" (APA, 1994; Tolin and Foa, 2006).

Other potentially long-term mental health consequences of exposure to
traumatic events include major depression; substance abuse; and more generalized anxiety or overwhelming worry, panic attacks, and phobias (Hoge, et
al., 2004; Najavits, 2002, Armstrong et al., 2006). While grief and "survivor's
guilt"[14] are not clinical disorders, these feelings, if they persist, can portend a
serious depression and may indicate a need for professional help (Sherman,
2006; Gray et al., 2004). Family disruption and financial problems are also
stress factors that may place an individual at risk for developing psychiatric
post-trauma disorders (Hobfall et al., 1991; Bray et al., 2006).

A further complication of wartime trauma involves soldiers being both victims of trauma and agents trained to inflict trauma on others (Elhai, North, and
Frueh, 2005). The latter is critical for those returning to police work because a
need to control others' behavior goes beyond their wartime experience and, in
effect, is a feature of their jobs. This has implications for police departments in
monitoring complaints and use-of-force rates among returning reservists.

Prevalence of PTSD

In 2004, the *New England Journal of Medicine* published a groundbreaking
study that examined the mental health of soldiers and Marines involved in

---

13. Prospective studies look for outcomes that occur during the study period (e.g., development of a disease). In contrast, retrospective studies look backward to examine outcomes that were already known when the study began.

14. The term "survivor's guilt" is sometimes used to describe feelings of guilt or shame
associated with having survived a tragedy while others did not. It is not a psychiatric disorder, nor is it among the diagnostic criteria for PTSD.

combat operations in Iraq and Afghanistan. This was "the first time there had been such an early assessment of the prevalence of psychiatric disorders, reported while the fighting continues" (Friedman, 2004). The researchers administered an anonymous survey to members of four combat infantry units either before their deployment or 3 to 4 months after their return. Outcomes included major depression, generalized anxiety, and PTSD. As Friedman (2004) observes, the study results "force us to acknowledge the psychiatric cost of sending young men and women to war." Further, "perceptions of stigma[15] among those most in need" was identified as an important barrier to receiving mental health services" (Hoge et al., 2004).

A follow-up study published in the *Journal of the American Medical Association* examined help-seeking among soldiers and Marines (Hoge et al., 2006). Again, the results raised concern:

- The prevalence of reporting a mental health problem was 19.1 percent among service members returning from Iraq and 11.3 percent among those returning from Afghanistan.
- 35 percent of Iraq veterans accessed mental health services in the year after returning home; 12 percent were diagnosed with a mental health problem.
- Fewer than 10 percent of service members who received mental health services were referred through the DOD screening program (discussed later).

A report published in early 2005 by the Operation Iraqi Freedom (OIF-II) Mental Health Advisory Team (MHAT-II), which is chartered by the U.S. Army Surgeon General, concluded that mental health and wellbeing showed improvements compared to an earlier assessment but that "[a]cute or posttraumatic stress symptoms remain the top MH [mental health] concern, affecting at least 10 percent of OIF-II Soldiers" (MHAT-II, 2005, 3).[16]

---

15. Stigma in this context refers to fears that disclosing a mental illness will result in negative consequences—for example, harm to one's career or perceptions by supervisors, unit members, or others of being different or weak.

16. Another study of the health and mental health of military service members is the DOD-sponsored "Survey of Health Related Behaviors Among Active Duty Military Personnel." Conducted nine times since 1980, the December 2006 survey report (based on 2005 data) provides detailed findings on substance abuse, stress, PTSD, help-seeking behaviors, and other concerns but did not report findings specific to service members in Iraq and Afghanistan (the sample involved more than 16,000 service members randomly selected from throughout the world).

Clearly, there are pronounced differences between serving in a combat zone and surviving other traumatic events, and it is difficult to compare results from studies of PTSD prevalence among survivors of different wars and survivors of other events involving mass casualties. Researchers have used diverse survey instruments and methods, and they have conducted the surveys within a variety of time frames (e.g., weeks or months after the event compared to years later). Nevertheless, the reported prevalence of PTSD symptoms and depression associated with Hurricane Katrina—among first responders as well as other survivors—appears to be similar to that reported among Iraq veterans. Hurricane Katrina hit the U.S. Gulf Coast in August 2005, and in mid-October 2005 the Centers for Disease Control and Prevention (CDC) conducted a survey of randomly selected adults returning to Orleans Parish and Jefferson Parish, Louisiana. The CDC determined that of the 166 respondents, 33 percent had a probable need for mental health assistance and 50 percent had a "possible" need for such assistance (Weisler, Barbee, and Townsend, 2006).[17]

Seven to 13 weeks after Katrina, the CDC conducted another assessment, this time of New Orleans Police Department and Fire Department personnel.[18] Of the 912 police officers who completed the questionnaire, 19 percent reported PTSD symptoms and 26 percent reported major depressive symptoms.[19] Of the 525 firefighters who completed the same questionnaire, 22 percent reported PTSD symptoms and 27 percent reported major depressive symptoms (Weisler, Barbee, and Townsend, 2006).[20]

Nature and Duration of Exposure

"BAGHDAD, May 9—Attracting a crowd by hawking flour at half-price from a pickup truck, a suicide attacker in the northern city of Tall Afar on Tuesday detonated bombs hidden beneath the flour sacks, killing at

---

17. Later, Harvard Medical School researchers found similar results after polling 1,043 adults between January 19 and March 31, 2006. The researchers concluded that 31 percent suffered some type of mental illness (compared to 16 percent in a 2003 general population survey); and that 11 percent suffered a serious mental illness such as PTSD or depression. See Kessler, R. C., et al., "Mental Illness and Suicidality After Hurricane Katrina," Bulletin of the World Health Organization, 2006. www.who.int/bulletin/volumes/84/10/06-033019.pdf.

18. This assessment used the Center for Epidemiologic Studies Depression Scale and the VA checklist to identify symptoms of PTSD.

19. 888 of the police officers responded to questions about depression.

20. 494 of the firefighters responded to the questions about depression.

least 19 people, many of them women shopping with children, police said.[21]

The nature of a person's exposure to war is one of the critical determinants of combat stress and PTSD (Schlenger et al., 1999). Exposure to casualties and the types of casualties to which a person is exposed—particularly dead and wounded civilians and soldiers— have been linked to higher distress scores for symptoms of posttraumatic stress. The prevalence of PTSD symptoms among veterans of the 1991 Persian Gulf war, for example, (Kang et al., 2003; Southwick 1995; Alder et al., 1996) appears to be relatively low compared to findings about Iraq and Afghanistan veterans, Hurricane Katrina responders, or survivors of the genocide in Rwanda in 1994 (24.8 percent, according to a recent study [Pham et al., 2004]). Clearly, exposure to the death and injury of children is difficult under any circumstances and a potential risk factor for PTSD.

Historically, personnel deployed to Iraq have exhibited significantly higher rates of PTSD than those deployed to Afghanistan, a difference that has been linked to trauma exposure and strongly associated with intense and prolonged combat (Hoge, 2004; GAO, 2006). In addition, deployment length and multiple deployments place military personnel at significantly higher risks for developing mental health problems (MHAT-V, 2008).

Many service personnel in Iraq and Afghanistan have little respite from daily exposure to death and life-threatening events, and many serve several tours of duty or must stay longer than expected.

For first responders to catastrophes like Hurricane Katrina and the September 11 attacks, the intensity and duration of exposure to trauma are factors, as well. Casualties may include family members, friends, and coworkers. Responders may work long hours for weeks or months afterward, at the same time dealing with the disaster's personal impact on their own life circumstances.

Both the military and law enforcement stand to gain from future research on reducing the risk of PTSD and other long-lasting psychological problems associated with traumatic experiences, keeping in mind both the differences and similarities between exposure to trauma in combat zones and in other environments with multiple casualties. For example, what lessons can be applied from research on resilience and on specific protective factors, such as train-

---

21. Knickmeyer, Ellen and Dlovan Brwari. "Deadly Deception at an Iraqi Market: Attacker Posing as Vendor Kills 19 in City Called Model by Bush." *Washington Post Foreign Service*, May 10, 2006, A17.

ing, personality type, age, gender, prior traumatic experiences, and other possible factors, singularly and in combination?

Important messages for police agencies based on what we do know are that (1) we cannot predict with certainty who will develop PTSD or other potentially long-term mental health problems, and (2) assumptions that those things happen only to weaklings have no basis in fact. We do have some knowledge of protective factors, but it is not safe to assume that police officers in National Guard or Reserve units will be spared by virtue of their age or maturity alone (MHAT-II, 2005). Not every memory of a crisis is painful, and not every painful memory is debilitating, but PTSD can affect anyone experiencing traumatic events.

Intervention and Treatment

Efforts to reduce the risk of PTSD related to combat and disasters are grouped into three categories: (1) primary prevention—the selection, preparation, and training of people who are likely to be exposed to traumatizing events; (2) secondary prevention—a number of techniques that are offered immediately or shortly after such events; and (3) tertiary interventions, which include various treatments for PTSD (Deahl et al., 2000).

Military Interventions, Screening Processes, and Treatment Resources

The DOD's combat stress control program includes components for training service members on early signs and symptoms of combat stress. DOD teams of mental health professionals also travel to units to reinforce this information and help identify persons at risk. According to the Army's MHAT-II in January 2005, two-thirds of soldiers in Iraq "reported receiving training in handling the stresses of deployment and/or combat," although only 41 percent said this training was adequate (MHAT-II, 2005, 4).

To provide immediate interventions after trauma, the military has increased the number of behavioral health professionals deployed to the front lines, although shortages of these personnel, difficulty reaching soldiers, and burnout among behavioral health personnel are significant obstacles (MHAT-V, 2008). The philosophy of Proximity, Immediacy, and Expectancy (PIE) has long driven the provision of front-line interventions in the military. Essentially this involves treating distressed soldiers close to the battlefield (proximity), as soon as possible (immediacy), and with the expectation that they will return to duty (expectancy).[22]

Postdeployment, the DOD uses a "postdeployment health assessment questionnaire," followed by an interview, to identify both physical and mental health problems. In practice, however, the required postdeployment interview process varies from base to base and may be done in a group setting led by a chaplain or senior officer, rather than a one-on-one interview.

The DOD postdeployment questionnaire includes this screening question for PTSD:

Have you ever had any experience that was so frightening, horrible, or upsetting that, in the past month, you

- have had any nightmares about it or thought about it when you did not want to?
- tried hard not to think about it or went out of your way to avoid situations that remind you of it?
- were constantly on guard, watchful, or easily startled?
- felt numb or detached from others, activities, or your surroundings?[23]

Other postdeployment identification efforts are needed for several reasons. First, problems may not emerge until much later (Grieger et al., 2006), indicating a role for employers in identifying signs of PTSD and other mental health issues. Second, the DOD postdeployment questionnaire is a brief self-report. Service members may believe that checking "yes" to PTSD symptoms (or any other item related to mental health) will have negative consequences, or they may be unwilling to risk retention at the base while others leave to reunite with loved ones.[24] Third, responses on the screening questionnaire indicating PTSD symptoms may not result in referrals for additional assessments; or service members may not follow up on referrals. Among service members back from Iraq who reported either three or four PTSD symptoms on the screening questionnaire, only 23 percent of soldiers and 15 percent of Marines received referrals for further mental health evaluations (GAO, 2006). Further, 50 per-

---

22. For an overview of the Army's Combat and Operational Stress program, see "Army Behavioral Health: Combat and Operational Stress General Information," www.behavioralhealth.army.mil/provider/general.html#cosr. For more specific information about frontline interventions, see "Army Behavioral Health: Traumatic Event Management," www.behavioralhealth.army.mil/provider/traumatic.html.

23. Question # 12, DOD Post-Deployment Health Assessment (Form DD 2796).

24. Also see the section in this report on "barriers to treatment."

cent of those referred were not found to have sought treatment within the first year of their referral (Hoge et al., 2006).

The DOD has recognized these issues and has begun to address them. Current policy is to conduct a second post-deployment screening for health and mental health concerns after 90 days but no later than 180 days (Guard and Reserve members may still be eligible for military health and mental health benefits for up to 180 days post deployment). All service members who complete the first post-deployment screening form—not just those who identified concerns at that time—are asked to participate in the second screening.[25] Even with this additional screening process, however, employers cannot be certain that all issues will have been identified and addressed through military channels because, again, individuals may be reluctant to report a problem, or problems may not emerge until a later date.

All branches of the U.S. military, as well as the VA and its National Center for PTSD, have been developing additional resources to treat PTSD and other mental health concerns. Through the military health care system, service members can receive mental health evaluations and treatment for PTSD while on active duty and for specific periods after discharge or release from active duty. The VA also provides mental health benefits to veterans through more than 200 Vet Centers, and through its hospitals and clinics. At the Vet Centers, multidisciplinary staff teams include many professionals who are also combat veterans. In addition to counseling and referrals for mental health services, Vet Center services include help with applications for benefits and with troubleshooting related to eligibility issues, paperwork delays, and other concerns.[26]

Treatment Approaches

Effective treatment for PTSD is available, but approaches and programs are not all alike. It may take some time for an individual to find the right fit. The National Center for PTSD offers a short list of questions that those seeking mental health care should ask of a potential therapist (e.g., treatment approaches, provider qualifications and experience, fees).[27]

---

25. DD Form 2900 is completed for the second screening. For a description of this new Post-Deployment Health Reassessment (PDHRA) Program, see www.pdhealth.mil/dcs/pdhra.asp.

26. See the GAO report noted under "Resources" for a summary of DOD and VA mental health evaluation and treatment resources.

27. See "Choosing a therapist," in the National Center for PTSD Fact Sheet, Finding a Therapist, available at www.ncptsd.va.gov/ncmain/ncdocs/fact_shts/fs_finding_a_therapist.html#choosing.

The type of intervention proven most effective for treating PTSD is cognitive behavioral, exposure-based therapy (Foa et al., 2004). "Prolonged imaginal exposure" carefully exposes the individual to "prolonged and repeated imagined images of the trauma until the images no longer cause severe anxiety,"[28] while "in vivo"[29] interventions expose the individual to situations or objects they avoid or fear because of their association with the trauma (for example, highway underpasses, which some Iraq veterans may avoid because they remind them of times when they were under sniper attack). The exposure treatments are combined with other cognitive behavioral approaches that focus on learning to change patterns of thinking about the traumatic event and the person's relationship to it. These approaches may be combined with others, such as eye movement desensitization and reprocessing; teaching coping skills such as relaxation techniques, anger management, and sleep hygiene; traumatic grief treatment; and prescribing medications, such as antidepressants (Ruzek, 2001).

Researchers continue to explore other approaches to PTSD treatment, as well as new means to deliver treatment services. The field of telemedicine, for example, may hold promise as a service delivery option, although more needs to be learned about the effectiveness of "telemental health services" for assessing and treating PTSD. As the National Center for PTSD explains, the term refers to "behavioral health services that are provided using communication technology;" and include clinical assessments, individual therapy, group therapy (e.g., via videoconferencing), and other interventions that may benefit those who are isolated from in-person services (Morland et al., 2003).[30] Another example is research on the role of adrenaline in PTSD, which may offer hope for new medications that permit more timely interventions.[31]

Police administrators and managers, while not expected to become mental health treatment or research experts, need some familiarity with research results on effective interventions and treatment. "Psychological debriefings" or "stress debriefings," for example, although used by some military and civilian

---

28. For a brief explanation, see "Exposure Therapy Helps PTSD Victims Overcome Trauma's Debilitating Effects," American Psychological Association, www.psychology matters.org/keane.html.

29. Latin for "in life."

30. Also see "Virtual Training's No Game," a public radio program aired November 23, 2006, that discusses adapting video gaming software, including "America's Army," as part of critical incident management training, including stress management (http://marketplace. publicradio.org/shows/display/web/2006/11/23/virtual_trainings_no_game).

31. See CBS News, "A Pill to Forget? Can a Medication Suppress Traumatic Memories?" November 26, 2006, www.cbsnews.com.

mental health workers, have not been proven effective in reducing the risk of PTSD, depression, or anxiety and, for some individuals, may be harmful.[32] Another example is peer support programs, including law enforcement programs and "vets helping vets" programs developed by veterans' organizations. These programs may be a resource for some police officers returning from combat zones; however, they are not a form of treatment and should follow strict guidelines.[33] None of these findings suggest that persons distressed by traumatic events should be left alone; rather, they suggest that police administrators need to consult with mental health experts to stay current about effective interventions and treatment methods. A resource for police is the International Association of Chiefs of Police (IACP) Psychological Services Section, which has offered presentations at recent IACP annual conferences on police officers' return from combat zones (Ritchie and Curran, 2006; Best, 2006).

Military and Police Cultures

Nancy Sherman, author of *Stoic Warriors* (2005), refers to "a culture of suck it up" (Sherman, 2006) when discussing military organizations' historical reluctance to admit that their members may need help coping with the ravages of war. Police agencies and officers, steeped in paramilitary traditions, also have a vested interest in being perceived as always in control—able to withstand trauma by sheer will and get on with the job. Beyond providing for a short break from extremely stressful duties—what the military calls "three hots and a cot"—organizational resources for maintaining mental health and dealing with stress have been slow to evolve in both the military and in policing.

Barriers to PTSD recognition and treatment for military service members and veterans are often reported in the news and, in some cases, are being investigated. They include instances of supervisors ridiculing officers with PTSD

---

32. The value of various forms of stress debriefings is still debated; however, the VA's National Center for PTSD has concluded that psychological debriefing is "inappropriate for acutely bereaved individuals" and cautions: " .... the best studies suggest that for individuals with more severe exposure to trauma, and for those who are experiencing more severe reactions such as PTSD, [stress] debriefing is ineffective and possibly harmful." emphasis in original]. See National Center for PTSD Fact Sheet: "Types of debriefing following disasters," www. ncptsd.va.gov/ncmain/ncdocs/fact_shts/fs_type_debriefings_disaster.html.

33. See the IACP Psychological Services Section's 2006 "Peer Support Guidelines," www.theiacp.org/div_sec_com/sections/PeerSupportGuidelines.pdf.

or refusing to release them from drills for appointments; and allegations that some officers with PTSD, including those who served with distinction in combat zones, are purposely being discharged on less than honorable grounds— for example, for a pattern of misconduct.[34] In addition, there are concerns that officers with extreme combat stress or PTSD are being kept on duty in combat zones because of a shortage of personnel.

At the same time, the military and the VA have acknowledged and made efforts to address the stigma that many service members associate with seeking help for mental health concerns. One example is a video CD developed by the Navy[35] that directly addresses some of the most difficult barriers: fears that difficulties in coping are, or will be viewed as, weakness and will be ridiculed; or that prospects for a promotion, a security clearance, or an entire career will be sacrificed because of asking for help. Materials and outreach efforts by other branches of the military also seek to convey the message that combat stress is normal and that effective treatments for PTSD are available if needed. Some of the materials are geared to the particular needs of reservists in Iraq, some target their civilian employers, and other outreach efforts target military families.

A reluctance to seek help for mental health concerns has also been prevalent among police (Delprino, 2002). Over the years, however, many police agencies have come to recognize a need for mental health resources, as evidenced by the psychological or behavioral services units in some departments; and by the growth of city, county, and police department employee assistance programs and police peer support teams in the 1990s (Finn, 2000).

Employee assistance and behavioral services programs also have been a cornerstone of police organizations' efforts to assist their officers when they return from combat zones. The next section of this report illustrates a range of department responses to assist returning police officers and their families. In addition, some law enforcement agencies have developed related training. A partnership in Wisconsin of the Dane County Sheriff's Department, Madison Police Department, and the state's Department of Veterans Affairs resulted in a new, required 1-hour training session for all enforcement officials. Its purpose is to heighten police officers' awareness of veterans' experiences in combat zones, whether the veterans are police officers, their family members,

---

34. For example, see the National Public Radio report by Daniel Zwerdling, "Soldiers Say Army Ignores, Punishes Mental Anguish," www.npr.org/templates/story/story.php?story Id=6576505.

35. Called *Combat Stress Reactions: Normal Responses to Abnormal Conditions*, it has segments geared to Marines and Navy service members, their families, and command staff.

or citizens who come to police attention.[36] In Holyoke, Massachusetts, veterans' advocates, mental health experts, and prosecutors held a training program for police, dispatchers, and other emergency workers, in part to help police identify troubled veterans in the community and refer them to appropriate services.[37]

Law Enforcement Agency Responses

One limitation of this report is that it leaves many important questions unanswered about the nature and extent of specific problems that returning police officers are experiencing. The study was too small to survey police officers who have returned from combat zones, and most of the agency representatives who were interviewed on the telephone provided only general observations. For example, one said that some officers had difficulty transitioning from the "go-go-go mindset" of active duty to the slower pace of in-service training or routine police duties. Another said "signs of stress" had been reported regarding a few officers. Several emphasized the importance of outreach to deployed police officers' families, while others suggested that equal or greater attention be paid to potential problems among combat veterans who apply for police work. Similarly, psychologists who reviewed a draft of this report expressed concerns about the adequacy of current psychological screening instruments for identifying unresolved, combat-related mental health issues among police recruits. Finally, several interview participants emphasized the importance of recognizing the benefits that military veterans can bring to policing, such as leadership skills, teamwork experiences, and weapons training.

The study did find a wide range of police department responses to officers returning from combat zones. In some departments, officers simply go back to work. As one police officer and SWAT team member explained, his return from combat to law enforcement was essentially a matter of "here's your gun back," no questions asked.[38] Other departments required some type of reorientation, training, and/or a conversation about the availability of personal

36. Jones, M. "Police Learn to Help Vets with Cultural Shift: Home Front Presents New Battle," April 15, 2007, *Milwaukee Journal Sentinel/JS Online.* www.jsonline.com/story/index.aspx?id=591503.

37. Reitz, Stephanie, "1st Responders Trained to Spot Troubled Vets," Associated Press, February 4, 2008. www.armytimes.com/news/2008/02/ap_troubledvets_080202.

38. Discussion at "PTSD: The Newest Community Issue, A Roundtable Discussion for Service Providers," Washington, D.C., March 23, 2005.

and family assistance. They required, for example, firearms retraining and recertification, and a meeting with a supervisor (but not with a professional mental health or family services counselor). At various departments, the supervisor brought the officer up to date on policies and procedures that had changed and/or reminded the officer that personal and family resources were available if needed, such as through the department's (or a city/county) employee assistance program, psychological or behavioral services unit, or a peer assistance team.

In other departments, the screening and intervention process for mental health or family concerns is more deliberate and formal: officers returning from combat zones are required to meet with a mental health professional before resuming their duties. The police departments in Dallas, Louisville, Houston, Los Angeles, Kansas City (Missouri), New York City, and Chicago are among those with this requirement.

The New York City Police Department, which has approximately 40,000 members, reports that between September 11, 2001, and November 2005, approximately 800 officers were called up for Guard or Reserve duties. The department did not report developing any new policies related to these officers; however, they must meet the same requirements as officers who leave and return for other reasons. This includes a debriefing with a staff psychologist and a 2-week training course for firearms requalification.

Several departments also mentioned making concerted efforts to stay in touch with officers while they are on military duty. The Chicago Police Department, for example, reports that "the union helps a lot with keeping in contact" with police officers overseas, and the department includes their families as honored guests in special events such as holiday celebrations.

One police department member interviewed for this study said his own agency might do more simply by consulting with members who had been deployed (about 10 to 12 a year), asking them more specifically about their needs and concerns, and then determining whether there were commonalities that the department could address. Another much larger department with a retraining and assessment process in place suggested that "any department could always do more" but may have to work within budget constraints and draw on existing department services.

The Los Angeles Police and Sheriff's Departments, the Kansas City Police Department, and the Richland County (South Carolina) Sheriff's Department are among agencies that have implemented comprehensive, proactive approaches to address officers' transitions from combat zones.

Los Angeles Police Department Military Liaison Program

The Los Angeles Police Department (LAPD) reported having about 500 officers who are reservists, about 200 of whom were called to active duty soon after September 11, 2001. The department's military liaison officer position was created during that period,[39] in part to handle the many inquiries from, and concerns of, deployed officers' families.

Assistance to families is still a significant part of the military liaison officer's job, but it has evolved to include assisting officers before, during, and after their deployment with any of their needs, including issues related to pay, promotions, and transfers. The chief of police and the organizational culture generally were described as very supportive of officers on military deployments, and commanders are encouraged to stay in contact with officers' families during that time. While officers are out, the LAPD provides pay differential and annual pay step advances, continues benefits, and provides accumulated annual vacation and tenure for the duration of their military service. Officers are still eligible for promotional consideration and can take promotional exams while on military leave.

As of February 2005, each officer returning from military duty is required to complete a confidential interview with Behavioral Sciences Services personnel, who provide resource materials and extend offers of individual or family assistance. Also within the past 2 years, the department developed a new reintegration program for officers separated from the department for more than 1 year for various reasons, including military service. Returning officers are assigned to the police academy for a month of retraining; receive both physical and mental health assessments; and undergo background checks.

In 2005, the LAPD was one of 15 employers nationwide to receive a Freedom Award from Employer Support of the Guard and Reserves (ESGR) (www.esgr.mil). ESGR is a DOD organization created in 1972 to promote cooperation between Reserve members and their civilian employers. One of the LAPD officers who helped nominate the department was a Marine Corps Reserve sergeant who had been injured in Iraq by an IED. He described the department and the military liaison officer as having given him "the utmost support."[40]

---

39. In October 2005, about 60 police officers were on leave for active duty, with 6 to 12 leaving or returning every pay period.

40. "The Department of Defense Honors the Los Angeles Police Department for Its Support of Employees Serving in National Guard and Reserves," Los Angeles Police Department. www.lapdonline.org/inside_the_lapd/content_basic_view/6578.

Los Angeles Sheriff's Department Military Activation Committee

In September 2004, the Los Angeles Sheriff's Department (LASD) was also a winner of the ESGR Freedom Award for its military repatriation program. At the time of the award, 151 of the department's 365 military reservists had been called to active duty.

The Military Activation Committee (MAC) was created after the September 11, 2001 terrorist attacks to address the needs of employees who were military reservists called to active duty. A key goal of the MAC is to ensure that department members return to a welcoming environment.[41] Each key unit in the department has a military liaison officer.

While department members are on leave, the LASD continues benefits, makes up the difference between military and department pay, provides support to families, and keeps in touch with personnel deployed overseas. Returning department members are partnered with a mentor for 3 days, primarily to receive updates on policies, procedures, and job skills. They also meet with their unit commander and military liaison officer. In addition, the program includes a confidential, informational briefing by a psychologist, who offers counseling assistance to the returning officer and his or her family, with periodic follow-up.

A recent news article provides one example of LASD support. A new LASD deputy's Marine Reserve unit was called to Iraq after he had spent only a few days on the job. While overseas, he suffered a brain aneurism and was transported to Walter Reed Hospital in Bethesda, Maryland. The LASD raised enough money to allow several family members to visit him, and the sheriff called the officer personally to assure him he would have a job waiting for him when he returned.[42] Another example is a yard sale held in 2005 at the sheriff's training academy and at a retail parking lot. The sale raised nearly $5,000, a portion of which was used to purchase equipment requested by the MAC—special holsters designed for drawing a sidearm while seated in a military vehicle and wearing body armor.[43]

---

41. Tempest, R. "The Hidden Cost of Iraq War," *Los Angeles Times*, May 23, 2004.
42. "Local Hero." *Los Angeles Garment & Citizen*, February 23, 2006. http://garment andcitizen.com/category/archives/archived-local-herostories/2006-02-23-2.php.
43. County of Los Angeles Sheriff's Department, "Year in Review 2005." www.lasd.org/sites/yr2005web/22text.htm.

Kansas City (Missouri) Police Department

In the past few years, about 35 to 50 Kansas City police officers have been called to Guard or Reserve duty in combat zones. A representative of the department's employee assistance program (EAP) explained that each officer participates in an interview with a critical incident psychologist upon returning to the department.

New within the past few years is a military support group made up of officers who have served in combat. In addition, other services—chaplains, peer counseling, psychological services, EAP—are available to employees and their families.

Police officers' families continue to receive insurance benefits while officers are deployed; upon their return, vacation time that officers may have missed is reinstated, and they have an opportunity to request time off. The EAP representative notes that the department is very supportive of the officers, and that if it could do more, she would like to see it make up lost pay.

Richland County (South Carolina) Sheriff's Department

The president of Post Trauma Resources, a firm that contracts with the Richland County Sheriff's Department (RCSD), reports that approximately 5 to 10 officers a year are called to active duty from the RCSD. The sheriff recognizes that their experiences could have some effect on their ability to do their jobs and wants to make sure that officers are ready to return to work.

Beginning in 2005, an RCSD policy made it mandatory for returning officers to meet with a Post Trauma Resources psychologist before returning to work. The psychologist does not do a full assessment but has a conversation with the returning officer to determine whether further assessments are needed and makes referrals to other services, if needed. Post Trauma Resources cautions against relying on military resources to meet the mental health needs of returning police officers. One reason is that members of the Guard or Reserves' eligibility to access these resources may run out before PTSD symptoms occur.

Conclusions and Recommendations

Brief Review of Findings and Issues

We do not know how many police officers have unresolved mental health concerns when they return to work from combat zones. We do not fully understand the ways in which people officers may be different from others who serve in combat zones—the extent to which their personal characteristics, training, experience, support systems, or age, for example, may serve as protective factors.

We do know, however, that police who have unresolved mental health concerns—whether or not those concerns are associated with their combat-related experiences—are at risk of harming themselves or others because of the nature of their jobs. Police officers' occupational tools include vehicles often driven at high speeds, and weapons. Police are governed by use-of-force policies that differ greatly from military Standing Rules for Use of Force and Rules of Engagement in the combat environment. Further, it is far more likely that police officers will be exposed to, or involved in, work-related trauma than will veterans who return to or enter many other occupations.

This study identified a wide range of police department responses to officers returning to work from combat zones. The proactive and comprehensive services that were found represent practices that other departments can consider.

The study also identified several issues that were not fully explored but may have important implications for police department. One is the concern among some in law enforcement about recruits who have served in Iraq or Afghanistan. Many police departments are in a hiring crisis (Woska, 2006), unable to attract qualified applicants for unfilled positions. Is there more that departments can do to assist Iraq and Afghanistan veterans who apply for police work, for example, those who are well qualified but have minor, unresolved issues related to combat stress?

In addition, this report has not discussed the potential impact on police organizations of returning vets and potential hires who have physical limitations because of injuries sustained in Iraq and Afghanistan. If physical injuries prevent a returning vet from performing previous job functions, what accommodations can be made? Can the department offer assignments that are equivalent to the predeployment work and level of responsibility, benefits, and promotional opportunities.

Before developing programs to assist returning police officers or veterans applying for police work, police departments should obtain legal advice from experts in employment law. Programs should be consistent with federal laws providing important protections for veterans, including the Uniformed Services Employment and Reemployment Rights Act (USERRA)[44] and Title I of

---

44. 38 U.S.C. § 4301-4334. The USERRA statute is available from www.justice. gov/crt/military/statute.htm. USERRA is enforced by the U.S. Department of Labor, Veterans Employment and Training Service (VETS). See www.dol.gov/vets/programs/userra/main.htm. Also see VETS' "USERRA Advisor," www.dol.gov/elaws/userra.htm. Another resource for USERRA information is Employer Support of the Guard and Reserve (ESGR), a U.S. De-

the Americans with Disabilities Act (ADA).[45] USERRA prohibits employers (regardless of number of employees) from discriminating against applicants or employees based on military status or obligations, and it also provides reemployment rights for persons who leave civilian jobs for military service. The ADA prohibits employers with 15 or more employees from discrimination against individuals on the basis of disability. Both USERRA and the ADA require employers to make reasonable accommodations for individuals with disabilities, "however, USERRA requires employers to go further than the ADA by making reasonable efforts to assist a veteran who is returning to employment in becoming qualified for a job."[46] Although legal definitions of disability vary, veterans who were wounded or became ill while on active duty may meet both the definitions of "disabled veteran" and the ADA's definition of "individual with a disability."[47]

Finally, police departments may need to examine their procedures for handling certain misdemeanors involving veterans in the community and expand their referral sources to included specialized services for veterans.

Recommendations for Police Departments

Police departments should do more to create a "welcome-home" environment and serve police officer reservists who return to work from assignments in Iraq or Afghanistan, whether or not the department is large enough to have its own EAP military liaison position. Many people are reluctant to ask for mental health services, and considerable time may pass before PTSD or other mental health concerns begin to interfere with work and daily life. Every department should consider the following questions:

- Is the department's organizational culture supportive of officers' transitions back to work after being in a combat zone or experiencing any type of traumatic event?

---

partment of Defense program, which provides assistance to employers and an extensive list of frequently asked questions at www.esgr.org/userrafaq.asp.

45. 42 U.S.C. § 12111-12117. See www.eeoc.gov/policy/ada.html. The ADA is enforced by the U.S. Equal Employment Opportunity Commission. Section 501 of the Rehabilitation Act applies the ADA's nondiscrimination and reasonable accommodation standards to federal agencies and the U.S. Postal Service.

46. U.S. Equal Employment Opportunity Commission, "Veterans with Service-Connected Disabilities and the Americans with Disabilities Act (ADA): A Guide for Employers," 1, www.eeoc.gov/facts/veteransdisabilities-employers.html.

47. U.S. Equal Employment Opportunity Commission, 2.

- Are supervisors and managers advocates of employee assistance programs and similar resources? Do they recognize that these resources can provide them with tools to be better managers?
- Have department supervisors and other members received sufficient education and training about traumatic stress?
- Is someone from the department or a department-affiliated volunteer organization staying in touch with department members and their families, while they are on military duty?
- Is a specific supervisor or officer, trained in issues to combat stress, assigned to welcome returning officers, update them on training and procedures, and remind them of available sources of confidential assistance?
- Do supervisors and department members know what to watch for in others who have lived through traumatic events (e.g., heavy drinking, taking unnecessary risks, incivility in dealing with community members, warning signs associated with suicide risk)?

Individual police departments, at a minimum, can make sure that returning officers have information about confidential sources of help for themselves and their family members. We recommend that departments go well beyond the minimum.

- Police departments should have experienced mental health professional conduct a confidential meeting with each officer returning from the military duty. The purpose is to assess the individual's wellbeing and need for assistance, if any, including family support. This is not the same as a fitness for duty examination. Departments should obtain legal advice to ensure that the assessment does not violate USERRA or the ADA's employment provisions.

  Family members should also be included in this process or should have a similar meeting with an experienced counselor, social worker, psychologist, or psychiatrist. Periodic follow-up should be done with veterans for the first two years after deployment.

- Depending on the size of the agency and number of returning officers affected, departments should consider implementing a special reintegration program for officers separated from the department for military tours of duty.

  In addition to the initial and follow-up confidential meetings noted above, program components to consider include a review of police use-of-force policies, firearms and other recertifications, a means to make up missed in-service training, and physical health assessments. Again, departments should consult with their legal advisors in developing such a program to ensure that it does not violate USERRA or other employment laws. In addition, human resources experts, psychological services experts, and employee representatives (e.g., unions) should be consulted.

- Departments should develop partnerships with other state, county, and local agencies to share resources for the reintegration program, such as veterans' support groups, law enforcement peer support groups, employee assistance programs, or behavioral health services.
- Departments should rate supervisors' awareness of potential problems that returning officers may face and train supervisors in early identification and in appropriate interventions.

Recommendations for Research and Policy Development

Police organizations should partner with the Department of Defense and the Department of Veterans Affairs and convene a special working group to develop additional recommendations. The group should identify areas of mutual concern in program development, training, and research. Potential funding for joint projects should be explored, and a plan for following-up should be developed and implemented.

Partnerships among police organizations, agencies like the National Institute of Justice and IACP Psychological Services Section, as well as relevant associations of mental health professionals, the National Center for PTSD, and other organizations should be established to identify research priorities related to policing and combat zone duty, natural disasters, and other events with mass casualties. Research questions to consider include the following:

- What are the implications of military service in combat zones for the psychological screening of police recruits? What influence, if any, should the current shortage of applicants for police work have on the screening process?
- What do police officers who have served in combat zones identify as unmet needs? What do they believe their agencies might do to better assist them and their families? Confidential interviews or survey should be conducted.
- What specific issues are police agencies facing related to police officers who return from combat zone deployments? More extensive research is needed to answer this question.

- What are the differences, if any, between the mental health needs and concerns of returning police officers and those of reservists returning to other occupations?
- Are police officers and other emergency responders at reduced risk, compared to reservists in other occupations, of PTSD and other combat-related mental health problems? Conversely, are police officer reservists at equal or greater risk for certain problems (for example, stress related to long periods of separation from their spouses, children, or jobs)?
- What protective factors are most important for reducing the risk of PTSD or for reducing the risk of other mental health problems associated with combat and disasters? How can this knowledge be translated into practical, effective police agency practices?
- Are police agencies nationwide implementing a broader range of proactive programs to assist returning officers than those identified in this study? Are the programs meeting their objectives? Can a matrix of the best practices be developed?

Law enforcement officers being deployed to law enforcement agencies have a long history of recruiting new police officers with military backgrounds and will continue to do so. While it is not clear how many current police officers are returning to work with unresolved combat-related problems, most will face stressful and potentially dangerous situations back on the job. At a minimum, they should be brought up to date about training policies, and they and their families should be assured that confidential sources of help are available if needed upon their return or in the future. Our preliminary study indicated that while some departments are responding in special ways, many are not. Only a concerted effort among law enforcement, mental health, and veterans' organizations can have a significant impact on the safety of returning officers, their families, and their communities.

References

Adler, A. B., M. A. Vaitkus, and J.A. Martin, "Combat Exposure and Post-traumatic Stress Symptomatology among U.S. Soldiers Deployed to the Gulf War." *Military Psychology*, 8(1), 1–14, 1996.

American Psychiatric Association. *Diagnostic and Statistical Manual of Mental Disorders, 4th edition.* (DSM-IV). 1994. www.psych.org/MainMenu?Research?DSM-IV.aspx.

American Psychiatric Association. *Let's Talk Facts About Posttraumatic Stress Disorder.* 2005. www.healthyminds.org.

Armstrong, K., S.R. Best, and P. Domenici. *Courage After Fire.* Berkeley, California: Ulysses Press, 2006.

Bentley, S., "A Short History of PTSD: From Thermopylae to Hue Soldiers Have Always Had a Disturbing Reaction to War." Reprinted in *The VVA Veteran.* Vietnam Veterans of America. 1991. www.archive.vva.org/The Veteran/2005_03/feature_HistoryPTSD.htm.

Best, S.R. *Common Issues in Returning Veterans: What Is a "Normal" Response to Combat?* Presentation to the International Association of Chiefs of Police, Police Psychological Services Section, Boston, 2006.

Bray, R. M., L.L. Hourani, et al. *2005 Department of Defense Survey of Health Related Behaviors Among Active Duty Military Personnel.* RTI [Research Triangle Institute] International, December 2006. www.ha.osd.mil/special _reports/2005_Health_ Behaviors_Survey_-07.pdf.

Deahl, M., M. Scrinivasan, N. Jones, J. Thomas, C. Neblett, and A. Jolly. "Preventing Psychological Trauma in Soldiers: The Role of Operational Stress Training and Psychological Debriefing," *British Journal of Medical Psychology* 73(2000), 77–85.

Delprino, R. P. *Lessons Learned from Early Corrections and Law Enforcement Family Support (CLEFS) Programs. Report to the U.S. Department of Justice, National Institute of Justice, 2002.* www.ncjrs.org/pdffiles1/nij/ grants/192287. pdf.

Elhai, J.D., T.C. North, and B.C. Frueh. "Health Service Use Predictors Among Trauma Survivors: A Critical Review," *Psychological Services* 2(1)(2005), 3–19.

Finn, P. "On-the-Job-Stress in Policing—Reducing It and Preventing It." (NCJ 180079). *National Institute of Justice Journal,* January 2000, 18–24.

Foa, E.B., T.M. Keane, and M.J. Friedman, eds. *Effective Treatment for PTSD.* New York: Guilford Press, 2004.

Friedman, M.J. "Acknowledging the Psychiatric Cost of War," *The New England Journal of Medicine* 351 (2004), 75–77.

Government Accountability Office. *Post Traumatic Stress Disorder: DOD Needs to Identify the Factors Its Providers Use to Make Mental Health Evaluation Referrals for Service Members.* Washington, D.C.: Government Accountability Office Report to Congressional Committees, 2006.

Gray, M. J., S. Maguen, and B.T. Litz. "Acute Psychological Impact of Disaster and Large-Scale Trauma: Limitations of Traditional Interventions and Future Practice Recommendations," *Prehospital and Disaster Medicine* 19 (2004):1. http://pdm.medicine.wisc.edu/19-1%20pdfs/Gray.pdf.

Grieger, T.A., S.J. Cozza, R.J. Ursano, C. Hoge, P.E. Martinez, C.C. Engel, and H.J. Wain. "Posttraumatic Stress Disorder and Depression in Battle-Injured Soldiers," *American Journal of Psychiatry* 163(2006): 1777–1783.

Hobfoll, S.E., C.D. Spielberger, S. Breznitz, C.R. Figley, S. Folkman, B.L. Green, D. Meichenbaum, N.A. Milgram, I.N. Sandler, I.G. Sarason, and B. A. Van Der Kolk. "War-Related Stress: Addressing the Stress of War and Other Traumatic Events," *American Psychologist* 46 (1991), 848–855.

Hoge, C.W., C.A. Castro, S.C. Messer, D. McGurk, D.I. Cotting, and R.L. Koffman. "Combat Duty in Iraq and Afghanistan, Mental Health Problems, and Barriers to Care," *The New England Journal of Medicine* 351(1)(2004), 13–22.

Hoge, C. W., J.L. Auchterlonie, and C.S. Milliken. "Mental Health Problems, Use of Mental Health Services, and Attrition from Military Service After Returning from Deployment to Iraq or Afghanistan," *The Journal of the American Medical Association* 295 (2006), 1023–1032.

Kang, H.K., B.H. Natelson, C.M. Mahan, K.Y. Lee, and F.M. Murphy. "Post-Traumatic Stress Disorder and Chronic Fatigue Syndrome-Like Illness among Gulf War Veterans: A Population-Based Survey of 30,000 Veterans," *American Journal of Epidemiology* 157(2003), 141–148.

Kessler, R.C., "Posttraumatic Stress Disorder: The Burden to the Individual and to Society," *Journal of Clinical Psychiatry*, 61 Suppl. 5:4-12, 2000.

Kessler, R. C., S. Galea, R.T. Jones, and H.A. Parker "Mental Illness and Suicidality After Hurricane Katrina," *Bulletin of the World Health Organization*, 2006. www.who.int/bulletinvolumes/84/10/06-033019.pdf.

Mental Health Advisory Team (MHAT-II). *Operation Iraqi Freedom-II Report*. Washington, D.C.: Office of the U.S. Army Surgeon General, January 30, 2005.

Mental Health Advisory Team (MHAT-V) *Operation Iraqi Freedom 06-08: Iraq; Operation Enduring Freedom 8: Afghanistan*. Washington, DC: Office of the U.S. Army Surgeon General, February 14, 2008.

Morland, L., C. Greene, J. Ruzek, and L. Godleski. *PTSD and Telemental Health: A National Center for PTSD fact sheet*. 2003. www.ncptsd.va.gov/facts/treatment/fs_telemental_health.html.

Najavits, L.M. *Seeking Safety: A Treatment Manual for PTSD and Substance Abuse*. New York: Guilford Press, 2002.

Neylan, T.C., A. Brunet, N. Pole, S.R. Best, T.J. Metzler, R. Yehuda, and C.R. Marmar, "PTSD Symptoms Predict Waking Salivary Cortisol Levels in Police Officers," *Psychoneuroendocrinology* 30(2005); 373–381.

Otte, C., T.C. Neylan, N. Pole, T. Metzler, S.R. Best, C. Henn-Haase, R. Yehuda, and C.R. Marmar, "Association Between Childhood Trauma and

Catecholamine Response to Osychological Stress in Police Academy Recruits," *Biological Psychiatry* 57(2005): 27–32.

Pham, P.N., H.M. Weinstein, and T. Longman, "Trauma and PTSD Symptoms in Rwanda: Implications for Attitudes Toward Justice and Reconciliation." *The Journal of the American Medical Association,* 292 (2004), 602-612.

Pole, N., T.C. Neylan, S.R. Best, S. Orr, and C.R. Marmar, "Effects of Fear-Potentiation on Physiologic Response to Acoustic Startle in Urban Police Officers with Posttraumatic Stress Symptoms," *Journal of Traumatic Stress* (9)(2005), 471–479.

Price, J.L. *Findings from the National Vietnam Veterans Readjustment Study.* National Center for PTSD Fact Sheet, 2006. www.ncptsd.va.gov/nemain/ ncdocs/ fact_shts/fs_nvvrs.html .opm=1&rr=rr45&srt=d&ech orr=true.

Ritchie, E.C. and S. Curran. *Warrior Transition by Army Reserve and National Guard Personnel from Combat Operations in Iraq to Policing in the United States.* Presented to the International Association of Chiefs of Police, Police Psychological Services Section, Boston, 2006.

Ruzek, J. and Watson, P., "Early Intervention to Prevent PTSD and Other Trauma-Related Problems," *PTSD Research Quarterly* 12(2001), 4. White River Junction, Vermont: The National Center for Post-Traumatic Stress Disorder, 2001.

Schlenger, W.E., J.A. Fairbank et al. "Epidemiology of Combat-Related Posttraumatic Stress Disorder," in *Posttraumatic Stress Disorder: A Comprehensive Text,* ed. P.A. Saigh and J.D. Bremner. Boston: Allyn and Bacon, 1999.

Sherman, N. *Stoic Warriors: The Ancient Philosophy Behind the Military Mind.* New York: Oxford University Press, 2005.

Sherman, N., Interview, CBS Evening News, July 6. 2006. http://audio.cbsnews.com/2006/ 07/12/audio1797914.mp3.

Southwick, S.M., C.A. Morgan, A. Darnell, J.D. Bremner, A.L. Nicolaou, L.M. Nagy, and D.S. Charney, "Trauma-Related Symptoms in Veterans of Operation Desert Storm: A 2-year Follow-Up," *American Journal of Psychiatry* 152 (1995), 1150–1155.

Tolin, D. F. and E.B. Foa, "Sex Differences in Trauma and Posttraumatic Stress Disorder: A Quantitative Review of 25 years of Research," American Psychological Association. *Psychological Bulletin* 132 (6)(2006), 959–992.

Woska, W. J., "Police Officer Recruitment: A Public-Sector Crisis," *The Police Chief.* Alexandria, Virginia: International Association of Chiefs of Police, October 2006.

Weisler, R. H., J.G. Barbee IV, and M.H. Townsend, "Mental Health and Recovery in the Gulf Coast After Hurricanes Katrina and Rita," *The Journal of the American Medical Association* 296 (5)(2006), 585–588.

Discussion Questions

1. When was the first time that the concept of the posttraumatic stress disorder was included in the American Psychiatric Association's Diagnostic and Statistical Manual of Mental Disorders (DSM)?
2. What historical evidence did the author provide to show that PTSD is a new name for an old story?
3. The formal diagnosis of PTSD involves assessing three clusters of symptoms and behaviors. What are they?
4. How have the diagnostic criteria for PTSD changed since 1980?
5. What are some other potentially long-term mental health consequences of exposure to traumatic events?
6. The philosophy of the military as it relates to intervention after trauma is described as Proximity, Immediacy, and Expectancy. What does this mean?
7. What are the elements of the Department of Defense postdeployment questionnaire as they relate to screening for PTSD?
8. What type of intervention has proven most effective for treating PTSD?
9. What does it mean when the police and military are described as "a culture of suck it up"?
10. What evidence is there that the military and the Veterans Administration have acknowledged and made efforts to address the stigma that many service members associate with seeking help with mental health concerns?

Military and Law Enforcement Psychology: Cross-Contributions to Extreme Stress Management

Laurence Miller

Introduction:
Military and Law Enforcement Psychology

Like siblings separated at birth, military psychology and law enforcement psychology have, for decades, each independently addressed the cognitive, perceptual, emotional, and behavioral challenges facing the men and women who perform extreme service in defense of their communities—whether this "community" be a specific neighborhood or the nation as a whole. In fact, many law enforcement officers have had military experience and many military service members utilize tactics and strategies derived from patrol and special unit policing to carry out their assigned duties (Barrett et al., 2011; IACP, 2009; IACP/USDJ, 2010; Miller, 2008b, 2010; Ralph & Sammons, 2006). Accordingly, this chapter will highlight the recent advances in law enforcement psychology (Miller, 2006d, 2008b, 2008c, 2008d) that have both drawn from, and can contribute to, the work of our military colleagues and improve the clinical and operational services we provide to men and women in uniform, wherever they may serve.

Combat and Critical Incident Stress

The history of the field of critical incident stress, combat stress, and posttraumatic stress disorder has been covered in Part One. Clearly, the most stressful aspect of both military service and police work is the prospect of being injured or killed, closely followed by the act of killing another (Grossman, 1996; Miller, 2006c). Other stresses have to do with enduring the loss of compatriots and generally confronting the human cruelty and carnage of warfare and violent criminal activity (Nordland & Gegax, 2004; Henry, 2004; Miller, 2007b). Law enforcement and military psychologists both have made important contributions to the assessment and amelioration of these traumatic stress syndromes.

Law Enforcement and Military Stress: Vulnerability and Resilience Factors

Some authorities (Henry, 2004; Violanti, 1999) have characterized police work as "civilian combat," and, as in all areas of psychology, there are individual differences in the ability to cope with combat stress and critical incident stress (Almedom, 2005; Bonanno, 2004; Borders & Kennedy, 2006; Bowman, 1997; Carlier & Gersons, 1995; Carlier et al., 1997; Corneil et al., 1999; Friedman et al., 2004; Gentz, 1991; Haas, 2007; Higgins & Leibowitz, 1999; Holbrook, 2011; Maddi, 2007; McNally, 2003; Miller, 1995, 1998, 2007b, 2007c; 2008c; Nordland & Gegax, 2004; Orasanu & Backer, 1996; Toch, 2002; Winerman, 2006). Increased stress resilience has been found to be associated with higher IQ, especially verbal IQ, active problem-solving, utilization of productive denial, rationalization, and compartmentalization, dispositional optimism, self-efficacy and self-confidence, and the ability to access and utilize social supports. Increased vulnerability to stress is associated with younger age of service and fewer years of experience, lower educational level (which is correlated with verbal intelligence), prior history of substance abuse or psychopathology, prior history of trauma, and poor social support systems.

Psychological Interventions for Military Combat Stress: PIES and BICEPS

Many of the principles of managing both combat stress and law enforcement critical incident stress incorporate the same basic elements. The primary goal is to depathologize these stress responses by framing them as normal responses of normal people to abnormal or "extra-normal" events (Brickman, 1982; Campsie et al., 2006; Mitchell & Everly, 1996, 2003), as well as to reinforce resilience by proper training and a positive service philosophy which has variously been characterized as *battlemind* for the military (Brusher, 2007) or *METTLE* for law enforcement (Miller, 2008d), among other terms. To this end, beginning in World War I, the military has relied on the *PIE* concept (Artiss, 1963; Jones et al., 2007; Ritchie & Owens, 2004; Salmon, 1919), where:

P = *Proximity:* Provide care as close to the unit as possible.
I = *Immediacy:* Offer treatment as soon as possible.
E = *Expectancy:* Convey the expectation of return to full duty.

Currently, the U.S. Department of Defense's protocol for management of combat stress (Brusher, 2007; Campsie et al., 2006; Munsey, 2006) is based on the *BICEPS* model, where:

B = *Brevity:* Treatment is short-term, addresses the problem at hand, and is focused on return to service.
I = *Immediacy:* Intervention begins as soon as possible, before symptoms have a chance to worsen.
C = *Centrality:* Psychological treatment is set apart from medical facilities to reduce the stigma soldiers might feel about seeking mental health services.
E = *Expectancy:* A service member experiencing problems with combat stress is expected to return to full duty.
P = *Proximity:* In order to enhance expectations of recovery, soldiers are treated as close to their units as possible and are not evacuated from the area of operations.
S = *Simplicity:* Besides formal therapy, the basics of a good meal, hot shower, and a comfortable place to sleep ensure that a soldier's fundamental physical needs are met.

Psychological Interventions for Law Enforcement Critical Incident Stress: CISD/CISM

To address the special needs of civilian law enforcement and emergency services personnel, the concept of *critical incident stress management* (CISM) has incorporated the basic philosophy and methodology of the PIE and BICEPS models and has expanded and refined the methodology, which has, in turn, been adopted back into the military. *Critical incident stress debriefing* (CISD) is a structured group intervention designed to promote the emotional processing of traumatic events through the ventilation and normalization of reactions, as well as to facilitate preparation for possible future crisis experiences (Campsie et al., 2006; Dyregrov, 1989, 1997; Everly & Boyle, 1999; Everly & Mitchell, 1997; Everly et al., 2000; Miller, 1995, 1998, 1999a, 1999b, 2000, 2005a, 2006b, 2006d; 2007d; Mitchell & Everly, 1996, 2003).

A CISD debriefing is a peer-led, clinician-guided, group process, although the individual roles of clinicians and peers may vary from setting to setting. A typical debriefing takes place within 24 to 72 hours of the critical incident and consists of a single group meeting that lasts two to three hours, although shorter or longer meetings may be dictated by circumstances. Where large numbers of workers are involved, such as in mass disaster rescues or large-scale demobilizations, several debriefings may be held successively over the course of days to accommodate all the personnel involved (Everly & Mitchell, 1997; Mitchell & Everly, 1996, 2003).

The formal CISD process consists of seven key phases, designed to assist cognitive and emotional integration and mastery, beginning with more objective and descriptive levels of processing, progressing to the more personal and emotional, and back to the educative and integrative levels. These include:

(1) *Introduction.* The team leader introduces the CISD process, encourages participation by the group, and sets the ground rules of confidentiality, attendance for the full session, unforced participation in the discussions, and the establishment of a noncritical atmosphere.

(2) *Fact phase.* The group members are asked to briefly describe their activity during the critical incident and some facts about what happened; the basic question is: "What did you do?"

(3) *Thought phase.* Group members discuss their initial and subsequent thoughts during the critical incident: "What was going through your mind?"

(4) *Reaction phase.* This begins to move the group from a predominantly cognitive mode of processing to a more expressive emotional level: "What was the worst part of the incident for you?"

(5) *Symptom phase.* This begins the movement back from the predominantly emotional processing level toward the cognitive processing level. Participants are asked to describe their cognitive, physical, emotional, and behavioral signs of distress: "What have you been experiencing since the incident?"

(6) *Education phase.* Continuing the move back toward intellectual processing and normalization of the experience, didactic information is provided about the nature of the stress response and the expected physiological and psychological reactions to critical incidents.

(7) *Re-entry phase.* During this wrap-up, any additional questions or statements are addressed, referral for individual follow-ups are made, and general group bonding is reinforced: "What have you learned?"

A number of specialized adaptations of the basic CISD/CISM model have been developed for both military and law enforcement personnel. In the military sphere, these include the U.S. Navy's *Special Psychiatric Response Intervention Teams (SPRINT)*; the U.S. Army's *Special Medical Augmentation Response Team-Stress Management (SMART-SM)*; the U.S. Air Force's *Critical Incident Stress Teams (CIST)*; the British Royal Marines' *Trauma Risk Management (TRiM) program;* and the Canadian Forces' *Operational Stress Injury Social Support Program* (Campsie et al., 2006; Grenier et al., 2007; March & Greenberg, 2007); For civilian law enforcement and emergency services personnel, special adaptations include *law enforcement debriefing* (Bohl, 1995); *integrative debriefing* (Regehr, 2001; Regehr & Bober, 2004; Ruzek, 2002); *line-of-duty death debriefing* (Mitchell & Levenson, 2006); *individual debriefings* (Solomon, 1991, 1995); *critical incident peer support seminars* (Solomon, 1995); *salutogenic debriefing* (Dunning, 1999; Stuhlmiller & Dunning, 2000; Violanti, 2000); *California Peace Officer Commission Peer Counselor Training* (Linden & Klein, 1986); *Salt Lake City Police Department Traumatic Incident Corps* (Nielsen, 1991); the FBI's *Critical Incident Stress Management Program* (McNally & Solomon, 1999); and the US Secret Service's *Critical Incident Support Team* (Britt, 1991).

Whether explicitly or tacitly, all of these programs incorporate the fundamental elements of the military PIE/BICEPS and law enforcement CISD/CISM models, that is: (1) nonpathological conceptualization of the stress response; (2) expectation of quick and full recovery with return to service; and (3) provision of targeted techniques and strategies to foster recovery and future resilience.

Psychotherapy for Law Enforcement and Military Service Members

Mental health services in law enforcement and the military are not limited to critical incident or combat stress (Budd & Kennedy, 2006; Miller, 2006d; 2008b; 2010; in press). Police officers and soldiers can be affected by a wide variety of problems that include depression, suicidality (see below), substance abuse, work stress, and relationship problems. Here again law enforcement and military psychologists can cross-contribute valuable therapeutic strategies for treating these specialized personnel.

Basic Principles of Psychotherapy with the "Wounded Warrior"

As noted above, law enforcement stress has been characterized as "civilian combat" (Violanti, 1999). Surveying the literature on both military and law enforcement psychotherapy, therefore, one should not be surprised by the convergences of theory and technique across domains. In general, the effectiveness of any therapeutic strategy will be determined by the timeliness, tone, style, and intent of the intervention. Effective psychological interventions with military and law enforcement personnel share in common the following elements (Ball & Peake, 2006; Blau, 1994; Budd & Kennedy, 2006; Fullerton et al., 1992; Miller, 1995, 1998, 1999b, 2000, 2006d, 2007d, 2008b, 2008c, 2008d, 2011b, in press; Peake et al., 2000; Rudofossi, 2007; Wester & Lyubelsky, 2005) some of which are already familiar from the PIES/BICEPS model discussed above:

Brevity: Utilize only as much therapeutic contact as necessary to address the present problem; the service member does not need to become a "professional patient."

Limited focus: Related to the above, the goal is not to solve all the service member's problems, but to assist in restabilization and provide stress-inoculation for future crises.

Directness: Therapeutic efforts are focused on resolving the current conflict or problem to reach a satisfactory short-term conclusion, while planning for the future if necessary.

Law Enforcement Psychotherapy Techniques: Lessons for Military Psychology

The following models and techniques from the field of law enforcement psychotherapy can be productively adapted to the military setting. This approach begins with Blau's (1994) recommendation that the first meeting between the therapist and the service member establish a safe and comfortable working atmosphere, fostered by the therapist's articulating a positive endorsement of the service member's decision to seek assistance (or obedience of an order to do so), a clear description of the therapist's responsibilities and limitations with respect to confidentiality and privilege, and an invitation to the service member to state his or her concerns.

A straightforward, goal-directed, problem-solving therapeutic intervention style includes the following elements:

Create a sanctuary. The service member should feel safe that what he or she says will be used primarily for the purposes of his or her healing and strengthening, not as part of a disciplinary process.

Focus on critical areas of concern. Therapy should be goal-directed and focused on resolving specific adaptation and recovery issues related to the crisis at hand.

Specify desired outcomes. In the early phases, the clinician may have to help the service member sort out, focus, and operationalize his or her goals so that there will be a way of measuring whether the therapy process is accomplishing them.

Develop a general plan. From the first session, develop an initial game plan that can be modified as you go along.

Identify practical initial implementations. Begin intervention as soon as possible to induce confidence and to allow the clinician to get feedback from treatment efforts that will guide further interventions.

Review assets and encourage self-efficacy. Consistent with the overarching aim of military and law enforcement psychotherapy as a strengthening, not weakening, process, it is vital to assist the service member in identifying and utilizing his or her strengths and capabilities as coping resources.

Blau (1994) delineates a number of effective individual psychotherapeutic strategies for police officers that can be applied to therapy with military service members:

Attentive listening. This includes good eye contact, appropriate body language, genuine interest, and interpersonal engagement.

Being there with empathy. This conveys availability, concern, and awareness of the disruptive emotions being experienced by the distressed service member.

Reassurance. This means realistically reassuring the service member that routine matters will be taken care of, deferred responsibilities will be handled by others, and that the member has administrative and command support.

Supportive counseling. This includes active listening, restatement of content, clarification of feelings, and validation.

Interpretive counseling. While still keeping the process short-term and focused on the immediate problem, interpretive counseling can stimulate the service member to explore underlying emotional or psychodynamic issues that may be intensifying a naturally stressful traumatic event (Horowitz, 1986).

Humor. When used appropriately and respectfully, therapeutic humor may help to bring a sense of balance, perspective, and clarity to a world that seems to be warped by malevolence and horror (Fry & Salameh, 1987; Fullerton et al., 1992; Henry, 2004), as long as the therapist keeps a lid on destructive types of self-mockery or inappropriate projective hostility and is careful that well-intentioned kidding and cajoling not be interpreted as dismissive of the seriousness of the service member's plight.

Utilizing Cognitive Defenses

In psychology, *defense mechanisms* are the mental stratagems the mind uses to protect itself from unpleasant thoughts, feelings, impulses, and memories. While the normal use of such defenses enables the average person to avoid conflict and ambiguity and maintain some consistency to their personality and belief system, most psychologists would agree that an overuse of defenses to wall off too much unpleasant thought and feeling leads to a rigid and dysfunctional approach to coping with life. Accordingly, much of the ordinary psychotherapeutic process involves carefully helping the patient to relinquish pathological defenses so that he or she can learn to deal with internal conflicts more constructively.

However, in the face of the kinds of immediately traumatizing critical incidents that confront military and law enforcement personnel, the last thing the affected service member needs is to have his or her defenses stripped away. If you sustain a broken leg on the battlefield in the middle of a firefight, the medic doesn't stop to clean the wound, put you under anesthesia, set the bone, wrap you in a cast, and nurse you back to health. Hell no: he binds and braces the limb as best and as fast as he can—with a dirty tree branch and fishing tackle if necessary—and helps you hobble out of there, double-time. If that helps you live through the emergency, then more extensive treatment can be applied, once you have the luxury of time and safety.

In the same way, for an acute psychological trauma, the proper utilization of psychological defenses can serve as an important cognitive splint or emotional field dressing that enables the service member to function during the crisis and in the immediate posttraumatic aftermath and eventually be able to resolve and integrate the traumatic experience when the luxury of therapeutic time can be afforded (Janik, 1991; Miller, 2008b, 2008c, 2008d). In fact, in their regular military and law enforcement work, most service members usually need little help in applying defense mechanisms on their own.

Examples of adaptive cognitive defense strategies (Durham et al., 1985; Henry, 2004; Taylor & Brown, 1988; Taylor et al., 1983) include:

Denial: "Put it out of my mind; focus on other things; avoid situations or people who remind me of it."

Rationalization: "I had no choice; things happens for a reason; it could have been worse; other people have it worse; most people in the same situation would react the way I'm doing."

Displacement/projection: "It was Command's fault for issuing such a stupid order; I didn't have the right backup; they're all trying to blame me for everything."

Refocus on positive attributes: "Hey, that miss was a fluke—I'm usually a great marksman; I'm not going to let one mistake jam me up."

Refocus on positive behaviors: "Okay, I'm going to get more training, increase my knowledge and skill so I'll never be caught with my thumb up my ass like this again."

Janik (1991) proposes that, in the short term, clinicians actively support and bolster psychological defenses that temporarily enable the service member to continue functioning. Just as a physical crutch is an essential part of orthopedic rehabilitation when the leg-injured patient is learning to walk again, a psychological crutch is perfectly adaptive and productive if it enables the service member to get back on his emotional feet as soon as possible after a traumatic critical incident. Only later, when he or she is making the bumpy transition back to normal life, are potentially maladaptive defenses revisited as possible impediments to progress. It is thus only when defenses are used inappropriately and for too long—past the point where the service member should be walking on his or her own two feet—do they constitute a "crutch" in the unhealthy and pejorative sense.

Suicide Prevention and Intervention

Arguably, the single most devastating personal mental health crisis is suicide. Considering that both military service and law enforcement are high-demand, high-stress professions that attract personnel who tend to have commensurately high expectations of themselves, little tolerance for weakness, and a black-and-white, all-or-nothing view of success and failure, it is not surprising that self-perceived failure may lead to depression and suicidality, often fueled by alcohol and substance abuse. Law enforcement officers and military service members may become despondent and suicidal for a variety of reasons related to their service or their family life (Jones et al., 2007; Miller, 2005b, 2006a, 2006d, 2007a; 2011b; Miller et al., 2010; Norcross, 2003; Rodgers, 2006).

Military and Law Enforcement Suicide: Basic Facts

One area of disparity between military service and law enforcement may be in the actual rate of suicide. While suicide is the third leading cause of non-battle-related deaths in the military, the actual suicide rate for military personnel is lower than that of the nation as a whole (Jones et al., 2007). In contrast, several surveys have identified the suicide rate among civilian police officers as higher than that of the general population (Allen, 1986; Cummings, 1996; Mohandi & Hatcher, 1999; Rudofossi, 2007; Violanti, 1995, 1996), although this is still controversial (Abrams et al., 2011; Curran, 2003).

Whatever the comparative statistics, suicidal crises rarely occur in isolation, but are most commonly seen in law enforcement officers with prior histories of depression, or in those who have recently faced an overwhelming crush of debilitating stressors, leading to feelings of hopelessness and helplessness. A typical pattern consists of a slow, smoldering build-up of tension and demoralization, which reaches a "breaking point," and then rapidly nosedives into a suicidal crisis (Allen, 1986; Blau, 1994; Cummings, 1996; Heiman, 1975; Henry, 2004; Mohandie & Hatcher, 1999; Rodgers, 2006). Similarly, the most frequent precipitating factors in suicides among active-duty military personnel include feelings of shame, disgrace, isolation, worthlessness, and hopelessness related to service performance failures, disciplinary charges, professional and personal relationship problems, substance abuse, or prior suicide attempts (Finley, 2011; Jones et al., 2006; Moore et al., 2009). Curiously, higher rates of suicide are seen in military personnel who work in security or law enforcement specialties (Jones et al., 2007).

Suicidal crises tend to be short, which means that timely intervention can literally make a life-or-death difference. With appropriate treatment, the vast majority of depressed, potentially suicidal subjects improve considerably within a few weeks (Bongar, 2002; Maris, 1981; Reinecke et al., 2007). This hardly means that depressed moods and suicidal thoughts won't ever occur again, but a history of successful psychological treatment provides a support resource that the individual can rely on if and when the next crisis begins to brew.

Preventing Military and Law Enforcement Suicide

One of the persisting problems in dealing with police officer suicide is the pervasive code of silence that characterizes these personnel. Officers are reluctant to report depression or other problems for fear of being seen as weak or, worse, of having restrictions placed on their activities (e.g. weapon carrying). Fellow officers are equally reluctant to "rat out" a distressed comrade, even though they may strongly suspect he or she needs help. Thus, there is a need for every law enforcement agency to have an efficient, nonstigmatized referral system for dealing with officers in psychological distress, so that any problems noted can receive appropriate treatment in a supportive atmosphere (Anderson et al., 1995; Blau, 1994; Miller, 2005b, 2006d; in press; Rodgers, 2006; Russell & Biegel, 1990; Toch, 2002).

In this regard, police psychologists can learn from their military colleagues, who have been proactive in education and training around mental health issues such as depression and suicide. One advantage of military organizations is that programs generated by the Department of Defense, or even within an individual service branch, can achieve rapid, wide dissemination among service personnel, whereas the fragmented nature of literally thousands of municipal, county, regional, state, and federal law enforcement agencies in the U.S. makes such information-sharing a daunting task.

One example of such a military program is the U.S. Air Force's *LINK* (Staal, 2001), which stands for:

L = *Look* for possible concerns or signs of distress.
I = *Inquire* about those concerns.
N = *Note* the level of risk.
K = *Know* the appropriate referral sources and strategies.

Similarly, the U.S. Navy and Marine Corps have adopted a program called *AID LIFE* (Jones et al., 2007), which stands for:

A = *Ask*, "Are you thinking of hurting yourself?" or "Are you thinking about suicide?" Remember that asking a suicidal person about his or her thoughts will not impel them to do it, and may in fact save their life.

I = *Intervene immediately*. Don't wait to take action. Let the person know that he or she is not alone and that someone cares enough to do something.

D = *Don't keep it secret*. Silence can only lead to increasing isolation and deterioration.

L = *Locate help*. Seek out a superior officer, chaplain, medical or mental health corpsman, crisis line worker, or other person who can intervene.

I = *Inform* the chain of command, so that they can arrange for long-term assistance, if necessary.

F = *Find* someone. Don't leave the person alone.

E = *Expedite*. Get help now. You may save someone's life.

Warning Signs of Suicide

In turn, one area where the military can learn from law enforcement is in the development and implementation of specific protocols for prevention, response, and follow-up treatment of service members in distress. One of the most important prevention factors involves recognizing the warning signs of suicide (Allen, 1986; Cummings, 1996; Mohandie & Hatcher, 1999; 2005b, 2006a, 2006d, 2011a; Quinnett, 1998; Rodgers, 2006), which include the following:

Threatening self. Verbal self-threats can be direct: "I'd be better off eating my gun;" or indirect: "Enjoy the good times while you can—they never last."

Threatening others. Verbal threats against others can be direct: "I oughta cap that damn lieutenant for writing me up;" or indirect: "People with that kind of attitude deserve whatever's coming to them."

Nothing to lose. The service member behaves insubordinately, without regard to career repercussions: "I'll drink or smoke what I want, on or off duty. What are they gonna do—shoot me?" Or he recklessly puts himself in danger on the job—a kind of "passive suicide."

Weapon surrender. The service member may fear his own impulses, but may be reluctant to admit it: "As long as I'm on desk duty this week, can I keep my gun in my locker? It's a pain to lug it around the building."

Weapon overkill. This is the opposite pattern: the service member begins carrying more than one backup weapon, or begins to keep especially powerful weapons in his vehicle, at home, or on his person.

Cry for help. "Things are getting too hairy out here; I think I may need to check into the Bug Hilton to get my act together."

Brotherhood of the damned. "You know the news story about that double-tour corporal who fragged his CO in Iraq? I know how that poor bastard felt."

Overwhelmed. "My wife just left me, my checks are bouncing, I'm drinking again, and the investigative ferrets are crawling up my butt. I just can't take all this."

No way out. "If that Review Board burns me again, that's my last strike. No friggin' way I'm going to jail for just trying to do my job."

Final plans. The service member may be observed making or changing a will, paying off debts, showing an increased interest in religion, giving away possessions, making excessive donations to charities, and other "end-of-days" activities.

Intervention with the Actively Suicidal Service Member

If the warning signs have been missed, the first chance a clinician or peer may get to intervene with a depressed, suicidal service member may be when the crisis is already peaking. The task now is to keep him or her alive long enough to get appropriate follow-up care, and this can be accomplished by adapting and applying some fundamental principles of civilian, law enforcement, and military crisis intervention (Gilliland & James, 1993; Greenstone & Leviton, 2001; Jones et al., 2007; Kleepsies, 1998; Miller, 1998, 2006d, 2008b, 2008c, 2008d, 2010, 2011a; Moore et al., 2009; Rudd et al., 1999):

Define the problem. While some personal crises relate to a specific incident, many evolve cumulatively as the result of a number of overlapping stressors, until they hit the proverbial "breaking point." In such cases, the service member himself may be unclear as to what exactly led to the present suicidal state. By helping the member clarify what's disturbing him, nonlethal options and coping resources may be explored. It also shows that you're listening and trying to understand.

Ensure safety. You're not going to solve all of the service member's problems in this one encounter. What you want to do is make sure he survives this crisis so he can avail himself of whatever follow-up services are necessary. For now, try to encourage the service member to put even a few short steps between the thought of a self-destructive action and its implementation. For example, if he has a gun, ask him to unload it or decock it. If he's got a knife to his throat, see if he'll put in on the table or at least lower it to his lap. If he's holding a bottle of pills, encourage him to keep the cap on while you're talking. If he's standing on a building ledge or on a curb beside heavy traffic, maybe you can get him to take a step or two back. And so on.

Provide support. Keep the conversation focused on resolving the present crisis, perhaps gently suggesting that the larger issues can be dealt with later—which subtly implies that there will indeed be a "later." In the meantime, just "being there with empathy" (see above) with the service member helps.

Examine alternatives. Often, people in crisis are so fixated on their pain and hopelessness that their cognitive tunnel vision prevents them from seeing any way out. What you want to do is to gently expand the range of nonlethal options for resolving the crisis situation. Typically, this takes one of two forms: (1) *accessing practical supports:* persons or groups immediately available to help the service member through the crisis until he or she can obtain follow-up care; and (2) *coping mechanisms:* cognitive strategies, distracting activities, positive images and memories of family, religious faith, or review of successful handling of crises in the past, that show the service member that hope is at least possible.

Make a plan and obtain commitment. Again, this involves a combination of both practical supports and coping mechanisms, as well as both short-term and longer-term plans. Clarify what the service member will do in the next minutes, hours, and days, and what role other people will play. Confirm that he or she agrees with the plan and set up a system to monitor and ensure its implementation.

Arrange for follow-up. When the acute crisis has passed, referral to a mental health clinician is crucial for two reasons. First, the military or police psychologist may have to perform a fitness-for-duty evaluation to determine if the officer or service member is able to return to work; and if not, what treatment or other measures will be required to restore him or her to active duty (Fischler et al., 2011; Miller, 2007e). Second, specialized psychotherapeutic techniques may be applied, that involve a combination of emotional exploration, realistic confidence-building, and practical problem-solving approaches, often combined with medication (Barrett et al., 2011; Miller, 2006d, in press).

Killing

Many professionals—firefighters, paramedics, rescue workers, airline pilots, construction workers, and so on—undertake dirty, demanding, and/or dangerous work. But only police officers and soldiers share the distinction of having the ability, authority, and in many cases the mandated obligation to kill other human beings as part of their job description. One important difference is that, while police officers may have to fire their weapon in the line of duty, killing another person in these circumstances is perceived as a last resort and the overall emphasis in civilian public safety is on maintaining order without the use of deadly force. Military service members, however, know that they are trained precisely to kill the enemy and may have to do so on a regular and large-scale basis. Even for highly trained soldiers, the taking of human life can be a profound experience that can contribute to combat stress and behavioral problems (Campsie et al., 2006; Clary, 2005; Corbett, 2004; Friedman, 2004; Galvoski & Lyons, 2004; Jelinek, 2007; Murphy, 2007; Nordland & Gegax, 2004). Thus, there may be much that law enforcement and the military can learn from each other in dealing with the effects of killing as a vocation.

Deadly Force in Policing: Officer-Involved Shootings

Among all public safety and emergency service workers, the unique and ultimate symbol of the law enforcement officer is the gun. No other nonmilitary service group is mandated to carry a lethal firearm as part of their daily equipment, nor charged with the responsibility to use their own discretion and judgment in making split-second decisions to employ deadly force when called for. Yet, in reality, the firing of one's weapon in the line of duty is a rare event, and most officers spend their entire careers without a single service-related weapon discharge.

Available data indicate that about 600 criminals are killed each year by law enforcement officers in the United States. Some of these killings are in self-defense, some are accidental, and others are to prevent harm to others. The sources of stress attached to an *officer-involved shooting* (OIS) are multiple, and include the officer's own psychological reaction to taking a life, the responses of his or her law enforcement peers and the officer's family, rigorous examination by departmental investigators and administrators, possible disciplinary action or change of assignment, possible criminal and civil court action, and unwanted attention and sometimes outright harassment by the media (Baruth, 1986; Bohrer, 2005; Cloherty, 2004; Henry, 2004; Honig & Roland, 1998; Honig & Sultan, 2004; Horn, 1991; IACP, 2004; McMains, 1986a,1991; Miller, 2006c, 2006d, 2008a, 2008b, 2009, 2011b; Perrou & Farrell, 2004; Regehr & Bober, 2005; Russell & Beigel, 1990; Zeling, 1986).

Shooting: Perceptual, Cognitive, and Behavioral Disturbances

Many police officers who have been involved in a deadly force shooting episode have described one or more alterations in perception, thinking, and behavior that occurred during the event (Artwohl, 2002; Honig & Roland, 1998; Honig & Sultan, 2004; Solomon & Horn, 1986; Wittrup, 1986), and these are similar to those reported in military personnel following a firefight. Most of these reactions can be interpreted as natural adaptive defensive reactions of an organism under extreme emergency stress.

Most common are *distortions in time perception*. In the majority of these cases, service members recall the shooting event as occurring in slow motion, although a smaller percentage report experiencing the event as speeded up.

Sensory distortions are also common and most often involve *tunnel vision*, in which the service member is sharply focused on one particular aspect of the visual field, typically, the suspect's gun or weapon, while blocking out everything in the periphery. Similarly, *tunnel hearing* may occur, in which the service member's auditory attention is focused exclusively on a particular set of sounds, most commonly the adversary's voice, while background sounds are tuned out. Sounds may also seem muffled or, in a smaller number of cases, louder than normal. Police officers have reported not hearing their own or other officers' gunshots. Overall perceptual clarity may increase or diminish.

Some form of *perceptual and/or behavioral dissociation* may occur during the firefight. In extreme cases, the shooter will describe feeling as though he or she were standing outside or hovering above the scene, observing it "like it was happening to someone else." In milder cases, the service member may report that he or she "just went on automatic," performing whatever actions were necessary with a sense of robotic detachment. Some shooters report intrusive distracting thoughts during the scene, often involving loved ones or other personal matters, but it is not known if these substantially affected their actions during the event.

A *sense of helplessness* may occur during the shooting exchange, but this may be underreported due to the potential stigma attached. A small proportion of service members report that they "froze" at some point during the event; again, either this is an uncommon response or personnel are understandably reluctant to report it. In a series of interviews with police officers, Artwohl (2002) found that most of these instances of "freezing" really represented the normal *action-reaction gap* in which officers make the decision to shoot only after the suspect has engaged in clearly threatening behavior. In most cases, this brief subliminal cognitive evaluation interval is a positive precaution, to prevent a premature and unnecessary shooting. But in situations where this ostensibly prudent action led to a tragic outcome, this cautious hesitation may well be viewed retrospectively as a fault: "If I hadn't waited to see the bad guy draw, maybe my partner would still be alive." Very similar situations are encountered by military personnel who patrol civilian areas.

Disturbances in memory are commonly reported in shooting exchanges. About half of these involve impaired recall for at least some of the events during the shooting; the other half involve impaired recall for at least part of the service member's own actions; this, in turn, may be associated with the going-on-automatic response. More rarely, some aspects of the scene may be recalled with unusually clarity—a *flashbulb memory*. Over a third of cases involve not a total loss of recall but a distortion of memory, to the extent that the shooter's account of what happened differs markedly from the report of other observers at the scene; in such cases, officers may be accused of lying or deliberate distortion of events (Miller, 2004, 2006c, 2009, 2011b).

Military and Law Enforcement Shooting and Post-Shooting Reaction Phases

The stages of response that both soldiers and civilian police officers go through following a service-related taking of a human life are similar. Campsie, Geller and Campsie (2006) summarize Grossman's (1996) description of five basic phases often seen in response to killing in combat, which is quite similar to the reactions reported by police officers in civilian law enforcement shootings (Nielsen, 1991; Williams, 1999).

The first phase occurs prior to the shooting itself and consists of *concern about being actually able to pull the trigger* when the time comes, of not freezing up and letting one's comrades down.

The second phase is the *actual killing experience,* which is often done re-flexively, with the service member describing him/herself as "going on auto-matic."

Elated at having survived the deadly encounter, and having proven to him-self that he can do the deed, there is a third stage, *exhilaration* that comes from having "popped my cherry" and from having been able to put one's training into action. This exhilaration, fueled by the release of large amounts of adrenalin, can create a high or rush, which in some cases can give rise to combat addic-tion. Rodgers (2006) describes a kind of "adrenalin overdosing" that can poi-son a police officer's nervous system and lead to adverse reactions later on.

Remorse and nausea, Grossman's (1996) fourth phase—or what police psy-chologists (Nielsen, 1991; Williams, 1999) have called the *recoil and remorse* phase—follows the rush of exhilaration and is often associated with a close-range kill; this may be the more common type of response experienced by civilian law enforcement officers who tend to confront their adversaries in close quarters, as opposed to the experience of many soldiers who often fire from a distance. Even among military service members, a sense of identification and empathy for the dead adversary may set in, especially if the slain combatant was a fel-low enemy soldier "just doing his job like I was," as opposed to an insurgent bomber or assassin, for whom there will be far less sympathy or identification. The service member may be creeped out by his own initial response: "I en-joyed killing that guy too much—is there something wrong with me?"

For civilian law enforcement officers, feelings of guilt or self-recrimination may be especially likely in cases where the decision to shoot was less than clear-cut or where the suspect's actions essentially forced the hand of the officer into using deadly force, such as in botched robberies, domestic disputes, or suicide-by-cop scenarios (Kennedy et al., 1998; Lindsay & Dickson, 2004; Miller, 2006e; Perrou & Farrell, 2004; Pinizzotto et al., 2005). Military service members may be able to feel more justification in killing on a traditional battlefield, but may experience many of the same kinds of self-recriminations in the nontraditional fighting arenas that have characterized most wars since the Vietnam era, in which targets are often elusive and ambiguous, with blurred lines between combatants and civilians.

During this recoil/remorse phase, the military or law enforcement service member may seem detached and preoccupied, spacily going through the mo-tions of his job duties, and operating on behavioral autopilot. He may be sen-sitive and prickly to even well-meaning probing and congratulations by his peers ("How close was the enemy?" "Way to go, killer—you got the bad guy"), and especially to accusatory-like interrogation and second-guessing from of-ficial investigators or the media: "Officer Jackson, did you really believe you were in fear for your life from a confused teenager?" or, "Sergeant, did you really believe that the slain civilian family was hiding a group of insurgents?"

Also, during this recoil phase, a variety of posttraumatic symptoms may be seen, most of which will resolve in a few days or weeks (Anderson et al., 1995; Blum, 2000; Cohen, 1980; Geller, 1982; Honig & Sultan, 2004; Russell & Beigel, 1990; Williams, 1999). Some of these will represent general posttraumatic reactions familiar to psychological trauma workers (Gilliland & James, 1993; Greenstone & Leviton, 2001; Miller, 1998, 2006d; Regehr & Bober, 2004), while others will have a specific military or law enforcement line-of-duty shooting focus.

Physical symptoms may include headaches, stomach upset, nausea, weakness and fatigue, muscle tension and fasciculations (muscular twitching involving the simultaneous contractions of contiguous groups of muscle fiber), and changes in appetite and sexual functioning. Sleep is typically impaired, with frequent awakenings and often nightmares. Typical posttraumatic reactions of intrusive imagery and flashbacks may occur, along with premonitions, distorted memories, and feelings of déjà vu. Some degree of anxiety and depression is common, often accompanied by panic attacks. There may be unnatural and disorienting feelings of helplessness, fearfulness, and vulnerability, along with self-second-guessing and guilt feelings. Substance abuse may be a risk.

Service members may show a pervasive irritability and low frustration tolerance, along with anger and resentment toward the enemy, their unit, their police department or military branch in general, unsupportive peers or superiors, or uncomprehending family members or civilians. Service members may long for support, but at the same time reject helping efforts, leading to an alternating *control-alienation syndrome* (McMains, 1986b, 1991) which is offputting and irritating to everyone concerned. All this, combined with increased hypervigilance and hypersensitivity to threats of all kinds, may result in overaggressive policing or soldiering, leading to abuse-of-force complaints (Miller, 2004, 2009, 2011b).

Grossman's (1996) final phase, *rationalization and acceptance,* can be a long process and many military veterans wrestle with their war experiences for a lifetime. Similarly, in law enforcement (Miller, 2006d, 2008b, 2008c; Nielsen, 1991; Williams, 1999), as the officer begins to come to terms with the shooting episode, a similar resolution or acceptance phase may be ensue, wherein he or she assimilates the fact that the use-of-force-action was necessary and justified in this particular instance of the battle for survival that often characterizes law enforcement deadly encounters. Even under the best of circumstances, resolution may be partial rather than total, and psychological remnants of the experience may continue to haunt the officer periodically, especially during future times of crisis. But overall, he or she is eventually able to return to work with a reasonable sense of confidence.

In the worst case, sufficient resolution may never occur, and the officer enters into a prolonged posttraumatic phase, which may effectively end his or her law enforcement career. In less severe cases, a period of temporary stress disability allows the officer to seek treatment, to eventually regain his or her emotional and professional bearings, and to ultimately return to the job. Still other officers return to work right away, but continue to perform marginally or dysfunctionally until their actions are brought to the attention of superiors (Bender et al., 2005; Miller, 2004, 2009, 2011b; Rudofossi, 2007). Similar posttraumatic reactions can be seen in military service members (Campsie et al., 2006).

Post-Shooting Psychotherapeutic Strategies

One thing we know from civilian officer-involved shootings is that most officers can be successfully returned to service with minimum psychological intervention. Psychotherapeutic strategies in these cases will follow the short-term intervention model described in a previous section of this chapter. Some specific principles apply to law enforcement post-shooting stress (Miller, 2006c, 2006d, 2008d, in press), and these can be productively adapted to the military setting.

First, review the facts of the case with the service member. This allows for a relatively nonemotional narrative of the traumatic event. But in the case of a shooting episode, it serves a further, specific function. Precisely because of the cognitive and perceptual distortions that commonly occur in these kinds of incidents, what may be particularly disturbing to the service member is the lack of coherence in his or her own mind as to the actual nature and sequence of events. Just being able to review what is known about the facts of the case in a relatively safe and non-adversarial environment may provide a needed dose of mental clarity and sanity to the situation. Solomon (1991, 1995) describes one such therapeutic format as going over the incident "frame by frame," which allows the service member to verbalize the moment-to-moment thoughts, perceptions, sensory details, feelings, and actions that occurred during the shooting incident. This format helps the service member become aware of, sort out, and understand what happened.

Next, review the service member's thoughts and feelings about the shooting incident itself. This resembles the thought and reaction phases of a critical incident debriefing, but may not be as cut-and-dried as with a typical group debriefing. Remember, killing another person represents a special kind of critical incident and it may take more than one attempt for the service member to productively untangle and express what's going on in his mind. Give him/her extra time or extra sessions to express his/her thoughts and feelings, and be sure to monitor the reaction so as not to encourage unproductive spewing or loss of control. One of the most important things the military or police psychologist can do at this stage is to help modulate emotional expression so that it comes as a relief, not as an added burden, and the service member learns that he/she can express feelings without fear of losing control.

Provide authoritative and factual information about psychological reactions to a law enforcement or military shooting incident. The kinds of cognitive and perceptual distortions that take place during the incident, the posttraumatic symptoms and disturbances, and the sometimes offputting and distressing reactions of colleagues and family members, are likely to be quite alien to the service member's ordinary experience, and might be interpreted by him or her as signs of going soft or crazy. Normalize these responses for the service member, taking a somewhat more personal and individualistic approach than might be found in the typical group debriefing's information-education phase. Often, just this kind of authoritative reassurance from a credible mental health professional (and who, in the military setting, is also likely to be a superior officer) can mitigate the service member's anxiety considerably.

Finally, provide the opportunity for follow-up services, which may include additional individual sessions, group or family therapy, referral to support services, possible medication referral, and so on. For both military and law enforcement personnel, the seeking of psychological services must be destigmatized and supported at all levels (Blau, 1994; Friedman, 2004). In addition, both military and police psychologists can utilize the powerful social bonding forces of unit cohesion and morale to bolster stress-resilience and aid in recovery from shootings and other traumatic incidents (Brusher, 2007; Campsie et al., 2006; Maddi, 2007; Miller, 2006d, 2008b, 2008c, 2008d; Rodgers, 2006).

As with most cases of critical incident psychological intervention, follow-up psychotherapy for shooting episodes tends to be short-term, although additional services may be sought later for other problems partially related or unrelated to the incident. Indeed, any kind of critical incident may often be the stimulus to explore other troublesome aspects of the service member's professional or personal life and the success in resolving the present incident with the psychologist may give the service member confidence to pursue these other issues in an atmosphere of trust, thus potentially avoiding an adversarial disciplinary process (Blau, 1994; Miller, 1998, 2006d, 2009, 2011b).

Conclusions

Military and police psychology are siblings that need to be reintroduced and reunited, along with their firefighter, paramedic, rescue and recovery, and other emergency services cousins, to form a comprehensive system of clinical and operational psychology for personnel in high-danger, high-demand professions. This article has offered a glimpse into that collaboration and cross-fertilization which will hopefully spur further research into the art and science of helping our men and women in uniform, whatever their stripes and colors may be.

References

Abrams, A.A., Liang, A., Stevens, K. & Frechette, B. (2011). Suicide and law enforcement: What do we know?. In J. Kitaeff & K. Cather (Eds.), *Handbook of police psychology* (pp. 469–475). New York: Psychology Press.

Allen, S.W. (1986). Suicide and indirect self-destructive behavior among police. In J.T. Reese & H.A. Goldstein (Eds.), *Psychological services for law enforcement* (pp. 413–417). Washington DC: USGPO.

Almedom, A.M. (2005). Resilience, hardiness, sense of coherence, and posttraumatic growth: All paths leading to "light at the end of the tunnel"? *Journal of Loss and Trauma, 10,* 253–265.

American Psychiatric Association (2000). *Diagnostic and statistical manual of mental disorders* (4th ed., text revision). Washington DC: APA.

American Psychological Association (2007). *The psychological needs of U.S. military service members and their families: A preliminary report.* Washington, DC: APA.

Anderson, W., Swenson, D. & Clay, D. (1995). *Stress management for law enforcement officers.* Englewood Cliffs: Prentice Hall.

Artiss, K.L. (1963). Human behavior under stress: From combat to social psychiatry. *Military Medicine, 128,* 1469–1475.

Artwohl, A. (2002). Perceptual and memory distortion during officer-involved shootings. *FBI Law Enforcement Bulletin,* October, pp. 18–24.

Ball, J.D. & Peake, T.H. (2006). Brief psychotherapy in the U.S. military. In C.H. Kennedy & E.A. Zillmer (Eds.), *Military psychology: Clinical and operational applications* (pp. 61–73). New York: Guilford.

Barrett, J.E., Johnson, W.B., Johnson, S.J., Sullivan, G.R., Bongar, B., Miller, L. & Sammons, M.T. (2011). Psychology in extremis: Preventing problems of professional competence in dangerous practice settings. *Professional Psychology: Research and Practice, 42,* 94–104.

Baruth, C. (1986). Pre-critical incident involvement by psychologists. In J.T. Reese & H.A. Goldstein (Eds.), *Psychological services for law enforcement* (pp. 413–417). Washington DC: USGPO.

Bender, L.G., Jurkanin, T.J., Sergevnin, V.A. & Dowling, J.L. (2005). *Critical issues in police discipline: Case studies.* Springfield, IL: Charles C Thomas.

Blau, T.H. (1994). *Psychological services for law enforcement.* New York: Wiley.

Blum, L.N. (2000). *Force under pressure: How cops live and why they die.* New York: Lantern Books.

Bohl, N.K. (1995). Professionally administered critical incident debriefing for police officers. In M.I. Kunke & E.M. Scrivner (Eds.), *Police psychology into the 21st century* (pp. 169–188). Hillsdale, NJ: Erlbaum.

Bohrer, S. (2005). After firing the shots, what happens? *FBI Law Enforcement Bulletin,* September, pp. 8–13.

Bongar, B. (2002). *The suicidal patient: Clinical and legal standards of care* (2nd ed.). Washington, DC: American Psychological Association.

Bonanno, G.A. (2004). Loss, trauma, and human resilience. *American Psychologist, 59,* 20–28.

Borders, M.A. & Kennedy, C.H. (2006). Psychological interventions after disaster in trauma. In C.H. Kennedy & E.A. Zillmer (Eds.), *Military psychology: Clinical and operational applications* (pp. 331–352). New York: Guilford.

Bowman, M. (1997). *Individual differences in posttraumatic response: Problems with the adversity-distress connection.* Mahwah: Erlbaum.

Brickman, P. (1982). Models of helping and coping. *American Psychologist, 37,* 368–384.

Britt, J.M. (1991). U.S. Secret Service critical incident peer support team. In J. Reese, J. Horn & C. Dunning (Eds.), *Critical incidents in policing* (pp. 55–61). Washington DC: US Government Printing Office.

Brusher, E.A. (2007). Combat and operational stress control. *International Journal of Emergency Mental Health, 9,* 111–122.

Budd, F.C. & Kennedy, C.H. (2006). Introduction to clinical military psychology. In C.H. Kennedy & E.A. Zillmer (Eds.), *Military psychology: Clinical and operational applications* (pp. 21–34). New York: Guilford.

Campsie, R.L., Geller, S.K. & Campsie, M.E. (2006). Combat stress. In C.H. Kennedy & E.A. Zillmer (Eds.), *Military psychology: Clinical and operational applications* (pp. 215–240). New York: Guilford.

Carlier, I.V.E. & Gersons, B.P.R. (1995). Partial PTSD: The issue of psychological scars and the occurrence of PTSD symptoms. *Journal of Nervous and Mental Disease, 183,* 107–109.

Carlier, I.V.E., Lamberts, R.D. & Gersons, B.P.R. (1997). Risk factors for posttraumatic stress symptomatology in police officers: A prospective analysis. *Journal of Nervous and Mental Disease, 185,* 498–506.

Clary, M. (2005). War vets besieged by stress. *South Florida Sun-Sentinel,* March 28, pp. 1–2.

Cloherty, J.J. (2004). Legal defense of law enforcement officers in police shooting cases. In V. Lord (Ed.), *Suicide by cop: Inducing officers to shoot* (pp. 85–150). Flushing: Looseleaf Law Publications.

Cohen, A. (1980). "I've killed that man 10,000 times." *Police, 3*, 4.

Corbett, S. (2004). The permanent scars of Iraq. *New York Times Magazine*, February 15, pp. 34–41, 56–61.

Corneil, W., Beaton, R., Murphy, S., Johnson, C. & Pike, K. (1999). Exposure to traumatic incidents and prevalence of posttraumatic stress symptomatology in urban firefighters in two countries. *Journal of Occupational Health Psychology, 4*, 131–141.

Cummings, J.P. (1996). Police stress and the suicide link. *The Police Chief*, October, pp. 85–96.

Curran, S. (2003). Separating fact from fiction about police stress. *Behavioral Health Management, 23*, 1–2.

Dunning, C. (1999). Postintervention strategies to reduce police trauma: A paradigm shift. In J.M. Violanti & D. Paton (Eds.), *Police trauma: Psychological aftermath of civilian combat* (pp. 269–289). Springfield: Charles C Thomas.

Durham, T.W., McCammon, S.L. & Allison, E.J. (1985). The psychological impact of disaster on rescue personnel. *Annals of Emergency Medicine, 14*, 664–668.

Dyregrov, A. (1989). Caring for helpers in disaster situations: Psychological debriefing. *Disaster Management, 2*, 25–30.

Dyregrov, A. (1997). The process in psychological debriefing. *Journal of Traumatic Stress, 10*, 589–605.

Evans, R.W. (1992). The postconcussion syndrome and the sequelae of mild head injury. *Neurologic Clinics, 10*, 815–847.

Everly, G.S. & Boyle, S. (1999). Critical incident stress debriefing (CISD): A meta-analysis. *International Journal of Emergency Mental Health, 1*, 165–168.

Everly, G.S., Flannery, R.B. & Mitchell, J.T. (2000). Critical incident stress management: A review of the literature. *Aggression and Violent Behavior, 5*, 23–40.

Everly, G.S. & Mitchell, J.T. (1997). *Critical incident stress management (CISM): A new era and standard of care in crisis intervention.* Ellicott City: Chevron.

Finley, E.P. (2011). *Fields of combat: Understanding PTSD among veterans of Iraq and Afghanistan.* Ithaca, NY: Cornell University Press.

Fischler, G.L., McElroy, H.K., Miller, L., Saxe-Clifford, S., Stewart, C.O., & Zelig, M. (2011). The role of psychological fitness-for-duty evaluations in law enforcement. *The Police Chief*, August, pp. 72–78.

Frazier, F. & Wilson, R.M. (1918). The sympathetic nervous system and the "irritable heart of soldiers." *British Medical Journal, 2*, 27–29.

Freud, S. (1920). Beyond the pleasure principle. In J. Strachey (Ed. & Transl.), *The standard edition of the complete psychological works of Sigmund Freud* (Vol. XVIII, pp. 7–64). New York: Norton.

Friedman, M.J. (2004). Acknowledging the psychiatric cost of war. *New England Journal of Medicine, 351,* 75–77.

Friedman, M.J., Hamblen, J.L., Foa, E.B. & Charney, D.S. (2004). Fighting the psychological war on terrorism. *Psychiatry: Interpersonal and Biological Processes, 67,* 123–136.

Fry, W.F. & Salameh, W.A. (Eds.) (1987). *Handbook of humor and psychotherapy.* Sarasota: Professional Resource Exchange.

Fullerton, C.S., McCarroll, J.E., Ursano, R.J. & Wright, K.M. (1992). Psychological responses of rescue workers: Firefighters and trauma. *American Journal of Orthopsychiatry, 62,* 371–378.

Galovski, T. & Lyons, J.A. (2004). Psychological sequelae of combat violence: A review of the impact of PTSD on the veteran's family, and possible interventions. *Aggression and Violent Behavior, 9,* 477–501.

Geller, W.A. (1982). Deadly force: What we know. *Journal of Police Science and Administration, 10,* 151–177.

Gentz, D. (1991). The psychological impact of critical incidents on police officers. In J. Reese, J. Horn & C. Dunning (Eds.), *Critical incidents in policing* (pp. 119–121). Washington DC: US Government Printing Office.

Gilliland, B.E. & James, R.K. (1993). *Crisis intervention strategies* (2nd ed.). Pacific Grove: Brooks/Cole.

Greenstone, J.L. & Leviton, S.C. (2001). *Elements of crisis intervention: Crises and how to respond to them.* New York: Wadsworth.

Grossman, D.A. (1996). *On killing: The psychological cost of learning to kill in war and society.* New York: Little, Brown.

Haas, F. (2007). Stress in policing. *Training Wheel,* April–June, pp. 4–6.

Heiman, M.F. (1975). The police suicide. *Journal of Police Science and Administration, 3,* 267–273.

Henry, V.E. (2004). *Death work: Police, trauma, and the psychology of survival.* New York: Oxford University Press.

Higgins, R.L. & Leibowitz, R.Q. (1999). Reality negotiation and coping: The social construction of adaptive outcomes. In C.R. Snyder (Ed.), *Coping: The psychology of what works* (pp. 20–49).

Holbrook, J. (2011). Veterans' courts and criminal responsibility: A problem-solving history and approach to the liminality of combat trauma. In D.C. Kelly, S. Howe-Barksdale & D. Gitelson (Eds.), *Treating young veterans: Promoting resilience through practice and advocacy* (p. 259–300). New York: Springer.

Honig, A.L. & Roland, J.E. (1998). Shots fired: Officer involved. *The Police Chief,* October, pp. 65–70.

Honig, A.L. & Sultan, E. (2004). Reactions and resilience under fire: What an officer can expect. *The Police Chief,* December, pp. 54–60.

Horn, J.M. (1991). Critical incidents for law enforcement officers. In J.T. Reese, J.M. Horn & C. Dunning (Eds.), *Critical Incidents in Policing* (rev. ed., pp. 143–148). Washington DC: Federal Bureau of Investigation.

Horowitz, M.J. (1986). *Stress response syndromes* (2nd ed.). New York: Jason Aronson.

International Association of Chiefs of Police (2004). *Officer-involved shooting guidelines.* Los Angeles: IACP.

International Association of Chiefs of Police (2009). *Employing returning combat veterans as law enforcement officers: Supporting the integration or reintegration of military personnel into federal, state, local, and tribal law enforcement.* Alexandria, VA: IACP.

International Association of Chiefs of Police & United States Department of Justice (2010). *Combat veterans and law enforcement: A transition guide for veterans beginning or continuing careers in law enforcement.* Washington DC: IACP/USDOJ.

Janik, J. (1991). What value are cognitive defenses in critical incident stress? In J. Reese, J. Horn & C. Dunning (Eds.), *Critical incidents in policing* (pp. 149–158). Washington DC: US Government Printing Office.

Jelinek, P. (2007). Troops' ethics studied. *South Florida Sun-Sentinel,* May 5, p. 10A.

Jones, E., Thomas, A. & Ironside, S. (2007). Shell shock: An outcome study of a First World War PIE unit. *Psychological Medicine, 37,* 215–223.

Kardiner, A. (1941). *The traumatic neuroses of war.* Washington DC: National Research Council.

Karlsson, I. & Christianson, S.A. (2003). The phenomenology of traumatic experiences in police work. *Policing: An International Journal of Police Strategies and Management, 26,* 419–438.

Kennedy, D.B., Homant, R.J. & Hupp, R.T. (1998). Suicide by cop. *FBI Law Enforcement Bulletin,* August, pp. 21–27.

Kleepsies, P.M. (Ed.) (1998). *Emergencies in mental health practice: Evaluation and management.* New York: Guilford.

Linden, J.I. & Klein, R. (1986). Critical issues in police peer counseling. In J.T. Reese & H.A. Goldstein (Eds.), *Psychological services for law enforcement* (pp. 137–139). Washington DC: Federal Bureau of Investigation.

Lindsay, M.S. & Dickson, D. (2004). Negotiating with the suicide-by-cop subject. In V. Lord (Ed.), *Suicide by cop: Inducing officers to shoot* (pp. 153–162). Flushing: Looseleaf Law Publications.

Maddi, S.R. (2007). Relevance of hardiness assessment and training to the military context. *Military Psychology, 19,* 61–70.

March, C. & Greenberg, N. (2007). The Royal Marines' approach to psychological trauma. In C.R. Figley & W.P. Nash (Eds.), *Combat stress injury: Theory, research, and measurement* (pp. 247–260). New York: Routledge.

Maris, R.W. (1981). *Pathways to suicide: A study of self-destructive behaviors.* Baltimore: Johns Hopkins University Press.

McMains, M.J. (1986a). Post-shooting trauma: Demographics of professional support. In J.T. Reese & H. Goldstein (Eds.), *Psychological services for law Enforcement* (pp. 361–364). Washington DC: US Government Printing Office.

McMains, M.J. (1986b). Post-shooting trauma: Principles from combat. In J.T. Reese & H. Goldstein (Eds.), *Psychological services for law enforcement* (pp. 365–368). Washington DC: US Government Printing Office.

McMains, M.J. (1991). The management and treatment of postshooting trauma. In J.T. Horn & C. Dunning (Eds.), *Critical incidents in policing* (rev ed., pp. 191–198). Washington DC: Federal Bureau of Investigation.

McNally, R.J. (2003). Progress and controversy in the study of posttraumatic stress disorder. *Annual Review of Psychology, 54,* 229–252.

McNally, V.J. & Solomon, R.M. (1999). The FBI's critical incident stress management program. *FBI Law Enforcement Bulletin,* February, pp. 20–26.

Mearburg, J.C. & Wilson, R.M. (1918). The effect of certain sensory stimulations on respiratory and heart rate in cases of so-called "irritable heart." *Heart, 7,* 17–22.

Miller, H.B., Miller, L. & Bjorklund, D. (2010). Helping military parents cope with parental deployment: Role of attachment theory and recommendations for mental health clinicians and counselors. *International Journal of Emergency Mental Health, 12,* 231–235.

Miller, L. (1995). Tough guys: Psychotherapeutic strategies with law enforcement and emergency services personnel. *Psychotherapy, 32,* 592–600.

Miller, L. (1998). *Shocks to the system: Psychotherapy of traumatic disability syndromes.* New York: Norton.

Miller, L. (1999a). Critical incident stress debriefing: Clinical applications and new directions. *International Journal of Emergency Mental Health, 1,* 253–265.

Miller, L. (1999b). Tough guys: Psychotherapeutic strategies with law enforcement and emergency services personnel. In L. Territo & J.D. Sewell (Eds.), *Stress management in law enforcement* (pp. 317–332). Durham, NC: Carolina Academic Press.

Miller, L. (2000). Law enforcement traumatic stress: Clinical syndromes and intervention strategies. *Trauma Response, 6*(1), 15–20.

Miller, L. (2004). Good cop–bad cop: Problem officers, law enforcement culture, and strategies for success. *Journal of Police and Criminal Psychology, 19,* 30–48.

Miller, L. (2005a). Critical incident stress: Myths and realities. *Law and Order,* April, p. 31.

Miller, L. (2005b). Police officer suicide: Causes, prevention, and practical intervention strategies. *International Journal of Emergency Mental Health, 7,* 101–114.

Miller, L. (2006a). Practical strategies for preventing officer suicide. *Law and Order,* March, pp. 90–92.

Miller, L. (2006b). Critical incident stress debriefing for law enforcement: Practical models and special applications. *International Journal of Emergency Mental Health, 8,* 189–201.

Miller, L. (2006c). Officer-involved shooting: Reaction patterns, response protocols, and psychological intervention strategies. *International Journal of Emergency Mental Health, 8,* 239–254.

Miller, L. (2006d). *Practical police psychology: Stress management and crisis intervention for law enforcement.* Springfield, IL: Charles C Thomas.

Miller, L. (2006e). Suicide by cop: Causes, reactions, and practical intervention strategies. *International Journal of Emergency Mental Health, 8,* 165–174.

Miller, L. (2007a). Police families: Stresses, syndromes, and solutions. *American Journal of Family Therapy, 35,* 21–40.

Miller, L. (2007b). Line-of-duty death: Psychological treatment of traumatic bereavement in law enforcement. *International Journal of Emergency Mental Health, 9,* 13–23.

Miller, L. (2007c). Stress management and crisis intervention for law enforcement and mental health professionals. In F.M. Dattilio & A. Freeman (Eds.), *Cognitive-behavioral strategies in crisis intervention* (3rd ed., pp. 93–121). New York: Guilford.

Miller, L. (2007d). Law enforcement traumatic stress: Clinical syndromes and intervention strategies. In L. Territo & J.D. Sewell (Eds.), *Stress management in law enforcement* (2nd ed., pp. 381–397). Durham, NC: Carolina Academic Press.

Miller, L. (2007e). The psychological fitness-for-duty evaluation. *FBI Law Enforcement Bulletin,* August, pp. 10–16.

Miller, L. (2008a). The ultimate use of force: The psychology of killing. *ILEETA Use of Force Journal, 8*(2), 7–11.

Miller, L. (2008b). Military psychology and police psychology: Mutual contributions to crisis intervention and stress management. *International Journal of Emergency Mental Health, 10,* 9–26.

Miller, L. (2008c). Stress and resilience in law enforcement training and practice. *International Journal of Emergency Mental Health, 10,* 109–124.

Miller, L. (2008d). *METTLE: Mental toughness training for law enforcement.* Flushing, NY: Looseleaf Law Publications.

Miller, L. (2009). You're it! How to psychologically survive an internal investigation, disciplinary proceeding, or legal action in the police, fire, medical, mental health, legal, or emergency services professions. *International Journal of Emergency Mental Health, 11,* 185–190.

Miller, L. (2010). Psychotherapy with military personnel: Lessons learned, challenges ahead. *International Journal of Emergency Mental Health, 12,* 179–192.

Miller, L. (2011a). Suicide intervention: Basic processes and strategies. *International Journal of Emergency Mental Health, 13,* 37–41.

Miller, L. (2011b). Cops in trouble: Helping officers cope with investigation, prosecution, or litigation. In J. Kitaeff & K. Cather (Eds.), *Handbook of police psychology* (pp. 479–490). New York: Psychology Press.

Miller, L. (in press). *Practical police psychology: Stress management and crisis intervention for law enforcement* (2nd ed.). Springfield, IL: Charles C Thomas.

Mitchell, J.T. & Everly, G.S. (1996). *Critical incident stress debriefing: Operations manual.* (rev. ed.). Ellicott City: Chevron.

Mitchell, J.T. & Everly, G.S. (2003). *Critical incident stress management (CISM): Basic group crisis intervention* (3rd ed.). Ellicott City: ICISF.

Mitchell, J. & Levenson, R.L. (2006). Some thoughts on providing effective mental health critical care for police departments after line-of-duty deaths. *International Journal of Emergency Mental Health, 8,* 1–4.

Mohandie, K. & Hatcher, C. (1999). Suicide and violence risk in law enforcement: Practical guidelines for risk assessment, prevention, and intervention. *Behavioral Sciences and the Law, 17,* 357–376.

Moore, B.A., Hopewell, C.A. & Grossman, S. (2009). After the battle: Violence and the warrior. In S.M. Freeman, B.A. Moore & A. Freeman (Eds.), *Living and surviving in harm's way: A psychological treatment handbook for pre- and post-deployment of military personnel* (pp. 307–327). New York: Routledge.

Munsey, C. (2006). Soldier support. *Monitor on Psychology,* April, pp. 36–38.

Murphy, B. (2007). Combat ethics report concerns commander. *South Florida Sun-Sentinel,* May 8, p. 13A.

Nielsen, E. (1991). Traumatic incident corps: Lessons learned. In J. Reese, J. Horn & C. Dunning (Eds.), *Critical incidents in policing* (pp. 221–226). Washington DC: US Government Printing Office.

Norcross, R.H. (2003). The "modern warrior." A study in survival. *FBI Law Enforcement Bulletin,* October, pp. 20–26.

Nordland, R. & Gegax, T.T. (2004). Stress at the front. *Newsweek*, January 12, pp. 34–37.

Orasanu, J. & Backer, P. (1996). Stress and military performance. In J. Driskell & E. Salas (Eds.), *Stress and human performance* (pp. 89–125). Hillsdale: Erlbaum.

Paton, D. & Smith, L. (1999). Assessment, conceptual and methodological issues in researching traumatic stress in police officers. In J.M. Violanti & D. Paton (Eds.), *Police trauma: Psychological aftermath of civilian combat* (pp. 13–24). Springfield: Charles C Thomas.

Peake, T.H., Bourdin, C.M. & Archer, R.P. (2000). *Brief psychotherapies: Changing frames of mind* (3rd ed.). Northvale, NJ: Jason Aronson.

Perrou, B. & Farrell, B. (2004). Officer-involved shootings: Case management and psychosocial investigations. In V. Lord (Ed.), *Suicide by cop: Inducing officers to shoot* (pp. 239–242). Flushing: Looseleaf Law Publications.

Pinizzotto, A.J., Davis, E.F. & Miller, C.E. (2005). Suicide by cop: Defining a devastating dilemma. *FBI Law Enforcement Bulletin*, February, pp. 8–20.

Pizarro, J., Silver, R.C. & Prouse, J. (2006). Physical and mental health costs of traumatic experiences among Civil War veterans. *Archives of General Psychiatry*, *63*, 193–200.

Quinnett, P. (1998). QPR: Police suicide prevention. *FBI Law Enforcement Bulletin*, July, pp. 19–24.

Ralph, J.A. & Sammons, M.T. (2006). Future directions of military psychology. In C.H. Kennedy & E.A. Zillmer (Eds.), *Military psychology: Clinical and operational applications* (pp. 371–386). New York: Guilford.

Regehr, C. (2001). Crisis debriefings for emergency responders: Reviewing the evidence. *Journal of Brief Treatments and Crisis Intervention*, *1*, 87–100.

Regehr, C. & Bober, T. (2004). *In the line of fire: Trauma in the emergency services*. New York: Oxford University Press.

Reinecke, M.A., Washburn, J.J & Becker-Weidman, E. (2007). Depression and suicide. In F.M. Dattilio & A. Freeman (Eds.) *Cognitive-behavioral strategies in crisis intervention* (3rd ed., pp. 25–67). New York: Guilford.

Ritchie, E.C. & Owens, M. (2004). Military issues. *Psychiatric Clinics of North America*, *27*, 459–471.

Rodgers, B.A. (2006). *Psychological aspects of police work: An officer's guide to street psychology*. Springfield, IL: Charles C Thomas.

Rosen, G. (1975). Nostalgia: A forgotten psychological disorder. *Psychosomatic Medicine*, *5*, 342–347.

Rudd, M.D., Joiner, T.E., Jobes, D.A. & King, C.A. (1999). The outpatient treatment of suicidality: An integration of science and recognition of its limitations. *Professional Psychology: Research and Practice*, *30*, 437–446.

Rudofossi, D. (2007). *Working with traumatized police officer-patients: A clinician's guide to complex PTSD syndromes in public safety personnel.* Amityville, NY: Baywood.

Russell, H.E. & Beigel, A. (1990). *Understanding human behavior for effective police work* (3rd ed.). New York: Basic Books.

Ruzek, J.I. (2002). Providing "brief education and support" for emergency response workers: An alternative to debriefing. *Military Medicine, 167,* 76–78.

Salmon, T.W. (1919). The war neuroses and their lesson. *New York State Journal of Medicine, 51,* 993–994.

Sherman, N. (2005). *Stoic warriors: The ancient philosophy behind the military mind.* New York: Oxford University Press.

Solomon, R.M. (1991). The dynamics of fear in critical incidents: Implications for training and treatment. In J.T. Reese, J.M. Horn & C. Dunning (Eds.), *Critical incidents in policing* (pp. 347–358). Washington DC: Federal Bureau of Investigation.

Solomon, R.M. (1995). Critical incident stress management in law enforcement. In G.S. Everly (Ed.), *Innovations in disaster and trauma psychology: Applications in emergency services and disaster response* (pp. 123–157). Ellicott City: Chevron.

Solomon, R.M. & Horn, (1986). Post-shooting traumatic reactions: A pilot study. In J.T. Reese & H. Goldstein (Eds.), *Psychological services for law enforcement* (pp. 383–393). Washington DC: US Government Printing Office.

Southard, E. (1919). *Shell-shock and other neuropsychiatric problems.* Boston: Leonard.

Staal, M.A. (2001). The assessment and prevention of suicide for the 21st century: The Air Force's community awareness training model. *Military Medicine, 169,* 301–306.

Stuhlmiller, C. & Dunning, C. (2000). Challenging the mainstream: From pathogenic to salutogenic models of posttrauma intervention. In J. Violanti, D. Paton & C. Dunning (Eds.), *Posttraumatic stress intervention: Challenges, issues, and perspectives* (pp. 10–42). Springfield: Charles C Thomas.

Taylor, S.E. & Brown, J.D. (1988). Illusion and well-being: A social psychological perspective on mental health. *Psychological Bulletin, 103,* 193–210.

Taylor, S.E., Wood, J.V. & Lechtman, R.R. (1983). It could be worse: Selective evaluation as a response to victimization. *Journal of Social Issues, 39,* 19–40.

Toch, H. (2002). *Stress in policing.* Washington DC: American Psychological Association.

Trimble, M.R. (1981). *Post-traumatic neurosis: From railway spine to whiplash.* New York: Wiley.

Tyre, P. (2004). Battling the effects of war. *Newsweek,* December 6, pp. 68–70.

Violanti, J.M. (1995). The mystery within: understanding police suicide. *FBI Law Enforcement Bulletin,* July, pp. 19–23.

Violanti, J.M. (1996). *Police suicide: Epidemic in blue.* Springfield: Thomas.

Violanti, J.M. (1999). Death on duty: Police survivor trauma. In J.M. Violanti & D. Paton (Eds.), *Police trauma: Psychological aftermath of civilian combat* (pp. 139–158). Springfield: Charles C Thomas.

Violanti, J.M. (2000). Scripting trauma: The impact of pathogenic intervention. In J. Violanti, D. Paton & C. Dunning (Eds.), *Posttraumatic stress intervention: Challenges, issues, and perspectives* (pp. 153–165). Springfield: Charles C Thomas.

Wester, S.R. & Lyubelsky, J. (2005). Supporting the thin blue line: Gender-sensitive therapy with male police officers. *Professional Psychology: Research and Practice, 36,* 51–58.

Williams. M.B. (1999). Impact of duty-related death on officers' children: Concepts of death, trauma reactions, and treatment. In J.M. Violanti & D. Paton (Eds.), *Police trauma: Psychological aftermath of civilian combat* (pp. 159–174). Springfield: Charles C Thomas.

Wilson, J.P. (1994). The historical evolution of PTSD diagnostic criteria: From Freud to DSM-IV. *Journal of Traumatic Stress, 7,* 681–698.

Winerman, L. (2006). Coping through cognition. *Monitor on Psychology,* November, 16–17.

Wittrup, R.G. (1986). Police shooting–An opportunity for growth or loss of self. In J.T. Reese & H. Goldstein (Eds.), *Psychological services for law enforcement* (pp. 405–408). Washington DC: US Government Printing Office.

Zeling, M. (1986). Research needs in the study of post-shooting trauma. In J.T. Reese & H.A. Goldstein (Eds.), *Psychological services for law enforcement* (pp. 409–410). Washington DC: US Government Printing Office.

Discussion Questions

1. What are major stressors associated with both military service and police work?
2. What personal characteristics have been shown to be positively associated with increased stress resiliency?
3. What qualities have been shown to be associated with increased vulnerability to stress?
4. What are the elements of the PIE concept?
5. What are the elements of the BICEPS model?

6. What is Critical Incident Stress Debriefing (CISD)?
7. What are the elements of a Critical Stress Debriefing?
8. The formal CISD process consists of seven key phases. What are they?
9. What explicitly or tacitly are the fundamental elements of the military PIE/BICEPS and law enforcement CISD/CISM models?
10. In general, what elements determine the effectiveness of any therapeutic strategy?
11. What are the goals of a straightforward, goal-directed, problem-solving therapeutic intervention style?
12. What are examples of cognitive defense strategies?
13. What are the elements of the United States Air Force *LINK* program?
14. What are the elements of the US Navy and Marine Corps program called *AID LIFE*?
15. What are the warning signs of suicide?
16. In what important ways are the mandated obligations of police officers and soldiers different from other professionals such as firefighters, paramedics, rescue workers, airline pilots or construction workers?
17. What specific alterations in perception, cognitive, and behavioral changes occur when police officers are involved in a deadly force shooting episode?
18. What are the stages that responsible soldiers and civilian police officers go through following a service-related taking of a human life?

Part Eight

What Are the Tools That a Cop Can Use to Better Handle Stress?

By now, the reader should have developed an understanding of the nature, severity, and complexity of police stress. The solutions to this complicated problem, especially assuring that the individual officer learns and utilizes successful coping strategies, are equally complex.

Many researchers and practitioners have identified a variety of mechanisms that can be used to control or reduce law enforcement stress. Increased stress management training, professional counseling for officers and their families, peer advisement, and required fitness standards and programs have been identified as important measures at the department level. The use of relaxation responses and neutralization techniques, proper nutrition and diet, and regular exercise, particularly of an aerobic nature, have been offered as remedies for the individual officer.

So what works? How can police officers effectively cope with the effects of stress? What are the tools that a cop can use to better handle stress on and off the job? Our authors in Part Eight offer some suggestions.

In 1963, two Los Angeles Police Officers were kidnapped and one later killed. This crime, which became the basis for author Joseph Wambaugh's *The Onion Field*, was one of the first to document the symptoms and ultimate effects of Post-Traumatic Stress Disorder and is a key part of the effort of Harpold and Feemster to learn from the past. As they discuss ways to deal with the impact of stress, they recommend that agencies examine the success of other approaches, i.e., the Crime Prevention Model and the Disease Prevention Model, not necessarily connected with stress management, to provide a framework for enhanced and more effective programs of stress management.

Over a number of years, psychologists and others working in the field of stress management have focused on the importance of resilience in allowing an individual to successful confront specific stressors and stressful events. Paton and his co-authors have developed the Stress Shield as a model of resiliency for police officers, positing that an individual officer's capacity to "render challenging experiences meaningful, coherent, and manageable reflects the interaction of person, team, and organizational factors." Their ultimate goal is the promulgation of a model based on empirically tested theories that offers practical utility to law enforcement agencies in the selection, training, assessment, and stress preparation of their personnel.

Miller applies the concept of resilience in a slightly different manner, examining methods of fostering mental toughness and resilience in preparation for the incidents and stressors a law enforcement officer will confront. He then explores the psychological approaches, such as critical incident stress debriefing, mental health counseling, and specific therapeutic strategies, that may be appropriate for fostering recovery from critical incidents and traumatic events.

Much of Parts Eight and Nine deals with the psychological mitigation of stress, especially following critical incidents, in conceptual terms or in recognition of specific programs or approaches. Cipriano, a retired law enforcement command officer with one of Florida's largest sheriff's office who, after retirement, returned to school full-time to earn his doctorate in psychology, offers a different tack. He provides a more hands-on approach to the reader, suggesting specific exercises, including relaxation techniques and meditation, which can be applied immediately, by a law enforcement officer or a student of criminal justice, to reduce stress.

Further Reading

Anshel, Mark H. (2000). "A Conceptual Model and Implications for Coping with Stressful Events in Police Work," *Criminal Justice and Behavior*, 27(3), 375–400.

Band, Stephen R., and Vasquez, I. John (1991). "The Will to Survive," *FBI Law Enforcement Bulletin*, 60(8), 1–4.

Feemster, Samuel L. (2009). "Spirituality: An Invisible Weapon for Wounded Warriors," *FBI Law Enforcement Bulletin*, 78(1) 1–12.

Kureczka, Arthur W. (1996). "Critical Incident Stress in Law Enforcement," *FBI Law Enforcement Bulletin*, 65(8) 11–16.

Sewell, James D. (2003). "Handling the Stress of the Electronic World," *FBI Law Enforcement Bulletin*, 72(8), 11–16.

Key Terms in Part Eight

Alarm Reaction Stage: The first stage in the General Adaptation Syndrome. During this stage, the body's physiological defenses mobilize to recognize and respond to the assault by the stressor.

Comprehensibility: Refers to the events deriving from a person's internal and external environments in the course of living that are structured, predictable, and explicable. Things "make sense" and therefore seem less overwhelming.

COMPSTAT: The computerized statistical program adopted by the New York Police Department to ensure the accountability of its commanders in responding to crime in the City.

Confidentiality: A professional standard holding that, with some limited restrictions, what is discussed between licensed mental health professionals and their clients is privileged.

Crime prevention model: The National Crime Prevention Institute has long held that crime prevention is the "anticipation, recognition, and appraisal of crime risk and the initiation of some action to remove or reduce it." This model could be used to develop a parallel working definition of stress reduction.

Disease prevention model: Public health medicine identifies three stages of disease prevention: education of people about healthy lifestyles; targeting healthy persons who have a potential for the disease; and treating persons who are ill. Such a prevention model offers a basis for efforts in dealing with stress among law enforcement officers.

General Adaptation Syndrome: The manner in which the body responds to stress. Selye held that it occurs in three stages: the alarm reaction; the stage of resistance; and the stage of exhaustion.

Manageability: Refers to the idea that the individual possesses the resources to meet the demands posed by the adverse events. The person feels realistically in control, not helpless.

Meaningfulness: The person conceptualizes the adversity as a challenge worthy of his or her investment and engagement. There is an intellectual and emotional satisfaction in tackling a tough problem and seeing it through to conclusion.

Organizational climate: Describes officers' perceptions of how their organization functions; and how these perceptions influence both their well-being and their performance within their organizational role.

Project Shield: A research project funded by the National Institute of Justice that examined the negative effects of law enforcement stress according to its effects on psychological, physical, behavioral, and organizational health.

Resiliency: The capacity of agencies and officers to draw upon their own individual, collective, and institutional resources and competencies to cope with, adapt to, and develop from the demands, challenges, and changes encountered during and after a critical incident, mass emergency, or disaster; it includes the traits, characteristics, and circumstances that make some people more resistant to traumatic stress effects.

Sense of coherence: A stress/health-mediating personality construct proposed by Antonovsky. Within it, three component orientations (comprehensibility, manageability, and meaningfulness) contribute to an individual's ability to understand and effectively deal with a particular stressor.

Stage of Exhaustion: The third stage in the General Adaptation Syndrome. At this stage, the body has been unsuccessful in its response and is unable to respond or adjust to the stressor. In dealing with the stress of most occupations, the "worst case scenario" is death, either through physical disease or suicide.

Stage of Resistance: The second stage in the General Adaptation Syndrome. At this point, the body draws upon its natural and learned skills to confront or adjust to the stressor.

31

Negative Influences of Police Stress

Joseph A. Harpold and Samuel L. Feemster

> *Ian Campbell believed that what most policemen shared was an abhor-*
> *rence of the predictable, a distaste for the foreseeable experiences of work-*
> *ing life. … He felt that the job was not particularly hazardous physically*
> *but was incredibly hazardous emotionally and too often led to divorce,*
> *alcoholism, and suicide. … Never mind whether they could interpret,*
> *never mind if it was potentially hazardous to the soul. To be there was*
> *the thing.*
>
> — Joseph Wambaugh,
> The Onion Field[1]

Many variables exist in the battle against the negative influences of stress. While people can control some variables more easily than others, choice remains the one that they can exercise the most influence over. Officers have *chosen* a career in law enforcement, rather than having someone force them to join the profession. Other decisions, such as living with a mate, having a family, or attending college, represent examples of controlled choices that officers make.

However, choosing to live as healthy a life as possible remains one of the most important choices that officers *should* make. Deciding to battle the negative influences of life by developing and accentuating positive influences reduces stress in officers' daily activities. Research has shown that negative influences increase distress (negative stress), which, in large enough quantities, may cause some individuals to become sick.[2]

---

1. Joseph Wambaugh, *The Onion Field* (New York, NY: Delacorte Press, 1973), 3–4.

2. Edward A. Charlesworth and Ronald G. Nathan, *Stress Management: A Comprehensive Guide to Wellness*(New York, NY: Ballantine Books, 1984).

Defining Stress

What is stress? One researcher defined stress as "a nonspecific response of the body to any demand placed on it."[3] What does that really mean? It simply means that each person responds differently to internal and external demands of life, but that each person *does* experience stress. Denying its existence does not alleviate the body's response to daily stress.

The day-to-day stress of dealing with people and their problems, especially the deeply disturbing aspects of dealing with critical incidents, can traumatize officers and poison their spirits. Friederich Nietzsche said, "Whoever fights monsters should see to it that in the process he does not become a monster. And, when you look into an abyss, the abyss also looks into you."[4] This aptly applies to the law enforcement profession because officers look into the abyss of evil and negative behavior every day. The quote at the beginning of this article provides insight into what happens to police officers who, during the course of their duties, daily look into the abyss. Although they may face physical jeopardy, their souls remain constantly susceptible to poisoning with each encounter at the edge of the abyss.

Historically, the law enforcement profession has not acknowledged the negative stress related to being an officer. For example, law enforcement academies throughout the United States rarely have addressed stress in police work. Notwithstanding unmistakable cries for help disclosed in internal reviews, academies have been particularly lax in suggesting appropriate methods for identifying this potentially debilitating disorder. In addition, until recently, many law enforcement agencies did not implement programs to assist officers struggling with stress-related issues. One case, in particular, illustrates this problem all too well.

Examining *The Onion Field*

In *The Onion Field*, author Joseph Wambaugh described the horrible tale of two Los Angeles police officers' abduction while on duty one night in 1963. Criminals took the officers to an onion field outside of Bakersfield, California, and murdered one officer at the feet of the other. Somehow, miraculously,

---

3. Ibid.

4. Friedrich Nietzsche, *Beyond Good and Evil*, quoted in Margaret Miner and Hugh Rawson, *The New International Dictionary of Quotations*, 2nd ed. (New York, NY: A Signet Book, 1994), 111.

the second officer escaped and survived, only to experience second-guessing by his colleagues and the criminal justice system and incredible effects of negative stress without any assistance or support.

The surviving officer not only was victimized by watching his partner murdered but was second-guessed by his colleagues because he escaped and survived. The result was a second victimization. However, in 1963, no critical incident stress management debriefings or employee assistance programs existed, so he had no place to turn for support within his agency. His family members could not support him because no family education programs existed to teach them about the job and its negative stressors. He could not communicate with a police chaplain because his agency had no chaplain program. To make matters worse, a main aspect of the police personality dictated that officers, regardless of traumatic experiences, must endure repeated emotional and physical exposure to the abyss as if nothing had happened. In such an environment, the surviving officer's agency would not have had meaningful peer discussions or formal peer support programs in place to encourage him to talk about his problems.

The case ultimately went to court. For the next 9 years, the surviving officer had to recount the horror of the night over and over again during all of the hearings and appeals of the case. This left an open and infected psychological wound that never properly healed so that he could return to duty as a fully functional officer.

> The gardener was a thief. That's the thing that bothered him the most .... It was getting so hard to remember ... something flashed in his mind. ... He began getting afraid for no reason .... a throbbing pain started at the base of his skull. ... The fear was weakening him and the pain was ferocious. He wanted to work it off. ... Even the pain would not stop the gardener from thinking about his crimes. ... He used to think about the night in the onion field... before he became a thief.[5]

In recounting this true story, Wambaugh described the effects of what has come to be known as posttraumatic stress disorder (PTSD) along with some of the symptoms that someone with PTSD may exhibit. Tragically, the surviving officer ultimately was lost to PTSD and to the law enforcement profession because he became a thief himself by shoplifting some tools that he could have paid for but did not.

Fortunately, the law enforcement profession has made great strides since 1963 in the development of programs to treat officers exposed to such horrific

---

5. Supra note 1, 1–2.

incidents. However, room exists for improving these treatment efforts and for enhancing the credibility of such programs so that officers will participate in them. Most important, however, the law enforcement community must remind officers of the negative effects of stress and provide them with the skills to deal with the demands of their profession.

Learning from the Past

The U.S. Department of Justice's National Institute of Justice conducted research involving one of the major law enforcement agencies in the United States.[6]

Through an anonymous survey of the officers in this agency, researchers discovered that, apparently, the law enforcement profession had not learned from the history of negative influences of job stress and what that stress does to officers exposed to it. The study, Project Shield, provided information about the negative effects of stress and broke these down into categories of psychological, physical, behavioral, and organizational public health.

During this research project, officers admitted anonymously to increased vulnerability to alcohol abuse and anxiety within the first 5 years of employment. Project Shield also found that officers experienced increased risk of mortality and morbidity from cancer, heart disease, hypertension, acute migraine headaches, reproductive problems, chronic back problems, foot problems, and insomnia.

Project Shield showed that profound emotional effects from stress occurred most often when officers attended a police funeral, were the subject of an internal affairs investigation, experienced a needle stick or exposure to body fluids, made a violent arrest, or personally knew victims. In addition, the study discovered that officers experienced organizational, or job-related, stress most often when making split-second decisions with serious consequences; hearing media reports of police wrongdoing biased against police; having administrators who did not support their officers; putting work ahead of anything, including family; and not having enough time for personal or family responsibilities.

In the psychological area, Project Shield revealed that officers lost energy or interest, including loss of sexual interest, along with experiencing pound-

---

6. Robin Gershon, U.S. Department of Justice, National Institute of Justice, *Public Health Implication of Law Enforcement Stress*, video presentation, March 23, 1999.

ing in their chests and feelings of impending doom. Most important, 1 percent of these officers considered ending their lives.[7]

Regarding behavioral problems due to negative job stress, officers reported smoking and drinking problems; more injuries; and physical abuse of spouses, children, and even their police partners. Based on the laws associated with police officers convicted of domestic violence having to give up their guns, the potential exists to lose officers to this problem if they are convicted of domestic violence or child abuse. Of course, physically abusing their police partners also can result in tragedy in the workplace.

Project Shield demonstrated that whereas only a small percentage of officers in this agency reported these problems, they also were 30 percent more likely to report health problems than other officers in the agency, 3 times more likely to abuse their spouses, 5 times more likely to report alcoholism, 5 times more likely to have somatization (multiple, recurrent, and long-term physical complaints apparently not due to any physical disorder),[8] 6 times more likely to have anxiety, 10 times more likely to be depressed, and the least likely to seek help.

Reducing and Preventing Stress

More important than discovering that the negative impact of stress still exists is developing a comprehensive strategy to prevent or reduce it. Sadly, little is being done to inoculate new law enforcement personnel against the poisonous effects of negative stress. One story illustrates the need for action. "There were two doctors standing in the middle of a river. Gradually, dead bodies began coming toward them. At first, there were only a few, and the doctors were successful in pulling them out of the river. Later though, more bodies were coming downstream, and it was becoming impossible to get them all out of the river. At that point, one of the doctors got out of the water and went up on the bank. The other doctor, still in the river, said, 'Hey, where are

---

7. A presentation at a national conference on police suicide held at the FBI Academy in September 1999 indicated that police officers are three to four times more likely to kill themselves than to be killed in the line of duty. Given the predisposition to suicide that a few officers harbor, there seems to be a real potential for violence in the workplace of a police station by an officer who turns from suicidal to homicidal thoughts. See U.S. Department of Justice, Federal Bureau of Investigation, *Suicide and Law Enforcement* (Washington, DC, 2001).

8. *American Psychiatric Glossary*, 6th ed., s.v. "somatization."

you going? I can't get all of these bodies out of the water by myself.' With that, the doctor on the bank replied, 'I am going upstream to find out who is throwing all of these bodies in the river.' "[9]

Likewise, the law enforcement profession must go upstream to prevent the negative impact of stress. Prevention, or at least the reduction, of the negative impact of stress proves crucial to the health of law enforcement officers. Comparing stress prevention or reduction to similar efforts, such as crime or disease prevention and reduction, can lead to a better understanding of how to approach the problem.

Crime Prevention Model

Since 1970, the National Crime Prevention Institute (NCPI) in Louisville, Kentucky, has taught that crime prevention is "the anticipation, recognition, appraisal of a crime risk; and the initiation of some action to remove or reduce it."[10] Prior to the advent of a formal crime prevention philosophy at NCPI in 1970, a basic example of such action would have involved officers who worked the midnight shift checking for unlocked or open doors of businesses. When they found a door open or unlocked, they surmised that a thief could enter and steal what was inside. Recognizing this as a crime risk, officers understood that something had to be done to remove this opportunity from the criminal. Therefore, officers would have called the business owner to come and secure the business, which would have removed or at least reduced the opportunity for theft.

The law enforcement community can apply this definition of crime prevention to the concept of negative stress reduction by simply substituting "negative stress," or, more correctly, "distress" (as opposed to eustress or positive stress, such as winning the lottery), in the place of "a crime risk." Now, officers have a working definition of stress reduction: "the anticipation, recognition, appraisal of distress; and the initiation of some action to remove or reduce it." Anticipation means that anyone can experience distress. The importance of recognition lies in the awareness of the particular distress that bothers someone the most. Appraisal relates to understanding stress and how it affects people in general and why certain distress bothers a person. With these concepts in mind, the law enforcement community can begin to "initiate some action to remove or reduce it (distress)."

9. Presentation given by Deborah Prothrow-Stith, M.D., FBI Academy, October 15, 1991.

10. National Crime Prevention Institute, *Understanding Crime Prevention* (Stoneham, MA: Butterworth, 1986), 2.

To bring the reduction or prevention of negative stress about, however, law enforcement officers first must consider some contributing factors inherent in their profession. For example, research in criminal victimization has shown that those who have become victims are never the same as they were prior to their criminal victimization.[11] Likewise, officers are never the same as they were prior to entering the law enforcement profession. When they come in contact with individuals who have been victimized by criminals, officers also are victimized because people naturally relate to the pain of others. Victims of crime have experienced a violation of their inner selves, and officers can easily empathize because of the realization that this could have happened to anyone. Each time officers encounter this poisonous contact, the potential exists for their spirits to erode. After a period of time, the mind begins to build a wall to protect itself from experiencing any more pain. When this occurs, officers may display cold, unfeeling, or cynical attitudes, even though they do not mean to. To prevent this from occurring, officers need the skills to combat this exposure and avoid becoming sick and dispirited. Anticipation through education may develop a better understanding of how this distress may be contagious and will help to initiate action to guard against this phenomenon.

Disease Prevention Model

Just as with the crime prevention comparison, the law enforcement community can borrow the three phases of disease prevention from public health medicine to help in the battle against stress.

In the primary phase of disease prevention, doctors focus on educating people who live healthy lifestyles about unhealthy behaviors so that they will not *choose* to engage in those behaviors and become ill. For example, they teach people who do not smoke about the dangers of smoking so that they will *choose* not to smoke and, thus, reduce their chances of becoming ill.

In the secondary phase of disease prevention, doctors target those individuals engaged in behavior that may lead to disease, but who are still healthy. The doctors attempt to educate these people so that they will stop the dangerous behavior (e.g., smoking) before they contract such ailments as lung cancer, emphysema, or heart disease. The final, or tertiary, prevention phase involves treating sick individuals and educating them to choose not to continue the behavior that resulted in their illness. This represents the most costly

---

11. Interview of Morton Bard, Ph.D., in *Because You Need to Know*, prod. Federal Law Enforcement Training Center, July 5, 1988, video.

phase of the three, and the one that stands the least chance of being effective because treatment usually offers no guarantee of success once a serious illness has developed.[12]

If the law enforcement community applies the three phases of public health medicine's concept of prevention to developing a stress reduction model, then choosing the primary phase makes the most sense. Why wait until the negative influences have broken into a healthy lifestyle and the individual is so sick with stress that the tertiary phase is required to attempt to restore health?[13]

However, even in the secondary phase, officers can choose to "initiate some action to remove or reduce" the negative influences of stress by employing various coping methods. Some of these include deep breathing, muscle relaxation, meditation/prayer, positive thinking and self-talk, and mental imagery.[14] Officers can choose one of these or use them in combination, whatever works the best. Each person is different and what might work well for one might not work for another. These various techniques do work, and when officers find a technique that works the best, they have to practice it to increase its effectiveness. Most important, officers can refine these coping skills to the point that they can employ them as stressful situations occur.[15] Using these techniques gives a hopefulness in dealing with most stressful situations and even preventing them from becoming destructive to an officer's overall health.

Practicing stress management also must be used in the context of practicing a healthy lifestyle, including regular exercise, wholesome nutrition and diet, spiritual renewal, and enriching social interactions. Officer choices determine the health of the body, mind, spirit, and social interactions. If any one of these four areas sickens, other areas can become ill as well. Conversely, if officers choose to practice a healthy lifestyle in these four areas, then they choose to take care of their bodies.

Finally, officers also can choose to think positive thoughts.[16] Plato said that "thinking is the soul talking to itself."[17] This should be a positive dialogue. Officers should choose to cultivate an energetic, positive, and loving spirit. To

12. Supra note 8.

13. Supra note 8.

14. Supra note 2.

15. Patricia Carrington, *How to Relax* (New York, NY: Warner Audio Publishing, 1985).

16. For additional information, see Norman Vincent Peale, *The Power of Positive Thinking* (New York, NY: Fawcett Columbine Trade paper ed., 1996).

17. Plato, *The Republic*, retrieved from *http://www.ag.wastholm.net/aphorism/A-1993*, on June 18, 2001.

help in this effort, they also should choose to associate or interact with others who think and act in a positive manner as well.

Conclusion

As law enforcement officers become healthier, their agencies need to consider their health as well. "Police agencies need to be healthy before they can treat the community's illnesses and injuries. Signs of good health include pride, self-esteem, quality leadership, comprehensive training, and board certification."[18] Also, "… they always should demonstrate an appropriate bedside manner and always practice what they preach."[19]

Choosing to be healthy is the best weapon against the negative influences of stress. Once a commitment is made to fight back against the negative factors of stress, life becomes healthier and more enjoyable. Fighting back includes the deliberate adoption and implementation of stress reduction techniques and the vigilance of the law enforcement community to protect its members from the effects of negative stress as vigorously as officers protect society from lawlessness.

Suggested Reading and Resources

Aumiller, Gary, *Keeping It Simple* (Holbrook, MA: Adams Publishing, 1995).

Charlesworth, Edward A. and Ronald G. Nathan, *Stress Management: A Comprehensive Guide To Wellness* (New York, NY: Ballantine Books, 1984).

Chopra, Depak, *The Seven Spiritual Laws Of Success* (San Rafael, CA: Amber-Allen Publishing, 1993).

Covey, Stephen R., *Seven Habits of Highly Efficient People* (New York, NY: Simon & Schuster, 1990); *Principle Centered Leadership* (New York, NY: Summit Books, 1991); and *First Things First* (New York, NY: Simon & Schuster, 1995).

Dossey, Larry, *Healing Words* (New York, NY: Harper Collins Paper Backs, 1993).

Ellison, Katherine W., and John L. Genz, *Stress and the Police Officer* (Springfield, IL: Charles C Thomas Publisher, 1983).

---

18. Joseph A. Harpold, "A Medical Model for Community Police," *FBI Law Enforcement Bulletin*, June 2000, 26.

19. Ibid, 27.

Peale, Norman Vincent, *The Power of Positive Thinking* (New York, NY: Fawcett Columbine Trade paper ed., 1996).

Smalley, Gary, *Loving Each Other For Better and For Better* (New York, NY: Inspirational Press, 1993).

Mitchell, Jeffrey T., and George S. Everly, Jr., *Critical Incident Stress Management: The Basic Course Workbook*, 2nd edition (Ellicott City, MD: International Critical Incident Stress Foundation, 1998).

Discussion Questions

1. The US National Institute of Justice conducted research involving one of the major law enforcement agencies in the United States. The study was called Project Shield. What was it intended to do?
2. What were some of the findings of this research project?
3. It has been suggested that the law enforcement community can borrow ideas from the three phases of the disease prevention model used in public health medicine in order to help in their battle against stress. What do these three phases involve?

Stress Shield: A Model
of Police Resiliency

*Douglas Paton, John M. Violanti, Peter Johnston,
Karena J. Burke, Joanna Clarke, and Denise Keenan*

Police officers are regularly exposed to critical incidents. Although this work traditionally is viewed as a precursor to the development of acute and chronic posttraumatic stress reactions, growing evidence for it to be associated with adaptive and positive (e.g., posttraumatic growth, enhanced sense of professional efficacy) outcomes (Aldwin, Levenson, & Spiro, 1994; Armeli, Gunthert, & Cohen, 2001; Paton, Violanti, & Smith, 2003) calls for a reappraisal of this aspect of police work. While not denying the potential for pathological outcomes, growing evidence for resilient (adaptive and growth) outcomes introduces the need to identify predictors of resilience.

First, it is pertinent to consider what is meant by "resiliency." The term resilience is often used to imply an ability to "bounce back." Being able to bounce back is an important capability. However, because police officers are called upon repeatedly to deal with increasingly complex and threatening incidents, it is appropriate to expand the scope of this definition to include the development of one's capacity to deal with future events. Consequently, the definition adopted here embodies the notion of "adaptive capacity" (Klein, Nicholls, & Thomalla, 2003). Resiliency thus defines the capacity of agencies and officers to draw upon their own individual, collective, and institutional resources and competencies to cope with, adapt to, and develop from the demands, challenges, and changes encountered during and after a critical incident, mass emergency, or disaster.

Understanding and managing resilience involves adopting a perspective that assumes that salutary outcomes occur when individuals and groups can use their psychological and physical resources and competencies in ways that allow them to render challenging events coherent, manageable, and meaningful

(Antonovsky, 1990). In emergency populations, "critical" incidents create a sense of psychological disequilibrium that represents that period when the existing interpretive frameworks or schemas that guide officers' expectations and actions have lost their capacity to organize experience in meaningful and manageable ways (Janoff-Bulman, 1992; Paton, 1994). The challenge is to identify those factors that can be developed prior to exposure that predict officers' capacity to develop a schema that broaden the range of (unpredictable) experiences that officers can render coherent, meaningful, and manageable (Fredrickson, Tugade, Waugh, & Larkin, 2003; Paton, 1994, 2006). Building on recent empirical research into how protective services officers adapt to highly challenging circumstances (Burke & Paton, 2006; Johnston & Paton, 2003), in this paper we outline a new model of adaptive capacity. In constructing the Stress Shield model of resilience, it is essential that the theories used to inform its development can integrate personal, team, and organizational levels of analysis.

Integrating Officer, Team, and Organizational Factors

Although typically investigated at the level of the individual officer, this paper argues that the comprehensive understanding of resilience must integrate organizational, team, and individual perspectives, with the organizational level of analysis having greater influence in this process than has hitherto been acknowledged. This argument is based on the fact that the police organization defines the context within which officers experience and interpret critical incidents and their sequelae and within which future capabilities are nurtured or restricted (Paton, 2006). Officers respond to incidents as members of law enforcement agencies in which the organizational culture influences their thoughts and actions, representing the context in which challenging experiences (using a schema whose nature derives from patterns of interaction with colleagues, senior officers, and organizational procedures over time) are interpreted (Paton, Smith, Ramsay, & Akande, 1999; Paton, Smith, Violanti, & Eranen, 2000; Weick & Sutcliffe, 2007). However, the organization is not the only influence. Several person- and team-level factors (e.g., coping, social support) have also been implicated as playing complementary roles in predicting resilience (Paton, 2006), and they must be included in any comprehensive model.

Modeling Resilience

The development of models of resilience faces several conceptual challenges. Although resilience is evident when officers successfully adapt to actual critical incident demands, research into resilience must be undertaken prior to such events occurring to ensure that intervention can be undertaken to arm officers with a capability to adapt before they experience critical incidents. This would not be a problem if it were possible to predict exactly what officers will be called upon to confront. However, because critical incidents are characterized by considerable diversity (e.g., mass casualty incidents, school shootings, biohazard attack), police agencies cannot predict what their officers will encounter. Consequently, any model used to guide this activity must identify the resources and competencies that facilitate the proactive development of a general capacity to adapt (i.e., render any future experience meaningful and manageable) to unpredictable circumstances.

This introduces a second conceptual problem. There is currently no measure capable of capturing the diverse ways in which police officers can experience meaningfulness and manageability in the context of their work. Until such measures are developed, what is needed is a measure that can capture the experience of coherent, meaningful, and manageable outcomes irrespective of the specific outcomes officers' experience. The construct of job satisfaction can fulfill this role.

Satisfaction and Resilience

Thomas and Tymon (1994) found a relationship between perceptions of meaning found in work tasks ("meaningfulness") and enhanced job satisfaction. Spreitzer, Kizilos, and Nason (1997) observed a positive relationship between competence ("manageability") and job satisfaction. These findings have been echoed in the critical incident literature, with finding meaning and benefit in emergency work being manifest in changes in levels of job satisfaction (Britt, Adler, & Bartone, 2001; Hart & Cooper, 2001; North et al., 2002).

Because the job satisfaction construct can capture changes in the meaningfulness and manageability facets of resilience, as well as the implications of the coexistence of positive and negative aspects of officers' experience, it represents a construct capable of acting as an indicator of officers' resilience and their future capacity to adapt to unpredictable and challenging critical incidents. Having identified a means of measuring adaptive outcomes, the next task is to identify the personal, team, and organizational level factors that influence resilience.

Organizational Characteristics, Coping, and Resilience

Hart and Cooper (2001) proposed a conceptual model of organizational health that predicts that interaction between individual and organizational factors influences the experience of salutary outcomes. Of particular relevance for the present paper was the central role that Hart and Cooper afforded organizational climate. "Organizational climate" describes officers' perceptions of how their organization functions, and these perceptions influence both their well-being and their performance within their organizational role (Hart & Cooper).

Burke and Paton (2006) tested the ability of this model to predict satisfaction in the context of emergency responders (police, fire, paramedic) experience of critical incidents. The model tested how interaction between organizational climate (measured using the Team Climate Inventory [Anderson & West, 1998]), officers' experience of organizational and operational practices prescribed by the organizational culture (measured using the Police Daily Hassles and Uplifts Scale [Hart, Wearing, & Headey, 1993]), and officers' problem-focused and emotion-focused coping styles (measured using the COPE Inventory (Carver, Scheier, & Weintraub, 1989). Job Satisfaction was measured by the Job Satisfaction Inventory (Brayfield & Rothe, 1987). The results are summarized in Figure 1.

The model accounted for 44% of the variance in job satisfaction. Organizational climate was the best single predictor of job satisfaction (Figure 1) and, by inference, represents a significant influence on officers' ability to render their critical incident experiences meaningful and manageable. The relationship between organizational climate and how officers deal with the consequences of critical incidents was evident in the influence of climate on coping (Figure 1). Organizational climate had a negative influence on emotion-focused coping, resulting in an increase in negative work experiences. Similarly, climate had a direct positive influence on problem-focused coping, resulting in an increase in positive work experiences. Organizational climate also demonstrated a direct negative influence on negative ("hassles") work experiences and a direct positive influence on positive ("uplifts") work experiences. Positive and negative work experiences made relatively equal and separate contributions to job satisfaction.

Given that satisfaction assesses perceived meaning, the culture or climate of an organization represents one source of officers' ability to impose and sustain coherence and meaning on critical incident outcomes. The important role played by organizational climate indicates that police agencies have a key role in facilitating staff adaptability and resilience.

This model (Figure 1) accounted for 44% of the variance in job satisfaction, leaving a substantial portion of the variance to be explained. Hart and Cooper (2001) argued that the inclusion of individual (e.g., personality, hardiness) and group (e.g., peer and supervisor support) constructs could help account for additional variance. There are other reasons for developing the model further.

Figure 1. The relationship between personal characteristics, organizational climate, work experiences and job satisfaction. Adapted from Burke and Paton (2006).

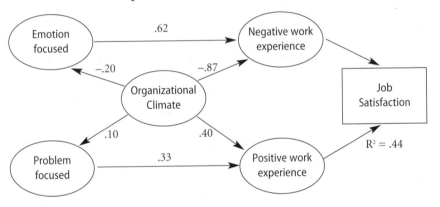

Developing the Model

Although this model (Figure 1) provides a sound basis for the relationship between organizational culture and officer resilience, additional elements are required to account for how officers' experiences of the work environment and critical incidents are translated into schemas that contribute to or detract from the officers' capacity to learn from experience in ways that facilitate their future capacity to adapt.

As outlined above, any theory used must meet certain criteria. First, it must encompass personal, team, and organizational levels of analysis. Secondly, it must contribute toward explaining how challenging experiences are rendered meaningful and manageable (by predicting change in satisfaction). One such construct is empowerment. In the next section, reasons why empowerment represents a construct that informs an understanding of resilience are discussed.

Empowerment

The first issue is whether a relationship between empowerment and satisfaction can be demonstrated. Several studies have demonstrated that empowerment predicts satisfaction in individuals and teams (Kirkman & Rosen, 1999; Koberg, Boss, Senjem, & Goodman, 1999). The second issue is whether empowerment theories can encapsulate the individual, team, and organizational influences in ways that positively influence the meaningfulness and manageability of experiences (captured by job satisfaction). It is to a discussion of how empowerment satisfies this criterion that this paper now turns.

Empowerment as an Enabling Process

Empowerment is a well-used construct in the management literature, usually in relation to processes such as participation and delegation (Conger & Konungo, 1988). Because delegation, as an attribute of organizational culture, can influence resilience (e.g., delegating responsibility for crisis decision making) (Paton & Flin, 1999), this facet of empowerment may contribute to increasing resilience. However, it is the finding that empowerment has demonstrated strong links to motivating action under conditions of uncertainty (Conger & Konungo; Spreitzer, 1997) that renders the concept of empowerment capable of providing valuable insights into how resilience can be developed and sustained.

Motivational interpretations of empowerment derive from a theoretical perspective that argues that if people have sufficient resources (psychological, social, and physical) and the capacity to use them, they will be able to effectively confront the challenges presented by events and the environment (Conger & Konungo, 1988; Spreitzer, 1997). Empowerment theories argue that the potential to use resources to accomplish tasks derives from the relationship between the organization and the officer. Empowerment theories thus afford opportunities to develop models that integrate personal, team, and organizational factors.

Conger & Konungo (1988) conceptualize empowerment as an enabling process that facilitates the conditions necessary to effectively confront (i.e., develop meaning, competence, etc.) future challenges. Conger and Konungo argue that individual differences in meaning and competence reflect the degree to which the environment (i.e., the police organization) enables actions to occur. Empowerment thus describes a process that uses organizational strategies to remove conditions that foster powerlessness (e.g., organizational hassles) and encourage organizational practices (e.g., organizational and operational uplifts, self-efficacy information, competencies) that develop officers' learned resourcefulness (Johnston & Paton, 2003).

Thomas and Velthouse (1990) complement this position by adding that beliefs about future competence derive from the schema or interpretive framework, developed through the enabling process of empowerment, which provides meaning to officers' experiences and builds their capacity to deal with future challenges. In addition to its ability to inform an understanding of resilience directly, the notion of enabling through the development of an empowering schema means that the empowerment construct can help explain how officers' experiences of their organizational culture (e.g., the hassles and uplifts that reflect how it is enacted) and critical incidents are translated in meaningful and manageable ways (manifest as changes in levels of satisfaction; see Figure 4).

By providing a mechanism that offers an explanation for the relationship between the organizational environment and the schema that underpins future adaptive capacity, empowerment theories have considerable potential to inform an understanding of how resilience is enacted in police agencies. This capability is further bolstered by the fact that empowerment is conceptualized as an iterative process involving a cycle of environmental events, task assessments, and behavior (Figure 2). Consequently, empowerment theories can accommodate the repetitive nature of police involvement in critical incidents in ways that demonstrate how it contributes to the learning process required to maintain adaptive capacity in the changing environment of contemporary policing (Paton & Violanti, 2008).

Critical Incidents, Incident Assessment, and Behavior

Environmental events (critical incidents) provide information to officers about both the consequences of their previous task behavior and the conditions they can expect to experience in future task behavior (Conger & Konungo, 1988). In addition to it emanating from their own experiences, task information (e.g., the assessment of critical incident experiences) can also be provided by peers, subordinates, and superiors at work in the context of, for example, performance appraisals, training programs, and meetings (Figure 2).

Through each progressive cycle of event (i.e., following a challenging critical incident), assessment (of specific critical incident experiences), and feedback, officers develop, maintain, and change the operational schema they use to plan for, interpret, and respond to critical incidents. This process is depicted in Figure 2. For it to inform the development of resilience, it is necessary to identify how empowerment cycles contribute to the development of future adaptive capacity. The environmental assessment process translates into two outcomes: task assessment and global assessment.

Figure 2. The cycle of environmental events, task assessments, and behavior. Adapted from Johnston and Paton (2003). The hashed line indicates the input into organizational learning.

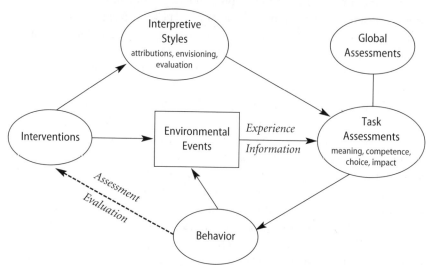

According to Thomas and Velthouse (1990), officers' task assessments comprise several components. The first component, meaningfulness (or meaning), describes the degree of congruence between the tasks performed and one's values, attitudes, and behaviors. Empowered individuals feel a sense of personal significance, purpose, and commitment to their involvement in work activities (Spreitzer, 1997; Thomas & Velthouse). Meaningfulness is increased by experiencing uplifts, such as receiving recognition and being given responsibility, but is constrained by organizational hassles (e.g., "red tape") that shift the emphasis from meaningful role performance to meeting administrative expectations.

The second component, competence, is analogous to Bandura's (1977) notion of self-efficacy. Competence is fundamental to the belief of officers in their ability to perform their operational roles successfully (Spreitzer, 1997). This outcome is comparable to the manageability component of resilience. Importantly, Bandura points out that there is a direct relationship between the level of self-efficacy (i.e., competence) and the level of effort and persistence that officers invest in facing challenging events, thus making an important contribution to officers' capacity to adapt to the unexpected.

The third component, choice, reflects the extent to which officers perceive that their behavior is self-determined (Spreitzer, 1997). A sense of choice is achieved when officers believe they are actively involved in defining how they perform their role (a prominent item when officers report uplifts) rather than just being passive recipients (as is often the case when officers describe hassles). The sense of choice is enhanced when the organization delegates responsibility for planning and task performance to officers. This facet of empowerment is comparable to the coherence component of resilience. A sense of choice is particularly important for dealing with emergent, contingent, emergency demands and for creative crisis decision-making and the development and maintenance of situational awareness when responding to critical incidents (Paton & Flin, 1999). An ability to exercise choice also facilitates learning from training and operational experiences and, in an empowering climate, facilitates others to do likewise and pass on learning.

The final component, impact, describes the degree to which officers perceive that they can influence important organizational outcomes (Spreitzer, 1997). Where choice concerns control over one's work behaviors, impact concerns the notion of personal control over organizational outcomes. Parallels can be drawn between the choice and impact elements of empowerment and perceived control, another factor that has been widely implicated in thinking on stress resilience and adaptability.

The ability to draw a direct comparison between the components of task assessment and the concepts of meaningfulness, manageability, and coherence adds weight to the argument that empowerment can encapsulate resilience in police organizations. This comparison also illustrates how hassles and uplifts can affect core empowerment processes such as meaning and choice (see Figure 4), thus affording an opportunity to see that empowerment research complements the earlier model (see Figure 1) and how their integration contributes to the development of a comprehensive model of police resilience.

Before continuing to advance this argument, there is one final form of assessment that remains to be discussed: global assessment, which further establishes empowerment as a construct that plays an important role in informing the understanding of officers' resilience and their capacity to adapt to future incidents.

Although task assessments are localized within a singular task and time period, global assessments refer to an outcome of empowerment that embodies a capacity to generalize expectancies and learning across tasks and over time. Thomas and Velthouse (1990) observed that global assessments describe a capacity to fill in gaps when faced with new and/or unfamiliar situations. This aspect of empowerment is essential for adaptive capacity in a profession where one cannot predict what he or she will be called upon to confront and thus must be able to use current experiences as a basis for preparing to deal with future risk and uncertainty.

Both global and task assessments, and thus the capacity to adapt, are influenced by officers' interpretive styles (Figure 2), with these schemas comprising separate but related components (Thomas & Velthouse, 1990). According to Thomas and Velthouse, interpretive frameworks are influenced by the work context, with management practices (intervention; see Figure 2) having an important influence on how the schemas are developed and sustained.

Empowerment Schema and Resilience

The first schema component concerns the attributions made by officers to account for success or failure. Empowerment is greater when officers attribute causes for failure to external (i.e., other than personal shortcomings), transient (i.e., likely to change over time), and specific (e.g., limited to a specific day or event) factors.

The role of this schema component is consistent with findings in the literature of critical incident stress. For example, Paton and Stephens (1996) discuss how an officer's frequent experience of successful outcomes under normal circumstances can lead to the development of the helper stereotype. The schema of the helper stereotype fuels officers' expectations that they will always be resourceful, in control, and able to put things right. The suddenness, scale, and complexity of mass emergencies and disasters make it inevitable that officers will have to deal with failure at some point or with not being able to perform at their expected level (Paton, 1994). Under these circumstances, the helper stereotype results in officers' internalizing failure (Raphael, 1986) rather than, more correctly, attributing a given problem to environmental complexity. Similarly, organizational hassles such as reporting practices that supersede concern for officers' well-being or that project blame on officers increase the likelihood that officers will perceive problems as emanating from internal sources (MacLeod & Paton, 1999). In contrast, feedback processes that differentiate personal and environmental influences on outcomes contribute to the development of attributional schemas that sustain adaptive capacity (MacLeod & Paton).

A second schema component, envisioning, refers to how officers anticipate future events and outcomes. It influences the quality of the attributional processes brought to bear on critical incident experiences. Officers who anticipate positive rather than negative outcomes experience stronger task and global assessments and, thus, empowerment. With regard to response problems, the existence of a learning culture in police agencies that interprets problems as catalysts for future development and not as failure (Paton, 2006; Paton & Stephens, 1996) will increase positive expectations regarding performance and well-being.

The final schema component, evaluation, refers to the standards by which one evaluates success or failure. Thomas and Velthouse (1990) argue that individuals who adopt less absolutist and more realistic standards experience greater empowerment. This observation is reinforced by findings in the critical incident literature. Officers who have realistic performance expectations, and who acknowledge environmental limitations on their outcomes, are better able to adapt to highly threatening circumstances (Paton, 1994; Raphael, 1986).

In addition to being able to predict satisfaction and thus inform understanding of how meaning and manageability develop, by mediating the relationship between organizational characteristics and satisfaction, empowerment represents a mechanism that illustrates how an officer's experience of organizational culture (e.g., hassles and uplifts) is translated, via the above schema components, into resilience and future adaptive capacity. Having identified the potential of empowerment theories to inform understanding of resilience, the next issue involves identifying its organizational predictors.

Several antecedents to psychological empowerment have been identified. Prominent among these are social structural variables (access to resources and information, organizational trust, peer cohesion, and supervisory support) and personal characteristics (personality). This literature can contribute to identifying the predictors of empowerment that can be included in the Stress Shield model.

Access to Resources

Having insufficient, inadequate, or inappropriate resources to perform response tasks contributes to critical incident stress risk (Carafano, 2003; Paton, 1994). Having resources (physical, social, and informational) allows individuals to take initiative and enhance their sense of control (impact) and self-efficacy (competence) over environmental challenges (Gist & Mitchell, 1992; Lin, 1998; Paton, 1994). One resource that plays a pivotal role in predicting empowerment is information.

Crisis information management systems capable of providing pertinent information in conditions of uncertainty are essential to adaptive capacity in emergency responders (Paton & Flin, 1999) and play an important role in creating a sense of purpose and meaning (Conger & Konungo, 1988) among officers (Figure 3). However, information itself is not enough. The social context in which information is received is an equally important determinant of empowerment. In this context, one aspect of the agency-officer relationship becomes particularly important, and that is trust.

Trust

Trust is a prominent determinant of the effectiveness of interpersonal relationships, group processes, and organizational relationships (Barker & Camarata, 1998; Herriot, Hirsh, & Reilly, 1998), and it plays a crucial role in empowering officers (Spreitzer & Mishra, 1999). People functioning in trusting, reciprocal relationships are left feeling empowered and are more likely to experience meaning in their work. Trust has been identified as a predictor of a person's ability to deal with complex, high-risk events (Siegrist & Cvetkovich, 2000), particularly when relying on others to provide information or assistance.

Trust influences one's perception of other's motives, their competence, and the credibility of the information they provide (Earle, 2004). People are more willing to commit to acting cooperatively in high-risk situations when they believe those with whom they must collaborate or work under are competent, dependable, and likely to act with integrity (in the present and in the future) and care for their interests (Dirks, 1999). Organizations functioning with cultures that value openness and trust create opportunities for officers to engage in learning and growth, thus contributing to the development of officers' adaptive capacity (competence) (Barker & Camarata, 1998; Siegrist & Cvetkovich, 2000) (Figures 3 and 4). The quality of this aspect of the interpersonal environment is also influenced by officers' dispositional characteristics.

Dispositional Influences

Although less extensively researched than other variables, one dispositional factor that has attracted interest is the personality dimension of conscientiousness, particularly with regard to its attributes of achievement orientation and dependability (McNaus & Kelly, 1999). Conscientious individuals experience a stronger sense of meaning and competence in their work, particularly during times of change and disruption (e.g., responding to critical incidents in which officers need to adapt to unpredictable, emergent demands) (Thomas

& Velthouse, 1990), demonstrate greater levels of perseverance in these efforts (Behling, 1998), and are more committed to contributing to collective efforts (Hough, 1998). This contributes positively to both the level of cooperation with and support for coworkers that they demonstrate in work contexts and to sustaining a cohesive team response to complex events.

Modeling Empowerment and Resilience

Using these variables, Johnston and Paton (2003) described how empowerment mediated the relationship between the above predictors and resilience (job satisfaction) in hospital staff dealing with critical incidents. Psychological empowerment was measured using Spreitzer's (1995a) empowerment scale. Trust was measured using the interpersonal trust at work scale (Cook & Wall, 1980). Access to resources and information was assessed using Spreitzer's (1995b) social structural measures. Conscientiousness was assessed using Costa and McCrae's (1992) conscientiousness scale. The results are summarized in Figure 3.

The model shown in Figure 3 provided good support for the role of empowerment as a predictor of resilience, accounting for some 51% of the variance in job satisfaction. It also supports the inclusion of empowerment in the Stress Shield model. However, before doing so, other social structural (e.g., senior officer attitudes and behavior, levels of peer cohesion and support) and dispositional (e.g.., hardiness) variables capable of predicting adaptive capacity through empowerment can be identified.

Figure 3. The relationship between empowerment and job satisfaction. Adapted from Johnston (2002) and Johnston and Paton (2003).

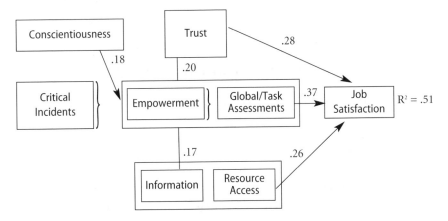

Senior Officer Support and Empowerment

Senior officers play a central role in developing and sustaining empowering environments (Liden, Wayne, & Sparrow, 2000; Paton & Stephens, 1996). They have a major role in creating and sustaining a climate of trust and empowerment as a result of their being responsible for translating the organizational culture into the day-to-day values and procedures that sustain the schema officers engage to plan for and respond to critical incidents.

Leadership practices such as positive reinforcement help create an empowering team environment (Manz & Sims, 1989; Paton, 1994). This is particularly true when senior officers focus on constructive discussion of response problems and how these problems can be resolved in the future; this type of approach from both coworkers and senior officers empowers employees (Quinn & Spreitzer, 1997). It does so by drawing one's emphasis away from personal weaknesses in a difficult or challenging situation and placing it on an active approach of anticipating how to exercise control in the future (Paton & Stephens, 1996). In this way, the behavior of senior officers contributes to the development of the attributional, envisioning, and evaluative schema components (see above) that are instrumental in translating officers' organizational experiences into resilient beliefs and competencies.

Quality supervisor-subordinate relationships, of which supportive supervisor behavior is a crucial factor (Liden, Sparrow, & Wayne, 1997), create the conditions necessary for personal growth (Cogliser & Schriesheim, 2000) by enhancing general feelings of competence (global assessment) (see Figure 4). Additionally, quality supervisor-subordinate relationships encourage the creation of similar value structures between officers (Cogliser & Schriesheim), building shared schema, enabling employees to find increased meaning in their task activities, and contributing to the development of a sense of cohesion between colleagues.

Peer Cohesion and Empowerment

The quality of relationships between coworkers predicts the meaning that officers' perceive in their work (Major, Kozlowski, Chao, & Gardner, 1995; Liden et al., 2000; Mullen & Cooper, 1994; Paton & Stephens, 1996; Perry, 1997) and increases the level of social support provided to coworkers (George & Bettenhausen, 1990). Members of cohesive work teams are more willing to share their knowledge and skills, an essential prerequisite for the development and maintenance of the learning culture that is fundamental to agency and officer resilience. Cohesive networks are also less dependent on senior officers for obtaining important resources. Peer relationships are an alternative source for such resources (Liden et al., 1997), contributing to a greater sense of self-determination in one's work (see Figure 4).

Taken together, the social structural variables of senior officer support and peer cohesion can make a valuable contribution to a model of resilience (see Figure 4). In the earlier discussion of the choice and impact components of empowerment (see above), a comparison was made between them and the construct of perceived control. Consequently, the final variable proposed for the model, hardiness, is a dispositional one that informs an understanding of the relationship between perceived control and resilience.

Hardiness and Empowerment

Hardiness has a long history as a predictor of resilience, one which embraces the officer-agency relationship (Bartone, 2004). Hardiness may be an important adjunct to empowerment. Portraying empowerment as a multi-level process introduces another issue. Although organizational decisions can provide the conditions necessary to enable officers, this does not automatically imply that officers will be able to fully utilize these opportunities. It is necessary to have an enabling (empowering) environment and officers with the dispositional characteristics to be empowered (see Figure 4).

The control, challenge, and commitment facets of hardiness represent a dispositional indicator of officers' potential to utilize environmental opportunities to learn from an empowering environment. For this reason, hardiness is included in the model. It has an advantage over conscientiousness in that hardiness is open to change through team and organizational intervention (Bartone, 2004).

Integrating the occupational health and empowerment models (Figure 1 and 3) with the additional factors described above provides the foundation for the Stress Shield model of resiliency. The Stress Shield model is depicted in Figure 4. Paths contributing to the development of empowerment are shown as solid lines. Paths proposed to reduce empowerment are illustrated as hatched lines. Because it can capture changes in perceived coherence, meaningfulness, and manageability, satisfaction is retained as an outcome measure. However, because the occupational health and empowerment literatures have not examined posttrauma outcomes specifically, a measure capable of capturing this aspect of officers' experience must be included in any test of the model. For this reason, posttraumatic growth has been included as an outcome measure in the model (Figure 4).

Figure 4. The Stress Shield model of resilience. Solid lines indicate positive influences on adaptive capacity and growth. Dash lines indicate pathways with a negative influence on empowerment.

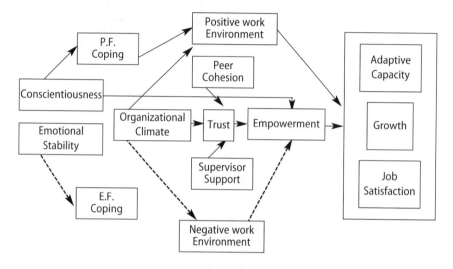

Conclusion

Recognition of the fact that critical incidents can result in resilient (adaptive and growth-oriented) outcomes for police officers means that exercising duty of care requires that police agencies have at their disposal a model that they can use to guide the development and maintenance of resilience. Furthermore, because police officers will encounter unpredictable and challenging circumstances repeatedly, it is important that resilience programs be designed as learning strategies and that any model used to guide this activity identify the resources and competencies that facilitate the proactive development of officers' general capacity to adapt (i.e., render any future experience meaningful and manageable) to unpredictable circumstances. The Stress Shield model was proposed as a means of achieving this goal.

The Stress Shield model was developed by integrating and building on theoretically robust and empirically tested work. This approach increases the expected utility of the model. The Stress Shield model describes resilience as resulting from the interaction between person, team, and organizational factors. However, the benefit of any model is a function of its being theoretically rigorous and capable of informing the design of practical programs in police agencies. All model components (with the exception of conscientiousness, and its influence can be accommodated in selection or assessment procedures) are amenable to change through organizational intervention and change strategies. Guidelines for changing hardiness, peer support, supervisor support, organizational hassles and uplifts, trust, and empowerment are available in the literature (Bartone, 2004; Cogliser & Schriesheim, 2000; Hart et al., 1993; Herriot et al., 1998; Perry, 1997; Quinn & Spreitzer, 1997). The fact that the proposed Stress Shield model is derived from empirically validated theories and includes variables that can be acted upon and influenced by police agencies to influence selection, training, assessment, and strategies for change confers upon the model both theoretical rigor and practical utility.

References

Aldwin, C. M., Levenson, M. R., & Spiro, A., III. (1994). Vulnerability and resilience to combat exposure: Can stress have lifelong effects? *Psychology and Aging, 9*, 34–44.

Antonovsky, A. (1990). Personality and health: Testing the sense of coherence model. In H. S. Friedman (Ed.), *Personality and disease* (pp. 155–177). New York: John Wiley & Sons.

Anderson, N.R., & West, M.A. (1998). Measuring climate for work group innovation: Development and validation of the team climate inventory. *Journal of Organizational Behavior, 19*, 235–258.

Armeli, S., Gunthert, K. C., & Cohen, L. H. (2001). Stressor appraisals, coping, and post-event outcomes: The dimensionality and antecedents of stress-related growth. *Journal of Social and Clinical Psychology, 20*, 366–395.

Bandura, A. (1977). Self-efficacy: Toward a unifying theory of behavioural change. *Psychological Review, 84*, 191–215.

Barker, R.T., & Camarata, M.R. (1998). The role of communication in creating and maintaining a learning organization: Preconditions, indicators, and disciplines. *Journal of Business Communication, 35*, 443–467.

Bartone, P. (2004). Increasing resiliency through shared sensemaking: Building hardiness in groups. In D. Paton, J. Violanti, C. Dunning, & L.M. Smith (Eds.), *Managing traumatic stress risk: A proactive approach* (pp. 129–140). Springfield, IL: Charles C Thomas.

Behling, O. (1998). Employee selection: Will intelligence and personality do the job? *Academy of Management Executive, 12*, 77–86.

Brayfield, A.H., & Rothe, H.F. (1987). Job satisfaction index. In B. Stewart, G. Hetherington, & M. Smith (Eds.), *Survey item bank* (Vol. 1, pp. 21–31). Harrowgate: University Press.

Britt, T.W., Adler, A.B., & Bartone, P.T. (2001). Deriving benefits from stressful events: The role of engagement in meaningful work and hardiness. *Journal of Occupational Health Psychology, 6,* 53–63.

Burke, K., & Paton, D. (2006). Well-being in protective services personnel: Organisational Influences. *Australasian Journal of Disaster and Trauma Studies,* 2006-2. http://trauma.massey.ac.nz/issues/2006-2/burke.htm

Carafano, J.J. (2003). *Preparing responders to respond: The challenges to emergency preparedness in the 21st Century* (Heritage Lecture No. 812). Washington, DC: The Heritage Foundation.

Carver, C.S., Scheier, M.F., & Weintraub, J.K. (1989). Assessing coping strategies: A theoretically based approach. *Journal of Personality and Social Psychology, 56,* 267–283.

Cogliser, C.C., & Schriesheim, C.A. (2000). Exploring work unit context and leader-member exchange: A multi-level perspective. *Journal of Organizational Behavior, 21,* 487–511.

Conger, J.A., & Konungo, R. (1988). The empowerment process: Integrating theory and process. *Academy of Management Review, 13,* 471–482.

Cook, J., & Wall, T. (1980). New work attitude measures of trust, organizational commitment and personal need non-fulfilment. *Journal of Occupational Psychology, 53,* 39–52.

Costa, P.T, & McCrae, R.R. (1992). *Revised NEO Personality Inventory (NEO PI-R) and NEO Five-Factor Inventory (NEO-FFI) professional manual.* Odessa, FL: Psychological Assessment Resources.

Dirks, K.T (1999). The effects of interpersonal trust on work group performance. *Journal of Applied Psychology, 84,* 445–455.

Earle, T. C. (2004). Thinking aloud about trust: A protocol analysis of trust in risk management. *Risk Analysis, 24,* 169–183.

Fredrickson, B. L., Tugade, M. M., Waugh, C. E., & Larkin, G. (2003). What good are positive emotions in crises?: A prospective study of resilience and emotions following the terrorist attacks on the United States on September 11th, 2001. *Journal of Personality and Social Psychology, 84,* 365–376.

George, J.M., & Bettenhausen, K. (1990). Understanding prosocial behavior, sales and turnover: A group level analysis in a service context. *Journal of Applied Psychology, 75,* 698–709.

Gist, M., & Mitchell, T.N. (1992). Self-efficacy: A theoretical analysis of its determinants and malleability. *Academy of Management Review, 17,* 183–211.

Hart, P.M., & Cooper, C.L. (2001). Occupational Stress: Toward a more integrated framework. In N. Anderson, D.S. Ones, H.K. Sinangil, & C. Viswesvaren (Eds.), *International handbook of work and organizational psychology, Vol. 2: Organizational psychology* (pp. 27–48). London: Sage Publications.

Hart, P. M., Wearing, A. J., & Headey, B. (1993). Assessing police work experiences: Development of the Police Daily Hassles and Uplifts Scales. *Journal of Criminal Justice, 21,* 553–572.

Herriot, P., Hirsh, W., & Reilly, P. (1998). *Trust and transition: Managing today's employment relationship.* Chichester: John Wiley & Sons.

Hough, L.M. (1998). Personality at work: Issues and evidence. In M.D. Hakel (Ed.), *Beyond multiple choice: Evaluating alternatives to traditional testing for selection* (pp. 131–166). Mahwah, NJ: Lawrence Erlbaum.

Janoff-Bulman, R. (1992). *Shattered assumptions.* New York: Free Press.

Johnston, P. (2002). Psychological empowerment as a mediating and multidimensional construct. Unpublished master's thesis, Massey University, Albany, New Zealand.

Johnston, P., & Paton, D. (2003). Environmental resilience: Psychological empowerment in high-risk professions. In D. Paton, J. Violanti, & L. Smith (Eds.), *Promoting capabilities to manage posttraumatic stress: Perspectives on resilience* (pp. 136–151). Springfield, IL: Charles C Thomas.

Kirkman, B.L., & Rosen, B. (1999). Beyond self-management: Antecedents and consequences of team empowerment. *Academy of Management Journal, 42,* 58–74.

Klein, R., Nicholls, R., & Thomalla, F. (2003). Resilience to natural hazards: How useful is this concept? *Environmental Hazards, 5,* 35–45.

Koberg, C.S., Boss, R.W., Senjem, J.S., & Goodman, E.A. (1999). Antecedents and outcomes of empowerment. *Group & Organization Management, 24,* 71–91.

Liden, R.C., Sparrow, R.T., & Wayne, S.J. (1997). Leader-member exchange theory: The past and potential for the future. *Research in Personnel and Human Resources Management, 15,* 47–119.

Liden, R.C., Wayne, S.J., & Sparrow, R.T. (2000). An examination of the mediating role of psychological empowerment on the relations between the job, interpersonal relationships, and work outcomes. *Journal of Applied Psychology, 85,* 407–416.

Lin, C.Y. (1998). The essence of empowerment: A conceptual model and a case illustration. *Journal of Applied Management Studies, 7,* 223–238.

MacLeod, M.D., & Paton, D. (1999). Police officers and violent crime: Social psychological perspectives on impact and recovery. In J.M. Violanti and D. Paton (Eds.), *Police trauma: Psychological aftermath of civilian combat.* Springfield, IL: Charles C Thomas.

Major, D.A., Kozlowski, S.W., Chao, G.T., & Gardner, P.D (1995). A longitudinal investigation of newcomer expectations, early socialization outcomes, and the moderating effects of the role development factors. *Journal of Applied Psychology, 80*, 418–431.

Manz, C.C., & Sims, H. (1989). *Super-leadership: Teaching others to lead themselves.* New York: Prentice Hall.

McNaus, M.A., & Kelly, M.L. (1999). Personality measures and biodata: Evidence predicting their incremental predictive value in the life insurance industry. *Personnel Psychology, 52*, 137–148.

Mullen, B., & Cooper, C. (1994). The relation between group cohesiveness and performance: An integration. *Psychological Bulletin, 115*, 210–227.

North, C.S., Tivis, L., McMillen, J.C., Pfefferbaum, B., Cox, J., Spitznagel, E.L., Bunch, K., Schorr, J., & Smith, E.M. (2002). Coping, functioning, and adjustment of rescue workers after the Oklahoma City bombing. *Journal of Traumatic Stress, 15*, 171–175.

Paton, D. (1994). Disaster relief work: An assessment of training effectiveness. *Journal of Traumatic Stress, 7*, 275–288.

Paton, D. (2006). Posttraumatic growth in emergency professionals. In. L. Calhoun and R. Tedeschi (Eds.), *Handbook of posttraumatic growth: Research and practice.* Mahwah, NJ: Lawrence Erlbaum Associates.

Paton, D., & Flin, R. (1999). Disaster stress: An emergency management perspective. *Disaster Prevention and Management, 8*, 261–267.

Paton, D., & Jackson, D. (2002). Developing disaster management capability: An assessment centre approach. *Disaster Prevention and Management, 11*, 115–122.

Paton, D., Smith, L.M., Ramsay, R., and Akande, D. (1999). A structural reassessment of the Impact of Event Scale: The influence of occupational and cultural contexts. In R. Gist and B. Lubin (Eds.), *Response to disaster* (pp. 83–100). Philadelphia: Taylor & Francis.

Paton, D., Smith, L.M., Violanti, J., & Eranen, L. (2000). Work-related traumatic stress: Risk, vulnerability and resilience. In D. Paton, J.M. Violanti, & C. Dunning (Eds.), *Posttraumatic stress intervention: Challenges, issues and perspectives* (pp. 187–204). Springfield, IL: Charles C Thomas.

Paton, D., & Stephens, C. (1996). Training and support for emergency responders. In D. Paton & J. Violanti (Eds.), *Traumatic Stress in critical occupations: Recognition, consequences and treatment.* Springfield, IL: Charles C Thomas.

Paton, D., & Violanti, J.M. (2008). Law enforcement response to terrorism: The role of the resilient police organization. *International Journal of Emergency Mental Health, 10*, 125–135.

Paton, D., Violanti, J.M., & Smith, L.M. (2003). *Promoting capabilities to manage posttraumatic stress: Perspectives on resilience.* Springfield, IL: Charles C Thomas.

Perry, I. (1997). "Creating and empowering effective work teams." *Management Services, 41,* 8–11.

Quinn, R.E., & Spreitzer, G.M. (1997). "The road to empowerment: Seven questions every leader should consider." *Organisational Dynamics,* Autumn, 37–49.

Raphael, B. (1986) *When disaster strikes.* London: Hutchinson.

Siegrist, M., & Cvetkovich, G. (2000). "Perception of hazards: The role of social trust and knowledge." *Risk Analysis, 20,* 713–719.

Spreitzer, G.M. (1995a). "An empirical test of a comprehensive model of intrapersonal empowerment in the workplace." *American Journal of Community Psychology, 23,* 601–629.

Spreitzer, G.M. (1995b). "Psychological empowerment in the workplace: Dimensions, measurement, and validation." *Academy of Management Journal, 38,* 1442–1465.

Spreitzer, G.M. (1996). "Social structural characteristics of psychological empowerment." *Academy of Management Journal, 39,* 483–504.

Spreitzer, G.M. (1997). "Toward a common ground in defining empowerment." *Research in Organizational Change and Development, 10,* 31–62.

Spreitzer, G.M., Kizilos, M.A., & Nason, S.W. (1997). "A dimensional analysis of the relationship between psychological empowerment and effectiveness, satisfaction and strain." *Journal of Management, 23,* 679–704.

Spreitzer, G.M., & Mishra, A.K. (1999). "Giving up control without losing control: Trust and its substitutes' effect on managers involving employees in decision making." *Group & Organization Management, 24,* 155–187.

Thomas, K.W., & Tymon, W. (1994). "Does empowerment always work?: Understanding the role of intrinsic motivation and interpretation." *Journal of Management Systems, 6,* 84–99.

Thomas, K.W., & Velthouse, B.A. (1990). "Cognitive elements of empowerment: An 'interpretive' model of intrinsic motivation." *Academy of Management Review, 15,* 666–681.

Weick, K.E., & Sutcliffe, K. M. (2007). *Managing the unexpected: Resilient performance in an age of uncertainty* (2nd ed.). San Francisco: Jossey-Bass.

Discussion Questions

1. What is meant by resiliency?
2. What conceptual challenges face the development of models of resilience?
3. How is "organizational climate" described?
4. What studies have been conducted to demonstrate whether or not there is a relationship between empowerment and satisfaction?
5. Motivational interpretations of empowerment derive from a theoretical perspective that argues that if people have sufficient resources (psychological, social, and physical) and the capacity to use them, they will be able to effectively confront the challenges presented by events and the environment. What are these resources?
6. According to Thomas and Velthouse, officers' task assessments comprise several components. What are they?
7. What antecedents to psychological empowerment have been identified?
8. What is the relationship between information and predicting empowerment?
9. What role does trust play in the crucial role of empowering officers?
10. What is the relationship between the dimension of conscientiousness and job satisfaction?
11. In what ways do leadership practices help create an empowering team environment?
12. In what ways does the quality of the relationship between coworkers predict the meaning that officers' perceive in their work and increase the level of social support provided to coworkers?
13. What is the relationship between hardiness and empowerment?

33

Stress and Resilience in Law Enforcement Training and Practice

Laurence Miller

Most productive people would describe their jobs as stressful to some degree, and a certain degree of coping and resilience is useful to navigate the daily challenges of any high-demand occupation (Maddi & Khoshaba, 2005; Miller, 2008c). Yet, in only a few professions—police, firefighting, emergency medical services, disaster management, search and rescue, the military—does this stress literally involve making critical decisions in life-and-death situations for oneself and others. In these cases, stress and resilience are not academic topics or luxuries; they are essential to the physical and mental health, as well as to the optimum job functioning, of the personnel concerned. Accordingly, while the material in this article is directed mainly to the challenges of law enforcement work, it can be readily applied to all of the high-demand professions noted above.

History of Stress and Trauma in Psychology, the Military, and Law Enforcement

Historically, the pendulum of interest in stress syndromes has swung back and forth between military and civilian traumas (Evans 1992; Pizarro, Silver, & Prouse, 2006; Rosen, 1975; Trimble, 1981; Wilson, 1994). During warfare, rulers and generals have always had an interest in knowing as much as possible about factors that might adversely affect their fighting forces. To this end, clinicians have been pressed into service to diagnose and treat soldiers with the aim of getting them back to the front lines as quickly as possible.

The ancient Greeks and Romans wrote eloquently about the trials and travails that could afflict the warrior mind (Sherman, 2005) and these writings are echoed to the present day (Grossman & Christensen, 2007). One of the first modern conceptualizations of posttraumatic stress was put forth in 1678 by the army surgeon Hoffer, who described what he called *nostalgia*, defined as a deterioration in the physical and mental health of homesick soldiers. This was attributed to the formation of abnormally vivid images in the affected soldier's brain by battle-induced overexcitation of the "vital spirits."

The American Civil War introduced a new level of industrialized killing and, with it, a dramatic increase in reports of stress-related nervous ailments. Further advances in weapons technology during the First World War produced an unprecedented accumulation of horrific battlefield casualties from machine guns, poison gas, and long-range artillery. The latter led to the widely applied concept of shell shock, initially believed to be caused by the brain-concussive effects of exploding shells, but later understood to be a form of psychological incapacitation resulting from the trauma of battle. Indeed, the failure to confirm any definitive organic basis for many of these debilitating stress syndromes led to the eventual replacement of shell shock by the more mentalistic-sounding term, war neurosis (Southard, 1919).

Kardiner's (1941) long-term study of soldiers with war neuroses led him to conclude that severe war trauma produced a constriction of the ego that prevented these patients from adapting to and mastering life's subsequent challenges. Kardiner elaborated a conceptualization of trauma termed *physioneurosis* that is quite close to the modern concept of posttraumatic stress disorder (see below). The features of this syndrome included: persistence of the startle response, irritability and proneness to explosive behavior, fixation on the trauma, constriction of the personality, and a disturbed dream life, including vivid nightmares.

The experiences of the Second World War contributed surprisingly little to the development of new theories and treatments for wartime trauma, except for its renaming as battle fatigue. In fact, resistance to the very concept of battle fatigue, with its implications of mental weakness and lack of moral resolve, was widespread in both medical and military circles. There was a war on, plenty of good Joes were getting killed and wounded, and the army had little sympathy for the whinings of a few slackers and nervous nellies who couldn't buck up and pull their weight—an attitude that persists among today's military and civilian fighting forces.

However, it was becoming apparent that wartime psychological trauma could take place in circumstances other than the actual battlefield. In WWII, then Korea and Vietnam, and most recently in the Persian Gulf wars, clinicians began to learn about disabling stress syndromes associated with large-scale bombings of civilian populations, prisoner of war and concentration camps, "brainwashing" of POWs, civilian atrocities, terrorism, and the threat of wholesale nuclear annihilation. In 1980, traumatic stress syndromes were finally codified as an identifiable type of psychopathological syndrome—*posttraumatic stress disorder* (PTSD)—in the American Psychiatric Association's official Diagnostic and Statistical Manual of Mental Disorders (APA, 1980) and it remains there in the current edition (APA, 2000). Well known to trauma clinicians, the symptoms include heightened physiological arousal, alternating intrusive and numbing symptomatology, flashbacks and nightmares, and general restriction of life activities.

In law enforcement and emergency services, this became incorporated into the concept of critical incident stress (Mitchell & Everly, 1996, 2003), and some authorities have gone so far as to characterize police trauma as the psychological aftermath of "civilian combat" (Violanti, 1999).

A *critical incident* is defined as any event that has an unusually powerful, negative impact on personnel. In the present context, it is any event that a law enforcement officer may experience that is above and beyond the range of the ordinary stresses and hassles that come with the job. Major classes of critical incidents include: a line-of-duty death; serious injury to police personnel; a serious multiple-casualty incident such as a multiple school shooting or workplace violence incident; the suicide of a police officer; the traumatic death of children, especially where irresponsible or frankly malevolent adults were involved; an event with excessive media interest; or a victim who is a family member or otherwise well-known to one or more responding officers (Everly & Mitchell, 1997). Recent times have multiplied exponentially the range and scope of horrific law enforcement critical incidents to include acts of mass terror and destruction, involving multiple deaths of civilians, fellow officers, and other emergency personnel (Henry, 2004; Karlsson & Christianson, 2003; Miller, 1998b, 2006).

Risk and Resiliency Factors for Traumatic Stress Responses

Not everyone who experiences a traumatic critical incident develops the same degree of psychological disability; there is significant variability among individuals in terms of their degree of susceptibility and resilience to stressful events. While many individuals are able to resolve acute critical incident stress through the use of informal social support and other adaptive activities (Bowman, 1997, 1999; Carlier & Gersons, 1995; Carlier, Lamberts, & Gersons, 1997; Gentz, 1991), in other cases, critical incident stress that is not resolved adequately or treated appropriately in the first few days or weeks may evolve into a number of disabling psychological traumatic disability syndromes (Miller, 1998b, 2006, 2008a, 2008b).

Risk Factors for PTSD and Traumatic Disability

Risk factors for PTSD or other traumatic disability syndromes in law enforcement officers (Carlier, Lamberts, & Gersons, 1997; Paton, Smith, Violanti, & Eranen, 2000) may be:

- *Biological,* including genetic predisposition and inborn heightened physiological reactivity to stimuli.
- *Historical,* such as prior exposure to trauma or other coexisting adverse life circumstances.
- *Psychological,* including poor coping and problem-solving skills, learned helplessness, and a history of dysfunctional interpersonal relationships.
- *Environmental/contextual,* such as inadequate departmental or societal support.

Resiliency or Protective Factors for PTSD and Traumatic Disability

Resiliency or protective factors are traits, characteristics, and circumstances that make some people more resistant to traumatic stress effects (Bowman, 1997, 1999; Hoge, Austin, & Pollack, 2007; Miller, 1990, 1998a). As a general trait factor, features associated with resilience to adverse life events in children and adults (Bifulco, Brown, & Harris, 1987; Brewin, Andrews, & Valentine, 2000; Garmezy, 1993; Garmezy, Masten, & Tellegen, 1984; Luthar, 1991; Miller, 1990, 1998a; Rubenstein, Heeren, Houseman, Rubin, & Stechler, 1989; Rutter, 1985, 1987; Rutter, Tizard, Yule, Graham, & Whitman, 1976; Werner, 1989; Werner & Smith, 1982; Zimrin, 1986) include:

- Good cognitive skills and intelligence, especially verbal intelligence, and good verbal communication skills.
- Self-mastery, an internal locus of control, good problem-solving skills, and the ability to plan and anticipate consequences.
- An easy temperament, not overly-reactive emotional style, good sociability, and positive response to and from others.
- A warm, close relationship with at least one caring adult or mentor, other types of family and community ties and support systems, and a sense of social cohesion as being part of a larger group or community.

Indeed, on close inspection, these appear to be virtually the opposite of the traits of impulsivity, neuroticism, and poor social connection and support that characterize those most vulnerable to trauma.

Kobasa (1979a, 1979b; Kobasa, Maddi, & Cahn, 1982) introduced the concept of *hardiness*, which has been defined as a stable personality resource consisting of three psychological attitudes and cognitions (Maddi & Khoshaba, 1994):

- *Commitment* refers to an ability to turn events into something meaningful and important, something worth working for and seeing through to completion.
- *Control* refers to the belief that, with effort, individuals can influence the course of events around them, that they are not helpless, but effective influencers of their fate and the responses of others.
- *Challenge* refers to a belief that fulfillment in life results from the growth and wisdom gained from difficult or challenging experiences, a realistically confident but not reckless "bring-'em-on" attitude.

Similarly, Antonovsky (1979, 1987, 1990) has proposed a stress/health-mediating personality construct termed *sense of coherence*, or SOC, which is expressed in the form of three component orientations or beliefs:

- *Comprehensibility* refers to the events deriving from a person's internal and external environments in the course of living that are structured, predictable, and explicable. Things "make sense" and therefore seem less overwhelming.
- *Manageability* refers to the idea that the individual possesses the resources to meet the demands posed by the adverse events. The person feels realistically in control, not helpless.
- *Meaningfulness* means that the person conceptualizes the adversity as a challenge worthy of his or her investment and engagement. There is an intellectual and emotional satisfaction in tackling a tough problem and seeing it through to conclusion.

The higher a person's SOC, the better able he or she will be to clarify the nature of a particular stressor, select the resources appropriate to that specific situation, and be open to feedback that allows the adaptive modification of behavior when necessary.

Applying these concepts specifically to police officers, Paton and colleagues (2000) have delineated a core set of resiliency factors that enable officers to withstand and even prevail in the face of seemingly overwhelming trauma. These include:

- Superior training and skill development—what I have characterized as the ITTS ("It's The Training, Stupid") principle (Miller, 2006).
- A learning attitude toward the profession—I have referred to this as building a "culture of knowledge" (Miller, 2006).
- Higher intelligence and problem-solving ability.
- Good verbal and interpersonal skills.
- Adequate emotional control and adaptive coping mechanisms.
- A sense of optimism.
- The ability and willingness to seek help and support where necessary.

The practical application of these concepts occurs in their incorporation into intervention services for PTSD and other critical incident stress reactions in law enforcement and emergency services personnel (Miller, 1998b, 2006, 2008a). This will be elaborated further, below.

Psychophysiology of Stress and Resilience

We know that the mental and the physical are not separate categories: we think and feel with our brains and we react with our bodies. Accordingly, the study of stress has always been linked with the study of resilience, and a psychophysiological model that encompasses both, while not essential to clinical practice, does provide a scientific model to guide further theory and application.

The modern study of the psychophysiology of stress is generally regarded as beginning with Claude Bernard's (1865) concept of the *milieu internal*, a term he used to describe the self-regulating mechanism that every healthy organism utilizes to maintain a constant state of adaptive functioning. This equilibrium can be disrupted by stress or disease, but as long as the organism survives, it will endeavor to restore and maintain this optimal internal state.

In the early 20th century, Walter Cannon (1914, 1939) used the term *homeostasis* to refer to a state of biological equilibrium that could be derailed by stress, but that the organism typically attempts to re-regulate back into health. Cannon urged physicians to consider the effects of psychological stress on physiological functioning, ushering in the modern study of psychosomatic illness (Alexander, 1950; Weiner, 1977, 1992).

Probably the most well-known account of the stress response comes from the work of Hans Selye (1956, 1973, 1975) whose active research spanned the decades from the 1930s to the 1970s. Selye developed the model of the *general adaptation syndrome*, or GAS, which he believed to define the physiological response to stressors of almost every type—from infections and toxins to social stress and interpersonal power struggles. Selye's GAS is said to consist of three overlapping but distinct stages.

In the *stage of alarm*, the organism marshals its physiological resources to cope with the stressor. For Selye, this involves activation of the hypothalamo-pituitary-adrenal axis, resulting in the increased production of cortisol by the adrenal cortex. This hormone has an anti-inflammatory effect on the body and also has neuroactive and psychoactive effects on the brain. The alarm-stage stress response also mobilizes the sympathetic nervous system and increases secretion of adrenalin from the adrenal medulla.

In the *stage of resistance*, the body goes into a kind of extended overdrive, as all systems stay on high alert while the organism is coping with the stressor, which may be anything from a bad flu to a bad divorce. In the best case, the organism rallies and the crisis is eventually passed, with the individual becoming more resilient in the process. In this case, Nietzsche (1969) is right: "Whatever doesn't kill me makes me stronger." Indeed, in some instances, adaptive responding to stress can lead to what has been called transcendent coping and posttraumatic growth (Calhoun & Tedeschi, 1999; Tedeschi & Calhoun, 1995, 2004; Tedeschi & Kilmer, 2005).

But no organism can stay on red alert forever. If the crisis is not resolved, at some point the individual reaches the *stage of exhaustion*, in which physiological reserves are finally depleted and the organism begins to deteriorate and may even die. Sorry, Nietzsche, but in this case, "Whatever doesn't kill me ... can make me really, really sick—and I might die later, anyway."

More recent research has revealed that the stress response may be more graded and nuanced, depending on the individual, and in this may lie the psychophysiological basis for differences in coping and resilience. Dienstbier (1989) has used the term *toughness* to refer to a distinct psychophysiological reaction pattern that characterizes animals and humans who cope effectively with stress. Two main physiological systems underlie the toughness response.

The first involves a pathway from the brain's hypothalamus to the sympathetic branch of the autonomic nervous system, and from there to the adrenal medulla. The sympathetic nervous system, or SNS, is responsible for the heart-pounding, fight-or-flight response that mobilizes body and mind to deal with challenging situations. As part of this response, the adrenal gland releases its main hormone, adrenalin.

The second system involved in the toughness response also begins with the hypothalamus but acts through the pituitary gland which in turn stimulates the adrenal cortex to release cortisol—the chief stress hormone involved in Selye's triphasic GAS response, discussed above. Together, the pattern of SNS-adrenal medulla and pituitary-adrenal cortex responses to stressful events characterizes the nature of the toughness trait.

It is the flexibility and gradedness of response of these two interrelated systems that defines an individual's physiological resilience or toughness. In resiliently tough organisms— animal or human—the normal, everyday activity of the two systems is low and modulated; tough individuals are at relative ease under most ordinary circumstances and their physiological responses reflect this relative quiescence. But when faced with a stressful challenge or threat, the SNS-adrenal medulla system springs into action quickly and efficiently, while the pituitary-adrenal cortex system remains relatively stable. As soon as the emergency is over, the adrenalin response returns quickly to normal, while the cortisol response stays low. The smoothness and efficiency of the physiological arousal pattern is what characterizes the psychophysiological toughness response—a response that has important aftereffects on the brain. Such a restrained reaction prevents depletion of catecholamines, important brain neurotransmitters that affect mood and motivation.

Not so with the "untough." The physiological reactions of less resilient individuals tend to be excessive and longer lasting, even in the face of everyday hassles. The result is more intense and disorganizing arousal, less effective coping, and faster depletion of brain catecholamines, which can lead to helplessness and depression. With each tribulation, major or minor, less resilient individuals tend to over-respond, their arousal levels overwhelming them and rendering them unable to do much about the current situation, leading to little confidence in their future ability to cope.

That's where the real psychological significance of psychophysiological toughness comes in. Humans can do one thing animals can't: we can reflect on our own thoughts, feelings, and actions, conceptualize our responses in terms of what kind of person that makes us, and thereby anticipate how we'll react to future challenges. Dienstbier (1989) points out that the toughness response— or its absence—interacts with a person's psychological appraisal of his or her own ability to cope with challenge. This in turn contributes to the person's self-image as an effective master of adversity or a helpless reactor—a self-assessment that influences later psychophysiological reactions to stress.

This, then, is the psychophysiological rationale of most "mental conditioning" or "mental toughness training" programs for law enforcement, emergency services, and the military (Asken, 1993; Blum, 2000; Doss, 2007; Duran, 1999; Grossman & Christensen, 2007; Miller, 2008a): by learning to control one's perceptions, feelings, thoughts, and reactions in advance, through progressive practice and rehearsal, and in combination with proper operational training, the individual can hopefully develop a core of resilient toughness—a kind of flexible psychological armor—that will enable the person to face any challenge with improved confidence and effectiveness. Although individuals differ naturally in their innate resilience, just as they do in physical strength, virtually any service member can reinforce his or her psychological armor and ramp up their toughness skills by appropriate training and practice. Additionally, there are effective resilience-based intervention strategies that peers and clinicians can apply to the treatment of service members following their exposure to a potentially traumatic critical incident.

Toughness on the Field:
Mental Conditioning in Competitive Sports

From the time of ancient Sparta, when athletic competition served as actual preparation for warfare, sports have always represented a form of ritualized combat (Sherman, 2005)—that's why we take it so seriously. Accordingly, much of the research and practical advice on mental toughness in the public safety and emergency services professions comes from the domain of sports psychology (Bull, Shambrook, James, & Brooks, 2005; Goldberg, 1998; Gould, Hodge, Peterson, & Petlinchkoff, 1987; Jones, Hanton, & Connaughton, 2002; Loehr, 1995; Thelwell, Weston, & Greenlees, 2005). In reviewing this literature, I have been able to distill the diverse components and conceptual constructs of this field down to four primary qualities that characterize resilience and mental toughness in sports that, in turn, can be applied to the practical task of inculcating stress-resistance in law enforcement, emergency services, and military personnel (Miller, 2008a). These are confidence, motivation, focus, and resilience.

Confidence. A professional athlete puts him- or herself on the line with every game or competition. Excellent performers don't just do their craft, they are their craft. This orientation is probably familiar to those police officers, doctors, soldiers, performance artists, and others who view their occupations as more of a calling than a job (Hays & Brown, 2004). This takes confidence. Confident athletes have an unshakable belief in their own abilities and, more pointedly, that these abilities are up to the task of beating their opponent. They thrive on the pressure of competition because they possess the skills and temperament to cope adaptively with the stresses and anxieties of competition. Their resoluteness cannot be shaken by the performance or intimidation of the other players. Confident athletes are able to overcome their inevitable self-doubts by a variety of intuitive and learned coping mechanisms. Their confidence is stable and unbreakable precisely because it is based on a track record of honest appraisal, real accomplishment, and continual training that allows them to draw strength from their own physical conditioning which, in turn, generates further confidence, in a positive cycle (Bandura, 1977, 1986; Doss, 2006). And the development of positive performance expectations is a crucial factor in preparing personnel to operate under high-demand conditions (Locke, Frederick, Le, & Bubko, 1984; Salas, Driskell, & Hughes, 1996). In short, attitude does matter.

Motivation. While confidence sustains the athlete's performance, motivation spurs it forward. Confidence and motivation are reciprocal and mutually reinforcing: motivation impels performance which builds confidence which further increases motivation and so on. Motivated athletes have an insatiable desire to succeed and excel, a desire that comes from within and cannot be compelled or coerced. They strive to make the most of their abilities, to self-actualize (Maslow, 1968). They are willing to take risks and embrace new challenges and the pressure of competition only heightens their drive to succeed (Hays & Brown, 2004). They can tie short-term performance to long-term goals in order to sustain their motivation over bad stretches because they are committed to their craft for the long haul. Their motivation produces a powerful work ethic that impels them to "go the extra mile" in training and practice; they never coast, they're always moving forward. They compete with themselves as well as with others. As with confidence, motivation must be based on reality, and these athletes use their stumbles and failures as learning experiences to do better next time.

Focus. If motivation is the fuel that drives the performance engine, focus is the guidance system that allows the engine to stay on track toward the athlete's goals. As used here, the term focus has two meanings: focus on the moment-to-moment, here-and-now aspects of a particular training exercise or performance, and a more long-term, event-spanning focus on career goals. Being fully focused on a particular performance task enables the athlete to persevere in the face of external distractions. Focus is also internal, and skilled athletes have learned to monitor their inner physical and mental states, to be able to run a self-system check as needed, both to assess ongoing performance during a competition and to check themselves between performances. Focus also includes clarity of thinking, and many athletes will describe states of almost supernatural mental sharpness during intense competitions. This comes about through intensive and protracted training, so that when critical situations arise, the athlete is not overwhelmed by anxiety and complexity, but can switch into a smooth, efficient performance mode as needed (cf. the psychophysiological toughness response discussed earlier, Dienstbier, 1989).

Resilience. As used here, the term resilience describes the bounce-back that enables skilled athletes and other professionals to endure and prevail over physical injuries, mental shocks, and performance failures without burning out or melting down. Resilient athletes don't fold under pressure. They adapt to extreme conditions by using their training and experience to devise and implement moment-to-moment corrections of their performance in response to rapidly-changing circumstances. Even when knocked down, they quickly regain equilibrium and self-control without being overwhelmed. They can endure physical pain and emotional distress and maintain technique and sustained effort by what seems to be sheer force of will, but which is really a tough resilience that grows out of confidence and determination borne of training, perseverance, and expertise.

The core components of mental toughness are reciprocal and interactive. Resilience partly depends on confidence which, in turn, is based on a track record of accomplishment. Specifically with law enforcement, Doss (2006) notes that when an officer's confidence is degraded because of poor training or a negative outcome despite utilizing techniques he thought would work, this may have a deteriorative effect on subsequent performance and the recovery process may be painfully slow. This explains the seemingly obsessive nature of training that characterizes all high-performance fields. Proper training not only helps build skill and proficiency itself, it also helps inoculate the professional against corrosive self-doubt and feelings of failure in the case of a bad outcome (Miller, 2006, 2008a).

Fostering Recovery and Resilience Following Traumatic Events

While mental toughness training and psychological conditioning techniques can serve to inure and inoculate service members to many kinds of potentially traumatizing stressful events, there will always be some critical incidents so extreme that they overwhelm or attenuate the coping mechanisms of even some of the most resiliently tough personnel. In other cases, a particular event may have specific meaning to a particular officer and thus have a much greater impact than it would on someone else. In all these cases, we need additional strategies we can apply after the fact for maximizing resilient recovery and return to normal functioning in these service members.

Critical Incident Stress Debriefing

Well-known to emergency response clinicians, the intervention of critical incident stress debriefing (CISD) will only be summarized here. CISD is a structured group intervention designed to promote the emotional processing of traumatic events through the ventilation and normalization of reactions, as well as to facilitate preparation for possible future crisis experiences. CISD is one component of an integrated, comprehensive crisis intervention program spanning the critical incident continuum from pre-crisis, to crisis, to post-crisis phases, and subsumed under the heading of critical incident stress management (CISM), which has been adopted and modified for law enforcement and emergency services departments throughout the United States, Great Britain, Europe, Australia, and other parts of the world (Dyregrov, 1989, 1997; Everly & Mitchell, 1997; Everly, Flannery, & Mitchell, 2000; Mitchell & Everly, 1996, 2003).

The full CISM program includes: individual and organizational pre-crisis preparation; large-scale demobilization procedures following mass disasters; on-scene, one-on-one supportive counseling for acute, individual crisis reactions; defusings, which represent a shorter, compressed stress debriefing protocol for small groups under acute stress; critical incident stress debriefing, described more extensively below; family crisis intervention and supportive counseling; and referral for follow-up mental health services as needed (Everly & Mitchell, 1997; Mitchell & Everly, 1996, 2003).

A CISD debriefing is a peer-led, clinician-guided process that takes place within 24 to 72 hours of the critical incident and consists of a single group meeting of approximately 6–20 personnel that lasts about two to three hours. The formal CISD process consists of seven key phases, designed to assist psychological integration, beginning with more objective and descriptive levels of processing, progressing to the more personal and emotional, and back to the educative and integrative levels, focusing on both cognitive and emotional mastery of the traumatic event. These are introduction, fact, thought, reaction, symptom, education, and re-entry phases. Throughout the process, reactions to critical incident stress are conceptualized as normal responses to an abnormal situation and recovery and return to duty are emphasized, although the possible presence of residual symptoms is acknowledged.

Salutogenic Debriefing

One group of practitioners (Dunning, 1999; Paton & Smith, 1999; Paton et al., 2000; Stuhlmiller & Dunning, 2000; Violanti, 2000) has advocated a radical shift in the theory and practice of critical incident debriefing. Their criticism of the standard CISD model views it as pathologing stress reactions and offering debriefing as a quick-fix, one-size-fits-all package of therapeutic intervention. These authors propose an alternative salutogenic debriefing model that views critical incident reactions as opportunities for adaptive coping and personal growth.

Consistent with the concepts of resilience and posttraumatic growth, these authors propose that interventions for critical incidents should not foster the learned helplessness of a traumatized victim mentality but should encourage a sense of competence, confidence, resilience, hardiness, and learned resourcefulness (Almedom, 2005; Antonovsky, 1987; Higgins, 1994; Kobasa et al., 1982; Tedeschi & Calhoun, 1995; Tedeschi & Kilmer, 2005).

In fairness, the purpose of all traumatic stress interventions, including CISD, is to reduce hopelessness and helplessness and to foster adaptive and resilient coping in the face of a potentially overwhelming event. But going too far in the other direction and adopting a "Clarence the Angel" approach to intervention (Miller, 1998b) may only serve to put too much pressure on distressed officers who understandably may not be able to bring themselves to the point of turning a horrific episode into a personal growth experience, and may therefore feel like they're failures if they can't meet this excessively high bar of recovery and growth (see below). As always, clinicians and law enforcement administrators alike have to use their professional judgment.

More broadly, most authorities would endorse the idea that CISD, or any other systemized approach to intervention, should supplement and enhance—not replace—each individual's natural coping resources (McNally, Bryant, & Ehlers, 2003; Sheehan, Everly, & Langlieb, 2004). In other words, all psychological services for law enforcement should be in the direction of empowering officers to deal with challenges as independently and effectively as possible (Miller, 2006, 2008a). While many critical incidents will not require any special intervention, and while the majority of those that do will be well served by a CISD approach, it is the responsibility of departmental administrators, and the mental health professionals who advise them, to ensure that debriefing modalities are used responsibly and that other forms of clinically appropriate psychotherapeutic intervention are available to those who need them. CISD, like all successful treatment modalities, must be a living, evolving organism. Continued research and clinical ingenuity will hopefully further texturize and expand the stress debriefing approach into new and different applications (Mitchell & Levenson, 2006).

Mental Health Services for Recovery and Resilience

For some traumatized service members, a CISD debriefing may not suffice and more extensive, intensive, and individualized approaches to fostering recovery may be required, involving the services of mental health professionals.

Unfortunately, sometimes for good reason (Max, 2000), police officers have traditionally shunned these services, often perceiving its practitioners as ferrets and shills who are out to dig up dirt that their departments can use against them. Other cops may fear having their "head shrunk," harboring a notion of the psychotherapy process as akin to brainwashing, a humiliating and emasculating experience in which they are forced to lie on a couch and sob about their inner child. Less dramatically and more commonly, the idea of needing any kind of "mental help" implies weakness, cowardice, and lack of ability to do the job. In the environment of many departments, some officers realistically fear censure, stigmatization, ridicule, thwarted career advancement, and alienation from colleagues if they are perceived as the type who "folds under pressure." Still others in the department who may have something to hide may fear a colleague "spilling his guts" to the clinician and thereby blowing the malfeasor's cover (Miller, 1998b, 2006).

But the goal of law enforcement psychological services following a critical incident should always be to make officers stronger, not weaker. Sometimes a broken bone that has begun to heal crookedly has to be re-broken and reset properly for the individual to be able to walk normally again and, while the re-breaking may hurt, the pain is temporary and the effect is to restore and re-strengthen the limb. In the same way, an officer who is responding to critical incident stress with an ossified, malformed defensive mindset that's impeding his or her job performance and personal life may need to have those defenses challenged in a supportive atmosphere, so he or she can benefit from a healthy resetting of his mental state to deal with life more adaptively and courageously. He or she needs to regain the psychological strength to learn to walk the path of life again (Miller, 2006; Rudofossi, 2007; Toch, 2002).

Therapeutic Strategies for Recovery and Resilience

Psychotherapeutic strategies for law enforcement officers have been covered in detail elsewhere (Miller, 2006; 2008a). For purposes of the present discussion, the effectiveness of any therapeutic strategy in fostering resilient recovery will be determined by the timeliness, tone, style, and intent of the intervention. Effective psychological interventions with law enforcement officers and other service personnel share the following common elements (Blau, 1994; Fullerton, McCarroll, Ursano, & Wright, 1992; Wester & Lyubelsky, 2005).

- *Briefness.* Utilize only as much therapeutic contact as necessary to address the present problem. The officer does not want to become a "professional patient."

- *Limited focus.* Related to the above, the goal is not to solve all the officer's problems, but to assist in restabilization from the critical incident and provide stress-inoculation for future incidents.
- *Directness.* Therapeutic efforts are directed to resolve the current conflict or problem to reach a satisfactory short-term conclusion, while planning for the future if necessary.

In light of Violanti's (1999) conceptualization of police work as "civilian combat," it is interesting that a very similar intervention model has recently been articulated by military psychologist and U.S. Army Captain Bret Moore for dealing with soldiers experiencing combat stress (Munsey, 2006). The program goes under the acronym, BICEPS, which stands for

- *Brevity.* Treatment is short, addressing the problem at hand.
- *Immediacy.* Intervention takes place quickly, before symptoms worsen.
- *Centrality.* Psychological treatment is set apart from medical facilities, as a way to reduce the stigma soldiers might feel about seeking mental health services (although it could be argued that putting mental health treatment in a special category might make some soldiers feel alienated from their colleagues who've suffered "real" injuries; accordingly, clinicians should use their judgment).
- *Expectancy.* A soldier experiencing problems with combat stress is expected to return to duty.
- *Proximity.* Soldiers are treated as close to their units as possible and are not evacuated from the area of operations.
- *Simplicity.* Besides therapy, the basics of a good meal, hot shower, and a comfortable place to sleep ensure a soldier's basic physical needs are met.

Utilizing Cognitive Defenses for Resilience

In psychology, defense mechanisms are the mental stratagems the mind uses to protect itself from unpleasant thoughts, feelings, impulses, and memories. While the normal use of such defenses enables the average person to avoid conflict and ambiguity and maintain some consistency to their personality and belief system, most psychologists would agree that an overuse of defenses to wall off too much unpleasant thought and feeling leads to a rigid and dysfunctional approach to coping with life. Accordingly, much of the ordinary psychotherapeutic process involves carefully helping the patient to relinquish pathological defenses so that he or she can learn to deal with internal conflicts more constructively.

However, in the face of immediately traumatizing critical incidents, the last thing the affected person needs is to have his or her defenses stripped away. If you sustain a broken leg on the battlefield, the medic binds and braces the limb as best he can and helps you quickly hobble out of the danger zone, reserving more extensive medical treatment for a later, safer time and place. Similarly, for an acute psychological trauma, the proper utilization of psychological defenses can serve as an important psychological splint that enables the person to function in the immediate posttraumatic aftermath and eventually be able to productively resolve and integrate the traumatic experience when the luxury of therapeutic time can be afforded (Janik, 1991).

Indeed, whether in their regular daily work or following critical incidents, law enforcement and public safety personnel usually need little help in applying defense mechanisms on their own. Examples (Durham, McCammon, & Allison, 1985; Henry, 2004; Taylor, Wood, & Lechtman, 1983) include:

- *Denial.* "Put it out of my mind; focus on other things; avoid situations or people who remind me of it."
- *Rationalization.* "I had no choice; things happen for a reason; it could have been worse; other people have it worse; most people would react the way I'm doing."
- *Displacement/projection.* "It was Command's fault for issuing such a stupid order; I didn't have the right backup; they're all trying to blame me for everything."
- *Refocus on positive attributes.* "Hey, this was just a fluke—I'm usually a great marksman; I'm not gonna let this jam me up."
- *Refocus on positive behaviors.* "Okay, I'm gonna get more training, increase my knowledge and skill so I'll never be caught with my pants down like this again."

Janik (1991) proposes that, in the short term, clinicians actively support and bolster psychological defenses that temporarily enable the officer to continue functioning. Just as a physical crutch is an essential part of orthopedic rehabilitation when the leg-injured patient is learning to walk again, a psychological crutch is perfectly adaptive and productive if it enables the officer to get back on his emotional two feet as soon as possible after a traumatic critical incident. Only later, when he or she is making the bumpy transition back to normal life, are potentially maladaptive defenses revisited as possible impediments to progress.

And just as some orthopedic patients may always need one or another kind of assistive walking device, like a special shoe or a cane, some degree of psychological defensiveness may persist in officers so they can otherwise productively pursue their work and life tasks. Indeed, rare among us is the person who is completely defense-free. Only when defenses are used inappropriately and for too long—past the point where we should be walking on our own psychological two feet—do they constitute a "crutch" in the pejorative sense.

Survival Resource Training

As noted earlier, a recently evolving trend in trauma psychotherapy emphasizes the importance of accessing and bolstering the patient's natural powers of resilience, and the constructive marshalling of strength and resistance to stress and disability (Calhoun & Tedeschi, 1999; Dunning, 1999; Stuhlmiller & Dunning, 2000; Tedeschi & Calhoun 1995; Tedeschi & Kilmer, 2005; Violanti, 2000). In this vein, Roger Solomon (1988, 1991, 1995) has been ahead of the curve in capitalizing on the idea that constructive denial of vulnerability and mortality can be an adaptive response for law enforcement officers coping with ongoing critical incidents and their immediate aftermath.

Solomon (1988, 1991) points out that, following critical incidents characterized by fear, danger, injury, or death, officers often dwell on their mistakes and overlook what they did right in terms of coping with their emotions and getting the job done. Thus, being realistically reminded by the clinician of their own adaptive coping efforts may prove especially empowering because it draws upon strengths that came from the officer him- or herself. Termed survival resource training, this intervention allows officers to utilize the fear response to tap into a state of controlled strength, increased awareness, confidence, and clarity of mind—many of the features, noted earlier, that characterize high-performance athletes.

In this technique, the clinician encourages the officer to view the critical incident from a detached, objective point of view, "like you were watching a movie of yourself," and to go through the incident "frame-by-frame." At the point where he imagines himself fully engaging in this activity (negotiating with a hostage-taker, arresting a dangerous felon, taking cover, firing his weapon, etc.), the officer is instructed to "focus on the part of you enabling you to respond."

In most cases, the survival resource training procedure leads to a mental reframe characterized by controlled strength, heightened awareness, confidence, and mental clarity, as the officer mentally zooms in on his capability to respond, instead of focusing on the immobilizing fear, perceptions of weakness, loss of control, or perceptual distortions. Often, this results in the officer's being reminded of how he put his fear on hold and rose to the occasion in order to get the job done. The reframing thus focuses on resiliency instead of vulnerability, strength instead of weakness.

In addition to processing past critical incidents, realistic feelings of efficacy and competence can also shade over into future incidents, as officers have reported increased confidence and ability to handle subsequent calls, such as arrests, shooting incidents, domestic disturbances, and traffic chases. In addition, officers have felt more confident in other non-emergency but stressful situations, such as court testimony, and personal matters, such as resolving family conflicts (Solomon, 1988, 1991, 1995). It is especially gratifying to clinicians and officers alike when their mutual efforts can turn vicious cycles of demoralization and despair into positive cycles of confidence and optimism. Indeed, this is the essence of the resilience model of psychotherapy.

Finding Meaning in Adversity: "Existential Toughness"

As useful as salutogenic and growth-oriented therapeutic approaches may sometimes be, trying to force-feed a "positive meaning" or "life lesson" from a noxious experience can sometimes be counterproductive: some bad things in life just plain suck and no amount of philosophical sugar-coating is going to make a turdball taste like a jelly donut. But human beings are meaning-making creatures, and people will naturally grope to find reasons or messages hidden in even the most grotesque catastrophes. When this comes from the officer him- or herself, it must be respected and nurtured in the psychotherapy process because a consolidation of one's worldview is, in itself, a resiliency-enhancing process (Miller, 1998b).

In general, existential treatment strategies that focus on a quest for meaning, rather than just alleviation of symptoms, may productively channel the worldview conflicts generated by the traumatic event. This may include helping the officer to formulate an acceptable "survivor mission" or "professional purpose" (Henry, 2004; Rudofossi, 2007; Shalev et al., 1993). In the best cases, the rift and subsequent reintegration of the personality may lead to an expanded self-concept, a renewed sense of purpose, and a new level of psychological, spiritual, and career growth (Bonanno, 2005; Calhoun & Tedeschi, 1999; Luthar, Cicchetti, & Becker, 2000; Tedeschi & Calhoun, 1995, 2004; Tedeschi & Kilmer, 2005). Of course, not all traumatized service members will be able to achieve this successful reintegration of their ordeal and many will struggle with at least some vestige of emotional injury for a long time, perhaps for life (Everstine & Everstine, 1993; Matsakis, 1994; McCann & Pearlman, 1990; Miller, 1998b).

Therefore, my main caution about these transformational therapeutic conceptualizations is that they be presented as an opportunity, not an obligation. The extraction of meaning from adversity is something that must ultimately come from the officer him- or herself, not be foisted upon him or her by the clinician. Such existential "forced conversions" are often motivated by a need to reinforce the clinician's own meaning system, or they may be part of what I call a therapeutic "Clarence-the-Angel fantasy" (Miller, 1998b), wherein the enlightened clinician swoops down and, by dint of the therapist's brilliantly insightful ministrations, rescues the hapless patient from his or her darkest hour.

Realistically, as mental health clinicians, we can hardly expect all or even most of our traumatized patients to miraculously transform their tragedy and acquire a fresh, revitalized, George Bailyean outlook on life—how many of us would respond that well? But, as noted above, human beings do crave meaning (Yalom, 1980) and if a philosophical or religious orientation can nourish the officer in his or her journey back to the land of the living, then the therapeutic role must sometimes stretch to include some measure of guidance in affairs of the spirit.

Organizational and Departmental Support

Not all interventions involve psychotherapy or debriefings. Following a department-wide critical incident, such as a line-of-duty death, serial homicide investigation, or mass casualty rescue and recovery operation, the departmental psychologist or consulting mental health professional can advise and guide law enforcement agencies in encouraging and implementing several organizational response measures (Alexander, 1993; Alexander & Walker, 1994; Alexander & Wells, 1991; DeAngelis, 1995; Fullerton et al., 1992; Palmer, 1983). Many of these strategies are proactively applicable as part of training before a critical incident occurs. Others apply even when there is no specific incident, but just involve cops in a jam seeking support and relief. Some specific organizational and leadership measures that can promote recovery and resilience include those that follow.

- *Encourage mutual support among peers and supervisors.* The former typically occurs anyway; the latter may need some explicit reinforcement. Although not typically team workers like firefighters or paramedics, police officers frequently work as partners and understand that some degree of shared decision-making and mutual reassurance can enhance effective performance on the job, as well as helping to deal with tragedy.
- *Utilize humor as a coping mechanism to facilitate emotional insulation and group bonding.* The first forestalls excessive identification with victims, the second encourages mutual group support via a shared language. Of course, as noted earlier, mental health clinicians and departmental supervisors need to carefully monitor the line between adaptive humor that encourages healing and gratuitous nastiness that only serves to entrench cynicism and despair.
- *Make use of appropriate rituals that give meaning and dignity to an otherwise existentially disorienting experience.* This includes not only reli-

gious rites related to mourning, but such respectful protocols as a military-style honor guard to attend bodies before disposition, and the formal acknowledgement of actions above and beyond the call of duty.
- *Make productive use of grief leadership.* This involves the commanding officer demonstrating by example that it's okay to express grief and mourn the death of fallen comrades or civilians, and that the dignified expression of one's feelings about the tragedy will be supported, not denigrated. Indeed, this healthy combination of masterful task-orientation and validated expression of legitimate grief has largely characterized the response of rescue and recovery personnel at the New York World Trade Center and other mass-casualty disaster sites (Henry, 2004; Regehr & Bober, 2004).
- *Show respect for psychological issues and psychological services.* If the departmental brass don't believe that encouraging the appropriate utilization of psychological services is a valid way of expressing their concern and support for their troops' welfare, then the rank and file won't buy it, either. Psychological referrals should be destigmatized and supported as a health and safety measure, the same as with medical referrals and general fitness maintenance.

In summary, law enforcement officers and other service members who cope resiliently with critical incidents prepare their minds and bodies proactively through rigorous training, and avail themselves of legitimate support services during and after a critical incident. In this way, they become tough, act tough, and stay tough, while retaining the mental agility, flexibility, resiliency, and humanity that are necessary for top-notch law enforcement and emergency services work.

References

Alexander, D.A. & Walker, L.G. (1994). "A study of methods used by Scottish police officers to cope with work-related stress." *Stress Medicine, 10,* 131–138.

Alexander, D.A. & Wells, A. (1991). "Reactions of police officers to body-handling after a major disaster: A before-and-after comparison." *British Journal of Psychiatry, 159,* 547–555.

Alexander, F. (1950). *Psychosomatic medicine: Its principles and applications.* New York: Norton.

Almedom, A.M. (2005). "Resilience, hardiness, sense of coherence, and post-traumatic growth: All paths leading to 'light at the end of the tunnel'?" *Journal of Loss and Trauma, 10,* 253–265.

American Psychiatric Association (2000). *Diagnostic and statistical manual of mental disorders* (4th ed., text revision). Washington DC: American Psychiatric Association.

Antonovsky, A. (1979). *Health, stress, and coping.* San Francisco: Jossey-Bass.

Antonovsky, A. (1987). *Unraveling the mystery of health: How people manage stress and stay well.* San Francisco: Jossey-Bass.

Antonovsky, A. (1990). "Personality and health: Testing the sense of coherence model." In H.S. Friedman (Ed.), *Personality and disease* (pp. 155–177). New York: Wiley.

Asken, M.J. (1993). *PsycheResponse: Psychological skills for optimal performance by emergency responders.* Englewood Cliffs: Regents/Prentice Hall.

Bandura, A. (1977). "Self-efficacy: Toward a unifying theory of behavioral change." *Psychological Review, 84,* 191–215.

Bandura, A. (1865). *Introduction a l'etude de la medecine experimentale.* Paris: Bailliere et Fils.

Bernard, C. (1994). *Psychological services for law enforcement.* New York: Wiley.

Bifulco, A.T., Brown, G.W. & Harris, T.O. (1987). "Childhood loss of parent, lack of adequate parental care and adult depression: A replication." *Journal of Affective Disorders, 12,* 115–128.

Blau, T.H. (1994). *Psychological services for law enforcement.* New York: Wiley.

Blum, L.N. (2000). *Force under pressure: How cops live and why they die.* New York: Lantern Books.

Bonanno, G.A. (2005). "Resilience in the face of potential trauma." *Current Directions in Psychological Science, 14,* 135–138.

Bowman, M. (1997). *Individual differences in posttraumatic response: Problems with the adversity-distress connection.* Mahwah, NJ: Erlbaum.

Bowman, M.L. (1999). "Individual differences in posttraumatic distress: Problems with the DSM-IV model." *Canadian Journal of Psychiatry, 44,* 21–33.

Brewin, C.R., Andrews, B., Valentine, J.D. (2000). "Meta-analysis of risk factors for posttraumatic stress disorder in trauma-exposed adults." *Journal of Consulting and Clinical Psychology, 68,* 748–766.

Bull, S.J., Shambrook, C.J., James, W. & Brooks, J.E. (2005). "Towards an understanding of mental toughness in elite English cricketers." *Journal of Applied Sport Psychology, 17,* 209–227.

Calhoun, L.G. & Tedeschi, R.G. (1999) *Facilitating posttraumatic growth.* Mahwah, NJ: Erlbaum.

Cannon, W.B. (1914). "The interrelations of emotions as suggested by recent physiological researchers." *American Journal of Psychology, 25,* 256–282.

Cannon, W.B. (1939). *The wisdom of the body.* Philadelphia: Norton.

Carlier, I.V.E. & Gersons, B.P.R. (1995). "Partial PTSD: The issue of psychological scars and the occurrence of PTSD symptoms." *Journal of Nervous and Mental Disease, 183,* 107–109.

Carlier, I.V.E., Lamberts, R.D., & Gersons, B.P.R. (1997). "Risk factors for posttraumatic stress symptomatology in police officers: A prospective analysis." *Journal of Nervous and Mental Disease, 185,* 498–506.

DeAngelis, T. (1995). "Firefighters' PTSD at dangerous levels." *APA Monitor,* February, pp. 36–37.

Dienstbier, R.A. (1989). "Arousal and physiological toughness: Implications for mental and physical health." *Psychological Review, 96,* 84–100.

Doss, W. (2006). }Exercising emotional control." *Police,* March, pp. 68–73.

Doss, W. (2007). *Condition to win: Dynamic techniques for performance oriented mental conditioning.* Flushing, NY: Looseleaf Law Press.

Dunning, C. (1999). "Postintervention strategies to reduce police trauma: A paradigm shift." In J.M. Violanti & D. Paton (Eds.), *Police trauma: Psychological aftermath of civilian combat* (pp. 269–289). Springfield, IL: Charles C Thomas.

Durham, T.W., McCammon, S.L. & Allison, E.J. (1985). "The psychological impact of disaster on rescue personnel." *Annals of Emergency Medicine, 14,* 664–668.

Dyregrov, A. (1989). "Caring for helpers in disaster situations: Psychological debriefing." *Disaster Management, 2,* 25–30.

Dyregrov, A. (1997). "The process in psychological debriefing." *Journal of Traumatic Stress, 10,* 589–605.

Evans, R.W. (1992). "The postconcussion syndrome and the sequelae of mild head injury." *Neurologic Clinics, 10,* 815–847.

Everly, G.S., Flannery, R.B. & Mitchell, J.T. (2000). "Critical incident stress management: A review of the literature." *Aggression and Violent Behavior, 5,* 23–40.

Everly, G.S. & Mitchell, J.T. (1997). *Critical incident stress management (CISM): A new era and standard of care in crisis intervention.* Ellicott City: Chevron.

Everstine, D.S. & Everstine, L. (1993). *The trauma response: Treatment for emotional injury.* New York: Norton.

Fullerton, C.S., McCarroll, J.E., Ursano, R.J. & Wright, K.M. (1992). "Psychological responses of rescue workers: Firefighters and trauma." *American Journal of Orthopsychiatry, 62,* 371–378.

Garmezy, N. (1993). "Children in poverty: Resilience despite risk." *Psychiatry, 56,* 127–136.

Garmezy, N., Masten, A.S. & Tellegen, A. (1984). "The study of stress and competence in children: A building block for developmental psychopathology." *Child Development, 55,* 97–111.

Gentz, D. (1991). "The psychological impact of critical incidents on police officers." In J. Reese, J. Horn & C. Dunning (Eds.), *Critical incidents in policing* (pp. 119–121). Washington DC: U.S. Government Printing Office.

Goldberg, A.S. (1998). *Sports slump busting: 10 steps to mental toughness and peak performance.* Champaign, IL: Human Kinetics.

Gould, D., Hodge, K., Peterson, K. & Petlichkoff, L. (1987). "Psychological foundations of coaching: Similarities and differences among intercollegiate wrestling coaches." *The Sport Psychologist, 1,* 293–308.

Grossman, D. & Christensen, L.W. (2007). *On combat: The psychology and physiology of deadly conflict in war and in peace.* Millstadt, IL: PPCT Research Publications.

Hays, K.F. & Brown, C.H. (2004). *You're on! Consulting for peak performance.* Washington DC: American Psychological Association.

Henry, V.E. (2004). *Death work: Police, trauma, and the psychology of survival.* New York: Oxford University Press.

Hoge, E.A., Austin, E.D. & Pollack, M.H. (2007). "Resilience: Research evidence and conceptual considerations for posttraumatic stress disorder." *Depression and Anxiety, 24,* 139–152.

Higgins, G.O. (1994). *Resilient adults: Overcoming a cruel past.* San Francisco: Jossey-Bass.

Janik, J. (1991) "What value are cognitive defenses in critical incident stress?" In J. Reese, J. Horn & C. Dunning (Eds.), *Critical incidents in policing* (pp. 149–158). Washington DC: U.S. Government Printing Office.

Jones, J.G., Hanton, S. & Connaughton, D. (2002). "What is this thing called mental toughness? An investigation of elite performers." *Journal of Applied Sport Psychology, 14,* 205–218.

Kardiner, A. (1941). *The traumatic neuroses of war.* Washington DC: National Research Council.

Karlsson, I. & Christianson, S.A. (2003). "The phenomenology of traumatic experiences in police work." *Policing: An International Journal of Police Strategies and Management, 26,* 419–438.

Kobasa, S.C. (1979a). "Personality and resistance to illness." *American Journal of Community Psychology, 7,* 413–423.

Kobasa, S.C. (1979b). "Stressful life events, personality, and health: An inquiry into hardiness." *Journal of Personality and Social Psychology, 37,* 1–11.

Kobasa, S.C., Maddi, S. & Cahn, S. (1982). "Hardiness and health: A prospective study." *Journal of Personality and Social Psychology, 42,* 168–177.

Locke, E.A., Frederick, E., Lee, C., & Bubko, P. (1984). "Effect of self-efficacy goals and task strategy on task performance." *Journal of Applied Psychology, 64,* 241–251.

Loehr, J.E. (1995). *The new toughness training for sports.* New York: Penguin.

Luthar, S.S. (1991). "Vulnerability and resilience: A study of high-risk adolescents." *Child Development, 62,* 600–616.

Luthar, S.S., Cicchetti, D. & Becker, B. (2000). "The construct of resilience: A critical evaluation and guidelines for future work." *Child Development, 71,* 543–562.

Maddi, S.R. & Khoshaba, D.M. (1994). "Hardiness and mental health." *Journal of Personality Assessment, 63,* 265–274.

Maddi, S.R. & Khoshaba, D.M. (2005). *Resilience at work: How to succeed no matter what life throws at you.* New York: Amacom.

Maslow, A.H. (1968). *Toward a psychology of being* (2nd ed.). Princeton: VanNostrand.

Matsakis, A. (1994). *Post-traumatic stress disorder: A complete treatment guide.* Oakland, CA: New Harbinger.

Max, D.J. (2000). "The cop and the therapist." *New York Times Magazine,* December 3, pp. 94–98.

McCann, I.L. & Pearlman, L.A. (1990). *Psychological trauma and the adult survivor: Theory, therapy, and transformation.* New York: Brunner/Mazel.

McNally, R.J., Bryant, R.A. & Ehlers, A. (2003). "Does early psychological intervention promote recovery from posttraumatic stress?" *Psychological Science in the Public Interest, 4,* 45–79.

Miller, L. (1990). *Inner natures: Brain, self, and personality.* New York: St. Martin's Press.

Miller, L. (1998a). "Ego autonomy and the healthy personality: Psychodynamics, cognitive style, and clinical applications." *Psychoanalytic Review, 85,* 423–448.

Miller, L. (1998b). *Shocks to the system: Psychotherapy of traumatic disability syndromes.* New York: Norton.

Miller, L. (2006). *Practical police psychology: Stress management and crisis intervention for law enforcement.* Springfield, IL: Charles C Thomas.

Miller, L. (2008a). *METTLE: Mental toughness training for law enforcement.* Flushing, NY: Looseleaf Law Publications.

Miller, L. (2008b). *Counseling crime victims: Practical strategies for mental health professionals.* New York: Springer.

Miller, L. (2008c). *From difficult to disturbed: Understanding and managing dysfunctional employees.* New York: Amacom.

Mitchell, J.T. & Everly, G.S. (1996). *Critical incident stress debriefing: An operations manual for the prevention of traumatic stress among emergency services and disaster workers* (2nd ed.). Ellicott City: Chevron.

Mitchell, J.T. & Everly, G.S. (2003). *Critical incident stress management (CISM): Basic group crisis intervention* (3rd ed.). Ellicott City: ICISF.

Mitchell, J. & Levenson, R.L. (2006). "Some thoughts on providing effective mental health critical care for police departments after line-of-duty deaths." *International Journal of Emergency Mental Health, 8,* 1–4.

Munsey, C. (2006). "Soldier support." *Monitor on Psychology,* April, pp. 36–38.

Nietzsche, F. (1969). *Twilight of the gods.* London: Penguin.

Palmer, C.E. (1983). "A note about paramedics' strategies for dealing with death and dying." *Journal of Occupational Psychology. 56,* 83–86.

Paton, D. & Smith, L. (1999). "Assessment, conceptual and methodological issues in researching traumatic stress in police officers." In J.M. Violanti & D. Paton (Eds.), *Police trauma: Psychological aftermath of civilian combat* (pp. 13–24). Springfield, IL: Charles C Thomas.

Paton, D., Smith, L., Violanti, J.M. & Eranen, L. (2000). "Work-related traumatic stress: Risk, vulnerability, and resilience." In J. Violanti, D. Paton & C. Dunning (Eds.), *Posttraumatic stress intervention: Challenges, issues, and perspectives* (pp. 187–203). Springfield, IL: Charles C Thomas.

Pizarro, J., Silver, R.C. & Prouse, J. (2006). "Physical and mental health costs of traumatic experiences among Civil War veterans." *Archives of General Psychiatry, 63,* 193–200.

Regehr, C. & Bober, T. (2004). *In the line of fire: Trauma in the emergency services.* New York: Oxford University Press.

Rosen, G. (1975). "Nostalgia: A forgotten psychological disorder." *Psychosomatic Medicine, 5,* 342–347.

Rubenstein, J.L., Heeren, T., Houseman, D., Rubin, C. & Stechler, G. (1989). "Suicidal behavior in "normal" adolescents: Risk and protective factors." *American Journal of Orthopsychiatry, 59,* 59–71.

Rudofossi, D. (2007). *Working with traumatized police officer-patients: A clinician's guide to complex PTSD syndromes in public safety professionals.* Amityville, NY: Baywood.

Rutter, M. (1985). "Resilience in the face of adversity: Protective factors and resistance to psychiatric disorder." *British Journal of Psychiatry, 147,* 598–611.

Rutter, M. (1987). "Psychosocial resilience and protective mechanisms." *American Journal of Orthopsychiatry, 57,* 316–331.

Rutter, M., Tizard, J., Yule, W., Graham, P. & Whitmore, K. (1976). "Research report: Isle of Wight studies, 1964–1974." *Psychological Medicine, 6,* 313–332.

Salas, E., Driskell, J.E., & Hughes, S. (1996). "The study of stress and human performance." In J.E. Driskell & E. Salas (Eds.), *Stress and human performance* (pp. 1–45). Mahwah, NJ: Erlbaum.

Selye, H. (1956). *The stress of life.* New York: McGraw-Hill.

Selye, H. (1973). "The evolution of the stress concept." *American Scientist, 61,* 692–699.

Selye, H. (1975). *Stress without distress.* New York: Signet.

Shalev, A.Y., Galai, T. & Eth, S. (1993). "Levels of trauma; A multidimensional approach to the treatment of PTSD." *Psychiatry, 56,* 166–167.

Sheehan, D.C., Everly, G.S. & Langlieb, A. (2004). "Current best practices: Coping with major critical incidents." *FBI Law Enforcement Bulletin,* September, pp. 1–13.

Sherman, N. (2005). *Stoic warriors: The ancient philosophy behind the military mind.* New York: Oxford University Press.

Solomon, R.M. (1988). "Mental conditioning: The utilization of fear." In J.T. Reese & J.M. Horn (Eds.), *Police psychology: Operational assistance* (pp. 391–407). Washington DC: U.S. Government Printing Office.

Solomon, R.M. (1991). "The dynamics of fear in critical incidents: Implications for training and treatment." In J.T. Reese, J.M. Horn & C. Dunning (Eds.), *Critical incidents in policing* (pp. 347–358). Washington DC: Federal Bureau of Investigation.

Solomon, R.M. (1995). "Critical incident stress management in law enforcement." In G.S. Everly (Ed.), *Innovations in disaster and trauma psychology: Applications in emergency services and disaster response* (pp. 123–157). Ellicott City: Chevron.

Southard, E. (1919). *Shell-shock and other neuropsychiatric problems.* Boston: Leonard.

Stuhlmiller, C. & Dunning, C. (2000). "Challenging the mainstream: From pathogenic to salutogenic models of posttrauma intervention." In J. Violanti, D. Paton & C. Dunning (Eds.), *Posttraumatic stress intervention: Challenges, issues, and perspectives* (pp. 10–42). Springfield, IL: Charles C Thomas.

Taylor, S.E., Wood, J.V. & Lechtman, R.R. (1983). "It could be worse: Selective evaluation as a response to victimization." *Journal of Social Issues, 39,* 19–40.

Tedeschi, R.G. & Calhoun, L.G. (1995). *Trauma and transformation: Growing in the aftermath of suffering.* Thousand Oaks, CA: Sage.

Tedeschi, R.G. & Calhoun, L.G. (2004). "Posttraumatic growth: Conceptual foundations and empirical evidence." *Psychological Inquiry, 15,* 1–18.

Tedeschi, R.G. & Kilmer, R.P. (2005). "Assessing strengths, resilience, and growth to guide clinical interventions." *Professional Psychology: Research and Practice, 36,* 230–237.

Thelwell, R.C., Weston, N. & Greenlees, I. (2005). "Defining and understanding mental toughness within soccer." *Journal of Applied Sport Psychology, 17,* 326–332.

Toch, H. (2002). *Stress in policing.* Washington DC: American Psychological Association.

Trimble, M.R. (1981). *Post-traumatic neurosis: From railway spine to whiplash.* New York: Wiley.

Violanti, J.M. (1999). "Death on duty: Police survivor trauma." In J.M. Violanti & D. Paton (Eds.), *Police trauma: Psychological aftermath of civilian combat* (pp. 139–158). Springfield, IL: Charles C Thomas.

Violanti, J.M. (2000). "Scripting trauma: The impact of pathogenic intervention." In J. Violanti, D. Paton & C. Dunning (Eds.), *Posttraumatic stress intervention: Challenges, issues, and perspectives* (pp. 153–165). Springfield, IL: Charles C Thomas.

Weiner, H. (1977). *Psychobiology and human disease.* New York: Elsevier.

Weiner, H. (1992). *Perturbing the organism: The biology of stressful experience.* Chicago: University of Chicago Press.

Werner, E.E. (1989). "High-risk children in young adulthood: A longitudinal study from birth to 32 years." *American Journal of Orthopsychiatry, 59,* 72–81.

Werner, E.E. & Smith, R.S. (1992). *Overcoming the odds: High risk children from birth to adulthood.* Ithaca, NY: Cornell University Press.

Wester, S.R. & Lyubelsky, J. (2005). "Supporting the thin blue line: Gender-sensitive therapy with male police officers." *Professional Psychology: Research and Practice, 36,* 51–58.

Wilson, J.P. (1994). "The historical evolution of PTSD diagnostic criteria: From Freud to DSM-IV." *Journal of Traumatic Stress, 7,* 681–698.

Yalom, I.D. (1980). *Existential psychotherapy.* New York: Basic Books.

Zimrin, H. (1986). "A profile of survival." *Child Abuse and Neglect, 10,* 339–349.

Discussion Questions

1. As a general trait factor, there are certain features associated with resilience to adverse life events in children and adults. What do these include?

2. Kobasa introduced the concept of *hardiness*, which has been defined as a stable personality resource consisting of three psychological attitudes and cognitions. What are they?

3. Antonovsky has proposed a stress/health-mediating personality construct termed *sense of coherence*, which is expressed in the form of three component orientations or beliefs. What are they?

4. Paton and colleagues have delineated a core set of resiliency factors that enable officers to withstand and even prevail in the face of seemingly overwhelming trauma. What do these include?

5. The modern study of the psychophysiology of stress is generally regarded as beginning with Claude Bernard's concept of the *milieu internal*. What does this mean?

6. In the early 20th century, Walter Cannon used the term *homeostasis*. To what does this refer?

7. Probably the most well-known account of the stress response comes from the work of Hans Selye, whose active research spanned the decades from the 1930s to the 1970s. He developed the model of the *general adaptation syndrome*, which consists of three overlapping but distinct stages. What are these three stages? What occurs at each stage?

8. What two main physiological systems underlie the toughness response?

9. How do the "untough" react to stress?

10. The author has identified four primary qualities that characterize resilience and mental toughness in sports and can be applied to the practical task of inculcating stress-resistance in law enforcement, emergency services, and military personnel. What are these four primary qualities?

11. How does the author define critical incident stress debriefing?

12. What does the full critical incident stress management program include?

13. Effective psychological interventions with law enforcement officers and other service personnel share certain common elements. What are they?

14. How are defense mechanism defined in psychology?

15. In their regular daily work or following critical incidents, law enforcement and public safety personnel usually need a little help in applying defense mechanisms on their own. What examples were provided by the author?

16. What organizational and leadership measures can promote recovery?

34

Stress Management Techniques: A Practical Approach

Richard F. Cipriano

As has already been discussed in this text, stress is your body's response to any stimulus. In law enforcement, that stress can be any adaptive change that you must make, ranging from a real or perceived physical threat in the field to achieving a promotion or long desired duty assignment. Especially for a cop on patrol, routine everyday events can also create a continuous flow of potentially stressful events.

Stress can be set off by one or a combination of internal and external triggers. Physiologically, adrenaline output increases, your heart pumps faster, and your breathing rate becomes elevated. These bodily responses are normal and positive if properly channeled for a short period of time; however, if there is no release, then these stress responses may have a negative impact. This negative effect may produce symptoms such as chronic fatigue, headaches, sleeping and eating problems, inability to focus or concentrate, and general irritability, as well as other physical problems.

Law enforcement is an especially stressful profession, one in which your nervous system is always ready to react to a crisis, which in itself may create a constant state of tension. As such, enforcement officers are routinely poised in this mode and may react to small stresses in the same manner they would react to real emergencies. The cumulative energy created in the body to meet these conditions subsequently must be discharged in order to bring your body back into a state of homeostasis.

Ongoing and repeated episodes of the "fight or flight" reaction deplete your energy and, if not addressed, may result in a downward spiral that can lead to emotional burnout and varying degrees of exhaustion. Therefore, proactive steps to break this downward spiral can be achieved by learning techniques to manage stress and to protect and increase your energy bank.

It is less important whether the stress is from a significant life event or an accumulation of chronic daily stressors. Rather, it is your response to these episodes that, in the long run, will determine the overall impact these stressors will have on your personal and professional life.

Your interpretation of an experience sets the stage for how you deal with the event. For example, on the one hand, interpreting a frown on your supervisor's face while he reads your report to mean a substandard report may be stress provoking. On the other hand, interpreting the same look on your supervisor's face as discomfort from a muscle strain he/she has suffered will not be as stressful.

Perception becomes reality; it is therefore imperative that you gather as much information as possible to make a logical and rational decision as well as be willing to incorporate any new information when making a judgment.

Measuring Stress

The identification and study of stress within the law enforcement community have been on-going. The hope is that through prevention and early intervention, officers will be less likely to suffer from stress related disorders. There are a number of stress measures that have been used for law enforcement. Two early instruments specifically developed for law enforcement professionals are the Police Stress Survey (Spielberger et al., 1981), a 60-item measurement of stress, and the Law Enforcement Critical Life Events Scale (Sewell, 1983), a 144-item instrument.

More recently, the Law Enforcement Officer Stress Survey (LEOSS) is a brief, early-warning stress-screening measure for law enforcement officers. This scenario-based, 25-item scale was developed by FBI Supervisory Special Agent Donald Sheehan and Dr. Vincent Van Hasselt and is discussed in Part Two of this book.

Techniques for Relief of Stress

The hands-on techniques discussed here are not an exhaustive list of approaches; there are a number of mind-body alternative exercises beyond the scope of this chapter. The description of each technique provides a brief overview of the process and is for illustrative purposes only. As such, the interested reader is encouraged to seek additional information and professional guidance prior to engaging in these techniques.

Guided Imagery/Visualization

Guided Imagery uses your imagination to direct your thoughts toward a stress-free and soothing scene. The mind-body connection makes it possible to use your senses to visualize a scene as if you are really there. This technique uses your imagination to help you relax and reduce tension. In visualization, you mentally transport yourself to a scene or time of tranquility, inducing the state of relaxation or homeostasis.

- To begin, loosen your clothing, sit in a comfortable chair or lie down in a quiet place, and close your eyes.
- Relax your muscles as much as possible.
- Create a mental image using all of your senses: sight, hearing, smell, touch and taste. Imagine a pleasant, peaceful scene, such as a lush green forest with trees, sunlight beaming through the tree limbs, blue sky, soft clouds and groundcover of leaves and rocks. Incorporate the sounds of wind in the trees, a running brook and the rustling of rabbits and squirrels. Then add the smell of pine trees, the touch of tree bark and the taste of spring water.
- As you picture yourself in this setting, use affirmations that reinforce your ability to relax. Use the present tense and positive statements, such as "I am letting go of stress" and "I feel relaxed and refreshed."

I'd encourage the reader to practice visualization three times a day. Visualization exercises are easiest while lying in bed in the morning and at night, especially after a trying day.

Meditation

Meditation helps you clear your mind of stressful thoughts. Meditation has a long-standing history with many Eastern religions but, for most Westerners, it is viewed with some degree of skepticism. Meditation is a technique that involves entering a trance state by focusing on a word or sound (mantra), an object (e.g. burning candle), or a movement (e.g., a ceiling fan). It has physiological effects, all associated with decreased stress.

In the 1960's, Dr. Herbert Benson at Harvard Medical School tested subjects who utilized Transcendental Meditation to see if meditation did in fact reduce the physiological effects of stress. The test results proved that signs of relaxation were evident as the heart rate, respiratory rate, and blood pressure all decreased. Skin resistance to electrical current and increased brain wave patterns were also recorded. Benson concluded that any meditational practice could replicate these physiological changes as long as four factors were present: (1) a quiet environment, (2) a constant mental focal point, (3) a comfortable position, and (4) a passive attitude.

The primary goal of meditation is to pay attention to the things that are happening in the here and now. You should mentally note what you experience without trying to alter it. If your mind wanders, just acknowledge that your thoughts are wandering and return to the present moment.

Meditation techniques may vary; however, in general the steps are as follows:

- Find a quiet place. Wear loose, comfortable clothing. Select a seated position that is comfortable for you.
- Close your mouth and breathe through your nose.
- Close your eyes.
- Take slow, deep breaths.
- Concentrate on a single word, object or calming thought.
- Don't worry if other thoughts or images enter your mind while you are doing this. Just relax and return to what you were focusing on.
- Continue until you feel relaxed and refreshed.

Progressive Muscle Relaxation

Progressive muscle relaxation is another method to help you relax. Relaxation produces physiological effects opposite those of stress and anxiety. Relaxation slows the heart rate, respiration rate, blood pressure and skin conductance. There are a variety of relaxation techniques, but most methods utilize progressive relaxation.

In progressive muscle relaxation, you should tense and relax each muscle group, starting at your head and working your way down to your toes.

The actual process is as follows:

- Wear loose comfortable clothing; sit in a comfortable chair or lie down.
- Tense the muscles in your face for 5–10 seconds, then relax them for about 20 seconds.
- Tense the muscles in the back of your forehead for 5–10 seconds, then relax them for about 20 seconds. Notice the difference in how your muscles feel when relaxed.
- Move to your eyes and nose muscles. Tense and relax the muscles the same way you did with your forehead.

- Repeat the same steps with the other muscle groups in your body:
  Cheeks and jaws
  Neck and throat
  Dominant hand and forearm
  Dominant bicep and tricep
  Dominant hand and forearm
  Non-dominant bicep and tricep
  Chest, shoulders, upper back
  Stomach
  Lower back
  Buttocks — one at a time
  Dominant thigh
  Dominant calf
  Dominant foot and toes
  Non-dominant thigh
  Non-dominant calf
  Non-dominant foot and toes

Deep-Breathing Exercise

Your way of breathing affects your whole body. Deep breathing is a very good way to lower stress and reduce tension in your body. When you breathe deeply, the brain sends a message to your body to calm down and relax. As you perform this exercise and as you breathe deeply to relax, your heart rate, breathing rate and blood pressure will decrease.

These steps help keep stress from getting out of control:

- Sit comfortably or lie on your back.
- Breathe in slowly and deeply for a count of 5.
- Hold your breath for a count of 15.
- Breathe out slowly for a count of 5, pushing out all the air.
- Repeat several times until you feel calm and relaxed.

Diaphragmatic Breathing

Diaphragmatic breathing can be beneficial during highly stressful events. Diaphragmatic breathing, also known as belly-breathing, has well-established benefits for reducing stress, tension and anxiety by calming the "fight or flight" response.

Belly-breathing is not a magic bullet or cure, and the benefits are not an immediate solution to highly charged or emotional incidents. Rather, as you practice, you will become accustomed to this type of breathing and begin to incorporate this technique into many aspects of your everyday life. Essentially, the goal is to make the diaphragmatic technique your normal way of breathing. Deep breathing described earlier is shallow, fast and does not permit your lungs to fully expand. Hence, your lungs may not receive a sufficient amount of oxygen to fuel the blood during times of stress. By contrast, diaphragmatic breathing utilizes a greater range of movement of your diaphragm.

Diaphragmatic breathing activates the relaxation response by supplying an excess of oxygen to the blood during time of stress or emotional turmoil. This increase in oxygenated blood aids in the restoration of the body to a homeostatic state.

The following are basic steps to belly-breathing:

- Find a quiet place where you know you won't be disturbed.
- Lie down on your back on a flat surface.
- Place the palm of one hand on your upper chest and the palm of the other hand on your belly, just below your rib cage.
- Close your eyes.
- Breathe in slowly through your nose. The hand on your belly will rise noticeably, while the hand on your chest will remain stationary.
- Tighten up your stomach muscles and slowly exhale, allowing the air to gradually pass through your lips. The hand on your stomach will fall quite a bit, while the hand on your upper chest will hardly move.
- By placing a book on your belly, you can watch it rise and fall while you practice. This will let you know that you are breathing deeply with the diaphragm and not with your chest.
- Pay attention to the flow of your breathing.
- The goal is to breathe smoothly and softly. Try to find a steady rhythm in your breathing.

As you become accustomed to belly breathing, you can try it in a seated position.

The Department of Defense has released the Breathe2Relax (http://t2health. org/apps/breathe2relax) mobile application for smart phone users designed by the National Center for Telehealth & Technology (T2). Breathe2Relax is a diaphragmatic breathing trainer that uses a smart phone's interactive learning capabilities to teach deep-breathing exercises through video instruction and interactive demonstrations. This free application allows you to learn and practice diaphragmatic breathing on your own or in conjunction with a supervised stress management program. You can further customize the Breathe2Relax experience, using the application's preference settings to select breath duration and number of cycles, as well as selecting your choice of music and background images.

Final Notes

In conclusion, as noted earlier in this article and throughout the book, stress is your body's response to any stimulus. It is a dynamic variable to which the body must adapt in order to navigate the demands of everyday living. Stress can be useful; however, if left unchecked, stress can lead to deleterious physical and emotional consequences. Stress reducing techniques are useful approaches in helping the body to return to homeostasis, the body's desired state of equilibrium. However, stress reducing techniques are but one type of intervention and should be viewed as an adjunct to professional treatment when stress, tension and anxiety are adversely impacting your normal day-to-day functioning. It is imperative that law enforcement officers be proactive rather than reactive when dealing with the episodic and on-going stressful conditions that occur on a daily basis, both on-duty and off-duty over the course of their entire career.

References

Benson, Herbert, with Klipper, Miriam Z. (1976). *The Relaxation Response*. New York: William Morrow and Company, Inc.

Davis, D., Eshelman, E.R., & McKay, M. (1995). *The Relaxation and Stress Reduction Workbook (4th ed.)*. Oakland, CA: New Harbinger Publications, Inc.

National Center for Telehealth & Technology (2011). National Center for Telehealth & Technology (T2). Retrieved from http://t2health.org/apps/breathe2relax.

Sewell, J. D. (1983). "The Development of a Critical Life Events Scale for Law Enforcement," *Journal of Police Science and Administration*, 11, 109–116.

Sheehan, D. C. (1999). "Stress Management in the Federal Bureau of Investigation: Principles for program development," *International Journal of Emergency Mental Health*, 1, 30–42.

Spielberger, Charles D.; Westberry, L.G.; Grier, K.S.; and Greenfield, G. (1981). *The Police Stress Survey: Sources of Stress in Law Enforcement*. Tampa, FL: University of South Florida Human Resources Institute.

Van Hasselt, V. B., Sheehan, D. C., Malcolm, A.S., Sellers, A. H., Baker, M. T., & Couwels, J. (2008). "The Law Enforcement Officer Stress Survey (LEOSS) Evaluation of Psychometric Properties," *Behavior Modification*, 12, 133–151.

Discussion Questions

1. What were two early stress measurements instruments specifically developed for law enforcement professionals?
2. How does the technique of Guided Imagery/Visualization work as a stress reducer?
3. How often was it recommended that visualization be practiced? At what location was it recommended that it be employed?
4. How does meditation reduce stress?
5. What did Dr. Herbert Benson conclude regarding Transcendental Meditation and its ability to reduce the physiological effects of stress?
6. Meditation techniques may vary; however, in general there are certain steps that are recommended. What are they?
7. How does progressive muscle relaxation work as a stress reducing method?
8. What are the basic steps in diaphragmatic breathing (belly breathing)?

Part Nine

What Support Is Available for Cops?

But what if diet, exercise, and emotional and recreational outlets just don't work? What if an officer's emotional stress is so deep and his or her manifestations are so severe that routine coping techniques are not successful? What support is available for cops? How do we deal with officers following major traumatic events? What comprehensive services are or should be available to assure that "good" officers remain high performers and their life outside of law enforcement is relatively stable? There are, of course, professional resources available to support an agency's efforts to mitigate the stress experienced by its police personnel. Many departments have developed their own psychological services units, and others have contracted with outside providers. Increasingly, psychological services are becoming a more important and common part of the organization, with recognized success stories accepted within the police subculture. Oftentimes, these approaches are supplemented by the use of trained peer support personnel ... other cops who "have been there, done that, and have more than just the t-shirt." In Part Nine, then, our authors explore the successful utilization of psychological services in policing today.

Miller has an extensive history as a police psychologist and as an author of practical police psychology books and articles. This article discusses the sources of stress within individual areas of a law enforcement agency and outlines a number of critical intervention and psychotherapeutic strategies which are both useful and effective in dealing with law enforcement officers under stress. Important in successfully dealing with stress are a number of parallel issues, including trust in the psychotherapist, support for intervention within the department and its organizational culture, and administrative actions which affect the provision of psychological services within an agency.

Increasingly, stress experts are seeking out new alternatives to traditional therapy to resolve traumatic stress experienced by police officers and other professionals. In a piece written specifically for this book, Logan discusses the advances made in neurosciences over the last several years, linking changes in the brain with traumatic experiences and suggesting that a memory malfunction may underlie post-traumatic stress disorder. Our increased knowledge about the brain's information processing activities also brings forth alternative treatment modalities, and Logan focuses her attention on the benefits offered by eye movement desensitization and reprocessing (EMDR).

For many agencies, peer support teams, as Kamena and his colleagues note, "fill an emotional void." Recognizing that the police subculture commonly is resistant to outside, and at times internal, psychologists, trained peer support personnel offer emotional, social, and practical support to other officers during times of stress and crisis. As this work discusses, it is critical that such officers are carefully selected and trained, that the policies and procedures governing their operation are clear, and that their relationship with licensed mental health professionals is specified.

In their short piece, Dowling, Genet, and Moynihan discuss the Police Organization Providing Peer Assistance, a confidential, nondepartmental assistance program associated with the New York Police Department and better known by its acronym, POPPA. Created after a significant number of suicide within NYPD over a two-year period in the mid-1990s, POPPA uses trained volunteer NYPD officers as peer support personnel to provide both telephone and face-to-face assistance to officers in crisis. They are supplemented by a cadre of independent mental health professionals in New York City and its surrounding counties who are available for referral from the peer officers.

Recognizing that suicide in law enforcement is a severe problem, the Badge of Life Psychological Survival for Police Officers Program was founded on January 1, 2008, to develop an effective law enforcement officer suicide primary and secondary prevention program. Critical to the success of its efforts is the Emotional Self-Care (ESC) training program, focused on the officer's ability and responsibility to care for his or her own emotional well-being. Levenson, O'Hara, and Clark, all involved in the leadership of the BOL Program, discuss some of its key elements, including its website, its use of peer support officers, and its applicability among Canadian, as well as American, police officers.

On November 5, 2009, a gunman entered the Soldier Readiness Processing site at Fort Hood, Texas, and opened fire with a handgun, killing 13, including 12 soldiers, and wounding 31. Strand, Felices, and Williams conduct a case study on the critical incident response, discussing the types and results of the interventions initiated, while also acknowledging the initial concerns by some of the military leadership and line personnel about the use of critical incident stress management in this particular situation. As part of their discussion, they offer a number of policy and training recommendations which should be of use to both military and civilian law enforcement agencies.

Nationally known leaders in critical incident stress management and emergency mental health, Mitchell and Levenson acknowledge that there is no more stressful or emotionally painful event in the professional lives of police officers than a fellow officer's death in the line of duty. In discussing the appropriate response to such incidents, they warn against some common mistakes made by newly formed Critical Incident Stress Management teams and suggest a strategic framework within which teams should work with law enforcement agencies following a line of duty death.

Further Reading

Arendt. M., and Elklit, A. (2001). "Effectiveness of Psychological Debriefing," *Acta Psychiatrica Scandinavica*, 2001, 104, 423–437.

Delprino, Robert P., and Bahn, Charles (1988). "National Survey of the Extent and Nature of Police Psychological Services in Police Departments," *Professional Psychology: Research and Practice*, 19(4), 421–425.

Dyregrov, Atle (1998). "Psychological Debriefing: An Effective Method?" *Traumatology*, 4(2), 1–10.

Everly, George S. (2000). "Crisis Management Briefings (CMB): Large Group Crisis Intervention in Response to Terrorism, Disasters, and Violence, *International Journal of Emergency Mental Health*, 2(1), 53–57.

Everly, George S., and Mitchell, Jeffrey T. (1996). *Innovations in Disaster and Trauma Psychology*. Ellicott City, MD: Chevron Publishing.

Finn, Peter, and Tomz, Julie Esselman (1998). "Using Peer Supporters to Help Address Law Enforcement Stress," *FBI Law Enforcement Bulletin*, 67(5), 10–18.

IACP Police Psychological Services Section (2007). "Peer Support Guidelines," *The Police Chief*, 74(8), 90–93.

Janik, James (1995). "Who Needs Peer Support," *Police Chief*, 62(1), 38–41.

Madonna, John M., and Kelly, Richard E. (2002). *Treating Police Stress: The Work and the Words of Peer Counselors*. Springfield, IL: Charles C Thomas.

McNally, Vincent J., and Solomon, Roger M. (1999). "The FBI's Critical Incident Stress Management Program," *FBI Law Enforcement Bulletin*, 68(2), 20–26.

Miller, Laurence (1995). "Tough Guys: Psychotherapeutic Strategies with Law Enforcement and Emergency Services Personnel," *Psychotherapy*, 32(4), 592–600.

Reese, James T. and Goldstein, Harvey A. (Eds.) (1986). *Psychological Services for Law Enforcement*. Washington, DC: U.S. Government Printing Office.

Sheehan, Donald C., Everly, George S., and Langlieb, Alan (2004). "Current Best Practices: Coping with Major Critical Incidents," *FBI Law Enforcement Bulletin*, 73(9), 1–13.

Key Terms in Part Nine

Amygdala: Parts of the brain located within the medial temporal lobes which are involved in the processing and memory of emotional reactions.

Core competency: The basic and most critical feature(s) of a curriculum, a model policy, or a best practices model.

Critical Incident: "An event which is outside the usual range of experience and challenges one's ability to cope ... and has the potential ... to overwhelm one's usual psychological defenses and coping mechanisms" (Everly & Mitchell, 2000, p. 212).

Critical Incident Peer Support (CIPS): The U.S. Army Military Police School program for training MPs and CID agents to serve as peer supporters following critical incidents.

Critical Incident Stress: the intense emotional reaction to experiencing a critical incident.

Critical Incident Stress Debriefing (CISD): A group process of psychological crisis intervention specifically designed for emergency service personnel. It is recommended to take place within 24 and 48 hours after an event and promotes emotional processing of traumatic events through ventilation and normalization of reactions and through recognition of and preparation for recurrence of symptoms in the future.

Critical Incident Stress Management (CISM): A comprehensive approach to dealing with stress resulting from critical incidents, including pre-crisis preparation and training, post-operation intervention (referred to as *demobilization* in civilian arenas), crisis management brief, defusing, CISD, one-on-one intervention, pastoral crisis intervention, family intervention, organizational consultation, and post-crisis follow-up and referral.

Crisis Management Briefing (CMB): Considered a component of the Critical Incident Stress Management system, Crisis Management Briefing is a group psychological intervention designed to mitigate the levels of felt crisis and traumatic stress in the wake of large-scale crises.

Defusing: A structured small group discussion provided within hours of a crisis for purposes of assessment, triaging, and acute symptom mitigation.

Early Warning Screening: A process to immediately identify acute problems within emergency workers, at the first signs of maladaptive responses, following a critical incident.

Eye movement desensitizing and reprocessing (EMDR): developed by Francine Shapiro, this form of psychotherapy holds that individuals suffering from post-traumatic stress disorder have inadequately processed the traumatic memories and uses an eight-stage approach, centering on eye movement, to reprocess those memories.

Hippocampus: Part of the limbic system, the hippocampus is located in the medial temporal lobe of the brain. It plays a major role in an individual's memory and in consolidation of information.

One-on-one Intervention: The most-used element of CISM interventions, it involves contact by a trained professional or paraprofessional with an individual who is in crisis.

Peer Support: The provision of crisis intervention services by those other than mental health clinicians and directed toward individuals of similar key characteristics or responsibilities.

Peer counselor/peer supporter: Law enforcement officers who have received additional training in counseling skills and stress recognition to allow them to better provide support and assistance, including referral to mental health professionals, to other officers during times of stress. Peer support personnel do not conduct any clinical therapy, but, instead, focus on three major responsibilities: listening, assessing and referring.

Prefrontal cortex: Part of the frontal lobes of the brain, the prefrontal cortex affects decision-making, cognitive behaviors, and social behavior.

Thalamus: Located between the cerebral cortex and midbrain, the thalamus relays sensations and motor signals to the cortex and regulates consciousness and sleep.

Therapeutic relationship: The interaction between a mental health professional and an officer in a therapeutic setting. Miller holds that an effective relationship is built upon accurate empathy, genuineness, availability, respect, and concreteness.

35

Law Enforcement Traumatic Stress: Clinical Syndromes and Intervention Strategies

Laurence Miller

Introduction

Every time we dial 911, we expect that our emergency will be taken seriously and handled competently. The police will race to our burgled office, the firefighters will speedily douse our burning home, the ambulance crew will stabilize our injured loved one and whisk him or her to the nearest hospital. We take these expectations for granted because of the skill and dedication of the workers who serve the needs of law enforcement, emergency services, and public safety.

These "tough guys" (Miller, 1995) — the term includes both men and women — are routinely exposed to special kinds of traumatic events and daily pressures that require a certain adaptively defensive toughness of attitude, temperament, and training. Without this resolve, they couldn't do their jobs effectively. Sometimes, however, the stress is just too much, and the very toughness that facilitates smooth functioning in their daily duties now becomes an impediment to these helpers seeking help for themselves.

This article first describes the types of critical incidents and other stresses experienced by law enforcement personnel. Many of these challenges affect all personnel who work in public safety and the helping professions, including police officers, firefighters, paramedics, dispatchers, trauma doctors, emergency room nurses, and psychotherapists (Miller, 1995, 1997, 1998a, 1998b, 1999, in press); however, the focus here will be on the stressors most relevant to police officers, criminal investigators, and other law enforcement personnel. Secondly, this article will describe the critical interventions and psychotherapeutic strategies that have been found most practical and useful for helping cops in distress.

The target audience for this article is a dual one. This article is for law enforcement supervisors and administrators who want to understand how to provide the best possible psychological services to the men and women under their command. It is also for mental health clinicians who may be considering law enforcement consultation and therefore want some insight into the unique challenges and rewards of working with these personnel.

Stress and Coping in Law Enforcement

Police officers can be an insular group, and are often more reluctant to talk to outsiders or to show "weakness" in front of their own peers than are other emergency service and public safety workers. Officers typically work alone or with a single partner, as opposed to firefighters or paramedics, who are trained to have more of a team mentality (Blau, 1994; Cummings, 1996; Kirschman, 1997; Reese, 1987; Solomon. 1995). This presents some special challenges for clinicians attempting to identify and help those officers in distress.

The Patrol Cop

Even those civilians who have no great love for cops have to admit that theirs is a difficult, dangerous, and often thankless job. Police officers regularly deal with the most violent, impulsive, and predatory members of society, put their lives on the line, and confront cruelties and horrors that the rest of us view from the sanitized distance of our newspapers and TV screens. In addition to the daily grind, officers are frequently the target of criticism and complaints by citizens, the media, the judicial system, adversarial attorneys, social service personnel, and their own administrators and law enforcement agencies (Blau, 1994).

Police officers generally carry out their sworn duties and responsibilities with dedication and valor, but some stresses are too much to take, and every officer has his or her breaking point. For some, it may come in the form of a particular traumatic experience, such as a gruesome accident or homicide, a vicious crime against a child, a close personal brush with death, the death or serious injury of a partner, the shooting of a perpetrator or innocent civilian, or an especially grisly or large-scale crime; in some cases, the traumatic critical incident can precipitate the development of full-scale post-traumatic stress disorder, or PTSD (Miller, 1994, 1998c). Symptoms may include numbed responsiveness, impaired memory alternating with intrusive, disturbing images of the incident, irritability, hypervigilance, impaired concentration, sleep disturbance, anxiety, depression, phobic avoidance, social withdrawal, and substance abuse.

For other officers, there may be no singular trauma, but the mental breakdown caps the cumulative weight of a number of more mundane stresses over the course of the officer's career. Most police officers deal with both the routine and exceptional stresses by using a variety of situationally adaptive coping and defense mechanisms, such as repression, displacement, isolation of feelings, humor—often seemingly callous or crass humor—and generally toughing it out. Officers develop a closed society, an insular "cop culture," centering around what many refer to as *The Job*. For a few, *The Job* becomes their life, and crowds out other activities and relationships (Blau, 1994).

In the United States, two-thirds of officers involved in shootings suffer moderate or severe problems and about 70 percent leave the force within seven years of the incident. Police are admitted to hospitals at significantly higher rates than the general population and rank third among occupations in premature death rates (Sewell et al., 1988). Interestingly, however, despite the popular notion of rampantly disturbed police marriages, there is no evidence for a disproportionately high divorce rate among officers (Borum & Philpot, 1993).

Perhaps the most tragic form of police casualty is suicide (Cummings, 1996; Hays, 1994; McCafferty et al., 1992; Seligman et al., 1994). Twice as many officers, about 300 annually, die by their own hand as are killed in the line of duty. In New York City, the suicide rate for police officers is more than double the rate for the general population. In fact, these totals may actually be even higher, since such deaths are sometimes underreported by fellow cops to avoid stigmatizing the deceased officers and to allow families to collect benefits. Most suicide victims are young patrol officers with no record of misconduct, and most shoot themselves off-duty. Often, problems involving alcohol or romantic crises are the catalyst, and easy access to a lethal weapon provides the ready means. Cops under stress are caught in the dilemma of risking confiscation of their guns or other career setbacks if they report distress or request help.

Special Assignments and Units

Aside from the daily stresses and hassles of patrol cops, special pressures are experienced by higher-ranking officers, such as homicide detectives, who are involved in the investigation of particularly brutal crimes, such as multiple murders or serial killings (Sewell, 1993). The protective social role of the police officer becomes even more pronounced, at the same time as their responsibilities as public servants who safeguard individual rights become compounded with the pressure to solve the case.

Moreover, the sheer magnitude and shock effect of many murder scenes, and the violence, mutilation, and sadistic brutality associated with many serial killings, especially if they involve children, often overwhelm the defense mechanisms and coping abilities of even the most seasoned officers. Revulsion may be tinged with rage, all the more so when fellow officers have been killed or injured. Finally, the cumulative effect of fatigue results in case errors, impaired work quality, and deterioration of home and workplace relationships. Fatigue also further wears down defenses, rendering the officer even more vulnerable to stress and impaired decision-making.

Dispatchers and Support Personnel

In addition to line-of-duty officers, a vital role in law enforcement is played by the workers who operate "behind the scenes," namely the dispatchers, complaint clerks, clerical staff, crime scene technicians, and other support personnel (Holt, 1989; Sewell & Crew, 1984). Although rarely exposed to direct danger (except where on-scene and behind-scene personnel alternate shifts), several high-stress features characterize the job descriptions of these workers. These include: (1) dealing with multiple, sometimes simultaneous, calls; (2) having to make time-pressured life-and-death decisions; (3) having little information about, and low control over, the emergency situation; (4) intense, confusing, and frequently hostile contact with frantic or outraged citizens; and (5) exclusion from the status and camaraderie typically shared by on-scene personnel who "get the credit."

After particularly difficult calls, dispatchers may show many of the classic post-traumatic reactions and symptoms, but they are often overlooked by police supervisors and consulting mental health clinicians alike. As with other tough jobs, these individuals deserve the proper treatment and support.

Intervention Services and Strategies

To avoid overly "shrinky" connotations, mental health intervention services with law enforcement personnel are often conceptualized in such terms as "stress management" or "critical incident debriefing" (Anderson et al., 1995; Belles & Norvell, 1990; Mitchell & Bray, 1990; Mitchell & Everly, 1996). In general, one-time, incident-specific interventions will be most appropriate for handling the effects of overwhelming trauma on otherwise normal, well-functioning personnel. Where post-traumatic sequella persist, or where the psychological problems relate to a longer-term pattern of maladaptive functioning, more extensive individual psychotherapeutic approaches are called for. To have the greatest impact, intervention services should be part of an integrated program within the department, and have full administrative commitment and support (Blau, 1994; Sewell, 1986).

Critical Incident Stress Debriefing (CISD)

Although components of this approach comprise an important element of all therapeutic work with traumatized patients, critical incident stress debriefing, or CISD, has been organizationally formalized for law enforcement and emergency services by Jeff Mitchell and his colleagues (Mitchell, 1983, 1988, 1991; Mitchell & Bray, 1990; Mitchell & Everly, 1996), and the "Mitchell model" of CISD is now implemented in public safety departments throughout the United States, Britain, and other parts of the world (Davis, 1998/99; Dyregrov, 1989). CISD is a structured intervention designed to promote the emotional processing of traumatic events through the ventilation and normalization of reactions, as well as preparation for possible future experiences. CISD is an essential technique associated with efficient and effective Critical Incident Stress Management (CISM).

According to the Mitchell model, following a critical incident, there are a number of criteria on which peer support and command staff might decide to provide a debriefing to personnel. These include: (1) many individuals within a group appear to be distressed after a call; (2) the signs of stress appear to be quite severe; (3) personnel demonstrate significant behavioral changes; (4) personnel make significant errors on calls occurring after the critical incident; (5) personnel request help; and (6) the event is unusual or extraordinary.

The structure of a CISD usually consists of the presence of one or more mental health professionals and one or more peer debriefers, (i.e. fellow police officers or emergency service workers who have been trained in the CISD process and who may have been through critical incidents and debriefings themselves.) A typical debriefing takes place within 24–72 hours after the critical incident, and consists of a single group meeting that lasts approximately 2–3 hours, although shorter or longer meetings are determined by circumstances.

The formal CISD process consists of seven standard phases:

Introduction: The introduction phase of a debriefing is when the team leader introduces the CISD process and approach, encourages participation by the group, and sets the ground rules by which the debriefing will operate. Generally, these guidelines involve issues of confidentiality, attendance for the full duration of the group, however with nonforced participation in discussions (no "hot seat"), and the establishment of a supportive, noncritical atmosphere.

Fact Phase: During this phase, the group is asked to describe briefly their job or role during the incident and, from their own perspective, some facts regarding what happened. The basic question is: "What did you do?"

Thought Phase: The CISD leader asks the group members to discuss their first thoughts during the critical incident: "What went through your mind?"

Reaction Phase: This phase is designed to move the group participants from the predominantly cognitive level of intellectual processing into the emotional level of processing: "What was the worst part of the incident for you?"

Symptom Phase: This begins the movement back from the predominantly emotional processing level toward the cognitive processing level. Participants are asked to describe their physical, cognitive, emotional, and behavioral signs and symptoms of distress which appeared (1) at the scene or within 24 hours of the incident, (2) a few days after the incident, and (3) are still being experienced at the time of the debriefing: "What have you been experiencing since the incident?"

Education Phase: Information is exchanged about the nature of the stress response and the expected physiological and psychological reactions to critical incidents. This serves to normalize the stress and coping response, and provides a basis for questions and answers: "What can we learn from this experience?"

Re-entry Phase: This is a wrap-up, in which any additional questions or statements are addressed, referral for individual follow-ups are made, and general group solidarity and bonding are reinforced: "How can we help one another the next time something like this occurs?" "Was there anything that we left out?"

For a successful debriefing, timing and clinical appropriateness are important. The consensus from the literature and my own clinical experience support scheduling the debriefing toward the earlier end of the recommended 24–72 hour window (Bordow & Porritt, 1979; Solomon & Benbenishty, 1988). To keep the focus on the event itself and to reduce the potential for singling-out of individuals, some authorities recommend that there be a policy of mandatory referral of all involved personnel to a debriefing or other appropriate mental health intervention (Horn, 1991; McMains, 1991; Mitchell, 1991; Reese, 1991; Solomon, 1988, 1990, 1995). However, in other cases, mandatory or enforced CISD may lead to passive participation and resentment among the conscripted personnel (Bisson & Deahl, 1994; Flannery et al., 1991), and the CISD process may quickly become a boring routine if used indiscriminately after every incident, thereby diluting its effectiveness in those situations where it really could have helped. Departmental supervisor and mental health consultants must use their common sense and knowledge of their own personnel to make these kinds of judgment calls.

Special Applications of CISD for Law Enforcement

To encourage participation and reduce fear of stigmatization, the administrative policy should strongly and affirmatively state that debriefings and other post-incident mental health and peer-support interventions are confidential. The only exceptions to confidentiality are a clear and present danger to self or others, or disclosure of a serious crime by the officer. Where only one officer is involved, as in a shooting, or as a follow-up or supplement to a formal group debriefing, individual debriefings may be conducted by a mental health clinician or trained peer (Solomon, 1995).

In an officer-involved shooting, when there is an ongoing or impending investigation, Solomon (1988, 1995) recommends that the group debriefing be postponed until the initial investigation has been completed and formal statements have been taken by investigators. Otherwise, debriefing participants may be regarded as witnesses who are subject to subpoena for questioning about what was said. For particularly sensitive or controversial situations or complicated internal affairs investigations, it may be advisable to postpone the group debriefing until the investigation has been officially resolved. Individual interventions can be provided for the primarily involved officer(s) in the meantime, and/or a group debriefing may proceed with other, nonprimarily involved personnel who may have been affected by the incident, especially where the response team was multidisciplinary and multidepartmental (police, firefighters, paramedics, etc.).

Finally, as a follow-up measure, Solomon (1995) recommends holding a critical incident peer support seminar, in which the involved officers come together for two or three days in a retreat-like setting, several months post-incident, to revisit and reflect upon their experience. The seminar is facilitated by mental health professionals and peer support officers.

Sewell (1993, 1994) has adapted a CISD-like stress management model to the particular needs of detectives who investigate multiple murders and other violent crimes. The major objectives of this process are: (1) ventilation of intense emotions; (2) exploration of symbolic meanings; (3) group support under catastrophic conditions; (4) initiation of the grief process within a supportive environment; (5) dismantling of the "fallacy of uniqueness;" (6) reassurance that intense emotions under catastrophic conditions are normal; (7) preparation for the continuation of the grief and stress process over the ensuing weeks and months; (8) preparing for the possible development of physical, cognitive, and emotional symptoms in the aftermath of a serious crisis;

(9) education regarding normal and abnormal stress response syndromes; and (10) encouragement of continued group support and/or professional help.

Perhaps the most comprehensive adaptation of the CISD process comes from the work of Bohl (1995) who explicitly compares and contrasts the phases in her own program with the phases of the Mitchell model.

In Bohl's program, the debriefing takes place as soon after the critical incident as possible. A debriefing may involve a single officer within the first 24 hours, later followed by a second, with a group debriefing taking place within one week to encourage group cohesion and bonding. This addresses the occupationally lower team orientation of most police officers who may not express feelings easily, even—or especially—in a group of their fellow cops.

The Bohl model makes no real distinction between the cognitive and emotional phases of a debriefing. If an officer begins to express emotion during the fact or cognitive phase, there is little point in telling him or her to stifle it until later. To be fair, the Mitchell model certainly does allow for flexibility and common sense in structuring debriefings, and both formats recognize the importance of responding empathically to the specific needs expressed by the participants, rather than following a rigid set of rules.

In the emotion phase itself, what is important in the Bohl model is not the mere act of venting, but rather the opportunity to validate feelings. Bohl does not ask what the "worst thing" was, since she finds the typical response to be that "everything about it was the worst thing." However, it often comes as a revelation to these law enforcement "tough guys" that their peers have had similar feelings.

Still, some emotions may be difficult to validate. For example, guilt or remorse over actions or inactions may actually be appropriate, as when an officer's momentary hesitation or impulsive action resulted in someone getting hurt or killed. In the Bohl model, the question then becomes: "Okay, you feel guilty—what are you going to do with that guilt?" That is, "What can be learned from the experience to prevent something like this from happening again?"

The Bohl model inserts an additional phase, termed the "unfinished business" phase, which has no formal counterpart in the Mitchell model. Participants are asked, "What in the present situation reminds you of past experiences? Do you want to talk about those other situations?" This phase grew out of Bohl's observation that the incident that prompted the current debriefing often acts as a catalyst for recalling past events. The questions give participants a chance to talk about incidents that may arouse strong, unresolved feelings. Bohl finds that such multilevel debriefings result in a greater sense of relief and closure than might occur by sticking solely to the present incident. In many cases, it has also been my own experience that feelings and reactions to past critical incidents will sometimes spontaneously come up during a debriefing about a more recent incident, and this must be dealt with and worked through as it arises, although team leaders must be careful not to lose too much of the structure and focus of the current debriefing.

The education phase in the Bohl model resembles its Mitchell model counterpart, in that participants are schooled about normal and pathological stress reactions, how to deal with coworkers and family members, and what to anticipate in the days and weeks ahead. Unlike the Mitchell model, the Bohl model does not ask whether anything positive, hopeful, or growth-promoting has arisen from the incident. Officers who have had to deal with senseless brutality might be forgiven for failing to perceive anything positive about the incident, and expecting them to extract some kind of "growth experience" from such an event may seem like a sick joke.

A final non-Mitchell phase of the debriefing in the Bohl model is the "round robin" in which each officer is invited to say whatever he or she wants. The statement can be addressed to anyone, but others cannot respond directly; this is supposed to give participants a feeling of safety. My own concern is that this may provide an opportunity for last-minute gratuitous sniping, which can quickly erode the supportive atmosphere that has been carefully crafted during the debriefing. Additionally, in practice, there doesn't seem to be anything particularly unique about this round robin phase to distinguish it from the standard re-entry phase of the Mitchell model. Finally, adding more and more "phases" to the debriefing process may serve to decrease the forthrightness and spontaneity of its implementation. Again, clinical judgment and common sense should guide the process.

Law Enforcement Psychotherapy

As noted above, police officers have a reputation for shunning mental health services, often perceiving its practitioners as "softies" and "bleeding hearts" who help criminals go free with over complicated psychobabble excuses. Other cops may fear being "shrunk," having a notion of the psychotherapy process as akin to brainwashing, a humiliating and emasculating experience in which they lie on a couch and sob about their dysfunctional childhoods. More commonly, the idea of needing "mental help" implies weakness, cowardice, and lack of ability to do the job. In the environment of many departments, some officers realistically fear censure, stigmatization, ridicule, thwarted career advancement, and alienation from colleagues if they are perceived as the type who "folds under pressure." Still others in the department who may have something to hide may fear a colleague "spilling his guts" to the shrink and thereby blowing the malfeasor's cover (Miller, 1995, 1998c).

Administrative Issues

There is some debate about whether psychological services, especially therapy-type services, should be provided by a psychologist within the department, even a clinician who is also an active or retired sworn officer, or whether such matters are best handled by outside therapists who are less involved in departmental politics and gossip (Blau, 1994; Silva, 1991).

On the one hand, the departmental clinician is likely to have more knowledge of, and experience with, the direct pressures faced by the personnel he or she serves; this is especially true if the psychologist is also an officer or has had formal law enforcement training or ride-along experience. On the other hand, in addition to providing psychotherapy services, the departmental psychologist is likely to also be involved in performing work status and fitness-for-duty evaluations, as well as other assessments or legal roles which may conflict with that of an objective helper. An outside clinician may have less direct experience with departmental policy and pressures, but may enjoy more therapeutic freedom of movement.

My own experience has been that officers who sincerely come for help are usually less interested in the therapist's extensive technical knowledge of *The Job* and more concerned that he or she demonstrate a basic trust and a willingness to understand the officer's situation—the cops will be more than happy to provide the grim details. These officers expect mental health professionals to "give 100 percent" in the psychotherapy process, just as the officers do in their own jobs; they really don't want us to be another cop, they want us to be a skilled therapist—that's why they're talking to us in the first place.

Many cops are actually glad to find a secure haven away from the "fishbowl" atmosphere of the department and relieved that the therapeutic sessions provide a respite from shop talk. This is especially true where the referral problem has less to do with direct job-related issues and more with outside pressures, such as family or alcohol problems, that may impinge on job performance. In any case, the therapist, the patient, and the department should be clear at the outset about the issues relating to confidentiality and chain of command, and any changes in ground rules should be clarified as needed.

Trust and the Therapeutic Relationship

Difficulty with trust appears to be an occupational hazard for workers in law enforcement and public safety who typically maintain a strong sense of self-sufficiency and insistence on solving their own problems. Therapists may therefore frequently find themselves "tested," especially at the beginning of the treatment process. As the therapeutic alliance begins to solidify, the officer will begin to feel more at ease with the therapist and may actually find comfort and sense of stability from the psychotherapy sessions. Silva (1991) has outlined the following requirements for establishing therapeutic mutual trust:

> *Accurate Empathy:* The therapist conveys his or her understanding of the officer's background and experience (but beware of premature false familiarity and phony "bonding").
>
> *Genuineness:* The therapist is as spontaneous, tactful, flexible, and nondefensive as possible.
>
> *Availability:* The therapist is accessible and available (within reason) when needed, and avoids making promises and commitments he or she can't realistically keep.
>
> *Respect:* This is both gracious and firm, and acknowledges the officer's sense of autonomy, control, and responsibility within the therapeutic relationship. Respect is manifested by the therapist's general attitude, as well as by certain specific actions, such as signifying regard for rank or job role by initially using formal departmental titles, such as "officer," "detective," "lieutenant," until trust and mutual respect allow an easing of formality. Here it is important for clinicians to avoid the dual traps of overfamiliarity, patronizing, and talking down to the officer on the one hand, and trying to "play cop" or force bogus camaraderie by assuming the role of a colleague or commander.
>
> *Concreteness:* Therapy should, at least initially be goal-oriented and have a problem-solving focus. Police officers are into action and results, and to the extent that it is clinically realistic, the therapeutic approach should emphasize active, problem-solving approaches before tackling more sensitive and complex psychological issues.

Therapeutic Strategies and Techniques

Since most law enforcement and emergency services personnel come under psychotherapeutic care in the context of some form of post-traumatic stress reaction, both clinical experience and literature (Blau, 1994; Cummings, 1996; Fullerton et al., 1992; Kirschman, 1997) reflect this emphasis. In general, the effectiveness of any intervention technique will be determined by the timeliness, tone, style, and intent of the intervention. Effective interventions share in common the elements of briefness, focus on specific symptomatology or conflict issues, and direct operational efforts to resolve the conflict or to reach a satisfactory conclusion.

In working with police officers, Blau (1994) recommends that the first meeting between the therapist and the officer establish a safe and comfortable working atmosphere by the therapist's articulating: (1) a positive endorsement of the officer's decision to seek help; (2) a clear description of the therapist's responsibilities and limitations with respect to confidentiality and privilege; and (3) an invitation to state the officer's concerns.

A straightforward, goal-directed, problem-solving therapeutic intervention approach includes the following elements: (1) creating a sanctuary; (2) focusing on critical areas of concern; (3) specifying desired outcomes; (4) reviewing assets; (5) developing a general plan; (6) identifying practical initial implementations; (7) reviewing self-efficacy; and (8) setting appointments for review, reassurance, and further implementation (Blau, 1994).

Blau (1994) delineates a number of effective individual intervention strategies for police officers, including the following:

> *Attentive Listening:* This includes good eye contact, appropriate body language, and genuine interest, without inappropriate comment or interruption. Clinicians will recognize this intervention as "active listening."
>
> *Being There With Empathy:* This therapeutic attitude conveys availability, concern, and awareness of the turbulent emotions being experienced by the traumatized officer. It is also helpful to let the officer know what he or she is likely to experience in the days and weeks ahead.
>
> *Reassurance:* In acute stress situations, this should take the form of realistically reassuring the officer that routine matters will be taken care of, deferred responsibilities will be handled by others, and that the officer has administrative and command support.
>
> *Supportive Counseling:* This includes effective listening, restatement of content, clarification of feelings, and reassurance, as well as community referral and networking with liaison agencies, when necessary.
>
> *Interpretive Counseling:* This type of intervention should be used when the officer's emotional reaction is significantly greater than the circumstances that the critical incident seem to warrant. In appropriate cases, this therapeutic strategy can stimulate the officer to explore underlying emotional stresses that intensify a naturally stressful traumatic event. In a few cases, this may lead to ongoing psychotherapy.

Not to be neglected is the use of humor, which has its place in many forms of psychotherapy, but may be especially useful in working with law enforcement and emergency services personnel. In general, if the therapist and patient can share a laugh, this may lead to the sharing of more intimate feelings. Humor serves to bring a sense of balance, perspective, and clarity to a world that seems to have been warped and polluted by malevolence and horror. Humor—even sarcastic, gross, or callous humor, if handled appropriately and used constructively—may allow the venting of anger, frustration, resentment, or sadness, and thereby lead to productive, reintegrative therapeutic work (Fullerton et al., 1992; Miller, 1994; Silva, 1991).

Departmental Support

Even in the absence of formal psychotherapeutic intervention, following a department-wide critical incident, such as a line-of-duty death or a particularly stressful rescue or arrest, the mental health professional can advise and guide law enforcement departments in encouraging and implementing several organizational response measures, based on the available literature on individual and group coping strategies for public safety personnel (Alexander, 1993; Alexander & Walker, 1994; Alexander & Wells, 1991; DeAngelis, 1995; Fullerton et al., 1992; Palmer, 1983). Many of these measures are applicable proactively as part of training before a critical incident occurs. Some specific measures include the following:

(1) Encourage mutual support among peers and supervisors. The former typically happens anyway; the latter may need some explicit reinforcement. Police officers frequently work as partners and understand that shared decision-making and mutual reassurance can enhance effective job performance.

(2) Utilize humor as a coping mechanism to facilitate emotional insulation and group bonding. The first forestalls excessive identification with victims, the second encourages mutual group support via a shared language. Of course, the mental health clinician needs to monitor the line between adaptive humor and unproductive gratuitous nastiness that only serves to entrench cynicism and despair.

(3) Make use of appropriate rituals to give meaning and dignity to an otherwise existentially disorienting experience. This includes not only religious rites related to mourning, but such respectful protocols as a military-style honor guard to attend bodies before disposition, and the formal acknowledgment of actions above and beyond the call of duty. Important here is the role of "grief leadership," in which the commanding officer demonstrates by exam-

ple that it's okay to express grief and mourn the death of fallen comrades or civilians and that the dignified expression of one's feelings about the incident will be supported, not denigrated.

Conclusion

Psychotherapy with law enforcement and emergency services personnel entails its share of frustration as well as satisfaction. A certain flexibility is called for in adapting traditional psychotherapeutic models and techniques for use with this group and clinical work frequently requires both firm professional grounding and "seat-of-the-pants" maneuverability. Incomplete closures and partial successes are to be expected, but in a few instances, the impact of successful intervention can have profound effects on morale and job effectiveness that may be felt department-wide. Working with these "tough guys" takes skill, dedication, and sometimes a strong stomach, but for mental health clinicians who are not afraid to tough it out themselves, this can be a fascinating and rewarding area of clinical practice.

References

Alexander, D.A. (1993). Stress among body handlers A long-term follow-up." *British Journal of Psychiatry, 163,* 806–808.

Alexander, D.A. & Walker, L.G. (1994). "A study of methods used by Scottish police officers to cope with work-related stress." *Stress Medicine, 10,* 131–138.

Alexander, D.A. & Wells, A. (1991). "Reactions of police officers to body-handling after a major disaster: A before-and-after comparison." *British Journal of Psychiatry, 159,* 547–555.

Anderson, W., Swenson, D. & Clay, D. (1995). *Stress Management for Law Enforcement Officers.* Englewood Cliffs, NJ: Prentice Hall.

Belles. D. & Norvell, N. (1990). *Stress Management Workbook for Law Enforcement Officers.* Sarasota: Professional Resource Exchange.

Bisson, J.I. & Deahl, M.P. (1994). "Psychological debriefing and prevention of post-traumatic stress: More research is needed." *British Journal of Psychiatry, 165,* 717–720.

Blau,T.H. (1994). *Psychological Services for Law Enforcement,* New York: Wiley.

Bohl, N. (1995). "Professionally administered critical incident debriefing for police officers." In M.1. Kunke & E.M. Scrivner (Eds.), *Police Psychology Into the 21st Century*(pp. 169–188). Hillsdale: Eribaum.

Bordow, S. & Porritt, D. (1979). "An experimental evaluation of crisis inter-vention." *Psychological Bulletin, 84,* 1189–1217.

Borum, R. & Philpot, C. (1993). "Therapy with law enforcement couples: Clinical management of the 'high-risk lifestyle.'" *American Journal of Family Therapy, 21,* 122–135.

Cummings, J.P. (1996). "Police stress and the suicide link." *The Police Chief,* October, pp. 85–96.

Davis. J.A. (1998/99). "Providing critical incident stress debriefing (CISD) to in-dividuals and communities in situational crisis," *Trauma Response, 5,* 19–21.

DeAngelis, T. (1995). "Firefighters' PTSD at dangerous levels." *APA Monitor,* February, pp. 36–37.

Dyregrov, A. (1989). "Caring for helpers in disaster situations: Psychological debriefing." *Disaster Management, 2,* 25–30.

Flannery, R.B., Fulton, P. & Tausch, J. (1991). "A program to help staff cope with psychological sequelae of assaults by patients." *Hospital and Community Psychiatry, 42,* 935–938.

Fullerton, C.S., McCarroll, J.E., Ursano, R.J., & Wright, K.M. (1992). "Psy-chological responses of rescue workers: Firefighters and trauma." *American Journal of Orthopsychiatry, 62,* 371–378.

Hays, T. (1994). "Daily horrors take heavy toll on New York City police offi-cers." *The* News, September 28, pp. 2A–3A.

Holt, F.X. (1989). "Dispatchers' hidden critical incidents." *Fire Engineering* No-vember, pp. 53–55.

Horn, J.M. (1991). "Critical incidents for law enforcement officers." In J.T. Reese, J.M. Horn & C. Dunning (Eds.), *Critical Incidents in Policing* (rev. ed., pp. 143–148). Washington DC: U.S. Government Printing Office.

Kirschman, E. (1997). *I Love a Cop: What Police Families Need to Know.* New York. Guilford.

McCafferty, R.L., McCafferty, E. & McCafferty, M.A. (1992). "Stress and sui-cide in police officers: Paradigms of occupational stress." *Southern Medical Journal, 85,* 233.

McMains, M.J. (1991). "The management and treatment of postshooting trauma." In J.T. Horn & C. Dunning (Eds.), *Critical Incidents in Policing* (rev ed., pp. 191–198). Washington DC: U.S. Government Printing Office.

Miller, L. (1994). "Civilian posttraumatic stress disorder: Clinical syndromes and psychotherapeutic strategies." *Psychotherapy, 31,* 655–664.

Miller, L. (1995). "Tough guys: Psychotherapeutic strategies with law en-forcement and emergency services personnel." *Psychotherapy, 32,* 592–600.

Miller, L. (1997). "Workplace violence in the rehabilitation setting: How to prepare, respond, and survive." *Florida State Association of Rehabilitation Nurses Newsletter*, 7, 4–6.

Miller, L. (1998a). "Our own medicine: Traumatized psychotherapists and the stresses of doing therapy." *Psychotherapy*, 35, 137–146.

Miller, L. (1998b). "Psychotherapy of crime victims: Treating the aftermath of interpersonal violence." *Psychotherapy*, 35, 336–345.

Miller, L. (1998c). *Shocks to the System: Psychotherapy of Traumatic Disability Syndromes*. New York: Norton.

Miller, L. (1999). "Treating posttraumatic stress disorder in children and families: Basic principles and clinical applications." *American Journal of Family Therapy*, 27, 21–34.

Miller, L. (in press). "Workplace violence: Prevention, response, and recovery." *Psychotherapy*.

Mitchell, J.T. (1983). "When disaster strikes … . The critical incident stress process." *Journal of the Emergency Medical Services*, 8, 36–39.

Mitchell, J.T. (1988). "The history, status, and future of critical incident stress debriefings." *Journal of the Emergency Medical Services*, 13, 47–52.

Mitchell, J.T. (1991). "Law enforcement applications for critical incident stress teams." In J.T. Reese, J.M. Horn & C. Dunning (Eds.), *Critical Incidents In Policing*(rev. ed., pp. 201–212). Washington DC: U.S. Government Printing Office.

Mitchell. J.T. & Bray, G.P. (1990). *Emergency Services Stress: Guidelines for Preserving the Health and Careers of Emergency Services Personnel*. Englewood Cliffs, NJ: Prentice-Hall.

Mitchell, J.T. & Everly, G.S. (1996). *Critical Incident Stress Debriefing: Operations Manual.*(rev. ed.). Ellicott City, MD: Chevron.

Palmer, C.E. (1983). "A note about paramedics' strategies for dealing with death and dying." *Journal of Occupational Psychology*, 56, 83–86.

Reese, J.T. (1987). "Coping with stress: It's your job." In J.T. Reese (Ed.), *Behavioral Science in Law Enforcement* (pp. 75–79). Washington DC: FBI.

Reese. J.T. (1991). "Justifications for mandating critical incident aftercare." In J.T. Reese, J.M. Horn & C. Dunning (Eds.), *Critical Incidents in Policing* (rev. ed., pp. 213–220). Washington DC: U.S. Government Printing Office.

Seligmann, J., Holt, D., Chinni, D. & Roberta, E. (1994). "Cops who kill— themselves." *Newsweek*, September 26, p. 58.

Sewell, J.D. (1986). "Administrative concerns in law enforcement stress management." *Police Studies: The International Review of Police Development*, 9, 153–159.

Sewell, J.D. (1993). "Traumatic stress of multiple murder investigations." *Journal of Traumatic Stress*, 6, 103–118.

Sewell, J.D. (1994). "The stress of homicide investigations." *Death Studies*, 18, 565–582.

Sewell, J.D. & Crew, L. (1984). "The forgotten victim: Stress and the police dispatcher." *FBI Law Enforcement Bulletin*, March, pp. 7–11.

Sewell, J.D., Ellison, K.W. & Hurrell, J.J. (1988). "Stress management in law enforcement: Where do we go from here?" *The Police Chief*, October, pp. 94–98.

Silva, M.N. (1991). "The delivery of mental health services to law enforcement officers." In J.T. Reese, J.M. Horn & C. Dunning (Eds.), *Critical Incidents in Policing*(rev ed., pp. 335–341). Washington, DC: U.S. Government Printing Office.

Solomon, R.M. (1988). "Post-shooting trauma." *The Police Chief*, October, pp. 40–44.

Solomon. R.M. (1990). "Administrative guidelines for dealing with officers involved in on-duty shooting situations." *The Police Chief*, February, p. 40.

Solomon, R.M. (1995). "Critical incident stress management in law enforcement." In G.S. Everly (Ed.), *Innovations in Disaster and Trauma Psychology: Applications in Emergency Services and Disaster Response*(pp. 123–157). Ellicott City, MD: Chevron.

Solomon, Z. & Benbenishty, R. (1988). "The role of proximity, immediacy, and expectance in frontline treatment of combat stress reactions among Israelis in the Lebanon war." *American Journal of Psychiatry*, 143, 613–617.

Discussion Questions

1. When the author refers to "tough guys" in his article, to whom is he referring?

2. In what ways are police officers different from other emergency workers in their reluctance to show any weakness?

3. What is done by police agencies to avoid the overly "shrinky" connotations associated with programs of mental health intervention services for law enforcement personnel?

4. According to the Mitchell model, following a critical incident there are a number of criteria on which peer support and command staff might decide to provide a debriefing to personnel. What do these criteria include?

5. The formal critical incident stress debriefing (CISD) process consists of seven standard phases. What are they?

6. Why do police officers have a reputation for shunning mental health services and practitioners?

7. What requirements are outlined by the author for establishing therapeutic mutual trust?

8. What did the author recommend for the first meeting between the therapist and the officer?

9. One researcher delineated a number of effective individual strategies for assisting police officers. What do these include?

36

PTSD Treatment for Law Enforcement Personnel: An Information Processing Perspective

Carol Logan

Over the past twenty years, important developments in the understanding of Post Traumatic Stress Disorder (PTSD) have provided a greater understanding of the origins of trauma, the specific aspects of its development, and what can be done to resolve it. The most compelling information comes not from psychology but from the neurosciences which have linked trauma to the brain's mechanics of information processing and memory formation. These findings directly impact the understanding of common areas of struggle for much of law enforcement personnel in their constant exposure to high stress in the form of danger, high risk, violence, death, and loss.

This article will summarize these neurophysiological developments and discuss their implications for professionals who are working with police officers and others in the law enforcement setting. Additionally, it will also discuss treatment for law enforcement officers that seems to develop directly from this new understanding of brain physiology.

The Brain's Task: Processing Information

According to neurophysiologists, of all the brain's many jobs, one of its most important functions is to process the large inflow of sensory information, delete what is unnecessary, and store for future use what is possibly beneficial for survival. This information processing function of the brain is also one of the most crucial for police officers facing critical incidents. At any given moment the brain takes in a massive amount of information: visual, auditory, somatic (body sensations), cognitive (thoughts), and affective (emotion). This information goes through various stages of processing, resulting in the overwhelming majority getting deleted, and the remaining stored and linked with other information similarly categorized.

This is true even when the experience is emotionally charged. To the brain, emotion is just another form of information. In fact there's consistent data that show that emotionally elevated experiences are remembered more clearly (Siegel, 1997) from the increase in stress hormones and neurotransmitters, which is likely a basic survival mechanism of the body. Successful processing and integration of emotionally charged experiences allows for the use of important related information in the future.

For example, let's imagine that these are ancient times, mankind's hunter/gatherer days, when walking through the countryside, we pass by a dense grove of trees and hear a low, unfamiliar growl. A predatory cat then leaps out. We respond by waving our arms and yelling, and the cat runs off. We process through the emotional distress by talking about what happened, expressing emotion about it, thinking about it, dreaming about— and, under most circumstances, the disturbing aspects of the experience process through, and the experience is integrated into the memory-linked body of related information already stored. Any valuable information remains available for future use: these cats possibly hide in dense groves; the sound of a low growl is linked to this predatory cat and means danger; the waving of hands to ward off this attack was successful as was the case when we previously encountered other similar predatory cats.

What Happens When the Experience Is Traumatic?

Neurophysiological studies are finding that events characterized by extreme trauma do not follow this same course of information processing. These studies are showing that this extreme arousal disrupts the normal information processing of the experience, dramatically interrupting the functioning of each of the critical neurostructures. When this disruption occurs, the individual may develop the symptoms of PTSD.

An understanding of the nature of this breakdown in the brain has distinct implications for the treatment of PTSD. Since one of the occupational hazards for law enforcement workers is frequent exposure to trauma and therefore the possibility of developing PTSD, such an understanding can be crucial for professionals who oversee programs or who offer treatment to these front-line law enforcement workers.

Two Separate Pathways: Explicit and Implicit Information

In order to understand the nature of this breakdown, it is important to recognize the two separate layers of information processing that occur in the brain prior to an incident being committed to memory. These layers follow two separate and divergent pathways through the brain. One of these pathways comprises the processing of the *explicit* information and the other is composed of processing the *implicit* information in any given situation. These two split processes follow their separate neurological pathways until they join together at the end of the process and are consolidated into one complete memory.

It takes the consolidation of both these aspects for there to be an integrated memory where the event is clearly understood, including the factors that led to it, facts about when it happened, and the ultimate outcome. This consolidation ensures that the individual's recollection of the event is grounded firmly in the past and is experienced as a memory rather than a "here and now" physical and sensory event.

In order to fully grasp the significance of this neurophysiological process, it is necessary to understand the characteristics of explicit versus implicit categories of information.

Explicit Information — Defined

Explicit information consists of two components: First, facts and general information and second, autobiographical data. The explicit layer provides the contextual information of the event — the how, where and what. The autobiographical aspect places self in the event in space and time. For example, if an officer was attacked by a suspect, the facts and general information would be: A man in his late 30s, with short brown hair, wearing a blue t-shirt, swung his right arm. The autobiographical information would be, "I was hit; it occurred last Sunday around 2:30 p.m."

Implicit Information — Defined

On the other hand, implicit information is composed of emotions, body sensations, reflexes, and classical conditioned responses. Implicit information is raw sensory data devoid of information regarding the context within. In the assault exampl,e the implicit information is anger and fear, tightness in the chest, pain in the jaw, and an impulse to reach for a weapon.

Information Processing

There are several different neurostructures that are primarily involved in the information processing of these two pathways and that finally consolidate the pathways into one comprehensive memory.

The Explicit Information Processing Layer

Two neurostructures in particular seem to be centrally involved in the processing of the explicit information. One of these is the *prefrontal cortex* which is the center for higher reasoning and focused attention. It is this brain structure that provides the ability to observe (mindfulness), know, and predict and that has access to the stores of processed, categorized, information that has accumulated over a lifetime of experiences. This allows it to be the balancing point for our emotional selves in part by inhibiting, organizing, and modulating the automatic emotional responses coming from the limbic brain.

With regard to information processing, the prefrontal cortex is especially involved with linking of new information to previously stored related information and with assessing the context of such information. For example, if I am an officer on a patrol shift, when my sergeant loudly and unexpectedly reprimands me, my prefrontal cortex can access my background history and the specific context of the current situation and let me know that: 1) this is my sergeant, not my grandfather who used to yell at me like that; 2) I am an adult and I am perfectly capable of protecting myself through a variety of sophisticated methods; and 3) since this is a work setting, it's not appropriate for me to yell back or to burst into tears like I did when I was three years old.

A second neurostructure that is instrumental in processing explicit data is the *hippocampus*. This structure is involved with the sorting, processing and storing of explicit layers of information. It moves the vast information that is obtained from any incident though a series of stages such as sensory memory, working memory, long-term memory.

The Implicit Information Processing Layer

Two other neurostructures are primarily concerned with the processing of implicit information. One of these is the *thalamus*, located in the forebrain. This location positions it to act as a relay station between the higher cortical centers and the lower limbic centers. The thalamus has multiple functions outside of the information process, but with regard to information processing, it initially receives the vast inflow of information and conducts the first level of sorting.

The other neurostructure is the *amygdala* which serves as the brain's "smoke detector". It is always scanning for danger, tagging incoming stimuli, identifying emotional significance, and determining if there is an emotional response or if an emotionally driven action is to be immediately taken (fight, flight or freeze). The amygdala is largely responsible for the sorting, processing, and encoding of implicit information. It is considered to be the structure that provides emotional meaning to the inflow of information from the senses.

Consolidation of the Two Layers

The final stage of information processing is cortical consolidation which combines and integrates the separately processed explicit and implicit information of a situation. It also links this integrated data with the body of previously acquired related knowledge and information and it allows the entire memory to move into permanent memory storage. It is relevant to note that research over the years has also shown that rapid eye movement (REM) sleep is critical to the moving of this information from one stage of information processing to the next. In the case of extreme trauma, however, this cortical consolidation does not occur.

Explicit Information — Illustration

An illustration of explicit information for an officer-involved incident would be as follows:

> *Tuesday evening at 2:00 a.m., traffic stop on the north-bound Interstate near the first main exit into town, I approach the vehicle, the suspect steps out of the driver side door, right arm raises to point a handgun in my direction. Suspect is a white male, in his late 30s, approximately 6' with short brown hair. I am wearing my protective vest under my uniform. Suspect fires two rounds, one round striking me in the chest area. I return fire. The subject falls to the ground, I report "shots fired, suspect down." Back-up officers arrive.*

Implicit Information — Illustration

By contrast, an illustration of implicit information of the same officer-involved event follows:

Terror, heart pounding, can't breathe, heat flashing through my body, stomach sinking like on a roller coaster, chest tight.

When the brain's information processing system is functioning properly, these two layers of information would be processed through separate pathways and then be consolidated and integrated into a complete memory. This memory then can be efficiently stored and calmly and appropriately retrieved at any time in the future when it may be needed.

Thus the raw emotion of the implicit aspect of the experience would be combined and integrated with the rational, step-by-step linear understanding of the facts and embedded within the time-line from beginning to end. The individual would have, at most, a frightening memory, but it would be experienced clearly as a *memory* that occurred in the past and not as a concurrent event to be experienced in the present moment.

What Happens When There Is Trauma?

When officers are exposed to extreme trauma, there is an instant cascade of neurochemical changes. Hormones and neurotransmitters are stimulated and flood the nervous system and the structures of the brain. As a result, neither the *explicit* nor the *implicit* information is properly processed.

With regard to the EXPLICIT information pathway, the hippocampus in particular is sensitive to cortisol levels; it is cortisol that serves as one of the primary stress hormones. When it reaches a critical level, the hippocampus shuts down, thus sending the entire chain of explicit information "off line" entirely. So the explicit information is not properly processed, integrated, and stored.

Meanwhile, during a high trauma situation, the IMPLICIT INFORMATION goes unprocessed as well. Implicit information is left stored in the amygdala as fragmented raw sensory data in the form of feelings, body sensations, and images. It remains separate from the related explicit information. This raw emotional fragment of implicit data stays stranded in the nervous system, separated from all other related information, frozen without reference to time and detached without reference to location.

Because there are no retrievable data regarding the time frame, the event is not anchored in time and other contextual data. In the absence of this data, the only thing the individual can do is to go to the default timeframe which is RIGHT NOW. Because there are no anchoring data indicating the location, the only thing the individual can do is to go to the default location which is RIGHT HERE.

A memory that has not been integrated is just an incomplete fragment and not a total entity. It usually consists of only that most terrifying moment, that one snapshot of time, where the individual honestly doesn't know if he or she will live, die, or be seriously injured. This memory fragment is not connected to the outcome that may have occurred as soon as only a few moments later, and it does not have a working connection to those unique, singular events that led up to the terrifying moment. The rational brain understands that a myriad of antecedent events must occur for this same horrific event to occur again, but a fragmented implicit memory is not associated with any of the necessary antecedent events.

Of course another, more rational, separate area of the officer's brain knows that he or she is in a different location and at a different point in time than when the incident occurred, but that crucial information is not connected to the neurological bundle that contains the trauma memory.

All of this has direct implications for treatment because it becomes apparent why therapeutic efforts to verbally provide corrective factual data into the officer's rational brain are often not at all helpful. That information already exists in the cognitive area of the officer's brain, the prefrontal cortex and it is the *connection* that needs to be made. The neurological bundle that contains the raw sensory data of the traumatic experience needs to be integrated with the explicit contextual data and this can only happen through neurological processing, information processing between the two areas of the brain.

Linkage to General Knowledge

Not only is the information prevented from being appropriately processed, but normal encoding and linkage to previously acquired adaptive information and general background knowledge does not occur. With the explicit information disrupted from moving through the normal processing stages, the autobiographical, related facts, and general information from the experience goes missing.

To summarize, during a traumatic experience, both the explicit and the implicit information are stored in the brain, but in separate areas with no means of communication between the two. This state of affairs has several implications.

1. There are no corrective experiences that are added to nor integrated with a trauma memory.

This memory is isolated from any additional life experiences. Unfortunately this stored sensory information commonly remains stable over any length of time and is largely unchanged by other experiences that might ordinarily provide counterbalancing corrective information.

For example, if 20 years ago I was assaulted walking out of movie theatre at night into a dark parking lot, I can gather two decades of experience of walking out of movie theatres at night into dark parking lots and not being harmed and still feel fear. All those years of experiences and the knowledge they contain does not alter the fear that remains unprocessed in my amygdala. If I am taking the trash to the street at night and a jogger unexpected runs out of the shadows the memory from that 20-year-old assault can get activated, bringing forth a feeling of terror and the experience of the heart pounding but, because the explicit information from that memory is not connected, it does not register as a memory. Since it has no anchor in time and no anchor in a specific past location reference, my mind believed the time is NOW and the location is HERE.

2. The trauma memory can be unexpectedly triggered by associated stimuli.

The implicit information that is tied to the experience can be triggered by any stimuli the brain perceives as similar, whether it be that same specific location, or any similar nondescript dark parking lot. The amygdala holding the unprocessed emotional data quickly activates this information by any real or imagined potential harm.

As a result, the officer who has been previously involved in a shooting may suddenly experience symptoms when she fires her weapon at the firing range during her routine quarterly firearm qualification. As another example, a police accident investigator who is off duty and driving his daughter to gymnastics class might experience symptoms as he approaches the railroad crossing where he had previously had the gruesome task of processing the body parts of a decapitated victim.

3. The individual often cannot verbally articulate any rational reason for this anxiety.

When a traumatic memory is triggered, it is not generally the stored explicit information that presents itself unexpectedly, but it is the unprocesssed implicit-only information that springs forward consisting of emotions, visual images, and other sensory information. The moment in which the extreme trauma first registers is widely referred to in law enforcement circles as the "Oh Shit!" moment. This label can actually be considered quite accurate. Because the rational verbal part of the brain that contains the explicit information is not functionally connected to it, and because the verbal labels have not been integrated with the raw sensory data, the person finds it difficult to articulate what he or she is thinking or feeling. Additionally, there is little or no access to the related body of stored information that would balance out the emotional/somatic response such as the following:

> *I am an adult and I have handled this many times before. Even though for a few terrifying moments I felt trapped and powerless in that situa-*

tion, I have actually handled dozens of other situations like this very well, and I was successful.

PTSD as a Memory Disorder

All this neurophysiological data then raise the question of how PTSD is officially classified. It is currently classified as a psychological disorder and, more specifically, an anxiety disorder. Robert Stickgold and others point out that this may be appropriate in a clinical sense, but the anxiety is actually only a symptom of the underlying memory malfunction. When the memory processing is given the chance to correct the information processing, the anxiety problem no longer exists. This neurophysiological material suggests that PTSD may actually more appropriately be called a memory disorder. (Stickgold, 2009.)

Treatment of PTSD

Of all the challenges for which individuals come to therapists for help, PTSD is one of the most treatable. Two treatment methods, Eye Movement Desensitization and Reprocessing (EMDR) and Cognitive Behavioral Therapy (CBT), have been researched for over 20 years, accumulating a breadth of data showing a high level of effectiveness of treatment. (Shapiro, 2002; Carlson, Chemtob, and Rusnak , et al., 1998; Edmond, Rubin, and Wambach, 1999; Ironson, Freund, and Strauss, et al., 2002; Lee, Gavriel, and Drummond, et al., 2002; Marcus, Marquis, and Sakai, 1997; Power, McGoldrick, and Brown, et al., 2002; Soberman, Greenwald, and Rule, 2002.)

Here we will focus on the former, as research shows EMDR to be the more efficient of the two, requiring fewer sessions and no homework outside of sessions, and more quickly producing symptom relief.

EMDR Treatment

EMDR treatment responds directly to the problem in the brain's previously described information processing system. The explanatory theory for the effectiveness of EMDR is referred to as the Adaptive Information Processing Model and was developed by Shapiro (2001).

Quite simply, EMDR treatment provides the brain with another opportunity to process traumatic memories or disturbing life events that remain frozen in the nervous system. Through the EMDR approach a conscious link is created to the traumatic memory and the fragmented aspects stored in their respective parts of the brain. That link is created by the individual recalling the worst aspects of the trauma and describing them to the EMDR therapist. Eye movements then are initiated with the individual moving his or her eyes from side to side, guided by the therapist's hand, a hand-held wand, or light bar equipment designed specifically for this purpose. (Some police officers have compared this to the "horizontal gaze nystagmus" procedure they use in field testing drunk drivers.)

This eye movement has the effect of "jump starting" the innate processing system that had shut down due to being overwhelmed by the intensity of the disturbance. At this point in the treatment, the brain's own natural system begins to do its job of reprocessing the disturbing aspects of the memory. Discussion with the therapist between sets of eye movement helps to keep the therapeutic process on track with the brain's natural process and monitors the progress of the brain's natural healing mechanism. With each set of eye movements, the unprocessed information from the memory moves further along the appropriate neurological pathways and does so at an accelerated rate of speed. The EMDR therapist then continues sets of eye movements until full consolidation of the memory occurs and all related disturbance is eliminated.

Once that memory is reprocessed, any valuable information tied to the experience becomes available for future use. It is now thought that the repairing of dysfunctional linkage to the broader body of knowledge and experience is a central aspect of the healing process.

Using the example of the previous assault at age 20, once that memory is fully addressed, this experience then no longer triggers any reactive response. That traumatic memory then is connected to all other related experiences of walking in dark areas, coming out of movie theatres and being safe. That old memory is no longer isolated and fragmented in the nervous system.

Once the trauma is reprocessed, the officer more fully remembers even some previously lost aspects of the event and is more fully aware of the contextual data. The memory is firmly anchored in a time and place, and that point is firmly rooted in the *past*. The officer is truly aware that the feelings are not happening right here and right now. The memory of the instance of controlled terror is also not floating by itself in a timeless place, but is anchored along with the memories of the direct aftermath, including the knowledge that "I survived." The officer's thought process becomes something similar to the following:

> *I remember that as a scary moment, but it is only a memory. Although, at that past moment, I thought I was going to die, in reality, I did not die, and I am not in danger right now. I took effective action and went home to my family. Yes, it is an unpleasant memory, but it is only a memory. I also realize that many other times I have been in situations that may have had some similarities to the trauma situation, and those occasions have turned out just fine.*

PTSD as an Accumulation of Painful Events

The general issue of cumulative stress is particularly relevant to law enforcement since officers on patrol, as well as on other specialized assignments, are frequently and even routinely exposed to trauma. PTSD results from two types of stressors. One is the single event, the overwhelming experience that in law enforcement is typically connected to a critical incident such as an officer-involved shooting or officers working in the aftermath of a multiple casualty incident.

But PTSD can also result from a second type of stressor, painful life experiences that accumulate over time. Mol et al. (2005) looked at the severity of PTSD symptoms and these two types of trauma. They found that people who had experienced a major traumatic event had slightly less severe symptoms than those whose PTSD resulted from an accumulation of disturbing life events.

In law enforcement, this might explain why officers can be exposed to horrific experiences over the course of years without an obvious struggle, then one relatively minor event triggers a post trauma response.

Cumulative trauma within the EMDR treatment process also suggests that some more recent trauma memories may be directly linked to other trauma memories that occurred earlier in the person's career or life. Sometimes it is necessary to clear all the "feeder memories" that are linked within the network of trauma memories.

This corresponds with clinical observations in the treatment of law enforcement officers in EMDR treatment. Frequently during the process of resolution of the most recent trauma, other past traumas, or "feeder memories," pop into consciousness. This actually presents a useful window of opportunity not only to clear out the most obvious recent trauma, but to clean out other traumas that have accumulated during the past and that continue to subliminally affect behavior. Since the information processing was disrupted during the original critical incident, the individual, working with the EMDR therapist, often will spontaneously go back weeks, months, or even years later and reprocess this information, in the way it was originally intended to be processed.

It may seem that individuals who have experienced a trauma should obviously be aware that it is affecting them. Yet, because police officers may store multiple trauma memories over the course of a career or a lifetime, they are sometimes unaware that past incidents are still affecting them. Let's look at an example of the unique way that trauma can unexpectedly be triggered, even decades after the events. An officer, in the top level rank of his agency's command staff, routinely represented his department at public events because of his great skill at talking in public to large gatherings. After years of successful speaking engagements, he suddenly and quite inexplicably began experiencing severe anxiety symptoms whenever he had to speak in public. Over several months, he tried many things to overcome this, even resorting to taking prescription anti-anxiety medication. Finally, he worked with an EMDR therapist who helped him target his feelings of anxiety during public events.

Several sets of eye movement were used to clarify and isolate the source of his trauma. As he focused upon the circumstances that seemed to trigger the anxiety symptoms, his focus gradually began to narrow upon the video cameras in the audience that sometimes recorded his speech. More sets of eye movement focused not only upon the cameras but oddly, on the small red dot of light that indicated that the camera was recording. As the EMDR process continued, it was during the next set of eye movements that a traumatic memory broke through and, with accompanying emotion, he recalled his experience decades earlier when he was a young soldier on patrol in Viet Nam one wet and rainy night. In the miserable weather, he was sorely tempted to sneak a cigarette even though his squad leader had forbidden it. Suddenly in the thick, wet, darkness, it became clear that there was an enemy sniper hiding in the bushes across a clearing. Immediately, he and his buddies responded with a thundering volley of automatic fire in a cloud of smoke, decisively eliminating the threat. Terror shot through him as he realized that this could just as easily been his own fate. For the sign that tipped them off to the deadly sniper threat in that night years in the past, was the glowing red ember that became visible as the enemy Viet Cong soldier softly lit up his cigarette. Thus the process of EMDR had not only served to make this emotional connection to the cause of the anxiety, but after a few more sets of eye movement sessions, was able to resolve it as well.

EMDR Similarity to REM Sleep

Numerous theories have been developed as to why EMDR works. The most frequently presented theory links EMDR to Rapid Eye Movement (REM) sleep. The theory is that EMDR creates a similar brain/mind state as REM which, as previously mentioned, has been identified as a critical element in certain aspects of information processing and memory formation. It is further theorized that EMDR is simply using the same mechanism in a more focused way and in a clinical setting.

Currently there are over 71 studies that have been done using EMDR in the treatment of trauma, resulting in it being the ranked on the recommended list, among many others, by the Substance Abuse and Mental Health Services

Administration (SAMHSA) within the U.S. Department of Health and Human Services, the National Registry of Evidence-based Programs and Practices (2011), and the American Psychiatric Association (2004). The Department of Veterans Affairs and Department of Defense (2004) have placed EMDR in the "A" category as "strongly recommended" for the treatment of trauma. Additionally, five meta-analyses (Bisson and Andrew (2007); Bradley et al. (2005); Davidson and Parker, (2001); Maxfield and Hyer (2002), and Seidler and Wagner (2006)) have been done regarding EMDR.

Indicators of Measurable Physical Changes in the Brain

One study that focused on Vietnam veterans found that soldiers who were exposed to the chronic stress of combat had smaller hippocampi compared to soldiers who had non-combat duties. (Bremner, et al., 1995) This study was replicated in 1996 and also found that the smaller a soldier's hippocampus, the more likely he was to have had combat exposure and more severe PTSD. The same result was also found in a 1997 study on women chronically sexually abused as children.

The assertion that EMDR responds directly to the new neuropsychological view of information processing is supported by other important studies. One, by Bossini et al. (2007) at the University of Siena Medical School, found that not only did EMDR treatment eliminate PTSD symptoms but also resulted in an increase in hippocampal volume, underscoring not only the effectiveness of this treatment approach but also the amazing healing capacity of the brain.

EMDR Research with Police Officers

As previously noted, many studies have documented the use of EMDR as a treatment for PTSD, as well as many other disorders, Two main research studies (Lansing, Amen, Hanks, and Rudy, 2005. and Wilson, Logan, Becker, and Tinker 2001) have investigated the use of EMDR for treatment of stress and PTSD specifically for police officers. These studies complement each other very well, providing a more comprehensive picture of how EMDR can be used in a law enforcement setting. The study by Lansing and his colleagues demonstrates the use of EMDR with officers who had moderate to severe PTSD symptoms as the result of on-duty, officer-involved shootings. This study not only reflects the successful use of the treatment but also documents the actual physical changes that occurred in the brain as a result of the treatment.

The study by Wilson et al. (2001) demonstrates the use of EMDR for a much larger sample of police officers (N=60), with 30 officers assigned to a traditional stress management treatment group, and 30 officers assigned to an EMDR treatment group. This study investigated the use of EMDR as a stress management technique for officers who were not necessarily experiencing clinical level of PTSD symptoms. It supports the use of the treatment for a subclinical population, regular officers who presumably are exposed to the standard level of trauma experienced by normal police officers over the course of their career. The outcome measures fell into four groups: Five Personal and Job Stress measures; a Marital Relationship measure which involved the officers' significant others; a Posttraumatic Stress Disorder Diagnostic Scale; and a Symptom Check List.

The EMDR treatment focused upon officers' designation of stress in three separate areas of their own lives: 1) stress from the nature of police work, e.g., (critical incidents); 2) stress due to organizational and administrative factors; and 3) stress due to personal factors. Each officer in the EMDR treatment condition was scheduled for three, two-hour EMDR sessions following the standard protocol (Shapiro, 1995) and using his/her own designated areas of stress as the target.

Officers in the stress management condition were provided a six-session, professionally prepared, video course of the type used in police departments as a tool for reducing stress. Each of the six sessions took about an hour. Each topic is accompanied by a workbook which provides an overview for the videotape and includes "stop and reflect" questions that focus attention on the issues covered. A number of critical topics were covered in the program: Handling Workplace Pressure; Clarifying Roles and Expectations; Controlling the Workload; Managing People Pressures; Surviving the Changing Workplace; and Balancing Work and Home.

Upon completion, officers in the EMDR condition showed greater improvements on measures of PTSD symptoms, subjective distress, job stress, anger, and marital satisfaction ratings, than those who were in the Stress Management conditions. The curative effects of EMDR were maintained at the 6-month follow-up indicating enduring gains from a relatively brief treatment regimen for these officers.

The research by Lansing et al. (2005) studied six police officers who had been involved in on-duty shootings and who had also developed delayed-onset PTSD. Three to four EMDR treatment sessions were conducted with each officer, and sessions averaged from two to three hours in length. Because of the intensity of this type of treatment, the sessions were spaced three to four weeks apart. After treatment with EMDR, all officers showed marked clinical improvement not only in PTSD symptoms, but also as measured by a high-resolution brain single photon emission computed tomography (SPECT) imaging scan, reflecting physical changes in the brain. There were decreases in the left and right occipital lobe, left parietal lobe, and right precentral frontal lobe, as well as significant increased perfusion in the left inferior frontal gyrus —all linked to trauma experiences. In this study, EMDR was an effective treatment for PTSD in this police officer group, showing both clinical and brain imaging changes.

As this area of research has shown, the understanding of PTSD as a memory disorder based on an information processing model seems to be useful in understanding PTSD in a law enforcement setting. Professionals in law enforcement settings should continue to investigate the use of an information processing model in understanding the effects of PTSD and stress upon law enforcement workers and in selecting interventions for the treatment of their symptoms.

References

American Psychiatric Association (2004). *Practice Guideline for the Treatment of Patients with Acute Stress Disorder and Posttraumatic Stress Disorder.* Arlington, VA: American Psychiatric Association Practice Guidelines.

Bisson, J., and Andrew, M. (2007). Psychological treatment of post-traumatic stress disorder (PTSD). *Cochrane Database of Systematic Reviews* 2007, Issue 3. Art. No.: CD003388. DOI: 10.1002/14651858.CD003388. pub3.

Bossini, L.; Tavanti, M.; Lombardelli, A.; Calossi, S.; Polizzotto, N.R. Galli, R.; Vatti, G.; Pieraccini, F., and Castrogiovanni, P. (2007). Changes in Hippocampal Volume in Patients With Post-Traumatic Stress Disorder After Sertraline Treatment. *Journal of Clinical Psychopharmacology*, (April) *Volume 27*, Issue 2, 233–235.

Bradley, R., Greene, J., Russ, E., Dutra, L., and Westen, D. (2005). A multi-dimensional meta-analysis of psychotherapy for PTSD. *American Journal of Psychiatry, 162*, 214–227.

Bremner, J.D., et al. (1995). MRI-based measurements of hippocampal volume in combat-related post-traumatic stress disorder. *American Journal of Psychiatry, 152*, 973–978.

Carlson J., Chemtob C.M., Rusnak K., et al. (1998). Eye movement desensitization and reprocessing (EMDR): Treatment for combat-related post-traumatic stress disorder. *J Trauma Stress, 11*, 3–24.

CREST (2003). *The management of post traumatic stress disorder in adults.* A publication of the Clinical Resource Efficiency Support Team of the Northern Ireland Department of Health, Social Services and Public Safety, Belfast.

Davidson, P.R. and Parker, K.C. (2001). Eye movement desensitization and reprocessing (EMDR): A meta-analysis. *Journal of Consulting and Clinical Psychology*, 69, 305-316.

Department of Veterans Affairs and Department of Defense (2004). *VA/DoD Clinical Practice Guideline for the Management of Post-Traumatic Stress.* Washington, DC: Veterans Health Administration, Department of Veterans Affairs and Health Affairs, Department of Defense. Office of Quality and Performance publication 10Q-CPG/PTSD-04.

Edmond T., Rubin A., and Wambach K. (1999). The effectiveness of EMDR with adult female survivors of childhood sexual abuse. *Soc Work Res, 23*, 103–116.

Foa, E.B., Keane, T.M., Friedman, M.J., and Cohen, J.A. (2009). *Effective treatments for PTSD: Practice Guidelines of the International Society for Traumatic Stress Studies.* New York: Guilford Press.

Ironson G.I., Freund B., Strauss J.L., et al. (2002). Comparison of two treatments for traumatic stress: A community-based study of EMDR and prolonged exposure. *J Clin Psychol, 58*, 113–128.

Lansing, K., Amen, D.G., Hanks, C., and Rudy, L. (2005). High–resolution brain SPECT imaging and Eye Movement Desensitization and Reprocessing in police officers With PTSD. *The Journal of Neuropsychiatry and Clinical Neurosciences, 17*, 526–532.

Lee C., Gavriel H, Drummond P, et al. (2002). Treatment of post-traumatic stress disorder: A comparison of stress inoculation training with prolonged exposure and eye movement desensitization and reprocessing. *J Clin Psychol, 58*, 1071–1089.

Marcus S., Marquis P., and Sakai C. (1997). Controlled study of treatment of PTSD using EMDR in an HMO setting. *Psychotherapy, 34*, 307–315.

Maxfield, L., and Hyer, L.A. (2002). The relationship between efficacy and methodology in studies investigating EMDR treatment of PTSD. *Journal of Clinical Psychology, 58*, 23–41.

Miller, L. (1999). Psychotherapeutic intervention strategies with law enforcement and emergency services personnel. In L. Territo and J.D. Sewell (Eds.), *Stress management in law enforcement.* Durham: Carolina Academic Press (pp. 317–332).

Mol, S.S. L., Arntz, A., Metsemakers, J.F. M., Dinant, G., Vilters-Van Montfort, P.A.P, and Knottnerus, J.A. (2005). Symptoms of post-traumatic stress disorder after non-traumatic events: Evidence from an open population study. *British Journal of Psychiatry, 186*, 494–499.

National Institute for Clinical Excellence (2005). *Post traumatic stress disorder (PTSD): The management of adults and children in primary and secondary care.* London: NICE Guidelines.

Power K.G., McGoldrick T., and Brown K., et al. (2002). A controlled comparison of eye movement desensitization and reprocessing versus exposure plus cognitive restructuring, versus waiting list in the treatment of post-traumatic stress disorder. *J Clin Psychol and Psychotherapy, 9*, 299–318.

Rodenburg, R., Benjamin, A., de Roos, C, Meijer, A.M., and Stams, G.J. (2009). Efficacy of EMDR in children: A meta-analysis. *Clinical Psychology Review, 29*, 599–606.

SAMHSA's National Registry of Evidence-based Programs and Practices (2011). The Substance Abuse and Mental Health Services Administration (SAMHSA) Is an agency of the U.S. Department of Health and Human Services (HHS).

Seidler, G.H., and Wagner, F.E. (2006). Comparing the efficacy of EMDR and trauma-focused cognitive-behavioral therapy in the treatment of PTSD: a meta-analytic study. *Psychological Medicine, 36*, 1515–1522.

Siegel, D.J. (1997). Working with the memories of trauma. In B.S. Mark & J.A. Incorvaia (Eds.), *Psychotherapy with Children and Adolescents*, 221–278.

Shapiro, F. (1995). *Eye Movement Desensitization and Reprocessing: Basic Principles, Protocols, and Procedures*. New York: Guilford Press.

Shapiro, F. (2001). *Eye Movement Desensitization and Reprocessing: Basic Principles, Protocols, and Procedures* (2nd edition). New York: Guilford Press.

Shapiro F. (2002). EMDR 12 years after its introduction: Past and future research. *J Clin Psychol 58*, 1–22.

Soberman G.B., Greenwald R., and Rule D.L. (2002). A controlled study of eye movement desensitization and reprocessing (EMDR) for boys with conduct problems. *J Aggression, Maltreatment, and Trauma, 6*, 217–236.

Stickgold, R. (2009). Sleep-Dependent Memory Processing and EMDR Action, *Keynote Address*, EMDR Conference 2009.

Wilson, S.A., Tinker, R.H., Becker, L.A., and Logan, C.R. (2001). Stress management with law enforcement personnel: A controlled outcome study of EMDR versus a traditional stress management program. *International Journal of Stress Management, 8(3)*, 179–200.

Discussion Questions

1. According to neurophysiologists, the brain has many functions. What has the author identified as one of the most important?
2. What type of massive information does the brain take in at any given moment?

3. What happens in the brain when it is exposed to extreme trauma?
4. There are two separate layers of information processing that occur in the brain prior to an incident being committed to memory. What are they and how do they operate?
5. Explicit information consists of two components. What are they?
6. There are two neurostructures in particular that seem to be centrally involved in the processing of the explicit information. What are they and how do they work?
7. Two neurostructures are primarily concerned with the processing of implicit information. What are they and how do they work?
8. What happens to the brain when it is exposed to extreme trauma?
9. During a traumatic experience both explicit and implicit information are stored in the brain but in separate areas with no means of communication between the two. This state of affairs has several implications. What are they?
10. How is post-traumatic stress disorder officially classified?
11. Eye Movement Desensitization and Reprocessing (EMDR) treatment provide the brain with an opportunity to process traumatic memories of disturbing life events that remain frozen in the nervous system. How is this done?
12. Post-traumatic stress disorder results from two types of stressors. What are they?
13. What theories have been developed to explain why Eye Movement Desensitization and Reprocessing (EMDR) works?

Peer Support Teams Fill an Emotional Void in Law Enforcement Agencies

Mark D. Kamena, Douglas Gentz, Virginia Hays,
Nancy Bohl-Penrod, and Lorraine W. Greene

Psychologically healthy police officers are far more likely to provide high-quality, professional services to the members of their communities. Police departments make a significant investment in selecting mentally and emotionally healthy individuals as part of their hiring process. Police chiefs can protect and enhance that investment by various methods aimed at promoting wellness. One effective strategy for stimulating a culture of psychological wellness within an agency is the development and maintenance of a peer support program. Such programs need not be the exclusive purview of large departments with behavioral health sections; small departments would also greatly benefit from the training of their staff in peer support techniques.

The mission of a peer support program is to provide emotional, social, and practical support to police personnel during times of personal or professional crisis. It may also offer peer-to-peer assistance in anticipating and addressing other potential personal challenges or difficulties. Consider the following scenario:

> *Officer Bob Tasker (not his real name) had recently completed probation in a large, cosmopolitan police department. He was no longer under the watchful eye of his field training officer and felt proud to be a patrol officer. Soon after, he was dispatched to a motor vehicle accident and expected to see the usual fender bender, but when he arrived on scene, he did not see a crash. Instead, he saw two young boys—one eight years old and one nine years old—lying in the street. While running across the street, they were hit by a car. The nine-year-old boy was moving; the*

younger one was not. Tasker decided to attend to the little boy who was not moving. He tried to rouse him by moving his shoulder. The little boy was unresponsive. Then, Tasker looked into the eight-year-old boy's eyes. They were blank. And, in looking back, he began to believe that was the moment when he "froze."

Tasker knows that he froze for less than one minute and had no awareness until the paramedics arrived. He then took names of witnesses, protected the scene, and gave information to the accident investigators, doing all that was required to do a good job. The nonresponsive eight-year-old boy died. The nine-year-old survived.

After completing his duties at the accident scene, Tasker resumed his patrol. Later, he felt bad about not doing what he had been taught in the academy: airway, breathing, circulation. He had trouble sleeping, started drinking to fall asleep, and felt incredibly guilty. He never told anyone about his reaction to this incident. He suffered with his guilt for 10 years. It was only when a newly formed peer support team was established in his department that he asked for help.

Franklin, the officer who assisted as part of the peer support team, was a 22-year veteran of the agency. Franklin listened attentively to members of the peer support team and thought about the times that he, himself, had paused when assessing a crime scene. He recognized Tasker's distress and the inappropriate guilt. Tasker knew and respected Franklin, who said, "So you have been carrying this guilt for 10 years, thinking that you 'froze' and are afraid that you might do that again, despite the evidence that you have not frozen or even come close to doing so since this incident. Is that right?"

Tasker replied, "That about sums it up."

Franklin then disclosed some of his own stories and said, "I wonder if you simply 'paused' like I have so many times. I don't think of it as 'freezing.' It makes sense to pause when confronted by an overwhelming scene."

Tasker replied, "I never thought of it that way." Hearing this from someone who had been in a similar situation was different than hearing it from his wife or other members of his supportive family. It was then that Tasker began his journey to healing.

Although a peer support program is an effective tool for influencing healthy responses to the psychological challenges of working in the public safety profession, it should be seen as augmenting, not replacing, psychological services or other employee assistance programs. Sworn or nonsworn peer support members are specifically trained colleagues, not counselors or therapists. Consider the following scenario:

Sergeant Smith and his wife had been arguing for several years. She claimed that he had abused her and their children. She wanted a divorce and full custody of the children. She threw him out of the house, and he was temporarily bunking with Jones, a single coworker. Smith needed to find more permanent housing and hire an attorney. He was not sleeping well, was drinking more than usual, and felt like he was going crazy. Jones suggested that Smith contact the peer support team, but he refused. He thought he could handle it on his own and did not want to discuss his home affairs with coworkers. He was not making any progress on his goals and was barely able to get to work. Finally, Smith's captain pulled him into her office and told him that she had noticed that his work was suffering and that some of his subordinates had been making mistakes that needed to be addressed, but that Smith was letting them slide. This intervention prompted him to agree to see a fellow sergeant who was a member of the peer support team. Smith was able, for the first time, to talk about what was going on in his life. While Smith's problems were not miraculously solved, the peer was able to steer him to appropriate professional resources and stayed in touch with him as he worked his way through the situation.

Policies and Procedures

Agencies that do not yet have a peer support program but are in the process of forming one would be wise to create a steering committee to provide organizational guidance and structure. The ongoing utilization and viability of a peer support team depends on buy-in from sworn and nonsworn employee organizations, supervisors, communications personnel, administrators, and licensed mental health professionals. A representative steering committee will help to integrate the different groups' concerns into the peer support team's policies and standard operating procedures. The IACP Police Psychological Services Section recommends that a licensed mental health professional with experience working with public safety personnel be included to provide ongoing professional consultation to the peer support team.[1]

---

1. IACP Psychological Services Section, "Peer Support Guidelines," ratified at the 113th Annual Conference of the International Association of Chiefs of Police (Boston, Massachusetts, 2006), may be found online at http://www.theiacp.org/psych_services_section/pdfs/Psych-PeerSupportGuidelines.pdf (accessed June 8, 2011).

The policies and procedures for a peer support program will inevitably vary from agency to agency; however, it is recommended that each agency create a policy and procedures handbook. This handbook should contain a description of the program and a listing of procedures for practical administrations of the program. It should also describe the skills and techniques that may be used by a peer supporter to assist persons who are faced with stressful situations.

A program coordinator should serve to ensure that the peer supporters participating in the program act in accordance with the goals and objectives established for the program. Major duties of the program coordinator include supervising the program on a daily basis, serving as a member of the peer support advisory committee, recruiting and coordinating the screening of the peer support applicants, and coordinating peer supporter training. Duties also include developing resources to assist individuals when problem areas are identified, maintaining statistical data of reported contacts by peer supporters, and offering guidance to peer supporters when problems occur. The program coordinator may also coordinate follow-up response of peer supporters when referrals are made. Peer supporters who are on duty and have been assigned by the program coordinator to assist fellow peers should be compensated as part of their normal workweeks. The program coordinator or a designee must approve any off-duty emergencies in order to be compensated. A peer support advisory committee should act as the policy setting board for the program's operation and future direction, subject to review and approval by the agency's peer support program coordinator. The committee also participates in the selection process of peer supporters.

Selection

Prospective peer supporters should meet the following criteria:

- agree to maintain confidentiality within the guidelines provided in the handbook,
- be empathic and possess excellent interpersonal and communication skills,
- be motivated and willing to manage time effectively,
- successfully complete the selection process,
- attend and successfully complete the minimum training program, and
- agree to participate in any necessary ongoing training.

The peer support advisory committee should recommend candidates suited for appointment as peer supporters to the peer support coordinator for final approval. Agencies should select peer support volunteers who are in good standing with their departments and who have received recommendations from their superiors or peers. The peer support advisory committee may provide guidance about what groups should be represented in the interview panel, but it is strongly encouraged that one of the members be the mental health professional who will be working with the program.

The selection process may include a review of applicants' interests and motivations for being team members, such as their previous education and training, as well as personal exposure to traumatic experiences and the responses to those experiences. There are desirable personal qualities such as maturity, good judgment, empathy, teamwork, and personal and professional credibility that should be evaluated through the interview process. It can be useful to provide applicants with scenarios to gauge applicants' empathy, interpersonal skills, and judgment.

One of the most difficult aspects of maintaining a peer support program is deciding when a member should no longer be part of the program. It is crucial to have a procedure in place that establishes criteria and a process for deselection from the program. Quality control is essential for the health and viability of the program. Possible criteria include a breach of confidentiality, the failure to attend training, or the loss of one's good standing with the department.

Members of the peer support team are volunteers and may have situations develop in their own personal or professional lives that interfere with their abilities to effectively participate in the program. From the outset, members should be advised that the option is always available to take a leave of absence if and when personal issues or obligations require.

Training

Initial training should focus on skill development in such areas as communication, active listening, and problem assessment. Continuing training is necessary to enhance problem-solving skills, provide a venue for group sharing, and allow for an exchange of experiences among program participants. Most initial training sessions last a minimum of three days to one week, and continuing trainings are daylong mandatory programs held quarterly. It is important for program fidelity that peer supporters attend all initial and quarterly training sessions. The program's manual should clearly state the training expectations and outcomes should peer supporters fail to attend training sessions.

Initial training should provide information on privacy; confidentiality; role conflict (for example, multiple relationships); and ethical issues. Each peer supporter should be given the opportunity to demonstrate the skill that is being taught. Additionally, conflict management and stress management are critical topics that should be covered during the initial training program. Assistance with critical traumatic incidents, alcohol and substance abuse, suicide assessment, and crisis intervention must be strongly emphasized in the training program. Onsite visits by the peer supporters to local alcohol and substance abuse treatment facilities and mental health facilities are encouraged. Familiarity with these programs may facilitate quick access when services are needed. A licensed mental health professional should assist in developing a training program that provides information and scenarios for actual role plays, an ongoing assessment process to determine skill sets, and continuing training to address ongoing needs.

Confidentiality

Peer support programs are designed to provide emotional support during and after times of professional and personal crisis to employees, by employees; consequently, there is a need to promote trust and ensure privacy. Preserving confidentiality of persons using the services of peer supporters is critical. Peer supporters must be able to convey trust and anonymity and assure confidentiality within the program guidelines to all personnel.

To assure colleagues using the program that the peer supporters will be able to ensure privacy, each department must provide a formal policy statement from the chief of police. The statement should state that the department believes that police personnel must be free to express themselves about any job-related or personal problems and that trust, anonymity, and privacy will be maintained. To that end, no peer supporter should be questioned or ordered to divulge information for the purpose of general inquiry or to subject any employee to ridicule or embarrassment. No information obtained through the peer support program should be conveyed to supervisors or be used for investigations. Peer supporters are, however, affected by departmental policy, legal mandates, and state-imposed limitations and regulations. In some states, peer support personnel are granted legally privileged communication, but the confidentiality in most programs is by agency policy. Privileged or not, examples of exceptions to confidentiality can include making an immediate report of any information communicated by an employee that involves the commission of a crime, a serious violation of a departmental policy or procedure, a threat of violence toward a known third party, or suicidal intent. It is essential that the peer supporter inform the employee seeking assistance, prior to initiating discussions, what the limitations and exceptions are regarding the confidentiality of information disclosed.

To manage the program effectively, the program director or administrator should collect statistical information to measure the number and type of contacts between program personnel and the type of service or referral offered.

To best preserve confidentiality, no formal or private records should be maintained outside of the anonymous statistical records for program management. All peer supporters should be required to sign a confidentiality agreement to affirm their commitment to ensure the confidentiality of the program participants for both their issues and their identities.

Critical Incidents and Officer-Involved Shootings

Officers or other public safety personnel can be seen as having experienced a critical incident when two, interwoven conditions have been met:

1. The officer has been involved in an event that is sudden, unexpected, unusual, and includes the loss or the threat of loss of life; and
2. Involvement in that event requires a much greater than normal degree of psychological and, perhaps, physical adjustment.

For example, many officer-involved shootings become critical incidents for not only the officer who is directly involved but also the officers and other public safety personnel who are peripheral to the shooting, such as backup and cover officers, dispatchers, and fellow squad members who may arrive after the event. Peer support response in the form of immediate, positive social support is aimed at assisting the officer to decrease physical and emotional overarousal. This calming, social support is precisely what a peer supporter is trained to provide. A few examples of some of those actions might include encouraging the officer to step away from the scene and any media attention, providing the necessary transportation, ensuring against isolation, previewing the investigative process, making sure a firearm is replaced if necessary, facilitating contact with family members, and helping with any physical or equipment needs.

Peer support provides a lot more than providing support after a shooting. Consider the following scenario:

> *Officer Fields did not get a wanted promotion. He started taking it out on his family by being argumentative and abusive. He became overly aggressive on the job and began to slack off. Eventually he had to be suspended. If peer support had been available, a peer could have made a preemptive intervention before Field's behavior and attitude became problematic at home and at work to the degree that disciplinary action had to be taken.*

Other critical incidents may be more difficult to detect because the "event" element of the incident may seem more routine and the public safety personnel are exposed after, not during, the situation. Examples include horrific car wrecks, extraordinarily grotesque crime scenes, and crimes and accidents involving children. The members of a peer support program can serve as the agency's designees to stay alert to the possibility that these types of calls may evolve into critical incidents for the involved personnel. The peer support organization can initiate contact with personnel in these sorts of situations as appropriate to the circumstances.

Some "events" are not work-related. Consider the following scenario:

> *Officer Rich received a call that she needed to contact her domestic partner. She thought that one of her kids might have stubbed a toe, sprained a wrist, or even broke an arm—something that she could easily take care of with a phone call. Instead, she was told that her mother had unexpectedly been taken to the hospital. She did not know why or what her mother's condition was. Soon, she was met by her lieutenant and the police chaplain and was told that her mother had suffered a massive stroke and had passed away. Members of her peer support team, of which she was an active peer supporter, met her. Rich had been a member since the support team began and never thought that she would need the services herself. Her designated peer was able to normalize her grief and help her to arrange her work schedule to accommodate her temporary needs.*

The distress experienced by employees in critical incidents or personal events is exacerbated at times by how they are treated by their departments following the event. For example, if the only contact an injured officer has is the lieutenant asking when the officer expects to be returning to work, the assumption may be that no one cares about the officer's welfare—the "police family" has let the officer down. Instead, a peer supporter could be assigned to keep in contact with the officer and allow for an experience of the police family being a resource and helping to promote the officer's recovery.

In these tough fiscal times, chiefs of police face difficult decisions. Departmental requirements for equipment purchases are relatively easy choices. However, choosing to establish a new peer support program that will increase morale and hopefully save highly trained personnel may be the more fiscally sound choice. It is likely more expensive to replace an officer than a police car.

Consultation with Licensed Mental Health Professionals

There are many situations that law enforcement personnel may experience, both personally and professionally, that will elicit the need for licensed mental health professionals. Many agencies offer assistance with these stressors through peer support programs, chaplains, and licensed mental health professionals. In an ideal world, all three assisting factors would work as a team to improve the mental health of the affected individual. Law enforcement personnel vary greatly in their willingness to talk to others about the heavy emotional demands placed on them as part of their employment in a law enforcement agency. Some are comfortable talking exclusively to peers about certain situations because they are operating under the belief that their peers are the only ones who will understand what they are experiencing. Others believe that the spiritual support of a chaplain is what is needed to reduce the negative emotional demands. Still others feel secure talking only to a licensed mental health professional. In an approach that involves all three entities, there will undoubtedly be sufficient support for all involved personnel.

In accordance with the peer support program, a licensed mental health professional should be one of the members on the peer support advisory committee and should assist in the selection process of peer supporters. Members of the IACP Police Psychological Services Section, psychologists specifically trained in the area of law enforcement, are available to assist in the establishment of a peer support program. Such licensed mental health professionals should be available to supervise, guide, and assist peer supporters with any concerns they may have as they continue through the program and should be available and on-call 24 hours a day, 7 days a week. Licensed mental health professionals also should design the necessary peer support training curriculum and assist in teaching peer supporters basic and continuing (updated) curricula. Experienced law enforcement mental health professionals should conduct the quarterly meetings among members of the peer support team, any involved chaplains, and other mental health professionals to ensure that all entities are working together to assist the agency in a positive manner.

Discussion Questions

1. What is the mission of the peer support program?
2. What should be the relationship between a peer support program, psychological services, and other employee assistance programs?
3. The policies and procedures for a peer support program will inevitably vary from agency to agency; however, it is recommended that each agency create a policy and procedures handbook. What kind of information should be incorporated in this handbook?
4. What criteria should be met by prospective peer supporters?

5. One of the most difficult aspects of maintaining a peer support program is deciding when a member should no longer be part of the program. What elements are involved in the process of deselection of a team member from the program?
6. What type of training should be provided to peer support members?
7. What policy elements should be imposed upon peer supporters to maintain confidentiality of information they receive?
8. What role does the licensed mental health specialist play in the peer support program?

38

A Confidential Peer-Based Assistance Program for Police Officers

Frank G. Dowling, M.D., Bill Genet, and Gene Moynihan

Posttraumatic stress is an understandable complication of police work. Despite stereotypes that portray police officers as heroic and invincible, about one-third of police officers who are exposed to diverse work-related traumatic events develop significant posttraumatic stress symptoms. Many suffer from additional complications, including high rates of alcohol abuse, marital and family problems, domestic violence, and suicide.

Police officers with psychological or personal problems are reluctant to seek assistance from internal departmental services. Fears of stigmatization, adverse job consequences (such as modified work assignments, altered career paths, or loss of one's weapon), and perceptions of personal weakness or failure prevent police officers from seeking help. As a closed group, police officers are unwilling to share their problems with mental health professionals, who are seen as outsiders who cannot understand the police culture.

After 26 suicides in the New York Police Department (NYPD) over two years (1994 and 1995), it was determined that a confidential, nondepartmental assistance program was needed to assist NYPD officers. In addition, peers would be needed to help officers overcome the personal and cultural barriers to seeking professional assistance. With the endorsement of the NYPD and Police Unions, the Police Organization Providing Peer Assistance (POPPA) was created.

POPPA is a confidential, voluntary, independent, nondepartmental assistance program for the NYPD that uses trained volunteer NYPD officers as peer support officers. Volunteers have been recruited and trained from all ranks and backgrounds of the NYPD. Since 1995 POPPA has run a 24-hour help line. An officer can call any time about any personal or job-related stress problem and talk to a trained volunteer peer support officer. Calls are self-referred, and all assistance is voluntary. Within 24 hours (the same day if necessary), the peer support officer will meet with the officer face to face. About 75 percent of calls to the help line result in a face-to-face peer meeting.

To protect privacy, such meetings take place outside departmental facilities, and no records are maintained. The peer support officer provides an empathic ear and screens for major safety issues, such as suicidal or homicidal ideation, alcohol abuse, and risk of violence. The peer support officer also helps the officer accept that a personal or stress-related problem is not a sign of weakness or personal failure. Asking for help is discussed as a sign of strength. Often this peer meeting provides the support that officers need to be able to use their own personal resources to cope more effectively.

When necessary, the officer is provided with a referral to a mental health professional who is trained and experienced in working with police officers. Peer support officers do not provide ongoing counseling. Their role is to screen, support, and act as a bridge toward professional assistance. Clients who need further assistance are advised to see a professional. The responding peer support officer discusses each call and referral with a senior peer team coordinator who has several years of experience working with POPPA. All at-risk or questionable cases are reviewed with the clinical director, a retired police officer and clinical social worker (C.S.W.), and, when needed, with the medical advisor, a psychiatric physician.

POPPA has developed and trained a panel of more than 110 independent mental health professionals in New York City and the surrounding counties. Alleviating fears of job-related consequences, all assistance provided is confidential and is not reported to the NYPD. Officers of the NYPD have gradually accepted POPPA's peer support officers and the reality that sometimes even they need assistance for personal problems. In the first year, there were about 250 calls to the help line. Since 2001, the number of calls has increased to between 900 and 1,200 per year. The proportion of callers who accept a referral for professional assistance has also increased, from about 30 percent to 45 percent of callers. Because of confidentiality issues, detailed information is unavailable. However, the primary reasons for calls over the years 2003 and 2004 were in the areas of stress or anxiety (34 percent), alcohol problem (26 percent), marital problem (24 percent), traumatic stress (18 percent), depression (14 percent), and bereavement issues (7 percent).

It is encouraging to see that many police officers can overcome stigmatization issues and view mental health problems as normal complications of their work that can be addressed. Other emergency services and professional organizations whose members also fear the consequences of seeking assistance—such as physicians, nurses, and other mental health professionals—may also benefit from a similar independent, voluntary, confidential peer-based assistance program.

Discussion Questions

1. Why are police officers with psychological personal problems reluctant to seek assistance from internal departmental services?
2. What resulted from a study of 26 suicides in the New York City Police Department over a two-year period?
3. What is the Police Organization Providing Peer Assistance (POPPA)?
4. What steps are taken to protect the privacy of officers seeking assistance from the Police Organization Providing Peer Assistance (POPPA)?

The Badge of Life Psychological Survival for Police Officers Program

Richard L. Levenson Jr., Andrew F. O'Hara, and Ron Clark Sr.

Overview

That police officer stress is unique in its intensity and duration is widely known in research on law enforcement personnel (Anderson, Litzerberg, & Plecas, 2002; Brown & Campbell, 1994; Collins & Gibbs, 2003; Copes, 2005; Van Hasselt, Sheehan, Sellers, Baker, & Feiner, 2003). It is not only a significant problem in the United States and Canada but in other countries as well (McNally, 2006). In fact, worldwide, there are no more consistently stressful jobs than that of the police officer (Chamberlain, 2000; Delprino & Bahn, 1988; Greenstone, 2000; Henry, 2004; Levenson, 2009; Levenson & Dwyer, 2003; Miller, 1995; Miller, 2006; Mitchell & Levenson, 2006; Violanti, 1999; Violanti & Aron, 1994). Evidence suggests police officers lead shorter and sicklier lives than the general population (Gershon, Lin, & Li, 2002; Kerley, 2005; Mayhew, 2001; Violanti, 2005; Richmond, Kehoe, Hailstone, Wodak, & Uebel-Yan, 1999; Stellman, 1998; Violanti, 2009). Shift work alone is associated with an increased incidence of stroke, cardiovascular disease, metabolic-syndrome, memory problems, fatigue, and decreased family and community activities, productivity, and morale (Violanti, 2009).

In that regard, police officers may take more time off from work than those in the private sector as a result of anxiety disorders and related issues (Levenson & Dwyer, 2003) and engage in more illegal or deviant behaviors related to occupational stress (Arter, 2008). It is not atypical for officers to describe a lifestyle in which they are maintaining a family, working rotating shifts, experiencing the well-known "nights of boredom and sudden moments of terror," and the challenges of masking problems and resultant marital issues.

Upon graduation from the police academy, officers are, in some ways, psychologically healthier and better prepared in general, for stress and trauma than the general population (Ghazinour, Lauritz, Du Preez, Cassimijee, & Richter, 2009). Academy and subsequent police training emphasize the legal aspects of policing (i.e. search and seizure, laws of arrest, etc.) and surviving lethal force encounters. While these areas are important for officers to carry out their sworn duties, there is a pervasive lack of training addressing the impact a career in law enforcement has on officers and their families. As a result, officers are woefully unprepared to manage the stress of "the job."

Police officers gravitate toward *avoidant* coping strategies (Levenson & Dwyer, 2003), such as consumption of alcohol, in an attempt to block out the unpleasant feelings associated with stress and trauma. In police officers, avoidant coping has been associated with anxiety, trauma, depression, perceived work stress, health problems, risk-taking behaviors, and partner abuse (Burke, 1998; Essex & Scott, 2008; Gershon, Barocas, Canton, Li, & Vlahov, 2009). Police culture dictates that one "suck-it-up" if something happens, and talking about it and the "touchy-feely, warm and fuzzy" approach is definitely not the way to go. Rather, after the shift is over, congregating at the local bar to tell war stories and drink excessively to hide the pain by self-medicating through alcohol is tantamount to a faulty group "therapy" where no one gets better—ever.

Avoidant coping does not offer a solution for managing ongoing work-related stressors or traumatic events and is, therefore, reactionary rather than of a proactive nature. This distinction is important because one's subjective sense of wellness and objective health are strongly influenced by how officers manage, or fail to manage, the stress in their lives. While most would believe that stress would be caused alone by the police officer's role and function, informal contacts with literally thousands of police officers indicate that the most severe stress comes from "the job" itself, and that the internal work environment is the most potent, negative stressor affecting attitudes, family relationships, abuse of alcohol, and physical and mental health. One might imagine that the more typical every-day stressors tax an officer's positive outlook, coping skills, and professional training. Yet, even the lack of appreciation in their role, disrespect, lack of common courtesy, undercover assignments, crime scene investigations, repeated exposure to homicide, violence, and countless forms of human misery, violent and sex crimes against children, the prospect of using deadly physical force and/or being killed on the job do not compare to a work environment where favoritism, "higher-up" contacts, vengeful superiors—all components of a caustic work environment—make equal contributions to negativity, isolation, and withdrawal into a police-only culture that serves to alienate officers from interacting with civilians who just don't understand their everyday life. Still, officers' perception of potentially traumatic incidents can differ, too (Colwell, 2009).

Suicide among police officers is a serious problem and, as Miller (2006) noted, one that has been on the increase since data collection began in the 1920s. Current data suggest that, on average, 145 police officers commit suicide every year (O'Hara & Violanti, 2009), but this number is likely to be an underestimate. As Miller (2006) stated, police officers are more likely to die by suicide than by any type of criminal or criminal activity.

Regardless, the number of police suicides is thought to be higher than those reported, since in police culture such behavior represents cowardice and brings shame on the officer's department. Attitudes toward suicide in general may lead some departments to offer an alternative explanation to the family and to keep the news of such a death out of the media. A 1998 study found that 17% of police officer suicides later reviewed by medical examiners were misclassified, compared to 8% of other municipal workers (Violanti, Vena, & Petralia, 1998). Worse, departments do not take responsibility for an officer's suicide, preferring to state the cause was due to marital or financial difficulties or alcohol abuse. O'Hara and Violanti (2009) found, in their two-year study of police suicides in the United States during 2008–2009, no single case in which a department acknowledged that work-related stress, trauma, or PTSD was involved. On the positive side, as Miller (2006) reports, about 70% of people (including police officers) suffering from depression and thoughts of suicide recover, indicating that "mental health critical care" (Levenson, 2005) may avert a tragedy of epic proportions to the office, work colleagues, and family members.

If "the best form of crisis intervention is crisis prevention" (Miller, 2006, p. 9), then stress management and proactive efforts to prepare for stressful and traumatic life events in policing must be at the forefront of training. This statement has implications for training recruits when they step foot in the academy, with mental well-being seen in a matter-of-fact way, and on the same level of importance as general policing procedures.

The Role of Peer Support

Peer Support in law enforcement has been widely accepted but only rarely utilized and is still not a regular part of accepted practice in law enforcement training and response (Levenson, 2007; 2009). Peer Support has its roots in "paraprofessional" work (Carkhuff and Truax, 1965), wherein officers who have an interest in mental health and wellness as applied to law enforcement learn the basic skills of dealing with other law enforcement officers who experience severe duress or show signs of inadequate coping. With respect to law enforcement, active- and retired-duty officers become "peers" after attending training programs typically run by psychologists with backgrounds in law enforcement together with more experienced officers with extensive training and experience in peer support programs.

The role of the Peer Support Officer is to listen, assess, and refer (Finn & Tomz, 1998), with *active listening* being a key technique for the peer support officer (Slatkin, 2010). Training consists of learning the basic signs of job-related psychopathology (e.g., anxiety, depression, burnout, alcohol and substance abuse, excessive sick leave, and stress-related physical illnesses, such as ulcers and migraine headaches). Signs and symptoms of posttraumatic stress disorder (PTSD) and other severe conditions are also taught, and peer support officers come to learn the warning signs that signal more serious dysfunction warranting immediate intervention, such as those who are at risk for suicide and homicide. Acceptance of the tenets of Critical Incident Stress Management (CISM; Mitchell & Everly, 1995) and an understanding of the continuum of services, from a quiet, confidential conversation all the way to referral for in-patient treatment is key. When confronted with an officer in severe crisis, peer officers often work in teams and schedule a personal visit with the officer requesting intervention. It is accepted that peer support in law enforcement is effective because, in police departments that utilize peer support officer programs, the number of sick days has decreased while specific indicators of job performance have increased (Freeman, 2002). Most importantly, peer support officers bring credibility to their roles as both officers and helpers, and there is less stigma attached to speaking with a peer rather than with a licensed mental health professional, sometimes referred to as a "shrink." If a referral is needed, peer support officers can act as a "bridge to professionals" (Finn & Tomz, 1998, p. 10) for officers needing more in-depth intervention and mental health care. Police peer support programs are in existence in the United States, and have been cited for positive practices and improvements in officers' mental well-being, job satisfaction, and job performance (Levenson & Dwyer, 2003). Having roots in the Federal Bureau of Investigation's Behavioral Science Unit, Sheehan (1999) showed that stress management and stress reduction helped Special Agents work through critical incidents. In addition, peer support programs utilizing techniques of CISM (Mitchell & Everly, 1995) have been overwhelmingly accepted. Estimates are that well over 10,000 law enforcement personnel have undergone such techniques as a CISM debriefing following their involvement in a large-scale critical incident (e.g., Dowling, Moynihan, Genet, & Lewis, 2006; Levenson & Dwyer, 2003). Peer support officers need support, too, after they have had a formal encounter with a police officer in crisis, as proximity in crisis work may affect those in the helping professions (Dimaggio, Galea, & Emch, 2010; Gill & Gershon, 2010).

The Badge of Life Psychological Survival for Police Officers Program

The Badge of Life Psychological Survival for Police Officers Program (BOL) was founded on January 1, 2008. Its date of foundation followed ten months, during 2007, of organization, discussion, meetings, and evolving presentations made with the support of the National Alliance on Mental Illness (NAMI), the Sacramento County Sheriff's Health and Wellness Program, and the Star 6 Memorial Foundation. A 501(c) (3) nonprofit organization, BOL was formed by two retired California Highway Patrol officers whose careers had ended as a result of critical incidents and formal diagnoses of posttraumatic stress disorder. In one of these cases, there was a near suicide.

Immediately, the goal of the BOL founders was to develop an effective law enforcement officer suicide primary and secondary prevention program. Such a program was not, and still is not, a regular entity within most law enforcement agencies. Based on personal experience and that of other police officers, it seemed increasingly apparent that a far more proactive approach to mental health in law enforcement was needed, instead of merely waiting for officers to reach the point of crisis in order to act. At the same time, BOL staff found that one of its most effective tools was the internet. Because all of the organization's services and materials are free, its website became more than merely an advertising or attention-getting medium. In a short time, through effective use of linking as well as the addition of satellite websites, BOL began giving website users free videos, power point presentations, lesson plans, and articles on a wide variety of useful topics that included not only its own programs but those from multiple other resources. Materials that were too large for inclusion on the website were provided free by DVD/mail on request. In short, the Badge of Life website (www.badgeoflife.com) became not only an introduction to the organization's program, but a "virtual classroom" on mental health and emotional well-being, suicide prevention, survivor care, peer support, and retirement issues.

In the BOL program development phase, it was decided that peer support officers would be utilized to achieve credibility and acceptance with active-duty and retired officers who contacted the program. Emotional decompensation as a result of ongoing or cumulative job stress remains a potential danger in a career fraught with tension and conflict, and peer support officers have already proven their value as guides and pathfinders through which troubled officers can find access to mental health assistance.

What was found lacking in police culture, however, was a meaningful focus on long-term career emotional health for police officers. Instead of teaching officers to deal more effectively with potential emotional stressors and traumas *before* they occurred, suicide prevention programs focused exclusively on those officers who were already in a severe emotional crisis. Case after case illustrated that the "old" model was often too late. Further, for every police suicide, there are many hundreds of police officers still working and suffering either from undiagnosed depression, posttraumatic stress disorder, and/or other anxiety disorders as a result of their work experiences.

To address these concerns, BOL developed the *Emotional Self-Care* (ESC) Training Program. Along with standard suicide prevention protocols typically used in other programs, ESC was designed to focus on the officer's ability and responsibility to care for his/her own emotional well-being. The model relies on teaching the factor of resilience as a significant component of stress-resistance (Everly, Welzant, & Jacobson, 2008). A "cradle-to-the-grave" program (i.e., rookies to retirees), ESC calls upon departments to begin teaching their personnel about the effects of job-related stress and trauma while they are still in the academy, emphasizing the importance of voluntary, confidential "annual mental health checks." Through these health checks, officers are encouraged to schedule an annual visit with a licensed mental health clinician. The purpose of these sessions is to review the past year, apply its lessons to the next, and work on personal strengths and resiliencies. Employee assistance programs are offered as an option, but those officers who are suspicious (Miller, 2006) of that option are encouraged to seek their own private therapist, preferably one with experience working with law enforcement officers. The key element is the importance of "healthy choices" and the preventive nature of the process ("whether you think you need it or not"). The goal is that officers will be well prepared for difficulty and emotional crisis *before* they arise—and not be left floundering for help afterward.

Peer support officers were identified as key players in the success of the Emotional Self-Care training program and its practice. Selected for their credibility and trust level, peer support officers conduct the actual annual training workshops, set the example, and encourage involvement at all levels. Management participation and support is also a key to the success of the program as leadership by example is always a necessary component. To this end, countless examples of the cost-effectiveness of maintaining employee health, in addition to the cost of replacing officers, are provided to management by BOL as encouragement for the importance and adoption of the program.

During the formative stage of BOL, an additional concern was the lack of valid information on police suicides. Throughout the law enforcement culture, and promoted by numerous speakers, were a plethora of "urban myths" about suicide numbers, causes, rates of substance abuse and divorce. In plain terms, departments did their best to deflect the responsibility of "the job" as a cause of officer suicide. A significant worry was that popular but overinflated statistics had the potential for misleading program planners and causing harm to those in need of help. BOL staff carefully identified these myths, researched them, and published the findings (O'Hara & Violanti, 2009). Additionally, with the assistance of John Violanti, Ph.D. of the University of New York at Buffalo, BOL staff embarked upon an intensive national study to determine, as closely as possible, a scientifically-based approximation of police suicides occurring annually. A follow-up study was conducted in 2009 and confirmed the results of O'Hara & Violanti (2009).

BOL also committed itself to the fair and compassionate treatment of survivors of law enforcement suicide. Believing that a large percentage of police suicides are clearly related to work-related stress and trauma, BOL has provided a voice to the families and children that have been shunned and ignored by departments so undeservingly.

Recognizing the active roles and value that police officer retirees were already playing in its own training activities, BOL began developing two programs that focused on effective utilization of police officer retirees by departments and academies. First, a *Retiree Mentoring Program* matches a newly hired officer with a selected retired officer in the community (whether from the same department or not) to act as a support resource—a mentor, if you will—prepared by the department to act as an independent and confidential resource that the officer can turn to for emotional, stress-related, adjustment, and non-policy issues during the formative adjustments of a training period, or for as long as that officer wishes. In addition, based on the experience that many police academies are reluctant to utilize retirees in recruit training, BOL began long-term efforts to bridge the gap by demonstrating not only their wealth of value in mental health programs, but by providing a structured means by which departments can feel more comfortable taking advantage of these rich-in-experience resources.

Since its formation, BOL has grown with alacrity. Its Board of Directors is a diverse one, and includes police officers, both active-duty and retired, a psychiatrist, psychologist, social worker, marriage and family therapist, and survivors of police suicide attempts. BOL's membership is represented by police administrators, "road cops," officers who suffer from PTSD, and parents and wives who have lost their loved ones to suicide.

BOL in Canada

From the outset, it was apparent that Canadian law enforcement shared a close kinship with its American counterpart, not only in contiguity, culture, and heritage, but in the nature of their work and the problems confronting personnel in the area of police mental health. In only a short time, Canadian police officers contacted BOL and formed a branch of the organization in order to provide Emotional Self-Care training and other elements of the BOL emotional health program to their country's city and provincial police officers.

The influence of BOL in Canada has grown rapidly as representatives speak before prestigious groups such as the Alberta Federation of Police Associations, the Tema Conter Memorial Foundation, and many other police groups. Recognizing the important interrelationships of American and Canadian law enforcement and the mutual value each has to the other, a significant portion of the BOL website and educational materials are directed at that country's police personnel.

Because the Toronto Workers Compensation Board was the first in North America to recognize a police suicide as "a line of duty death," BOL representatives arranged for the Commissioner of the Ontario Provincial Police Force to travel to the United States to address a conference on the topic of police officer suicide resulting from work-related trauma. Promotion of this issue, the recognition of officer deaths due to the stress and trauma of their work, is the organization's primary mission in both countries.

Representatives of BOL now lecture regularly across the United States and Canada. All consultations, lectures, educational and training workshops, services, and referrals are free, as are original training materials developed and approved by the BOL Board of Directors. Among the materials regularly requested are lesson plans, videos on a variety of topics, and power point presentations. BOL continues to be a strong, innovative voice in the formulation of new ideas to improve the emotional well-being of law enforcement officers throughout the United States and Canada. Training and education in police officer suicide prevention remains the core of BOL, while parallel issues currently under study are the recognition and acceptance of what we term the *Line of Duty Suicide* (LODS) by police administrators and police officers, in general.

References

Anderson, G.S., Litzenberger, R., & Plecas, D. (2002). Physical evidence of police officer stress. *Policing: An international journal of police strategies and management, 25*(2), 399–420.

Arter, D. (2008). Stress and deviance in policing. *Deviant Behavior, 29*(1), 43–69.

Brown, J.M., & Campbell, E.A. (1994). *Stress and policing: Sources and strategies.* NY: Wiley.

Burke, R.J. (1998). Work and non-work stressors and well-being among police officers: The role of coping. *Anxiety, Stress, & Coping, 11*(4), 345–362.

Carkhuff, R.R., & Truax, C.B. (1965). Lay mental health counseling: The effects of lay group counseling. *Journal of Consulting Psychology, 29*(5), 426–431.

Chamberlain, J. (2000). Cops trust cops, even one with a Ph.D. *APA Monitor, 31*(1), 74.

Collins, P.A., & Gibbs, A.C. (2003). Stress in police officers: A study of origins, prevalence and severity of stress-related symptoms within a county police force. *Occupational Medicine, 53*, 256–264.

Colwell, L.H. (2009). Police officers' experience with trauma. *International Journal of Emergency Mental Health, 11*(1), 3–16.

Copes, H. (2005). *Policing and stress.* Englewood Cliffs, NJ: Prentice Hall.

Delprino, R.P., & Bahn, C. (1988). National survey of the extent and nature of psychological services in police departments. *Professional Psychology: Research and Practice. 19*(4), 421–425.

Dimaggio, C., Galea, S., & Emch, M. (2010). Spatial proximity and the risk of psychopathology after a terrorist attack. *Psychiatry Research, 176*(1), 55–61.

Dowling, F.G., Moynihan, G., Genet, B., & Lewis, J. (2006). A peer-based assistance program with the New York City Police Department: Report of the effects of Sept. 11, 2001. *American Journal of Psychiatry, 163*, 151–153.

Essex, B., & Scott, L.B. (2008). Chronic stress and associated coping strategies among volunteer EMS personnel. *Prehospital Emergency Care, 12*(1), 69–75.

Everly, G.S., Jr., Welzant, V., & Jacobson, J.M. (2008). Resistance and resilience: The final frontier in traumatic stress management. *International Journal of Emergency Mental Health, 10*(4), 261–270.

Finn, P., & Tomz, J.E. (1998). Using peer supporters to help address law enforcement stress. *FBI Law Enforcement Bulletin, 67*(5), 10–18.

Freeman, G. (2002). 9/11 one year later, ACFE members reflect: What have we learned? *The Forensic Examiner, 11*(9–10), 10–15.

Gershon, R.R., Lin, S., & Li, X. (2002). Work stress in aging police officers. *Journal of Occupational and Environmental Medicine, 44*(2), 160–67.

Gershon, R., Barocas, B., Canton, A., Li, X., & Vlahov, D. (2009). Mental, physical, and behavioral outcomes associated with perceived stress in police officers. *Criminal Justice and Behavior, 36*(3), 275–289.

Ghazinour, M., Lauritz, L.E., Du Preez, E., Cassimijee, N., & Richter, J. (2009). An investigation of mental health and personality in Swedish police trainees upon entry to the police academy. *Journal of Police and Criminal Psychology, 25*(1) 34–42.

Gill, K.B., & Gershon, R.R. (2010). Disaster mental health training programmes in New York City following September 11, 2001. *Disasters, 34*(3), 608–618.

Greenstone, J.L. (2000). Peer support in a municipal police department. *The Forensic Examiner, 9*(3–4), 33–36.

Henry, V.E. (2004). *Death work: Police, trauma, and the psychology of survival.* New York, NY: Oxford University Press.

Kerley, K.R. (2005). The costs of protecting and serving: Exploring the consequences of police officer stress. In H. Copes (Ed.), *Policing and stress.* NJ: Prentice Hall.

Levenson, R. L., Jr. (2005). On the cutting edge of mental health critical care. *International Journal of Emergency Mental Health, 7*(1), 59.

Levenson, R.L., Jr. (2007). Prevention of traumatic stress in law enforcement personnel: A cursory look at the roles of peer support and critical incident stress management. *The Forensic Examiner, 16*(3), 16–19.

Levenson, R.L. (2009). Issues in line-of-duty suicides: Stress, coping, and defense mechanisms. August, 2009, http://www.lemha.org/id27.html.

Levenson, R.L., Jr., & Dwyer, L.A. (2003). Peer support in law enforcement: past, present, and future. *International Journal of Emergency Mental Health, 5*(3), 147–52.

Mayhew, C. (2001). Occupational health and safety risks faced by police officers. *Australian Institute of Criminology, Trends and Issues. 196,* 1–6.

McNally, V.J. (2006). The impact of posttraumatic stress on Iraqi police. *International Journal of Emergency Mental Health, 8*(4), 275–281.

Miller, L., (1995). Tough guys: Psychotherapeutic strategies with law enforcement and emergency services personnel. *Psychotherapy, 32*(4), 592–600.

Miller, L. (2006). *Practical police psychology: Stress management and crisis intervention for law enforcement.* Springfield, IL: Charles C Thomas.

Mitchell, J.T., & Everly, G.S., Jr. (1995). *Critical Incident Stress Debriefing: An operations manual for the prevention of traumatic stress among emergency and disaster workers.* Ellicott City, MD: Chevron.

Mitchell, J.T., & Levenson, R.L., Jr. (2006). Some thoughts on providing effective mental health critical care for police departments after line-of-duty deaths. *International Journal of Emergency Mental Health, 8*(1), 1–5.

O'Hara, A.F., & Violanti, J.M. (2009). Police suicide—A web surveillance of national data. *International Journal of Emergency Mental Health, 11*(1), 17–24.

Richmond, R.L., Kehoe, L., Hailstone, S., Wodak, A., Uebel-Yan, M. (1999). Quantitative and qualitative evaluations of brief interventions to change excessive drinking, smoking and stress in the police force. *Addiction, 94*(10), 1509–1521.

Sheehan, D.C. (1999). Stress management in the Federal Bureau of Investigation: Principles for program development. *Internationals Journal of Emergency Mental Health, 1*, 39–42.

Slatkin, A.A. (2010). *Crisis and communication in hostage negotiations* (2nd Ed.), Springfield, IL: Charles C Thomas.

Stellman, J.M. (1998). *Encyclopaedia of Occupational Health and Safety* (pp. 95, 10-95-12). International Labour Organization. Retrieved June 16, 2009 from the Trauma Central. http://www.massey.ac.nz/~trauma/issues/1997-1/cvs1.htm.

Van Hasselt, V.B., Sheehan, D.C., Sellers, A.H., Baker, M.T., & Feiner, C.A. (2003). A behavioral-analytic model for assessing stress in police officers: Phase I. Development of the Law Enforcement Officer Stress Survey (LEOSS). *International Journal of Emergency Mental Health, 5*(2), 77–84.

Violanti, J.M. (1999). Death on duty: Police survivor trauma. In J.M. Violanti & D. Paton (Eds.), *Police trauma: Psychological aftermath of civilian combat* (pp. 139–158). Springfield, IL: Charles C Thomas.

Violanti, J. (2005). Dying for the Job: Psychological Stress Disease and Mortality in Police Work. In Policing and Stress. In H. Copes (Ed.), *Policing and Stress* (p. 94). NJ: Prentice Hall.

Violanti, J. (2009). *Shift work may be hazardous to your health*. Retrieved July 7, 2010, Jimston Journal web site: http://www.jimstonjournal.com/id136. html.

Violanti, J.M., & Aron, F. (1994). Ranking police stressors. *Psychological Reports, 75*(2), 824–826.

Violanti, J.M., Vena, J.E., & Petralia, S. (1998). Mortality of a Police Cohort, 1950–1990. *American Journal of Industrial Medicine, 33*, 366–373.

Discussion Questions

1. What are the negative physical and psychological factors associated with shift work?
2. What are some examples of avoidant coping strategies?
3. Literally thousands of police officers indicate that the most serious stress comes from the job itself. What examples were provided?
4. What alternative explanations were provided by police agencies to the family and to keep the news of suicides out of the media?
5. What is the role of the Peer Support Officer?
6. What type of training is provided to Peer Support Officers?
7. What is the immediate goal of the Badge of Life Psychological Survival for Police Officer Program (BOL)?
8. What the elements of the BOL Emotional Self-Care (ESC) Training Program?
9. What two BOL programs were developed to focus on effective utilization of police retirees by departments and academies?

40

Critical Incident Stress Management (CISM) in Support of Special Agents and Other First Responders Responding to the Fort Hood Shooting: Summary and Conclusions

Russell Strand, Karina Felices, and Kenneth Williams

On November 5, 2009, a lone gunman entered the Soldier Readiness Processing (SRP) site at Fort Hood, Texas and began to fire a handgun at personnel inside and outside the site. The results of the gunman's actions were 12 Soldiers and one civilian killed and 31 wounded. This has been described as the worst mass killing on a military installation in the history of the United States Department of Defense. On November 6 and 7, the United States Army Military Police School (USAMPS) received a request from the Commander of the 11th Military Police (MP) Battalion, Criminal Investigation Division (CID) for Critical Incident Peer Support (CIPS) for the unit. On November 7, US-AMPS also received a request from the Fort Hood Director of Emergency Services (DES) for CIPS support. These requests were strongly supported by the Commander of the 6th MP Group (CID) and the Commandant of USAMPS. This paper provides a description of the actions of the CIPS team during the days that followed the shooting. The description includes a discussion of the interventions that were conducted, the results of the interventions, and provides recommendations for establishing policies, procedures, and programs of Critical Incident Stress Management (CISM) and peer support programs, such as CIPS, in preparation for critical incidents.

Description of Interventions

A two-person CIPS team from USAMPS arrived at Fort Hood on the evening of November 6. The CIPS team provided an initial in-brief to the Commander of the 11th MP Detachment (CID). The in-brief included roles, responsibilities, and capabilities of the CIPS team. Following the in-brief, the Commander mandated all Battalion personnel, including CID agents, support personnel and unit leaders, participate in a critical incident stress debriefing (CISD) led by the CIPS team.

The CIPS team coordinated with several organizations at Fort Hood, including Department of Social Services and the III Corps Mental Health cell that was activated following the shootings. As a result of this coordination, III Corps included the USAMPS CIPS team in their mental health operational plan (OPLAN). The team also coordinated with the Chief, Fort Hood Social Work Services who was informed the USAMPS CIPS support team was on the ground augmenting their mission. This coordination was important to assist local mental health experts in understanding the CIPS team role and to obtain support for additional mental health referrals should the need arise during CIPS one-on-one interventions and debriefings. The team also coordinated with the Chief, DES who requested CIPS for firefighters, emergency medical services (EMS) personnel, and other first responders. On November 7, 2009, the CIPS team received a guided briefing through the crime scene to obtain a sense of understanding of the nature of the incident. This walk-through turned out to be crucial for the CIPS team during subsequent debriefings and individual interventions as agents and other first responders described where they were when the events unfolded. It was also essential for the CIPS team to have a better sense of the magnitude of the tragedy in preparation for the debriefings and one-on-one interventions, and also provided a good basis for follow-on questions during the thought and reaction phases of the debriefings. This walk-through also assisted the CIPS team in gaining credibility with the participants of the debriefings and the one-on-one interventions because they knew the team shared some of their experiences and understanding of the events that transpired.

Definitions of Key Terms

Critical Incident: "an event which is outside the usual range of experience and challenges one's ability to cope ... and has the potential ... to overwhelm one's usual psychological defenses and coping mechanisms" (Everly & Mitchell, 2000, p. 212).

Critical Incident Peer Support (CIPS): the U.S. Army Military Police School program for training MPs and CID agents to serve as peer supporters following critical incidents.

Critical Incident Stress: the intense emotional reaction to experiencing a critical incident.

Critical Incident Stress Debriefing (CISD): "a highly structured form of group crisis intervention and represents a discussion of the traumatic, or critical, incident" (Everly & Mitchell, 2000, p. 212). The CISD model follows seven phases —introduction, fact, thought, reaction, symptom, teaching, re-entry (Mitchell & Everly, 1997).

Critical Incident Stress Management (CISM): pre-crisis preparation and training, post-operation intervention (referred to as *demobilization* in civilian arenas), crisis management brief, defusing, CISD, one-on-one intervention, pastoral crisis intervention, family intervention, organizational consultation, and follow-up and referral (Everly & Mitchell, 1999, 2000).

Defusing: "a 3-phase, 45-minute, structured small group discussion provided within hours of a crisis for purposes of assessment, triaging, and acute symptom mitigation" (Everly & Mitchell, 2000, p. 215).

One-on-one Intervention: the most-used element of CISM interventions, it consists of "1 to 3 contacts with an individual who is in crisis [and] may last 15 minutes to more than 2 hours depending upon the nature and severity of the crisis" (Everly & Mitchell, 2000, p. 215).

Peer Support: "the provision of crisis intervention services by those other than mental health clinicians and directed toward individuals of similar key characteristics as those of the providers, e.g., emergency services peer support, student peer support, etc." (Everly, 2004, p. 43).

Peer Supporter: "a member of the workplace who has been specially selected and trained to provide a first line of assistance and basic crisis intervention to fellow workers" (Robinson & Murdoch, 2003, p. 1); "any person who is engaged in the provision of mental health support, but does not possess a professional degree in mental health services" (Everly, 2002, p. 91).

Between November 7 and 12, the CIPS team conducted numerous interventions which are listed in Table 1.

Table 1
Interventions Conducted by the CIPS Team

Intervention	Target Group	# of Events/Attendees	Duration
CISD	CID/DES	32/135	60–150 min
One-on-one intervention	CID	114	10–60 min
CISD	Spouses	2/6	60 min

Efficacy of Critical Incident Stress Management

A detailed analysis of the efficacy of CISM is beyond the scope of this paper. However, it is appropriate to present an overview. The use of CISDs is controversial and has been highly scrutinized. Several studies (Devilly & Cotton, 2003; Mitchell, 2003) have questioned its efficacy. However, it has been noted that these studies have utilized questionable research procedures (Mitchell, 2003, 2004; Robinson, 2004) such as using subjects that CISD was not designed to support and conducting CISDs inconsistent with standardized guidelines and protocols. This brings into question those studies that are critical of the use of CISD and CISM. Based on these studies, some mental health professionals in the Army have discounted the effectiveness of CISD and CISM for use with Army personnel. However, the other branches of service (Air Force, Navy, Marines, and Coast Guard) have used CISD and CISM with success (Department of Defense, 2010).

The efficacy of CISM is based on its use as a comprehensive system of interventions. CISD is not intended to be a stand-alone intervention, but is to be used in conjunction with other elements of CISM (Everly & Mitchell, 1999). When implemented as a comprehensive system, CISM has proven to be highly effective in mitigating CIS and facilitating a return to normal functioning (Mitchell, 2003). Several organizations have developed programs and policies that implement CISM, such as the Federal Bureau of Investigation (Kureczka, 2002; McNally & Solomon, 1999), emergency medical services (EMS) (Volkmann, 2003), fire departments (Fire Engineering, 2004), law enforcement (Levenson, 2007; Ussery & Waters, 2006; Waters & Ussery, 2007), Employee Assistance programs (EAP) (Masi, 2006; Tyler & Rogers, 2005), Assaulted Staff Action programs (ASAP) (Flannery, Hanson, Rego, & Walker, 2003), and other entities and workplaces exposed to critical incidents (Everly et al., 2006). Numerous local agencies ranging in size from small towns to large cities have adopted policies and procedures for implementing CISM as a multicomponent system (Levenson & Dwyer, 2003). The comprehensive use of the components of CISM has been shown to increase resiliency and mitigate intense CIS reactions (Freeman & Carson, 2006; Roberts & Everly, 2006).

In addition to conducting interventions, the CIPS team provided literature to all the participants of interventions. The team sent literature overnight from USAMPS to Fort Hood. Other literature was obtained from local social work services. Literature that provided information on typical reactions, coping skills, and local support agencies was highly beneficial. The materials provided by the CIPS team provided personnel with referral information they otherwise may not have received. Several participants reported that they read through the materials and self-referred themselves to other helping agencies.

Results of the Interventions

Timing

Initially, leaders expressed concern about the timing of CIPS support. The concern focused on the possibility that interventions would interfere with the investigation. The CIPS team noted the concerns and presented to the chain of command the premise that early intervention could serve to mitigate intense stress reaction and restore rational thinking. The result could be a higher quality investigation. The CIPS team made every effort to be accessible and to coordinate interventions at times that were convenient to personnel. Numerous agents, first responders, and support personnel commented on how important it was for them to see peer supporters in the area doing an initial assessment. The visibility of the CIPS team developed trust between personnel and the team, and laid the foundation for subsequent debriefings and one-on-one interventions. In fact, the mere presence of the team in the investigative work areas and at the crime scene encouraged several agents to seek out immediate one-on-one interventions which had a direct positive impact on their ability to continue with their emotionally difficult mission.

Additionally, personnel stated that it was essential for them to receive the support earlier rather than later and that early intervention assisted them in continuing their difficult tasks. The CIPS team was proactive, present, and accessible. The timing of the team's arrival and early intervention facilitated emotional and mental adaptive response which was necessary for effective debriefing. Early intervention also provided personnel the opportunity to process what happened as soon as possible and to be made aware of signs and symptoms they might not yet be experiencing.

Location

Due to the ongoing nature of the investigation, meeting space was limited. All available space was being used by additional CID agents, Texas Rangers, and FBI agents. The CID Battalion arranged for the delivery of a portable building (MILVAN) to be used for the specific purpose of conducting CISDs. The MILVAN was placed adjacent to the CID detachment. The location of the MILVAN, near but separate from the unit's operation, greatly facilitated access by personnel to the CIPS team and decreased disruptions to the investigation.

Comfort with Peer Supporters

The CIPS team consisted of two experienced individuals, both retired from the military after more than 20 years of service. One is a retired CID agent, and the other is a retired MP. Both have extensive experience in critical incidents and criminal investigations. Both are trained in Critical Incident Stress Management (CISM). The use of trained, experienced peer supporters fosters a high level of trust in responders, which in turn facilitates seeking help (Levenson, 2007).

The personnel being supported (firefighters, EMS, MPs, DA Police, CID agents, and other first responders) demonstrated openness and a high level of comfort in interacting with the CIPS team. CID agents stated that they would not have shared as much information with someone who did not have CID experience. Due to the sensitive nature of this particular investigation, many agents related they would have been hesitant to share information with someone who wasn't an agent or former agent. Numerous personnel stated that their experience with participating in "text-book" type debriefings was not beneficial. In the case at hand, participants stated that the interventions conducted by trained peers were much more practical and beneficial. In fact, following the debriefings conducted by the CIPS team, most of the participants of the debriefings were required to undergo mental health screenings. Following the mental health screenings, several participants of both the CIPS debriefings and mental health screenings commented the debriefings were more helpful in contextualizing the critical incidents they experienced. Some commented the mental health screening was too clinical impersonal, making them feel like they were merely being examined which made them suspicious of that process.

It was beneficial for the CIPS team to have specific first responder experience. The team was seen as approachable and capable of understanding. Several DES personnel returned for a second CISD. These personnel commented that the CISDs conducted by the CIPS team had more meaning and made a significant difference in their ability to cope with the critical incident. Numerous personnel sought out CIPS team members to talk repeatedly about some of the difficulties they were having as a result of this event. In some cases, supervisors brought personnel to the CIPS team and asked the team to talk with them again.

Relationship

Having the CIPS team on the site was very beneficial. Close proximity enhanced the development of caring relationships. Accessibility was of utmost importance in that all personnel who received support were working shifts and found it much easier to attend CISDs anytime throughout the day or evening versus being forced into a scheduled time slot. Numerous participants commented that it was very helpful for them to get to know the CIPS team prior to the CISD instead of being placed in a room and introduced to the peer supporters for the first time at the beginning of the CISD.

Mandatory Attendance

Leaders and personnel expressed some initial concern about mandatory attendance at CISDs. After participation in a CISD, many of the personnel commented that they would not have attended debriefings unless it was mandated and all but a few stated they were glad that they attended. Mandatory attendance may reduce the stigma associated with seeking help. If all those who have been involved in a critical incident are required to participate in a CISD, then no one is singled out as "having a problem." Also, even if someone does not need an intervention, that person's presence may provide support to the others in the group, as well as build cohesion within the group. Participants reported that the confidential nature of the debriefings was beneficial.

Multicomponent

The CIPS team conducted two types of interventions—CISDs and one-on-one interventions. CISM is not a unilateral activity but is a multicomponent system. The combination of interventions conducted by the CIPS team served to facilitate adaptive rational thinking and to mitigate intense stress reactions. The team practiced flexibility and intentionality as they conducted the appropriate intervention given the availability and needs of personnel.

Trauma and grieving is a process—not an event. Numerous personnel disclosed some trauma before, during, and after CISDs. Peer support availability between debriefings was essential for personnel who needed to share some of their trauma response individually. Small debriefing groups were preferred to larger groups by the participants. Due to the nature of the investigation, some personnel desired but did not have time for a CISD. These personnel participated in a one-on-one intervention.

Homogenous Groups

A key element of crisis intervention is conducting interventions with homogenous groups. The term *homogenous group* indicates that those with similar level of contact with the crisis or those having similar roles are grouped together for the intervention. For example, a group formed for an intervention should consist of all CID agents, or all firefighters, or those directly involved versus those indirectly involved. The CIPS team was careful to follow this principle. Also, the team conducted separate debriefings for supervisors and non-supervisors.

Several participants stated that they were more at ease discussing their reactions to the event being in the room with "peers" as opposed to being in a mixed group of supervisors and non-supervisors. Senior personnel received separate debriefings which enabled them to disclose more information. The first debriefing included leaders and subordinates which appeared to hinder disclosure and discussion even though all agreed to keep matters shared confidential. The CIPS team observed increased interaction and discussion when leaders and subordinates were debriefed separately. The subordinates appeared to speak more freely without the fear that their supervisor may see them as weak or problematic. Additionally, the leaders opened up more without fear that their subordinates may see them in a more negative light because of their emotional and physical reactions to the critical incidents they experienced.

Spouse Response

At the request of several agents and leaders, the CIPS team provided interventions for spouses who had intense reactions to the crisis. The spouses who attended the CISDs were open and expressive in disclosing their significant reactions to the event. All spouses who attended stated that the CISDs were of great benefit, saying that the discussion of their reactions provided understanding, insight, and instilled a better sense of teamwork and partnership with their spouse. The CISD was the first time that many of the spouses had met each other. They committed to developing relationships and to creating a phone chain in the event of another critical incident.

Stigma

The actions of the CIPS team and unit leaders reduced the stigma of seeking help, according to feedback stated by the participants. The presence, visibility, and accessibility of the CIPS team served to promote the fact that crisis intervention is an integral element of a critical incident. The team's presence reinforced the notion that there was nothing wrong with those who were involved with the event. The team's presence did promote the principle that those who were involved in the event would most likely have a typical reaction to an atypical event.

Initially, several personnel voiced their perception that the presence of the CIPS team would be just another "check the block" suicide awareness class. However, once participants attended one-on-one interventions and CISDs, they stated that it was clear that the CIPS team was there because their supervisors cared for the participants' well-being. As stated above, making attendance at interventions mandatory served to reduce stigma, according to statements of the participants. Since all were required to attend, no one was singled out as having a problem. It was also very important for the participants to know that their supervisors and leaders also attended debriefings.

Team Facilitated and Mitigated

The various interventions conducted by the CIPS team had a positive impact on personnel and their continuing mission, according to the participants. Many participants shared their traumatic experiences, both from this event and previous critical incidents. Participants began learning and attempting to cope with the effects of this event as well as previous incidents. Participants shared their experiences and reactions with each other which began their process of providing mutual support with their coworkers. The vast majority of participants who participated in interventions reported the following benefits:

- Debriefings provide understanding of individual emotional, psychological, and physical impact of trauma.
- Personnel who have undergone previous debriefings from previous incidents reported that the information they received helped them prepare for future stress and trauma.

The Director of Emergency Services offered positive feedback regarding the support of the CIPS team. He stated, "From my perspective the USAMPS CIPS support team was very responsive to the needs of the DES from the very instant that I contacted them. They were extremely flexible and understanding of our work schedule and in fact spent the better part of three days (working from at least 0900–2100 [9 a.m.–9 p.m.]) in our building ensuring all large and small groups of personnel received CIPS debriefs."

One of the key actions of the CIPS team was referring personnel for additional support. A secondary goal of crisis intervention is the identification of those who need a higher level of care. The CIPS team identified several personnel who needed a higher level of care. These individuals were referred in a confidential and respectful manner to local mental health providers.

Care of the CIPS Team

Conducting CIPS/CISM can be very demanding and draining on the emotional reservoirs of peer supporters. Just as those who experience a critical incident first-hand need crisis intervention, so do those who provide support experience *secondary traumatization*, the trauma that occurs when being exposed to and hearing the experiences of others who have been involved in a critical incident. Upon the return to USAMPS, the CIPS team received a debriefing, referred to as Post Action Staff Support, from an experienced, trained professional in CIPS/CISM. This intervention enabled the CIPS team to diffuse the stress they had accumulated in the course of providing support.

Summary of Results

The effectiveness of the interventions conducted by the CIPS team was due to several key factors. The CIPS team was available and accessible due to a focus on early intervention and establishing a base of operations in close proximity to the personnel being supported. The CIPS team provided a level of comfort and reduced stigma by having credibility as experienced peer supporters and by focusing on developing relationships with those they were supporting. Unit leaders further reduced stigma by requiring attendance at interventions and by participating in intervention themselves. The CIPS team demonstrated effectiveness and competence in providing individual and small group interventions, by forming homogenous groups, and by being flexible and adaptable. The care that the team provided to spouses served to nurture family relationships, to provide insight, and to mitigate the stress reaction of spouses. The overall results of the support provided by the CIPS team include facilitating the expression of emotional and mental reaction to the event and the mitigation of intense stress reaction. This enabled the personnel to continue with their mission.

Recommendations

Policy

It was the consensus of unit leaders and personnel that CIPS and CISM should be official policy. Addressing the emotional and mental reactions of critical incident stress should be a normal and intentional element of the operational response to a critical incident. The incorporation of multicomponent interventions should be an automatic response such that personnel become comfortable with and accustomed to the use of crisis interventions. The interventions should not be an isolated, singular activity. Instead, interventions should utilize the full range of interventions in a tiered response according to need, the quality of the reaction, and the nature of those involved. A policy should also provide for interventions for family members of affected personnel.

Policy, procedures, and programs of CISM must outline a proactive stance toward addressing CIS. Rather than waiting for a critical incident to occur and providing only counseling by mental health professionals, units and installations must implement all elements of CISM. A policy should include establishing a unit or installation Critical Incident Stress Team (CIST) to oversee the program and the training of personnel, establishing procedures for response to a critical incident, establishing guidelines for selection and training of peers, and establishing guidelines for coordination among the various agencies on an installation (Everly & Mitchell, 1999; Robinson & Murdoch, 2003).

This recommendation addresses the concern and mirrors the recommendation of the Department of Defense (DOD) study of the Fort Hood shooting. The DOD study identified the lack of policy regarding implementing strategies for addressing traumatic stress as the result of critical incidents. The DOD study recommends developing and implementing policy, programs, and procedures that provide preventive and restorative care for traumatic events in domestic environments, using "best practices inside and outside the Department of Defense" (Department of Defense, 2010, p. 50). As mentioned above, the principles of CISM have been shown to be effective in mitigating CIS reaction and enhancing resilience among personnel affected by traumatic events.

Trained Peer Supporters

A policy of CIPS or CISM should include the provision of trained peers at various levels of a unit, organization, or command structure. Peer supporters have been highly effective in addressing mental health issues, reducing absenteeism, providing support for families, and reducing the suicide rate of personnel in the civilian arena (Levenson, 2007). Several studies have demonstrated the benefits of peer supporters among federal (Sheehan, 1999) and local law enforcement (Chamberlin, 2000; Freeman, 2002; Greenstone, 2000).

Trained peer supporters should be utilized at platoon, company, battalion, and Group levels. Just as units have combat lifesavers trained in first aid for physical injuries, units need peer supporters trained in first aid for mental injuries. These trained peers would function as support to others within their unit on a one-on-one basis. However, in the event of a critical incident, trained peers should not facilitate interventions for their own units. This key principle of CISM ensures that personnel who are experiencing a stress reaction themselves can deal with their own issues and not have to deal with others' issues as well. A trained peer must be able to focus on the needs of others and not be influenced by their own stress reaction.

Stigma and Confidentiality

A policy of CIPS or CISM should include provisions for addressing the stigma of seeking help. While some may resist mandatory attendance at interventions, such a policy serves to reduce stigma as no one is singled out as being weak or having a problem. Also, facilitators and participants must stress confidentiality. Participants must be sure that the thoughts and reactions that they share will not become public knowledge. A key to restoring rational thinking and mitigating the stress reaction is personal discussion in small groups. The fear of being singled out as having a problem, coupled with the fear of having one's personal reactions shared in public may create a barrier to open sharing and hinder the intervention process. The focus of interventions should be on the critical incident stress reaction, not the operation. A CISD is not an operational after action review (AAR) in which personnel's actions are scrutinized. Personnel must not be required to critique one another's performance during interventions. Information disclosed in CISDs should be exempt from being reported in investigations of agent misconduct.

Training

Another key to the effectiveness of CIPS and CISM is pre-incident training. Just as units conduct operational rehearsals of critical incidents such as mass casualty and active shooter, units should also rehearse and conduct training on the psychological interventions that will be used following a critical incident. As one element of the CISM, trained peers and personnel should conduct mock CISM interventions, such as debriefings and defusings, in order to become familiar with the processes. Such rehearsals and training will provide information on typical stress reactions and expectations of interventions. Also, those who are selected to serve as peer supporters must receive specialized training in crisis intervention. They should be skilled in providing the multiple components of CIPS and CISM, including CISDs, defusings, one-on-one interventions, pre-incident training, and family interventions.

Follow-up

Follow-up is essential. The CISD process enables peer supporters to identify those who need additional support. Crisis intervention in general, and CISM specifically, are not isolated, singular actions. Both are most effective when CISM Team members use multiple interventions at various times in the aftermath of a critical incident. (Everly, 2004; Everly & Mitchell, 2003; Robinson & Murdoch, 2003.) Therefore, peer supporters must plan for the ability to contact personnel following specific interventions for assessment and referral if necessary.

Summary of Policy Recommendations

The CIPS team recommends that the U.S. Army Provost Marshal General (PMG) and the U.S. Army Criminal Investigation Division Command (USACIDC) develop an official policy for CIPS/CISM. A policy should include:

- Mandated CISM interventions following specific types of critical incidents.
- Confidentiality of information disclosed during interventions.
- Critical incident peer support team program management and implementation.
- Mandated critical incident peer support cells.
- Incorporation of lessons learned in policy.
- Required attendance of the USAMPS CIPS course for all peer supporters.
- USAMPS further develop and maintain CIPS support team deployment capability in the event of major critical incidents.
- Provide on-scene support within 8–12 hours following event if possible.
- Permanent funding for USAMPS CIPS training and direct unit support program.
- Recognition of CIPS/CISM as an essential element in supporting the Army Human Capital capabilities in promoting Soldier, Family, and Civilian well-being and resilience.

Conclusion

The use of CIPS and CISM may be an intentional and effective response to address the potentially intense stress reactions of personnel and their family members to critical incidents. This paper has outlined the specific actions of the USAMPS CIPS team in providing support to the CID unit and DES members who responded to the Fort Hood shooting and the subsequent investigation. The results of the actions and interventions of the CIPS team demonstrated that, when conducted according to the principles of crisis intervention and CISM, such interventions may have a significant effect on facilitating the restoration of rational thinking and normal functioning, and on mitigating the effects of critical incident stress reaction.

Note: CISDs were conducted for CID special agents, CID support personnel, CID leadership, firefighters, EMS, DA Police, MPs, detectives, and one FBI analyst. The one-on-one interventions included an extremely traumatized shooting victim and a witness, as well as several CID agents who were attending the memorial service for the victims.

References

Chamberlin, J. (2000). Cops must trust cops, even one with a Ph.D. *APA Monitor, 31*, 1.

Department of Defense. (2010). *Protecting the force: Lessons from Fort Hood.* Washington, DC: Department of Defense.

Devilly, G.D., & Cotton, P. (2003). Psychological debriefing and the workplace: Defining a concept, controversies and guidelines for intervention. *Australian Psychologist, 38*, 144–150.

Everly, G. (2002). Thoughts on peer (paraprofessional) support in the provision of mental health services. *International Journal of Emergency Mental Health, 4*(2), 89–90.

Everly, G. (2004). *Assisting individuals in crisis.* 3rd Ed. Ellicott City, MD: International Critical Incident Stress Foundation.

Everly, G. & Mitchell, J. (1999). *Critical incident stress management: A new era and standard of care in crisis intervention,* 2nd Ed. Ellicott City, MD: Chevron Publishing.

Everly, G. & Mitchell, J. (2000). The debriefing "controversy" and crisis intervention: A review of lexical and substantive issues. *International Journal of Emergency Mental Health, 2*(4), 211–225.

Everly, G. & Mitchell, J. (2003). *Critical incident stress management (CISM): Individual crisis intervention and peer support.* Ellicott City, MD: International Critical Incident Stress Foundation, Inc.

Everly, G., Sherman, M., Stapleton, A., Barnett, D., Hiremath, G., & Links, J. (2006). Workplace crisis intervention: A systematic review of effect sizes. *Journal of Workplace Behavioral Health, 21*(3–4), 153–170.

Fire Engineering. (2004). *Critical incident stress management. Fire Engineering, 157*(12), 22–30.

Flannery, R., Hanson, A., Rego, J., & Walker, A. (2003). Precipitants of psychiatric patient assaults on staff: Preliminary empirical inquiry of the Assaulted Staff Action Program (ASAP). *International Journal of Emergency Mental Health, 5*(3), 141–146.

Freeman, D. & Carson, M. (2006). Developing workplace resilience: The role of the peer referral agent diffuser. *Journal of Workplace Behavioral Health, 22*(1), 113–121.

Freeman, G. (2002). 9/11 one year later, ACFE members reflect: What have we learned? *The Forensic Examiner, 11*(9–10), 10–15.

Greenstone, J. (2000). Peer support in a municipal police department. *The Forensic Examiner, 9*(3–4), 33–36.

Kureczka, A. (2002). Surviving assaults: After the physical battle ends, the psychological battle begins. *FBI Law Enforcement Bulletin, 71*(1), 18–21. Jan 2002.

Levenson, R. (2007). Prevention of traumatic stress in law enforcement personnel: A cursory look at the roles of peer support and critical incident stress management. *Forensic Examiner, 16*(3), 16–19.

Levenson, R. & Dwyer, L. (2003). Peer support in law enforcement: Past, present, and future. *International Journal of Emergency Mental Health, 5*(3), 147–152.

Masi, D. (2006). New initiatives in the EAP field. *Behavioral Healthcare, 26*(4), 23–24.

McNally, V. & Solomon, R. (1999). The FBI's Critical Incident Stress Management Program. *FBI Law Enforcement Bulletin, 68*(2), 20–25.

Mitchell, J. (2003). *Crisis intervention and CISM: A research summary.* Ellicott City, MD: International Critical Incident Stress Foundation.

Mitchell, J. (2004). A response to the Devilly and Cotton article, "Psychological Debriefing and the Workplace … ." *Australian Psychologist, 39*(1), 24–28.

Mitchell, J., & Everly, G. (1997). *Critical incident stress debriefing,* 3rd Ed. Ellicott City, MD: Chevron Publishing.

Roberts, A. & Everly, G. (2006). A meta-analysis of 36 crisis intervention studies. *Brief Treatment and Crisis Intervention, 6*, 10–21.

Robinson, R., & Murdoch, P. (2003). *Establishing and maintaining peer support programs in the workplace,* 3rd Ed. Ellicott City, MD: Chevron Publishing.

Robinson, R. (2004). Counterbalancing misrepresentations of Critical Incident Stress Debriefing and Critical Incident Stress Management. *Australian Psychologist, 39*(1), 29–34.

Sheehan, D. (1999). Stress management in the Federal Bureau of Investigation: Principles for program development. *International Journal of Emergency Mental Health, 1*(1), 39–42.

Tyler, M., & Rogers, J. (2005). A federal perspective on EAPs and emergency preparedness. *International Journal of Emergency Mental Health, 7*(3), 179–186.

Ussery, W., & Waters, J. (2006). COP-2-COP Hotlines: Programs to address the needs of first responders and their families. *Brief Treatment and Crisis Intervention, 6*(1), 66–78.

Volkmann, P. (2003). When traumatic events affect the EMS worker: The role of the CISM team. *Fire Engineering, 156*, 51–54.

Waters, J., & Ussery, W. (2007). Police stress: History, contributing factors, symptoms, and interventions. *Policing, 30*(2), 169–188.

Discussion Questions

1. Define "critical incident."
2. What is the function of Critical Incident Peer Support (CIPS)?
3. What are the elements of a Critical Incident Stress Debriefing?
4. What is the function of Critical Incident Stress Management?
5. Define the term "defusing."
6. What are the elements of the "one-on-one intervention"?
7. What is a "peer supporter"?
8. What is the efficacy of Critical Incident Stress Management?
9. What concerns did the leaders discussed in this article express concerning the timing of the critical incidents peer support?
10. What counter arguments were presented by the Critical Incident Peer Support team about the concern that interventions would interfere with an investigation?
11. What were the backgrounds of the personnel who served as members of the Critical Incident Peer Support team in this incident?
12. What types of personnel were being supported by the Critical Incident Peer Support team?
13. What was the final reaction to the requirement that there be mandatory attendance at the Critical Incident Stress Debriefing?
14. The Critical Incident Peer Support (CIPS) team conducted two types of interventions—Critical Incident Support Debriefings and one-on-one interventions. What were the advantages of using this combination?

15. What were some of the generalized reactions of the participants in the Critical Incident Stress Debriefing?

16. A key element of crisis intervention is conducting interventions with homogenous groups. How was a "homogeneous group" defined in this article?

17. What benefits were reported by the vast majority of the participants following the interventions after this incident?

41

Some Thoughts on Providing Effective Mental Health Critical Care for Police Departments after Line-of-Duty Deaths

Jeffrey T. Mitchell and Richard L. Levenson Jr.

In 2005, approximately 153 police officers were killed in the line-of-duty in the United States. According to the National Law Enforcement Officers Memorial Fund (http://www.nleomf.com), Line-of-Duty-Deaths (LODD) occurred as a result of traffic accidents (n=62); shootings (n=62); medically-related incidents, such as heat stroke, myocardial infarction, and other medical conditions including one New York City police officer who died of illnesses acquired as a result of his participation in search, rescue, and recovery efforts at Ground Zero of the World Trade Center (n=20); a helicopter crash (n=2); an explosive device (n=1); stabbing (n=1); drowning (n=2); and falls (n=3). These separate, but related LODDs not only resulted in creating emotional trauma in deceased officers' peers, but also in re-awakening temporarily dormant, traumatic, job-related experiences in those indirectly affected by the original events.

Because a LODD can have such far-reaching implications, the Critical Incident Stress Management (CISM) team must have a large repertoire of *tactics* ready to deal effectively with the many levels of these very personal and emotionally painful psychological traumas.

The aims of this brief article are to: 1) enhance overall learning in the CISM field; 2) caution crisis team members about problematic situations and mistakes that can occur especially, but not only, when newly trained people are making decisions in the face of challenging and emotionally painful events; and, 3) encourage teams to develop strategic plans before choosing crisis intervention tactics to apply in a complex situation.

The circumstance least desirable for a newly formed CISM team is a LODD. It is an extremely emotionally painful and complex jolt to organizations and to the support teams that attempt to provide assistance. Crisis response teams find themselves caught up in a swirling tornado of new traumatic experiences combined with old memories, previous traumas, raw human pain, political issues, anger, resentments, anxiety, sadness, misinterpretations, and frustrations.

A newly formed team can be completely overwhelmed by such circumstances. The cognitive demands alone of sorting out the **Target** groups (e.g., motorcycle officers, detectives, command personnel, special operations teams) within the department can be mentally exhausting. Add to that the choices of psychological first aid and mental health critical care **Tactics** (e.g., defusing, crisis management briefing, CISD, individual support, family support, follow-up services, referrals) and properly **Timing** those interventions, and a team can be stretched to its limits. But the problems do not end when a crisis team makes those decisions. **Themes** then enter the picture. Themes, such as more than one LODD at a time, can complicate decision making under crisis conditions. There is one final consideration and that is **Team**. Who is assigned to do what? Does your team handle it all by itself or call for outside help? What if there are insufficient personnel on the team—what do you do then? What if your team members are part of the department impacted by the tragedies?

As outlined above, there are five major considerations in handling any crisis response. They are:

- Target
- Tactics
- Timing
- Themes
- Team

If a crisis team is inexperienced in linking these considerations into an overall strategic plan, mistakes are more likely. Common mistakes can be made easily by teams in complex situations. We will elaborate on two of these common mistakes.

- *Not utilizing peer support personnel.* The presence of well trained and experienced peers, who are not personally involved in the tragedy, is vital to providing mental health critical care and psychological first aid. Peer support personnel from the same profession have a decided advantage in providing emotional support to their colleagues. They have instant credibility. They know the "language" of the personnel and they can more easily generate discussion of painful emotional material. The use of properly trained peers cannot be overemphasized. They are essential.

- *Confusion in definitions, terminology and choice of tactics.* New teams typically are still becoming familiar with the definitions of tactics and are sometimes unsure of what-to-do-when.

Let us clarify some of the Tactics that have been emphasized within the CISM model. There are two large group interventions and there are two small group crisis intervention tactics that are commonly used in CISM. The large group interventions are the Demobilization and the Crisis Management Briefing. Small group interventions include Defusing and the Critical Incident Stress Debriefing.

Demobilizations are rarely used and are reserved for operations personnel working at massive events such as major disasters. In a demobilization ten minutes of information are given to the large group. There is no group discussion of the situation.

Crisis Management Briefings are very versatile. They can be used in a variety of circumstances. They allow several question and answer segments to clarify the situation and to provide information. They may be used in a LODD situation, but only to brief a large and heterogeneous group or one that is too emotionally charged to engage in a discussion.

A Defusing is a small group process and it really serves as an "emotional band aid" that buys time to set up more sophisticated interventions. It is provided only within the first 8 to 12 hours after an event and quickly loses its utility after that time because people re-establish their natural defense systems and do not want to open up emotionally in a group for about another 24 hours. Once the opportunity for the Defusing is lost, it is gone. It should *not* be employed several days after the event. Additionally, the Defusing process is *almost never used in a line-of-duty death*. It is not a very powerful form of intervention and is not robust enough to use in such a circumstance. In LODD situations, the Defusing is *not the right choice of tactics*.

The Critical Incident Stress Debriefing (CISD) is a small group process that is designed to be used only with homogeneous groups who have had the same traumatic experience. However, on the day of a line-of-duty death, a full seven-phase CISD can be just too much. It goes deeper than most law enforcement personnel can manage when they are only a few hours past the death of a colleague and friend. The full seven-phase CISD process should be held back for three to seven days following the funeral.

Instead, the CISD process is modified into a five phase process in a LODD situation. The modified CISD is used instead of the Defusing and it is conducted on the day of the death. It usually lasts between 30 and 45 minutes. Its objectives are to equalize the information that some group members have and others do not, and to prepare people to face the turmoil of the next few days as they approach and go through the funeral. Additionally, it is helpful in guiding people in self care and "buddy support" as they deal with the loss of a colleague. The phases of the modified CISD are:

- *Introduction*: A very brief introduction.
- *Fact*: Those who were present are asked to briefly describe what happened so that those who were not present in the situation can at least know the most basic and pertinent facts of the situation.
- *Reaction*: The participants are asked "What are you having the most difficulty with right now?" (The overall worst part of the situation cannot yet be questioned because at this early point most people do not even know what the overall worst part is. For many, the worst part will occur during or even after the funeral.)
- *Teaching*: The teaching phase is used to prepare people for the funeral and to encourage them to do things that will help them to take care of themselves as they deal with the loss.
- *Reentry*: For the most part, this is a question, answer, and summarization process to give final directives as people are moving into the next phases of the tragedy.

A full seven-phase CISD is usually provided as a follow-up mechanism to the five-phase CISD that was provided on the day of the death. It usually occurs between three and seven days after the funeral. This is the point in time when the overall worst part is discussed and information is provided on the long-range grief process.

Attendance by line officers (e.g., sergeants, lieutenants and sometimes captains) is usually not a problem if they were part of the response in the field. High ranking officers (e.g., majors, deputy inspectors, deputy chiefs, assistant chiefs and chiefs) who were not part of the incident typically become a problem for lower ranking personnel in a CISD process. Sometimes it is best to provide separate CISD services for higher ranking personnel. A possible exception exists when an LODD occurs in a small department. In such a case everyone is seriously impacted by a line-of-duty death, and all should be included in the same CISD. This is a judgment call. Team members should think about it carefully and make rational decisions based upon all the available information regarding an organization and its personnel interactions. In this regard, it is both important and helpful to ask department members how they would like the intervention to be managed.

Line-of-duty death situations generate more one-on-one interventions than almost any other situation. CISM teams need to get their members out to contact individuals who are struggling with a great loss. Some people isolate themselves from their colleagues and are in enormous emotional pain. A friendly, supportive contact with these individuals can be helpful to them in reconnecting with their group. Such contact enhances group cohesion. It is especially helpful in assisting the individual through a difficult time.

A word of caution is in order here regarding CISM team member participation in funerals. There are positives and negatives that must be considered. On the positive side, team members present at funerals see first hand what has happened. They can use that information to more carefully reach out to those who need additional contact and support. On the down side, exposure to a funeral causes emotional contamination for CISM team members who may now have a hard time maintaining their objectivity as they try to assist others. It is generally not recommended that the primary CISM team leader attend the funeral services. They need to remain distant enough from the intense emotions in order to be able to make clear decisions about Targets, Tactics, Timing of interventions, Themes, and Team resources.

When an event is too overwhelming for a single CISM team to manage, such as in medium-to-large police departments, the team should connect with resources in other localities. A local CISM team should call the International Critical Incident Stress Foundation to arrange for other police-focused CISM teams to participate in the support processes. They should not rely solely on their own CISM team's abilities to reach the best strategic plan. Teams that can swallow their pride and ask for assistance generally tend to shine as a beacon of hope in a sea of chaos. They grow from the knowledge, experience, and skills of others and they become more capable of helping other teams on mutual aid requests in the future.

Referrals of individuals in law enforcement to outside mental health professionals can sometimes be a source of frustration, disappointment, and anger. Often command personnel suggest that one of their personnel needs a referral. We have personally found that one or two brief meetings with one of the mental health professionals on the CISM team may be all that is necessary to help a person recover. We would suggest that CISM teams not be too quick with referrals to licensed mental health personnel, even those who have been trained to work with police officers. The team should further assess a person before proceeding with a blanket referral. When a referral is necessary, seek mental health professionals whom you know or who are familiar with law enforcement personnel and their work. It is best if those mental health professionals have been trained in CISM. We should avoid therapists who have little or no experience with law enforcement personnel. Such lack of experience is a formula for a failed therapy process and much unresolved anger. It can result in an officer feeling misunderstood or as if the therapist is speaking a foreign language.

Another caution to keep in mind is that some "friendly fire" incidents in which an officer has been killed have resulted in the suicide death of the shooter. One-on-one assessment and crisis support is essential for the shooter. Always keep individual contacts in mind as a fall-back position after you have achieved whatever is possible with group interventions.

The International Critical Incident Stress Foundation has developed a new course on Strategic Planning. It is an essential course and CISM team members should take it as soon as possible. It provides clear guidelines for managing many of the problems encountered in law enforcement deaths. The course material will help in the decision making required by police departments enmeshed in tragedy. It will also help CISM teams to avoid some of the pitfalls discussed in this article.

Perfection is a rarely achieved goal in any human endeavor. We all strive, however, to do the very best we can for the people we meet. We strive to have the best CISM training and to stick with commonly accepted standards of practice. We learn from our mistakes and we correct our performance for the next crisis that crosses our paths. We know that when we are committed to improving our crisis intervention skills we substantially reduce the potential to make future mistakes. Most notably we make a positive difference in the lives of others. How do we know that? The people we have served have been our teachers, our mentors, our guides, and our critics. They tell us what worked and what did not work very well. They tell us that, despite our mistakes, we have made their lives a little easier during some very tough times. Police agencies continue to call upon CISM teams and frequently express their gratitude for the people who care for them and provide relief under duress. Police culture has been altered to the extent that crisis intervention provided by trained peers is now an acceptable alternative to living with debilitating and life-threatening psychological stress from traumatic circumstances occurring on the job.

Discussion Questions

1. What were the aims of the article?
2. What are the two common mistakes made by inexperienced crisis team members?

3. What process is involved in the group intervention called "demobilization?"
4. What process is involved in the small group interactions called "defusing?"
5. Why was it recommended that the full seven-day Critical Stress Incident Debriefing (CISD) not be used on the day of a line-of-duty death?
6. What are some of the positive and negative aspects of the Critical Incident Stress Management (CISM) team members participating in the funerals involving line-of-duty deaths?
7. What course of action should be taken when an event is too overwhelming for a single (Critical Incident Stress Management) CISM team to manage?
8. What type of therapist should be avoided when referring police officers for professional assistance?
9. The International Critical Incident Stress Foundation has developed a new course on Strategic Planning. What were the recommendations made regarding the involvement of CISM team members with this group?

Part Ten

How Can the Bosses
Better Help Their Cops?

Ayres (1990) has emphasized that the creation and maintenance of a healthy workplace is critical as an organizational goal within a law enforcement agency and serves as an effective barrier against organizational and individual stress damage. Of particular importance is recognition by the law enforcement organization's administration that it has a responsibility for the mitigation and management of the stress of its employees.

Administrative support takes a variety of forms. An environment that encourages communication and facilitates an officer's ability to access stress management services is, perhaps, the most important. Well-defined missions and goals, clear policies and procedures, and state of the art training, equipment and management techniques are equally important. Above all else, the actions and practices of the administration must bring life to its well-meaning words.

Here in Part Ten, our authors expand on the interaction between the police administration and stress management. Their core questions: How can the bosses better help their cops? Can we learn better from our mistakes of the past? How can administrators better "walk the talk"? What specific action, even more than on-going support, needs to clearly come from the top of the organization?

The Police Psychological Services Section of the International Association of Chiefs of Police has been a leader in developing the professional standards for psychological support for America's law enforcement personnel. Gupton and his co-authors reflect on a number of critical issues, including confidential counseling, training, traumatic incidents, the police family, and military deployments and return to duty, which are necessary to emotionally and psychologically support and sustain the personnel within a given agency. Their bottom line emphasizes the importance of the use of police psychologists as one tool in ensuring a healthy law enforcement workforce.

Yet, not all agencies comply with the best practices outline by Gupton and his colleagues in IACP's Police Psychological Services Section. Teresa Tate has experienced and professionally observed the good and bad that a police administration can do in dealing with one of the worst consequences of police stress—a police officer suicide. As a 28-year-old wife, she lost her police officer husband, a six-year veteran of his department, to suicide. Her experience during that ordeal, and her observations as President of the Survivors of Law Enforcement Suicides (S.O.L.E.S.) organization, offer the reader insight into the treatment of a survivor and suggest specific actions that a law enforcement agency should both take and avoid during such times of tragedy.

The role of an undercover employee (UCE) is highly stressful, physically and psychologically demanding, and, oftentimes, dangerous. To many law enforcement agencies, the experience of utilizing UCEs has been negative at best, with officers forming inappropriate relationships with the criminal element, bending the rules which govern legal and ethical law enforcement conduct, or simply burning out. Personnel can be left in an assignment for too long, and reintegration into the "normal" police role and routine can be difficult. Krause stresses the importance of an agency's implementation of a comprehensive safeguard process and focuses on its six phases (selection, training, operational planning, deployment, decompression, and reintegration). As she emphasizes, "to effectively execute the critical functions, the safeguard process must be anchored by an unwavering commitment to the primary well-being of the UCE."

An officer-involved shooting is one of the most stressful events for both officers and the law enforcement agency. As part of its Model Policy Center, the International Association of Chiefs of Police has developed one governing best practices in officer-involved shootings. An essential component of this model policy is the recognition of the impact of post-shooting emotional trauma and the need for the availability of employee mental health services. Trompetter and his colleagues discuss in detail the features of this model policy from a psychological perspective, as well as some of the potential legal ramifications, especially surrounding the use of a fitness-for-duty examination following a shooting event.

Over the last several years, research into law enforcement stress has dramatically underscored the problems experienced by police officers throughout this country and the significant efforts devoted to programs of stress awareness identification and management. The key to any successful agency program lies in the strength, knowledge and practices of its first-line supervisors and middle managers. It remains an issue in many agencies that, far from helping their employees, the management style and actions of some managers actually contribute to the stress of their employees and foster an unhealthy work environment. In the book's closing article, Sewell discusses specific stress-causing practices of supervisory personnel and identifies methods by which agency executives and managers can reduce stress within an organization.

Further Reading

Ayres, Richard M. (1990). *Preventing Law Enforcement Stress: The Organization's Role*. Alexandria, VA: National Sheriffs' Association.

Band, Stephen R., and Sheehan, Donald C. (1997). "Managing Undercover Stress: The Supervisor's Role," *FBI Law Enforcement Bulletin*, 68(2),1–32.

Finn, Peter (1997). "Reducing Stress: An Organization-Centered Approach," *FBI Law Enforcement Bulletin*, 66(8), 20–26.

Miller, Laurence (2003). "Police Personalities: Understanding and Managing the Problem Officer," *The Police Chief*, LXX(5), 53–60.

Scrivner, Ellen M. (1994). *Controlling Police Use of Excessive Force: The Role of the Police Psychologist*. Washington, DC: National Institute of Justice.

Sewell, James D. (1986). "Administrative Concerns in Law Enforcement Stress Management," *Police Studies*, 9(3), 153–159.

Sewell, James D. (2002). "Managing the Stress of Organizational Change," *FBI Law Enforcement Bulletin*, 71(3), 14–20.

Sheehan, Donald C. (1999). "Stress Management in the Federal Bureau if Investigation: Principles for Program Development." *International Journal of Emergency Mental Health*, 1, 39–42.

Takasato, Joanne (2009) *In Search of Truth and Honor: Reflections of an Undercover Journey though the Dark Side of the Badge*. Charleston, SC: Booksurge Publishing Company.

Violanti, John M. (2011). "Police Organizational Stress: The Impact of Negative Discipline," *International Journal of Emergency Mental Health*, 13(1), 31–36.

Key Terms in Part Ten

Fitness-for-duty evaluation: According to guidelines promulgated by the Police Psychological Services Section of the International Association of Chiefs of Police, a psychological fitness-for-duty evaluation (FFDE) is a formal, specialized examination of an incumbent employee that results from (1) objective evidence that the employee may be unable to safely or effectively perform a defined job and (2) a reasonable basis for believing that the cause may be attributable to psychological factors. The central purpose of an FFDE is to determine whether the employee is able to safely and effectively perform his or her essential job functions.

Person-job fit analysis: The process of assuring that persons chosen for entry-level positions in an agency or for special assignments, e.g., SWAT, UCE, or child abuse investigations, are psychologically, physically, emotionally and maturity-wise suited for the requirements and demands of the particular job.

Undercover employee (UCE): An employee of a law enforcement agency tasked with performing an undercover assignment, using a covert identity, and having no apparent law enforcement affiliation.

UCE Reintegration: An effort to successfully bring an undercover employee back into the law enforcement agency and effectively deal with the psychological and emotional issues that may have resulted from the assignment.

42

Support and Sustain: Psychological Intervention for Law Enforcement Personnel

Herbert M. Gupton, Evan Axelrod, Luz Cornell,
Stephen F. Curran, Carol J. Hood, Jennifer Kelly, and Jon Moss

Law enforcement executives develop and implement policies and procedures that are directed at enforcing the law, protecting the public, and promoting safety within their communities. They also have a responsibility to implement programs designed to address the emotional well-being of the men and women who work for them. An agency's employees are its most expensive, most valuable, and most vulnerable assets. Even police officers who are typically strong of character, stress tolerant, and flexible are still fallible and susceptible to injury.

By working with psychologists who are familiar with law enforcement, law enforcement executives are better able to develop and implement programs that prevent or mitigate potential problematic behaviors. Intervention programs can be direct (e.g., counseling and response to critical incidents); indirect (e.g., training and wellness programs); or targeted to specific populations (e.g., military readjustment and police families).

The authors recognize the resistance to seek psychological intervention—or, for that matter, any other assistance—because it conveys a stigma that the officer is somehow weak and cannot handle stress. It is also sometimes true that executives use "seeing the psych" as a "hammer," or a mandated action, which it should not be. The authors invite executives to rethink this issue and support employee participation in voluntary programs.

This article familiarizes police executives with examples of psychological intervention services available from police psychologists. These services include confidential counseling, counseling family members, dealing with traumatic incidents, reintegrating police officers following discharge from active military service, and training. A more comprehensive listing of police psychology services and a description of those services can be found at the IACP Police Psychological Services Section website at http://psych.theiacp.org, under the heading Domains.[1]

Confidential Counseling

Research supports the fact that psychological treatment works,[2] and its success is augmented when it is tailored to the client and to the client's culture and preferences. Counseling services offer support to law enforcement employees who are experiencing professional, personal, emotional, or behavioral problems that may affect their job performance or productivity. Such services can be accessed through multiple pathways such as self-initiated and department referrals to in-house psychologists, contract psychologists, employee assistance programs, or community psychologists who are specifically trained to work with law enforcement personnel.

Ensuring that the counseling is confidential and that the provider has substantive experience working with public safety personnel are two particularly important elements for the success of counseling with law enforcement personnel. Savvy police administrators develop relationships with departmental and community psychologists who have a proven level of knowledge and expertise as it pertains to the unique experiences of law enforcement personnel and in whom they have confidence.

Regardless of the type of service provided or the nature of the referral, employees seeking services should expect privileged communication and confidentiality.[3] Any notion that their reported difficulties could be repeated back to the employer would significantly undermine the therapeutic process. There are limits to confidentiality, however. Traditional statutory limits (e.g., when

---

1. Gary S. Aumiller et al., "Defining the Field of Police Psychology: Core Domains and Proficiencies," *Journal of Police and Criminal Psychology* 22, no. 2 (November 2007): 65–76.

2. U.S. Department of Health and Human Services, *Mental Health: A Report of the Surgeon General* (Rockville, MD: Substance Abuse and Mental Health Services Administration, Center for Mental Health Services, National Institutes of Health, National Institute of Mental Health, 1999), http://www.surgeongeneral.gov/library/mentalhealth/home.html (accessed June 15, 2011); and Barry L. Duncan et al., ed., *The Heart and Soul of Change: Delivering What Works in Therapy*, 2nd ed. (Chicago: American Psychological Association, 2009).

3. *Jaffee v. Redmond* 518 U.S. 1; 116 S. Ct. 1923 (1996).

there is an admission of a plan to harm oneself or others, a report of child or elder abuse, or as otherwise provided by law) should be the only exceptions to confidentiality. Even under those circumstances, it is preferable that the provider engage the employee in seeking appropriate remedies, whenever possible.

By the very nature of the job, law enforcement personnel are routinely exposed to ordinary as well as extraordinary stressors. In the past, all too often the solution was to use unhealthy coping mechanisms such as alcohol to deal with troubles or stress, sometimes causing officers to not only find solace but also find camaraderie. This included drinking at home or at a bar. Historically, peer pressure to join the group has been powerful and difficult to avoid, causing many officers to feel intimidated or socially ostracized if they resist. Consequently, police culture, social values, customs, and occupational stress often foster alcohol use, which contributes to the potential development of problems associated with alcohol use, abuse, or dependence.

Generalized stress comes in many forms and is often associated with the physical demands of the job, including long hours and variable shifts that result in sleep deprivation, the perceived lack of support often associated with the job, and organizational stressors.[4] In addition, traumatic experiences, such as exposure to violent deaths, near death incidents, and injuries involving the employee, are equally traumatizing. Psychological difficulties also arise through the indirect experience of others' trauma,[5] thus compounding the already heavy burden experienced by law enforcement personnel. Long-term cumulative exposure to these general stressors, as well as to the employee's personally experienced traumas, can result in emotional and behavioral difficulties.

Stress encountered by law enforcement personnel is not restricted to sworn agency members. Civilian employees in police agencies are tasked with stressful and traumatic duties including answering and dispatching emergency calls for service; photographing and collecting evidence from crime scenes; transcribing suspect and victim interviews; and the reading, the classifying, and the redacting of police case report information. Additionally, because of the growing numbers of layoffs or long delays in filling vacated positions, sworn and civilian support staff personnel are being tasked with an increasing number of responsibilities.

The psychological and behavioral difficulties of law enforcement personnel may be transitory and quickly improved through a supportive contact with a

---

4. Rebecca M. Pasillas, Victoria M. Follette, and Suzanne E. Perumean-Chaney, "Occupational Stress and Psychological Functioning in Law Enforcement Officers," *Journal of Police and Criminal Psychology* 21, no. 1 (March 2006): 41–53.

5. Charles R. Figley, *Compassion Fatigue: Coping with Secondary Traumatic Stress Disorder in Those Who Treat the Traumatized* (New York: Brunner Mazel, 1995), 23.

police psychologist, or they may be more chronic in nature. For those seeking services, some of the most commonly identified reasons for doing so include marital or relationship problems; parent-child difficulties; difficulties managing schedule changes; family responsibilities; substance abuse; anxiety; on-the-job trauma; and organizational stressors, including a perceived lack of administration support.

Police psychologists identify these reactions in law enforcement personnel and use a variety of counseling techniques designed to assist in the recognition and understanding of the reactions. The police psychologist then assists in relieving the negative psychological or behavioral issues the officer may be experiencing. A variety of task-oriented and problem-focused tools are frequently implemented to reduce symptoms, including stress and anger management training, focus on self-care and wellness, and substance abuse treatment. Implied and concrete evidence of departmental support leads to improved responses by law enforcement personnel experiencing psychological difficulties and a reduction in reported stress.[6] When psychological and behavioral difficulties persist over the long term, ongoing counseling will be required with the ultimate goal of reducing symptoms and minimizing the negative impact on job performance.

Family Impact

Since the 1970s, researchers and psychologists have examined the causes and the consequences of stress in law enforcement. Their work provides a framework for understanding the multidimensional nature of occupational, organizational, personal relationship, and familial sources of stress impacting officers' and civilian employees' functioning and performance. Their efforts have resulted in increasingly more sophisticated and ambitious programs that address the widespread need for interventions for sworn and civilian personnel. Similarly, the negative or sometimes debilitating effects of stress on the health and well-being of officers and civilians may also have a detrimental effect on their families. This often sets up a cycle of stress and conflict resulting in officers and civilian employees, their loved ones, and the police organization all paying a toll of increased emotional or physical difficulties, impaired coping, marital or family discord, decreased personal and work satisfaction, and diminished work performance.

---

6. Philip E. Carlan and Lisa S. Nored, "An Examination of Officer Stress: Should Police Departments Implement Mandatory Counseling?" *Journal of Police and Criminal Psychology* 23, no. 1 (June 2008): 8–15.

Although it is common for police officers to want to shelter their families by not sharing the details of their daily experiences, they nonetheless take their work home with them in some form. Officers may need to put considerable energy into maintaining their composure at work, especially when dealing with the public—suspects included—but they may have difficulty maintaining the same composure when at home. Even under the most favorable of circumstances, having a law enforcement officer in the family changes that family's dynamics. For example, consider that police officers tend to favor structure and rules and have high expectations. Through their exposure to the dangers of police work and the elements of society that pose potential threats not commonly experienced by the average person, police officers tend to be more conservative and cautious, bringing a level of suspiciousness into a family.[7] Additionally, shift work is stressful for families. Officers are commonly not present in the home because of their work schedules and time required in court. Consequently, officers often forfeit the opportunity for time with their families, and this is especially noticed when work takes precedence on special occasions and during holidays.

Increasingly, agencies are implementing programs recommended by police psychologists aimed at providing clinical services, peer support services, and training seminars or academies for the family members of police officers and of civilian employees. Attending to the psychological health of an employee's home and family life has progressively been recognized as beneficial to the agency as well as to the employee. Such programs are powerful and valuable ways of serving employees by improving their home environments and, therefore, benefiting the law enforcement agency and the communities they serve.

The IACP recommends programs tailored to meet the needs of officers' family members. According to the IACP, although the financial costs of implementing these programs may be regarded as prohibitive, the "return benefits to the officer, the family, the department, and the community can be immense in stimulating positive public relations, reducing stress, promoting marital harmony, and improving job performance."[8] While officers and civilian employees are often the primary benefactors of psychological serv-

---

7. Kevin M. Gilmartin, "Hypervigilance: A Learned Perception Set and Its Consequences on Police Stress," in J.T. Reese and H.A. Goldstein, ed., *Psychological Services for Law Enforcement*, Library of Congress no. 85-600538, (Washington, D.C.: U.S. Government Printing Office, 1986), 445–448.

8. Peter Finn and Julie Esselman Tomz, "Developing a Law Enforcement Stress Program for Officers and Their Families," *National Institute of Justice Issues and Practices* (Washington, D.C.: U.S. Department of Justice, Office of Justice Programs, 1997), 138.

ices or counseling within their organizations, police psychologists also may provide services to spouses or significant others of employees or other family members, without the participation of the employee themselves. Police psychologists provide information to spouses and other family members about the unique working conditions of law enforcement, the types of stresses experienced by police officers, effective ways to support and interact with the family member who is a law enforcement officer, and other information intended to facilitate positive and satisfying interactions within the couple or the family. For example, the IACP Officer-Involved Shooting Guidelines,[9] developed by the Police Psychological Services Section (IACP-PPSS), while primarily created to provide public safety agencies and police psychologists with recommendations to support officers involved in shootings and other critical incidents, make it a point to include recommendations for family members.

Services for family members can take many forms, including individual or family counseling, the formation of family support groups that provide assistance to families experiencing stress, and spouse academies designed to increase the spouse's knowledge of an officer's work responsibilities and organizational environment. Officers appreciate the availability of counseling and supportive services when their family members are interested or in need of using these services. Officers readily recognize that services benefiting their family members and resulting in positive outcomes in turn decrease their own levels of stress. By providing services to employees *and* their families, departments enhance support to personnel, promote professionalism, and enhance the quality of service to citizens.

Traumatic Incidents

Shell shock, war neurosis, battle fatigue, combat stress, and posttraumatic stress disorder are just some of the monikers that psychological trauma has garnered over the years. The first evidence of psychological trauma as it is understood today can be found in Homer's epic poems *The Iliad* and *The Odyssey*,[10]

---

9. IACP Police Psychological Services Section, "Officer-Involved Shooting Guidelines," ratified at the 116th Annual Conference of the International Association of Chiefs of Police (Denver, Colorado, 2009), http://theiacp.org/psych_services_section/pdfs/Psych-Officer-Involved Shooting.pdf (accessed June 15, 2011).

10. Homer, *The Iliad and The Odyssey*, ed. James H. Ford, trans. Samuel Butler (El Paso, TX: Norte Press, 2006).

where Homer describes soldiers who, after having survived combat, experience damaged character, long-standing changes, and difficulty returning to their normal lives.

The impact of trauma on individuals, particularly those charged with protecting the public, continued to be observed historically through the experience of soldiers during the First and Second World Wars. Exposure to traumatic events and stimuli caused some soldiers to develop intense feelings of fear, anger, grief, horror, emotional numbness, and disbelief. Today, police officers and other public safety personnel are at risk for similar reactions. Being a police officer can be an incredibly stressful job. Beyond the daily stressors, police officers can be both directly and indirectly exposed to danger, violence, disasters, and death.

Exposure to a critical incident or other traumatic stress can cause periods of psychological instability. In fact, after potentially traumatic events, it is expected that many people will experience at least some level of distress. A smaller portion of people exposed to traumatic and critical incident stress will develop more persistent problems that may require specific psychological treatment. For the majority of people who are experiencing normal, expected levels of distress after a traumatic incident, providing them with immediate adjustment strategies and assistance with coping is helpful.

Psychological intervention following traumatic incidents first became popular for use in military combat where there was a need to help soldiers in distress effectively cope with the impact of trauma so they could quickly return to duty. Trauma interventions were and continue to be facilitated by military commanders and mental health professionals after a battle, wherein soldiers share personal stories about their experiences with like-minded listeners in an effort to improve morale and better prepare them for future combat. These early interventions were aimed at maintaining group cohesion, promoting rest and education, reducing stigma, and triaging individuals for more intensive intervention. The official U.S. Army doctrine developed during the Vietnam conflict required treatment to be rendered in proximity to the combat operation immediately following the traumatic experience, with the expectation that the soldier would be returned to full duty as soon as possible, thus avoiding a prolonged patient identity. The treatment strategy is similar to the initial response to law enforcement critical incidents in practice today.

Beginning in the early 1980s, trauma intervention was more frequently applied to public safety settings. Modern trauma intervention at its core is a form of crisis intervention. Based on IACP PPSS guidelines, trauma intervention is usually conducted within the first week of a precipitating event.[11] It is semi-structured, often involving only a single initial session lasting from one to several hours. Trauma intervention can be applied to both individuals and groups. It is designed to provide psychological education to personnel about normal, usually temporary or short-term reactions to critical incidents. During the intervention, personnel are educated about general reactions to stress and are given tips about adaptive coping strategies. Effective trauma intervention serves to normalize an individual's reactions and experiences, as well as to promote emotional processing. It provides an opportunity to address other helpful interventions while also providing information about further potential resources, if needed.

Although there is some variation in the exact delivery method and style of post-trauma interventions, law enforcement agencies should strive to ensure that the services the agency selects include the following components based on IACP guidelines. The intervention should

- address the need for acute symptom reduction while not interfering with the natural recovery processes;
- preclude the development of maladaptive responses or maladaptive problem solving;
- facilitate social support and effective communication;
- restore individuals to a pre-crisis, independent level of functioning;
- provide closure, if possible; and
- refer for more advanced care and intervention as necessary.

IACP guidelines suggest that posttrauma interventions be conducted by a licensed mental health professional. The involvement of peer support teams also is encouraged and may serve as beneficial components to the intervention, although not in isolation.[12]

Assuming that intervention strategies continue to follow the lead of the military, the importance of contacting personnel following a traumatic experience and a post-trauma intervention during the subsequent months cannot be overemphasized. Such follow-up contact not only demonstrates continued concern for the employee but can be decisive in assisting an employee in avoid-

---

11. IACP Psychological Services Section, "Peer Support Guidelines," ratified at the 113th Annual Conference of the International Association of Chiefs of Police (Boston, Massachusetts, 2006), http://theiacp.org/psych_services_section/pdfs/Psych-PeerSupportGuidelines.pdf (accessed June 15, 2011).

12. IACP Psychological Services Section, "Peer Support Guidelines."

ing the development of serious posttrauma symptoms such as depression, anxiety, and posttraumatic stress disorder.

Also, following the military's lead, programs may be developed to build resilience in advance of a traumatic experience. Programs designed to promote healthy lifestyles, problem-solving skills, psychological well-being, and stress and anger inoculation promote resiliency, better equip employees to effectively confront stressful situations, and decrease the likelihood of a lasting adverse reactions to trauma.

Police Officer — Citizen Soldiers and Military Deployments

Since 9/11, nearly 800,000 deployment orders have been issued for the National Guard and the U.S. military reserves to support various military operations, including combat in Iraq and Afghanistan.[13] Law enforcement professionals represent 10 percent of those activated, thus posing unique challenges and opportunities for public safety agencies.[14] For example, on December 21, 2010, there were 92,860 active guard and reserve members, of which thousands were employed as police officers and related public safety personnel, such as correctional officers, emergency medical services workers, and emergency communications. Chiefs often ask the following questions:

- How can I support my officers while they are deployed?
- There have been so many department policy and procedure changes while my officer was deployed; how can I efficiently manage the information upon the officer's return to duty?
- My officer is on orders for deployment, so how can patrol duties be assigned if subsequent court dates may be affected?
- Are my officers going to be OK? Will they interact with the public appropriately since they saw serious action and dealt with hostile combatants and citizens while deployed?

---

13. Reserve Components: Noble Eagle/Enduring Freedom/New Dawn, Contingency Tracking System (CTS) Daily Processing Files, Defense Manpower Data Center, last modified December 21, 2010, http://www.defense.gov/news/d20101221ngr.pdf (accessed June 15, 2011).

14. Stephen F. Curran and Ritchie C. Elspeth, "Warrior Transition by Army Reserve and National Guard Personnel from Combat Operations in Iraq to Policing in the United States" (presentation, IACP 2006, Boston, Mass., October 2006).

Recognizing the need to address the emotional and behavioral effects of combat deployment on the returning citizen soldier-police officer, the IACP, with the substantial assistance of the IACP-PPSS, published guides to assist law enforcement leaders[15] and the returning citizen soldier-police officer.[16] Lessons learned about the needs of the employee, the employee's family, and the agency during the officer's deployment have led to several approaches incorporating best practices. Many of these programs are facilitated by psychologists. Among the agencies that demonstrate the most effective programs is the Honolulu, Hawaii, Police Department (HPD).

The HPD provides an array of psychological services to department personnel, including assessment, consultation, operational support, and clinical intervention. Clinical intervention services incorporate caring for police officers and civilian employees who also serve in the National Guard or U.S. military reserves by using a variety of strategies to address the unique needs of military warriors-civilian officers and their family members during all phases of the deployment cycle. Such services include

- predeployment identification and management of the individual needs of employees and their family members (e.g., informal surveys and psychological education regarding preparing for deployment);
- review of departmental policies and procedures to ensure that they comply with the Uniformed Services Employment and Reemployment Rights Act (USERRA)[17] and the Americans with Disabilities Act (ADA),[18] with amendments;

---

15. IACP and the Bureau of Justice Assistance, Office of Justice Programs, U.S. Department of Justice, *Law Enforcement Leader's Guide on Combat Veterans: A Transition Guide for Veterans Beginning or Continuing Careers in Law Enforcement* (July 2010), http://www.theiacp.org/PublicationsGuides/ContentbyTopic/tabid/216/Default.aspx?id=1298&v=1 (accessed June 15, 2011).

16. IACP and the Bureau of Justice Assistance, Office of Justice Programs, U.S. Department of Justice, *Combat Veterans and Law Enforcement: A Transition Guide for Veterans Beginning or Continuing Careers in Law Enforcement* (July 2010), http://www.theiacp.org/Publications Guides/ContentbyTopic/tabid/216/Default.aspx?id=1298&v=1 (accessed June 15, 2011).

17. Uniformed Services Employment and Reemployment Rights Act (USERRA) of 1994, Pub. L. No. 103-353, 38 U.S.C. 43 (2002), http://www.dol.gov/vets/usc/vpl/usc38.htm (accessed June 17, 2011).

18. Americans with Disabilities Act of 1990, as amended by the ADA Amendments Act of 2008, Pub. L. No. 110-325, http://www.ada.gov/pubs/adastatute08.htm (accessed June 9, 2011).

- support for deployed employees and their immediate family members during the deployment (e.g., sending emails and care packages to employees deployed to combat zones; maintaining contact with the deployed employee's family members to include them in police department celebrations and events and to assist them in meeting any identified psychological or support needs); and
- provision of a postdeployment reintegration program (e.g., each returning employee is given the voluntary opportunity to meet one-on-one with the chief of police in a "Welcome Home Meet-and-Greet with the Chief" individualized recognition ceremony).[19]

HPD psychologists receive feedback from HPD command and the formerly deployed employees in an effort to refine the psychological and educational services for the department's employees who serve in the military.

Training

Police psychologists develop and conduct a range of intervention-related training for individuals and groups and online education and training programs designed to prevent or mitigate problematic behaviors in employees. Although there are common psychologically based training modules that may be generalized to address the needs of most law enforcement agencies, training is most effective when tailored to the unique culture, the working conditions, and the critical issues of the specific agency and the community it serves. Educational programs are continually updated to reflect current psychological research and police psychology professional standards of practice,[20] accepted law enforcement standards of practice,[21] agency policies, and legal parameters and judicial decisions.[22] Typical spotlights for training law enforcement personnel

---

19. Major Cities Chiefs Association and the Federal Bureau of Investigation National Executive Institute, *Promoting Health and Wellness: Returning to Full Duty* (March 2008) http://www.neiassociates.org/health/fullduty.pdf (accessed June 15, 2011).

20. Aumiller et al., "Defining the Field of Police Psychology," 48.

21. CALEA, *Standards for Law Enforcement Agencies: A Management Improvement Model through Accreditation*, 5th ed. (Fairfax, VA: CALEA, 2006, as amended, Change Notice No. 5.9, enacted November 20, 2010).

22. *Walker v. City of New York*, 974 F.2d 293, 299–300 (2d Cir. 1992). Recognizing that a wrong course of action in limited situations is not enough for liability to attach to a city, which clarifies U.S. Supreme Court decision *City of Canton v. Harris*, 489 U.S. 378, 390 (1989).

include identifying, understanding, and managing or mitigating psychological risk factors associated with

- discipline trends that adversely affect the integrity and effectiveness of the agency,[23] such as social media (e.g., Facebook), police credibility issues, and the violence-prone police officer, including abuse of force and domestic violence,[24] anabolic steroid abuse, alcohol or substance abuse, driving under the influence, police prejudice and discrimination, deviant or corrupt police behavior, and police sexual misconduct;
- traumatic and workplace stress (e.g., sexual assault, child pornography, and child abuse investigations; working deep undercover; homicide or suicide investigations); and
- specialized policing responses (e.g., recognition of and dealing with persons with a mental illness,[25] psychological dynamics of interacting with persons in crisis, suicide assessment and prevention, dealing with juveniles and the elderly in crisis, and responding to domestic violence).

Other psychological training issues focus on the individual and the collective health and the holistic wellness of the agency and its personnel. Psychologists may provide workshops and continuing education designed to improve work productivity, transitional or organizational adjustment, and the general mental health and wellbeing of law enforcement personnel. Such training may include

- holistic wellness (i.e., mental, emotional, spiritual, and physical) and stress management (e.g., training police officers and civilian personnel regarding specific health-enhancing behaviors, coping strategies, and techniques aimed at preventing or reducing the negative impact of stress; and developing and delivering public safety psychological education and training materials to optimize personnel health and wellness);[26]

---

23. National Executive Institute Associates, Major Cities Chiefs Association, and Major County Sheriffs' Association, *Discipline Trends: Focus on Behavior Affecting the Integrity and Effectiveness of the Agency* (June 2010), http://www.neiassociates.org/disciplinetrends2010.pdf (accessed June 17, 2011).

24. IACP, *Discussion Paper on IACP's Policy on Domestic Violence by Police Officers: A Product of the IACP Police Response to Violence Against Women Project* (July 2003), http://www.vaw.umn.edu/documents/policedv.pdf (accessed June 15, 2011).

25. IACP and the Bureau of Justice Assistance, Office of Justice Programs, U.S. Department of Justice, *Building Safer Communities: Improving Police Response to Persons with Mental Illness* (June 2010), http://www.theiacp.org/PublicationsGuides/NationalPolicy-Summits/BuildingSafer Communities/tabid/664/Default.aspx (accessed June 15, 2011).

26. Peter White, ed., *Biopsychosocial Medicine: An Integrated Approach to Understanding Illness* (Oxford, U.K.: Oxford University Press, 2005).

- public safety personnel resiliency training (e.g., strength-based resiliency training for civilian personnel and police recruits, mental attitude preparation for special weapons and tactics and crisis response teams that work in high-stress environments); and
- early recognition for police supervisory personnel (e.g., teaching supervisory roles and responsibilities in the early identification of police officers or civilian personnel whose behavior signals potential problems that may prove detrimental to the employee or to the agency).

Psychologists also develop and implement online, agency intranet-based training modules that parallel and support law enforcement annual refresher training. The modules provide psychological education materials, articles, PowerPoint presentations, and website links relevant to police and public safety psychological services.

Police psychologists also develop and implement psychology training programs, strategically planning for the future of the profession. They supervise predoctoral and postdoctoral trainees in the specialty of police psychology as a cost-effective means to provide professional services and better train psychologists who can serve a community's police and public safety departments.

CALEA

An agency need not be vested in formal compliance with the Commission on the Accreditation of Law Enforcement Agencies (CALEA) for law enforcement executives to learn more. Law enforcement executives who are interested in the development and implementation of policies and procedures designed to assist in the maintenance or revitalization of the holistic health (i.e., physical, social, psychological, mental, and spiritual) of their law enforcement personnel and their family members may want to consider CALEA standards.[27] Three CALEA standards particularly relevant to intervention programs are Standard 22.2.3, Personnel Support Services Program; Standard 22.2.6, Employee Assistance Program; and Standard 22.3.3 Fitness and Wellness Program.

---

27. CALEA, *Standards for Law Enforcement Agencies.*

Summary

Psychological interventions, including programs to build resilience among law enforcement personnel and their family members, are readily available tools for executives to support and sustain their work force. Police psychologists offer numerous services to benefit employees and the agencies they serve. They strive to prepare law enforcement employees to be better prepared to deal with the stressors of their jobs, to make healthy adjustments when confronted with difficult situations, and to affect the culture of policing by likening therapy to going to a family physician or dentist. Psychological services to law enforcement personnel are unique when compared to traditional clinical practice. For example, police psychologists must be informed about multiple laws, statutes, and cases that guide their activities in providing intervention services. Police psychologists must also have a working knowledge of law enforcement organizational dynamics and be aware of and sensitive to police culture.

As the world economies struggle and municipal, state, and federal budgets suffer, executives are forced to conserve resources with the ever-present expectation to do more with less. Morale may be dropping, employee schedules and workloads may be impacted, and jobs may be threatened or lost. As declining financial resources impact individuals, morale is not the only area affected; tension might develop in officers' home lives, efforts to work more overtime might increase, and employees in general might feel under increased pressure. More consideration, not less, should be focused on supporting and sustaining employees to maintain a healthy workforce. Police psychologists can be a part of the solution.

Discussion Questions

1. Research supports the fact that psychological treatment works. What elements must be associated with it in order to be effective?
2. Regardless of the type of service provided or the nature of the referral, employees seeking services should expect privileged communication and confidentiality. Why is this essential?
3. What are among the most commonly identified reasons for law enforcement officers who seek supportive contact with a police psychologist?
4. Police psychologists use a variety of counseling techniques designed to assist in the recognition and understanding of police officers having psychological problems. What are they?

5. While officers and civilian employees are often the primary bene-factors of psychological services or counseling within their or-ganizations, police psychologists also may provide services to spouses or significant others of employees or other family mem-bers, without the participation of the employee. What type of in-formation is provided by police psychologists to these individuals?

6. Modern trauma intervention at its core is a form of crisis inter-vention. The Police Psychological Services Section of the Inter-national Association of Chiefs of Police provide certain guidelines for such intervention. What are they?

7. Although there is some variation in the exact delivery method and style of post-trauma interventions, IACP guidelines suggest that law enforcement agencies should strive to ensure that the services they select include certain components. What are they?

8. The authors tell us that typical "spotlights" for training law en-forcement personnel include identifying, understanding, and managing or mitigating psychological risk factors is associated with certain events. What are they?

43

Breaking the Silence of Law Enforcement Suicide: A Survivor's Perspective

Teresa T. Tate

> No one who has not experienced a severe episode of depression
> can really understand what it is.
> It's like a woman trying to explain childbirth to a man.
> Or a black man trying to explain to a white man
> what it is like to live with racism.
> Or the blind, the deaf or crippled trying to explain
> to a healthy person what it is like to live with a disability.
> You can explain, but the other person can't truly understand.
> So it is with depression.
> It is real and totally disabling.
> It is not merely feeling low or alone—it is overwhelming.
>
> —An excerpt from a suicide note written by J. Timothy Hogan
> with permission from his mother, Pat Scoones

SOS. Most people associate this acronym as Save Our Ship. There is an-other acronym—Survivor of Suicide. That is what I am—a survivor of my husband's suicide. Some people are confused when they hear that term be-lieving that a person survived a suicide attempt. That is not the case.

Depression, like cancer, diabetes, and other diseases, if left undiagnosed and untreated, can become deadly. People who end their life do so to end their pain, whether it is emotional or physical. They do not necessarily wish to die. They just want to be free of the hopelessness that has undoubtedly filled their life with darkness.

In September 1989, I went to work as a wife and came home a widow—a survivor of a police officer suicide. Two decades later, I can vividly recall every detail from the minute I walked into our house and found his note, to the moment that has forever changed my life. It is like watching a movie play out in my head. Every sight, every noise, every feeling, every detail forever imprinted in my brain. I do not remember simple things—like where I put my keys or where I parked my vehicle, but I can recall the events that happened to me on the night that my husband died.

My husband was 28 years old, had served in the U.S. Marine Corps, and had been a police officer for six years. He had received commendations including a Meritorious Action Award. He had a great sense of humor and was well liked by his peers and supervisors. The first four years of his law enforcement career was shift rotation. After four years, the department implemented permanent shifts. I wanted him assigned to the day shift so that we could have a "normal" family life. He wanted the afternoon shift. So, we compromised and he took the midnight shift. He worked the night shift for over a year. It was during this time that slow behavioral changes were occurring.

My husband eventually switched to the day shift to try and balance out his life. Night shift had caused sleep deprivation, especially on those days when he had to report to court after working a 10-hour shift. Although there were signs of depression—stomach aches, loss of appetite, headaches, joint aches, moodiness, and social withdrawal—I had no knowledge that these were signs of depression.

Studies have shown that people who work odd work schedules, such as the night shift, are more subject to chronic intestinal and heart disease and have been shown to have a higher incidence of some forms of cancer. If working the night shift can be so hazardous to one's physical health, then it would certainly make sense that it would impact a person's psychological well-being as well.

My husband left me a note stating where he would be, knowing that I would not be able to find him. I called a neighbor, who I knew could get me to where my husband was, and we drove the hour-long drive to get there. I would have never found the location nor would I have been able to provide the location to the police. This was an isolated fishing spot in another county where he and his friends would go periodically.

We arrived at the scene at dusk. We had enough daylight to find his truck and another note inside. At this point, I still wanted to forge ahead because I thought I could save him, but I was no longer in control. Our neighbor forced me back into his truck, and we drove to the nearest house to call 911.

Two law enforcement agencies responded—the state police and the local sheriff's office. By this time, night had fallen, and it was dark. The trooper and deputy walked a few steps ahead with flashlights, chatting about the calls they had responded to on their shift. After about a 15-minute walk, and two steps away, the flashlights illuminated his lifeless body. No one could console me at this point as I collapsed in despair.

Upon being released from the scene after midnight, I was driven home with one thought in mind. Who do I notify at his department? I did not know his supervisor and therefore called a rookie officer, who was also a friend.

Receiving a phone call from an officer's spouse at 1:30 a.m. set off a chain reaction that soon spiraled out of control. Not wanting to reveal to the rookie why I was calling, I asked for the contact information of my husband's supervisor. The rookie was persistent in questioning me as to why I needed this information, and I finally blurted out that he was dead. I needed to talk to someone in authority to notify them that my husband would not be at work the next day. Since I was not getting the information that I needed, I hung up the phone.

The events escalated through the night as the rookie arrived at my house after 2:00 a.m. He had called the local police, who did not approach my door, but contacted me on the telephone. During this time, I had called the state police to advise them as to what was happening and was instructed, through dispatch, that this was a state police investigation and I did not have to talk to anyone and therefore was not required to open the door. There were now three jurisdictions involved—the state police, my husband's department and my local police department.

By adhering to the state police's statement and not opening the door, the local police department had surrounded my house shining lights through the windows. I was curled up in a ball in a corner of a darkened house, not able to comprehend why this was happening, especially after finding my husband's body. I kept wondering when I was going to wake up from this nightmare. All I wanted was to notify my husband's supervisor that he would not be coming to work.

Through another telephone contact, I did tell the local police department that my husband had died outside of this jurisdiction and that the state police was working the investigation. They asked me to come to the door, which I did. The local police officer at my door said that I was part of the law enforcement family and asked to enter my home. Before I could, I said that I would put our dog in the backyard. The officer then asked me to wait while they cleared the officers out of the yard. I could not understand why my house was surrounded. I could not understand much since I had been up for almost 24 hours and in shock from knowing that my husband had died by suicide.

At this point, the state trooper called back and stated that the officers were preparing to kick in my door, and I needed to allow my husband's captain to approach the house. Unbeknownst to me, his captain had been sitting outside in his car the entire time watching the chaos unfold. If the captain had either called me or approached my door and identified himself, the additional trauma that I incurred by the police department would not have happened.

I have told this story countless times at law enforcement suicide prevention conferences and have been repeatedly asked why I just did not tell the rookie officer what happened early on. It is for one reason—I wanted to protect my husband, even in death. I, like many ignorant people, believed that people end their life because they had done something wrong. My husband did nothing wrong, and I did not want anyone thinking that he had. And now I was about to experience a journey of depression that possibly was similar to his. I was scared and I was alone. Could I survive this pain that had enveloped me so deeply?

The Suicide Note

My husband's note contained his last thoughts and his final words to me.

I was forced to surrender the note to the state police that night. Although the investigating trooper said I would get it back, I read it over and over, committing it to memory. It was the one piece of property that I so desperately needed to help me through my grief. It was the one piece of property that was the most difficult to have returned from the state police. How ironic that it was easier for me to obtain the firearm that ended his life than his final words of goodbye.

In the coming months, I repeatedly requested to have his note returned. I received his personal effects such as his keys, watch, wedding band, and driver's license. I also received items in a sealed brown paper bag with evidence tape across it. Inside the bag were the shotgun shell casing, an empty whiskey bottle, and discarded cans of beer, which, based on the brand, were not his. Not only were these items of no use to me, but there was evidence of blood splatter on everything. For whatever purpose the trooper had in returning the items in the evidence bag, additional trauma had been inflicted upon me months after my husband's death.

When I finally received his note, what was returned were two pieces of notebook paper that had been washed with a liquid that had erased my husband's last words. The letter had been ruined. Those last words had vanished from the paper. There was nothing, but a written word here and there. It was all gone. The state police had taken away the one piece of property that I so desperately needed to know that this was not my fault. Without that note, like so many survivors, I would fall victim to the feelings of guilt and blame. Guilt, for not having recognized the warning signs of suicide, even though I had no knowledge of these signs. Blame, because suicide is not understandable, and it is easier for others to blame someone than to think that they may be vulnerable to such an act.

It is imperative to understand the importance a suicide note can have on a family member. In my case, it contained the words of a husband who loved his wife, but could not get through the depth of depression that he was suffering. In cases where a note is left behind, provide a copy to the family. The original letter can be maintained in the case file, but allow the family the opportunity to keep a copy if it may help them in their grief. Many times, the letter becomes an issue with the family in needing to find clues as to why the suicide had occurred.

Notification

When an officer is injured or killed in the line of duty, the family is not a witness to the event. It is highly probable that notification of the officer's death will be made to the family by hospital personnel in a controlled setting. Rarely does a line-of-duty death involve the family witnessing or responding to the scene of the death of an officer.

In the cases of suicide, the family may have witnessed the suicide or may be the first on scene and will call 911. If the officer works in a different jurisdiction than where he/she has died, notification to the officer's department should be made by the investigating law enforcement agency. In hindsight, the state police should have been the agency to notify my husband's department. Upon my release from the scene, my husband's supervisor and a chaplain should have been waiting for me at my house. A survivor should never be left with the responsibility of notifying the officer's agency if a law enforcement agency is on scene.

If the officer died away from home, notification should be made by command personnel, along with a police chaplain, a crisis counselor or victim/witness advocate. Many victim/witness advocates have information on community resources that they can provide the family on the initial response.

Police departments may also consider having EMS personnel stationed a block or two away from the site of notification in case a family member experiences a panic or anxiety attack, and even a possible heart attack. Survivors have been transported to the hospital after receiving this tragic news. By parking the ambulance a few blocks away, you protect the family's privacy and avoid curious neighbors and potential media problems.

In cases where the officer was divorced with children, departments need to ensure that notification is made to the ex-spouse as well. The officer's children do not need to learn that their parent died by suicide from the media, classmates, or other police personnel. In a society where communication is relayed in lightening speed, it is essential that notification is made to all immediate family members prior to any information being released to neighbors or media or through a department-wide personnel notification.

Funeral Protocol

Funeral protocol for officers who died by suicide seem to be more controversial for some leaders than others. Protocol has ranged from mirroring that of a line-of-duty funeral to the minimal amount of participation from the police department. There are cases where not only did personnel from the officer's department attend, but governors, congressional representatives, city council members, and other law enforcement agencies were present as well.

And then there are cases on the complete opposite of the spectrum where law enforcement officers in attendance were instructed not to wear their uniform nor mourning bands, nor to drive their police vehicle to the funeral.

The night before my husband's memorial service, I received a telephone call from his police chief. He requested that he be allowed to wear his police dress uniform. I was puzzled as to why he would ask this question. He stated that my husband's captain had informed him that I requested that the officers not wear their uniform at the service. I had never made such a request.

Upon arriving at the memorial service, there were no marked police cruisers in the parking lot. Stunned and dismayed, I entered the chapel where I could only see two men in police uniforms—the chief and my neighbor, who worked for another law enforcement agency. If you had walked into the church, you would not have known that this was the funeral for a law enforcement officer. Through the entire service, I thought that not one police officer had attended. I thought that no one cared. My pain deepened.

Why the difference? For some leaders, they choose to limit the department's involvement in the funeral planning due to the way the officer died, not for how they lived. Based on one leader's opinion of suicide, the years of commendations or sacrifice that the officer made throughout his/her career is ignored.

It is essential that leaders consider each case of officer suicide prior to determining what involvement the department will partake. If the department is open to offering services, ask the family what they would like to have the department participate in. Most families will not know what is available to them regarding funeral protocol. Consideration must be made to avoid inflicting additional trauma on the family. If a family member heard the fatal gunshot, a firearm salute should be omitted from the funeral. If the officer lived and worked in two jurisdictions, planning transportation logistics could be remedied by offering school buses. In one case, a sheriff offered to transport deputies via an inmate bus to the funeral. Needless to say, the widow was quite upset when she heard this. What deputy would want to ride an inmate bus to a funeral? The sheriff not only lacked the sensitivity and compassion towards the family, but to his own personnel as well.

Leaders should not pass up the opportunity to allow the officer's peers to express their condolences to the family. This can be done privately before the memorial service or at a wake. It may be necessary to offer guidance to the officer's peers in expressing condolences if they have never attended a funeral or may be uncomfortable in not knowing what to say to the family. It is best to keep remarks simple, such as "I am sorry for your loss.\ " or "I will miss … ." Another avenue for his/her peers can be made by sending a sympathy card or mass card to the family. It should be at the discretion of the officer's peers in determining how they wish to offer their condolences, although guidance may be necessary.

Responding to the Media

In the past, the media could always be found on scene due to the broadcast of radio calls on police scanners. With the advancement of technology, calls are dispatched through computers, allowing officers to respond without the flurry of media activity. On scene communication can also be channeled through cell phones, ultimately eliminating the media. There have been cases where police officers from a separate jurisdiction had been able to seal off a perimeter without allowing the media access or providing information as to the nature of the call. The responding police department was able to close off several blocks surrounding the deputy's home by positioning their vehicles across the road. These cases never appeared in the media, allowing the family to grieve in private.

Notifying the media can be accomplished by simply sending a text message. A Texas police chief chose to send a briefly worded text to the local newspaper as well as news television stations upon the death of an officer. Two things were accomplished by handling the notification in this manner. First, the chief was not hiding that the suicide occurred, but second and most importantly, the media was unable to ask questions. Although the chief was on scene, he was able to keep the media at a distance.

If a press release is provided to the media, explain to the survivor why it was necessary. Be brief and offer your department's condolences. A simple statement such as, "Our thoughts and prayers are with the officer's family," not only shows support to the family, but to the community as well. Leaders should prevent officers from making anonymous comments that can be quoted as "an anonymous source" or "unofficial statements." Officers who make statements to the media, but hide behind a classification of anonymous source, tend to inflame the reason as to why the officer took his/her life. It is important to remember that the officer's children attend schools as well as live and work within the community.

It is recommended that if the department were to release a photo of the officer, the officer's attire should be in plain clothes and not the department uniform. This tends to ease the tension within the department among officers who have outspoken views on suicide.

How Can Leaders Support the Family?

Police administrators should show compassion to the family immediately after the death by providing departmental and community resources for counseling. To abandon the family in their most dire time is negligent. In cases where there may be animosity between the family and department, administrators should request a third party liaison, such as EAP personnel, police chaplain, or local suicide prevention organization, that has experience in dealing with survivor issues. It is imperative that the family feels the support of the department, which can be easily accomplished by home visitation or telephone calls, at least until the family has been able to receive therapeutic support.

In cases where both spouses work in law enforcement, one as a sworn officer and the other a civilian, administrators should be cognizant of the work place environment upon the surviving spouse returning to work. There have been instances of the surviving spouse returning to a hostile environment in which false rumors and innuendos are rampant. This response by co-workers projects shame and guilt onto the survivor which fuels the stigma associated with suicide.

Prior to returning to work, my agency conducted a meeting with my co-workers so that they would know how best to support me. This meeting was conducted by a division chief who would eventually coordinate the agency's peer support team. Although my immediate co-workers were supportive, I still had to interact with those outside my office. In one instance, I was subjected to an insensitive remark by a Federal agent who handed me a riot ball shell casing and stated, "We give these to agents so they won't hurt themselves."

In cases where both spouses are sworn law enforcement officers and one died by suicide, the surviving spouse is generally assigned light duty until he/she passes a fitness for duty exam. Administrators should ensure that the work environment is not causing the officer to feel ostracized by his/her peers. It is a double tragedy to have the surviving officer take his/her own life because of the lack of support within his/her own department.

Asking questions such as to what part of the body the officer was shot or what type of firearm was used is not only insensitive, but quite frankly, nobody's business. The family will need to process this information, including dealing with the visual effects of finding the officer after the fact, and will begin to talk about the scene when they are ready. Having friends or coworkers asking detailed questions soon after the death, will only cause more trauma. Departmental support will be needed in ways that are simplistic such as compassion, sensitivity, and privacy. Privacy does not mean isolation, but the skill to listen as the family processes what has become reality—losing a loved one to suicide.

Instruct police personnel not to make promises that they cannot keep, even if their intentions are good. Shortly after a deputy's funeral, a captain contacted the widow and asked how she could help. The widow said she would like to receive counseling, but could not afford it. The captain told the widow that she would set up counseling for her through the department's EAP office. Six months went by without any further contact from the captain. Through encouragement and insistence, the widow finally contacted the captain and asked about the counseling. Within the week, the widow had her first appointment with a counselor through EAP. Following up with survivors in a timely fashion is crucial when offering assistance. Many survivors who have witnessed the act of their loved one's suicide are diagnosed with Post Traumatic Stress Disorder (PTSD). Survivors who are unable to afford psychological counseling, may continue through life with complications from PTSD.

If a law enforcement agency has a victim advocate office, the resources that it provides to the community will be the same resources you may need to help the family. For instance, if the suicide occurs in the home, the department should ensure that a disaster cleanup service has been called to clean the area where the officer died. Never leave the family to clean up the scene. There have been cases where co-workers of the officer have cleaned the scene so the family would not have to endure this task. In reality, this should not be done by either the family or co-workers. Most homeowner insurance policies will cover this claim. Allow the company to remove linens, furniture, carpeting, walls, etc., but have someone supervise the process, perhaps a chaplain, family friend, or even an officer. Ask the spouse who he/she would like to be present in the home when this is being done. It is best to either have the spouse leave while the area is being cleaned or suggest being in another area of the house without a view of the cleanup process.

It may be necessary to ask the spouse if he/she would like to have other firearms in the home removed, either permanently or temporarily. This question may be a relief to the spouse depending on the age of any children, as well as whether the firearms are in a secure area. Administrators should not demand or assume that all firearms within the home should be surrendered. Although the family will be understandably distraught with the death of their spouse, they will, most likely, not be suicidal.

Secondary Trauma

The responding police department, as well as the officer's department, should avoid inflicting secondary trauma on the family. This can happen in several ways. Survivors have experienced 911 operators instructing them to sit atop the officer and place pressure on the chest wound. The survivor is so traumatized by witnessing the act that they are not capable of rendering aid and, for the most part, it would not be life-saving.

Another instance of secondary trauma is the number of police personnel at the scene, especially if the suicide occurred in the officer's home. In most cases, the responding officer, homicide detectives, internal affairs, supervisors, crime scene technicians, and coroners, as well as emergency medical technicians will arrive at the scene. If the officer lived in one jurisdiction and worked in a different jurisdiction, the number of personnel on the scene could double.

In cases where the spouse was present when the suicide occurred, secondary trauma can happen when the spouse is fingerprinted and tested for gun powder residue. If possible, these tests should be done on scene. If the survivor must surrender the clothing that they were wearing at the time of death, allow the survivor to change at the home so that he or she is not wearing clothing with blood residue for any length of time. The clothing can be placed in an evidence bag prior to leaving the home. Transporting the survivor in blood stained clothing will cause additional stress and anxiety.

The residual effects of that night still remain for me. I do not like the dark. It took over 10 years before I was able to fall asleep without the noise and the light of the television being on. My house is never dark and is illuminated with both nightlights as well as lamps on timers. When traveling alone in hotel

rooms, I sleep with the bathroom light on. And if I travel to a survivor's conference, I always invite other survivors to share the room with me, so that I
do not have to be alone. This is the result of secondary trauma.

How Long Will I Grieve?

There are many skills in life that one must learn in order to survive. For law
enforcement officers, it is defensive driving, firearms training, and defensive
tactics. For survivors, it is learning how to cope with the intense feelings of
grief, anger, abandonment and isolation. Survivors can learn coping mechanisms through counseling and support groups.

Grieving the loss of a loved one who died by suicide is deeply painful and
complex. Survivors experience a sudden and unexplainable death compounded
by the aftermath associated with the stigma of mental illness and suicide. For
years, the family may continue to struggle with why the suicide happened. This
forever unanswered question then typically evolves into guilt and anger, among
many other emotions.

Somewhere along the way, society's timetable for grieving averages out to
one year. I met a woman whose son died by suicide. She told me that, due to
her religion, she could only grieve for 30 days. Her religion believes in mourning, but also sets boundaries so as not to become paralyzed by grief and unable to move forward in life. For me and the many survivors that I have
encountered, we were in a perpetual state of shock after 30 days.

Most people would be surprised to learn that decades after losing a loved one
to suicide can still bring about sadness, particularly on the anniversary date of
the death. Survivors admit that they have learned to cope with their loss, manage their grief, and suppress their emotions, but getting past the pain of losing someone to suicide is never ending. The raw emotion that is experienced
in the first few years eventually lies beneath the surface and can be triggered at
any moment in their life.

For the family members and a very short list of friends who do remember
the date, it is a quick phone call to say hello or to send the e-mail that says, "I
am thinking of you today" that can trigger the memory of the events of what
happened decades ago. Survivors never forget all that happened on that day
nor the events that continue to happen in the days, weeks, months and years
to come. It is difficult to explain to someone who has not experienced a loss
to suicide or the trauma that may have occurred by either witnessing the act
or by the actions of the police department. But it is a permanent imprint on
the lives of survivors as they continue their life.

On the eighth anniversary of his death, Ruth Benallie wrote a letter to her brother, Richard, who was an officer with the Navajo Nation Police Department in Arizona. Below is an excerpt from that letter recalling her thoughts and actions the last time she saw her brother alive.

Hi little brother,
Today is 8 years since you decided to end your life, though it seems a couple of days ago. Last night I was thinking you were alive 8 years ago, and probably going over what was going to happen in the next couple of hours. I could only imagine what you were going through. This morning, my first thoughts were of you again. That long night 8 years ago. I am so sorry that I didn't read between the lines and wasn't able to help you. Remember the last time I saw you? Thinking about it now, I was glad that I was home and gave you my last hug and kissed the top of your head, not knowing that would be the last ever. Tears still flow and my heart feels so sad remembering that again. We all miss you so much.

Whether it is a biological, marital, or law enforcement family, suicide leaves those behind questioning the relationship and wondering what could possibly drive a person to get to that point.

Stigma

There are a number of police organizations that offer emotional as well as financial assistance to families of officers killed in the line of duty. There is no shortage of members of the law enforcement family who rally around the family with fundraisers, friendship, mentoring for the officer's children, etc. But when it comes to suicide, most families are left in isolation. Neither child played a part in their parent's death, yet one group of kids are ignored. These children are in just as much need of counseling and support, yet the police department and police organizations turn their backs on them. What message are we sending the children within our police family?

On several occasions, I have been contacted by a national law enforcement survivor organization to ask if I could offer assistance to a family of an officer suicide. In one case, the widow of an officer who died by suicide requested that monetary donations be given to this particular organization, unaware that the organization does not provide assistance in a suicidal death. The chapter president was understandably conflicted in receiving the donations knowing that they could not provide assistance to the family.

We can stop the stigma by displaying compassion and support to the families of law enforcement suicide. When police officers ignore the family in public settings, it not only inflicts shame, but lowers the self-esteem of the surviving children. Police honor guards have been present at graduation ceremonies for children of officers killed in the line duty, but where are they for the children whose parent died by suicide?

Removing the stigma surrounding mental health and suicide can help reduce the suicide rate. In 2011, President Barack Obama reversed the policy of not sending condolence letters to the family of soldiers who died by suicide in a combat zone. President Obama stated that this new policy is part of a commitment to remove stigma and that service members who die by suicide, " ... didn't die because they were weak. And the fact that they didn't get the help they needed must change."[1] Law enforcement leaders must also recognize that it is healthy and courageous for police officers to ask for help.

A non-profit organization dedicated to law enforcement suicide prevention believes that the suicide of an officer should be classified as a line of duty death. Although there are a number of cases that should be classified as a line of duty death, this organization chooses to classify the death as a 'line of duty suicide.' In order to de-stigmatize a law enforcement suicide, it needs to be classified as line of duty without any further description. By adding the word 'suicide' to the classification, the stigma associated with suicide is still in place.

How Do We Prevent Suicide?

It is imperative that law enforcement officers learn how to survive their profession, not just physically, but psychologically as well. I received a phone call from a police department that had a second officer die by suicide within two months. They wanted me to answer one question: How do we know that another suicide is not going to happen again?

So, how do we prevent suicide? Implementing training programs that address stress management, mental health and suicide awareness in the police academy is a necessary beginning. In-service training can reinforce the ability to recognize the signs of suicide—depressed moods, change in appetite or weight, fatigue or loss of energy, inability to concentrate, indecisiveness, excess drug and alcohol use, and thoughts of suicide—as well as the availability of resources in seeking help. In the midst of the training, we must dispel the

---

1. "Statement by the President on Change of Condolence Letter Policy," The White House, Office of the Press Secretary, press release dated July 6, 2011.

myth that talking about suicide brings about the act of suicide. We need to eliminate the stigma, which is brought about through ignorance and fear. It is equally important that law enforcement officers feel comfortable in investigating issues dealing with anger, irritability, and aggression with a therapist so that these feelings do not culminate to a crisis situation.

Leadership qualities have changed over the years as education and training on law enforcement suicide prevention has been implemented. There are still those in leadership positions that have been candid with their feelings on peer support, including commenting that they do not believe " … in that touchy-feely stuff." For those leaders, I can only hope that they are nearer their time of retirement than in the midst of their career.

Stress can wreck havoc on a person both physically and emotionally. Neither the police chief nor the rookie is immune. Law enforcement officers who contemplate suicide rarely utilize any support systems that the department may have in place. By not reaching out for support, these officers are unable to see a resolution to their pain and the time it takes to recover.

Administrators should take notice of how the military is handling suicide prevention. Suicide prevention training is now taught at all levels of leadership. Leadership throughout the chain of command must be prepared to recognize, know the signs of behavioral problems, PTSD and traumatic brain injury. The military has been working to de-stigmatize the need of soldiers reaching out for help and no longer jeopardize their career by saying they have a problem.

As more survivors begin to speak out about the circumstances that led up to their loved one's death, there is one message that is conveyed—no spouse, parent, sibling, or child wants another family to endure this tragedy. To be standing before a room full of law enforcement officers talking about the most painful event in one's life is distressing, but also promotes the message that suicide can be prevented. They reveal their shattered life in hope of breaking the silence of this tragedy.

Conclusion

Suicide is a tragedy that rips families apart. The reason why suicide happens is complex. It most likely happens because of an accumulation of events and emotions that occur over a period of time. But there are also cases where the suicide was an impulsive act and occurred due to one specific incident.

It is important to understand that suicide is about ending one's pain, whether physical or emotional. The person contemplating suicide does not have the ability to think rationally and believes the only way to eliminate that feeling is to end his or her own life. Often, those who end their life believe that their family would be better off without them. Contrary to this belief, families are left in a tumultuous and devastating emotional state which may, or may not, be worse than what the officer was experiencing.

The military's approach to combating the increasing rate of suicide is to hold supervisors accountable for the mental well-being of the men and women in their command. How would law enforcement supervisors react to this responsibility? Would many of them forego promotions or would they take a personal interest into the well-being of each of their officers?

Leaders can no longer afford to ignore the inevitable elephant in the room. If the issue of law enforcement suicide is not openly discussed and psychological resources are not encouraged, then the suicide rate among law enforcement officers will never decline. General Ronald R. Fogleman, Air Force Chief of Staff (1994–1997) said, " … Suicide affects the Total Force and causes the loss of our most valuable resource, trained professionals. As leaders, we must take action to turn the tide on the needless tragedy of suicide. …"[2]

In 2002, Florida added law enforcement and corrections officers to the Florida Heart and Lung Bill, which had been in effect for firefighters for many years. This legislation, which is a worker's compensation law that may cover heart disease, tuberculosis and hypertension, gives the presumption that heart disease is the result of the stressful lives of emergency workers. It provides financial benefits to these professions which could not prove a link between employment and heart disease. We know that stress can cause heart disease, hypertension and other diseases, but we should also accept that stress causes brain diseases, such as depression and anxiety.

While we continue to learn why suicide occurs, it is important to acknowledge the growing number of widows being awarded death benefits through worker compensation claims after the suicide of their husband. This trend is proving that work-related stress, anxiety, PTSD, and physical injuries sustained in the line of duty are correlated to the psychological trauma that officers experience repeatedly throughout their careers.

Only when more police officers educate themselves as to why suicide may happen, how to prevent it from happening, and breaking the stigma that binds officers from seeking the help that they may need, will we be able to reduce the statistics. We have learned from the military and, more recently, NFL players that suicide can happen as a result of traumatic brain injuries. We have

---

2. The US Air Force Suicide Prevention Program: A description of program initiatives and outcomes. April 2001 AFPAM 44-160.

learned from family members that stigma associated with psychological counseling can lead to suicide. We have learned from police administrators that ignoring the signs of suicide can only lead to more suicides. It is time that the law enforcement profession step up to dispel the stigma associated with psychological trauma and promote better well-being for the men and women who are sworn to serve and protect.

Discussion Questions

1. What were the biographical data and background of the officer who committed suicide?
2. According to the author, what was the relationship between her husband's suicide and shift work?
3. How was the suicide note eventually returned to the author and why was it so important for her to have it returned?
4. What course of action should be taken if an officer dies away from his home jurisdiction?
5. What role can be played by emergency medical service personnel in relation to notifying the family about the death of an officer?
6. What type of photograph should be released to the media of the deceased officer if one is requested?
7. In what ways can leaders support the family?
8. What course of action should be taken when both spouses are sworn law enforcement officers and one dies by suicide?
9. What course of action should be taken if the officer commits suicide in his/her home?
10. What steps can be taken to prevent suicides?

Safeguarding Undercover Employees: A Strategy for Success

Meredith Krause

The selection, management, and retention of effective undercover employees (UCEs) pose significant challenges to local, state, federal, and international law enforcement agencies. UCEs face unique experiences and stressors that set them apart from their overt counterparts and place them at increased risk for psychological injury, disciplinary action, and other adverse personal and professional consequences. Growing awareness of these hazards among law enforcement managers and allied mental health professionals has resulted in the discussion and development of proactive policies and procedures intended to safeguard the well-being of UCEs.[1]

Some agencies have independent units or divisions dedicated to the recruitment, training, certification, and management of UCEs. In many other cases, however, managers, supervisors, or affiliated mental health providers must tend to the operational and psychological needs of their UCEs. Regardless of how an agency administers the safeguard process, the commitment of its leaders to the well-being of UCEs from the time of recruitment to their return to regular or overt duties determines the impact and effectiveness of the

---

1. Australian Institute of Police Management, *Managing the Risk of Psychological Injury Associated with Undercover Policing* (Manly, NSW: Australian Institute of Police Management, 2003); L. Miller, "Undercover Policing: A Psychological and Operational Guide," *Journal of Police and Criminal Psychology* 21 (2006): 1–24: Neil S. Hibler, "The Care and Feeding of Undercover Agents," in *Police Psychology—Into the 21st Century* eds. Neil S. Hibler, Martin I. Kurke, and Ellen M. Scrivner (Hillsdale, NJ: Lawrence Erlbaum Associates, Inc., 1995), 299–317; Stephen R. Band and Donald C. Sheehan, "Managing Undercover Stress: The Supervisor's Role," *FBI Law Enforcement Bulletin*, February 1999. 1–6.

initiative.[2] Such commitment and support prove essential to building a safeguard process that UCEs view as a credible, reliable, collaborative, and proactive program worthy of their trust and open and honest involvement.

Critical Functions of the Process

The undercover safeguard process addresses the needs of UCEs and their agencies throughout the six phases (selection, training, operational planning, deployment, decompression, and reintegration) of covert activity.[3] To accomplish this, the safeguard process exposes the UCE to a complementary team of personnel who shares a commitment to the undercover mission and possesses specialized skills, knowledge, and abilities. At a minimum, this team includes a qualified mental health professional (for selection and monitoring purposes) and one or more experienced UCEs (to provide input regarding operational or target-specific subjects) who answer to an administrator or supervisor experienced in undercover matters. Given the complex and phased nature of the safeguard process, this team frequently accesses local and federal resources for case- or UCE-specific needs or questions (e.g., tactical, technological, backstopping, or legal) and readily taps into these resources to maximize effectiveness and efficiency. In so doing, the safeguard team can provide critical selection, education, stress inoculation, monitoring, debriefing or reintegration support, and risk management services to UCEs and their department.

Selection

The selection of UCEs is one of the most critical functions of the safeguard team. During this phase, members must apply their knowledge of existing research regarding the personal and professional qualities that distinguish effective UCEs to determine the suitability of a candidate for a given operation. They can maximize the accuracy of such decision making by focusing on the goodness of fit between the candidate and a particular undercover operation (UCO) or activity; by administering psychological tests designed to assess specific traits and skills; and by completing in-depth interviews and role-plays that provide critical information regarding the candidate's personal style, interpersonal skills, professional experience, and operational competence.

---

2. I. John Vasquez and Sharon A. Kelly, "Management's Commitment to the Undercover Operative: A Contemporary View," *FBI Law Enforcement Bulletin*, February 1989, 3–12.

3. Supra note 1 (Hibler).

During the safeguard interviews, candidates meet independently with the mental health professional (assessor) to review the results of their psychological tests, relate their personal and professional histories, confirm their voluntary status, participate in a brief clinical interview, and discuss relevant personal and interpersonal issues (e.g., coping resources and personal, job, and family stressors). This psychological evaluation is complemented by an independent operational assessment conducted by an experienced UCE (counselor) focused on investigative knowledge, trade-craft issues, and problem-solving skills and includes role-play scenarios designed to elicit the candidate's responses to typical undercover experiences. Upon completion of these interviews, the assessor and counselor meet to share their impressions and form a final opinion regarding the suitability of the candidate to the operation. They communicate their findings in writing to the candidate's supervisor or the individual responsible for administering the UCO. The operation-specific nature of this assessment process is critical because it reminds the candidate and other involved parties of the reality that no *one* UCE can function effectively in every UCO. This case- or operation-specific orientation also is important in that it allows initially unsuccessful candidates to return for evaluation as new cases arise in the future.

Education

The safeguard team also provides an educational function during its interviews with candidates and its ongoing contacts with personnel involved in the administration of UCOs. Specifically, the assessor and counselor provide the candidate with information regarding the qualities and traits that distinguish effective UCEs, the stressors that they commonly face, the possible pitfalls of undercover work, and the skills and abilities critical to success in undercover roles. In addition, interactions with supervisors and other law enforcement personnel provide the safeguard team with opportunities to educate colleagues regarding risks and benefits of undercover work, effective strategies for managing undercover stress and operations, and other pertinent information. The safeguard team also participates in the training of new or inexperienced undercover employees by providing blocks of classroom-based instruction, creating and participating in role-play scenarios, and functioning as mentors for novice UCEs.

Inoculation

By speaking with candidates and novice UCEs openly and frankly regarding the hazards associated with undercover work, the safeguard team promotes the self-awareness and mental preparation needed for them to remain resilient in the face of expected and unexpected stressors. This process challenges the myths promulgated by popular culture portrayals of undercover operatives and inoculates, or protects, UCEs against the adverse impact of undercover stress. This proactive approach attempts to minimize long-term negative changes in personal, professional, health, and family or interpersonal functioning by enhancing their self-awareness, sensitivity to the impact of the work, and willingness to request respite from undercover duties on an as-needed basis.

Support, Monitoring, and Retention

Upon completion of required training and certification, the UCE is referred to the safeguard process at the beginning, midpoint, and end of every covert operation. In the case of extended UCOs, the UCE participates in the safeguard process at regular intervals determined by the safeguard team (typically every 6 months but more frequently if at increased risk due to the nature of personal stressors or assignment). At each time point, the UCE completes psychological testing and interviews with the assessor and counselor. The repeated administration of psychological tests provides objective information regarding changes in stress levels and personality, as well as emotional, health, and interpersonal functioning, over time.

The testing results often identify areas of concern and serve as an important tool for the safeguard team during one-on-one interviews with the UCE, who may be unaware of these changes or unwilling to disclose them. In these cases, the testing results open the door to discussion of sensitive personal issues, which the team can monitor over the course of subsequent safeguard assessments. In many cases, this added monitoring and support feature allows the UCE to remain in the assigned UCO without disruption. In more extreme cases, however, temporary or permanent removal from the project may be necessary to address problems in personal functioning that jeopardize the health and well-being of the UCE, the UCO, or the department.

Debriefing and Reintegration

Both research and practice have highlighted the difficulties that UCEs often face upon termination of their UCOs and return to regular duty.[4] Without

---

4. Supra note 1 (Miller and Hibler).

proper preparation and support prior to and during this period of reintegration, UCEs may manifest adjustment problems that significantly impair their ability to function in expected personal, familial, and professional roles. The safeguard team can ease the reintegration process by discussing the UCE's plan for return to regular duty even *before* the UCO begins and then again during each safeguard assessment. This approach reinforces undercover assignments as necessarily time limited and the return to regular duty as an expected outcome and not a punishment. Many agencies codify this expectation in policy guidelines that limit the time that any employee can spend undercover and provide for respite periods between undercover assignments.

Even with clear expectations and early preparation for reintegration, UCEs require careful support and monitoring during this phase. Debriefing at the close of the UCO is essential to determine their perspectives on the outcome of the investigation, the perceived level of support for their activity during the investigation, and their feelings about their return to regular duty. Particular attention must be paid to expressions of resentment, mistrust, or divided loyalty (i.e., identification with the target) or to lingering changes in appearance or behavior because these factors may impede successful reintegration.[5] When UCEs manifest these indicators, the safeguard team must work closely with departmental contacts to address and resolve them sensitively and directly. Successful resolution of reintegration-related issues is essential to long-term positive outcomes for both the UCE and the agency and constitutes a prerequisite for return to undercover work.

Risk Management and Liability Mitigation

The safeguard team's exclusive commitment to the health and well-being of the UCE serves a vital risk management and liability mitigation function for the agency. The initial selection process includes both objective and subjective measures of suitability that promote accurate decision making and minimize exposure to litigation related to negligent or unfair hiring or selection procedures. The education and ongoing monitoring and support components of the safeguard process reflect a commitment to prevention of duty-related injuries and early intervention when problems arise with undercover personnel. As such, the safeguard process provides an assertive risk management function that sensitively balances the needs of the UCE, the operation, and the agency.

---

5. Supra note 1 (Hibler) and note 2.

Critical Features of the Process

To effectively execute the critical functions, the safeguard process must be anchored by an unwavering commitment to the primary well-being of the UCE. In addition, it must adhere to and display seven critical features.

Research Based

The safeguard approach is based on more than 25 years of institutional research regarding the experiences, stressors, and outcomes typically associated with undercover assignments.[6] This research has enhanced the selection and monitoring functions performed by safeguard personnel by limiting reliance upon anecdotal information, myth, rules of thumb, and personal opinion or bias. While this empirical research has formed the foundation of the safeguard process, the changing nature of crime and criminal investigations has forced continued study and programmatic evolution.

For optimal effectiveness, the safeguard team must be well versed in the small but coherent body of empirical research and knowledge regarding undercover stress and the personal and professional characteristics of effective UCEs. In addition, the mental health professional included in the safeguard team must be trained and qualified to administer and interpret appropriate psychological tests that directly measure the characteristics and qualities outlined in this research. Without this knowledge and experience, the safeguard team cannot be expected to accurately select future UCEs, anticipate operational or personal issues among active ones, or intervene appropriately with troubled employees.

Organizationally Embedded

Given the nature of its mission, the safeguard team requires unfettered access to internal and external resources for training UCEs; for establishing and maintaining cover identities; for monitoring the status of the UCO; for resolving administrative issues; and for addressing health, personal, and emotional needs of UCEs. As such, the safeguard team must be empowered to

---

6. For additional information, see U.S. Department of Justice, Federal Bureau of Investigation, *The Special Agent in Undercover Operations: A Research Study* (Quantico, VA, 1980); Michael Arter, "Undercover and Under Stress: The Impact of Undercover Assignments on Police Officers" (Ph.D. diss., Indiana University of Pennsylvania, 2005); and Mark Pogrebin and Eric Poole, "Vice Isn't Nice: A Look at the Effects of Working Undercover," *Journal of Criminal Justice* 21 (1993): 383–394.

execute its mission and supported by agency personnel at all levels. Close and effective working relationships with agency command staff and federal law enforcement personnel also are essential to the safeguard mission.

Mission Oriented

To establish and maintain credibility among the UCE cadre, the safeguard team must focus on the primacy of the well-being of these employees over the outcome or progress of any given investigation. The team must reflect this primary allegiance to UCEs through the nonadversarial nature of the safeguard assessment process, regular contact with them to build rapport and trust, and written and oral communication with agency command staff regarding their suitability or status. Careful attention to the confidentiality of the information gleaned during safeguard assessments, maintained within a legally protected medical record, must guide all of these contacts. As such, communication regarding a given UCE to agency personnel must provide only essential information, such as the date and outcome of the assessment. In the absence of this type of unwavering commitment, UCEs may view the safeguard team as an adversarial tool of agency management that intends to strip them of their assignment, wantonly divulge their personal information, or intrude upon their lives.

Case Specific and Time Sensitive

To reduce errors in decision making, the safeguard process necessarily addresses very specific questions regarding the goodness of fit between a particular UCE and a particular case or assignment at a particular point in time.[7] This approach eliminates the need to make global conclusions in the face of insufficient information and, thus, enables the safeguard team to pinpoint the specific assets and liabilities the potential UCE brings to an assignment. This information is shared with the UCE during the safeguard assessment to enhance personal and professional functioning over the course of the UCO and to alert the employee to areas of risk and possible remediation. Given the case- and time-sensitive nature of this work, it remains imperative that safeguard personnel communicate their decisions to the necessary agency contacts in a timely manner because the UCE's status and suitability always can change.

---

7. David Faust and Jay Ziskin, "The Expert Witness in Psychology and Psychiatry," *Science* 41 (1988): 31–35.

Separate but Equal Assessment Process

At its core, the safeguard assessment process requires UCEs to undergo independent interviews with a mental health professional and an experienced UCE counselor on the same day. The unique content and structure of these promote broad coverage on a range of personal and operational issues. In addition, this bifurcated design often yields very different disclosures by UCEs based on their relationship and comfort level with the interviewer. This dynamic leads the safeguard team to generate two independent opinions based on different and unique sets of information, which members share and consider in rendering the final determination of suitability for undercover assignment. This approach proves critical in generating a well-rounded understanding of the undercover candidate and in reducing the potential impact of "group think" and other decision-making biases on determinations of suitability.

Broad Based

Decision making by the safeguard team is based on a host of objective and subjective information from multiple sources. This wide-ranging information-gathering method creates a holistic perspective of a given UCE that allows the safeguard team to render accurate decisions and provide tailored support and intervention as the need arises. Critical sources of information include objective personality testing; input from supervisors regarding the UCE's skills, achievements, behavior, and judgment; comments from family members or close contacts; and self-report information from the UCE.

Legally Minded

During the execution of their duties, team members must remain mindful of the legal issues possibly raised by the information they generate. The most pressing concern relates to the confidentiality of the records produced by the safeguard process. The agency should maintain these as confidential medical records apart from the UCE's personnel file and ensure that supervisory staff or other external parties cannot review them without written permission from the employee. Safeguard personnel may breach this confidentiality, however, should the UCE disclose homicidal or suicidal ideation, child or elder abuse, or significant criminal involvement. These caveats to confidentiality mirror those in traditional health-care settings and are clearly communicated to the UCE prior to participation in the safeguard process.

Given the content of safeguard records, some concerns have arisen regarding possible disclosure during the course of criminal legal proceedings in an attempt to discredit the testimony of UCEs. Although case law on this matter has been inconsistent, judges have typically ruled in favor of the protection of the UCE's personal information and service files in all but the most extreme cases of misconduct. Despite this overwhelming pattern, safeguard team members must remain cognizant of the possibility of future disclosure and discovery issues and must structure their documentation in keeping with established best practices related to medical record keeping.[8]

Conclusion

Undercover employees play a vital role in local and federal law enforcement agencies and experience a unique set of demands, stressors, and challenges in the execution of their duties. Case examples and research reports offer chilling evidence of the very real human toll of undercover investigations and emphasize the need for specialized selection, training, and support services suited to the needs of UCEs.[9] The safeguard process represents one integrated approach to addressing the selection, education, inoculation, monitoring, debriefing, and risk management and liability mitigation needs of both UCEs and law enforcement agencies. Effective implementation of an undercover safeguard program depends to a large extent upon organizational commitment to the primary well-being of UCEs and understanding of the well-documented consequences and correlates of undercover work.

Organizational commitment, support, and sensitivity are all necessary conditions for effective implementation of a safeguard program. But, the UCE's willingness to "buy in" to the program determines its ultimate success. Open, honest, and consistent participation in the safeguard process by the UCE cadre can be fostered by adherence to seven critical features that reflect and support the credibility, trustworthiness, responsiveness, reliability, and effectiveness of the safeguard staff.

---

8. Richard G. Schott, "The Discovery Process and Personnel File Information," *FBI Law Enforcement Bulletin*, November 2003, 25–32.

9. Supra note 1 (Hibler); Michel Girodo, "Health and Legal Issues in Undercover Narcotics Investigations: Misrepresented Evidence," *Behavioral Sciences and the Law* 3 (1985): 299–308; and Ric Kahn, "Secret Soldier in Drug War Lost Last Battle," *The Boston Globe*, February 27, 1994.

Discussion Questions

1. What can be done by law enforcement administrators to maximize the accuracy in the selection process of undercover employees?
2. What steps should be taken during the safeguard interview?
3. Why is case—or operation—specific orientation so important?
4. What issues are discussed by the safeguard team in their interview with candidates?
5. What is the goal of the safe team during the inoculation phase in the selection of undercover employees?
6. What was the reason for the repeated administration of psychological tests of undercover operations?
7. What specific recommendations were made regarding the reintegration of the undercover employee back into the organization?
8. What seven critical features must an effective safeguard process display?
9. What research is the safeguard approach based upon?
10. Decision making by the safeguard team is based upon a host of objective and subjective information from multiple sources. What are the specific sources of this information?

45

Psychological Factors after Officer-Involved Shootings: Addressing Officer Needs and Agency Responsibilities

Philip S. Trompetter, David M. Corey, Wayne W. Schmidt, and Drew Tracy

The police use of deadly force is a consequential event for all parties: the officers and their families, the agency, the community, and the suspects and their families and survivors. In light of these profound consequences, the most critical investigation in any law enforcement agency is that of an officer-involved shooting (OIS).[1] To ensure transparency and accountability, agencies have developed meticulous policies and procedures that address the administrative and criminal investigations of these events.

In recent years, many agencies also have devised strategies to attend to the psychological needs of the involved officers while maintaining the integrity of the investigative process. Many of the programs to support involved officers have become relatively uniform across agencies. Less consistent has been the manner in which agencies return the involved officers to work. This article suggests strategies for agencies to assist with the involved officers' psychological needs following an OIS, in addition to examining how agencies can responsibly and lawfully consider the officers' readiness to return to work.

Since 1985, the IACP has been host to the Police Psychological Services Section (PPSS). This section is dedicated to providing expertise to police agen-

---

1. Drew J. Tracy, "Handling Officer-Involved Shootings," *The Police Chief* 77 (October 2010): 38–48.

cies in psychological matters affecting law enforcement. Toward that end, the section has created five guidelines, each revised every five years and available at http://theiacp.org/psych_services_section by clicking Resources, and then Guidelines. The guidelines include Preemployment Psychological Evaluations, Psychological Fitness-for-Duty Evaluations (FFDE), OIS, Peer Support, and Consulting Police Psychologists. Pertinent to this article are the OIS[2] and FFDE Guidelines,[3] both revised in 2009 and approved by IACP in 2010.

The OIS guideline is consistent with the IACP Model Policy number 76, "Investigation of Officer-Involved Shootings," particularly section III. Model Policy number 76 reads:

1. *Supervisory, investigative and other sworn and nonsworn employees shall be familiar with and follow the provisions established by this agency in its policy on dealing with post-shooting emotional trauma in police personnel.*

2. *All personnel shall be familiar with the provisions of this agency's policy on employee mental health services and should avail themselves of these services following officer-involved shooting incidents where appropriate.[4]*

The OIS guideline is also consistent with the Concepts and Issues Paper by the IACP National Law Enforcement Policy Center[5] that accompanies the model policy. The Concepts and Issues Paper identifies several of the possible adverse or distressing psychological reactions experienced by many officers during and after an OIS (for example, perceived vulnerability during the event, perceptual distortions, or impaired recall).[6]

---

2. "Officer-Involved Shooting Guidelines," IACP Police Psychological Services Section (2009), http://theiacp.org/psych_services_section/pdfs/Psych-OfficerInvolvedShooting.pdf (accessed November 23, 2010).

3. "Psychological Fitness-for-Duty Evaluation Guidelines," IACP Police Psychological Services Section (2009), http://theiacp.org/psych_services_section/pdfs/Psych-Fitnessfor-DutyEvaluation.pdf (accessed November 23, 2010).

4. "Post-Shooting Incident Procedures," IACP National Law Enforcement Policy Center (1998). For more information on up-to-date model policies, and their related papers, please contact the National Law Enforcement Policy Center by e-mail at policycenter@theiacp. org or visit http://www.theiacp.org/policycenter.

5. Ibid. and "Investigation of Officer-Involved Shootings," IACP National Law Enforcement Policy Center (August 1999).

6. The following papers are excellent resources for discussions of specific psychological reactions during and following an OIS: Alexis Artwohl and Loren W. Christensen, *Deadly Force Encounters: What Cops Need to Know to Mentally and Physically Prepare for and Survive a Gunfight* (Boulder, Colorado: Paladin Press, 1997); Alexis Artwohl, "Perceptual and

This article targets how agencies can attend and respond to these reactions both to assist involved officers as well as to ensure that when they subsequently return to work, agencies are prepared to properly address the officers' psychological suitability to resume their public safety responsibilities.

Assisting the Involved Officers After an OIS

The IACP OIS guidelines were developed to provide information and recommendations to public safety agencies and mental health providers to constructively support officers involved in shootings and other use-of-force incidents that may trigger the investigative process. Many of these recommendations can also be applied to other potentially distressing critical events.

Before an OIS occurs, agencies should have a protocol to address the psychological needs of the involved officers. Arrangements should already be in place for the availability of a qualified, licensed mental health professional experienced with law enforcement culture and deadly force confrontations.

In addition, officers should be provided a companion officer as soon as possible, preferably a trusted colleague who has been through an OIS. Talking with peers who have had similar experiences can be quite helpful for officers involved in significant use-of-force incidents. Agencies should train potential companion officers in peer support techniques. The trained companion officer can provide guidance to the agency procedures, ensure the involved officer refrains from speaking about the incident except to those authorized to hear it, and offer support that is helpful and appropriate.

While officers may be asked to provide pertinent information soon after a shooting to aid the initial investigative process, it is suggested that they have some recovery time before providing a full, formal statement. Depending on the nature of the incident and the emotional status of the officers, this can range from a few hours to several days. The agency may wish to consider permitting a walkthrough while taking a statement from the officer to assist in gathering the most accurate information.

Memory Distortions in Officer Involved Shootings," *FBI Law Enforcement Bulletin* 158, no. 10 (October 2002): 18–24; Audrey L. Honig and Jocelyn E. Roland, "Shots Fired: Officer Involved," *The Police Chief* 65 (October 1998): 16–19; Audrey L. Honig and Steven E. Sultan, "Reactions and Resilience under Fire: What an Officer Can Expect," *The Police Chief* 71 (December 2004); Ellen Kirschman, *I Love a Cop: What Police Families Need to Know* (New York: The Guilford Press, 2006).

Similarly, the timing of when to offer a psychological debriefing is flexible and wide-ranging depending on the needs of the officer and the investigation; some debriefings occur before the officer secures from the shift during which the shooting occurred, where others prefer a debriefing within one week of the shooting.

After a life-threatening incident, officers frequently are most concerned about how they reacted physiologically and emotionally and whether these reactions were "normal." Post-shooting interventions should be primarily educative as this reassurance reduces worry, anxiety, and negative self-assessment. Some officers would choose not to participate in the post-shooting interventions provided by qualified mental health professionals, yet, when required to attend, they often find them helpful. In addition, some may be unaware of the potential impact of the incident and choose not to attend. For these reasons, it is recommended that officers be required to attend one individual post-shooting intervention so they can, at a minimum, be provided with basic education and coping skills to better manage their reactions.

While officers may be required to attend at least one mandatory session, this does not mean that it should be mandatory for them to discuss the event or how they feel with the mental health professional. Any participation beyond attendance should be voluntary on the part of the officers.

It would be helpful to provide officers and their significant others with written information that reviews physical and psychological reactions to shooting incidents. Topics covered should include what to expect, how to support each other, coping strategies, and whom to contact for further assistance.

The realities of deadly force confrontations have taught us that in these dynamic, rapidly unfolding, ambiguous, and dangerous situations there will be officers whose shots miss the target, or officers who for good reason decided not to discharge their weapons. It is not uncommon for these officers to struggle with a misperception that they failed to perform adequately. Intervening mental health professionals and agencies should be mindful to ensure these officers are included in mandatory interventions, too. The well-being of dispatchers, nonsworn personnel, and others centrally involved in the incident should also be considered.

Shooting incidents can result in heightened physical and emotional reactions for the participants. It is recommended that officers involved in such incidents be given a minimum three days leave, either administrative or through regular days off, in order to marshal their natural coping skills to manage the emotional impact of the incident prior to return to duty or the preparation of a use-of-force or incident report.

A single contact with a mental health professional may prove to be inadequate for officers who have been severely affected by an event. Also, a subset of officers may experience delayed onset of problems. The mental health professional should informally assess, for the sole purpose of voluntary referral, which officers may need additional or alternative types of support to further their recovery process. Follow-up sessions should be made available to every involved officer, and, if appropriate, referrals may be offered for further treatment and to peer support or chaplaincy programs.

Because delayed reactions may occur, all officers receiving an initial post-shooting intervention should receive follow-up contact by the intervening mental health professional either via phone or e-mail sometime within the first four months post-incident. In addition, contact should be made by the intervener prior to the first anniversary of the incident.

Life-threatening use-of-force incidents also have the potential to emotionally impact an officer's significant others, who often can provide valuable support to officers following these incidents. Therefore, it can be beneficial for all concerned to include significant others in the psychological debriefing process.

Issues Involving Readiness to Return

Police executives have a legal duty to ensure that police officers under their command are mentally and emotionally fit to perform their duties, and failure to do so can result in significant civil liability[7] and serious consequences to citizens, other officers, and an employing agency's reputation.[8] Various courts have interpreted this duty to include the authority to mandate psychological FFDE of police officers reasonably believed to be impaired in their ability to perform their job functions due to a known or suspected psychological condition.[9]

The employer's duty to ensure a psychologically fit workforce does not, however, allow an unrestrained right to require such evaluations of any police officer in any circumstance. Instead, the employer's duty must be balanced by the

---

7. *Bonsignore v. City of New York*, 683 F.2d 635 (2d Cir. 1982).

8. David M. Corey, "Principles for Fitness-for-Duty Evaluations for Police Psychologists," in *Handbook of Police Psychology*, ed. Jack Kitaeff (Oxford, England: Routledge Psychology Press, in press).

9. *Brownfield v. City of Yakima*, 612 F.3d 1140 (9th Cir. 2010); *Colon v. City of Newark*, 188 N.J. 490, 909 A. 2d 725 (2006); *Conte v. Horcher*, 50 Ill. App. 3d 151, 365 N.E. 2d 567 (1977); *Deen v. Darosa*, 414 F.3d 731 (7th Cir. 2005); *Kraft v. Police Commissioner of Boston*, 417 Mass. 235, 629 N.E. 2d 995 (1994); *McKnight v. Monroe Co. Sheriff's Dept.*, 90 FEP Cases (BNA) 35 (S.D. Ind. 2002); *Tingler v. City of Tampa*, 400 So. 2d 146 (Fla. App. 1981); *Watson v. City of Miami Beach*, 177 F.3d 932 (11th Cir. 1999).

public's interests and the employee's constitutional, civil, and property rights and interests.[10]

By law, an employer may require an FFDE of an incumbent police office only when objective facts pose a reasonable basis for concern about fitness. When making a disability inquiry or medical examination of an incumbent employee, the Americans with Disabilities Act of 1990 (ADA) requires the employer to meet a fact-specific, individualized threshold; namely, that the inquiry or examination is "job-related and consistent with business necessity" (42 U.S.C. §12112(d) (4) (A); 29 C.F.R. §1630.14(c)). In general, the ADA regards this threshold as having been met when an employer "has a reasonable belief, based on objective evidence, that (1) an employee's ability to perform essential job functions will be impaired by a medical condition; or (2) an employee will pose a direct threat due to a medical condition." In other words, legal justification for a compulsory mental health examination of an employee requires objective evidence of job-related performance problems or safety threats linked to a known or reasonably suspected mental condition. One of these in the absence of the other represents an insufficient basis for an FFDE.[11]

Accordingly, the IACP PPSS OIS Guidelines state

> 5.10 It should be made clear to all involved personnel, supervisors, and the community at large that an officer's fitness-for duty should not be brought into question by virtue of their involvement in a shooting incident. Post-shooting psychological interventions are separate and distinct from any fitness-for-duty assessments or administrative or investigative procedures that may follow. This does not preclude a supervisor from requesting a formal fitness-for-duty evaluation based upon objective concerns about an officer's ability to perform his or her duties. However, the mere fact of being involved in a shooting does not necessitate such an evaluation prior to return to duty.

Thus, a blanket policy of requiring an FFDE for an officer involved in an OIS, standing alone, appears to be inappropriate. Yet, a brief online survey of agency OIS policies finds some departments requiring an FFDE before involved officers may return to work based solely on their status of having been in an OIS. Such a policy may be inconsistent with federal law.[12]

---

10. *Denhof et al. v. City of Grand Rapids*, 494 F.3d 534 (6th Cir. 2007); *Holst v. Dept. of Veterans Affairs*, 298 Fed. Appx. 974 (Fed. Cir. 2008); *Jackson v. Lake County*, 14 AD Cases (BNA) 1609 (N.D. Ill. 2003); *McGreal v. Ostrov*, 368 F.3d 657 (7th Cir. 2004).

11. Liza H. Gold and Daniel W. Schuman, *Evaluating Mental Health Disability in the Workplace: Model, Process, and Analysis* (New York: Springer Science and Business Media, 2009).

12. The U.S. Equal Employment Opportunity Commission, "Enforcement Guidance on Disability-Related Inquiries and Medical Examinations of Employees under the Amer-

The licensed mental health professional providing the post-shooting intervention might appear to be in the best position to address the agency's interest in determining an officer's readiness to return to work. However, this intervention can only help to alleviate or mitigate readiness-to-return-to-duty concerns only if the officer is candid—an outcome made more likely by an assurance of confidentiality or privileged communication.[13] A requirement that the intervener report readiness concerns to the agency impedes the efficacy of the post-shooting intervention to the extent that it motivates officers to be less candid and forthcoming with the mental health professional. The post-shooting intervention should be off-limits as an agency source of readiness-to-return-to-duty information unless the disclosure is initiated at the request of, and with the informed consent and authorization of, the officer, or unless other exceptions to confidentiality pertain, as discussed below.

However, the agency may view its responsibility to the community as superseding the efficacy of the post-shooting intervention, and there is a legal basis to allow for disclosure of specified information to an employer from the intervener in limited circumstances. The federal Health Insurance Portability and Accountability Act of 1996 (HIPAA), Public Law 104-191, § 164.512 provides, in pertinent part

(j) Standard: Uses and disclosures to avert a serious threat to health or safety.

(1) Permitted disclosures. A covered entity may, consistent with applicable law and standards of ethical conduct, use or disclose protected health information, if the covered entity, in good faith, believes the use or disclosure:

(i)(A) Is necessary to prevent or lessen a serious and imminent threat to the health or safety of a person or the public; and

---

icans with Disabilities Act," *Compliance Manual*, volume II, section 902, no. 915.002 (Washington, D.C.: Equal Employment Opportunity Commission).

13. In *Jaffee v. Redmond*, 518 U.S. 1; 116 S. Ct. 1923 (1996), the U.S. Supreme Court majority held that the communications of Redmond, a police officer, to his psychotherapist in a post-OIS intervention were privileged. The Court observed, "Effective psychotherapy depends upon an atmosphere of confidence and trust, and therefore the mere possibility of disclosure of confidential communications may impede development of the relationship necessary for successful treatment. The privilege also serves the public interest, since the mental health of the Nation's citizenry, no less than its physical health, is a public good of transcendent importance."

(B) Is to a person or persons reasonably able to prevent or lessen the threat, including the target of the threat... .[14]

Moreover, the patient-therapist privilege is not absolute. Typical exceptions to medical confidentiality include a duty to:

1. report patients who express a desire to harm themselves or others;
2. report communicable diseases, such as STDs; and
3. report gunshot wounds.

In view of this, some agencies require the intervening mental health professional to recommend whether or not to return the officer to field duty. For example, the Los Angeles Police Manual Sec 794.40 explains that the commanding officer of an on- or off-duty employee who is involved in an officer-involved shooting resulting in an injury to any person or categorical use of force resulting in death or the substantial possibility of death shall "[c]onsult with the BSS (Behavioral Services Section) after the involved employee's mandated appointment to obtain their recommendation of whether or not to return the employee(s) to field duty. Other than the recommendation of BSS, matters discussed during the BSS evaluation shall be strictly confidential."[15]

Given the broad legal recognition of an employee's right to privacy, a mental health professional in this position must limit the unauthorized disclosure of confidential health information to a recommendation that the employee should or should not return to field duty.[16] Moreover, since such a policy provides an exception to privileged communication, the intervener is ethically bound to inform the officer of the exception and limit to confidentiality at the outset of the intervention.[17]

An intervening mental health professional is not prohibited from reporting readiness concerns directly to the officer and would be doing a disservice to the officer if such concerns were ignored. Honest feedback and a recommen-

---

14. *Health Insurance Portability and Accountability Act of 1996*, Public Law 104-191, § 164.512, "Uses and Disclosures for which an Authorization or Opportunity to Agree or Object Is Not Required," Title 45 Public Welfare § 164.512 (65 FR 82802, Dec. 28, 2000, as amended at 67 FR 53270, Aug. 14, 2002).

15. "Officer-Involved Shootings, Custodial, and In-Custody Deaths, and Use of Force Incidents Resulting in Injury," *Los Angeles Police Department Manual, Personnel Management*, volume 3, chapter 794, http://www.lapdonline.org/lapd_manual/volume_3.htm#794 (accessed November 23, 2010).

16. *Pettus v. Cole*, number A060253, 49 Cal.App. 4th 402 (Cal. App. 1st Dist. 1996).

17. Ethical Principles of Psychologist and Code of Conduct, 2010 Amendments, ethical standard 3.11, American Psychological Association, http://www.apa.org/ethics/code/index. aspx (accessed November 23, 2010).

dation to the officer for additional time off to voluntarily continue counseling should be an objective, and, with the officer's informed consent and authorization, the intervening mental health professional can communicate to the agency and coordinate a plan for addressing the noted concerns.

For agencies that wish to follow the PPSS OIS Guidelines to promote the efficacy of the post-shooting intervention without requiring the intervening mental health professional to disclose concerns to the agency about an officer's readiness to return to duty, several alternative strategies can be employed to address the agency's duty to protect the community. A commanding officer can interview the employee to assess the employee's readiness and suitability to return to field duty. Some agencies offer returning officers a modified duty assignment partly as a way to provide a safe vantage point to assess their readiness and suitability to return to their pre-incident positions. Other agencies train supervisors in the signs, both obvious and subtle, that might be apparent in returning officers who are not ready or suitable to resume their pre-incident roles.[18] Officers can also be evaluated in "shoot" and "don't shoot" scenarios to assess their readiness to return to their positions.[19]

These and other strategies provide platform from which an employer can monitor and identify reasonably objective signs, or credible third-party reports, that a returning officer may have a "medical condition" (that is, a mental health condition caused or aggravated by the shooting incident) that warrants a referral for mandatory FFDE from a licensed mental health professional experienced with law enforcement culture, deadly force confrontations, and other requirements for a psychological FFDE of an incumbent police officer. If an FFDE becomes necessary, it should not be conducted by the mental health professional that provided the post-shooting intervention.

Summary

Attending to an officer's psychological needs after an OIS is sound personnel management and good public policy. To accomplish this, agencies should require involved officers to undergo an intervention with a licensed mental health professional that is familiar with post-shooting intervention, law enforcement culture, and the realities of deadly force confrontations.

---

18. Philip S. Trompetter, "Assessing the Psychological Well-Being of Returning Officers following a Critical Incident," *The Journal of California Law Enforcement* 27, no. 3 (1993).

19. Drew J. Tracy, "Handling Officer-Involved Shootings."

The most effective post-shooting intervention occurs if the officer is offered privileged communication, barring a statutory exception, or an officer who authorizes the disclosure. Mental health professionals who are required by agency policy to recommend whether or not their client officers should return to duty after an OIS should be mindful of the ethical obligation to disclose that requirement prior to the initiation of service. A blanket requirement that officers involved in an OIS undergo an FFDE appears to violate the procedural requirements of the ADA.

Agencies that wish to optimize the efficacy of the post-shooting intervention can employ several strategies to address the agency's duty to protect the community. These mechanisms demonstrate the agency's due diligence by addressing the officer's readiness to return to public safety responsibilities while maximizing the efficacy of the psychological intervention.

The tension between offering the most efficacious post-shooting intervention to the officer and safeguarding the agency's duty to ensure the officer is ready and suitable to return to public safety responsibilities is manageable, but will differ between jurisdictions.

Discussion Questions

1. What services are provided by the Police Psychological Services Section?
2. Why were the International Association of Chiefs of Police (IACP) Officer Involved Shooting guidelines developed?
3. What arrangements should already be in place before an officer involved shooting occurs?
4. While officers may be asked to provide pertinent information soon after a shooting to aid the initial investigative process, the authors suggest that they have some recovery time before providing a full, formal statement. How much time is involved and what is the rationale for this recovery period?
5. The employer has duty to ensure that it has a psychologically fit workforce. What limitations exist as to how far they can go to make this assessment?
6. What difficulties were there with the provision that a licensed mental health professional counseling an officer involved in a post-shooting incident be required to report the officer's readiness to go back to work with his/her agency?

7. There are certain federal laws which allow disclosure of what would normally be considered confidential information. What are these laws and what are their provisions?

8. For agencies that wish to follow the Police Psychological Services Section's OIS Guidelines without requiring the intervening mental health professionals to disclose concerns to the agency about an officer's readiness to return to duty, what alternative strategies can be employed to address the agency's duty to protect the community?

46

Let's Drive 'Em Crazy: How Managers Contribute to Employee Stress

James D. Sewell

Introduction

Stress is, of course, a critical issue within contemporary organizations and society. For law enforcement agencies, stress can arise from a variety of sources. It may stem from circumstances or incidents occurring as a result of the unique nature of the law enforcement officer's job. It may result from issues within an individual's personal or family life. Finally, such stress may be caused by issues that develop in the workplace and are similar to those occurring in any organization.

Among the latter — and the focus of this article — are management practices which create stress in the life of the individual employee. While contemporary leadership and management courses foster effective management techniques, some managers, often trained in the "old school" or perhaps more interested in their own advancement, forget their own actions can create a stressful work environment and impact the success and organizational health of a work unit or organization.

So who are these stress-carrying managers?

Managers Who Confuse Urgency with Crisis

Especially in law enforcement, many assignments and responsibilities must carry a sense of urgency; they are important, necessary, and must be completed in a timely manner. Yet, particularly on the administrative side of an agency, not every action is—or needs to be portrayed as—a crisis. For many managers, however, all assignments are given as the "crisis du jour," and employees are forced to labor under unnecessary deadlines and under stressful conditions for assignments which should be considered routine.

Managers Who Micro-Manage

There is a clear distinction between knowing what is going on within an organization and among its personnel and trying to do—or dictate—the jobs of one's subordinates. This stress-carrier places too much emphasis on structuring and controlling the subordinate's workday and specifying the only acceptable response to assigned tasks. At the same time, he or she focuses too little on developing the knowledge, skills and abilities necessary for subordinates to work independently and achieve their own success.

Managers Who Give Incomplete Assignments

A frequent method by which managers can exert and maintain control over their employees and their work product is through assigning work in a piecemeal fashion. Employees are forced to return for additional information before any assignment can be successfully completed.

Managers Who Knee-Jerk or Are Inflexible

Effective law enforcement now, perhaps more than ever, demands managers who adopt a reasoned, flexible approach to the changing demands placed upon them and their resources. Community concerns, internal politics, and external political realities have frequently seen managerial responses which were inflexible, often a knee-jerk response to the immediate issue, and lacking adequate thought about anticipated or unintended consequences. Such ill-timed and ill-planned responses place the most significant stress upon those expected to carry out the decisions and who most directly live with their results.

Managers Who Set Unrealistic Expectations and Deadlines

Like the manager who confuses "crisis" with "urgency," some managers fail to understand the magnitude of the tasks they assign or appreciate the time, detail, and effort necessary to bring a project or assignment to its fruition. Unrealistic expectations and deadlines often act to add to the burden of staff or the assignments themselves and can increase the frustration of assigned personnel.

Managers Who Fail to Acknowledge Employee Performance and Workload

For most law enforcement personnel, a key to their emotional health is that their bosses appreciate their accomplishments and are aware of the volume and intensity of their workload. Yet, in spite of this accepted fact of personnel management, some managers still fail to acknowledge the impact of heavy workloads and the demands required of professional performance. It is those managers who have yet to learn to say "thank you" that cause stress in their employees and fail to reach the leadership potential we now expect in law enforcement agencies.

Managers Who Fail to Deal with Non-Performing Employees

While, in most agencies, the majority of employees respond appropriately to community or organizational expectations for their performance, some employees fail to meet the performance standards or display the professional values exhibited by their peers. Both the organization's administration and individual employees then expect managers to deal with such "problem" personnel. When managers fail to address such non-performance or when they seek to provide excuses for the failures of such employees without addressing the problem itself, they undermine morale and add to the stress and frustration of those who seek simply to "do right" and expect their bosses to do the same.

Managers Who Are Ineffective Communicators

Communication is, of course, a critical element in effective agency management. For some managers, interpersonal communication is difficult and they may avoid interaction with employees. Some managers choose to communicate only via written memoranda or email; others limit their face-to-face contact with their subordinates and prefer to stay in their offices. In all these cases, communication is less likely to be effective, and employees frequently fume with frustration.

Managers Who Are Inconsistent in Evaluations and Discipline

Law enforcement personnel recognize that discipline and performance evaluations are a necessary part of the job. They expect, however, that both be administered fairly and in a consistent manner. Organizational stress arises when managers show favoritism to certain subordinates, invoke discipline on an apparent whim, or evaluate employees against ill-defined or arbitrary standards.

Managers Who Refuse to Share Success or Accept Responsibility for Failure

Perhaps one of the greatest frustrations for an employee, whether in a law enforcement agency or any other public or private organization, is the manager who, on the one hand, refuses to give or share credit for a work unit's successes or, on the other, accepts no responsibility for its failures. As previously noted, people desire appreciation and acknowledgement of their contributions to an organization's success. At the same time, they respect that manager who acknowledges his or her own failures and recognizes that many failures within an organizational unit should not be laid solely at the feet of an individual employee.

So how can managers both become more effective as managers *and* reduce the stress they cause in the work lives of employees who report to them? Aside from concentrating heavily on understanding the impact of their actions on employees and continuing to learn—and apply—leadership and effective management skills,[1] there are a number of specific steps—the daily dozen if you will—a manager can take.

Communicate

The standard axiom for the sale of real estate is "location, location, location." Similarly, the axiom for effective leadership must be "communication, communication, communication." In many organizations, the breakdown in relations between labor and management occurs when there is a breakdown in communication. Within smaller organizational units, the failure of a manager to communicate with his or her employees or to encourage reciprocal communication with the manager produces negative results. Effective leadership within an agency and management of its human resources require effective and ongoing communication at all levels.

Be Fair, Open, and Honest

A corollary to the communication axiom is that, in dealing with subordinates and others within the organization, the manager must be viewed as fair, open, and honest. Trust between a manager and his subordinates is a necessity for the most successful operations. From the beginning, employees should understand the expectations of the manager, particularly in regards to the way they should approach their job and in the way he or she conducts discipline and performance evaluation.

Act as a Safety Valve

Times of great stress are, of course, emotional times for law enforcement employees. One of the important roles played by a manager during such times is that of safety valve, an emotional outlet through which employees can appropriately vent their anger, fear, frustration, and concerns. At the same time,

---

1. While there are many practical leadership books available, three can be particularly useful when applied to law enforcement: *Leadership Challenge* (3rd Edition) by James M. Kouzes and Barry Z. Posner; *Managing the Unexpected* by Karl E. Weick and Kathleen M. Sutcliffe; and *Good to Great* by Jim Collins.

it is equally important that the manager learn how to successfully buffer subordinates from the stress produced by those higher up in the chain of command, including elected and appointed officials outside the law enforcement agency.

Be Involved

While employees may grate at the manager who attempts to micro-manage or over-control their work, they look forward to the manager who takes a direct interest in their performance and is involved in the activities of the organization. In law enforcement agencies, the more respected leader is the manager who remembers his or her roots, who spends time "on the street" in spite of administrative demands, and who supports subordinates as they do their jobs.

Be Positive

Law enforcement is, by its nature, a negative experience. Law enforcement officers and their support personnel deal with people at their worst, in times of crisis and pain, and when human emotions are at their rawest. It is therefore critical that the manager realize the importance of their support of subordinates, especially when those personnel are the ones impacted by crisis. Such a role, akin to that of a cheerleader, becomes particularly necessary when the negative issues occur within the organization itself, rather than as a byproduct of the work, and managers are charged with maintaining the morale of the agency. Especially in the latter case, it is essential that managers themselves maintain an outwardly positive attitude, especially in the presence of their subordinates; for the health of the organization and its mission, managers can ill afford to be viewed as negative and anti-administration.

Lighten Up!

It is, of course, important to acknowledge the seriousness of contemporary law enforcement and its critical social mission. At the same time, managers should recognize that such seriousness does not require a Puritan work environment, devoid of humor and personality. The demands of this job require that, for their own mental health, personnel search for the "bright side," accepting that the seriousness of job tasks can be alleviated. Managers who not only take their jobs but also themselves too seriously risk damage to the emotional well-being of their personnel and themselves.

Accept Responsibility

Part of the maturation process for organizational leaders and managers is the realization that they must be willing to accept responsibility for the actions of their subordinates, actions which are not always under the manager's direct control, as well as for their own actions. It is, of course, easy to throw a subordinate "under the bus" and place blame on someone lower in the chain of command for failures which reflect on the organization. Absent criminal or ethical violations, it may be more appropriate for the manager to accept some of the responsibility when a subordinate fails to accomplish what is desired and use the situation as a learning experience for all.

Learn to Balance Life

Managers and personnel alike should realize that effective job performance requires a balance of professional demands, family responsibilities, and personal issues. Failure to acknowledge and accept the relationship between each can too frequently result in conflict, frustration, and anger which spill over throughout all the parts of one's life. To be effective on the job means simply that one learns to balance its demands with those of the other elements of one's life. For managers, this also means that they not only learn to apply such balance in their own lives, but that they also accept it as a necessity for the healthy work and personal lives of their employees.

Foster a Healthy Work Environment

Contemporary law enforcement is, by its nature, a stressful profession, and that stress permeates the law enforcement organization. Good leadership and effective management practices can, however, reduce the stress which can be attributed to the organization and its hierarchy. As Ayres (1990) has noted:

> Law enforcement leaders wanting to reduce the psychological stress caused by poor supervision and apathetic attitudes toward employees must be committed to making the workplace a 'worthplace' — where people care about people and where employee needs are emphasized .... and by developing a healthy environment that is perceived by the employees as a good place to work.[2]

Focus on Your Folks

Two areas are particularly key. The first is to know the people you work with: their strengths, their weaknesses, their families, and their career aspirations. Armed with that knowledge, a successful manager can both appropriately assign tasks and responsibilities and assure that employees perceive their work as both meaningful and valuable. With that also comes the recognition of the importance of family in stabilizing and supporting the professional life of today's law enforcement personnel.

The second is to work at the development of the people who serve in your organization, helping them do their jobs more effectively and with fewer distractions through programs in stress management, time management, and personal finance, for instance. Such development should be viewed as an investment in the future of the agency's people, rather than as training which has little relevance to one's job as a cop.

Plan Effectively

A sign which has appeared in many offices reads: "Failure to plan on your part does not constitute an emergency on mine!" As previously noted, the aura of crisis attached to many efforts is simply due to the manager's failure to adequately plan. To that end, managers who devote time to planning for their organization's operations and even for their own day reduce the stress that they cause for their subordinates.

---

2. Richard M. Ayres, *Preventing Law Enforcement Stress: The Organization's Role* (Alexandria, VA: National Sheriffs' Association, 1990), 33–35.

Display Organizational Loyalty

In a parallel to the case with divorced or battling parents, employees, rather than children, frequently become pawns between battling managers. In this context, managers have two primary considerations. First, within proper legal and ethical boundaries, they have an obligation to maintain loyalty to the organization and the persons for whom they work. Second, they have a responsibility to keep their own counsel. Employees do *not* need to hear their own bosses' emotional outbursts toward the organization, its hierarchy, or their own peers.

By the very nature of their chosen profession, with its high demands and heavy personal toll, law enforcement officers will continue to experience stress throughout their careers. Some of these stressors, however, frequently caused by organizational issues, poor leadership, and ineffective management, can be effectively mitigated. It is critical, then, that leaders and managers in law enforcement agencies recognize how they contribute to the stress of their employees and take aggressive steps to reduce their stress-causing practices.

Table 1
Stress Reducing Practices for Managers

1. Assure effective two-way communication with employees
2. Be fair and honest in communications with personnel and assure they understand your expectations
3. Act as a safety valve to allow employees to "emote" and to protect them from stress from "higher ups"
4. Be involved in employee assignments and available for guidance
5. Project a positive attitude
6. Lighten up!
7. Accept the responsibility of both leadership and management
8. Learn to balance home, office, and personal stress
9. Foster a healthy working environment
10. Learn to build and encourage the self-esteem of employees
11. Plan effectively
12. Display organizational loyalty and maintain your own counsel

---

Discussion Questions

1. What are some of the characteristics of managers who micro-manage?
2. What are the consequences of managers who fail to acknowledge employee performance and workload?
3. What are the consequences of managers who fail to deal with non-performing employees?
4. What happens within an organization when managers are inconsistent in evaluations and discipline?
5. How can managers become more effective and reduce the stress they cause in the working lives of the employees who report to them?

Index

Note: **Boldface** numbers indicate definitions of key terms; *n*, footnote; and *t*, table.